READING CRITICALLY
WRITING WELL

A READER AND GUIDE

EIGHTH EDITION

READING CRITICALLY
WRITING WELL

A READER AND GUIDE

Rise B. Axelrod
University of California, Riverside

Charles R. Cooper
University of California, San Diego

Alison M. Warriner
California State University, East Bay

BEDFORD/ST. MARTIN'S
Boston ◆ New York

For Bedford/St. Martin's

Senior Developmental Editor: John Elliott
Production Editor: Jessica Skrocki
Production Supervisor: Andrew Ensor
Senior Marketing Manager: Karita dos Santos
Art Director: Lucy Krikorian
Text Design: Linda M. Robertson
Copy Editor: Rosemary Winfield
Cover Design: Donna Lee Dennison
Cover Art: Mira Hecht, *Untitled #8* from the Full Circle Series, 2003. Oil on canvas,
   60 × 60 inches.
Composition: TexTech International
Printing and Binding: R. R. Donnelley & Sons Company

President: Joan E. Feinberg
Editorial Director: Denise B. Wydra
Editor in Chief: Karen S. Henry
Director of Development: Erica T. Appel
Director of Marketing: Karen Melton Soeltz
Director of Editing, Design, and Production: Marcia Cohen
Managing Editor: Shuli Traub

For information, write: Bedford/St. Martin's, 75 Arlington Street, Boston, MA 02116
(617-399-4000)

ISBN-10: 0-312-66776-0
ISBN-13: 978-0-312-66776-4

Acknowledgments

Natalie Angier. "Intolerance of Boyish Behavior." Originally titled, "The Debilitating Malady Called Boyhood" from The New York Times, July 24, 1994. Copyright © 1994 The New York Times Company. Reprinted by permission.

Acknowledgments and copyrights are continued at the back of the book on pages 703–05, which constitute an extension of the copyright page.

It is a violation of the law to reproduce these selections by any means whatsoever without the written permission of the copyright holder.

Preface

Read, read, read . . . Just like a carpenter who works as an apprentice and studies the master. Read!

—William Faulkner

I went back to the good nature books that I had read. And I analyzed them. I wrote outlines of whole books—outlines of chapters—so that I could see their structure. And I copied down their transitional sentences or their main sentences or their closing sentences or their lead sentences. I especially paid attention to how these writers made transitions between paragraphs and scenes.

—Annie Dillard

In these quotations, the Nobel Prize–winning novelist William Faulkner and the Pulitzer Prize–winning essayist Annie Dillard tell us what many authors know intuitively—that reading critically helps writers learn to write well. Reading closely and critically also helps students become analytical thinkers.

Now in its eighth edition, *Reading Critically, Writing Well* helps students see the connection between reading closely and critically and writing thoughtfully and effectively. By using the book's approach, students learn how texts work rhetorically to achieve their purposes with particular readers. They also learn an array of strategies for critical reading and thinking—strategies that contribute to enhanced comprehension of a text, inspire active engagement with it, and stimulate analysis of the text's as well as the reader's own assumptions, values, and beliefs.

This book brings critical reading and writing together by engaging students in two fundamental ways of reading: reading for meaning and reading like a writer. While Reading for Meaning sections give students insight into how readers construct meanings from what they read, Reading like a Writer sections teach students how to construct their own texts rhetorically to influence their readers' understanding and critical response. The two strategies are introduced in Chapter 1, developed further at the beginning of each subsequent chapter, and applied to every reading selection throughout the text. Through continued use of these two critical reading strategies, students gain confidence in their ability to read with a critical eye and to write effectively in different rhetorical situations.

FEATURES

The special features of *Reading Critically, Writing Well* include:

Engaging Readings Demonstrating Eight Different Types of Real-World Writing

Reading Critically, Writing Well includes 48 readings—four published essays and two student essays in each assignment chapter (Chapters 2–9). Each of these chapters focuses on a specific type of writing that students will encounter during college or on the job, including four expository genres (autobiography, observation, reflection, and explanation of concepts) and four argumentative genres (evaluation, speculation about causes or effects, proposal to solve a problem, and position on a controversial issue). Chosen to stimulate lively class discussion and to illustrate a variety of writing strategies, the readings provide students with provocative perspectives on many important topics. You will find many tried and true essays by distinguished professional and academic writers such as Annie Dillard, Brent Staples, David Quammen, Deborah Tannen, Stephen King, Amitai Etzioni, and Michael Pollan.

Uniquely Thorough Instruction in the Reading-Writing Connection

Reading Critically, Writing Well teaches students how to analyze the content and craft of successful writing and then shows them how to apply what they have learned to their own writing. Each assignment chapter begins with a Guide to Reading and ends with a Guide to Writing, both tailored to the distinctive features of the chapter's genre. These guides provide an array of flexible activities designed to help students learn to read a specific kind of writing with a critical eye and write it with a clear purpose for their own readers. The Guide to Reading introduces the two overall strategies for critical reading—Reading for Meaning and Reading like a Writer—that frame the questions following each reading selection. The Guide to Writing scaffolds the composing process, using concepts students have learned in their Reading like a Writer activities. These major structural elements of the book provide guidance for students in moving from critical reading to effective writing.

In addition, Appendix 1, A Catalog of Critical Reading Strategies, explains and applies to Martin Luther King Jr.'s "Letter from Birmingham Jail" seventeen additional strategies for critical reading, from annotating and summarizing to exploring the significance of figurative language and judging the writer's credibility.

"Reading for Meaning" Activities That Teach Students to Read Deeply and Critically

Three class-tested Reading Meaning activities following each selection give students three different kinds of help in understanding and interpreting what they are reading. The first activity, Read to Comprehend, helps students focus on an important aspect of the reading and summarize it. Students are also invited to think about word choice and to define any words they do not understand. The second activity, Read to Respond, engages students in exploring aspects of the reading that resonate for them or that stimulate strong reactions. The third activity, Read to Analyze Assumptions, leads students to think more critically about the cultural beliefs and values implicit in the reading's word choices and assertions. Students are also encouraged to examine the cultural bases for their own assumptions as readers. Each of these three Reading for Meaning activities concludes with a list of additional critical reading strategies from Appendix 1 that would most productively enhance the student's continued efforts to comprehend, respond to, or analyze the assumptions of the reading.

"Reading like a Writer" Activities That Teach Students to Read Rhetorically

The Reading like a Writer activities help students learn how to examine and assess the effectiveness of a writer's choices in light of the purpose and audience—that is, to read rhetorically. The Guide to Reading at the beginning of each chapter presents several Reading like a Writer activities that introduce the rhetorical strategies typical of the genre. Each subsequent essay in a chapter is followed by a Reading like a Writer activity inviting students to learn more about one of these strategies. Altogether, each chapter invites students to complete nine or ten focused rhetorical analyses of readings in the same genre.

Every Reading like a Writer activity directs students to a specific part of a reading—a few sentences or paragraphs—so that students lose no time wondering where to begin their analysis. Many activities show students the first step to take. Because they are focused and accessible, these activities make it possible for even the most inexperienced readers to complete them and engage in a serious program of rhetorical learning.

Guides to Writing That Support Students' Composing

As writing instructors, we know that students need help writing essays. To provide this support, each *Reading Critically, Writing Well* chapter concludes with a comprehensive Guide to Writing that escorts students through every stage of writing, from choosing a topic and gathering information and ideas to drafting and revising and then editing and proofreading an essay. In our experience, all students, from the most anxious to the most confident writers, benefit in some way from the Guides to Writing.

Grounded in research on composing as well as in genre and learning theory, each Guide to Writing scaffolds student learning about a genre, providing temporary support so that students can focus on one stage of writing at a time. In addition, it teaches students the kinds of questions they need to ask themselves as they write and helps them apply the rhetorical knowledge gleaned from reading to writing an essay in the genre. To provide students with practical help to increase their rhetorical prowess, a section in every Guide to Writing, Considering a Useful Sentence Strategy, explains and illustrates a specific sentence pattern that writers typically use when composing in that genre, such as rhetorical questions in proposals and appositives in explanations of concepts. In addition, a Guide to Critical Reading tailored to the genre helps students engage in constructive peer critique of their classmates' writing.

Intensive Coverage of Strategies for Research and Documentation

The Guides to Writing and the comprehensive discussions of strategies for research and documentation in Appendix 2 provide students with clear, helpful guidelines for evaluating sources, integrating them with one's own writing, and citing them using the most current MLA and APA styles. With eight different genres, students have an opportunity to practice the full gamut of research strategies, from memory search to the field research methods of observation and interview to library and Internet research. In recognition that many students now begin any writing assignment by going online, the first section of each Guide to Writing, Invention and Research, includes advice to help students make productive use of the Web in research for that specific genre, such as searching for memorabilia for autobiographical writing or researching opposing views in argumentative essays.

Activities That Ask Students to Reflect on Their Learning

Research has shown that when students reflect on their learning, they clarify their understanding and remember what they have learned longer. Reflecting also enables students to think critically about what they have learned and how they have learned it. *Reading Critically, Writing Well* now provides three opportunities for students to reflect on their learning and also to discuss what they have learned with others: Reflecting on Your Experience, Reviewing What Makes [the kind of essay] Effective, and Reflecting on What You Have Learned. These activities are placed at important transitions in each chapter, at points when looking back at what they have learned will help students move forward more productively.

NEW TO THIS EDITION

Twenty-Five New Readings on Engaging Topics

Half of the reading selections—25 of 48—are new, including seven new student essays and eighteen pieces by award-winning writers such as Carolina A. Miranda, Carl Safina, and Michael Pollan; social critics such as David Brooks and

David Moberg; and distinguished professors and researchers such as Steven Doloff and Chip and Dan Heath. The new readings engage students with current topics close to their daily lives, such as evaluations of the iPod, Wikipedia, and Web sites that rate professors, as well as proposals and position papers about giving college degrees in football, starting high school later in the day, letting girls attend single-sex public schools, and teaching contraception as part of sex-education classes. New paired essays by Brooks and Moberg offer contrasting perspectives on the value of hard work and discipline in achieving financial success in the United States.

More Help with Critical Reading

The first professional essay and the second student essay in each assignment chapter are now annotated with an analysis of specific words, phrases, sentences, and passages that makes it easier for students to see features and strategies in context and models the close, critical reading students must learn to do themselves. In addition, the Read to Analyze Assumptions activity that is part of the Reading for Meaning apparatus after each essay now provides more background explanation to help students understand and write about the assumptions, values, and attitudes that inform writers and readers.

New Attention to Online Writing

Each assignment chapter now includes a feature that shows students a specific way that the chapter's genre appears in online writing, such as a blog entry for reflection and a Wikipedia article for explaining concepts. In each case, annotations, questions, and writing prompts help students see and analyze how the genre's basic features and strategies are expressed in the online medium in ways that may both resemble and differ from their expressions in print.

New Advice on Working with Sources

Because using sources effectively is essential to good academic writing, the revision section in every Guide to Writing includes new advice and help for students on working with sources. Focused on the complex rhetorical choices that students have to make, these sections address topics such as introducing sources in a paragraph, addressing opposing points of view, and avoiding plagiarism.

Instructor's Manual with New Help for the Online Classroom

The Instructor's Manual has been supplemented with material on how to use the text in an online learning environment, including both courses taught completely online and those in which instructors use course management systems such as Blackboard or WebCT to enhance their on-campus teaching.

ACKNOWLEDGMENTS

We first want to thank our students and colleagues at the University of California, Riverside, and the University of California, San Diego; California State University, East Bay, and California State University, San Bernardino; and the University of Nevada, Reno, who have taught us so much about reading, writing, and teaching.

We also owe a debt of gratitude to the many reviewers and questionnaire respondents who made suggestions for this revision. They include Maribeth E. Anderson, Ivy Tech Community College of Indiana; David L. G. Arnold, University of Wisconsin–Stevens Point; Martha Bailie, Iowa Central Community College; Pat Barnes, Delaware County Community College; Tammie Bob, College of DuPage; Laurie E. Buchanan, Clark State Community College; Abby E. Freeland, West Virginia University; Judith Fourzan-Rice, University of Texas–El Paso; Tanya Grosz, Northwestern College; Ida Hagman, College of DuPage; Sarah Hamilton, West Virginia University; J. Paul Johnson, Winona State University; Keith Jones, Northwestern College; Janet Barnett Minc, The University of Akron, Wayne College; Renee Mizrahi, Kingsborough Community College; Loretta Navarra, Kingsborough Community College; Alison Smith, Middle Tennessee State University; Tim Taylor, St. Louis Community College at Meramec; and Mary Tohill, The University of Akron, Wayne College.

We want especially to thank our developmental editor, John Elliott. This book could not have been written without his insightful criticism, skillful editing, cheerful persistence, and good humor. Working with John all these years has been an unalloyed pleasure and wonderful learning experience. We also want to thank Joan Feinberg, Karen Henry, Denise Wydra, and Erica Appel for their leadership and support. Our deepest appreciation goes out to Nancy Perry, who has been our mainstay at Bedford/St. Martin's lo, these many years; thank you, Nancy, for your wise guidance and kind friendship. We are grateful for Jessica Skrocki's seamless coordination of the production process, Rosemary Winfield's skillful copy editing, Sandy Schechter's and Naomi Kornhauser's work on permissions and art research, and Karita dos Santos's help in marketing.

Rise wishes to dedicate the book to her husband, Steven, and their son, Jeremiah, in appreciation for their enduring support and love. Alison dedicates this book with love to her daughter, Dawn, and to her husband, Jeremiah.

Rise B. Axelrod
Charles R. Cooper
Alison M. Warriner

Contents

APPENDIX 1 A Catalog of Critical Reading Strategies 596

APPENDIX 2 Strategies for Research and Documentation 647

Paired Readings

The first reading in each of the following pairs is followed by an activity inviting students to compare and contrast the readings. In each pair, the page numbers in parentheses indicate the first pages of the readings; the boldface number at the end indicates the first page of the Comparing and Contrasting Related Readings activity.

READING CRITICALLY
WRITING WELL

A READER AND GUIDE

CHAPTER 1

Introduction

Reading Critically, Writing Well is designed to help prepare you for the special demands of learning in college, where all your reading should be critical reading—not only understanding but also analyzing, and evaluating what you read.

When you read a text critically, you alternate between two points of view: seeking to understand the text on its own terms and questioning the text's ideas and authority. Putting your questions aside even temporarily allows you to be open to new ideas. But reading critically requires that eventually you examine every idea—your own as well as those of others—skeptically.

Learning to read critically also helps you to write well. It leads you to a fuller understanding of the subject you plan to write about, enabling you to go beyond the obvious to avoid superficiality and oversimplification. In addition, reading critically helps you anticipate what readers will expect and what questions they may have in mind as they read your writing.

Knowing your readers' expectations for the kind of essay you are writing helps you plan your essay with readers in mind. For example, if you are explaining an unfamiliar concept, you can assume that your readers will expect concrete examples and comparisons to help them grasp the new and abstract idea. If you are arguing a position on a current issue, you know that readers will expect you not merely to assert your position but also to support it with facts, statistics, expert testimony, or other relevant evidence. In turn, knowing your readers' expectations will help you anticipate their questions. If you expect readers to accept certain of your ideas but to be skeptical about others, you can support with specific details, examples, or quotations those parts of your essay that present your most unfamiliar or controversial ideas.

Being able to anticipate how readers will respond does not mean that as a writer you always seek to please readers. In fact, good writing often challenges readers. But to challenge readers' assumptions, you need to know what they expect.

You will learn from the activities in this book that reading critically and writing well are intellectually demanding tasks that require your time and effort.

Speed-reading may be the best strategy when you need to get the gist of an article or sort through a pile of possible sources. But when you need to understand new ideas or to evaluate complex arguments, when you are reading to prepare for class discussion or to write an essay, then you need to read—and possibly also reread—more slowly and thoughtfully.

The same principles apply to writing. Some kinds of writing can be dashed off in a single draft. The more practiced you are in a given kind of writing, the more efficient your writing process will be. If you write a lab report every week for a term, you should be able to write one rather quickly. If you know how to study for essay exams and have written them often, you should become adept at them. But when you need to do a kind of writing that you have not mastered or to write about new and difficult material, then you will need more time to develop and organize your ideas.

Slowing down your reading and writing probably sounds like a bad idea to you right now, especially as you begin a new term and have just been told how much course work you will have to do. This book offers practical and efficient ways to meet this challenge by introducing easy-to-use strategies for reading critically and writing well.

■ Reading Critically

After you read each selection in *Reading Critically, Writing Well*, you will practice two basic strategies for reading critically: *reading for meaning* and *reading like a writer*. These strategies offer different but complementary ways of looking at a text.

When you read for meaning, you look at the ideas and information in a text to understand and respond critically to what is being said. When you read like a writer, your focus shifts from meaning to rhetoric—from *what* is being communicated to *why* and *how* it is communicated. Although experienced readers may combine these two ways of reading—simultaneously reading for meaning and reading like a writer—we separate them here to give you an opportunity to sharpen your critical reading skills.

In Chapters 2 through 9, you will be asked to read a variety of essays in these two ways. Strategies such as summarizing, outlining, and evaluating the logic of an argument will be introduced to extend and deepen your repertoire of sharpen reading skills. Appendix 1 presents a complete catalog of these strategies.

READING FOR MEANING

When you read, your primary effort is to make the characters on the page or computer screen meaningful. But as you know from your experience as a reader, a text may be more meaningful or less so depending on your familiarity with the words that are used, your knowledge of the subject, and the kind of text or genre you are reading. If you have some knowledge about an issue currently being debated, for example, then an essay arguing for a position on that issue is likely to be relatively easy to read and full of meaning for you. If, however, you know nothing about the issue or the positions people have been taking on it, then the essay will probably be more difficult to read and less obviously meaningful.

Reading for meaning requires you to use your knowledge and experience to create meaning. You must bring to the text your knowledge about the subject and genre, your beliefs and values, your personal experience, as well as the historical and cultural contexts you share with others. Reading with this rich context helps you to see many possibilities for meaning in a text. Therefore, what you find meaningful in a given reading may overlap to some extent with what others find meaningful in the same reading.

As a reader, you are not a passive receptacle into which meaning is poured. Instead, as your eyes move across a text, you actively construct meaning from it, contributing your own relevant knowledge and point of view while also assimilating the text's new ideas and information. This highly significant and culturally important activity is what we mean by reading for meaning.

Annotating as you read is a powerful method for making sure you have something relevant to say about a given text. It helps concentrate your attention on the text's language and leaves you with a record of the insights, reactions, and questions that occurred to you in the process of reading for meaning. Annotating simply involves marking the page as you read. You note what you think is important in a reading, what you think it means, and what ideas and questions it raises for you. Annotating is easy to do. All it takes is a text you can write on and something to write with. Here are a few ways to annotate a text:

- Highlight or underline key words and sentences.
- Bracket important passages.
- Connect related ideas with lines.
- Circle words to be defined.
- Outline the main ideas in the margin.
- Write brief comments and questions in the margin.

Some readers mark up the text extensively, while others mark only the parts they consider significant or problematic. What is important is not how you annotate or even how much you annotate but *that* you annotate. The simple act of marking the page as you read makes it more likely that you will read closely and attentively. There is no right or wrong way to annotate. You will find examples of annotating in Chapters 2 through 9 as well as in Appendix 1, pp. 597–603.

After annotating, *exploratory writing* is a helpful way of developing your ideas about an essay. You will find that the very act of composing sentences leads you to clarify and extend your ideas, discover new insights, and raise new questions.

The key to productive exploratory writing is to refrain from censoring yourself. Simply write at least a page. The goal at this stage is to allow ideas to flow freely.

We recommend, then, a two-step procedure: annotating as you read followed by exploratory writing that develops meanings for a text. You can extend your understanding by adding a third step—conversing with others who have also read the essay. Your instructor will likely give you opportunities, whether in class or online, to discuss the reading with other students.

Previewing the Reading for Meaning Activities

A set of three Reading for Meaning activities follows each reading in the book: (1) *Read to Comprehend*, (2) *Read to Respond*, and (3) *Read to Analyze Assumptions*. Turn to pages 19–22 to see one of these sets of activities. As you read for meaning, you may use all of these activities or focus on one that seems most useful for a particular selection and your purpose for reading it. Your instructor may ask you to do the Reading for Meaning activities as homework or in class, individually or with others. You may do these activities in any order; but when done in the order they appear in, they lead you from a basic understanding of what the text says to an exploration of your reactions to it and finally to a deeper understanding of the beliefs and values on which the text and your reactions are based. Each of the activities ends with an invitation for you to apply one or more of the critical reading strategies that are explained and illustrated in Appendix 1.

Read to Comprehend

This activity helps you gain a fuller understanding of the reading. It often begins by asking you to locate the author's thesis statement or main point and rewrite it in your own words. Several words that may be unfamiliar to you are defined, and then you are invited to define any other unfamiliar words you find. The activity ends with an invitation for you to expand your understanding by applying one or more of the critical reading strategies in Appendix 1 that are especially useful for increasing comprehension, such as outlining, summarizing, paraphrasing, and questioning to understand and remember.

Read to Respond

This activity helps you explore your reactions to the reading. It often begins by asking you to find a statement or passage that you have strong feelings about—perhaps because it resonates with your own experience, because you strongly agree or disagree with it, or because you question it or see it as contradicting other statements in the reading—and then to use exploratory writing to reflect on your reactions. The activity ends with an invitation for you to develop your response by applying one or more of the critical reading strategies in Appendix 1 that are especially useful for examining readers' responses, such as contextualizing, recognizing emotional manipulation, and judging the writer's credibility.

Read to Analyze Assumptions

This activity helps you probe the text more deeply to become aware of assumptions you find in the reading as well as your own assumptions. Every text has subtexts—what we call assumptions. These assumptions always include those of the writer and may also include those of other people mentioned in the text. Likewise, every reader comes to the text with certain assumptions. All of these assumptions include values and beliefs that often are ingrained in culture and family tradition, ethnic and religious background, or language itself as it expresses cultural values, ideology, and philosophy. Although assumptions may be stated directly in a text, they are more often only implied; in the same way, a reader may not be consciously aware of the assumptions he or she brings to the text. To understand a text fully and to understand your own as well as other readers' responses to the text, you need to analyze and evaluate the assumptions in the text and in your response to it. This activity helps you identify, analyze, and evaluate assumptions. It often begins by asking you to focus on the writer's word choices and use of examples or evidence and then to speculate about what has been left out. The activity provides a series of questions you can ask yourself to examine the assumptions with a critical eye. It ends with an invitation for you to probe assumptions more deeply by applying one or more of the critical reading strategies in Appendix 1 that are especially useful for analyzing and evaluating underlying assumptions, such as reflecting on challenges to your beliefs and values, exploring the significance of figurative language, looking for patterns of opposition, evaluating the logic of an argument, and performing a Toulmin analysis.

READING LIKE A WRITER

Reading like a writer shifts your focus from constructing meanings for a reading to analyzing and evaluating how its meanings are presented. Reading like a writer, you look closely at rhetoric—the ways that writers make their ideas understandable and seek to influence readers.

To read rhetorically, you need to think about writing in terms of its purpose and audience. Writers make many choices when they write, and these choices frequently depend on the writer's reason(s) for writing and the particular reader(s) being addressed. When you read like a writer, you examine the writer's choices and assess their effectiveness in light of the writer's purpose and audience. This kind of reading enhances your critical reading while helping you make rhetorically effective choices in your own writing.

When you read like a writer, you follow the same simple procedure as you do for reading for meaning: annotating followed by writing.

Previewing the Reading like a Writer Activities

A Reading like a Writer activity follows each selection in the book. Turn to pages 22–23 to see one of these activities. As you can see, each Reading like a Writer activity consists of one or two introductory paragraphs followed by two sections: *Analyze* and *Write*.

Analyze

The instructions in this section typically ask you to reread specific paragraphs in the reading and to underline or bracket certain words or sentences. These annotations, which you make as you read like a writer, focus on the characteristic textual features and rhetorical strategies of the genre—or type of writing—you are studying. Your aim is to use annotating as a way to begin analyzing the features and strategies typical of the genre and to begin evaluating how well they work in a particular reading.

Write

Here you are asked to write several sentences about what you discovered in analyzing and evaluating a reading's features and strategies in terms of how well they achieve the writer's purpose. Writing even a few sentences can help you develop your analysis and evaluation of a reading.

■ Writing Well

The following section introduces you to the essay-length writing you will do when you undertake the major assignments in Chapters 2 through 9 of *Reading Critically, Writing Well*. As you might guess, the briefer writing activities following every reading (Reading for Meaning and Reading like a Writer) prepare you to write your own full-length essay.

Before previewing the essay assignments, pause to think about your own writing experience in high school, in college, or on the job.

THE WRITING ASSIGNMENTS

As you work through the assignments in Chapters 2 through 9 of *Reading Critically, Writing Well*, you will learn how to write the following genres or types of essays:

Autobiography (Chapter 2): telling readers about important events and people in your life

THINKING ABOUT YOUR PAST WRITING EXPERIENCE

1. *Recall* the last time you wrote something fairly difficult, long, or complicated. It may have been an assignment at school or at work, or it may have been something you initiated yourself. Do not choose something written under strict time limits, such as an in-class essay exam.

2. *Write* several sentences describing how you went about planning and writing. Begin by briefly explaining your purpose for writing and identifying your intended readers. *Note* any assumptions you made about your readers' knowledge of the subject or their expectations of your writing.

You can use one or more of the following questions if you need help remembering how you went about completing the writing. But do not restrict yourself to answering these questions. Write down whatever comes to mind as you think about your past writing experience.

- How long did it take before you started putting your ideas on paper?

- What kind of plan did you have? How did your plan evolve as you worked?

- What did you change as you were writing? What changes, if any, did you make after completing your first draft?

- What role did other people play in helping you develop your ideas and plans?

Observation (Chapter 3): presenting to readers your firsthand reports about intriguing places, people, and activities

Reflection (Chapter 4): exploring for readers the larger social implications of your experience or observation

Explaining concepts (Chapter 5): defining for readers the meaning and importance of key ideas

Evaluation (Chapter 6): arguing to convince readers that your judgment of a movie, book, performance, essay, noteworthy person, or other subject is justifiable

Speculation about causes or effects (Chapter 7): arguing to convince readers that it is plausible that some event, trend, or phenomenon resulted from certain causes or will result in certain effects

Proposal to solve a problem (Chapter 8): arguing to convince readers to accept or seriously consider your proposed solution to a problem

Position paper (Chapter 9): arguing to convince readers to accept or seriously consider your position on a controversial issue

Each of these writing assignments identifies a genre of writing done every day by countless writers. More than mere school writing exercises, they are real-world writing situations like those you will encounter in college and at work. Each chapter includes essays written for school as well as for print publications and online Web sites. Pause now to learn a bit more about these assignments.

Previewing the Writing Assignments

Look at the different writing genres that are represented in this book. On the second or third page of each assignment chapter (Chapters 2 through 9) is a brief set of Writing Situations. Read this section in all of the chapters to get a quick sense of the different kinds of writing. Then write several sentences responding to the following questions:

1. Which of these genres have you already written?

2. With which of these genres have you had the most experience? Where and when did you do this kind of writing? What was most challenging about writing it?

THE GUIDES TO WRITING

Following the Readings section of Chapters 2 through 9 in *Reading Critically, Writing Well*, a Guide to Writing helps you complete the writing assignment. These guides reflect the fact that writing is a process of discovery. As writers, we rarely if ever begin with a complete understanding of the subject. We put together some information and ideas, start writing, and let the writing lead us to understanding. While writing helps us achieve greater understanding, it also raises questions and unexpected complexities, which, in turn, can inspire more writing and, nearly always, generate further ideas and insights.

Experienced writers have learned to trust this fascinating discovery process because they know that writing is an unsurpassed way of thinking. Writing helps you discover, explore, develop, and refine your ideas in a way that cannot compare with sitting around and thinking about a subject. Because writing leaves a record of your thinking, it reduces the burden of remembering and allows you to direct all your energy toward solving the immediate problem. By rereading what you have written, you can figure out where you became derailed or recall points that you forgot were important or see new possibilities you did not notice before.

The Guide to Writing for each assignment leads you through the complex, creative process of discovery: Invention and Research, Drafting, Reading a Draft Critically, Revising, and Editing and Proofreading. Because it helps to approach the first draft of an essay with some notes and other brief writings in hand, the first writing activity in each guide is called *invention*, a term used since classical Greek times to describe speakers' and writers' attempts to discover what they know and might say about a subject. Each Guide to Writing also includes advice about doing *research*, either to help you decide on a subject to write about or to learn more about your subject. Because *drafting* is most efficient and productive when you clarify your purpose and make even tentative plans in advance, the Guide to Writing helps you set goals and organize your draft. Also, because nearly any draft can benefit from the advice of thoughtful readers, guidelines are included to help you and your classmates *read each other's drafts critically*. And because *revising* gives you the opportunity to refine your ideas and to make your writing communicate more clearly and effectively, each Guide to Writing includes suggestions for improving your draft. Finally, because you want your finished essay to conform to the conventions of grammar, mechanics, punctuation, spelling, and style, each guide concludes with advice on *editing and proofreading* your essay.

Before reading about the resources offered to support your invention and research, drafting, critical reading, revising, and editing and proofreading, take time to preview a Guide to Writing.

Previewing a Guide to Writing

Turn to one of the Guides to Writing toward the end of any writing assignment chapter. Skim the guide, reading the headings and the first paragraph in each major section to get an idea of what the guide offers.

Invention and Research

Invention begins with finding a subject to write about. The Considering Ideas for Your Own Writing section following each reading, together with the suggestions in the Guide to Writing, will help you find a topic and understand the implications of developing it.

Because each writing situation makes unique demands on writers, the invention and research activities in each chapter differ. To see how, compare the activities under Invention and Research in two or three chapters—for example, in Chapter 2 on autobiography, Chapter 5 on explaining concepts, and Chapter 9 on arguing positions.

The immediate advantage of genre-specific invention is that it stimulates your thinking, getting you writing days before you begin drafting your essay. Although you will usually need no more than two hours to complete these invention and research activities, it is best to spread them over several days. As soon as you start writing the first few sentences about a subject, your mind goes to work on it, perhaps even offering ideas and insights when you are going about your daily activities, not consciously thinking about the subject. More invention writing will inspire more ideas. Your understanding of the subject will deepen and the possibilities will become more wide-ranging and subtle. An assignment that may have seemed daunting will become intellectually invigorating, and you will have pages of invention notes with which to launch your draft.

Drafting

After doing some invention, you may be eager to begin drafting your essay. If, however, you are having difficulty making the transition from jotting down invention notes to writing a first draft, the Guide to Writing in each chapter will show you how to set achievable goals and devise a tentative plan that will ease the process of drafting. The guide's Drafting section offers several activities, including Setting Goals, Organizing Your Draft, Considering a Useful Sentence Strategy, and Working with Sources. Setting Goals reminds you of the kinds of questions you need to ask yourself about your purpose and audience, such as how to interest readers in your subject, describe a person vividly, or counterargue effectively. You will also be reminded of the strategies that you saw other writers in the chapter use to accomplish similar goals and to organize their essays. The sections on sentences and sources recommend strategies that writers have found especially helpful for that chapter's type of writing and that you may want to use as well, and provides examples from the chapter's readings.

Reading a Draft Critically

The Reading a Draft Critically section invites you to make practical use of all you have learned about reading a genre. It also invites you to try out your newly acquired expertise—while doing a classmate a big favor. Part of the favor you provide is the written record of your critical reading that you give to your classmate, a record the classmate can refer to the next day or next week when revising his or her essay. You do yourself a favor as well. Like your classmate, you too will revise an essay in the same genre. As you read your classmate's essay critically, you will be reflecting intensely on your own just-completed draft. The more thoughtful and comprehensive your critical reading, the more likely you will be to discover ways to strengthen your own draft.

Revising

Revising offers the great opportunity of rethinking what you have written, given your evolving purpose and understanding of your readers' needs and expectations. Assume that you will want to make changes and add new material at this stage. Be prepared to cut sentences, move sentences, and reorder paragraphs. You provide the brainpower, and the computer provides the technology to make dramatic changes easy. The Revising section offers a range of suggestions for you to consider, along with the advice you received from your classmates and instructor.

Editing and Proofreading

Editing and proofreading are like taking a last look at yourself in the mirror before going out. You have given some thought to what you would wear and how you would look; now you check to make sure everything is the way you want it. When you write an essay, you spend a lot of time and energy planning, drafting, and revising. Now you want to check to make sure that there are no glaring mistakes in grammar, punctuation, word choice, spelling, or matters of style. If you are unsure whether you have made a mistake or how to fix it, consult a writer's handbook, a Web site, or your writing instructor.

Thinking about Your Learning

We know from research that if learning is not reviewed and reflected on, it soon fades and might not be available when new occasions arise for using or applying it. Therefore, in each assignment chapter, we provide two occasions for you to think about what you have learned.

Reviewing What Makes Essays Effective

The first occasion for thinking about your learning comes after the last reading in the chapter. For example, in Chapter 9, Position Paper, this section is titled Reviewing What Makes Position Papers Effective. You are asked to choose one reading from the chapter that seems to you a particularly good example of its genre, to reread it critically in light of all you have learned about the genre, and then to write a page or more justifying your choice. This activity enables you to review the characteristic features and rhetorical strategies of the genre you are about to write. Coming where it does, *before* the Guide to Writing, this activity helps you complete the transition from thinking like a reader to thinking like a writer.

Reflecting on What You Have Learned

This final occasion for thinking about your learning comes at the end of the chapter, where you are invited to describe what you are most pleased with in your final essay and to explain what contributed to this achievement. It reminds you that there is much you have learned and much to learn about writing—from reading others' work, from writing your own essays, and from collaborating with other writers.

CHAPTER 2

Autobiography

Autobiography involves telling stories about key events in your life and describing people who played important roles in it. Whether writing about an exhilarating childhood game or a difficult relationship, you should evoke for readers a vivid impression to help them see what you saw, hear what you heard, and feel what you felt. To write autobiography, therefore, you need to revisit the past, immersing yourself in the sights, sounds, and other sensations of memory. You also need to think deeply about the meaning of your experience—why it was and still is significant to you. Thinking deeply about the significance of important events and people in your life can help you discover something about the forces within yourself and within society that have helped to shape who you are and what is important to you.

While writing about your own life can be both enjoyable and instructive, so too can reading about other people's lives. As readers, we often take pleasure in seeing reflections of our own experience in other people's autobiographical writing. We enjoy recognizing similarities between the people and the events we have known and those that we read about. But sometimes the differences can be far more thought-provoking. For example, we may see how certain conditions—such as whether we grew up in the suburbs or the city; whether we are male or female; whether we are of African, European, Asian, Middle Eastern, or other descent—can profoundly affect our lives and perspectives. Autobiography sometimes affirms our preconceptions, but it is most effective when it leads us to question our certainties, challenging us to see ourselves and others in a new light.

Whether you are reading or writing autobiography, it is important to remember that autobiography is public, not private. While it involves self-presentation and contributes to self-knowledge, it does not require writers to make unwanted self-disclosures. Autobiographers compose themselves for readers; they fashion a self in words, much as a novelist creates a character. As readers, we come to "know" the people we read about by the way they are portrayed. Consequently, when you write autobiography, you have to decide how to portray yourself. This decision depends on whom you expect to read your essay (your audience) and what you want to communicate to readers (your purpose).

As you work through this chapter, you will learn more about autobiography by reading several different examples of it. You will see that some autobiographical essays center on a single event that occurred over a brief period of hours or days, while other essays focus on a person who played a significant role in the writer's life. Whether you decide to tell a story about a remembered event or to write about another person, you will practice two of the most basic writing strategies—narration and description. As you will see in later chapters of this book, narration and description can play roles not only in autobiography but also in providing explanations and advancing arguments.

The readings in this chapter will help you learn a lot about autobiography. From the readings and from the ideas for writing that follow each reading, you will get ideas for your own autobiographical essay. As you read and write about the selections, keep in mind the following assignment, which sets out the goals for writing an autobiographical essay. To support your writing of this assignment, the chapter concludes with a Guide to Writing Autobiography.

THE WRITING ASSIGNMENT

Autobiography

Write an autobiographical essay about a significant event or person in your life. Choose the event or person with your readers in mind. The subject should be one that you feel comfortable presenting to others and that will lead readers to reflect on their own lives or on the differences between your personal experiences and their own. Present your experience dramatically and vividly so that readers can imagine what it was like for you. Through a careful choice of words and details, convey the meaning and importance in your life—the autobiographical significance—of this event or person.

WRITING SITUATIONS FOR AUTOBIOGRAPHY

You may think that only scientists, novelists, politicians, movie stars, and other famous people write their autobiographies. But autobiographical writing is much more widespread, as the following examples indicate:

- As part of her college application, a high-school senior includes a brief autobiographical essay that conveys her reasons for wanting to study science and become a researcher. In the essay, she recalls what happened when she did her first scientific experiment on the nutritional effects of different breakfast cereals on mice.

- Asked to recall a significant early childhood memory for an assignment in a psychology class, a college student writes about a fishing trip he took as a nine-year-old. He reflects on the significance of the trip. It was the first trip he took alone with his father, and it began a new stage in their relationship.

- As part of a workshop on management skills, a business executive writes about a person who influenced his ideas about leadership. As he explores his memory and feelings, he realizes that he mistook fear for admiration. He recognizes that he has been emulating the wrong model, an autocratic leader who got people to perform by intimidating them.

THINKING ABOUT YOUR EXPERIENCE WITH AUTOBIOGRAPHY

Before studying a type of writing, it is useful to spend some time thinking about what you already know about it. You have almost certainly told stories about events in your life and described memorable people you have known, even if you have not written down these stories. When you tell such stories, you are composing autobiography. You also may have written autobiographically for school assignments, for a college application, and in letters or e-mails to family and friends.

To reflect on your experience with autobiography, you might recall one particular story you told orally or in writing and then consider questions like these: What made you choose this event or person? What did you want your audience members to think and feel? How did they react to your story? What in your story caught their attention or seemed significant?

Reflect also on the autobiographical stories that have been told to you or that you have read or seen in films or on television. What made these stories interesting? What did you expect from these stories? What do you think others expect from the autobiographical stories you relate to them?

Write at least a page about your experience with autobiography.

■ A Guide to Reading Autobiography

This guide introduces you to autobiographical writing. By completing all the activities in it, you will prepare yourself to learn a great deal from the other readings in this chapter about how to read and write an autobiographical essay. The guide focuses on a brief but powerful piece of autobiography by Annie Dillard. You will read Dillard's autobiographical essay twice. First, you will read it for meaning, seeking to grasp the significance of the event for Dillard—what it meant to her both at the time she experienced it and years later when she wrote about it—as well as the meaning it holds for you. Then you will reread the essay like a writer, analyzing the parts to see how Dillard crafts her essay and to learn the strategies she uses to make her autobiographical writing effective. These two activities—reading for meaning and reading like a writer—follow every reading in this chapter.

ANNIE DILLARD

An American Childhood

Annie Dillard (b. 1945) is a prolific writer whose first book, Pilgrim at Tinker Creek *(1974), won the Pulitzer Prize for nonfiction writing. Since then, she has written meditations on nature and religion, including* For the Time Being *(1999); several collections of poetry, most recently* Mornings Like This *(1996); novels, most recently* The Maytrees *(2007); an account of her work as a writer,* The Writing Life *(1989); and an autobiography,* An American Childhood *(1987), from which the following reading is excerpted. Dillard also coedited* Modern American Memoirs *(1995), a collection of autobiographical works originally published between 1917 and 1992.*

"An American Childhood" relates an event that occurred one winter morning when the seven-year-old Dillard and a friend were chased relentlessly by an adult stranger at whose car they had been throwing snowballs. Dillard admits that she was terrified at the time, and yet paradoxically she asserts that she has "seldom been happier since."

As you read, think about how this apparent contradiction helps you grasp the autobiographical significance of this experience for Dillard. The marginal annotations point to strategies writers of autobiography typically use. Add your own comments and questions, noting anything else you think is interesting.

1   Some boys taught me to play football. This was fine sport. You thought up a new strategy for every play and whispered it to the others. You went out for a pass, fooling everyone. Best, you got to throw yourself mightily at someone's running legs. Either you brought him down or you hit the ground flat out on your chin, with your arms empty before you. It was all or nothing. If you hesitated in fear, you would miss and get hurt: you would take a hard fall while the kid got away, or you would get kicked in the face while the kid got away. But if you flung yourself wholeheartedly at the back of his knees—if you gathered and joined body and soul and pointed them diving fearlessly—then you likely wouldn't get hurt, and you'd stop the ball. Your fate, and your team's score, depended on your concentration and courage. Nothing girls did could compare with it.

> Writers of autobiography sometimes begin by providing a context. As you read, think about how this context helps you grasp why this event is meaningful for Dillard.

Boys welcomed me at baseball, too, for I had, 2 through enthusiastic practice, what was weirdly known as a boy's arm. In winter, in the snow, there was neither baseball nor football, so the boys and I threw snowballs at passing cars. I got in trouble throwing snowballs, and have seldom been happier since.

On one weekday morning after Christmas, six inches 3 of new snow had just fallen. We were standing up to our boot tops in snow on a front yard on trafficked Reynolds Street, waiting for cars. The cars traveled Reynolds Street slowly and evenly; they were targets all but wrapped in red ribbons, cream puffs. We couldn't miss.

I was seven; the boys were eight, nine, and ten. The 4 oldest two Fahey boys were there—Mikey and Peter— polite blond boys who lived near me on Lloyd Street, and who already had four brothers and sisters. My parents approved Mikey and Peter Fahey. Chickie McBride was there, a tough kid, and Billy Paul and Mackie Kean too, from across Reynolds, where the boys grew up dark and furious, grew up skinny, knowing, and skilled. We had all drifted from our houses that morning looking for action, and had found it here on Reynolds Street.

It was cloudy but cold. The cars' tires laid behind 5 them on the snowy street a complex trail of beige chunks like crenellated castle walls. I had stepped on some earlier; they squeaked. We could not have wished for more traffic. When a car came, we all popped it one. In the intervals between cars we reverted to the natural solitude of children.

I started making an iceball—a perfect iceball, from 6 perfectly white snow, perfectly spherical, and squeezed perfectly translucent so no snow remained all the way through. (The Fahey boys and I considered it unfair actually to throw an iceball at somebody, but it had been known to happen.)

I had just embarked on the iceball project when we 7 heard tire chains come clanking from afar. A black Buick was moving toward us down the street. We all spread out, banged together some regular snowballs, took aim, and, when the Buick drew nigh, fired.

A soft snowball hit the driver's windshield right 8 before the driver's face. It made a smashed star with a hump in the middle.

Before narrating what happened, Dillard sets the scene with vivid description, including sensory detail and figurative language.

Setting the scene includes naming and describing the main characters. What do you learn about the narrator from knowing that she is the youngest and the only girl?

Most of Dillard's description is visual, but here the senses of touch and hearing are also evoked. What do these images add?

9   Often, of course, we hit our target, but this time, the only time in all of life, the car pulled over and stopped. Its wide black door opened; a man got out of it, running. He didn't even close the car door.

The man's getting out of the car is a surprising turning point, creating suspense (what will he do when he catches them?) and accelerating the action as the chase begins.

10   He ran after us, and we ran away from him, up the snowy Reynolds sidewalk. At the corner, I looked back; incredibly, he was still after us. He was in city clothes: a suit and tie, street shoes. Any normal adult would have quit, having sprung us into flight and made his point. This man was gaining on us. He was a thin man, all action. All of a sudden, we were running for our lives.

11   Wordless, we split up. We were on our turf; we could lose ourselves in the neighborhood backyards, everyone for himself. I paused and considered. Everyone had vanished except Mikey Fahey, who was just rounding the corner of a yellow brick house. Poor Mikey, I trailed him. The driver of the Buick sensibly picked the two of us to follow. The man apparently had all day.

12   He chased Mikey and me around the yellow house and up a backyard path we knew by heart: under a low tree, up a bank, through a hedge, down some snowy steps, and across the grocery store's delivery driveway. We smashed through a gap in another hedge, entered a scruffy backyard and ran around its back porch and tight between houses to Edgerton Avenue; we ran across Edgerton to an alley and up our own sliding woodpile to the Halls' front yard; he kept coming. We ran up Lloyd Street and wound through mazy backyards toward the steep hilltop at Willard and Lang.

Notice how Dillard makes her narrative vivid and intense, creating a motion picture in words.

13   He chased us silently, block after block. He chased us silently over picket fences, through thorny hedges, between houses, around garbage cans, and across streets. Every time I glanced back, choking for breath, I expected he would have quit. He must have been as breathless as we were. His jacket strained over his body. It was an immense discovery, pounding into my hot head with every sliding, joyous step, that this ordinary adult evidently knew what I thought only children who trained at football knew: that you have to fling yourself at what you're doing, you have to point yourself, forget yourself, aim, dive.

This personal perspective lets readers see what she saw and feel what she felt and enables them to identify with the young Dillard.

14   Mikey and I had nowhere to go, in our own neighborhood or out of it, but away from this man who was chasing us. He impelled us forward; we compelled

him to follow our route. The air was cold; every breath tore my throat. We kept running, block after block; we kept improvising, backyard after backyard, running a frantic course and choosing it simultaneously, failing always to find small places or hard places to slow him down, and discovering always, exhilarated, dismayed, that only bare speed could save us—for he would never give up, this man—and we were losing speed.

₁₅ He chased us through the backyard labyrinths of ten blocks before he caught us by our jackets. He caught us and we all stopped.

When the man catches Mikey and Dillard, the narrative reaches its climax—the high point of suspense leading readers to wonder what the man will do to them.

₁₆ We three stood staggering, half blinded, coughing, in an obscure hilltop backyard: a man in his twenties, a boy, a girl. He had released our jackets, our pursuer, our captor, our hero: he knew we weren't going anywhere. We all played by the rules. Mikey and I unzipped our jackets. I pulled off my sopping mittens. Our tracks multiplied in the backyard's new snow. We had been breaking new snow all morning. We didn't look at each other. I was cherishing my excitement. The man's lower pants legs were wet; his cuffs were full of snow, and there was a prow of snow beneath them on his shoes and socks. Some trees bordered the little flat backyard, some messy winter trees. There was no one around: a clearing in a grove, and we the only players.

₁₇ It was a long time before he could speak. I had some difficulty at first recalling why we were there. My lips felt swollen; I couldn't see out of the sides of my eyes; I kept coughing.

₁₈ "You stupid kids," he began perfunctorily.

The man's words are surprising, and Dillard repeats them in paragraph 20. Note the language (highlighted) she uses to describe how he speaks and how she felt about his actions.

₁₉ We listened perfunctorily indeed, if we listened at all, for the chewing out was redundant, a mere formality, and beside the point. The point was that he had chased us passionately without giving up, and so he had caught us. Now he came down to earth. I wanted the glory to last forever.

₂₀ But how could the glory have lasted forever? We could have run through every backyard in North America until we got to Panama. But when he trapped us at the lip of the Panama Canal, what precisely could he have done to prolong the drama of the chase and cap its glory? I brooded about this for the next few years. He could only have fried Mikey Fahey and me in boiling oil, say, or dismembered us piecemeal, or staked us to anthills. None of which I really wanted, and none

of which any adult was likely to do, even in the spirit of fun. He could only chew us out there in the Panamanian jungle, after months or years of exalting pursuit. He could only begin, "You stupid kids," and continue in his ordinary Pittsburgh accent with his normal righteous anger and the usual common sense.

21   If in that snowy backyard the driver of the black Buick had cut off our heads, Mikey's and mine, I would have died happy, for nothing has required so much of me since as being chased all over Pittsburgh in the middle of winter—running terrified, exhausted—by this sainted, skinny, furious redheaded man who wished to have a word with us. I don't know how he found his way back to his car.

Dillard looks back on the event from her present adult perspective, giving insight into why it was significant for her. Why do you think she calls the man "sainted"?

READING FOR MEANING

This section presents three activities that will help you reread Dillard's autobiographical essay with a critical eye. Done in sequence, these activities lead you from a basic understanding of the selection to a more personal response to it and finally to an analysis that deepens your understanding and critical thinking about what you are reading.

Read to Comprehend

Reread the selection, and write a few sentences briefly explaining what happened that winter morning when Dillard was seven years old. The following definitions may help you understand Dillard's vocabulary:

reverted: (paragraph 5): returned to a previous condition, often one considered less desirable or inferior.

perfunctorily (18): routinely, with little interest or care.

righteous (20): morally correct or proper.

Identify three or more additional words that you don't understand, and find the best definitions from the dictionary that work with their context.

To expand your understanding of this reading, you might use one or more of the following critical reading strategies that are explained and illustrated in Appendix 1: *outlining, summarizing, paraphrasing,* and *questioning to understand and remember.*

Read to Respond

Write several paragraphs exploring your initial thoughts and feelings about Dillard's autobiographical narrative. Focus on anything that stands out for you, perhaps because it resonates with your own experience or because you find a statement puzzling.

You might consider writing about the following:

- how a particular scene—such as the iceballing (paragraphs 5–8) or confrontation (15–21) scene—contributes to your understanding of the event's significance for Dillard;

- why you think Dillard uses such words as "hero" (16) and "sainted" (21) to describe the man who chased her, even though she dismisses what he said when he finally caught her as "redundant, a mere formality, and beside the point" (19); or

- how Dillard's experience reminds you of something you experienced.

To develop your response to Dillard's essay, you might use one or more of the following critical reading strategies that are explained and illustrated in Appendix 1: *contextualizing, recognizing emotional manipulation,* and *judging the writer's credibility.*

Read to Analyze Assumptions

Reread Dillard's autobiographical essay, and write a paragraph or two exploring one or more of the assumptions you find in the text. All writing contains *assumptions*—opinions, values, and beliefs that are taken for granted as commonly accepted truths by the writer or others. Personal or individual assumptions also tend to reflect the values and beliefs of a particular group or community, sometimes called *cultural ideology*, which shape the way those in the group think, act, and understand the world.

Analyzing assumptions is an important part of learning to read critically because assumptions tend to be unexamined and unquestioned (at least consciously) by those who hold them. When you read with a critical eye, you identify important assumptions in the text and ask questions about them. Sometimes assumptions are stated explicitly, but often they are only implied, so you may have to search for underlying assumptions in the word choices and examples. Here are some kinds of questions you should ask regarding the assumptions you find: Who holds this assumption? How does the assumption reinforce or critique the status quo? What alternative ideas, beliefs, or values would challenge this assumption? If the writer uses the assumption to appeal to readers, how effective do you think this appeal is, and why?

To help you get started reading for assumptions in Dillard's essay, notice her use of the ideas of courage and heroism. She refers to *courage* in paragraph 1 to describe what she values most in the fearless way she was taught to play football and *heroism* in paragraph 16 when she calls the man who chased her "our hero." These words are surprising to find in an essay about a man who jumped out of his car to chase kids who threw a snowball at his windshield. Together, they evoke a cultural ideology often associated with war and masculinity, assumptions that would benefit from critical scrutiny. Consider whether learning to play sports "fearlessly" in the way that Dillard was taught to play football trains children (especially boys, as Dillard says) to be valiant soldiers, willing to risk their lives and even enjoying the danger for its own sake. You might also ask yourself under what circumstances and for what goals the courage to risk life and limb is something to be valued. When does acting fearlessly become recklessness? Furthermore, aren't there other, quieter, less muscular and dramatic forms that courage and heroism can take—for example, when someone blows the whistle on wrongdoers or "speaks truth to power" by challenging a more powerful person on a moral issue? Which kind of courage do you think is most valued in our culture, and why?

You may want to examine Dillard's assumptions about the value of courage and heroism. Consider whether she seems to assume that her readers will agree with her or whether her story about the chase is designed to illustrate their value for skeptical readers. Or you might explore other assumptions in Dillard's essay that you may have touched on in one of the other Reading for Meaning or Reading Like a Writer activities, such as the following:

- **assumptions about rules and fair play.** Dillard asserts proudly that "[w]e all played by the rules" (paragraph 16) and that she and the Fahey boys "considered it unfair actually to throw an iceball at somebody" (6). Words like *rules* and *unfair* suggest there are principles of conduct or ethics that determine what is considered fair or right. To think critically about the assumptions in this essay related to rules and fairness, ask yourself: Whose rules are at issue in this essay? What typically happens when rules are broken or when different rules or values come into conflict? What rule do you think the man in this essay assumes that the kids have broken? What evidence is there that the kids—or at least the young Dillard—do or do not understand they have broken a rule?

- **assumptions about gender differences.** Dillard refers to gender differences when she describes the way the neighborhood boys taught her to play football and claims that "[n]othing girls did could compare with it" (paragraph 1). To think critically about the assumptions in this essay related to gender differences, ask yourself: What does Dillard seem to be saying about gender at the time (1950s) and place (Pittsburgh, an industrial city) that she is describing? Whose assumptions are they—Dillard's own assumptions during her childhood, those of mainstream American culture of the period, those of girls or women as well as boys or men? How has the situation changed, if at all?

- **assumptions about age or generational differences.** Dillard seems to make an assumption about the difference between children and adults when she writes: "Any normal adult would have quit, having sprung us into flight and made his point" (paragraph 10). She also reflects on the difference between her own childhood and adulthood when she asserts that "nothing has required so much of me since" (paragraph 21). What does she seem to be saying about the difference between childhood and adulthood here? To think critically about the assumptions in this essay related to age or generational differences, ask yourself: What do you think is "normal" and not normal about the man's actions? The word *normal* implies a standard that is customary or expected. What do you suppose most people would think if they saw the man chasing young kids after they had thrown a snowball at his car?

To probe assumptions more deeply, you might use one or more of the following critical reading strategies that are explained and illustrated in Appendix 1: *reflecting on challenges to your beliefs and values*, *exploring the significance of figurative language*, and *looking for patterns of opposition*.

READING LIKE A WRITER

This section leads you through an analysis of Dillard's autobiographical writing strategies: *narrating the story*, *presenting people*, *describing places*, and *conveying the autobiographical significance*. For each strategy, you will be asked to reread and annotate part of Dillard's essay to see how she uses the strategy to accomplish her particular purpose.

When you study the selections later in this chapter, you will see how different autobiographers use these same strategies for different purposes. The Guide to Writing Autobiography near the end of the chapter suggests ways you can use these strategies in your own writing.

Narrating the Story

Whether focusing on a single event or a person, writers nearly always tell a story or several brief stories called *anecdotes*. Stories are so pervasive in our culture, indeed in most cultures, that we are all familiar with what makes a story effective. A well-told story draws readers in by arousing their curiosity and often keeps them reading by building suspense or drama, making them want to know what will happen next.

Dillard's essay focuses on a single incident that occurred in a relatively short span of time. A chase is by nature dramatic because it is suspenseful. Readers want to know whether the man will catch the kids and, if he does, what will happen. Dillard heightens the drama in several ways. One strategy she uses is *identification*, letting us into her point of view. In addition, she uses *surprise*. In fact, Dillard surprises us from beginning to end. The first surprise is that the man gets out of the car. But when he chases the kids and then continues to chase them beyond the point that most reasonable people would do so, the suspense increases. We simply cannot know what such a man is capable of doing.

Another important strategy Dillard uses is *emphasizing action verb forms*. Here is a sentence with several action verbs (underlined): "We all spread out, banged together some regular snowballs, took aim, and, when the Buick drew nigh, fired" (paragraph 7). These verbs describe vividly a series of actions. Now look at the verbs in these two sentences: "This man was gaining on us. He was a thin man, all action" (paragraph 10). Both sentences use the verb *was*, but only the first sentence has an action verb (by combining *was* with the *-ing* form: "was gaining"). The verb in the second sentence is not an action verb; instead, it serves as a kind of equal sign describing a quality or characteristic of the subject ("a thin man"). As writers, we use both kinds of verbs, but in narrative writing action verbs tend to predominate. This activity will help you see how Dillard uses action verbs.

Analyze

1. *Reread* paragraphs 11 to 15 underlining as many of the action verbs as you can find. Do not worry if you miss some.

2. Also *underline* as many verbals as you can. Verbals are verb forms that usually end in *ing* as in "staggering" and "coughing" (paragraph 16), or *ed*, as in "blinded" (16) and "smashed" (8), or that begin with *to*, as in "to fling" and "to point" (13).

3. *Find* two or three sentences in which the action verbs and verbals help you imagine the drama of the chase.

Write

Write several sentences explaining what you have learned about Dillard's use of verbs and verbals to represent action and to make her narrative dramatic. *Use examples* from paragraphs 11 and 15 to support your explanation.

Presenting People

Autobiographers describe people by depicting what they look like, by letting readers hear how they speak, and by characterizing their behavior and personality. Often, one or two specific details about the way a person looks, dresses, talks, or acts will be sufficient to give readers a vivid impression of the person. As you will see when you read the essays later in this chapter by Anne Morgan Gray and Brad Benioff, even autobiographical essays that focus on a person rather than a single event tend to use only a few well-chosen details to present the person.

To see how Dillard presents people, let us look at the descriptions of the neighborhood boys in paragraph 4. Notice that she gives each boy a brief descriptive tag: "Mikey and Peter — polite blond boys who lived near me on Lloyd Street" and "Chickie McBride . . . a tough kid, and Billy Paul and Mackie Kean too, from across Reynolds, where the boys grew up dark and furious, grew up skinny, knowing, and skilled." The details "blond" and "skinny" create a visual image, whereas "polite," "tough," and "knowing" convey Dillard's characterizations or evaluations of the boys. These characterizations or evaluations contribute not only to the impression we get of each boy but also to our understanding of his significance in the writer's life. (As you will see later in the chapter, such characterizations are one way writers convey autobiographical significance.)

Analyze

1. In paragraphs 10, 16, and 21, *find* and *underline* words and phrases that visually describe the man. Also *put brackets around* words and phrases that characterize or evaluate the man.

2. *Look* at paragraph 18 and the last sentence of paragraph 20, where Dillard presents the man through dialogue. *Underline* the details used to describe how the man looks and sounds. Also *put brackets around* words and phrases used to characterize or evaluate what the man says and how he says it.

3. *Think about* how Dillard's presentation of the man in these five paragraphs helps you see him in your mind's eye and understand his role in the chase.

Write

Based on your analysis, *write* several sentences examining Dillard's use of descriptive details and characterizations to present the man. *Use examples* from the words and phrases you underlined and bracketed to support your ideas.

Describing Places

Whether autobiography centers on an event or a person, it nearly always includes some description of places. Writers make a remembered place vivid by naming memorable objects they want readers to see there and by detailing these objects. For examples of *naming* and *detailing,* look at paragraph 3, where Dillard describes what it looked like on that particular morning after Christmas. Notice that Dillard uses naming to point out the snow, Reynolds Street, and the cars. She also adds details that give information about these objects: "*six inches* of *new* snow," "*trafficked* Reynolds Street," "cars traveled . . . *slowly* and *evenly.*"

To make her description evocative as well as vivid, Dillard adds a third describing strategy: *comparing.* In paragraph 5, for example, she describes the trail made by car tires in the snow as being "like crenellated castle walls." The word *like* makes the comparison explicit and identifies it as a simile. Dillard also uses implicit comparisons, called metaphors, such as when she calls the cars "targets all but wrapped in red ribbons, cream puffs" (paragraph 3).

Analyze

1. *Examine* how Dillard uses naming and detailing to describe the "perfect iceball" in paragraph 6. What does she name it, and what details does she add to specify the qualities that make an iceball "perfect"?

2. Then *look closely* at the two comparisons in paragraphs 3 and 5. *Notice* also the following comparisons in other paragraphs: "smashed star" (8), "sprung us into flight" (10), "mazy backyards" (12), "every breath tore my throat" (14), and "backyard labyrinths" (15). Choose any single comparison—

simile or metaphor — in the reading, and *think about* how it helps you imagine what the place was like for Dillard on that day.

Write

Write a few sentences explaining how Dillard uses the describing strategies of *naming*, *detailing*, and *comparing* to help you imagine what the places she presents seemed like during the chase. *Give at least one example* from the reading of each describing strategy.

Conveying the Autobiographical Significance

Autobiographers convey the significance of an event or a person in two ways: by *showing* and by *telling*. Through your analyses of how Dillard narrates the story, presents people, and describes places, you have looked at some of the ways she *shows* the event's significance. This activity focuses on what Dillard *tells* readers.

When Dillard writes in the opening paragraphs about boys teaching her to play football and baseball, she is telling why these experiences were memorable and important. Autobiographers usually tell both what they remember thinking and feeling *at the time* and what they think and feel now *as they write about the past*. Readers must infer from the ideas and the writer's choice of words whether a phrase or sentence conveys the writer's past or present perspective, remembered feelings and thoughts or current ones. For example, look at the following sentences from paragraph 1: "You thought up a new strategy for every play and whispered it to the others. You went out for a pass, fooling everyone." The words "whispered" and "fooling" suggest that here Dillard is trying to reconstruct a seven-year-old child's way of speaking and thinking. In contrast, when she tells us that football was a "fine sport" and what was fine about it — "Your fate, and your team's score, depended on your concentration and courage" — we can infer from words such as "fate," "concentration," and "courage" that Dillard is speaking from her present adult perspective, telling us what she may have sensed as a child but now can more fully understand and articulate.

To determine the autobiographical significance of the remembered event or person, readers need to pay attention to what Dillard tells about the significance — both her remembered feelings and thoughts and her present perspective.

Analyze

1. *Reread* paragraphs 19 to 21, where Dillard comments on the chase and the man's "chewing out." *Put brackets around* words and phrases that tell what the adult Dillard is thinking as she writes about this event from her past. For example, in the first sentence of paragraph 19, "perfunctorily," "redundant," and "a mere formality" may seem to you to be examples of adult language, rather than words a seven-year-old would use.

2. Then *underline* words and phrases in the same paragraphs that seem to convey thoughts and feelings that Dillard remembers from when she was a child.

Write

Write several sentences explaining what you have learned about the event's significance for Dillard. What does she tell readers about the thoughts and feelings she had as a child as well as the thoughts and feelings she has now as an adult looking back on the experience? *Quote* selected words and phrases from your underlining and bracketing, indicating what identifies them as either remembered or present-perspective thoughts and feelings.

A SPECIAL READING STRATEGY

Comparing and Contrasting Related Readings: Dillard's "An American Childhood" and Rodriguez's "Always Running"

Comparing and contrasting related readings is a critical reading strategy useful both in reading for meaning and in reading like a writer. This strategy is particularly applicable when writers present similar subjects, as is the case in the autobiographical narratives in this chapter by Annie Dillard (p. 15) and Luis J. Rodriguez (p. 33). Both writers tell what happened when they broke the rules and were chased by adults. In both instances, their transgressions are relatively minor; however, the chase is viewed very differently by each writer and its results also differ dramatically. To compare and contrast these two autobiographies, think about issues such as these:

- Compare these essays in terms of their cultural and historical contexts. What seems to you to be most significant about the two versions of an American childhood represented in these essays?

- Compare how the two writers make their narratives dramatic. Compare the strategies Dillard uses in presenting the chase (paragraphs 11–14) with those Rodriguez uses (27–32). In addition to looking at the kinds of verbs each writer employs, you might also analyze how they construct sentences to push the action forward or slow it down. Notice also the length of the sentences and how much information the writers pack into sentences.

See Appendix 1 for detailed guidelines on using the comparing and contrasting related readings strategy.

■ Readings

SAIRA SHAH

Longing to Belong

> *Saira Shah (b. 1964) is a journalist and documentary filmmaker. The daughter of an Afghan father and Indian mother, she was born and educated in England. After graduating from the School of Oriental and African Studies at London University, Shah began her career as a freelance journalist in the 1980s, reporting on the Afghan guerrillas who were fighting the Soviet occupation; eventually she became a war correspondent for Britain's Channel 4 News. She is the recipient of the Courage under Fire and Television Journalist of the Year awards for her risky reporting on conflicts in some of the world's most troubled areas, including the Persian Gulf and Kosovo. She is best known in the United States for her undercover documentary films about the Taliban rule in Afghanistan,* Beneath the Veil *(2001) and* Unholy War *(2002).*
>
> *"Longing to Belong," originally published in the* New York Times Magazine *in 2003, is adapted from Shah's autobiography,* The Storyteller's Daughter *(2003), which relates her search to understand her father's homeland of Afghanistan. In this essay, Shah tells what happened when, at the age of seventeen, she visited her father's Afghan relatives living in Pakistan. As she explained in an interview, "I wanted this kind of romantic vision. This is the exile's condition, though, isn't it? If you grow up outside the place that you think of as your home, you want it to be impossibly marvelous. There is also the question of how Afghan I am. When I was growing up, I had this secret doubt — which I couldn't even admit to myself — that I was not at all an Afghan because I was born in Britain to a mixed family."*
>
> *As you read, think about Shah's search for her ethnic identity and the sense of cultural dislocation she experiences. Annotate the text, noting places where her sense of cultural dislocation is evident and anything else interesting about Shah's autobiographical writing strategies. (For help annotating, see the examples in this chapter on pages 15 and 58, as well as the advice on annotating on pages 597–603.)*

The day he disclosed his matrimonial ambitions for me, my   1
uncle sat me at his right during lunch. This was a sign of special favor, as it allowed him to feed me choice tidbits from his own plate. It was by no means an unadulterated pleasure. He would often generously withdraw a half-chewed delicacy from his mouth and lovingly cram it into mine — an Afghan habit with which I have since tried to come to terms. It was his way of telling me that I was valued, part of the family.

My brother and sister, Tahir and Safia, and my elderly aunt Amina and I were all attending the wedding of my uncle's son. Although my uncle's home was closer than I'd ever been, I was not yet inside Afghanistan. This branch of my family lived in Peshawar, Pakistan. On seeing two unmarried daughters in the company of a female chaperone, my uncle obviously concluded that we had been sent to be married. I was taken aback by the visceral longing I felt to be part of this world. I had never realized that I had been starved of anything. Now, at 17, I discovered that like a princess in a fairy tale, I had been cut off from my origins. This was the point in the tale where, simply by walking through a magical door, I could recover my gardens and palaces. If I allowed my uncle to arrange a marriage for me, I would belong.

Over the next few days, the man my family wished me to marry was introduced into the inner sanctum. He was a distant cousin. His luxuriant black mustache was generally considered to compensate for his lack of height. I was told breathlessly that he was a fighter pilot in the Pakistani Air Force. As an outsider, he wouldn't have been permitted to meet an unmarried girl. But as a relative, he had free run of the house. Whenever I appeared, a female cousin would fling a child into his arms. He'd pose with it, whiskers twitching, while the women cooed their admiration.

A huge cast of relatives had assembled to see my uncle's son marry. The wedding lasted nearly 14 days and ended with a reception. The bride and groom sat on an elevated stage to receive greetings. While the groom was permitted to laugh and chat, the bride was required to sit perfectly still, her eyes demurely lowered. I didn't see her move for four hours.

Watching this *tableau vivant* of a submissive Afghan bride, I knew that marriage would never be my easy route to the East. I could live in my father's mythological homeland only through the eyes of the storyteller. In my desire to experience the fairy tale, I had overlooked the staggeringly obvious: the storyteller was a man. If I wanted freedom, I would have to cut my own path. I began to understand why my uncle's wife had resorted to using religion to regain some control—at least in her own home. Her piety gave her license to impose her will on others.

My putative fiancé returned to Quetta, from where he sent a constant flow of lavish gifts. I was busy examining my hoard when my uncle's wife announced that he was on the phone. My intended was a favorite of hers; she had taken it upon herself to promote the match. As she handed me the receiver, he delivered a line culled straight from a Hindi movie: "We shall have a love-match, *ach-cha*?" Enough was enough. I slammed down the phone and went to find Aunt

Amina. When she had heard me out, she said: "I'm glad that finally you've stopped this silly wild goose chase for your roots. I'll have to extricate you from this mess. Wait here while I put on something more impressive." As a piece of Islamic one-upmanship, she returned wearing not one but three head scarves of different colors.

My uncle's wife was sitting on her prayer platform in the drawing room. Amina stormed in, scattering servants before her like chaff. "Your relative . . . ," was Amina's opening salvo, ". . . has been making obscene remarks to my niece." Her mouth opened, but before she could find her voice, Amina fired her heaviest guns: "Over the *telephone!*"

"How dare you!" her rival began.

It gave Amina exactly the opportunity she needed to move in for the kill. "What? Do you support this lewd conduct? Are we living in an American movie? Since when have young people of mixed sexes been permitted to speak to each other *on the telephone*? Let alone to talk—as I regret to inform you your nephew did—of love! Since when has love had anything to do with marriage? What a dangerous and absurd concept!"

My Peshawari aunt was not only outclassed; she was out-Islamed too. "My niece is a rose that hasn't been plucked," Amina said. "It is my task as her chaperone to ensure that this happy state of affairs continues. A match under such circumstances is quite out of the question. The engagement is off." My uncle's wife lost her battle for moral supremacy and, it seemed, her battle for sanity as well. In a gruff, slack-jawed way that I found unappealing, she made a sharp, inhuman sound that sounded almost like a bark.

READING FOR MEANING

This section presents three activities that will help you reread Shah's autobiographical essay with a critical eye. Done in sequence, these activities lead you from a basic understanding of the selection to a more personal response to it and finally to an analysis that deepens your understanding and critical thinking about what you are reading.

Read to Comprehend

Reread the selection, and write a few sentences briefly explaining what happened during Shah's visit with relatives in Pakistan. The following definitions may help you understand Shah's vocabulary:

unadulterated (paragraph 1): pure, not mixed; containing nothing that would detract from its effect.

tableau vivant (5): a scene or portrait that is acted out.

putative (6): generally regarded or accepted as being (something).

Identify three or more additional words that you don't understand, and find the best definitions from the dictionary that work with their context.

To expand your understanding of this reading, you might use one or more of the following critical reading strategies that are explained and illustrated in Appendix 1: *outlining, summarizing, paraphrasing,* and *questioning to understand and remember.*

Read to Respond

Write several paragraphs exploring your initial thoughts and feelings about Shah's autobiographical story. Focus on anything that stands out for you, perhaps because it resonates with your own experience or because you find a statement puzzling.

You might consider writing about the following:

- Shah's "longing to belong";

- Shah's experience of new and different cultural traditions—perhaps in relation to your own experience;

- her uncle's assumption that Shah and her sister were sent to Pakistan "to be married" (paragraph 2); or

- Shah's realization that "[i]f I wanted freedom, I would have to cut my own path" (5).

To develop your response to Shah's essay, you might use one or more of the following critical reading strategies that are explained and illustrated in Appendix 1: *contextualizing* and *reflecting on challenges to your beliefs and values.*

Read to Analyze Assumptions

Reread Shah's autobiographical essay, and write a paragraph or two exploring one or more of the assumptions you find in the text. The following suggestions may help:

- **assumptions about cultural differences.** Shah begins her story by describing her uncle's "Afghan habit" of feeding her "choice tidbits from his own plate," sometimes taken "from his mouth" (paragraph 1). Shah's word choices such as *generously withdraw* and *lovingly cram* might be read as ironic (suggesting these actions are not really generous or loving), but they may also signal that Shah is ambivalent, that she recognizes her uncle's affectionate intentions at the same time that she is somewhat repelled by his actions. To think critically about the assumptions in this essay related to these cultural differences, ask yourself: Where else in this reading do you find evidence of cultural differences? Which of these cultural differences cannot be bridged or at least pose the greatest challenge? What values, beliefs, ideas, or attitudes underlie these differences and make them so difficult to overcome?

- **assumptions about gender differences.** When Shah uses the phrase "romantic vision" (headnote) and describes herself as "a princess in a fairy tale" (paragraph 2), she is talking about the impact her father's stories about his "mythological homeland" had on her as a child (5). But watching her cousin and his "submissive Afghan bride" makes her realize that "[i]n my desire to experience the fairy tale, I had overlooked the staggeringly obvious: the storyteller was a man" (5). To think critically about the assumptions in this essay related to gender differences, ask yourself: Why does watching her cousin and his bride inspire this realization? What kinds of values, attitudes, and behaviors are girls taught by fairy-tale characters like Cinderella, Sleeping Beauty, Snow White, and the Little Mermaid?

To probe assumptions more deeply, you might use one or more of the following critical reading strategies that are explained and illustrated in Appendix 1: *reflecting on challenges to your beliefs and values*, *exploring the significance of figurative language*, and *looking for patterns of opposition*.

READING LIKE A WRITER
CONVEYING AUTOBIOGRAPHICAL SIGNIFICANCE

Shah conveys the autobiographical significance of the event through a combination of showing and telling. She begins the essay with a vivid image of her uncle: "He would often generously withdraw a half-chewed delicacy from his mouth and lovingly cram it into mine." This image conveys dramatically how she felt at the time, especially to Western readers who, like her, are inclined to be repelled by this particular cultural practice. The choice of the word *cram*, because it implies force, conveys a sense not only of disgust but also of violation. Yet by modifying *cram* with the adverb *lovingly*, Shah makes clear the ambivalence of her feelings. When she calls her uncle's behavior "an Afghan habit," she suggests to her Western readers that it should be read not as a sign of domination but of love and acceptance. In effect, by taking food from his own mouth, he is extending to her his protection and treating her as if she were his own daughter.

Analyze

1. Shah uses a vivid image to convey her remembered feelings when she describes herself as "a princess in a fairy tale" (paragraph 2). *Reread* paragraphs 2 and 3 to see how she imagines this fairy tale and what she feels about

the reality of her experience. *Underline* the words or phrases that show or tell you how Shah feels about the man with whom she has been matched.

2. *Reread* paragraphs 4 and 5 to see how the image of her uncle's son and his bride affect her fairy-tale fantasy. *Underline* words or phrases that show or tell how Shah feels about the role in which she has cast herself.

Write

Write several sentences explaining what you have learned about the autobiographical significance of this event for Shah. *Give two or three examples* from your underlining to support your explanation.

CONSIDERING IDEAS FOR YOUR OWN WRITING

Like Shah, consider writing about an event that you were looking forward to but that turned out differently than you had expected—perhaps a dreadful disappointment, a delightful surprise, or more likely a surprising combination of disappointment and delight. You might write about a time when you had thought you wanted something but then realized your desires were more complicated, when you were trying to fit in and discovered something about yourself or about the group to which you wanted to belong, or when you tried to conform to someone else's expectations for you or decided not to try to conform, but to rebel and go your own way. If, like Shah's, your experience involves a clash of cultures, you might write about that aspect of your experience and how it has affected you.

LUIS J. RODRIGUEZ
Always Running

Luis J. Rodriguez (b. 1954) is an award-winning writer who has published many books, including the short-story collection The Republic of East L.A.: Stories *(2002), the novel* Music of the Mill *(2005), the children's book* It Doesn't Have to Be This Way: A Barrio Story *(1999),* Poems across the Pavement *(1989), the CD* My Name's Not Rodriguez *(2002), and the best-selling autobiography* Always Running: La Vida Loca, Gang Days in L.A. *(1993), from which this selection is excerpted. Among the many honors bestowed upon Rodriguez are the Chicago Sun-Times Book Award, a New York Times Notable Book Award, the Lila Wallace-Reader's Digest Writers' Award, and the Hispanic Heritage Award for Literature. Rodriguez also occasionally writes essays for* The Nation, Los Angeles Weekly, *and* Americas Review. *In addition to writing, Rodriguez has helped found several arts organizations in Chicago and Los Angeles and a nonprofit community group that works with gang members and other young people. If you want to learn more about Rodriguez, visit his official Web site at http://www.luisjrodriguez.com.*

In this excerpt from his autobiography, which he began writing when he was fifteen years old, Rodriguez tells what happened at the age of ten when he trespassed to play basketball in a school yard. As you read, put yourself in the young Rodriguez's place. Would you have climbed the fence? When you were a child, where could you go to play? If you were caught playing in a school yard after hours, would you run, as Rodriguez and his friend did?

One evening dusk came early in South San Gabriel, with wind 1
and cold spinning to earth. People who had been sitting on porches or on metal chairs near fold-up tables topped with cards and beer bottles collected their things to go inside. Others put on sweaters or jackets. A storm gathered beyond the trees.

Tino and I strolled past the stucco and wood-frame homes of 2
the neighborhood consisting mostly of Mexicans with a sprinkling of poor white families (usually from Oklahoma, Arkansas and Texas). *Ranchera* music did battle with Country & Western songs as we continued toward the local elementary school, an oil-and-grime stained basketball under my arm.

We stopped in front of a chain-link fence which surrounded the 3
school. An old brick building cast elongated shadows over a basketball court of concrete on the other side of the fence. Leaves and paper swirled in tiny tornadoes.

"Let's go over," Tino proposed. 4

I looked up and across the fence. A sign above us read: NO ONE 5
ALLOWED AFTER 4:30 PM, BY ORDER OF THE LOS ANGELES COUNTY

SHERIFF'S DEPARTMENT. Tino turned toward me, shrugged his shoulders and gave me a who-cares look.

"Help me up, man, then throw the ball over." 6

I cupped my hands and lifted Tino up while the boy scaled the 7
fence, jumped over and landed on sneakered feet.

"Come on, Luis, let's go," Tino shouted from the other side. 8

I threw over the basketball, walked back a ways, then ran and 9
jumped on the fence, only to fall back. Although we were both
10 years old, I cut a shorter shadow.

"Forget you, man," Tino said. "I'm going to play without you." 10

"Wait!" I yelled, while walking further back. I crouched low to 11
the ground, then took off, jumped up and placed torn sneakers in
the steel mesh. I made it over with a big thud.

Wiping the grass and dirt from my pants, I casually walked up 12
to the ball on the ground, picked it up, and continued past Tino
toward the courts.

"Hey Tino, what are you waiting for?" 13

The gusts proved no obstacle for a half-court game of B-ball, 14
even as dark clouds smothered the sky.

Boy voices interspersed with ball cracking on asphalt. Tino's 15
lanky figure seemed to float across the court, as if he had wings
under his thin arms. Just then, a black-and-white squad car cruised
down the street. A searchlight sprayed across the school yard. The
vehicle slowed to a halt. The light shone toward the courts and
caught Tino in mid-flight of a lay-up.

The dribbling and laughter stopped. 16

"All right, this is the sheriff's," a voice commanded. Two depu- 17
ties stood by the fence, batons and flashlights in hand.

"Let's get out of here," Tino responded. 18

"What do you mean?" I countered. "Why don't we just stay 19
here?"

"You nuts! We trespassing, man," Tino replied. "When they get a 20
hold of us, they going to beat the crap out of us."

"Are you sure?" 21

"I know, believe me, I know." 22

"So where do we go?" 23

By then one of the deputies shouted back: "You boys get over 24
here by the fence—now!"

But Tino dropped the ball and ran. I heard the deputies yell for 25
Tino to stop. One of them began climbing the fence. I decided to
take off too.

It never stopped, this running. We were constant prey, and the 26
hunters soon became big blurs: the police, the gangs, the junkies,
the dudes on Garvey Boulevard who took our money, all smudged
into one. Sometimes they were teachers who jumped on us Mexi-

cans as if we were born with a hideous stain. We were always afraid. Always running.

Tino and I raced toward the dark boxes called classrooms. The rooms lay there, hauntingly still without the voices of children, the commands of irate teachers or the clapping sounds of books as they were closed. The rooms were empty, forbidden places at night. We scurried around the structures toward a courtyard filled with benches next to the cafeteria building.   27

Tino hopped on a bench, then pulled himself over a high fence. He walked a foot or two on top of it, stopped, and proceeded to climb over to the cafeteria's rooftop. I looked over my shoulder. The deputies weren't far behind, their guns drawn. I grabbed hold of the fence on the side of the cafeteria. I looked up and saw Tino's perspiring face over the roof's edge, his arm extended down toward me.   28

I tried to climb up, my feet dangling. But then a firm hand seized a foot and pulled at it.   29

"They got me!" I yelled.   30

Tino looked below. A deputy spied the boy and called out: "Get down here . . . you *greaser*!"   31

Tino straightened up and disappeared. I heard a flood of footsteps on the roof—then a crash. Soon an awful calm covered us.   32

"Tino!" I cried out.   33

A deputy restrained me as the other one climbed onto the roof. He stopped at a skylight, jagged edges on one of its sides. Shining a flashlight inside the building, the officer spotted Tino's misshapen body on the floor, sprinkled over with shards of glass.   34

READING FOR MEANING

This section presents three activities that will help you reread with a critical eye the selection from Rodriguez's autobiography. Done in sequence, these activities lead you from a basic understanding of the selection to a more personal response to it and finally to an analysis that deepens your understanding and critical thinking about what you are reading.

Read to Comprehend

Reread the selection, and write a few sentences briefly explaining what happened when Rodriguez and his friend Tino tried to play basketball in the school yard. The following definitions may help you understand Rodriguez's vocabulary:

elongated (paragraph 3): stretched out.

lay-up (15): a shot in basketball.

irate (27): showing or feeling extreme anger.

Find three or more additional words that you don't understand, and find the best definitions from the dictionary that work with their context.

To expand your understanding of this reading, you might use one or more of the following critical reading strategies that are explained and illustrated in Appendix 1: *outlining, summarizing, paraphrasing,* and *questioning to understand and remember.*

Read to Respond

Write several paragraphs exploring your initial thoughts and feelings about Rodriguez's autobiographical story. Focus on anything that stands out for you, perhaps because it resonates with your own experience or because you find a statement puzzling.

You might consider writing about the following:

- the shocking conclusion;

- the relationship between Rodriguez and Tino—perhaps reflecting on relationships you have had with friends;

- the sign posted on the school yard fence and the boys' reaction to it; or

- the behavior of the police and of the boys when the police arrive.

To develop your response to Rodriguez's essay, you might use one or more of the following critical reading strategies that are explained and illustrated in Appendix 1: *contextualizing, reflecting on challenges to your beliefs and values, recognizing emotional manipulation,* and *judging the writer's credibility.*

Read to Analyze Assumptions

Reread Rodriguez's autobiographical essay, and write a paragraph or two exploring one or more of the assumptions you find in the text. The following suggestions may help:

- **assumptions and stereotyping.** When Tino tells Luis that he won't do what the deputies ask because they will "beat the crap out of us" (paragraph 20), he assures Luis that he knows what he's talking about: "I know, believe me, I know" (22). Predicting how an individual will act based on how he or she has behaved in the past under similar circumstances may be fairly reliable. But it is much less reliable to predict how members of a group will act based on how others in that group have behaved in the past. Making this kind of generalization about members of a group is stereotyping. To think critically about the assumptions in this essay related to stereotyping, ask yourself: Is there any evidence in the text that Tino's stereotyping of the sheriff's deputies is accurate in this instance (26)? How does the essay explore a related cultural assumption—other people's stereotyping of Mexican Americans? How does the story's tragic ending comment on or imagine the possibility of escape from this destructive cycle of stereotyping and prejudice?

■ **assumptions about school.** This tragic conflict plays out in a school, and some of Rodriguez's language seems to suggest that the educational system bears some of the blame for what happens. To think critically about the assumptions in this essay related to schools, ask yourself: What does Rodriguez seem to be saying about teachers and their attitudes when he writes that they "jumped on us Mexicans as if we were born with a hideous stain" (26) and imagines them "irate" and issuing "commands" (27)? How does the fact that schools are "forbidden places" for neighborhood kids to play in worsen the situation?

To probe assumptions more deeply, you might use one or more of the following critical reading strategies that are explained and illustrated in Appendix 1: *reflecting on challenges to your beliefs and values*, *exploring the significance of figurative language*, and *looking for patterns of opposition*.

A SPECIAL READING STRATEGY

Contextualizing

Contextualizing is a special critical reading strategy. You can use it to read for meaning, to develop your analysis of the assumptions underlying "Always Running," and to compare your own assumptions with those of Rodriguez.

To contextualize an autobiographical essay like "Always Running," you need to explore the event's contexts:

■ *When* the event occurred and how the historical moment influenced what happened: paragraph 9 indicates that the event occurred when Rodriguez was ten years old. According to Rodriguez's official Web site, he was born in 1954. So the event he is writing about occurred in 1964 or 1965. You could do further Internet research to learn what was happening during this historical period.

■ *Where* the event occurred and how the location played a role: paragraph 1 identifies the location as "South San Gabriel," an area of Los Angeles, California. In paragraph 2, Rodriguez briefly describes the neighborhood. If you wanted to know more about this location during this period, you could read more of Rodriguez's autobiography or do further Internet research. If you do a Google search for "1960s Los Angeles ethnic," for example, you would learn about the area's ethnic makeup and political tensions, including the Watts riots of 1965.

> ■ *Who* was involved and how the power relationships among those
> involved affected what happened: Rodriguez identifies himself and
> Tino as "Mexicans" (26). He does not identify the officers' ethnicity,
> but the fact that one of them calls Tino "you *greaser*" suggests his
> attitude toward people of Mexican descent and may help explain
> Tino's assumption that if he didn't run away, the police would beat
> him.
>
> See Appendix 1 (pp. 614–16) for detailed guidelines on using con-
> textualizing as a critical reading strategy.

READING LIKE A WRITER
PRESENTING PLACES AND PEOPLE

Autobiographers typically use a combination of *naming* and *detailing* along
with *comparing* to present people and places. These descriptive strategies create
vivid images that enable readers to imagine what the experience was like for the
writer, and they also create a dominant impression that helps readers understand
the autobiographical significance.

In paragraph 3, for example, Rodriguez describes the school yard this way:

> We stopped in front of a chain-link fence which surrounded the
> school. An old brick building cast elongated shadows over a basketball
> court of concrete on the other side of the fence. Leaves and paper swirled
> in tiny tornadoes.

Rodriguez names features such as the "fence," "building," and "basketball court"
that he wants readers to notice about the scene. He also adds details to give readers information about these features. Descriptive details usually provide sensory
information indicating what the place looks, sounds, smells, tastes, and feels like.
Notice that Rodriguez chooses details like the "chain-link" of the fence, the
"brick" of the building, and the "concrete" of the basketball court that give visual
and tactile information. The brick and concrete suggest the hardness of these sur-
faces, an impression that is reinforced when we see how difficult it is for the
young Rodriguez to get over the chain-link fence.

Rodriguez also uses comparison when he metaphorically describes the
swirling leaves and papers as "tiny tornadoes." The word *tornadoes* reinforces
other descriptive language in this selection. For example, the opening paragraph
ends with a reference to a gathering storm, and the "gusts" and "dark clouds" of
the gathering storm are mentioned again in paragraph 14. The storm is literal in
that the weather actually is changing. But the storm is also figurative or

symbolic — that is, it stands for the tragedy of Tino's death. It may also suggest the social upheaval that was building toward the cataclysm of the Watts riots.

Analyze

1. *Reread* the selection, underlining the naming, detailing, and comparing used to describe Tino's body language (paragraph 5), the ease with which he scales the fence (7), his body in motion as he plays basketball (15), his actions as he runs away (28), and finally his body fallen to the floor (34).

2. *Notice*, in paragraph 15, that Rodriguez describes Tino figuratively as if he were flying: seeming "to float across the court, as if he had wings." *Review* the descriptive language you have underlined to see where this image of Tino flying, or not being weighed down by gravity, is reinforced. *Contrast* this image of Tino with the way the young Rodriguez is described; in paragraphs 9 to 12, for example, Rodriguez struggles to scale the fence that Tino seems to climb so effortlessly.

Write

Write several sentences explaining what you have discovered about Rodriguez's description of Tino. What dominant impression do these images of Tino suggest to you? How do they help you understand the significance of what happened? *Give two or three examples* from your underlining to support your explanation.

CONSIDERING IDEAS FOR YOUR OWN WRITING

In this autobiographical essay, Rodriguez writes about a traumatic event. If you feel comfortable sharing your memories of a traumatic experience with your instructor and classmates, consider writing about it for this occasion. Instead of writing about something that turned out worse than you expected, you could also consider writing about something that turned out better or significantly different than you anticipated. Rodriguez's essay also suggests the possibility of writing about a time when you did something uncharacteristic or when you followed someone else's lead. You might also think about people — like Tino — whom you knew as a child or as an early adolescent and the reasons that those people were significant in your life.

ANNE MORGAN GRAY
Daddy's Loss

Anne Morgan Gray is a psychotherapist in Bethesda, Maryland. "Daddy's Loss" is part of a work in progress on what she calls the "psychological inheritances" of her family. As she explained in an interview, "My father's imposed rule of not talking about the loss of his hand was a significant shaping aspect. I intend to trace the family inheritance of not talking about loss and grief. It's no coincidence that I am a psychotherapist, talking about the forbidden." "Daddy's Loss" was originally published in the journal Creative Nonfiction, *which describes its contents as "dramatic, true stories using scenes, dialogue, close, detailed descriptions, and other techniques usually employed by poets and fiction writers about important subjects" and as essays that "have purpose and meaning beyond the experiences related by the writers."*

Unlike the essays by Dillard, Shah, and Rodriguez, which focus on a significant event in the author's life, this autobiographical essay focuses on an important person. As you read, annotate the essay to note how Gray uses the autobiographical writing strategies of description, dialogue, and narrative to present her father and convey his significance to readers.

Daddy loved to tell stories, but he never told anyone the story of   1
his hand. We were forbidden to talk about his hand being gone, to
ask questions about what happened, to ever be able to offer help in
words. It just seemed easiest to not even see that it was missing, so to
make reasonable our having no words to describe it. It was a wrist
with a surprise ending, a puckering of skin that was sewn closed, the
seam forming the horizon. I never got to rub his wrist on purpose to
see how it felt, but the skin looked real soft, worn silk-like.

I have to stop even now and remember watching him to know   2
which hand was gone. I remember seeing him shaking hands with
somebody just fine, so I know he had a right hand. It was as if his
left hand was still there, only we couldn't see it.

I suppose I could refer to his wrist as a "stump"; as in "My   3
Daddy had a stump." Even as I practice saying that word it feels
unnatural; stumps are what we have in the yard when trees are
amputated, but Daddy was the tree, he wasn't cut off. There was
only a major branch stopped short.

I would look for the appearance of his wrist when he was sitting   4
at the kitchen table in his suit reading the newspaper and eating his
breakfast before he left for work; when he was driving our Buick
and I was in the back seat looking over his tall shoulder, seeing his

wrist directing the wheel; when he was teaching me how to shoot a rifle, his wrist steadying the barrel; or in the evening when his wrist was helping hold a book or keeping place on a page. On Saturday mornings he would sit at his desk to pay family bills, the huge accountant ledger open, his left wrist marking the item for his right hand to record dollars. It steadied me to see him that way, quietly taking care of his family.

I could feel the affection of Daddy's wrist pressure through my   5 spine in the morning when he would give me a quick hard back rub that would almost hurt, waking me up, teasing about my shoulder blade "buzzard wings" that needed to fly. Sometimes I would pretend to be asleep just for the pleasure of his affection. Daddy could do everything a daddy could possibly need to do with just one hand and two wrists, except possibly to teach us that we could talk about pain and loss.

I wonder if losing his hand is why Daddy wrote his name on   6 most all of his possessions, not just his initials but his first name, middle initial, last name. Wrote big. On anything he could lose. Maybe he wondered if he had written his name on his lost hand would it have been returned to him.

I remember when I was little, 3 or 4, I was sitting on the floor of   7 the living room in our house in Prescott, Ark. The early morning sun radiated air through the glass on the front door and the big front window. I loved touching empty air becoming full of flying haloed specks, looking like tiny gold spirits from Sunday School pictures.

Daddy walked from the kitchen into the living room, walking   8 right through the halos, ready to leave for work. "Daddy wait, what happened to your hand, Daddy? . . . I keep meaning to ask you and then I forget." He rushed out the living room door into the full sunlight, not saying anything about his hand, not even goodbye. He just left for work real fast.

Mama heard me ask, so she listened behind the door to see if   9 Daddy would tell me something he never told her. It gets confusing and competitive like that sometimes between mothers and daughters. Mama then went into the living room and sat down with me on the sofa to tell me the rule about not asking, which she thought she had told me before but evidently I wasn't listening at the time. And to tell me the secret of what happened to Daddy's hand, at least what his mama told her about what happened.

This is the story she was told.   10

———————————

As a boy Daddy was sitting on the old slanty-floored back porch   11
an early morning in fall, cleaning his still-warm rifle; a mound of
newly dead rabbits nearby, the heat rising from their bodies like
morning mist. The boy sold rabbits to poor people on the outskirts
of town, people who couldn't afford beef. His family needed his
money. He was 8 years old.

The boy always carefully cleaned anything that was his, even   12
then. Taking care of something so that it would last, so that he
would have more than if he had to keep starting over each time. He
had checked the gun to be sure it was empty, then put the cleaning
rod into the barrel. There was a bullet lodged in the chamber
somehow . . . the gun fired, blowing out the rod, the bullet ripping
through his hand.

His Mama came running out when she heard his scream. She   13
treated his wound the way they did on the farm, wrapping his hand
in a kerosene-soaked rag as antiseptic. The wound didn't heal;
kerosene wasn't medicine enough. It got infected, gangrene, hand
swollen large and tight like it would burst with red streaks up his
arm and a high fever. His Mama got her egg money out of its hid-
ing place, and she and his Daddy wrapped the boy in a blue quilt
she had made of feed sacks and put him in the back of the wagon.
The mule pulled the wagon over the dirt road of the farm, past the
sycamore tree where lightning had forked it into outspread arms,
slowly through country roads into the small town of Clarendon,
and the doctor.

His own Daddy held him down tight like he was tied on the   14
table while old Dr. Harvey sliced through the boy's infected flesh,
then sawed his left hand off at the wrist bone. Blood spurted out of
the severings, flushing the poison, soaking his Daddy with the wit-
ness of his son's blood. Then Dr. Harvey used a needle and boiled
thread to sew up the skin like it was a piece of cloth instead of
living tissue, and sent the boy back home wrapped in the quilt.
Dr. Harvey made it possible for the boy to live, if he could. The
doctor had nothing to offer to ease the pain, there was no anesthesia except whiskey and one shot of morphine; no antibiotic, just the
boy's will. It was up to the boy to figure out how to ride the pain.

MawMaw never could get all the blood washed out of that blue   15
quilt, but she had to keep using it anyway.

The boy never screamed since the surprising moment he was   16
shot. I don't know what happened to the hand that was cut off; I
reckon they threw it away in the back somewhere, though it is hard
to see a little boy's hand just lying in the tall grass. Maybe they
spaded a hole and buried it. I think that hand became more important in our lives than it ever would have if nothing had happened

to it, or if Daddy had been different. Daddy's being different is harder for me to imagine than to imagine his not having the accident, harder than to imagine Daddy with two hands.

I think about his being a little boy living on a farm where everybody worked hard, and never ever talking about losing his hand, never talking about being in pain, and nobody talking to him about it. I imagine him struggling to pour a bucket of water in the pump to prime it, to hoe the rows of cotton and corn . . . did he wrap his tender stump with a rag to protect it from the hoe handle until it could callous over? How did he work a pitchfork to feed the cows . . . did he ask his Mama's help to cut meat at dinner, or did she just know to quietly do it? The boy tried to figure out how to manage without, trying to be sure nobody would give him pity about his lost hand. Trying to be sure he never started crying.

His Mama decided the boy would have to use his head to make a living, since he couldn't use his hands. She devoted her will and the money she earned selling eggs and pecans to seeing that the boy got the most education and determination she could possibly teach him, and that was a great deal.

He still shot for rabbits to sell because his family still needed the money, and poor people still bought them with some regret and shame, because rabbits were poor people's meat, not the beef they wanted. Daddy told us the story of what would happen when his customers got a little prosperity: He would come to their door with the morning's kill to be informed "we don't eats rabbit." When their money got used up again he would be sent a message to return with the necessary. This prideful boy sold what people wished they didn't need to buy. Our family always used that phrase "we don't eats rabbit" to mean "putting on airs," as though a person could wisely deny his own history like yesterday doesn't write today.

The boy still left home six years later, somehow jumping into a moving freight train, holding himself against the frame of the open door with his endless arm so as he could wave goodbye with his good hand. He somehow did whatever he needed to do to stay alive and to leave home, and he did it all with never talking about just having one hand. He was heroic in that way.

He would often keep his arm bent with his wrist into the edge of his pants pocket, like his hand was in the pocket. People knew him for years without knowing he didn't have a hand in there, only a secret. I think about the effort that is a part of such concealment; keeping that secret was important enough to be aware of his body in that way all the time. When somebody was trusted not to ask questions, then Daddy would choose to reveal what could be seen. Daddy was so powerful he could control what people would see when he wanted to, which was most all of the time.

Daddy always looked down on complaining or blaming any- 22 body else for misfortune, "poor-mouthing." Said it showed little character. My brother and I wanted his approval more than we wanted the distant hope of comfort and support, so we tried to always hold ourselves accountable. He taught us it was an important part of character to work with what was given and bring it to its best. When something went wrong, Daddy said the first thing is to ask was whether it was a permanent problem or a temporary one. "Most worries in life are temporary, so should be treated as such," he said. I wonder if the permanence of losing his hand is what made most other problems seem more fleeting.

He did allow himself to cry at sad movies; Mama said after he 23 sobbed all the way through "The Sound of Music" that she didn't want to go to the theater with him anymore, it was just too hard.

Daddy mentioned his missing hand to me once in my whole 24 life. I was 20. He had been mowing the back yard when something got tangled in the lawn mower blade. As he tried to untangle it, his right hand got caught, cutting a finger real bad, almost off. He drove himself and Mama to the hospital, because Mama was too upset to drive. Daddy told me later, "I was worried, because I didn't have any extra fingers to lose." I listened real close in case he would say more, but he never did. That is as close as we ever got to talking about his missing hand.

I took the only photograph ever showing the evidence of 25 Daddy's amputation. I took it at the beginning of his last great battle before he died, when his handsome face was already swelling in protest against the invisible radiation. He and Mama had come to stay with me and my family, to have me take care of them while he wordlessly fought death. The statistics of medicine provided the war news of the day; how many X's of radiation can be borne; which would die first, Daddy or the cancer. My Daddy died first, but that came two months later.

In that last picture Daddy was sitting on the sofa in my living 26 room, talking to his grandchildren. It was the last evening he was able to sit up independently, he who never asked for help. He had a blanket folded over his lap. I knowingly, wordlessly, stole from him this forbidden image, stealing the evidence of his loss for my keeping. The photograph shows his left arm bent, elbow resting on his leg for support, his wrist propping his cheek. The cancer had already spread from his esophagus, wrapping itself like a kudzu vine around his carotid artery as it traveled up into his brain. He couldn't defend himself anymore. A year before he had lost his power to speak, when a doctor had again cut out a diseased part so the rest of him might live. Weeks after the photograph was taken, Daddy went blind from the radiation. He mouthed the words to us, "Am I blind?" He never cried, never mentioned it again. He lay on a bed trapped without speech or sight, without the strength to conceal his losses. Most of the time he went deep inside himself where no one could find him, where maybe he couldn't even feel what they could see. Especially where he couldn't see their grieving. He just couldn't abide grieving.

When I let myself really think about it, I reckon I've come by my 27 struggle against grief and the fear of pain quite naturally, like something I inherited from generations past, along with dark hair, brown eyes, an inward-turning foot. Like a chemist, I try to figure out just how much grieving I can have and still be sure I'll be all right the next morning. Titrate the dosage. So when I grieve for what I'll never have again with Daddy, I'll name it "the grief of never again being able to hear Daddy's stories." That sounds sad but OK, a luxury I don't have, and everybody can do all right without luxuries. That's why they are named that, and not necessities.

But I will grieve for the loss of the necessity of him my whole 28 life.

READING FOR MEANING

This section presents three activities that will help you reread Gray's autobiographical essay with a critical eye. Done in sequence, these activities lead you from a basic understanding of the selection to a more personal response to it and finally to an analysis that deepens your understanding and critical thinking about what you are reading.

Read to Comprehend

Reread the selection, and write a few sentences briefly summarizing what you learn about Gray's father from reading this portrait of him. The following definitions may help you understand Gray's vocabulary:

puckering (paragraph 1): something tightly pulled together, gathered into wrinkles.

character (22): the combination of qualities that determine a person's moral and ethical behavior.

Find three or more additional words that you don't understand, and find the best definitions from the dictionary that work with their context.

To expand your understanding of this reading, you might use one or more of the following critical reading strategies that are explained and illustrated in Appendix 1: *outlining* and *questioning to understand and remember.*

Read to Respond

Write several paragraphs exploring your initial thoughts and feelings about Gray's autobiographical portrait of her father. Focus on anything that stands out for you, perhaps because it resonates with your own experience or because you find a statement puzzling.

You might consider writing about the following:

- Gray's comparison of her father to a "tree" (paragraph 3);

- the image of Gray's father as "a little boy living on a farm where everybody worked hard, and never ever talking about losing his hand, never talking about being in pain, and nobody talking to him about it" (17);

- her father's habitual way of concealing his missing hand (21); or

- her father's philosophy that "[w]hen something went wrong . . . the first thing . . . to ask was whether it was a permanent problem or a temporary one" (22).

To develop your response to this essay, you might use one or more of the following critical reading strategies that are explained and illustrated in Appendix 1: *contextualizing* and *reflecting on challenges to your beliefs and values.*

Read to Analyze Assumptions

Reread Gray's autobiographical essay, and write a paragraph or two exploring one or more of the assumptions you find in the text. The following suggestions may help:

- **assumptions about expressing feelings.** Gray describes her psychotherapy as "talking about the forbidden." The so-called talking cure that has been the mainstay of most psychotherapy assumes that unconscious feelings, including "forbidden" ones, need to be made conscious for psychological healing to take place. To think critically about the assumptions in this essay related to talking about feelings, ask yourself: Is it possible that Gray's father has repressed and hidden even from himself his feelings of anger—for example, at himself for failing to clean his rifle properly, at his parents for the ignorance or poverty that led to his hand becoming infected, and at the doctor for amputating his hand and not giving him proper pain medication? Do you think expressing such feelings, even if they seem irrational and nothing can be done about them, would have made a difference for her father? He appears to have learned from his family culture that dwelling on or even expressing feelings is not helpful. What have you learned from your family culture and from American culture in general about dealing with negative feelings, traumatic experiences, and loss?

- **assumptions about self-reliance.** Gray describes her father as a self-reliant man whose strength of will and determination enable him to treat the permanent loss of his hand as a temporary problem. Self-reliance is often thought of as a fundamental American value, part of what made this country strong. To think critically about assumptions related to self-reliance, note that although Gray's father was self-reliant in many ways, his mother worked to give him an education because she knew he "would have to use his head to make a living, since he couldn't use his hands" (paragraph 18). What does this fact suggest about the ideology of self-reliance that assumes people can lift themselves up by their initiative and work without relying on help from others?

To probe assumptions more deeply, you might use one or more of the following critical reading strategies that are explained and illustrated in Appendix 1: *exploring the significance of figurative language,* and *looking for patterns of opposition.*

READING LIKE A WRITER
PRESENTING A PERSON THROUGH ANECDOTES AND RECURRING ACTIVITIES

Autobiography uses narrative in various ways. Some autobiographies, like those by Annie Dillard, Saira Shah, Luis J. Rodriguez, and Jean Brandt, focus on a single memorable event that occurred within a few hours or days, whereas others, like those by Anne Morgan Gray and Brad Benioff, focus on a person with whom the writer had an important relationship. Autobiographies that focus on a person may use two narrating strategies—anecdotes and recurring activities. *Anecdotes* present experiences that are one-time occurrences. Like a snapshot, an anecdote catches the person at a particular place and time, giving the reader a sense of what the person did and said on that occasion, such as one time when someone tripped and dropped the cake at a birthday party. *Recurring activities,* in contrast, present experiences that are typical and occur more than once, often on a regular basis with only a little variation over a period of time, such as several occasions when the same person tripped and dropped things, suggesting the person's clumsiness or nervousness. As you analyze Gray's use of anecdotes and recurring activities, you will see how they differ and what each contributes to the portrait of her father.

Analyze

1. Reread paragraphs 7 to 16, where Gray presents two anecdotes—each a one-time occurrence set in a specific time and place. The first anecdote (7–9)

reconstructs an incident that Gray experienced firsthand when she was three or four years old. The second (11–16) relates a story that her mother told and had heard from Gray's grandmother (called "MawMaw"). This anecdote presents an event that occurred many years earlier when Gray's father was eight years old. Notice how Gray uses a simple chronological organization in both anecdotes to help readers follow the sequence of actions that took place.

2. Reread paragraphs 4 and 5, where Gray presents recurring activities — things that her father typically did. Note the way Gray signals readers that she is narrating a recurring activity and not a one-time occurrence.

Write

Write several sentences describing how the recurring activities and anecdotes differ, pointing to specific ways that Gray presents these experiences and helps readers understand them. Then speculate about what the anecdotes and recurring activities contribute to Gray's portrait of her father.

CONSIDERING IDEAS FOR YOUR OWN WRITING

Autobiographers often write about people with whom they have close and somewhat complicated relationships. Like Gray, you might choose to present a person you are trying to figure out, perhaps a close friend or family member who behaved in a way that you think is harmful or unwise. Or you might consider writing about a person for whom you felt (and maybe still feel) strong and conflicting emotions, such as anger, disapproval, admiration, envy, disappointment, or hurt. Try to recall particular events or conversations with the person that you could use to help readers understand why the person aroused strong feelings or conflicting emotions in you. Another possibility is to write about a teacher, mentor, counselor, minister, or some other older person who influenced you deeply, for good or ill. Consider also someone who passed on to you a sense of your family history or culture.

Autobiography Online

Writers today have many places online to post their autobiographical writing, including personal blogs as well as Web sites like Memory Archive at http://www.memoryarchive.org, where we found this posting, titled "Playing B-Ball with Barack Obama, 1988/89." It was written by Marshall Poe, a history lecturer at Harvard University, who recalls playing pick-up basketball games with Obama when they were both graduate students at Harvard. The essay was posted on December 11, 2006, a month before Obama declared he was running for president. Autobiographers usually write about people who had a major impact on their lives, but here Poe writes about his brush with fame, giving readers an up-close and personal glimpse of a political "rock star," as he calls Obama. The marginal annotations point out the autobiographical writing strategies that readers expect to find in print versions as well as features that are characteristic of writing on the Web.

Playing B-Ball with Barack Obama, 1988/1989, by Marshall Poe

(1)
```
Who: Marshall Poe
What: Playing Basketball with Barack Obama
When: 1988/89
Where: Harvard University, Cambridge, MA
```

Playing B-Ball with Barack Obama, 1988/89

In 1988/89, I received a fellowship to work on my dissertation at Harvard ⊞ (I **(2)** was in a Ph.D. program at Berkeley). In those days I played basketball a lot more than I studied, which may have had something to do with the seven years it took me to complete my degree. As soon as I got to Cambridge ⊞, I **(3)** discovered "the Mac," as everyone calls the Malkin Athletic Center. As university rec centers go, the Mac is pretty much a disaster, though Harvard has made repeated and very costly attempts to put a better face on it. The basketball courts are particularly crappy: the gym is on the third floor, it's drafty in the winter, sweltering in the summer, and has only one regulation sized court, the other two courts being somewhat too narrow (and too narrow to allow any short of perimeter game). Despite the poor environs, the Mac is where all decent pick up basketball is played at Harvard.

And this is where I had the opportunity to play with Barack Obama ⊞—Senator **(4)** from Illinois ⊞, Democratic rock star, and possible presidential candidate. Barack played in the "afternoon game" (vs. the "noon game"). This game was particularly popular with undergrad jocks and competitive guys from the professional schools. Obama was, of course, in law school. I knew him as one of the "law school guys." This was a group of players that included Barack (a lanky forward—see more anon), Leon (a lithe diddling guard with big horn-rim

(1) Each Memory Archive entry begins with these four identifying headings.
(2) Poe begins by setting the time and place. The symbol following "Harvard" indicates a link.

(3) Poe inserts links to Wikipedia. Do you think these particular links are useful for the reader?

(4) Poe names and identifies the subject of his autobiographical post.

(5) glasses and a great sense of humor), Frank (great ups, tough inside—I'd played with him when he was a Berkeley undergrad), and a huge guy from the Caribbean whose name escapes me. There were also other regulars who should be mentioned: Jeff (a very strong off guard), Tom (tough forward with a surpassing jump shot), Sandy (fast guard, great handling skills, good shooter), Big Bill (a very athletic power forward, impossible to stop in the paint), Mark (another power forward good near the basket), Doug (a mathematician...), Curtis (yet another power forward with an excellent inside game and real stopping power), and "Jack Plastic Shirt" (an older guy who always but always wore one of those PVS weight loss shirts—he was a bit strange). I'm sure I've forgotten someone, but the years have taken their toll on my memory.

(6) We'd get together nearly everyday at 4:00 to "run" for a few hours. There was lots of yelling and fighting and misbehavior—which is to say it was an ordinary pick up game. It was competitive—there was no "next five" rule, that is, the guy who "next" could pick any players he wanted, even if they had just come off the floor. If you weren't good enough, you never got picked up. I remember asking new guys whether they had played high school ball. If they hadn't, they got passed over and had to play on the "side court." The "center court" was for good players only. In hindsight, that was cruel. But we didn't want to play with just anyone.

(7) And now to Barack. I remember him well for several reasons. First, his name. "Baruch" means "blessed" or something in Hebrew, and a Jewish friend of mine had just taught me the Shabbis blessing of the wine for fun (we used to drink a lot in those days, and a little ancient ritual made drinking that much better). I recall thinking it was an interesting name for an African American ⚐ to have, and wondered about Obama's background. Second, as I've said, he was part of a crew of "law school guys" (as opposed, say, to the "business school guys"). Finally, Barack had game, and he was even then a natural leader. He was tall (I'd say about six-four), but very thin, and this shaped his style of play. He couldn't really hold his own in the paint, but he had good ups and would snatch rebounds over slightly shorter and heavier players in a graceful motion that reminded me of Karem. He was relatively fast and agile, but had no outside game that I recall. I do remember him bringing up the ball from time to time, which was probably not a good idea (though I don't think he had a bad handle). It suggested that he wanted to be in charge (I did the same thing sometimes, much to the chagrin of my teammates).

(8) The game was full of what you might mildly call "personalities," and fights of various sorts often broke out (usually over bad calls). Lots of yelling and anger. Barack participated, as did pretty much everyone, but I don't recall him really going off on anyone. He was active in arguing, but he didn't loose his cool. He often played the role of conciliator. He had (and has) a great, rich baritone voice that commanded respect and a nearly continual fetching grin, a real "thousand watt" smile. He was a winning personality, and respected for his opinion, even though he wasn't one of the best players.

(5) Note that Poe describes other players as well as Obama.
(6) Poe tells what typically happened during these pick-up games, giving readers a context for what comes next.

(7) Note the specific description of Obama and his style of play. Should there be a link to Kareem Abdul-Jabbar?

(8) This is probably the most interesting section for readers who want to know about Obama as a potential president.

On the whole, Barack acted like everyone else: he was competitive, wanted to win, and he did what was necessary to achieve this end. On the center court at the Mac, picking players for anything other than skill usually lost you the game, and so Barack didn't do it and neither did most anyone else.

I recall fondly sitting on the sidelines of the court after we'd played until exhaustion. We'd rehearse every moment in the games, laugh at each other's bad play, and generally have a good time. It was very friendly and very enjoyable. I liked Barack, and I loved all of my b-ball comrades—even if I occasionally lost my cool (sorry, guys). It was a blast.

Categories: All Memoirs | Basketball | Harvard University | 1989 | Barack Obama

⑨ Poe concludes by returning to his remembered feelings and thoughts about the games.

Analyze

1. *Find* another example of online autobiography.

2. *Check* to see which basic features of autobiographical writing are displayed in the example you found. Look for narrating a one-time event or recurring activities, describing people and places, and conveying significance.

3. Also *look for* any special online characteristics, such as links, informal or specialized language, misspellings, and still or moving visuals.

4. In writing about Obama, Poe is not writing about a person who was an important influence in his own life. Instead, he is writing about someone who is famous and who is interesting to many readers. In the example of autobiography you find online, *note* whether the remembered person or event is significant because of its role in the author's life or for some other reason.

Write

Write several sentences explaining the features of the online autobiography that you found and the significance of the remembered event or person.

BRAD BENIOFF

Rick

> Brad Benioff was a first-year college student when he wrote the following essay for an assignment in his composition class. Like Anne Morgan Gray and Marshall Poe in the two preceding selections, Benioff focuses his essay on a memorable person: his high-school water-polo coach, Rick Rezinas.
>
> As you read, notice how Benioff uses dialogue to dramatize his relationship with Rick.

1   I walked through the dawn chill, shivering as much from nervousness as from the cold. Steam curled up from the water in the pool and disappeared in the ocher morning light. Athletes spread themselves about on the deck, lazily stretching and whispering to each other as if the stillness were sacred. It was to be my first practice with the high school water polo team. I knew nothing about the game, but a friend had pushed me to play, arguing, "It's the most fun of any sport. Trust me." He had awakened me that morning long before daylight, forced me into a bathing suit, and driven me to the pool.

2   "Relax," he said. "Rick is the greatest of coaches. You'll like him. You'll have fun."

3   The mythical Rick. I had heard of him many times before. All the older players knew him by his first name and always spoke of him as a friend rather than a coach. He was a math teacher at our school, and his classes were very popular. Whenever class schedules came out, everyone hoped to be placed in Mr. Rezinas's class. He had been known to throw parties for the team or take them on weekend excursions skiing or backpacking. To be Rick's friend was to be part of an exclusive club, and I was being invited to join. And so I looked forward with nervous anticipation to meeting this man.

4   My friend walked me out to the pool deck and steered me toward a man standing beside the pool.

5   "Rick," announced my friend, "I'd like you to meet your newest player."

6   Rick was not a friendly looking man. He wore only swim trunks, and his short, powerful legs rose up to meet a bulging torso. His big belly was solid. His shoulders, as if to offset his front-heaviness, were thrown back, creating a deep crease of excess muscle from his sides around the small of his back, a crease like a huge frown. His arms were crossed, two medieval maces placed carefully on their racks, ready to be swung at any moment. His

round cheeks and chin were darkened by traces of black whiskers. His hair was sparse. Huge, black, mirrored sunglasses replaced his eyes. Below his prominent nose was a thin, sinister mustache. I couldn't believe this menacing-looking man was the legendary jovial Rick.

He said nothing at first. In those moments of silence, I felt more inadequate than ever before in my life. My reflection in his glasses stared back at me, accusing me of being too skinny, too young, too stupid, too weak to be on his team. Where did I get the nerve to approach him with such a ridiculous body and ask to play water polo, a man's game? Finally, he broke the silence, having finished appraising my meager body. "We'll fatten him up," he growled. 7

Thus began a week of torture. For four hours a day, the coach stood beside the pool scowling down at me. I could do nothing right. 8

"No! No! No!" He shook his head in disgust. "Throw the damn ball with your whole arm! Get your goddamn elbow out of the water!" 9

Any failure on my part brought down his full wrath. He bellowed at my incompetence and punished me with pushups and wind sprints. Even when I was close to utter exhaustion, I found no sympathy. "What the hell are you doing on the wall?" he would bellow. "Coach . . . my side, it's cramped." 10

"Swim on it! If you can't take a little pain, then you don't play!" With this, he would push me off the wall. 11

He seemed to enjoy playing me against the older, stronger players. "Goddamn it, Brad! If someone elbows or hits you, don't look out at me and cry, 'It's not fair.' Push back! Don't be so weak!" I got elbowed around until it seemed that none of my internal organs was unscathed. He worked me until my muscles wouldn't respond, and then he demanded more. 12

"You're not trying! Push it!" 13

"Would you move? You're too slow! Swim!" 14

"Damn it! Get out and give me twenty!" 15

It took little time for me to hate both the game and the man who ruled it. 16

I reacted by working as hard as I could. I decided to deprive him of the pleasure of finding fault with me. I learned quickly and started playing as flawlessly as possible. I dispensed with looking tired, showing pain, or complaining of cramps. I pushed, hit, and elbowed back at the biggest of players. No matter how flawless or aggressive my performance, though, he would find fault and let me know it. He was never critical of other players. He would laugh and joke with the other players; but whenever he saw me, he frowned. 17

I decided to quit. 18

After a particularly demanding practice, I walked up to this 19
tyrant. I tried to hold his gaze, but the black glasses forced me to
look down.

"Coach Rezinas," I blurted, "I've decided that I don't want to 20
play water polo." His scowl deepened. Then after a moment he
said, "You can't quit. Not until after the first game." And he walked
away. The dictator had issued his command.

There was no rule to keep me from quitting. Anger flushed 21
through me. Somehow I would get revenge on this awful man. After
the first game? Okay. I would play. I would show him what a valuable player I was. He would miss my talents when I quit. I worked
myself up before the first game by imagining the hated face: the
black glasses, the thin mustache, the open, snarling mouth. I was
not surprised that he placed me in the starting lineup because I was
certain he would take me out soon. I played furiously. The ball, the
goal, the opposition, even the water seemed to be extensions of Rick,
his face glaring from every angle, his words echoing loudly in my
ears. Time and time again I would get the ball and, thinking of his
tortures, fire it toward the goal with a strength to kill. I forgot that
he might take me out. No defender could stand up to me. I would
swim by them or over them. Anger and the need for vengeance gave
me energy. I didn't notice the time slipping by, the quarters ending.

Then, the game ended. My teammates rushed out to me, con- 22
gratulating and cheering me. I had scored five goals, a school
record for one game, and shut out the other team with several key
defensive plays. Now I could get revenge. Now I could quit. I
stepped out of the pool prepared with the words I would spit into
his face: "I QUIT!"

As I approached him, I stopped dead. He was smiling at me, his 23
glasses off. He reached out with his right hand and shook mine
with exuberance.

"I knew you had it in you! I knew it!" he laughed. 24

Through his laughter, I gained a new understanding of the man. 25
He had pushed me to my fullest potential, tapping into the talent I
may never have found in myself. He was responsible for the way I
played that day. My glory was his. He never hated me. On the contrary, I was his apprentice, his favored pupil. He had brought out
my best. Could I really hate someone who had done that much for
me? He had done what he had promised: he had fattened me up
mentally as well as physically. All this hit me in a second and left me
completely confused. I tried to speak, but only managed to croak,
"Coach . . . uh . . . I, uh. . . ." He cut me off with another burst of
laughter. He still shook my hand.

"Call me Rick," he said. 26

READING FOR MEANING

This section presents three activities that will help you reread Benioff's autobiographical essay with a critical eye. Done in sequence, these activities lead you from a basic understanding of the selection to a more personal response to it and finally to an analysis that deepens your understanding and critical thinking about what you are reading.

Read to Comprehend

Reread the selection, and write a few sentences briefly explaining what you think Benioff wants readers to understand about Rick and why he was so important in Benioff's life. The following definitions may help you understand Benioff's vocabulary:

ocher (paragraph 1): reddish.

maces (6): weapons that resemble clubs.

unscathed (12): unhurt, untouched.

Identify three or more additional words that you don't understand, and find the best definitions from the dictionary that work with their context.

To expand your understanding of this reading, you might use one or more of the following critical reading strategies that are explained and illustrated in Appendix 1: *outlining, summarizing, paraphrasing,* and *questioning to understand and remember.*

Read to Respond

Write several paragraphs exploring your initial thoughts and feelings about Benioff's autobiographical essay about his relationship with Rick. Focus on anything that stands out for you, perhaps because it resonates with your own experience or because you find a statement puzzling.

You might consider writing about the following:

- Rick's coaching style, perhaps comparing it with other styles of coaching or teaching with which you are familiar;

- Benioff's effort to deprive Rick of "the pleasure of finding fault" with him and the surprising fact that Rick found fault with him "[n]o matter how flawless or aggressive [his] performance" (paragraph 17);

- the ways that being male or female may affect your response to Rick and to Benioff's attitudes toward Rick; or

- high-school students' desire to be "Rick's friend" and thus "part of an exclusive club" (3), perhaps in relation to your experience with exclusive groups in high school or college.

To develop your response to Benioff's essay, you might use one or more of the following critical reading strategies that are explained and illustrated in Appendix 1: *contextualizing, reflecting on challenges to your beliefs and values, recognizing emotional manipulation,* and *judging the writer's credibility.*

Read to Analyze Assumptions

Reread Benioff's autobiographical essay, and write a paragraph or two exploring one or more of the assumptions you find in the text. The following suggestions may help:

- **assumptions about coaching.** Benioff's friend describes Rick as "the greatest of coaches" (paragraph 2) and Benioff writes that "the older players . . . spoke of him as a friend rather than a coach" (3). But Benioff calls Rick a "tyrant" (19) and a "dictator" (20). He complains that Rick demands too much of him and works him too hard, always finding fault and never giving him praise—at least, until Benioff proves himself to be worthy. To think critically about the assumptions in this essay related to coaching, ask yourself: What does Benioff assume are the good and the bad qualities of coaching? Why does his attitude change after the game? What is your judgment of Rick's coaching? On what do you base your judgment? Do you think our culture values coaches like Rick? If so, why do you suppose being tough and critical rather than sympathetic and encouraging is valued in coaching?

- **assumptions about masculinity.** Benioff calls water polo "a man's game" and seems delighted that Rick "fattened [him] up mentally as well as physically" (25). For example, Benioff describes his own body before undergoing Rick's makeover as "too skinny . . . and too weak," "ridiculous," and "meager" (7). These images are in sharp contrast to those he uses to describe Rick's "powerful," "solid," "bulging" muscular body (6). To think critically about the assumptions in this essay related to masculinity, ask yourself: What assumptions about masculinity—both about the body and behavior—does Benioff come to share with Rick? Where else in our culture are these values celebrated? What alternative qualities, if any, does our culture (or another culture of which you are aware) associate with masculinity?

To probe assumptions more deeply, you might use one or more of the following critical reading strategies that are explained and illustrated in Appendix 1: *reflecting on challenges to your beliefs and values, exploring the significance of figurative language,* and *looking for patterns of opposition.*

READING LIKE A WRITER
DESCRIBING A PERSON THROUGH VISUAL DETAILS

Visual description enables readers to see the person and to get a sense of how that person appears to others. For example, providing vivid details of someone's facial features could show whether a person looks others directly in the eye or avoids eye contact. This activity will help you see how Benioff uses visual description to give readers a picture of Rick as well as an understanding of his significance to the writer.

Analyze

1. *Reread* paragraph 6, where Benioff describes Rick. *Notice* that the writer makes only two general statements characterizing Rick, in the first and last sentences of the paragraph. The remaining sentences in this paragraph offer visual details and images describing Rick's appearance. Because Rick is wearing only swim trunks and sunglasses, Benioff concentrates on the appearance of Rick's body.

2. *Underline* the parts of Rick's body that Benioff singles out, beginning with "legs" and "torso" in the second sentence. Then *put a wavy line* under each visual detail Benioff uses to describe the parts of Rick's body, beginning with "short, powerful" and "bulging" in sentence 2.

3. *Put a star* by the two comparisons: a simile in sentence 4 (a *simile* makes an explicit comparison by using the word *like* or *as*) and a metaphor in sentence 5 (a *metaphor* implicitly compares two items by describing one in terms of the other).

Write

Write several sentences explaining the impression that you get of Rick as seen through Benioff's eyes. *Quote* the visual details and comparisons that contribute most to this impression.

CONSIDERING IDEAS FOR YOUR OWN WRITING

Think about the coaches, teachers, employers, and other mentors who have influenced your life. Choose one of these people, and consider how you can describe what that person taught you and how he or she went about doing it. As a writer aiming to describe this individual's significance in your life, how would you reveal what you learned about the person and about yourself? Or as an alternative, you might consider someone with whom you have had continuing disagreements or conflicts and then speculate on how you can describe your relationship with that person.

JEAN BRANDT
Calling Home

Jean Brandt wrote this essay as a first-year college student. In it, she tells about a memorable event that occurred when she was thirteen. Reflecting on how she felt at the time, Brandt writes, "I was afraid, embarrassed, worried, mad." As you read, make your own marginal notes indicating where the writer's tumultuous and contradictory remembered feelings are expressed in the essay.

The other readings in this chapter are followed by reading and writing activities. Following this reading, however, you are on your own to decide how to read for meaning and read like a writer.

Brandt begins the action with the first sentence. Then she provides the context and identifies some of the people who play a role in the event.

Brandt shares her remembered feelings and thoughts at the time.

She summarizes a remembered conversation.

As we all piled into the car, I knew it was going to be a fabulous day. My grandmother was visiting for the holidays; and she and I, along with my older brother and sister, Louis and Susan, were setting off for a day of last-minute Christmas shopping. On the way to the mall, we sang Christmas carols, chattered, and laughed. With Christmas only two days away, we were caught up with holiday spirit. I felt light-headed and full of joy. I loved shopping—especially at Christmas.

The shopping center was swarming with frantic last-minute shoppers like ourselves. We went first to the General Store, my favorite. It carried mostly knick-knacks and other useless items which nobody needs but buys anyway. I was thirteen years old at the time, and things like buttons and calendars and posters would catch my fancy. This day was no different. The object of my desire was a 75-cent Snoopy button. Snoopy was the latest. If you owned anything with the Peanuts on it, you were "in." But since I was supposed to be shopping for gifts for other people and not myself, I couldn't decide what to do. I went in search of my sister for her opinion. I pushed my way through throngs of people to the back of the store where I found Susan. I asked her if she thought I should buy the button. She said it was cute and if I wanted it to go ahead and buy it.

When I got back to the Snoopy section, I took one look at the lines at the cashiers and knew I didn't want to wait thirty minutes to buy an item worth less than one dollar. I walked back to the basket where I found the button and was about to drop it when suddenly, instead, I took a quick glance around, assured myself no one could see, and slipped the button into the pocket of my sweatshirt. I hesitated for a moment, but once the item was in my pocket, there was no turning back. I had never before stolen anything; but what was done was done. A few seconds later, my sister appeared and asked, "So, did you decide to buy the button?"

4   "No, I guess not." I hoped my voice didn't quaver. As we headed for the entrance, my heart began to race. I just had to get out of that store. Only a few more yards to go and I'd be safe. As we crossed the threshold, I heaved a sigh of relief. I was home free. I thought about how sly I had been, and I felt proud of my accomplishment.

Notice how her remembered feelings help to create suspense.

5   An unexpected tap on my shoulder startled me. I whirled around to find a middle-aged man, dressed in street clothes, flashing some type of badge and politely asking me to empty my pockets. Where did this man come from? How did he know? I was so sure that no one had seen me! On the verge of panicking, I told myself that all I had to do was give this man his button back, say I was sorry, and go on my way. After all, it was only a 75-cent item.

A dramatic turning point. Brandt *tells* how she felt but also *shows* by her actions and remembered thoughts.

6   Next thing I knew, he was talking about calling the police and having me arrested and thrown in jail, as if he had just nabbed a professional thief instead of a terrified kid. I couldn't believe what he was saying.

What do the highlighted passages suggest Brandt assumes about how the law should apply to her? How does her attitude compare with that of Tino in "Always Running" (p. 33)?

7   "Jean, what's going on?"

8   The sound of my sister's voice eased the pressure a bit. She always managed to get me out of trouble. She would come through this time too.

This is the first of three extended dialogues in this essay. (The others are in paragraphs 19–24 and 26–34.) What do you learn from each? How do these dialogues help to *show* (rather than *tell*) readers the event's significance to Brandt?

9   "Excuse me. Are you a relative of this young girl?"

10   "Yes, I'm her sister. What's the problem?"

11   "Well, I just caught her shoplifting, and I'm afraid I'll have to call the police."

12   "What did she take?"

13   "This button."

14   "A button? You are having a thirteen-year-old arrested for stealing a button?"

15   "I'm sorry, but she broke the law."

16   The man led us through the store and into an office, where we waited for the police officers to arrive. Susan

had found my grandmother and brother, who, still shocked, didn't say a word. The thought of going to jail terrified me, not because of jail itself but because of the encounter with my parents afterward. Not more than ten minutes later, two officers arrived and placed me under arrest. They said that I was to be taken to the station alone. Then they handcuffed me and led me out of the store. I felt alone and scared. I had counted on my sister being with me, but now I had to muster up the courage to face this ordeal all by myself.

As the officers led me through the mall, I sensed a 17 hundred pairs of eyes staring at me. My face flushed, and I broke out in a sweat. Now everyone knew I was a criminal. In their eyes, I was a juvenile delinquent, and thank God the cops were getting me off the streets. The worst part was thinking my grandmother might be having the same thoughts. The humiliation at that moment was overwhelming. I felt like Hester Prynne being put on public display for everyone to ridicule.

That short walk through the mall seemed to take 18 hours. But once we reached the squad car, time raced by. I was read my rights and questioned. We were at the police station within minutes. Everything happened so fast I didn't have a chance to feel remorse for my crime. Instead, I viewed what was happening to me as if it were a movie. Being searched, although embarrassing, somehow seemed to be exciting. All the movies and television programs I had seen were actually coming to life. This is what it was really like. But why were criminals always portrayed as frightened and regretful? I was having fun. I thought I had nothing to fear—until I was allowed my one phone call. I was trembling as I dialed home. I didn't know what I was going to say to my parents, especially my mother.

"Hi, Dad, this is Jean." 19

"We've been waiting for you to call." 20

"Did Susie tell you what happened?" 21

"Yeah, but we haven't told your mother. I think you 22 should tell her what you did and where you are."

"You mean she doesn't even know where I am?" 23

"No, I want you to explain it to her." 24

There was a pause as he called my mother to the 25 phone. For the first time that night, I was close to tears.

These two highlighted passages let us know about Brandt's thoughts and feelings at the time and help clarify what is important to her.

At the end of this paragraph, Brandt compares her situation to that of the main character in Nathaniel Hawthorne's *The Scarlet Letter*. If you are familiar with the novel, how well does this comparison work?

Acknowledging that being arrested was "exciting" and "fun" risks losing readers' sympathy, but it shows that feelings can be contradictory.

The climax and resolution of the narrative begin here, revealed through reconstructed conversations and expressions of remembered feelings.

I wished I had never stolen that stupid pin. I wanted to give the phone to one of the officers because I was too ashamed to tell my mother the truth, but I had no choice.

26   "Jean, where are you?"

27   "I'm, umm, in jail."

28   "Why? What for?"

29   "Shoplifting."

30   "Oh no, Jean. Why? Why did you do it?"

31   "I don't know. No reason. I just did it."

32   "I don't understand. What did you take? Why did you do it? You had plenty of money with you."

33   "I know but I just did it. I can't explain why. Mom, I'm sorry."

34   "I'm afraid sorry isn't enough. I'm horribly disappointed in you."

35   Long after we got off the phone, while I sat in an empty jail cell waiting for my parents to pick me up, I could still distinctly hear the disappointment and hurt in my mother's voice. I cried. The tears weren't for me but for her and the pain I had put her through. I felt like a terrible human being. I would rather have stayed in jail than confront my mom right then. I dreaded each passing minute that brought our encounter closer. When the officer came to release me, I hesitated, actually not wanting to leave. We went to the front desk, where I had to sign a form to retrieve my belongings. I saw my parents a few yards away, and my heart raced. A large knot formed in my stomach. I fought back the tears.

Brandt tells us what she thought and felt, but she also shows it to us. How does doing both—showing and telling—help you understand the significance of the event?

36   Not a word was spoken as we walked to the car. Slowly, I sank into the back seat anticipating the scolding. Expecting harsh tones, I was relieved to hear almost the opposite from my father.

37   "I'm not going to punish you, and I'll tell you why. Although I think what you did was wrong, I think what the police did was more wrong. There's no excuse for locking a thirteen-year-old behind bars. That doesn't mean I condone what you did, but I think you've been punished enough already."

Endings, like beginnings, are always challenging to write. How effective is this ending? What does it add to your understanding of Brandt and her family?

38   As I looked from my father's eyes to my mother's, I knew this ordeal was over. Although it would never be forgotten, the incident was not mentioned again.

READING FOR MEANING

Reading for meaning involves three activities:

- reading to comprehend,
- reading to respond, and
- reading to analyze assumptions.

Reread Brandt's essay, and then write a page or so explaining your understanding of its basic meaning or main point, a personal response you have to it, and one of its assumptions.

READING LIKE A WRITER

Autobiographers who are focusing on a remembered event or person

- narrate the event or anecdotes,
- present people,
- present places, and
- convey autobiographical significance.

Focus on one of these strategies in Brandt's story, and analyze it carefully through close rereading and annotating. Then write several sentences explaining what you have learned, giving examples from the reading to support your explanation. Add a few sentences evaluating how successfully Brandt uses the strategy to dramatize the experience for her readers.

REVIEWING WHAT MAKES AUTOBIOGRAPHY EFFECTIVE

In this chapter, you have been learning how to read autobiographical essays for meaning and how to read them like a writer. Before going on to write a piece of autobiography, pause here to review and contemplate what you have learned about the elements of effective autobiography.

Analyze

Choose one reading from this chapter that seems to you especially effective. Before rereading the selection, *jot down* one or two reasons you remember it as an example of good autobiographical writing.

Reread your chosen selection, adding further annotations about what makes it a particularly successful example of autobiography. *Consider* the selection's purpose and how well it achieves that purpose for its intended readers. (You can make an informed guess about the intended readers and their expectations by noting the publication source of the essay.) Then *focus* on how well the essay

- narrates the story,

- presents people,

- describes places, and

- conveys the autobiographical significance.

You can review all of these basic features in the Guide to Reading Autobiography (p. 14).

Your instructor may ask you to complete this activity on your own or to work with a small group of other students who have chosen the same reading. If you work with others, allow enough time initially for all group members to reread the selection thoughtfully and to add their annotations. Then *discuss* as a group what makes the selection effective. *Take notes* on your discussion. One student in your group should then report to the class what the group has learned about what makes autobiographical writing effective. If you are working individually, write up what you have learned from your analysis.

Write

Write at least a page supporting your choice of this reading as an example of effective autobiographical writing. *Assume* that your readers— your instructor and classmates—have read the selection but will not remember many details about it. They also might not remember it as especially successful. Therefore, you will need to *refer* to details and specific parts of the essay as you explain how it works as autobiography and as you justify your evaluation of its effectiveness. You need not argue that it is the best reading in the chapter or that it is flawless, only that it is, in your view, a strong example of the genre.

■ A Guide to Writing Autobiography

The readings in this chapter have helped you learn a great deal about autobiographical writing. You have seen that some autobiographies tell dramatic stories, while others present vivid portraits of people who played a significant role in the writer's life. Whether the focus is on events or people, you have discovered that the overall purpose for writers of autobiography is to convey the significance—both the meaning and the importance—of their past experience. In so doing, autobiographers often present themselves as individuals affected by social and cultural influences.

As a reader of autobiography, you have examined how autobiographers convey through their writing drama and vividness as well as significance. But you may have also found that different readers interpret the significance of an autobiographical selection differently. In other words, you have seen how the meanings readers make are affected by their personal experience as well as their social and cultural contexts.

Having learned how autobiographers invest their writing with drama, vividness, and significance and how readers interpret and respond to autobiographical writing, you can now approach autobiography more confidently as a writer. You can more readily imagine the problems you must solve as a writer of autobiography, the materials and possibilities you have to work with, the choices and decisions you must make. This Guide to Writing offers detailed suggestions for writing autobiographical essays and resources to help you solve the special challenges this kind of writing presents.

INVENTION AND RESEARCH

The following activities will help you choose a memorable *event* or an important *person* to write about, recall details about your subject, and explore its significance in your life. Completing these activities will produce a record of remembered details and thoughts that will be invaluable as you draft your essay.

Choosing a Subject

Rather than limiting yourself to the first subject that comes to mind, take a few minutes to consider your options. By listing as many subjects as you can, you will have a variety of possible topics to choose from for your autobiographical essay. List the most promising subjects you can think of, beginning with any you listed for the Considering Ideas for Your Own Writing activities following the readings in this chapter. Here are some additional ideas to consider:

Events

- A difficult situation, such as when you had to make a tough choice, when someone you admired let you down (or you let someone else down), or when you struggled to learn or understand something

- An event that shaped you in a particular way or that revealed an aspect of your personality you had not seen before, such as your independence, insecurity, ambition, or jealousy

- An occasion when something did not turn out as you thought it would, such as when you expected to be criticized but were praised or ignored instead, or when you were convinced you would succeed but failed

- An event in which a single encounter with another person changed the way you view yourself, changed your ideas about how you fit into a particular group or community, or led you to consider seriously someone else's point of view

People

- Someone who helped you develop a previously unknown or undeveloped side of yourself

- Someone who led you to question assumptions or stereotypes you had about other people

- Someone who surprised or disappointed you

- Someone in a position of power over you or someone over whom you had power

- Someone who made you feel you were part of a larger community or had something worthwhile to contribute or someone who made you feel alienated or like an outsider

Choose a subject that you feel comfortable sharing with your instructor and classmates. The subject also should be one that you want to try to remember in detail and to think about in terms of what it means to you. You may find the choice easy to make, or you may have several equally promising possibilities. In making a final choice, it may help to think about your readers and what you would want them to learn about you from reading about the event or person.

Developing Your Subject

The following activities will help you develop your subject by recalling actions that happened during the event or by telling anecdotes that reveal something about the person. These activities will also help you recall details of the

RESEARCHING YOUR SUBJECT ONLINE

The Web offers sites that can help you write your autobiographical essay. Exploring Web sites where people write about their life experiences might inspire you by triggering memories of similar events and people in your own life. Moreover, the Web provides a rich repository of cultural and historical information, including photographs and music, that you might be able to use to prime your memory and create a richly detailed, multimedia text for your readers. As you search the Web, here are some possibilities to consider:

- Investigate sites such as citystories.com and storypreservation.com, where people post brief stories about their lives.

- Search for sites featuring the people and places you are writing about, as well as sites of friends, family members, or others who have been important to you.

- Look for sites related to places or activities—such as neighborhoods, schools, workplaces, sports events, or films—that you associate with the person or event you are writing about.

Make notes of any ideas, memories, or insights suggested by your online research. Download any visuals you might consider including in your essay—such as pictures of people and places you may want to include. Also be sure to download or record the information necessary to cite any online sources you may want to refer to in your essay. See Appendix 2 for help in citing sources.

place and people. Each activity takes only a few minutes but will help you produce a fuller, more focused draft.

Recalling the Event or Person.   *If you have chosen to write about an **event**, begin by writing for five minutes, simply telling what happened.* Do not worry about telling the story dramatically or even coherently.

*If you have chosen to write about a **person**, begin by listing anecdotes you could tell about the person.* Then choose one anecdote that reveals something important about the person or your relationship, and write for five minutes telling what happened.

Presenting Important People.   *If you have chosen to write about a **person**, list aspects of the person's appearance and dress, ways of walking and gesturing, tone of voice and mannerisms—anything that would help readers see the person as you remember her or him.*

*If you have chosen to write about an **event**, recall other people who were involved, and write a brief description of each person.*

Reconstructing Dialogue.   *Write a few lines of dialogue that you could use to convey something important about the event or to give readers an impression of the person you have chosen to write about.* You may use direct quotation, enclosing the words you remember being spoken in quotation marks, or you may use indirect quotation, paraphrasing and summarizing what was said. Try to re-create the give-and-take quality of normal conversation in the dialogue.

Describing Important Places.   *Identify the place where the event happened or a place you associate with the person, and detail what you see in the scene as you visualize it.* Try to recall specific sensory details — size, shape, color, condition, and texture of the scene or memorable objects in it. Imagine the place from the front and from the side, from a distance and from close up.

Considering Visuals.   *Consider whether visuals — photographs, postcards, ticket stubs — would strengthen your presentation of the event or person.* If you submit your essay electronically to other students and your instructor or if you post it on a Web site, consider including photographs as well as snippets of film or sound or other memorabilia that might give readers a more vivid sense of the time, place, and people about which you are writing. Visual and audio materials are not a requirement of an effective autobiographical essay, as you can tell from the readings in this chapter, but they could add a new dimension to your writing. If you want to use photographs or recordings of people, though, be sure to request their permission.

Reflecting on Your Subject

The following activities will help you think about the significance of your subject by recalling your remembered feelings and thoughts as well as exploring your present perspective. The activities will also help you consider your purpose in writing about this subject and formulate a tentative thesis statement.

Recalling Your Feelings and Thoughts.   *Write for a few minutes, trying to recall your thoughts and feelings when the event was occurring or when you knew the person.* What did you feel — in control or powerless, proud or embarrassed, vulnerable, detached, judgmental? How did you show or express your feelings? What did you want others to think of you at the time? What did you think of yourself? What were the immediate consequences for you personally?

Exploring Your Present Perspective.   *Write for a few minutes, trying to express your present thoughts and feelings as you look back on the event or person.* How have your feelings changed? What insights do you now have? What does your present perspective reveal about what you were like at the time? Try looking at the event or person in broad cultural or social terms. For example, consider whether you or anyone else upset gender expectations or felt out of place in some way.

Considering Your Purpose.   *Write for several minutes exploring what you want your readers to understand about the significance of the event or person.* Use the following questions to help clarify your thoughts:

- What will writing about this event or person enable you to suggest about yourself as an individual? What will it let you suggest about the social and cultural forces that helped shape you — for example, how people exercise power over one another, how family and community values and attitudes affect individuals, or how economic and social conditions influence our sense of self?

- What do you not understand fully about the event or relationship? What about it still puzzles you or seems contradictory? What do you feel ambivalent about?

- What about your subject do you expect will seem familiar to your readers? What do you think will surprise them, perhaps getting them to think in new ways or to question some of their assumptions and stereotypes?

Formulating a Tentative Thesis Statement.   *Review what you wrote for Considering Your Purpose, and add another two or three sentences that will help you convey to readers the significance of the event or person in your life.* Try to write sentences that do not just summarize what you have written but that also extend your insights and reflections. These sentences may be contradictory because they express ambivalent feelings. They also must necessarily be partial and speculative because you may never understand fully the event's or person's significance.

Keep in mind that readers do not expect you to begin your essay with the kind of explicit introductory thesis statement typical of argumentative essays. None of the readings in this chapter offers to readers an explicit thesis statement explaining the significance of the event or person. Instead, the readings convey the significance by combining showing with telling in their narration of events and descriptions of people and places. And yet it is possible for readers to infer from each reading an implied thesis or impression of the significance. For example, some readers might decide that Dillard wants readers to think that what was most significant and memorable about the event was the way the man threw himself into the chase, showing that childlike enthusiasm sometimes can survive into adulthood. Other readers might focus on the idea that what was significant was that the man as well as the children "all played by the rules" and that when people play by the rules they act with honor and nobility (paragraph 16). If, like you, Dillard had tried to write a few sentences about the significance she hoped to convey in writing about this small but memorable event in her life, she might have written sentences like these.

Nearly all first attempts at stating a thesis are eventually revised once drafting gets under way. Writing the first draft helps autobiographers discover what they think and feel about their subject and find ways to convey its significance without ever spelling it out directly. Just because there is no explicit thesis statement in an autobiography does not mean that the essay lacks focus or fails to convey significance.

DRAFTING

The following guidelines will help you set goals for your draft, plan its organization, choose relevant details, think about a useful sentence strategy, and decide how to begin.

Setting Goals

Establishing goals for your draft before you begin writing will enable you to make decisions and work more confidently. Consider the following questions now, and keep them in mind as you draft. They will help you set goals for drafting as well as recall how the writers you have read in this chapter tried to achieve similar goals.

- *How can I present my subject vividly and memorably to readers?* Should I rely on dialogue to present people and relationships, as so many of the writers in this chapter do, especially Brandt? Or should I concentrate on presenting action rather than dialogue, like Dillard and Rodriguez? Can I use visual or other sensory details, as Shah, Rodriguez, Gray, and Benioff do, to give readers a vivid impression of the person and place while also establishing the significance of my subject?

- *How can I help readers understand the meaning and importance of the event or person?* Can I build the suspense, as all of the writers do? Can I show how I changed, as Benioff does?

- *How can I avoid superficial or one-dimensional presentations of my experience and my relations with others?* Knowing that my readers will not expect easy answers about what makes the event or person significant, how can I satisfy their expectations for writing that has some depth and complexity? How might I employ one or more of the strategies illustrated by the writers I have read in this chapter—the paradox in Dillard's feeling both terror and pleasure as she is chased by the man in the black Buick; the contradictions Gray sees in relating the different attitudes toward talking she and her father have? Benioff's love-hate relationship with his coach? What contradictions, paradoxes, or ironies exist in my own story?

Organizing Your Draft

With these goals in mind, plan your draft by making a tentative outline. Although your plan may change as you write and revise your draft, outlining before you begin drafting can help you get organized. If you are uncertain about how to organize your material, review how some of the writers in this chapter organize their autobiographical essays.

For an *event*, outline the sequence of main actions, from the beginning to the end of the event.

For a *person*, outline the order of the recurring activities, or anecdotes you will use to present the person, interspersing relevant character traits, physical details, and dialogue.

WORKING WITH SOURCES

Using Memory and Memorabilia

In the essays that you will write in later chapters of this book, you will rely on interviews, observation, and print and online sources to support your explanations or arguments. In writing about a remembered event or person, however, you will rely almost entirely on memory—your own memory and that of others. You may also refer to memorabilia such as pictures, videos, letters, and documents. Anne Morgan Gray uses a variety of such sources to present her father in "Daddy's Loss."

Gray's primary source is her own memory, as she makes explicit in the following sentences: "I have to stop even now and remember watching him. . . . I remember seeing him shaking hands" (paragraph 2) and "I remember when I was little, 3 or 4" (7). None of the other writers is as direct as Gray is. Although they all relate what they remember, they do not say so because they present their memories in specific terms, often referring to a particular time and place, as we can see in these brief examples: "On one weekday morning after Christmas" (Dillard, paragraph 3) and "One evening dusk came early in South San Gabriel" (Rodriguez, paragraph 1).

In addition to recounting firsthand memory, writers may also relay what others have told them. Benioff, for example, introduces Rick as "The mythical Rick. I had heard of him many times before. All the older players knew him by his first name and always spoke of him as a friend" (paragraph 3). To explain how her father lost his hand, Gray has to report what she learned secondhand from her mother, to whom it was told by her father's mother. Gray introduces her narrative with the words "This is the story she [her mother] was told" (paragraph 10).

Gray is the only writer in this chapter who uses memorabilia to enhance her narrative. She explains that she took a photograph of her father shortly before he died and that it was "the only photograph ever showing the evidence of Daddy's amputation" (25). She describes it in detail: "The photograph shows his left arm bent, elbow resting on his leg for support, his wrist propping his cheek" (26). Although the photograph was not printed along with Gray's essay in the publication where it originally appeared, including visuals in print texts and other media such as audio and video in online texts can help bring memory to life.

Choosing Relevant Details

The invention and research activities helped you generate many details, probably more than you can use. To decide which details to include in your draft and which to leave out, consider how well each detail contributes to the overall impression you want to create. But before you discard any details that seem irrelevant, think again about what they might suggest about the significance of your subject. Sometimes, seemingly irrelevant details or ones that do not fit neatly can lead you to new insights.

Considering a Useful Sentence Strategy

As you draft your essay, you will need to present the details you have chosen in ways that help readers imagine the people, places, and events. One effective way to do so is to use sentences with participial phrases. These phrases begin with verb forms called participles: either present participles, ending in *ing* (*being, longing, grasping, drinking*), or past participles, usually ending in *ed, d, en, n,* or *t* (*baked, found, driven, torn, sent*). Participial phrases help you show simultaneous actions, make an action or image more specific or vivid, and relate what you or someone else was thinking or feeling at the time of an action.

- To show simultaneous actions:

  We kept running, block after block; we kept improvising, backyard after backyard, *running a frantic course* and *choosing it simultaneously, failing always to find small places or hard places to slow him down,* and *discovering always, exhilarated, dismayed, that only bare speed could save us*—for he would never give up, this man—and we were losing speed. (Dillard, paragraph 14)

  I whirled around to find a middle-aged man, dressed in street clothes, *flashing some type of badge* and *politely asking me to empty my pockets.* (Brandt, paragraph 5)

I would look for the appearance of his wrist when he was sitting at the kitchen table in his suit *reading the newspaper and eating his breakfast before he left for work*; when he was driving our Buick and I was in the back seat *looking over his tall shoulder, seeing his wrist directing the wheel*. (Gray, paragraph 4)

- To make a previously mentioned action or image (shown here in bold type) more specific and vivid:

  Shining a flashlight inside the building, the officer spotted **Tino's misshapen body on the floor**, *sprinkled over with shards of glass*. (Rodriguez, paragraph 34)

  Amina stormed in, *scattering servants before her like chaff*. (Shah, paragraph 7)

- To relate what you or someone else was thinking or feeling at the time:

  The boy tried to figure out how to manage without, *trying to be sure nobody would give him pity about his lost hand. Trying to be sure he never started crying*. (Gray, paragraph 17)

  Slowly, I sank into the back seat *anticipating the scolding*. (Brandt, paragraph 36)

Participial phrases are not required for a successful autobiographical essay, yet they do provide writers an effective sentence option. For another sentence strategy that can strengthen your autobiographical writing, the use of speaker tags in sentences with dialogue, see Chapter 3, pages 143–44.

Writing the Beginning

To engage your readers' interest from the start, consider beginning with a compelling graphic description (as Rodriguez and Benioff do), a startling action (as Dillard does), or a vivid memory (as Shah does) or by creating a sense of expectation (as Brandt does). You might have to try two or three different beginnings before finding a promising way to start, but do not agonize for too long over the first sentence. Try out any possible beginning, and see where it takes you.

READING A DRAFT CRITICALLY

Getting a critical reading of your draft will help you see how to improve it. Your instructor may schedule class time for reading drafts, or you may want to ask a classmate or a tutor in the writing center to read your draft. Ask your reader to use the following guidelines and to write out a response for you to consult during your revision.

Read for a First Impression

1. Read the draft without stopping to annotate or comment, and then write two or three sentences giving your general impression.

2. Identify one aspect of the draft that seems especially effective.

Read Again to Suggest Improvements

1. Recommend ways to make the narrative more dramatic and telling. For a draft presenting an *event*, try the following:

   - Point to any scenes where the action seems to drag or become confusing.

   - Suggest places where the drama might be intensified — by adding a close-up, using more active verbs, or shifting the placement of background information or descriptive detail, for example.

   - Indicate where dialogue could add drama to a confrontation scene.

   For a draft using anecdotes or recurring activities to present a *person*, try the following:

   - Note which anecdotes and recurring activities seem especially effective in illustrating something important about the person or the relationship.

   - Point to one weak anecdote or recurring activity, and suggest how it could be made more effective, such as by adding graphic details and dialogue or by telling how it relates to the person's significance.

   - Indicate any passages where direct quotations could be more effectively presented indirectly by paraphrasing, summarizing, or combining a striking quotation with summary.

2. Indicate any areas where improving dull or weak description could more vividly or effectively convey the dominant impression of the essay:

   - Describe the impression you get from the writer's description of the event or person.

   - Identify one or two passages where you think the description is especially vivid (for example, where the visual details and images help you picture the event or person).

   - Point to any passages where the description could be made more vivid or where it seems to contradict the impression you get from other parts of the essay.

3. Suggest how the autobiographical significance could be developed:

   - Briefly explain your understanding of the significance, indicating anything that puzzles or surprises you about the event or person.

- Note any word choice, contradiction, or irony—in the way people and places are described or in the way the story is told—that alerts you to a deeper meaning that the writer could develop.

- Point to any passages where the writer needs to clarify the historical, social, or cultural dimensions of the experience or relationship.

4. Suggest how the organizational plan could be improved. Consider the overall plan of the essay, perhaps by making a scratch outline (see Appendix 1 for an example):

- For an *event*, indicate any passages where narrative transitions or verb tense markers are needed to make the story unfold more logically and clearly.

- For a *person*, suggest where topic sentences or transitions could be added or where the writer could more clearly indicate what impression of the person the anecdotes or recurring activities are intended to convey.

5. Evaluate the effectiveness of visuals:

- Look at any visuals in the essay, and tell the writer what they contribute to your understanding of the event or person.

- If any visuals do not seem relevant or if there are too many visuals, identify the ones that the writer could consider dropping, explaining your thinking.

- If a visual does not seem to be appropriately placed, suggest a better place for it.

REVISING

This section offers suggestions for revising your draft. Revising means reenvisioning your draft, trying to see it in a new way, given your purpose and readers, to develop a more engaging, coherent autobiography.

The biggest mistake you can make while revising is to focus initially on words or sentences. Instead, first try to see your draft as a whole to assess its likely impact on your readers. Think imaginatively and boldly about cutting unconvincing material, adding new material, and moving material around. Your computer makes even drastic revisions physically easy, but you still need to make the mental effort and decisions that will improve your draft.

You may have received help with this challenge from a classmate or tutor who gave your draft a critical reading. If so, keep this feedback in mind as you decide which parts of your draft need revising and what specific changes you could make. The following suggestions will help you solve problems and strengthen your essay.

To Make the Narrative More Dramatic and Telling

- If the story seems to meander and have no point, focus the action so that it builds up more directly toward the climax.

- Where the narrative drags or the tension slackens, try using more active verbs, more dialogue, or shorter sentences.

- Where background information or descriptive detail interrupts the drama or slows the pace, consider cutting or moving it.

- If the purpose of an anecdote or a recurring activity is not clear, make explicit what it illustrates.

- If the exact words in a conversation are not striking or important, use indirect instead of direct dialogue or combine the two, paraphrasing or summarizing most of what was said but quoting a memorable phrase or word.

To Present People Vividly

- Where more graphic description is needed, give visual details showing what the person looks like or how the person gestures. Consider using participial phrases to show simultaneous actions by the person or to make your descriptions more specific and vivid.

- If any detail seems inconsistent or contradictory, cut it, or use it to develop the significance.

- If the description does not convey the impression you want it to convey, consider cutting some descriptive details and adding others or rethinking the impression you want your writing to convey and the significance it suggests.

To Describe Places Vividly

- If any details about an important place do not fit together well and do not contribute to the dominant impression or reinforce the significance, omit them from the essay.

- Where readers cannot visualize the place, add more sensory detail. Consider using participial phrases to make the images you present of the place more specific and vivid.

- Where the description distracts from the action, cut or move the description.

- Where the point of view is confusing, consider simplifying it.

To Convey the Autobiographical Significance

- If readers may not understand the significance of the person or event, look for passages where you could convey it more directly. Consider using participial phrases to reveal what you were thinking or feeling as you interacted with the person or as the event occurred.

- If the significance seems too pat or simplistic, consider whether you could develop contradictions or allow for ambivalence.

- If readers may not understand the importance of the social, cultural, or historical context, consider giving background information to reveal its influence.

To Make the Organizational Plan More Effective

- If readers may be confused about what happened when, add transitions or verb tense markers.

- If readers may not see clearly how the anecdotes or recurring activities contribute to the portrait of the person, add forecasting statements or topic sentences to clarify what those elements demonstrate.

EDITING AND PROOFREADING

After you have revised your essay, be sure to spend some time checking for errors in usage, punctuation, and mechanics and considering matters of style. If you keep a list of errors you typically make, begin by checking your draft against this list. Ask someone else to proofread your essay before you print out a copy for your instructor or send it electronically.

From our research on student writing, we know that essays dealing with autobiographical subjects have a high percentage of errors in verb tense and punctuation. You should proofread your narration for verb tense errors and your description for punctuation errors—such as comma splices and missing commas after introductory elements. Check a writer's handbook for help with these potential problems.

REFLECTING ON WHAT YOU HAVE LEARNED

Autobiography

In this chapter, you have read critically several pieces of autobiography and have written one of your own. To better remember what you have learned, pause now to reflect on the reading and writing activities you completed in this chapter.

1. *Write* a page or so reflecting on what you have learned. *Begin* by describing what you are most pleased with in your essay. Then *explain* what you think contributed to your achievement. *Be specific* about this contribution.

   ■ If it was something you learned from the readings, *indicate* which readings and specifically what you learned from them.

   ■ If it came from your invention writing, *point out* the section or sections that helped you most.

   ■ If you got good advice from a critical reader, *explain* exactly how the person helped you—perhaps by helping you understand a particular problem in your draft or by adding a new dimension to your writing.

   ■ *Try to write* about your achievement in terms of what you have learned about the genre.

2. Now *reflect* more generally on how you tend to interpret autobiographical writing, your own as well as other writers'. *Consider* some of the following questions: In reading for meaning, do you tend to find yourself interpreting the significance of the event or person in terms of the writer's personal feelings, sense of self-esteem, or psychological well-being? Or do you more often think of significance in terms of larger social or economic influences—for example, whether the writer is male or female, rich or poor, suburban or urban, African American or Anglo? Where do you think you learned to interpret the significance of people's stories about themselves and their relationships—from your family, friends, television, school?

CHAPTER 3

Observation

Certain kinds of writing are based on fresh observation or direct investigation. Travel writers, for example, profile places they have visited; naturalists describe phenomena they have observed undisturbed in nature. Investigative reporters or clinical psychologists write up interviews with individuals, while cultural anthropologists write ethnographies of groups they have studied in depth. Much of what we know about people and the world we learn from this kind of writing.

Writing about your own observations offers special challenges and rewards. It requires you to pay more attention than you normally do to everyday activities. You need to look with all your senses and give your curiosity free rein. Taking a questioning or inquiring stance will enable you to make discoveries in even the most mundane settings. In addition, it helps to take voluminous notes because you might not know what is significant until you begin to sort through the observations and quotations you have collected. That way, after the work of observing and interviewing is done, another kind of equally challenging and rewarding work can begin—making meaning of the bits and pieces you have gathered. Analyzing and synthesizing your notes, you interpret your subject and decide what you want to tell your readers about it. These activities of close observation and careful notetaking, combined with thoughtful analysis and imaginative synthesis, form the basic strategies of researching and learning in many areas of college study.

When writing about your observations, you will have an immediate advantage if you choose a place, an activity, or a person that is new to readers. But even if the subject is familiar, you can still intrigue and inform readers by presenting it in a new light or by focusing on a specific aspect of the subject. By focusing on certain details, you help readers imagine what the place looks, sounds, and smells like; picture how the people dress, gesture, and talk; and understand your idea or interpretation of the subject.

The readings in this chapter will help you learn a lot about observational writing. From the readings and from the ideas for writing that follow each reading, you will get ideas for your own observational essay. As you read and write about the selections, keep in mind the following assignment, which sets out the goals for writing an observational essay. To support your writing of this assignment, the chapter concludes with a Guide to Writing Observational Essays.

THE WRITING ASSIGNMENT

Observation

Write an observational essay about an intriguing place, person, or activity in your community. Your essay may be a brief profile of an individual based on one or two interviews; a description of a place or activity observed once or twice; or a longer, more fully developed profile of a person, place, or activity based on observational visits and interviews conducted over several days. Observe your subject closely, and then present what you have learned in a way that both informs and engages readers.

WRITING SITUATIONS FOR OBSERVATIONAL ESSAYS

As we indicated earlier, many people — including travel writers, investigative reporters, clinical psychologists, and cultural anthropologists — write essays based on observations and interviews. In your other college courses, you may have an opportunity to write an observational essay like one of the following:

- For an art history course, a student writes about a local artist recently commissioned to paint outdoor murals for the city. The student visits the artist's studio and talks with him about the process of painting murals, large pictures painted on walls or the sides of buildings. The artist invites the student to spend the following day as a part of a team of local art students and neighborhood volunteers working on the mural under the artist's direction. This firsthand experience helps the student profile the artist, present some of the students, and give readers a clear impression of the process of collaboration involved in mural painting.

- For a journalism course, a student profiles a typical day in the life of an award-winning scientist. He spends a day observing the scientist at home and at work, and he then interviews colleagues, students, and family, as well as the scientist herself. Her daily life, he learns, is very much like that of other working mothers — a constant effort to balance the demands of her career against the needs of her family. He conveys this idea in his essay by alternating between details about the scientist's work and those about her family life.

- For a sociology class, a student writes about a controversial urban renewal project to replace decaying but repairable houses with a library and park. To learn about the history of the project, she reads newspaper reports and interviews people who helped plan the project as well as some neighborhood residents and activists who oppose it. She also tours the site with the project manager to see what is actually being done. In addition to presenting different points of view about the project, her essay describes the library and park in detail, including pictures of the neighborhood before the project and drawings of what it will look like afterward. She seeks to give the impression that the project manager has succeeded in winning neighborhood support and that most residents will be pleased with the completed project.

THINKING ABOUT YOUR EXPERIENCE WITH OBSERVATION

Before studying a type of writing, it is useful to spend some time thinking about what you already know about it. You may have written about your firsthand observations, describing what you saw or heard, for a school assignment or during a trip. If you haven't written observational essays or reports, you have certainly made them orally to friends and family.

To analyze your experience composing observational essays, you might recall one occasion when you reported your observations orally or in writing and then consider questions like these: Why were you communicating what you saw and heard to members of this particular audience? Did you make your report primarily to teach them something, to show that you had learned something yourself, to entertain them, or for some other reason? What did you choose to emphasize? Why?

Consider also observational reports you have read, heard, or seen on television. If you recall one such report in some detail, try to identify what made it interesting to you. What tone did the narrator adopt? What descriptive details, dialogue, or commentary stood out for you?

Write at least a page about your experience with observational writing.

■ A Guide to Reading Observational Essays

This guide introduces you to observational writing. By completing all of the activities in it, you will prepare yourself to learn a great deal from the other readings in this chapter about how to read and write an observational essay. The guide focuses on "Soup," an intriguing profile of Albert Yeganeh and his unique New York City restaurant, Soup Kitchen International. You will read this observational essay twice. First, you will read it for meaning, looking closely at the essay's content and ideas. Then you will read the essay like a writer, analyzing it to see how the writer crafts the essay and to learn the strategies that make it vivid and informative. These two activities—reading for meaning and reading like a writer—follow every reading in this chapter.

THE NEW YORKER

Soup

"Soup" was published anonymously in a 1989 issue of the New Yorker, *a magazine read by many people across the country who enjoy its cartoons, short stories, music and art reviews, political and social commentary, and profiles of people and places. The subject of this essay is Albert Yeganeh, the creative and demanding owner/chef of a small take-out restaurant that serves only soup. In 1995, Yeganeh's restaurant inspired an episode of the then-popular television program* Seinfeld.

The writer of "Soup" relies extensively on dialogue quoted from the interview to keep the focus on Yeganeh's personality and ideas. Readers can readily imagine the reporter interviewing Yeganeh, writing down soup names and ingredients, observing people in line, and even standing in line for a bowl of soup.

As you read, notice the prominence given to reporting what Albert Yeganeh told the writer. The marginal annotations point to dialogue as well as other strategies writers of observation typically use. Add your own comments and questions to the annotations.

1   When Albert Yeganeh says "Soup is my lifeblood," he means it. And when he says "I am extremely hard to please," he means that, too. Working like a demon alchemist in a tiny storefront kitchen at 259-A West Fifty-fifth Street, Mr. Yeganeh creates anywhere from eight to seventeen soups every weekday. His concoctions are so popular that a wait of half an hour at the lunchtime peak is not uncommon, although there are strict rules for conduct in line. But more on that later.

> Yeganeh's arresting words, the image of him as "a demon alchemist," and mention of his "strict rules" create a strong impression and entice readers to go on.

2   "I am psychologically kind of a health freak," Mr. Yeganeh said the other day, in a lisping staccato of Armenian origin. "And I know that soup is the greatest meal in the world. It's very good for your digestive system. And I use only the best, the freshest ingredients. I am a perfectionist. When I make a clam soup, I use three different kinds of clams. Every other place uses canned clams. I'm called crazy. I am not crazy. People

> So far, the information comes mostly from the writer's interview with Yeganeh, interspersed with details describing the chef's appearance, voice, and gestures (highlighted through the rest of the essay).

don't realize why I get so upset. It's because if the soup is not perfect and I'm still selling it, it's a torture. It's *my* soup, and that's why I'm so upset. First you clean and then you cook. I don't believe that ninety-nine per cent of the restaurants in New York know how to clean a tomato. I tell my crew to wash the parsley *eight* times. If they wash it five or six times, I scare them. I tell them they'll go to jail if there is sand in the parsley. One time, I found a mushroom on the floor, and I fired that guy who left it there." He spread his arms and added, "This place is the only one like it in . . . in . . . the whole earth! One day, I hope to learn something from the other places, but so far I haven't. For example, the other day I went to a very fancy restaurant and had borscht. I had to send it back. It was *junk*. I could see all the chemicals in it. I never use chemicals. Last weekend, I had lobster bisque in Brooklyn, a very well-known place. It was *junk*. When I make a lobster bisque, I use a whole lobster. You know, I never advertise. I don't have to. All the big-shot chefs and the kings of the hotels come here to see what *I'm* doing."

As you approach Mr. Yeganeh's Soup Kitchen Inter- 3 national from a distance, the first thing you notice about it is the awning, which proclaims "Homemade Hot, Cold, Diet Soups." The second thing you notice is an aroma so delicious that it makes you want to take a bite out of the air. The third thing you notice, in front of the kitchen, is an electric signboard that flashes, saying, "Today's Soups . . . Chicken Vegetable . . . Mexican Beef Chili . . . Cream of Watercress . . . Italian Sausage . . . Clam Bisque . . . Beef Barley . . . Due to Cold Weather . . . For Most Efficient and Fastest Service the Line Must . . . Be Kept Moving . . . Please . . . Have Your Money . . . Ready . . . Pick the Soup of Your Choice . . . Move to Your Extreme . . . Left After Ordering."

"I am not prejudiced against color or religion," Mr. 4 Yeganeh told us, and he jabbed an index finger at the flashing sign. "Whoever follows that I treat very well. My regular customers don't say anything. They are very intelligent and well educated. They know I'm just trying to move the line. The New York cop is very smart — he sees everything but says nothing. But the young girl who wants to stop and tell you how nice you look and hold everyone up — *yah!*" He made a guillotining mo-

Is he crazy or arrogant, a perfectionist or a great chef—or all these things at once?

The writer shifts the topic to describe the restaurant from the outside, taking the perspective of an approaching customer who sees the sign and smells the soup.

The topic shifts again to Yeganeh's attitudes about customers. A reference to the sign described in the previous paragraph makes a smooth transition.

tion with his hand. "I tell you, I hate to work with the public. They treat me like a slave. My philosophy is: The customer is always wrong and I'm always right. I raised my prices to try to get rid of some of these people, but it didn't work."

5   The other day, Mr. Yeganeh was dressed in chef's whites with orange smears across his chest, which may have been some of the carrot soup cooking in a huge pot on a little stove in one corner. A three-foot-long handheld mixer from France sat on the sink, looking like an overgrown gardening tool. Mr. Yeganeh spoke to two young helpers in a twisted Armenian-Spanish barrage, then said to us, "I have no overhead, no trained waitresses, and I have the cashier here." He pointed to himself theatrically. Beside the doorway, a glass case with fresh green celery, red and yellow peppers, and purple eggplant was topped by five big gray soup urns. According to a piece of cardboard taped to the door, you can buy Mr. Yeganeh's soups in three sizes, costing from four to fifteen dollars. The order of any well-behaved customer is accompanied by little waxpaper packets of bread, fresh vegetables (such as scallions and radishes), fresh fruit (such as cherries or an orange), a chocolate mint, and a plastic spoon. No coffee, tea, or other drinks are served.

6   "I get my recipes from books and theories and my own taste," Mr. Yeganeh said. "At home, I have several hundreds of books. When I do research, I find that I don't know anything. Like cabbage is a cancer fighter, and some fish is good for your heart but some is bad. Every day, I should have one sweet, one spicy, one cream, one vegetable soup—and they *must* change, they should always taste a little different." He added that he wasn't sure how extensive his repertoire was, but that it probably includes at least eighty soups, among them African peanut butter, Greek moussaka, hamburger, Reuben, B.L.T., asparagus and caviar, Japanese shrimp miso, chicken chili, Irish corned beef and cabbage, Swiss chocolate, French calf's brain, Korean beef ball, Italian shrimp and eggplant Parmesan, buffalo, ham and egg, short rib, Russian beef Stroganoff, turkey cacciatore, and Indian mulligatawny. "The chicken and the seafood are an addiction, and when I have French garlic soup I let people have only one

The topic changes again, and readers are inside the kitchen, seeing the ingredients and equipment.

After another shift, readers are back in the position of a customer waiting in line and reading the sign. By now, readers can see that the essay is organized around topics instead of chronological events.

For the first time, the writer paraphrases instead of quoting Yeganeh. The examples show Yeganeh's creativity. Have you ever heard of soups like these?

small container each," he said. "The doctors and nurses love that one."

A lunch line of thirty people stretched down the block from Mr. Yeganeh's doorway. Behind a construction worker was a man in expensive leather, who was in front of a woman in a fur hat. Few people spoke. Most had their money out and their orders ready. 7

At the front of the line, a woman in a brown coat couldn't decide which soup to get and started to complain about the prices. 8

"You talk too much, dear," Mr. Yeganeh said, and motioned her to move to the left. "Next!" 9

"Just don't talk. Do what he says," a man huddled in a blue parka warned. 10

"He's downright rude," said a blond woman in a blue coat. "Even abusive. But you can't deny it, his soup is the best." 11

From here on, the writer switches to narration, showing Yeganeh's rules and customers' reactions to them.

READING FOR MEANING

This section presents three activities that will help you reread the observational essay "Soup" with a critical eye. Done in sequence, these activities lead you from a basic understanding of the selection to a more personal response to it and finally to an analysis that deepens your understanding and critical thinking about what you are reading.

Read to Comprehend

Reread the selection, and write a sentence or two explaining the kind of restaurant the Soup Kitchen International is. The following definitions may help you understand the *New Yorker* writer's vocabulary:

concoctions (paragraph 1): new and unusual combinations of ingredients.

staccato (2): a rapid burst of speech.

barrage (5): a torrent of words.

Find three or more additional words that you do not understand, and find the best definitions from the dictionary that work with their context.

To expand your understanding of this reading, you might use one or more of the following critical reading strategies that are explained and illustrated in Appendix 1: *summarizing* and *questioning to understand and remember*.

Read to Respond

Write several paragraphs exploring your initial thoughts and feelings about the observational essay "Soup." Focus on anything that stands out for you, perhaps because it resonates with your own experience or because you find a statement puzzling.

You might consider writing about the following:

- Yeganeh's ideas about food quality and health, perhaps in comparison to the quality at fast-food restaurants with which you are familiar;

- Yeganeh's work ethic for himself and his employees, perhaps in relation to your experience as an employee or a manager; or

- his customers' willingness to follow Yeganeh's strict rules and tolerate his rudeness.

To develop your response to "Soup," you might use one or more of the following critical reading strategies that are explained and illustrated in Appendix 1: *contextualizing* and *reflecting on challenges to your beliefs and values.*

Read to Analyze Assumptions

Reread the observational essay "Soup," and write a paragraph or two exploring one or more of the assumptions you find in the text. All writing contains *assumptions*—opinions, values, and beliefs that are taken for granted as commonly accepted truths by the writer or others. Personal or individual assumptions also tend to reflect the values and beliefs of a particular group or community, sometimes called *cultural ideology*, which shape the way those in the group think, act, and understand the world.

Analyzing assumptions is an important part of learning to read critically because assumptions tend to be unexamined and unquestioned (at least consciously) by those who hold them. When you read with a critical eye, you identify important assumptions in the text and ask questions about them. Sometimes assumptions are stated explicitly, but often they are only implied, so you may have to search for underlying assumptions in the word choices and examples. Here are some kinds of questions you should ask regarding the assumptions you find: Who holds this assumption? How does the assumption reinforce or critique the status quo? What alternative ideas, beliefs, or values would challenge this assumption? If the writer uses the assumption to appeal to readers, how effective do you think this appeal is, and why?

To help you get started reading for assumptions in "Soup," notice what the writer chooses to emphasize about the subject as well as what words the writer uses. For example, in the opening paragraph, the writer describes Yeganeh as "a demon alchemist," which amounts to calling him a mad scientist. An alchemist is a kind of magician supposedly capable of transforming worthless metal into gold. Moreover, the word *demon* suggests a person with enormous energy and also with something devilish or at least mischievous about him. Together, these word choices suggest a cultural ideology often associated with creativity, assumptions that would benefit from critical scrutiny. Consider, for example, whether the *New Yorker* writer, the restaurant's customers, and Yeganeh himself share the assumption that creativity is god-given—or in Yeganeh's case, inspired by the devil—and that artists may be mad or at least eccentric. Even an expression like *thinking outside the box* suggests that to be creative, you need to think differently—even unconventionally. From a more critical viewpoint, however, creative people may also be thought of as children who are to be indulged rather than respected. What, if any, evidence is there in "Soup" of these assumptions? To what extent do these assumptions about creativity lead artists to think of themselves as entitled to special privileges and lead us to grant them?

You may want to examine our cultural assumptions about creativity, or you may choose to explore other assumptions in "Soup," such as the following:

- **assumptions about power.** Yeganeh describes himself as a "perfectionist" (paragraph 2) and admits he's "extremely hard to please" (1). He brags about scaring his employees and tells how he fired someone for leaving a mushroom on the floor. In addition, he defends his rules and right to deny service to anyone who does not follow them. To think critically about the assumptions in this essay related to power, ask yourself: When Yeganeh scares and fires his employees, how much is he holding them to a high standard, and how much is he just showing off? Why does he tell the customer that she talks too much? Because she is disrupting the efficiency of his operation? Because she is complaining about his prices? Do you think Yeganeh is a tyrant who abuses power, or does he use his power appropriately?

- **assumptions about customer service.** When Yeganeh says, "The customer is always wrong and I'm always right" (4), he is reversing the popular saying that the customer is always right. To think critically about assumptions in this essay related to customer service, ask yourself: If most Americans expect business people to put on a friendly face, why is Donald Trump's television program *The Apprentice*—which shows Trump firing people who are competing for a job with his organization—popular? What in our culture might cause many Americans to be impressed by business people's power and arrogance as much as—or perhaps more than—by their friendliness and helpfulness? Consider whether there might be a class system at work in which employees and even managers are required to act as if the customer is always right but CEOs operate under a different set of assumptions. Consider also what seem to be the assumptions of the writer and Yeganeh's customers about service.

To probe assumptions more deeply, you might use one or more of the following critical reading strategies that are explained and illustrated in Appendix 1: *reflecting on challenges to your beliefs and values, exploring the significance of figurative language,* and *looking for patterns of opposition.*

READING LIKE A WRITER

This section guides you through an analysis of the observational writing strategies illustrated in "Soup": *describing places and people, presenting information about the subject, organizing the information, choosing a role,* and *conveying a dominant impression of the subject.* For each strategy, you will be asked to reread and annotate part of the essay to see how that particular strategy works in "Soup."

When you study the selections later in this chapter, you will see how different writers use these same strategies. The Guide to Writing Observational Essays near the end of the chapter suggests ways you can use these strategies in your own writing.

Describing Places and People

Observational writing, like autobiography (Chapter 2), succeeds by presenting the subject vividly and concretely. Writers of observation usually describe both places and people, although they may emphasize one over the other. Visual details usually predominate in an observational essay, but some writers complement these by describing sounds, smells, tastes, and even textures and temperatures.

Observational writers present people through visual details and action—how they look, how they dress, how they move, what they do. Notice, for example, that the author of "Soup" briefly describes the people waiting in line with a few choice visual details, mainly about their clothing—"a man in expensive leather" (paragraph 7), "a man huddled in a blue parka" (10), "a blond woman in a blue coat" (11). They also show how people talk and interact with one another, often including both direct quotations from their notes and paraphrases of what people have said. See, for example, the warning offered by the man in the parka and the blond woman's response. To gain a sense of an individual's personality, readers usually need only a few details indicating the person's tone of voice, facial expression, style of dress, or movements.

Analyze

1. Focus first on how Albert Yeganeh is described by *skimming* paragraphs 1, 2, and 4 to 6 and *underlining* the words and phrases that enable you to imagine what he looks and sounds like. Do not underline what he says, but do underline descriptions of how he looks and sounds as he says it. *Reflect on* how the description of Yeganeh's gestures and motions help you envision him as he talks. No Writing *

2. Next, focus on the way the place is described. *Skim* paragraphs 3 and 5, *putting brackets* around the words and phrases that enable you to imagine the Soup Kitchen International. Then *consider* which of the senses these descriptions bring to mind. Which of these descriptions of the place stays with you? No Writing *

Write

Paragraph

Write several sentences explaining how the author describes Yeganeh and his restaurant. *Give examples* from your analysis of the descriptive language to indicate the ways that Yeganeh stands out as an individual and that the Soup Kitchen International is different from other fast-food places you have visited. Also indicate any additional descriptive details that would have helped you imagine Yeganeh and his restaurant.

Presenting Information about the Subject

An observational essay—sometimes called a *profile, feature article,* or *ethnography*—seeks to inform readers about the subject but to present information in an engaging, even entertaining way. Because they are trying to interest as much as to enlighten readers, writers of observational essays integrate information gathered from field research—especially direct observation and interviews—to create a scene showing individuals moving, talking, and gesturing. In addition, observational writers sometimes do background library and Internet research about the subject or read materials offered at the place they are profiling and weave this secondhand information into their descriptions of the place and people.

Observational writers may also make good use of writing strategies to present information, such as giving examples, listing, comparing and contrasting, classifying, describing a process, and defining key terms. In "Soup," we can find many of these explanatory strategies. Paragraph 2, for instance, presents examples to illustrate Yeganeh's claim that he uses "only the best, the freshest ingredients." Paragraph 6 classifies soup into four categories—sweet, spicy, cream, and vegetable. The following analysis activity invites you to look for other explaining strategies and speculate about what they add to the essay.

Analyze

Just thinking

1. Skim "Soup," noting where the information came from—direct observation, interviews, or background research. Note if there are any places where you cannot identify the source of the information.

2. Reread paragraphs 3 and 6 to see how the explanatory strategy of listing is used. One or two soups could have been named. Consider why the *New Yorker* author chose to use listing twice in a brief essay instead of just naming a couple of the soups.

3. Look at paragraph 2, where the strategy of comparing and contrasting is used. Consider what this strategy adds to the essay.

Write

Paragraph

Write a few sentences describing the sources of the information included in "Soup." Add a sentence or two answering the following questions about the uses of listing and of comparing and contrasting: What do the long lists contribute to your understanding of the essay? What does contrasting his and another restaurant's lobster bisque tell you about Yeganeh?

Organizing the Information

Writers of observation typically rely on two basic organizational plans: *topical*, with related pieces of information grouped together; and *narrative*, with bits of information arranged into a chronological story line. Most observational essays use one or the other organization, but because narrative is so engaging for readers, a common strategy is to begin and end a topically organized essay with a bit of narrative. "Soup" is a good example of topical organization, but it concludes with a bit of narrative to illustrate a topic raised at the beginning of the essay. While a narrative plan offers the advantage of intriguing readers by arousing curiosity and even building suspense, a primarily topical plan keeps the focus firmly on the information.

Analyze

1. *Make a scratch outline* of paragraphs 1 to 6 of "Soup," identifying the topics in the order in which they appear. *Notice* that some paragraphs have more than one topic; paragraph 2, for instance, raises several topics — the health benefits of soup, Yeganeh's perfectionism, his emphasis on cleanliness, and the ways that his restaurant compares to others. You do not have to list every topic, but try to identify the most important ones in the paragraph. (For an example of scratch outlining, see Appendix 1.)

2. *Look closely* at paragraphs 7 to 11, where the writer presents a little narrative to show how customers respond to Yeganeh's rules. Consider how this bit of narrative helps bring the observational essay to a satisfying close.

Write

Write several sentences commenting on what types of topics are presented and how effectively they are sequenced. Then *write a few more sentences* answering these questions: How does the sequence of topics contribute to or inhibit your growing understanding of Soup Kitchen International as you read through the essay? Which topics does the writer introduce and then drop? Which topics does he or she return to later?

Choosing a Role

In making and writing up their observations, writers have a choice of roles to perform — as a *spectator observer* or as a *participant observer*. In the spectator role, the writer acts as a reporter, watching and listening but remaining outside of the activity. In contrast, participant observers become insiders for a time, joining in the activity with the people they are interviewing or observing. In most observational essays, the writer adopts the spectator role. The advantage of this role is that a writer who is in the same position as the reader knows what readers need to understand a new and unfamiliar subject. On the other hand, the participant observer role has the advantage of enabling the writer to reveal insider knowledge gained from intimate experience with the subject. But for observational writing, there is a danger in getting too involved in the subject. If writers know the subject too well, they tend to have difficulty anticipating what readers who are unfamiliar with the subject need to know. This is especially true of students who want to write about groups to which they belong or activities in which they excel. But as you will see later in the chapter, student Katie Diehm uses a participant observer role effectively to write about an activity she had never participated in before. You will also see in the next reading how John T. Edge alternates these roles, using the spectator role to present what he learned on his visit to a factory and using the participant observer role to give readers a close-up-and-personal perspective on a product the factory produces.

Analyze

1. *Reread* the essay, and *decide* which role the author of "Soup" adopts — a participant observer or a spectator observer role.

2. *Find* a passage that supports your analysis of the role that the author takes.

Write

Write a few sentences identifying the role that you think the *New Yorker* writer adopts in "Soup," and use the passage you have chosen to explain why you think so.

Conveying a Dominant Impression of the Subject

Readers want observational essays to communicate any insights into the subject that the writer gained by observing a place and interviewing people. But they do not expect such essays to make an argument asserting the writer's interpretation or evaluation of the subject. In fact, they would be surprised if the writer's ideas were more prominent than the presentation of people and places. In this regard, observational writing resembles autobiographical writing. In both genres, writers convey their perspective on what is significant and interesting about the subject primarily through showing with some telling interspersed. That is, the writer's word choices and selection of details and quotations create a dominant impression of the subject. Any explicit statements interpreting or evaluating the subject or expressing the writer's attitude toward it reinforce the dominant impression. For example, writers sometimes indicate what they had expected prior to observing the subject. They may also react to something that was said or done while they were on the scene. The author of "Soup" does not state a judgment about Yeganeh or analyze him, but as a careful reader you can infer what the writer thinks from the writer's word choices as well as from the details the writer decided to include in the essay.

Analyze

1. *Underline* any words or phrases that suggest the author's attitudes toward or feelings about Yeganeh as a human being, cook, and businessman.

2. *Note in the margin* any interpretation or evaluation of Yeganeh and his way of doing business that might be implied by what he says and does.

Write

Write several sentences identifying the dominant impression you have of Yeganeh and his Soup Kitchen International. *Quote* two or three phrases or sentences from the essay that convey this impression most strongly, and *identify* briefly the attitude, interpretation, or evaluation you see in each phrase or sentence.

A SPECIAL READING STRATEGY

Comparing and Contrasting Related Readings: "Soup" and John T. Edge's "I'm Not Leaving Until I Eat This Thing"

Comparing and contrasting related readings is a special critical reading strategy that is useful both in reading for meaning and in reading like a writer. This strategy is particularly applicable when writers present similar subjects, as is the case in the observational essays in this chapter by the *New Yorker* writer (p. 81) and John T. Edge (p. 93). Both writers describe a business they observed and report on their interview with the business owner. In both instances, the business involves food products and their preparation; however, Edge adopts the role of participant observer, whereas the author of "Soup" maintains a more "objective" distance. To compare and contrast these two observational essays, think about issues such as these:

- Compare these essays in terms of their cultural contexts. What seems to you to be most significant about the two business philosophies represented in these essays?

- Compare how the two writers organize the information derived from interview and observation. Highlight the places in each essay where information from interviews is quoted or summarized and places where information from direct observation is presented.

- Compare Edge's alternation between the participant-observer and spectator-observer roles to the *New Yorker* writer's consistent spectator-observer role. Note any places in "Soup" where you get a sense of the writer's point of view or judgment. What do the participant's observations add to Edge's essay?

See Appendix 1 for detailed guidelines on using the comparing and contrasting related readings strategy.

■ Readings

JOHN T. EDGE

I'm Not Leaving Until
I Eat This Thing

John T. Edge (b. 1962) earned a master's degree in Southern studies from the University of Mississippi and is director of the Southern Foodways Alliance at the university, where he coordinates an annual conference on Southern food. Food writer for the national magazine Oxford American, *he has also written for* Cooking Light *and* Food & Wine *and is a contributing editor at* Gourmet. *His essays are regularly included in* Best Food Writing *anthologies, and he coedits cookbooks and travel guides, such as* Lonely Planet: New Orleans *(2003). He has published many books of his own:* A Gracious Plenty: Recipes and Recollections from the American South *(1999);* Southern Belly *(2007), a portrait of Southern food told through profiles of people and places; and a series on iconic American foods, including* Fried Chicken: An American Story *(2004) and* Hamburgers and Fries: An American Story *(2005).*

This reading first appeared in a 1999 issue of Oxford American *(where the illustration on page 94 appeared) and was reprinted in 2000 in* Utne Reader. *Edge focuses his considerable observational writing skills on an unusual manufacturing business in rural Louisiana— Farm Fresh Food Supplier. He introduces readers to the company's workers and its pig products, a best-seller being pickled pig lips, which are sometimes bottled in vivid patriotic and special-events colors. Unlike the author of the previous reading, Edge participates in his subject—not by joining in the activities at Farm Fresh but by attempting to eat a pig lip at Jesse's Place, a nearby "juke" bar. You will see that the reading begins and ends with this personal experience.*

As you read, enjoy Edge's struggle to eat a pig lip, and pay attention to the information Edge offers about the history and manufacture of pickled pig lips at Farm Fresh.

It's just past 4:00 on a Thursday afternoon in June at Jesse's Place, a country juke 17 miles south of the Mississippi line and three miles west of Amite, Louisiana. The air conditioner hacks and spits forth torrents of Arctic air, but the heat of summer can't be kept at bay. It seeps around the splintered doorjambs and settles in, transforming the squat particleboard-plastered roadhouse into a sauna. Slowly, the dank barroom fills with grease-smeared mechanics from the truck stop up the road and farmers straight from the fields, the soles of their brogans thick with dirt clods. A few weary souls make their way over from the nearby sawmill. I sit alone at the bar, one empty bottle of Bud in front of me, a second in my hand. I drain the beer, order a third, and stare down at the pink juice spreading outward from a crumpled foil pouch and onto the bar.

I'm not leaving until I eat this thing, I tell myself. 2

Half a mile down the road, behind a fence coiled with razor 3 wire, Lionel Dufour, proprietor of Farm Fresh Food Supplier, is loading up the last truck of the day, wheeling case after case of pickled pork offal out of his cinder-block processing plant and into a semitrailer bound for Hattiesburg, Mississippi.

His crew packed lips today. Yesterday, it was pickled sausage; the 4 day before that, pig feet. Tomorrow, it's pickled pig lips again. Lionel has been on the job since 2:45 in the morning, when he came in to light the boilers. Damon Landry, chief cook and maintenance man, came in at 4:30. By 7:30, the production line was at full tilt: six women in white smocks and blue bouffant caps, slicing ragged white fat from the lips, tossing the good parts in glass jars, the bad parts in barrels bound for the rendering plant. Across the aisle, filled jars clatter by on a conveyor belt as a worker tops them off with a Kool-Aid-red slurry of hot sauce, vinegar, salt, and food coloring. Around the corner, the jars are capped, affixed with a label, and stored in pasteboard boxes to await shipping.

Unlike most offal—euphemistically called "variety meats"— 5
lips belie their provenance. Brains, milky white and globular, look
like brains. Feet, the ghosts of their cloven hoofs protruding,
look like feet. Testicles look like, well, testicles. But lips are different. Loosed from the snout, trimmed of their fat, and dyed a
preternatural pink, they look more like candy than like carrion.

At Farm Fresh, no swine root in an adjacent feedlot. No viscera- 6
strewn killing floor lurks just out of sight, down a darkened hall-
way. These pigs died long ago at some Midwestern abattoir. By
the time the lips arrive in Amite, they are, in essence, pig Popsicles,
50-pound blocks of offal and ice.

"Lips are all meat," Lionel told me earlier in the day. "No gristle, 7
no bone, no nothing. They're bar food, hot and vinegary, great
with a beer. Used to be the lips ended up in sausages, headcheese,
those sorts of things. A lot of them still do."

Lionel, a 50-year-old father of three with quick, intelligent eyes 8
set deep in a face the color of cordovan, is a veteran of nearly
40 years in the pickled pig lips business. "I started out with my
daddy when I wasn't much more than 10," Lionel told me, his shy
smile framed by a coarse black mustache flecked with whispers of
gray. "The meatpacking business he owned had gone broke back
when I was 6, and he was peddling out of the back of his car, selling
dried shrimp, napkins, straws, tubes of plastic cups, pig feet, pig
lips, whatever the bar owners needed. He sold to black bars, white
bars, sweet shops, snowball stands, you name it. We made the
rounds together after I got out of school, sometimes staying out till
two or three in the morning. I remember bringing my toy cars to
this one joint and racing them around the floor with the bar
owner's son while my daddy and his father did business."

For years after the demise of that first meatpacking company, 9
the Dufour family sold someone else's product. "We used to buy
lips from Dennis Di Salvo's company down in Belle Chasse,"
recalled Lionel. "As far as I can tell, his mother was the one who
came up with the idea to pickle and pack lips back in the '50s, back
when she was working for a company called Three Little Pigs over
in Houma. But pretty soon, we were selling so many lips that we
had to almost beg Di Salvo's for product. That's when we started
cooking up our own," he told me, gesturing toward the cast-iron
kettle that hangs from the rafters by the front door of the plant.
"My daddy started cooking lips in that very pot."

Lionel now cooks lips in 11 retrofitted milk tanks, dull stainless- 10
steel cauldrons shaped like oversized cradles. But little else has
changed. Though Lionel's father has passed away, Farm Fresh
remains a family-focused company. His wife, Kathy, keeps the
books. His daughter, Dana, a button-cute college student who has

won numerous beauty titles, takes to the road in the summer, selling lips to convenience stores and wholesalers. Soon, after he graduates from business school, Lionel's younger son, Matt, will take over operations at the plant. And his older son, a veterinarian, lent his name to one of Farm Fresh's top sellers, Jason's Pickled Pig Lips.

"We do our best to corner the market on lips," Lionel told me, his voice tinged with bravado. "Sometimes they're hard to get from the packing houses. You gotta kill a lot of pigs to get enough lips to keep us going. I've got new customers calling every day; it's all I can do to keep up with demand, but I bust my ass to keep up. I do what I can for my family—and for my customers.   11

"When my customers tell me something," he continued, "just like when my daddy told me something, I listen. If my customers wanted me to dye the lips green, I'd ask, 'What shade?' As it is, every few years we'll do some red and some blue for the Fourth of July. This year we did jars full of Mardi Gras lips—half purple, half gold," Lionel recalled with a chuckle. "I guess we'd had a few beers when we came up with that one."   12

Meanwhile, back at Jesse's Place, I finish my third Bud, order my fourth. *Now,* I tell myself, my courage bolstered by booze, *I'm ready to eat a lip.*   13

They may have looked like candy in the plant, but in the barroom they're carrion once again. I poke and prod the six-inch arc of pink flesh, peering up from my reverie just in time to catch the barkeep's wife, Audrey, staring straight at me. She fixes me with a look just this side of pity and asks, "You gonna eat that thing or make love to it?"   14

Her nephew, Jerry, sidles up to a bar stool on my left. "A lot of people like 'em with chips," he says with a nod toward the pink juice pooling on the bar in front of me. I offer to buy him a lip, and Audrey fishes one from a jar behind the counter, wraps it in tinfoil, and places the whole affair on a paper towel in front of him.   15

I take stock of my own cowardice, and, following Jerry's lead, reach for a bag of potato chips, tear open the top with my teeth, and toss the quivering hunk of hog flesh into the shiny interior of the bag, slick with grease and dusted with salt. Vinegar vapors tickle my nostrils. I stifle a gag that rolls from the back of my throat, swallow hard, and pray that the urge to vomit passes.   16

With a smash of my hand, the potato chips are reduced to a pulp, and I feel the cold lump of the lip beneath my fist. I clasp the bag shut and shake it hard in an effort to ensure chip coverage in all the nooks and crannies of the lip. The technique that Jerry uses—and I mimic—is not unlike that employed by home cooks mixing up a mess of Shake 'n Bake chicken.   17

I pull from the bag a coral crescent of meat now crusted with   18
blond bits of potato chips. When I chomp down, the soft flesh dis-
solves between my teeth. It tastes like a flaccid cracklin', unmistakably porcine, and not altogether bad. The chips help, providing
texture where there was none. Slowly, my brow unfurrows, my
stomach ceases its fluttering.

Sensing my relief, Jerry leans over and peers into my bag. "Kind   19
of look like Frosted Flakes, don't they?" he says, by way of describing the chips rapidly turning to mush in the pickling juice. I offer
the bag to Jerry, order yet another beer, and turn to eye the pig feet
floating in a murky jar by the cash register, their blunt tips bobbing
up through a pasty white film.

READING FOR MEANING

This section presents three activities that will help you reread Edge's observational essay with a critical eye. Done in sequence, these activities lead you from a
basic understanding of the selection to a more personal response to it and finally
to an analysis that deepens your understanding and critical thinking about what
you are reading.

Read to Comprehend

Reread the selection, and write a brief explanation of how Farm Fresh Food
Supplier obtains and packs pig lips. The following definitions may help you
understand Edge's vocabulary:

offal (paragraph 3): internal organs of an animal that are often regarded as
inedible.

euphemistically (5): worded in a manner considered less offensive than a
more direct wording might be.

abattoir (6): a slaughterhouse.

Identify three or more additional words that you don't understand, and find the
best definitions from the dictionary that work with their context.

To expand your understanding of this reading, you might use one or more of
the following critical reading strategies that are explained and illustrated in Appendix 1: *outlining, summarizing,* and *questioning to understand and remember.*

Read to Respond

Write several paragraphs exploring your initial thoughts and feelings about
Edge's observational essay. Focus on anything that stands out for you, perhaps
because it resonates with your own experience or because you find a statement
puzzling.

You might consider writing about the following

- Edge's description of the production line at Farm Fresh Food Supplier (paragraph 4), perhaps in relation to your own work experience;

- Lionel Dufour's story about how he "made the rounds" with his father after school (8), perhaps in relation to your own experience learning from a relative or mentor;

- your reaction to Edge's attempt to eat the pig lip, possibly in relation to your own experience trying an unusual food; or

- the ways that the photograph adds to your understanding of and response to the essay.

To develop your response to Edge's essay, you might use one or more of the following critical reading strategies that are explained and illustrated in Appendix 1: *contextualizing* and *reflecting on challenges to your beliefs and values.*

Read to Analyze Assumptions

Reread Edge's observational essay profiling Lionel Dufour and his business Farm Fresh Food Supplier, and write a paragraph or two exploring one or more of the assumptions you find in the text. The following suggestions may help:

- **assumptions about culture and food.** For many people, foods that they did not eat as children seem strange and sometimes even repulsive. Even though he is a Southerner, Edge is squeamish about eating a popular southern delicacy, pickled pig lip. To think critically about assumptions regarding culture and food, ask yourself: Why do you suppose Edge uses the words *courage* and *cowardice* to describe his hesitancy to try a new food? What might he assume about pig lips that makes him fearful? Remember that he has already visited Farm Fresh, so he knows a lot about pig lips and their production. Think of food anxieties that you or people you know have. What do you think causes them? What kinds of personal and cultural beliefs and values influence people's food preferences—and rejections?

- **assumptions about work.** In describing Jesse's Place, "a country juke" where locals come after work to drink and socialize (paragraph 1), and Farm Fresh Supplier, a factory where pig parts are cooked and prepared for shipping, Edge mentions many jobs, all of which involve tiring physical labor—mechanics, farmers, sawmill workers, cook, maintenance man, and assembly-line workers. To think critically about the assumptions in this essay related to work, ask yourself: Why are manual laborers not paid well or given much respect in our culture, while a strong work ethic is celebrated as a great American virtue? Lionel Dufour, the factory owner who gets to work at 2:45 a.m. and does "blue-collar" jobs such as loading trucks, seems to represent the work ethic for Edge. But unlike his employees, Dufour makes a lot of money.

Why do you suppose Edge does not interview one of the factory workers or the other customers at the bar?

To probe assumptions more deeply, you might use one or more of the following critical reading strategies that are explained and illustrated in Appendix 1: *reflecting on challenges to your beliefs and values* and *exploring the significance of figurative language.*

READING LIKE A WRITER

CHOOSING A ROLE AND ORGANIZING THE INFORMATION

Writers of observational essays can choose to adopt the role of a spectator or the role of a participant. The author of "Soup" chose to remain in the spectator role throughout the essay. He or she easily could have sampled the soups and included in the essay firsthand impressions of the taste and texture of different soups. The author might also have worked for an hour in Yeganeh's kitchen, participating in the soup preparation, and written about the experience of working under him rather than only quoting Yeganeh's criticism of his workers. But instead, the author chose to remain an outsider looking in, getting information only from interviews and observations. Edge, on the other hand, chose to use both roles. He acted as a spectator during his visit to Farm Fresh Food Supplier and as a participant when he tried to eat a pickled pig lip produced by Farm Fresh.

Another choice that writers have is to organize the information topically or narratively. As we saw, the author of "Soup" chose a topical organization. Edge uses both methods. He organizes the information that he gleaned from visiting at Farm Fresh under several topics and the information that he gained from trying to eat a pig lip as a narrative. Not all narratively organized profiles also involve participant observation (see, for example, Peggy Orenstein's "The Daily Grind: Lessons in the Hidden Curriculum" on p. 111). But if telling the story of the writer's participation would give the essay added interest and drama, writers should consider using a narrative plan or a combination of narrative and topical.

Analyze

1. *Reread* paragraphs 1 and 2, where Edge begins telling the story of his attempt to eat a pig lip. *Notice* how he sets up the time and place, describes the bar, and creates suspense.

2. *Skim* paragraphs 3 to 12, *identifying in the margin* where each new topic is introduced.

3. *Reread* paragraphs 13 to 19, where Edge returns to his story about eating the pig lip. *Reflect* on the relation of the bar story to the report of Edge's visit to Farm Fresh. What, if anything, do you learn from Edge's story about trying to eat a pig lip that you cannot find out from paragraphs 3 to 12?

Write

Write several sentences explaining how Edge's use of both roles—as spectator and as participant—contributes to the effectiveness of his observational essay. Add a few more sentences commenting on the effectiveness of Edge's way of organizing the information he learned about the Dufour family business.

CONSIDERING IDEAS FOR YOUR OWN WRITING

Consider writing about a place that serves, produces, or sells something unusual, perhaps something that, like Edge, you could try yourself to discover more about for the purpose of informing and engaging your readers. If no such place comes to mind, you could browse the online Yellow Pages of your local phone directory for ideas. One example is a company that produces or packages some special ethnic or regional food or a local café that serves it. There are many other possibilities—acupuncture clinic, caterer, novelty toy and balloon store, microbrewery, chain-saw dealer, boatbuilder, talent agency, ornamental iron manufacturer, bead store, manicure or nail salon, aquarium and pet fish supplier, auto-detailing shop, tattoo parlor, scrap-metal recycler, fly-fishing shop, handwriting analyst, dog- or cat-sitting service, photo restorer, burglar alarm installer, Christmas tree farm, wedding specialist, reweaving specialist, wig salon. You need not evaluate the quality of work at the place as part of your observational essay. Instead, keep the focus on informing readers about the service or product the place offers. Relating a personal experience with the service or product is a good idea but not a requirement of an observational essay.

WILLIAM L. HAMILTON
At Ole Miss, the Tailgaters Never Lose

William L. Hamilton is a reporter for the New York Times *who has written many observational articles, including profiles of the Virginia military post Fort Belvoir, a sleep clinic, and the canine star of the new film* Lassie. *His book* Shaken and Stirred: Through the Martini Glass and Other Drinking Adventures *(2004) is a collection of his observational writing about places where people gather to drink and socialize.*

"At Ole Miss, the Tailgaters Never Lose," which appeared in 2006 in the travel section of the Times, *profiles football-weekend partying at the Grove on the University of Mississippi (Ole Miss) campus. The title is taken from a remark by one of the people Hamilton interviewed and is a familiar saying at Ole Miss. Although the people Hamilton interviewed at the Grove attend the games and enthusiastically support the team, they seldom mention football. As you read, note in the margin what they say about why they spend game weekends at the Grove.*

Helen Craig, or Mrs. C. York Craig Jr., as she is more formally   1
known, leveled a well-seasoned eye at me as the bluegrass band set
up in the background. L. Rodney Chamblee, one of her 60 tailgating tent mates of friends and family, slipped a large bloody
mary into my hand. Mrs. Craig stood under a tall blue tent rapidly
filling with people and food, and underscored the eye with a smile

Brandi Inman, a member of the Rebellettes dance team, heads for the
football stadium after a pregame performance at the Grove at Ole Miss.

that held the history of the South, and its hospitality, wide and deep, behind it.

"We may not win every game," she said. "But we've never lost a party." 2

On the great American calendar of revelry and seasonal rites, fall equals football. And pigskin equals parties: tailgating parties, in particular. At the University of Mississippi in Oxford last Saturday, the Ole Miss Rebels, Mrs. Craig's team, lost 27–3 to Wake Forest. But the party, a 24-hour gale-force blowout held in the Grove, 10 acres of thick oak, elm and magnolia, was a victory. 3

The glory of the Grove is legend at all of Ole Miss's rival schools in the Southeastern Conference and beyond. It is the mother and 4

mistress of outdoor ritual mayhem. As Charles R. Frederick Jr., a folklorist at the University of Indiana, characterized it in his dissertation on the Ole Miss tailgating event, the call to "come on out Saturday and look us up" in the Grove is as basic, and born to a spot, as a human bond can get. And it is as deep as the root of a tree.

It is also as fresh and green as a leaf. "I love it," Molly Aiken, 19, a sophomore at Ole Miss, said on Saturday under a tent, under the trees, a party roar rising and dissipating into the whisper of a warm, humid wind above. "There's no place like it." Ms. Aiken, who is from Chattanooga, Tenn., said of the University of Tennessee in Knoxville, "I went to U.T. this past weekend, for the U.T.-Florida game, and I was, like, this just doesn't compare." 5

Ole Miss's stadium accommodates 60,580 people, and devotees of the Grove argue that the Grove accommodates more. It is every kind of party you can describe, at once: cocktail party, dinner party, tailgate picnic party, fraternity and sorority rush, family reunion, political handgrab, gala and networking party-hearty — what might have inspired Willie Morris, one of Mississippi's favorite sons, to declare Mississippi not a state, but a club. 6

On Saturday, David G. Sansing, a professor emeritus at Ole Miss who has written a history of the university, stood at the top of the Grove, watching the party. "Your college days are the fondest years of your life, and those memories of those years grow rosier as time recedes," he said. "When these alumni come back and walk 7

DRESSED TO PARTY The Grove look:
a new dress and pearls, a Colonel Reb
costume, or red and blue body paint.

through that grove, they're not just walking over land—ground—they're walking back through time."

That time has changed going forward. Ole Miss was not integrated until 1962. And though there were few black families partying in the Grove on Saturday, black players dominate the Rebels' football team.

The alumni join students for a walk back in time (always with a cup in hand). The hand-slapping between the partyers and the players as they took the "Rebel walk" through the Grove to the stadium was hard and full of heart. A police motorcycle escort preceded them.

There are seven home-game weekends at Ole Miss. And people in the Grove have how to have a good time down cold—they can stretch the party over three days, from Friday night into Sunday morning. It is pimento cheese sandwiches and silver trays, candelabra and fried chicken tenders, button-down shirts, reb ties and khaki shorts, pearls, expensive sunglasses and flip-flops in your purse for when your high heels become history. As Ms. Aiken explained, you show up in a new dress for each weekend, and you wear your hair curly if it's going to rain. Rain, like the thunderstorm that cracked the sky open late on Saturday, only throws fuel on the fire. When a bolt of lightning touched down at the edge of the Grove, blasting the trees with thunder, the crowd went crazy with approval.

The party is technically a picnic. Originally an informal tailgating get-together when most serious pregame socializing took place at Ole Miss's fraternity and sorority houses, by the 50's the Grove started to become its own pregame tradition. Cars have been kept out since a rainstorm in 1990 that reduced the Grove to a rutted swamp, and tents replaced them. With the tents began a dance of real estate that kicked off the rules and regulations, and like a ball in play, the interpretations of them, that characterizes the party in the Grove today.

The Grove Society, an alumni organization, posts a strict schedule for the event, which dictates that set-up will start at Friday midnight. Last Friday, at 11 p.m., the 15 university police officers assigned to orchestrate the arrival of people, pickups and vans unloading equipment at the road next to the Grove watched a gang of 60 picnickers, restless for territory and armed with tent poles and folding tables and chairs, sprint into the dark woods and disappear like a band of merry men into Sherwood Forest. White tents popped up like mushrooms, and the party was on.

"We've tried arresting the first two or three, and they still come out," said Officer Adam Peacock, standing beside his patrol car, its blue light bubble revealing more and more tents with each sweep. "They start yelling at each other, and then they just rush. I mean, we could arrest all of them, but that's not very right."

A woman in a black cocktail dress with a diamond buckle, Sheila Cowart, class of '83, approached the car to ask advice on beating the rush. "I know y'all say midnight, but if you really try to go by the rules, you got 200 that are in front of you, and you're kind of out of luck," Ms. Cowart said to Officer Peacock, shifting from heel to heel.

By midnight, most of the ground in the Grove was staked out by tents, circles of folding chairs and public squares of banquet tables. Christmas lights and camp lanterns were going up, satellite dishes pointed toward the stars and a boom box broke the stillness with thick, lazy Southern rock and roll.

A boy in white shorts and a polo shirt stepped out onto the Walk of Champions, the brick path where the Rebels would make their ceremonial march through the Grove on their way to the stadium the next day. "Are you READY?!" he called to the trees, prompting the Ole Miss cheer.

"HELLLLL YES! DAAAAMN RIGHT!" the trees yelled back. "Hotty Toddy gosh almighty who in the hell are we? Flim flam bim bam, OLE MISS by damn! WUUUUUUUUUUUUU!"

The Grove was now a tent city displaying the names of families, Mississippi towns and other states. "Good Times Here Are Not Forgotten," read one tent.

WHO NEEDS HALFTIME? The Ole Miss marching band plays in the Grove.

"Sometimes people encroach on your space, and you got to   19
kind of help them get in their correct spot, if you know what I
mean," said Johnnie Wade, class of '80, on Saturday at 10 a.m., with
a grin as friendly as a fried egg. "Bunch of rookies. There's a certain
place you want to be so everybody'll know where it is every year."
Mr. Wade's daughter cooked breakfast in their tent, beneath what
he called "our redneck chandelier"—an Ole Miss umbrella hung
upside down and wired with lights.

Many who attend the weekends, like Mr. Wade, hire students or   20
local people to set up the tent, stake out their spots and store the
setups between games. "The Walk of Champions is where the
prime real estate is," said Chip Trammell, a senior at Ole Miss,
whose business, the Rebel Tent Company, typically makes $25,000
a game, charging $150 a tent. "We don't guarantee it, but you will
be within a 10-yard radius." He worked from 3 p.m. Friday to 3 a.m.
Saturday to secure 40 tents for 30 clients.

By Saturday afternoon, people spilled everywhere, smoking, eat-   21
ing, talking, drinking. Red plastic cups bobbed in a sea of chest-
high hands, cigarettes tucked between two fingers. "Whiskey
Sprite," said Fred Vann, a sophomore and a Phi Delta, of his cup.
"Most of us get the Jim Beam plastic-bottle fifth." He produced one,
as did two of the four friends he was standing with. "If you drop it, it
doesn't break," he said. Susan Ashley Richburg, a sophomore standing with a group of sorority friends, when asked what was in
her cup, said, "Water—you want some?" The women exploded
shouting. "I'm 20 and I'll be 21 in September," Ms. Richburg said.
"WuuHUUU."

It is likely that Ms. Richburg will mark many events in her life   22
under the same trees. The Grove is a grove of generations of Mississippi families who went to Ole Miss and who send their children
there. Alumni and students, fathers and sons, old friends and new
acquaintances seemed inseparable last Saturday, as if they had
walked out of the halls ringing the Grove and were meeting between
classes, not between decades.

The confluence of a peaceful setting and the presence of the right   23
people is not ignored. "It is a tremendous network, that works,"
said Doug Hederman, class of '93, whose family not only owns a
commercial printing company but also dominated newspaper
publishing in the state for over 50 years. "What you'll find here on a
regular basis is presidents, C.E.O.'s of Fortune 500 companies," Mr.
Hederman said. "It's a great opportunity to meet somebody you're
not doing business with. Plus you start thinking of the political
influence here. Homecoming of last year, Senators Lott and Coch-
ran were both here, and Governor Barbour. It's pretty powerful."

It is the site of powerful history, too. When Ole Miss was inte- 24
grated at gunpoint in 1962 by federal troops, the rioting, during
which two people died, took its last stand in the Grove before leaving the campus for Oxford's square. James Meredith, the African-
American student whose admission precipitated the fighting,
graduated in the Grove. On Sunday, a monument to the chapter of
history opened by Mr. Meredith's admission, with a bronze figure
of him striding toward a small stone temple, will be dedicated. It is
placed behind the Lyceum, the school's oldest building, where bullet holes still mark the struggle in broken brick. A restoration in
2001 left them carefully in place. Professor Sansing, the historian,
called the day being commemorated "the last echo of the last battle
of the Civil War."

Down the hill from where he stood, the streets crowded as Ole 25
Miss's team made its march through the Grove. Five hours later,
the Rebels were defeated by Wake Forest in a blinding rain that
pushed a 5 p.m. kickoff back to 7 p.m. But the party in the Grove
held its ground until midnight.

READING FOR MEANING

This section presents three activities that will help you reread Hamilton's
observational essay with a critical eye. Done in sequence, these activities lead you
from a basic understanding of the selection to a more personal response to it and
finally to an analysis that deepens your understanding and critical thinking about
what you are reading.

Read to Comprehend

Reread the selection, and write a brief explanation of what is special about the
Grove. The following definitions may help you understand Hamilton's vocabulary:

revelry (paragraph 3): celebration, partying.

networking (6): making personal connections useful for business or some
other purpose.

encroach (19): to trespass.

Identify three or more additional words that you don't understand, and find the
best definitions from the dictionary that work with their context.

To expand your understanding of this reading, you might use one or more of
the following critical reading strategies that are explained and illustrated in Appendix 1: *outlining, summarizing*, and *questioning to understand and remember*.

Read to Respond

Write several paragraphs exploring your initial thoughts and feelings about Hamilton's observational essay. Focus on anything that stands out for you, perhaps because it resonates with your own experience or because you find a statement puzzling.

You might consider writing about the following:

- the Ole Miss school spirit and sense of camaraderie, perhaps as compared to the spirit at your college or high school;

- Officer Peacock's excuse for not doing anything to enforce the midnight starting time for setting up tents: "We've tried arresting the first two or three, and they still come out. . . . we could arrest all of them, but that's not very right" (paragraph 13);

- David G. Sansing's comment "Your college days are the fondest years of your life," perhaps in relation to your own experience in either college or high school (7); or

- the ways that the photographs add to your understanding of and response to the essay.

To develop your response to Hamilton's essay, you might use one or more of the following critical reading strategies that are explained and illustrated in Appendix 1: *contextualizing* and *reflecting on challenges to your beliefs and values*.

Read to Analyze Assumptions

Reread Hamilton's observational essay, and write a paragraph or two exploring one or more of the assumptions you find in the text. The following suggestions may help:

- **assumptions about drinking.** Drinking is obviously widespread at the Grove. Hamilton reports in the first paragraph that "a large bloody mary" was slipped into his hand, and he describes alumni and students at the Grove "always with a cup in hand" (paragraph 9). He also quotes sophomore Susan Ashley Richburg saying she will be "21 in September," revealing she is below the minimum drinking age. To think critically about the assumptions in this essay related to drinking, ask yourself: What assumptions about drinking at the Grove do the author and the people he interviewed seem to make? After a university police officer was killed in a recent drunk-driving accident, the Ole Miss chancellor apparently assumed drinking at the Grove was at least partly to blame. He denounced what he called the "culture of alcohol" on campus and instituted a "crackdown on tailgating activities in the famous grove." If your campus also has a "culture of alcohol," what assumptions do you suppose students and administrators hold about drinking?

- **assumptions about race.** Hamilton notes that "there were few black families partying in the Grove" even though "black players dominate the Rebels' football team" (paragraph 8). He also reminds readers about the civil rights struggle to integrate the university in 1962 (24). To think critically about the assumptions in this essay related to race, ask yourself: What is the significance of these observations by the author? What do Hamilton and the people he interviewed seem to assume or expect about racial representation at the Grove? Given that the Grove serves as a networking opportunity for business people and politicians—what Hamilton describes as "[t]he confluence of a peaceful setting and the presence of the right people" (23)—what do you suppose are some of the consequences of having only a few African Americans (and possibly no other ethnic minorities) participate in the partying there?

To probe assumptions more deeply, you might use one or more of the following critical reading strategies that are explained and illustrated in Appendix 1: *reflecting on challenges to your beliefs and values*, *exploring the significance of figurative language*, and *looking for patterns of opposition*.

READING LIKE A WRITER
PRESENTING INFORMATION ABOUT THE SUBJECT

Writers of observational essays present information from a variety of sources: interview, direct observation, and background reading. Hamilton uses all three sources. He also uses assorted strategies to present the information he has gathered from these sources. In paragraph 6, he classifies seven different kinds of parties, all of which occur "at once" during the Grove event. In paragraph 19, he defines a new term, "redneck chandelier," as "an Ole Miss umbrella hung upside down and wired with lights." He lists examples (paragraph 10), reports a comparison (5), describes a process (12), and narrates history (24). One special explanatory strategy used by Hamilton (and his editors) is to illustrate his observations with photographs. In this activity, you will examine this article's use of photographs.

Analyze

1. *Look* at the photographs, and consider how they work as a group to help you visualize the Grove.

2. *Choose* one photograph that you think is especially helpful, and *make notes* about the information it conveys.

Write

Write a few sentences explaining what you learned from analyzing the photograph you chose. What information do you get from this particular photograph? How does it add to the written text?

CONSIDERING IDEAS FOR YOUR OWN WRITING

You might write about a special site on your campus. Many campuses have research institutes or centers, art galleries, and specialized libraries where you could interview and observe visitors as well as people who work there. If you are interested in sports or performance, you might consider observing one of the athletic, theater, or musical groups on your campus. Campus programs (such as justice and crime studies, global studies), special services (counseling, job placement), and societies (Phi Beta Kappa, sororities, and fraternities) may also be interesting subjects for observational writing.

A SPECIAL READING STRATEGY

Comparing and Contrasting Related Readings: Edge's "I'm Not Leaving Until I Eat This Thing" and Hamilton's "At Ole Miss, the Tailgaters Never Lose"

Comparing and contrasting related readings is a special critical reading strategy useful both in reading for meaning and in reading like a writer. This strategy is particularly applicable when writers present similar subjects, as is the case in the observational essays in this chapter by John T. Edge (p. 93) and William L. Hamilton (p. 101). Both writers describe aspects of life in the Deep South. To compare and contrast these essays, think about issues such as these:

- Compare these essays in terms of their cultural contexts. What aspects of Southern culture does each essay focus on? What do you learn about Mississippi and Louisiana, such as social values or issues of economic class, from reading these essays side by side?

- Compare how these two writers use material from interviews to construct their essays. Note how many people each writer interviews, and what each chooses to quote or to summarize.

- Compare the two essays' use of photographs. In each case, what, if anything, do the photographs add to your understanding or appreciation of the subject? What is the effect of having one picture with no caption in one essay and five captioned pictures plus a map in the other? How might the differences be related to where the essays were originally published—one in a literary magazine and the other in the travel section of a newspaper? How might they be related to the essays' different subject matter? What would be the effect if the Edge essay illustrated more of what the writer observed or the Hamilton essay less?

See Appendix 1 for detailed guidelines on using the comparing and contrasting related readings strategy.

PEGGY ORENSTEIN

The Daily Grind: Lessons in the Hidden Curriculum

Peggy Orenstein has been a managing editor of Mother Jones, *a founding editor of the magazine* 7 days, *and a member of the editorial boards of* Esquire *and* Manhattan, inc. *and is now a contributing writer for the* New York Times Magazine. *Her essays have appeared in the* New Yorker, Vogue, *and many other nationally known publications and in many anthologies, including* The Best American Science Writing *(2004). Her 1994 book,* School Girls: Young Women, Self-Esteem, and the Confidence Gap, *won a New York Times Notable Book of the Year Award, and in 1996 the National Women's Political Caucus honored her for her contributions to literature and politics. She has since published* Flux: Women on Sex, Work, Kids, Love, and Life in a Half-Changed World *(2002) and* Waiting for Daisy: A Tale of Two Continents, Three Religions, Five Infertility Doctors, an Oscar, an Atomic Bomb, a Romantic Night and One Woman's Quest to Become a Mother *(2007). Orenstein also was featured in the documentary films* Crumb *(1994) and* Searching for Asian America *(2003) and was the executive producer of the Oscar-nominated documentary* The Mushroom Club *(2006).*

This observational essay, profiling an eighth-grade math class, comes from the opening chapter of School Girls. *Orenstein undertook the extensive research for this book after reading a study conducted by the American Association of University Women in 1991 that identified a gender gap in the achievements of male and female students in America. Her research concentrated on the ways in which some schools and teachers—often unwittingly—may inhibit girls' classroom experiences and constrain their opportunities to participate.*

As you read the essay, think about whether the story it tells is one you have witnessed firsthand.

Amy Wilkinson has looked forward to being an eighth grader forever—at least for the last two years, which, when you're thirteen, seems like the same thing. By the second week of September she's settled comfortably into her role as one of the school's reigning elite. Each morning before class, she lounges with a group of about twenty other eighth-grade girls and boys in the most visible spot on campus: at the base of the schoolyard, between one of the portable classrooms that was constructed in the late 1970s and the old oak tree in the overflow parking lot. The group trades gossip, flirts, or simply stands around, basking in its own importance and killing time before the morning bell.

At 8:15 on Tuesday the crowd has already convened, and Amy is standing among a knot of girls, laughing. She is fuller-figured than she'd like to be, wide-hipped and heavy-limbed with curly blond hair, cornflower-blue eyes, and a sharply upturned nose. With the help of her mother, who is a drama coach, she has become the school's star actress: last year she played Eliza in Weston's production of *My Fair Lady*. Although she earns solid grades in all of her subjects—she'll make the honor roll this fall—drama is her passion, she says, because "I love entertaining people, and I love putting on characters."

Also, no doubt, because she loves the spotlight: this morning, when she mentions a boy I haven't met, Amy turns, puts her hands on her hips, anchors her feet shoulder width apart, and bellows across the schoolyard, "Greg! Get over here! You have to meet Peggy."

She smiles wryly as Greg, looking startled, begins to make his way across the schoolyard for an introduction. "I'm not exactly shy," she says, her hands still on her hips. "I'm bold."

Amy is bold. And brassy, and strong-willed. Like any teenager, she tries on and discards different selves as if they were so many pairs of Girbaud jeans, searching ruthlessly for a perfect fit. During a morning chat just before the school year began, she told me that her parents tried to coach her on how to respond to my questions. "They told me to tell you that they want me to be my own person," she complained. "My mother *told* me to tell you that. I do want to be my own person, but it's like, you're interviewing me about who I am and she's telling me what to say—that's not my own person, is it?"

When the morning bell rings, Amy and her friends cut off their conversations, scoop up their books, and jostle toward the school's entrance. Inside, Weston's hallways smell chalky, papery, and a little sweaty from gym class. The wood-railed staircases at either end of the two-story main building are worn thin in the middle from the scuffle of hundreds of pairs of sneakers pounding them at forty-eight-minute intervals for nearly seventy-five years. Amy's mother, Sharon, and her grandmother both attended this school. So will her two younger sisters. Her father, a mechanic who works on big rigs, is a more recent Weston recruit: he grew up in Georgia and came here after he and Sharon were married.

Amy grabs my hand, pulling me along like a small child or a slightly addled new student: within three minutes we have threaded our way through the dull-yellow hallways to her locker and then upstairs to room 238, Mrs. Richter's math class.

The twenty-two students that stream through the door with us   8
run the gamut of physical maturity. Some of the boys are as small
and compact as fourth graders, their legs sticking out of their
shorts like pipe cleaners. A few are trapped in the agony of a
growth spurt, and still others cultivate downy beards. The girls'
physiques are less extreme: most are nearly their full height, and all
but a few have already weathered the brunt of puberty. They wear
topknots or ponytails, and their shirts are tucked neatly into their
jeans.

Mrs. Richter, a ruddy, athletic woman with a powerful voice, has   9
arranged the chairs in a three-sided square, two rows deep. Amy
walks to the far side of the room and, as she takes her seat, falls into
a typically feminine pose: she crosses her legs, folds her arms across
her chest, and hunches forward toward her desk, seeming to shrink
into herself. The sauciness of the playground disappears, and, in
fact, she says hardly a word during class. Meanwhile, the boys,
especially those who are more physically mature, sprawl in their
chairs, stretching their legs long, expanding into the available space.

Nate, a gawky, sanguine boy who has shaved his head except for   10
a small thatch that's hidden under an Oakland A's cap, leans his
chair back on two legs and, although the bell has already rung,
begins a noisy conversation with his friend, Kyle.

Mrs. Richter turns to him. "What's all the discussion about,   11
Nate?" she asks.

"*He's* talking to *me*," Nate answers, pointing to Kyle. Mrs.   12
Richter writes Nate's name on the chalkboard as a warning toward
detention and he yells out in protest. They begin to quibble over
the justice of her decision, their first—but certainly not their
last—power struggle of the day. As they argue, Allison, a tall,
angular girl who once told me, "My goal is to be the best wife and
mother I can be," raises her hand to ask a question.

Mrs. Richter, finishing up with Nate, doesn't notice.   13

"Get your homework out, everyone!" the teacher booms, and   14
walks among the students, checking to make sure no one has
shirked on her or his assignment. Allison, who sits in the front row
nearest both the blackboard and the teacher, waits patiently for
another moment, then, realizing she's not getting results, puts her
hand down. When Mrs. Richter walks toward her, Allison tries
another tack, calling out her question. Still, she gets no response, so
she gives up.

As a homework assignment, the students have divided their   15
papers into one hundred squares, color-coding each square prime
or composite—prime being those numbers which are divisible

only by one and themselves, and composite being everything else. Mrs. Richter asks them to call out the prime numbers they've found, starting with the tens.

Nate is the first to shout, "Eleven!" The rest of the class chimes in a second later. As they move through the twenties and thirties, Nate, Kyle, and Kevin, who sit near one another at the back of the class, call out louder and louder, casually competing for both quickest response and the highest decibel level. Mrs. Richter lets the boys' behavior slide, although they are intimidating other students. 16

"Okay," Mrs. Richter says when they've reached one hundred. "Now, what do you think of one hundred and three? Prime or composite?" 17

Kyle, who is skinny and a little pop-eyed, yells out, "Prime!" but Mrs. Richter turns away from him to give someone else a turn. Unlike Allison, who gave up when she was ignored, Kyle isn't willing to cede his teacher's attention. He begins to bounce in his chair and chant, *"Prime! Prime! Prime!"* Then, when he turns out to be right, he rebukes the teacher, saying, "See, I told you." 18

When the girls in Mrs. Richter's class do speak, they follow the rules. When Allison has another question, she raises her hand again and waits her turn; this time, the teacher responds. When Amy volunteers her sole answer of the period, she raises her hand, too. She gives the wrong answer to an easy multiplication problem, turns crimson, and flips her head forward so her hair falls over her face. 19

Occasionally, the girls shout out answers, but generally they are to the easiest, lowest-risk questions, such as the factors of four or six. And their stabs at public recognition depend on the boys' largesse: when the girls venture responses to more complex questions, the boys quickly become territorial, shouting them down with their own answers. Nate and Kyle are particularly adept at overpowering Renee, who, I've been told by the teacher, is the brightest girl in the class. (On a subsequent visit, I will see her lay her head on her desk when Nate overwhelms her and mutter, "I hate this class.") 20

Mrs. Richter doesn't say anything to condone the boys' aggressiveness, but she doesn't have to: they insist on — and receive — her attention even when she consciously tries to shift it elsewhere in order to make the class more equitable. 21

After the previous day's homework is corrected, Mrs. Richter begins a new lesson, on the use of exponents. 22

"What does three to the third power mean?" she asks the class. 23

"I know!" shouts Kyle. 24

Instead of calling on Kyle, who has already answered more than 25
his share of questions, the teacher turns to Dawn, a somewhat
more voluble girl who has plucked her eyebrows down to a few
hairs.

"Do you know, Dawn?" 26

Dawn hesitates, and begins "Well, you count the number of 27
threes and. . . ."

"*But I know!*" interrupts Kyle. "*I know!*" 28

Mrs. Richter deliberately ignores him, but Dawn is rattled: she 29
never finishes her sentence, she just stops.

"*I know! ME!*" Kyle shouts again, and then before Dawn recov- 30
ers herself he blurts, "*It's three times three times three!*"

At this point, Mrs. Richter gives in. She turns away from Dawn, 31
who is staring blankly, and nods at Kyle. "Yes," she says. "Three
times three times three. Does everyone get it?"

"*YES!*" shouts Kyle; Dawn says nothing. 32

Mrs. Richter picks up the chalk. "Let's do some others," she says. 33

"Let me!" says Kyle. 34

"I'll pick on whoever raises their hand," she tells him. 35

Nate, Kyle, and two other boys immediately shoot up their 36
hands, fingers squeezed tight and straight in what looks like a
salute.

"Don't you want to wait and hear the problem first?" she asks, 37
laughing.

They drop their hands briefly. She writes "8^4" on the board. 38
"Okay, what would that look like written out?"

Although a third of the class raise their hands to answer, includ- 39
ing a number of students who haven't yet said a word, she calls on
Kyle anyway.

"Eight times eight times eight times eight," he says trium- 40
phantly, as the other students drop their hands.

When the bell rings, I ask Amy about the mistake she made in 41
class and the embarrassment it caused her. She blushes again.

"Oh yeah," she says. "That's about the only time I ever talked in 42
there. I'll never do that again."

READING FOR MEANING

This section presents three activities that will help you reread Orenstein's
observational essay with a critical eye. Done in sequence, these activities lead you
from a basic understanding of the selection to a more personal response to it and
finally to an analysis that deepens your understanding and critical thinking about
what you are reading.

Read to Comprehend

Reread the selection, and write a brief explanation of what you learn from reading Orenstein's essay. The following definitions may help you understand Orenstein's vocabulary:

sanguine (paragraph 10): cheerful, confident.

shirked (14): avoided (a task or responsibility).

prime numbers (15): numbers that cannot be divided evenly by any number except themselves and 1 (such as 1, 3, 5, and 7).

Identify three or more additional words that you don't understand, and find the best definitions from the dictionary that work with their context.

To expand your understanding of this reading, you might use one or more of the following critical reading strategies that are explained and illustrated in Appendix 1: *outlining, summarizing, paraphrasing,* and *questioning to understand and remember.*

Read to Respond

Write several paragraphs exploring your initial thoughts and feelings about Orenstein's observational essay. Focus on anything that stands out for you, perhaps because it resonates with your own experience or because you find a statement puzzling.

You might consider writing about the following:

- cliques like the one Amy belongs to and which Orenstein describes as the "school's reigning elite" (paragraph 1);

- the contradictory images of Amy—the "bold," "brassy, and strong-willed" Amy (5), who is an honor roll student and actress, in contrast to the Amy in math class, "seeming to shrink into herself" and hardly saying a word (9); or

- the ways that your own school experiences add to your understanding of and response to the essay.

To develop your response to Orenstein's essay, you might use one or more of the following critical reading strategies that are explained and illustrated in Appendix 1: *contextualizing, reflecting on challenges to your beliefs and values,* and *judging the writer's credibility.*

Read to Analyze Assumptions

Reread Orenstein's observational essay, and write a paragraph or two exploring one or more of the assumptions you find in the text. The following suggestions may help:

- **assumptions about power struggles.** Orenstein describes Mrs. Richter's math class as the site of power struggles—between some boys and girls and between the teacher and two boys, Nate and Kyle. Even though she is the only adult and teacher in the room and presumably possesses power (she sets the rules and can send students to detention), Mrs. Richter seems unable to exercise it effectively or fairly. To think critically about the assumptions in this essay related to power struggles, ask yourself: In what ways do Mrs. Richter, Nate and Kyle, and even the girls assert power in the classroom? For example, how do you interpret the fact that the boys raise their hands most of the time or that Mrs. Richter is the one asking questions and presumably determining which answers are correct? How do the behaviors of Mrs. Richter and girls like Allison and Dawn create a space for Nate and Kyle to exercise power? What assumptions about power do you think Orenstein, Mrs. Richter, the boys, and the girls hold? What were your assumptions about power in the classroom when you first read this essay?

- **assumptions about gender differences.** In Mrs. Richter's math class, the boys seem to know all the answers. In the 1980s, standardized test scores showed that (at least in the United States) girls were significantly behind boys in math, but in recent years the gap seems to be narrowing. Nevertheless, many people continue to assume that boys are better than girls at math and science. Several theories have been put forward to explain this apparent gender difference: (1) boys are naturally endowed with better spatial abilities and logical thinking skills than girls, (2) boys are more interested in math and science careers, (3) boys, unlike girls, typically play games such as baseball that help them develop math skills, and (4) parents and teachers tend to treat girls stereotypically as weaker in math and therefore create a self-fulfilling prophecy.

  To think critically about assumptions in this essay related to gender differences, ask yourself: What do Orenstein, Mrs. Richter, the boys, and the girls seem to assume about who will be able to answer Mrs. Richter's questions? When you were in elementary or middle school, how common was the assumption that boys would do better in math and science than girls? Which of the four theories listed above do you think you or your teachers would have accepted? What are your assumptions about this issue now?

To probe assumptions more deeply, you might use one or more of the following critical reading strategies that are explained and illustrated in Appendix 1: *reflecting on challenges to your beliefs and values* and *looking for patterns of opposition*.

READING LIKE A WRITER
DESCRIBING PEOPLE

Writers of observational essays often focus their observations on people, whether alone or interacting with others. To present people, writers can choose from a repertoire of describing strategies. They may show us how people look and dress as well as how they gesture and move. They also may let us hear people talk, either to the interviewer or with other people. In this essay, we hear Amy talk to Orenstein, and we overhear the students and teacher talking with one another in the classroom. Dialogue functions in observational writing both to present people and to inform readers about a subject. To present the Weston School students' interactions and the teacher's role in the eighth-grade math classroom, Orenstein relies increasingly on dialogue beginning in paragraph 11. From paragraph 22 to the end, she relies mainly on dialogue.

Analyze

1. *Reread* paragraphs 1 to 5, 8 to 10, and 18, and *underline* the details that enable you to visualize Amy, Mrs. Richter, Nate, and Kyle.

2. *Reread* paragraphs 22 to 41, focusing on the dialogue (the material within quotation marks) and the descriptive speaker tags (*she asks, shouts Kyle*). *Think* about what you learn about the teacher and the students from this dialogue, and *make notes* about what you discover.

Write

Write several sentences explaining the kinds of details that Orenstein uses to describe people, giving examples from your annotations. Add another sentence or two explaining what the dialogue adds to your understanding of the people.

CONSIDERING IDEAS FOR YOUR OWN WRITING

Consider writing an observational essay about a group of people who interact with each other for a specific purpose. The essay might be about a teacher and students interacting in a classroom to learn a specific concept or practice a skill; a group of actors rehearsing for a play; a basketball team practicing for an upcoming game; employees working collaboratively on a project; committee members, businesspeople, or politicians debating a policy or proposal; or members of a club, sports team, or other interest group meeting to resolve a crisis.

A SPECIAL READING STRATEGY

Looking for Patterns of Opposition

Looking for patterns of opposition can be an especially useful strategy for reading observational essays like Peggy Orenstein's "The Daily Grind: Lessons in the Hidden Curriculum." Following the instructions in

Appendix 1, pp. 620–23, you will see that the first thing you need to do is reread the essay and mark the oppositions you find. "The Daily Grind," like the "Letter from Birmingham Jail" excerpt that we use to illustrate this strategy, is teeming with oppositions or binaries. In many instances, two opposing terms are obvious, such as *girls* versus *boys*. A less obvious opposition is the contrasting description *feminine pose . . . seeming to shrink into herself* versus *boys . . . expanding into the available space* (paragraph 9). Sometimes, one of the opposing terms is not introduced until later in the essay. For example, Amy is described in paragraph 5 as *bold*, but later, in paragraph 9, she is described as *say[ing] hardly a word during class*. You may even find instances where only one of the terms appears in the essay and you need to supply the missing opposite term. For example, Amy is described in paragraph 3 as someone who *loves the spotlight*, but in Mrs. Richter's class it is clear from her behavior that she doesn't want to be noticed. So you could present the opposition as *loves the spotlight* versus *tries to disappear* (or you could use the description *flips her head forward so her hair falls over her face* [paragraph 19]).

See Appendix 1 for detailed guidelines on using the *looking for patterns of opposition* strategy.

Observation Online

The Internet provides many sites where you can read and listen to observational profiles of interesting people, activities, and places and also can post your own. Some observational essays can be found on personal blogs, but there are also zines or online magazines that feature observations, such as American Profile, Outside Online, and WorldandI.com. Many of these Web sites, like the one illustrated below, are multimedia, including writing, audio, still photos, and motion pictures.

This example of an online observational essay comes from the site of the National Public Radio program All Things Considered. Originally posted on November 8, 2005, it was written by one of the hosts of the program, Michele Norris, a journalist whose writing has appeared in print (the Washington Post and Los Angeles Times) as well as on TV (ABC News) and radio. Her book, Ourselves among Others, is a compilation of pieces she wrote for the Washington Post on a child living in a crack house.

The marginal annotations point out the observational writing strategies that readers expect in print versions as well as features that are characteristic of writing on the Web. Notice, for example, the various clickable icons. Experienced Web users know they can click on text that is in color or underlined and automatically be linked to a new Web page. But unfamiliar icons may need to be explained. The NPR Web site is reader-friendly in this regard. For instance, it includes icons with a word or phrase to explain what the icon does: (◄» Listen) instructs readers that later in the piece, when they see the icon without the word listen, all they need to do is click and listen.

Behind the Scenes with Film Editor Walter Murch
(◄» Listen) by Michele Norris

The first photo caption provides *descriptive details* that help readers visualize Murch at his workplace.

⌕ Enlarge   Sean Cullen

Walter Murch at a New York postproduction facility where the final edit of *Jarhead* was made.

(◄») Murch discusses the system he uses to remember his initial reaction to scenes long after they've been shot.

All Things Considered, November 8, 2005 · In the world of filmmaking, actors and directors dominate the spotlight. The people who actually assemble the film frame by frame and beat by beat toil in relative obscurity. Walter Murch is one film editor whose profile is much higher than most.

Norris gives Murch's credits, establishing him as a person who should be interesting to readers.

Murch has won three Oscars. He has been nominated in sound and or editing categories eight times. His films include *Apocalypse Now,* all three *Godfather* films, *The English Patient, The Unbearable Lightness of Being, Ghost* and *The Talented Mr. Ripley.*

She tells where the interview took place and introduces Murch's latest film.

His latest film, *Jarhead,* is based on former Marine Anthony Swofford's best-selling book about the Persian Gulf War. Murch discussed that film, and his job as editor, in a New York postproduction facility where he had finished up work on *Jarhead.*

Murch is a man of many interests. He composes music, translates Italian poetry in his

Juliette Binoche in 1996's *The English Patient*. *Miramax Home Entertainment*

Watch the Scene

The helicopter attack scene, set to Wagner's "Ride of the Valkyries," from Frances Ford Coppola's *Apocalypse Now* (1979). *Copyright © 2000 Zeotrope Corp.*

Watch the Scene

This story was produced by Steve Lickteig.

spare time and if you spend enough time with him, you're likely to hear him quote French philosophers or string theorists. But his definition of what he does is simple.

"My job as an editor is to gently prod the attention of the audience to look at various parts of the frame," he says. "And I do that by manipulating, by how and where I cut and what succession of images I work with."

Sound is equally important to Murch's work. It's "a huge influence on people's attention," he says.

To demonstrate, Murch flips on his computer, clicks the mouse a few times and instantly pulls up a scene from *Jarhead*. Swofford's character, played by Jake Gyllenhaal, is in combat for the first time and there's an artillery barrage. Everyone else ducks for cover, but he stands up. And the camera moves closer to him. Then, in the distance, there's a muffled explosion followed by dead silence.

This fleeting silence is a golden moment for an editor -- a chance to put the audience right there on the battlefield. *Jarhead*'s director, Sam Mendes, originally wanted that silence to stretch for several seconds. But Murch came up with a better idea.

Pieces of dust and sand from the explosion hit the actor's face in slow motion. Then you hear the sound of the particles hitting his face. "My combat action has commenced," the character says.

Murch says the tiniest of sounds can help create the sense of silence in a film. "By manipulating what you hear and how you hear it -- and what other things you don't hear -- you can not only help tell the story, you can help the audience get into the mind of the character," Murch says.

Ironically, Murch begins the editing process with the sound turned off.

"If I had the sound up, it would tend to take all of my attention..." he says. "It would crowd out the possibilities for other sound. And then only after the scene has found its shape, then I turn the switch on and let the sound come in. And frequently there will be two sounds that come together, two lines of dialogue and I'll think, that's great that that happened by accident."

The editing process is tedious work -- viewing hours of footage, then assembling a film a half-second at a time. "I like to think this is sort of a cross between a short-order cook and a brain surgeon," Murch says. "Sometimes you're doing incredibly delicate things. Two frames different will mean whether the film is a success or not..."

Norris uses quotations to let Murch describe what he does as a film editor. Readers can click on the Watch the Scene icons below the film stills to see examples of Murch's editing.

She *narrates* what happened during the interview when Murch demonstrates how he edited the sound in a crucial scene.

Norris relates what she apparently learned from Murch, summarizing part of the interview.

She *describes* what a viewer sees and hears in the scene. By this point, it is clear that Norris has adopted a *spectator-observer role* and organized her essay *topically*.

She reveals part of Murch's editing process and follows with a quotation explaining it.

Norris selects Murch's witty comparisons of a film editor to a short-order cook and a brain surgeon and ends the piece with Murch's own memorable words.

Analyze

1. *Find* another example of online observational writing.

2. *Check* to see which basic features of observational writing the example that you found displays, such as describing people and places, presenting information about the subject, organizing the information narratively or topically, choosing a spectator-observer or a participant-observer role, and conveying a dominant impression.

3. Also *look for* any special online characteristics, such as links, audio, and still or moving visuals.

Write

Write several sentences explaining the features of the online observational writing you found.

BRIAN CABLE

The Last Stop

Brian Cable wrote the following observational essay when he was a first-year college student. His observations are based on a visit to a mortuary, or funeral home, a subject he views with both seriousness and humor. Hoping as he enters the mortuary not to end up as a participant that day, he records what he sees and interviews two key people, the funeral director and the embalmer. In reporting his observations, he seems equally concerned with the burial process—from the purchase of a casket to the display of the body—and the people who manage this process.

As you read, notice how the writer presents the place and people and how he attempts to heighten readers' interest in the mortuary by considering it in the larger, social context of people's beliefs about death and burial.

Let us endeavor so to live that when we come to die even the undertaker will be sorry.

—MARK TWAIN

Death is a subject largely ignored by the living. We don't discuss it much, not as children (when Grandpa dies, he is said to be "going away"), not as adults, not even as senior citizens. Throughout our lives, death remains intensely private. The death of a loved one can be very painful, partly because of the sense of loss, but also because someone else's mortality reminds us all too vividly of our own.

Thus did I notice more than a few people avert their eyes as they walked past the dusty-pink building that houses the Goodbody Mortuaries. It looked a bit like a church—tall, with gothic arches and stained glass—and somewhat like an apartment complex—low, with many windows stamped out of red brick.

It wasn't at all what I had expected. I thought it would be more like Forest Lawn, serene with lush green lawns and meticulously groomed gardens, a place set apart from the hustle of day-to-day life. Here instead was an odd pink structure set in the middle of a business district. On top of the Goodbody Mortuaries sign was a large electric clock. What the hell, I thought, mortuaries are concerned with time, too.

I was apprehensive as I climbed the stone steps to the entrance. I feared rejection or, worse, an invitation to come and stay. The door was massive, yet it swung open easily on well-oiled hinges. "Come in," said the sign. "We're always open." Inside was a cool and quiet reception room. Curtains were drawn against the outside glare, cutting the light down to a soft glow.

I found the funeral director in the main lobby, adjacent to the 5
reception room. Like most people, I had preconceptions about
what an undertaker looked like. Mr. Deaver fulfilled my expectations entirely. Tall and thin, he even had beady eyes and a bony
face. A low, slanted forehead gave way to a beaked nose. His skin,
scrubbed of all color, contrasted sharply with his jet black hair. He
was wearing a starched white shirt, gray pants, and black shoes.
Indeed, he looked like death on two legs.

He proved an amiable sort, however, and was easy to talk to. As 6
funeral director, Mr. Deaver ("call me Howard") was responsible
for a wide range of services. Goodbody Mortuaries, upon notification of someone's death, will remove the remains from the hospital
or home. They then prepare the body for viewing, whereupon features distorted by illness or accident are restored to their natural
condition. The body is embalmed and then placed in a casket
selected by the family of the deceased. Services are held in one of
three chapels at the mortuary, and afterward the casket is placed in
a "visitation room," where family and friends can pay their last
respects. Goodbody also makes arrangements for the purchase of a
burial site and transports the body there for burial.

All this information Howard related in a well-practiced, profes- 7
sional manner. It was obvious he was used to explaining the
specifics of his profession. We sat alone in the lobby. His desk was
bone clean, no pencils or paper, nothing—just a telephone. He did
all his paperwork at home; as it turned out, he and his wife lived
right upstairs. The phone rang. As he listened, he bit his lips and
squeezed his Adam's apple somewhat nervously.

"I think we'll be able to get him in by Friday. No, no, the family 8
wants him cremated."

His tone was that of a broker conferring on the Dow Jones. 9
Directly behind him was a sign announcing "Visa and Master Charge
Welcome Here." It was tacked to the wall, right next to a crucifix.

"Some people have the idea that we are bereavement specialists, 10
that we can handle the emotional problems which follow a death:
Only a trained therapist can do that. We provide services for the
dead, not counseling for the living."

Physical comfort was the one thing they did provide for the liv- 11
ing. The lobby was modestly but comfortably furnished. There
were several couches, in colors ranging from earth brown to pastel
blue, and a coffee table in front of each one. On one table lay some
magazines and a vase of flowers. Another supported an aquarium.
Paintings of pastoral scenes hung on every wall. The lobby looked
more or less like that of an old hotel. Nothing seemed to match,
but it had a homey, lived-in look.

"The last time the Goodbodies decorated was in '59, I believe. It still makes people feel welcome." 12

And so "Goodbody" was not a name made up to attract customers but the owners' family name. The Goodbody family started the business way back in 1915. Today, they do over five hundred services a year. 13

"We're in *Ripley's Believe It or Not*, along with another funeral home whose owners' names are Baggit and Sackit," Howard told me, without cracking a smile. 14

I followed him through an arched doorway into a chapel that smelled musty and old. The only illumination came from sunlight filtered through a stained glass ceiling. Ahead of us lay a casket. I could see that it contained a man dressed in a black suit. Wooden benches ran on either side of an aisle that led to the body. I got no closer. From the red roses across the dead man's chest, it was apparent that services had already been held. 15

"It was a large service," remarked Howard. "Look at that casket — a beautiful work of craftsmanship." 16

I guess it was. Death may be the great leveler, but one's coffin quickly reestablishes one's status. 17

We passed into a bright, fluorescent-lit "display room." Inside were thirty coffins, lids open, patiently awaiting inspection. Like new cars on the showroom floor, they gleamed with high-gloss finishes. 18

"We have models for every price range." 19

Indeed, there was a wide variety. They came in all colors and various materials. Some were little more than cloth-covered cardboard boxes, others were made of wood, and a few were made of steel, copper, or bronze. Prices started at $400 and averaged about $1,800. Howard motioned toward the center of the room: "The top of the line." 20

This was a solid bronze casket, its seams electronically welded to resist corrosion. Moisture-proof and air-tight, it could be hermetically sealed off from all outside elements. Its handles were plated with 14-karat gold. The price: a cool $5,000. 21

A proper funeral remains a measure of respect for the deceased. But it is expensive. In the United States the amount spent annually on funerals is about $2 billion. Among ceremonial expenditures, funerals are second only to weddings. As a result, practices are changing. Howard has been in this business for forty years. He remembers a time when everyone was buried. Nowadays, with burials costing $2,000 a shot, people often opt instead for cremation — as Howard put it, "a cheap, quick, and easy means of disposal." In some areas of the country, the cremation rate is now over 60 percent. Observing this trend, one might wonder whether 22 burials are becoming obsolete. Do burials serve an important role in society?

For Tim, Goodbody's licensed mortician, the answer is very definitely yes. Burials will remain in common practice, according to the slender embalmer with the disarming smile, because they allow family and friends to view the deceased. Painful as it may be, such an experience brings home the finality of death. "Something deep within us demands a confrontation with death," Tim explained. "A last look assures us that the person we loved is, indeed, gone forever." 23

Apparently, we also need to be assured that the body will be laid to rest in comfort and peace. The average casket, with its inner-spring mattress and pleated satin lining, is surprisingly roomy and luxurious. Perhaps such an air of comfort makes it easier for the family to give up their loved one. In addition, the burial site fixes the deceased in the survivors' memory, like a new address. Cremation provides none of these comforts. 24

Tim started out as a clerk in a funeral home but then studied to become a mortician. "It was a profession I could live with," he told me with a sly grin. Mortuary science might be described as a cross between pre-med and cosmetology, with courses in anatomy and embalming as well as in restorative art. 25

Tim let me see the preparation, or embalming, room, a white-walled chamber about the size of an operating room. Against the wall was a large sink with elbow taps and a draining board. In the center of the room stood a table with equipment for preparing the arterial embalming fluid, which consists primarily of formaldehyde, a preservative, and phenol, a disinfectant. This mixture sanitizes and also gives better color to the skin. Facial features can then be "set" to achieve a restful expression. Missing eyes, ears, and even noses can be replaced. 26

I asked Tim if his job ever depressed him. He bridled at the question: "No, it doesn't depress me at all. I do what I can for people and take satisfaction in enabling relatives to see their loved ones as they were in life." He said that he felt people were becoming more aware of the public service his profession provides. Grade-school classes now visit funeral homes as often as they do police stations and museums. The mortician is no longer regarded as a minister of death. 27

Before leaving, I wanted to see a body up close. I thought I could be indifferent after all I had seen and heard, but I wasn't sure. Cautiously, I reached out and touched the skin. It felt cold and firm, not unlike clay. As I walked out, I felt glad to have satisfied my curiosity about dead bodies, but all too happy to let someone else handle them. 28

READING FOR MEANING

This section presents three activities that will help you reread Cable's observational essay with a critical eye. Done in sequence, these activities lead you from a basic understanding of the selection to a more personal response to it and finally to an analysis that deepens your understanding and critical thinking about what you are reading.

Read to Comprehend

Reread the selection, and write a few sentences briefly explaining what you learned about the activities that take place at a funeral home. The following definitions may help you understand Cable's vocabulary:

mortality (paragraph 1): the state of being mortal or subject to death.

avert (2): turn away.

pastoral (11): representing nature in an idealized way as calm and peaceful.

Identify three or more additional words that you don't understand, and find the best definitions from the dictionary that work with their context.

To expand your understanding of this reading, you might use one or more of the following critical reading strategies that are explained and illustrated in Appendix 1: *outlining, summarizing, paraphrasing,* and *questioning to understand and remember.*

Read to Respond

Write several paragraphs exploring one or more of the assumptions, values, and beliefs underlying Cable's observational essay. As you write, explain how the assumptions are reflected in the text, as well as what you now think of them (and perhaps of your own assumptions) after rereading the selection with a critical eye.

You might consider writing about the following:

- Cable's preconceptions about what an undertaker would look like (paragraph 5), perhaps in relation to fictional representations with which you are familiar;

- Tim's claim that "[g]rade-school classes now visit funeral homes as often as they do police stations and museums" (27), perhaps in relation to the field trips you took in grade school; or

- Cable's curiosity "about dead bodies" and what one feels like (28), in relation to your own firsthand experience of death.

To develop your response to Cable's essay, you might use one or more of the following critical reading strategies that are explained and illustrated in Appendix 1: *contextualizing, reflecting on challenges to your beliefs and values,* and *recognizing emotional manipulation.*

Read to Analyze Assumptions

Reread Cable's observational essay, and write a paragraph or two exploring one or more of the assumptions you find in the text. The following suggestions may help:

- **assumptions about death.** Cable begins his essay by suggesting that we tend not to talk directly and openly about death and that the painfulness of a loved one's death may be in part "because someone else's mortality reminds us all too vividly of our own" (paragraph 1). Later, he also reports Tim's different idea that "[s]omething deep within us demands a confrontation with death" (23). To think critically about the assumptions in this essay related to death, ask yourself: How are Cable's and Tim's beliefs reflected in their comments elsewhere in the essay? Which attitude best represents your own? What cultural, family, and religious traditions affect your thinking about death? Comparing your assumptions with those of other students in your class, particularly students brought up with different traditions, what important differences do you see in the way people view death?

- **assumptions about funerals as a status symbol.** Comparing the coffin "display room" to a new car "showroom" and describing the top-of-the-line $5,000 "solid bronze casket" with "14-karat gold" handles, Cable suggests that "[d]eath may be the great leveler, but one's coffin quickly reestablishes one's status" (paragraph 17). To think critically about the assumptions in this essay related to funerals as a status symbol, ask yourself: It is fairly obvious why someone would want an expensive car (because of its luxury and performance, for example) or an expensive home (for its accommodations and location, for example), but why do you suppose so many people buy expensive caskets, cemetery plots, and newspaper death notices and spend as much money on a funeral as they do on a wedding? What messages does an expensive funeral send to the people who attend? What other kinds of assumptions besides those about status might motivate people to spend a lot of money for this purpose?

To probe assumptions more deeply, you might use one or more of the following critical reading strategies that are explained and illustrated in Appendix 1: *reflecting on challenges to your beliefs and values, exploring the significance of figurative language,* and *looking for patterns of opposition.*

READING LIKE A WRITER
CONVEYING A DOMINANT IMPRESSION OF THE SUBJECT

Writers of observational essays seek to inform readers about a subject, but they go further to convey to readers their impression of the subject. The observation essay's dominant impression is comparable to the autobiographical essay's autobiographical significance. It brings the many details into focus, letting readers know what the writer considers important and interesting about the subject. Writers create a dominant impression in several ways—by the attitude or preconceptions they reveal, by the information they include and leave out, and by the way they describe the subject. Readers may not find a sentence beginning "My impression is . . . ," but they will nevertheless get a distinct impression of the subject.

Analyze

1. *Underline* words and phrases in the essay that suggest Cable's attitudes toward or feelings about Goodbody Mortuaries. *Be selective.* In a successful essay, every detail reveals the author's attitude, but certain details will be especially revealing.

2. *Note in the margin* what your annotations seem to reveal about Cable's attitude toward his subject.

Write

Write several sentences explaining the impression you get about Goodbody Mortuaries, supporting your explanation with examples from the reading. Then *add a few sentences* evaluating how successful you think Cable is in conveying an impression of the funeral home.

CONSIDERING IDEAS FOR YOUR OWN WRITING

Think of places or activities that you have strong preconceptions about or that you have had little or no experience with and yet have been curious about or perhaps even put off by. Maybe in your neighborhood there is an upscale gym where you assume participants are interested primarily in posing for and competing with each other, a day-care center where you assume the teachers are idealistic and devoted to the children, a tattoo parlor where you assume all the clients are young, an acupuncture clinic where you doubt there is any scientific basis for the treatments, or a fast-food place where you expect that nearly all employees find their jobs onerous and unrewarding. Or perhaps on your campus there is a tutoring center where you assume tutors do students' work for them, a student counseling center where you have been led to believe that students are not treated with sympathy and understanding, or an office that seems to schedule campus events at times that make it difficult for commuter students to participate. Because many readers would likely share your preconceptions and curiosity, you would have a relatively easy time engaging their interest in the subject. How would you test your preconceptions through your observations and interviews? How might you use your preconceptions to capture readers' attention, as Cable does?

KATIE DIEHM

"Paddlers Sit Ready!" The Enduring Sport of Dragon Boating

Katie Diehm wrote this observational essay for a composition course at the Catholic University of America in Washington, D.C. Her profile of dragon boating takes us through a brief, action-packed race from the perspective of a paddler who is competing in the race. Diehm's participant-observer role allows her to offer readers the look, sound, and feel of the race. Readers experience the tug of the water as the paddlers struggle to hold their boats at the starting line; their rush of adrenaline at the command "GO!"; and the strain on their arms, stomachs, and baThe cks as they paddle through the rainy, windy weather. As you read the essay, notice these and other ways that her participation in the race enables Diehm to bring readers not just into the race but into the bodies of the racers.

The other readings in this chapter are followed by reading and writing activities. Following this reading, however, you are on your own to decide how to read for meaning and read like a writer.

From the first words, Diehm attracts readers' interest by adopting the participant-observer role and showing what it felt like to be in a boat at the beginning of a race.

As we bob up and down in the river, our arms begin 1 to shake in anticipation. Our hands grip our paddles tighter as we hold them down straight into the water, bracing the boat and willing it to stay still despite the rain blowing into us. From my seat on the left side of the sixth bench, I can see the call boat over the heads of my nervous teammates. The timer watches us intently until that exact moment when all four teams are lined up and he can give us the go.

This vivid description from the perspective of the boat adds to the visual image of the boats provided by the photograph.

Over the sound of water hitting the sides of the 2 boats, we can hear cheering from the excited spectators on the shore. From the other side of the river, the spectators appear as a long streak of moving color lined up in front of perhaps the most colorful of festivals. Tents with various Chinese wares, food, and music cover the lawn, all part of this joyous celebration of the Dragon Boat tradition.

Here Diehm shifts to relate historical information from her research. Even this information is presented dramatically.

Dragon Boats originated more than 2,000 years ago 3 in China when, as legend has it, disgruntled poet and scholar Qu Yuan committed suicide by jumping into a river after his village was overrun with enemies. As *Washington Post* journalist Paul Schwartzman tells us, "[L]ocal fishermen searched for him in their boats," "pounding drums and beating the waters furiously to ward off the water dragons they feared might eat him" (2). Dragon Boat racing soon developed in honor of this event, often as part of the Chinese Festival of the

Dragon, meant to honor and appease the dragon ruling over the river. Today's Dragon Boat races are often accompanied by a Dragon Festival, which generally begins with a flag-raising ceremony the day before the races. This ceremony, in which the Chinese flag is raised over the river, symbolizes China's lasting importance in the event. A far cry from the fishing boats of Qu Yuan's era, today's dragon boats are 45 feet long and made of fiberglass, complete with a dragon's head and tail at either end. Sixteen paddlers line both sides of the boat and paddle in synch in a way unique to Dragon Boating.

Diehm contrasts past and present and then describes modern dragon boats and the distinctive method of paddling.

4   "Boat Three draw left!" the timer yells over the wind, and the left-side paddlers on the boat in the third lane begin to work hard paddling sideways to move their boat farther away from the second lane.

She returns to narrating what happened on the day she participated in the race.

5   "Boat Four hold! Paddle back!" the timer yells as the wind shifts and their team begins to pull forward past the starting line. The paddlers strain to hold their paddles down in the water, keeping the boat still, and then slowly and steadily begin to paddle backwards.

6   The beginning of a Dragon Boat race is often the hardest due to elements like wind and the river current. Getting lined up often takes the better part of ten

Notice that even though she is one of the paddlers, Diehm writes about "their" (not "my") efforts. What do you think this strategy accomplishes?

Paddlers' arms are a blur of motion at the 2003 World Nations Dragon Boat Championships (Keplicz).

minutes—an ironic beginning for a race that lasts approximately three—and is grueling for the paddlers as they sometimes paddle constantly just to stay in one place. As the boats finally pull into place, the timer wastes no time in barking out orders.

"Paddlers sit ready!" he calls, signaling the time for all paddles to be removed from the water and proper grip on the paddle—the upper hand gripping the top of the paddle as if in a fist, the lower hand gripping the lower section of the paddle, directly above the wide part—to be assumed. 7

Notice that she first describes the paddlers' change in posture and then summarizes what she learned from a source about paddling posture.

"Attention!" At this call, the teams lean forward, arms extended and paddles raised about five inches above the water, ready to plunge with all intensity into the river. Mike Dojc, a Dragon Boat enthusiast, explains that the paddlers stretch their backs out straight, ready to pull at the paddle with the muscles from their arms, stomach, and back by twisting their bodies and keeping their arms straight (Dojc 1). 8

By now, Diehm's organizational plan is evident: information is interspersed into the narrative of the race. How well does she avoid losing momentum and drama?

"GO!" Instantly the teams spring into action. Simultaneously, my teammates and I drop our paddles down and forward and pull back with all our strength. The start time in Dragon Boat racing is extremely important—it's a 30-second chance to gain additional speed that will last even when the paddlers fall back into a slower and more constant pace. The tiller, the person in charge of steering the boat, stands at the back and grips the till, willing through long strokes or skillful dips of the till that the boat stay on course. The caller, standing on the front of the boat and struggling to keep her balance despite the surging of the boat, beats out a fast rhythm on a drum, shouting the counts over the beat. 9

"One! Two! Three! Four! Watch—your—lead! Two! Three! Four! Keep! It! Up! Two! Three! Four!" 10

This detail helps readers understand the pace and strenuous efforts of the paddlers.

As the boats leave the beginning of the race, the quick-start pace subsides, and the paddlers begin to pace themselves. At 90 strokes a minute, however, the pace is hardly relaxing. As arms begin to go numb, the paddlers begin to focus all their energy on keeping up with the rest of the paddlers in the boat, as they know that even the slightest delay on their paddle's entrance to the river can mean a demerit of a couple seconds. Suzanne Ma, a journalist from the *Hamilton Spectator*, tells us that their aim is for the "rhythm of the boat to be like one collective heartbeat" (1). 11

12   Each team has a unique way of keeping everyone in time using some division of the paddlers. My team divided the sixteen paddlers into two groups. The first ten paddlers (two per bench) watch the two paddlers in the front (called the lead strokes), the left-side paddlers watch the lead on the right, and the right-side paddlers watch the left. The paddlers on the fourth bench, called the mid-strokes, serve as pacers for the back half of the boat as they watch the lead-strokes and are then watched in the same way by the back paddlers. From my left-side fifth-bench position, I sit directly behind the mid-strokes and am dubbed a part of the "engine room," the part of the boat that is relied on for constant, steady paddling. The front of the boat is made up of paddlers who have long solid paddle strokes. These paddlers must also be very strong, as they are paddling dead water. The rear three benches are made up of powerful paddlers called rockets. These six paddlers are perhaps the most important on the boat, as it is their strength that propels the boat forward. Some describe the feeling of paddling in rhythm as entering a Zen state, and Schwartzman tells us that "if the boat is in tune, you can feel it gliding" (2). Paddling in unison with proper technique and a tailwind, our boat can get up to 6 miles per hour.

13   As the boat reaches the end of the 500-meter race, adrenaline kicks in to counteract our fatigue. At one minute to go, our designated flag catcher, chosen for her lightweight and gymnastlike frame, gets up, climbs behind the tiller, ties her feet into a strap secured from the neck of the dragon, and lies down prostrate over the dragon's head until she is extended a good two feet off the dragon's nose. Her outstretched arm directs the tiller toward the flag that she must catch or the team will receive a hefty demerit on their time.

Diehm describes the process that a team member follows to catch the flag.

14   The last 30 seconds of the race are often the hardest. Clearly fatigued and struggling to maintain the pace, the paddlers rely solely on adrenaline to get to the finish line. The pace accelerates to the beat of a drum, and the caller urges the paddlers to "Finish — it — now!" — a signal to paddle faster and firmer than before. As soon as the boats speed through the finish line and flags are caught, the callers waste no time in yelling.

Diehm uses the caller's words to help readers hear the beat of the drum.

15   "HOLD THE BOAT!" We thrust our paddles straight down into the water and attempt despite the

speed of the boat to hold them still. Our boat comes to a stop about eight feet away from the grassy shore, and the tiller rapidly begins to spin the boat around and back to the docks. With now-shaking arms and pounding hearts we slowly make our way back, where we unload and trade places with the next team waiting to go out. The races continue all day and into the next tournament-style until only four teams are left. These last four compete against each other in one final race, the last of the season.

This vivid detail (high-lighted) comes as no sur-prise as we can imagine the paddlers' physical effort.

As the competition narrows down, the festivities in-crease, and teams that are out of the running return to the shoreline to cheer for the teams that are still com-peting. The smell of Chinese foods cooking fills the air, and ethnic music explodes from all corners of the grounds, reminding the participants just how unique an experience the Chinese Dragon Festival really is.

Diehm ends with a descrip-tion of smells and sounds, giving us a sense of the festivities on the shore.

16

Following MLA style, Diehm documents the sources she cited parenthetically in her essay.

Works Cited

Dojc, Mike. "Blazing Paddles: Q&A with a Dragon Boat Enthusiast." *Toronto Sun* 26 June 2004: 1–3. *LexisNexis.* Web. 13 Oct. 2005.

Keplicz, Alik. Photograph of 2003 World Nations Dragon Boat Championships. "Pictures of the Week: August 30–September 4." *Time.* Time, 5 Sept. 2003. Web. 31 Oct. 2005.

Ma, Suzanne. "Pulling Together: Dragon Boat Racing Soothes the Mind, Energizes the Body." *Hamilton Spectator* 7 July 2005: 1–4. *LexisNexis.* Web. 13 Oct. 2005.

Schwartzman, Paul. "In Dragon Races, Team Spirit Sinks In, and That's Not All: Ancient Chinese Tradition Grows with Fourth Year of Competing on Potomac." *Washington Post* 29 May 2005: 1–3. *LexisNexis.* Web. 13 Oct. 2005.

READING FOR MEANING

Reading for meaning involves three activities:

- reading to comprehend,
- reading to respond, and
- reading to analyze assumptions.

Reread Diehm's essay, and then write a page or so explaining your under-standing of its basic meaning or main point, a personal response you have to it, and what you see as one of its underlying assumptions.

READING LIKE A WRITER

Writers of observational essays

- describe places and people,
- present information about the subject,
- organize the information,
- choose a role, and
- convey a dominant impression of the subject.

Focus on one of these strategies in Diehm's essay, and analyze it carefully through close rereading and annotating. Then write several sentences explaining what you have learned, giving specific examples from the reading to support your explanation. Add a few sentences evaluating how successfully Diehm uses the strategy to help readers unfamiliar with the sport of Dragon Boating learn about it.

REVIEWING WHAT MAKES OBSERVATIONAL ESSAYS EFFECTIVE

In this chapter, you have been learning how to read observational essays for meaning and how to read them like a writer. Before going on to write an observational essay, pause here to review and contemplate what you have learned about the elements of effective observational writing.

Analyze

Choose one reading from this chapter that seems to you especially effective. Before rereading the selection, *jot down* one or two reasons you remember it as an example of good observational writing.

Reread your chosen selection, adding further annotations about what makes it a particularly successful example of observation. *Consider* the selection's purpose and how well it achieves that purpose for its intended readers. (You can make an informed guess about the intended readers and their expectations by noting the publication source of the essay.) Then *focus* on how well the writer does the following:

- describes places and people,
- presents information about the subject,
- organizes the information,
- chooses a role, and
- conveys a dominant impression of its subject.

You can review all of these basic features in the Guide to Reading Observational Essays (p. 80).

Your instructor may ask you to complete this activity on your own or to work with a small group of other students who have chosen the same reading. If you work with others, allow enough time initially for all group members to reread the selection thoughtfully and to add their annotations. Then *discuss* as a group what makes the selection effective. *Take notes* on your discussion. One student in your group should then report to the class what the group has learned about the effectiveness of observational writing. If you are working individually, write up what you have learned from your analysis.

Write

Write at least a page supporting your choice of this reading as an example of effective observational writing. *Assume* that your readers — your instructor and classmates — have read the selection but will not remember many details about it. They also might not remember it as especially successful. Therefore, you will need to *refer* to details and specific parts of the essay as you explain how it works and as you justify your evaluation of its effectiveness. You need not argue that it is the best reading in the chapter or that it is flawless, only that it is, in your view, a strong example of the genre.

■ A Guide to Writing Observational Essays

The readings in this chapter have helped you learn a great deal about observational writing. You have seen that writers of observational essays present unfamiliar places and people. You have also seen that they collect large amounts of information and ideas from visits and interviews, which must be sorted, organized, and integrated into a readable draft. This Guide to Writing is designed to help you through the stages of invention and research, drafting, revising, and editing, as you gather the materials you will need and solve the problems you encounter as you write.

INVENTION AND RESEARCH

The following activities will help you choose a subject, research and reflect on your subject, plan and make observations, and decide on the impression you want your essay to convey to readers. Except for the visit or interview, each activity is easy to do and takes only a few minutes. If you can spread out the activities over several days, you will have adequate time to understand what you must do to present your subject in an engaging and informative way. Keep a written record of your invention work to use later when you draft and revise the essay.

Choosing a Subject

List the subjects you are interested in observing. To make the best possible choice and have alternatives in case the subject you choose requires too much time or is inaccessible, you should have a list of several possible subjects. You might already have a subject in mind, possibly one you listed for the Considering Ideas for Your Own Writing activities following the readings in this chapter. Here are some other suggestions that will help you think of possible topics:

People

- Anyone doing work that you might want to do—city council member, police officer, lab technician, computer programmer, attorney, salesperson
- Anyone with an unusual job or hobby—dog trainer, private detective, ham radio operator, race car driver, novelist
- A campus personality—coach, distinguished teacher, newspaper editor, oldest or youngest student
- Someone recently recognized for community service or achievement

Places

- Small-claims court, consumer fraud office, city planner's office
- Bodybuilding gym, weight-reduction clinic, martial arts school
- Hospital emergency room, campus health center, hospice, psychiatric unit
- Recycling center, airport control tower, theater, museum, sports arena

Activities

- Tutoring, registering voters, rehearsing for a play, repairing a car
- An unconventional sports event—dogs' frisbee tournament, chess match, amateur wrestling or boxing meet, dogsledding, log sawing and splitting, ice-fishing contest, Olympics for people with disabilities
- A team practicing a sport or other activity (one you can observe as a curious outsider, not as an experienced participant)
- A community improvement project—graffiti cleaning, tree planting, house repairing, church painting, road or highway litter collecting
- Special courses—rock climbing, folk dancing, dog training, truck driving

Choose a subject about which you are genuinely curious—and one that you think will appeal to your readers. Keep in mind that the more unfamiliar the subject is for readers, the easier it will be for you to interest them in it. If you choose a subject familiar to readers, try to focus on some aspect of it likely to be truly informative, even surprising, to them. In choosing a subject, be sure to check on accessibility, requesting permission to visit one or more times to make detailed observations and to interview key people.

Researching Your Subject

The writing and research activities that follow will enable you to gather information and ideas about your subject.

Considering Your Own Role. *Decide tentatively whether you will adopt a spectator-observer or participant-observer role to present your observations.* As a spectator observer, you would present what you learn from visiting the place and interviewing people there. As a participant observer, you would also take part in an activity at the place for a brief period so that you can insert your firsthand experience into your essay. To become a participant, you will need to ask permission and possibly arrange another visit.

Making a Schedule. *Set up a tentative schedule for your observational and interview visits.* If you could and want to participate for a time in the activity you are writing about, schedule that too. Figure out first the amount of time you have to complete your essay. Then determine the scope of your project—a onetime observation, an interview with follow-up, or multiple observations and interviews. Decide what visits you will need to make, whom you will need to interview, and what library or Internet work you might want to do to get background information about your subject. Estimate the time necessary for each, knowing you might need to schedule more time than anticipated.

Make phone calls to schedule visits or arrange interviews. When you write down your appointments, be sure to include names, addresses, phone numbers, dates and times, and any special arrangements you have made for each visit. (Consult the Field Research section in Appendix 2, pp. 647–52, for helpful guidelines on observing, interviewing, and taking notes.)

RESEARCHING YOUR SUBJECT ONLINE

One way to get a quick initial overview of the information available on the subject of your observational essay is to search for the subject online. Use Google <http://google.com> or Yahoo! Directory <http://dir.yahoo.com> to discover possible sources of information about the subject:

- For example, if you are writing about a beekeeper, you could get some useful background information to guide you in planning your interview by entering "bee keeping."

- If you are writing about a person, enter the full name to discover whether he or she has a personal Web site. If you are writing about a business or institution, the chances are even better that it offers a site. Either kind of site would orient and inform you prior to your interview or first visit.

Bookmark or keep a record of promising sites. After your interview with or visit to the subject, download any materials, including visuals, you might consider including in your own essay. If you find little or no information about your subject online, do not lose confidence in your choice. All of the information you need to develop your essay can come from your observations and interviews when you visit your subject.

Exploring Readers' and Your Own Preconceptions. *Write for several minutes about your readers' as well as your own assumptions and expectations.* For example, ask questions like these about your readers: Who are they? What are they likely to think about the subject? What would they want to know about it?

Also reflect on yourself: Why do you want to research this subject? What do you expect to find out about it? What aspects of it do you expect to be interesting or entertaining?

Visiting a Place.   *During your visit, take notes on what you observe.* Do not try to impose order on your notes at this stage; simply record whatever you notice. Pay special attention to visual details and other kinds of details (sounds, smells) as well as overheard conversations that you can draw on later to describe the place and people.

Interviewing a Person.   *Prepare for the interview by writing out some preliminary questions.* But do not be afraid of abandoning your script during the interview. Listen carefully to what is said and ask follow-up questions. Take notes; if you like and your subject agrees, you may also tape-record the interview.

Gathering Information.   *If you do background reading, take careful notes and keep accurate bibliographic records of your sources.* Try to pick up relevant fliers, brochures, or reports at the place you observe. In addition, you might conduct research on the Internet or in your college library. (For more information, see Researching Your Subject Online on p. 139; also see the sections on Library Research, pp. 652–63, and Internet Research, pp. 663–66, in Appendix 2.)

Reflecting on Your Subject

After you research your subject, consider your purpose in writing about it and formulate a tentative thesis statement.

Considering Your Purpose.   *Write for several minutes about the impression of the subject you want to convey to your readers.* As you write, try to answer this question: What makes this subject worth observing? Your answer to this question might change as you write, but a preliminary answer will give your writing a direction to follow, or what journalists commonly call an "angle," on the subject. This angle will help you choose what to include as well as what to emphasize in your draft. Use the following questions to help clarify the dominant impression you want your essay to convey:

- What visual images or other sensory details of the subject stand out in your memory? Think about the feelings these images evoke in you. If they evoke contradictory feelings, consider how you could use them to convey to readers the complexity of your feelings about the place, people, or activities you observed.

- What is most surprising about your observations? Compare the preconceptions you listed earlier with what you actually saw or heard.

- What interests you most about the people you interviewed? Compare the direct observations you made about them with the indirect or secondhand information you gathered about them.

Formulating a Tentative Thesis Statement. *Review what you wrote for Considering Your Purpose, and add two or three sentences that will bring into focus the dominant impression you want to give readers about the person, place, or activity on which you are focusing.* This impression is based on an insight into, interpretation of, or idea about the person, place, or activity you have gained while observing it. Try to write sentences that do not summarize what you have already written but that convey a deeper understanding of what dominant impression you want to make on your readers.

Keep in mind that readers do not expect you to begin your observational essay with the kind of explicit thesis statement typical of argumentative essays. None of the readings in this chapter offers to readers an explicit statement of the dominant impression the writer hopes to convey about the subject. Instead, the writers convey an impression through the ways they describe their subjects, select information to share with readers, or narrate the story of their experiences with the subject. And yet it is possible for readers to infer from each reading a dominant impression of the subject.

Nearly all first attempts to state a dominant impression to be conveyed, to focus a jumble of notes and remembered observations, or to state a thesis are eventually revised once drafting gets under way. Writing the first draft helps writers of observational essays discover their main impression and find ways to convey that impression without ever stating it directly. Just because there is no explicit thesis statement in an observational essay does not mean that it lacks focus or fails to convey an impression of its subject.

Considering Visuals. *Consider whether visuals—photographs you take, drawings you make, copies of revealing illustrative materials you picked up at the place observed—would strengthen your observational essay.* If you submit your essay electronically to other students and your instructor or if you post it to a Web site, consider including snippets of your interviews or sounds from the place (if you make use of a tape recorder in your project) or your own digital photographs or video. Remember to ask permission to make visual or audio records. Some persons may be willing to be interviewed or share printed material but reluctant to allow photographs or recordings. Visual and audio materials are not at all a requirement of an effective observational essay, as you can tell from the readings in this chapter, but they could add a new dimension to your writing.

DRAFTING

The following guidelines will help you set goals for your draft, plan its organization, and think about a useful sentence strategy.

Setting Goals

Establishing goals for your draft before you begin writing will enable you to make decisions and work more confidently. Consider the following questions now, and keep them in mind as you draft. They will help you set goals for drafting as well as recall how the writers you have read in this chapter tried to achieve similar goals.

- *How can I help my readers imagine the subject?* In addition to describing visual details, as all of the authors in this chapter do, should I evoke other senses, in the way that Edge describes how a pig lip smells and tastes and what its unusual texture is? Should I characterize people by their clothes, facial expressions, and talk, as Hamilton, Orenstein, and Cable do? Should I use surprising metaphors or similes, as the author of "Soup" does in describing Yeganeh's "working like a demon alchemist"?

- *How can I engage my readers?* Should I begin with a vivid image, as Diehm does? With an arresting statement, as Cable does? A surprising statement, as the author of "Soup" and Cable do? Should I begin by setting the stage, as Edge, Hamilton, and Orenstein do? Should I introduce the person, as Norris (in the Observation Online), Orenstein, and the author of "Soup" do? Can I use my experience as a participant observer to engage readers' interest, as Edge and Diehm do? Can I use humor, as Edge and Cable do?

- *How can I present and distribute the information?* Should I present some information through dialogue from interviews, as all the writers do? Can I also present overheard conversation, as in "Soup" and the essays by Orenstein, Hamilton, and Diehm? Should I present information I gathered from direct observations, as all the authors do, as well as from secondary research in the library and on the Internet, as Diehm does?

- *How can I organize and present the information?* Should I organize it topically in groups of related information, as the author of "Soup," Hamilton, Norris, and Cable do? Should I arrange it in a chronological narrative order, as Hamilton and Diehm do? Should I alternate between a narrative and a topical organization, as Edge does?

- *How can I convey a dominant impression?* Should I select information that focuses on one primary aspect of the subject, as the author of "Soup" and Norris do? Should I use my experience as a participant observer or as a guide to focus on what I think is important, as Edge, Diehm, Hamilton, and Orenstein do? Should I insert my own insights, as Orenstein and Cable do?

Organizing Your Draft

With your goals in mind, reread the notes you took about the place and people, and decide how to organize them—grouped into topics or put in chronological order. If you think a topical organization would work best, try grouping your observations and naming the topic of each group. If you think narrating what happened would help you organize your observations, make a time line and note where the information would go. You might want to try different kinds of outlines before settling on a plan and drafting your essay.

Writers who use a narrative structure usually follow a simple, straightforward chronology to present activities observed over a limited period—a few hours or a few days—in the order in which they occurred. Orenstein, for example, recounts what happened during a single class period.

Writers who organize their observations topically must limit the number of topics they cover. The author of "Soup," for example, focuses on Yeganeh's ideas about soup and his attitudes toward customers. In the topically organized section of his essay, Edge concentrates on the history and process of bottling and selling pig lips.

WORKING WITH SOURCES

Integrating Quotations from Interviews

In addition to describing people, your observation essay will also quote them. These quotations can be revealing because they let readers hear different people speaking for themselves rather than being presented through your voice. Nevertheless, the writer decides which quotations to use and how to use them. Therefore, one major task you face in drafting and revising your essay is to choose quotations from your notes, to present them in a way that reveals the character of the people you interviewed and the important information you learned from them, and to integrate these quotations smoothly into your sentences.

When you quote directly (rather than paraphrase or summarize) what someone said or wrote, you will usually need to identify the speaker. The principal way to do so is to create what is called a *speaker tag*. You may rely on a general or all-purpose speaker tag, using the forms of *say* and *tell*:

"We may not win every game," she *said*. "But we've never lost a party." (Hamilton, paragraph 2)

"My job as an editor is to gently prod the attention of the audience to look at various parts of the frame," he *says*. "And I do that by manipulating, by how and where I cut and what succession of images I work with." (Observation Online: Norris, paragraph 5)

"I love it," Molly Aiken, 19, a sophomore at Ole Miss, *said* on Saturday. . . . (Hamilton, paragraph 5)

"I am not prejudiced against color or religion," Mr. Yeganeh *told* us. . . . ("Soup," paragraph 4)

Suzanne Ma, a journalist from the *Hamilton Spectator, tells* us that their aim is for the "rhythm of the boat to be like one collective heartbeat" (1). (Diehm, paragraph 11)

Other speaker tags more precisely describe the speaker's tone or attitude:

"They told me to tell you that they want me to be my own person," she *complained.* (Orenstein, paragraph 5)

Kyle, who is skinny and a little pop-eyed, *yells out,* "Prime!" . . . (Orenstein, paragraph 18)

"It was a large service," *remarked* Howard. (Cable, paragraph 16)

"Something deep within us demands a confrontation with death," Tim *explained.* (Cable, paragraph 23)

Whether you use specific or general speaker tags, consider adding a word or phrase to identify or describe the speaker or to reveal more about *how, where, when,* or *why* the speaker speaks:

"We do our best to corner the market on lips," Lionel *told me, his voice tinged with bravado.* (Edge, paragraph 11)

"I'm not exactly shy," *she says, her hands still on her hips.* "I'm bold." (Orenstein, paragraph 4)

"It was a profession I could live with," he *told me with a sly grin.* (Cable, paragraph 25)

Don't forget to enclose all quotations in quotation marks and to separate the quotation from its speaker tag with appropriate punctuation, usually a comma.

Considering a Useful Sentence Strategy

As you draft your observation essay, you will need to help your readers imagine actions and objects. A sentence strategy called an *absolute phrase* enables writers to show simultaneous parts of a complex action or to detail observations of a person or object.

Here is an example, with the absolute phrase in italics:

Some of the boys are as small and compact as fourth graders, *their legs sticking out of their shorts like pipe cleaners.* (Orenstein, paragraph 8)

Orenstein could have presented her observation of the boys' skinny legs in a separate sentence, but the absolute phrase gives a visual image showing just how skinny they are. Here's another example:

> I offer the bag to Jerry, order yet another beer, and turn to eye the pig feet floating in a murky jar by the cash register, *their blunt tips bobbing up through a pasty white film.* (Edge, paragraph 19)

Again, Edge could have presented his observation in a separate sentence, but the absolute phrase lets him bring together his turning and looking with what he actually saw, emphasizing the at-a-glance instant of another possible stomach flutter.

Absolute phrases nearly always are attached to the end of a main clause, adding various kinds of details to it to create a more complex, informative sentence. They are usually introduced by a noun or a pronoun followed by a present participle (ending in *-ing*) or past participle (usually ending in *-ed*). Following are additional examples of absolute phrases from this chapter's readings. (Notice that the second example does not include a participle.)

> This was a solid bronze casket, *its seams electronically welded to resist corrosion.* (Cable, paragraph 21)

> "I'm not exactly shy," she says, *her hands still on her hips.* (Orenstein, paragraph 4).

> "I love it," Molly Aiken, 19, a sophomore at Ole Miss, said on Saturday under a tent, under the trees, *a party roar rising and dissipating into the whisper of a warm, humid wind above.* (Hamilton, paragraph 5)

Absolute phrases are certainly not required for a successful observation essay — experienced writers use them only occasionally — yet they do offer writers an effective sentence option. Try them out in your own writing.

READING A DRAFT CRITICALLY

Getting a critical reading of your draft will help you see how to improve it. Your instructor may schedule class time for reading drafts, or you may want to ask a classmate or a tutor in the writing center to read your draft. Ask your reader to use the following guidelines and to write out a response for you to consult during your revision.

Read for a First Impression

1. Read the draft without stopping to annotate or comment, and then write two or three sentences giving your general impression.

2. Identify one aspect of the draft that seems particularly effective.

Read Again to Suggest Improvements

1. Suggest ways of making descriptions of places and people more vivid.

   - Find a description of a place, and suggest what details could be added to objects in the scene (location, size, color, and shape) or what sensory information (look, sound, smell, taste, and touch) could be included to help you picture the place.

   - Find a description of a person, and indicate what else you would like to know about the person's dress, facial expression, tone of voice, and gestures.

   - Find reported conversation, and note whether any of the quotes could be paraphrased or summarized without losing impact.

   - Find passages where additional reported conversation could enhance the drama or help bring a person to life.

2. Recommend ways of making the organization clearer or more effective.

   - If the essay is organized chronologically, look for passages where the narrative seems to wander pointlessly or leaves out important information. Also suggest cues that could be added to indicate time sequence (*initially*, *then*, *afterward*).

   - If the essay is organized topically, mark topics that get too much or too little attention, transitions between topics that need to be added or clarified, and topics that should be placed elsewhere.

   - If the essay alternates narration with topical information, suggest where transitions could be made smoother or sequencing could be improved.

3. Suggest how the essay could be made more engaging and informative.

   - If the essay seems boring or you feel overwhelmed by too much information, suggest how the information could alternate with vivid description or lively narration. Also consider whether any of the information could be cut or simplified.

   - List any questions you still have about the subject.

4. Suggest ways to make the impression conveyed to you more focused and coherent.

   - Tell the writer what dominant impression you get of the subject.

   - Point to key information that supports this dominant impression, so that the writer knows how you arrived at it.

   - Point to any information that makes you doubt or question your impression.

5. Evaluate the effectiveness of visuals.

- Look at any visuals in the essay, and tell the writer what they contribute to your impression of the subject and your understanding of the observations.

- If any visuals do not seem relevant, or if there seem to be too many visuals, identify the ones that the writer could consider dropping and explain your thinking.

- If a visual does not seem to be appropriately placed, suggest a better place for it.

REVISING

This section offers suggestions for revising your draft. Revising means reenvisioning your draft and trying to see it in a new way, given your purpose and readers, in order to develop a more vivid, informative observational essay.

The biggest mistake you can make while revising is to focus initially on words or sentences. Instead, first try to see your draft as a whole to assess its likely impact on your readers. Think imaginatively and boldly about cutting unconvincing material, adding new material, and moving material around. Your computer makes even drastic revisions physically easy, but you still need to make the mental effort and decisions that will improve your draft.

You may have received help with this challenge from a classmate or tutor who gave your draft a critical reading. If so, keep this feedback in mind as you decide which parts of your draft need revising and what specific changes you could make. The following suggestions will help you solve problems and strengthen your essay.

To Make Your Description of Places and People More Vivid

- Cull your notes for additional details you could supply about people and objects in the scene.

- If your notes are sparse, consider revisiting the place to add to your visual observations, or try imagining yourself back at the place and write about what you see.

- Consider where you could add details about sounds, smells, or textures of objects.

- Identify where a simile or metaphor would enrich your description.

- Review reported conversations to make sure you directly quote only the language that conveys personality or essential information; paraphrase or summarize other conversations.

- Show people interacting with each other by talking, moving, or gesturing.
- Consider using more specific speaker tags to show how or in what circumstances people spoke.

To Make the Organization Clearer and More Effective

- If the essay is organized chronologically, keep the narrative focused and well paced, adding time markers to clarify the sequence of events.
- If the essay is organized topically, make sure it moves smoothly from topic to topic, adding transitions where necessary.
- If the essay alternates narration with topical information, make sure the sequence is clear and easy to follow.

To Make the Essay More Engaging and Informative

- If the essay bores or overwhelms readers, cut information that is obvious or extraneous, and consider alternating blocks of information with descriptive or narrative materials.
- If readers have questions about the subject, try to answer them.
- If the essay seems abstract, provide specific definitions, examples, and details.

To Strengthen the Impression Your Essay Conveys

- If readers get an impression of the subject you did not expect, consider what may have given them that impression. You may need to add or cut material.
- If readers are unable to identify an impression, look for ways to make clearer the impression you want to convey.

EDITING AND PROOFREADING

After you have revised your essay, be sure to spend some time checking for errors in usage, punctuation, and mechanics and considering matters of style. If you keep a list of errors you typically make, begin by checking your draft against this list. Ask someone else to proofread your essay before you print out a copy for your instructor or send it electronically.

From our research on student writing, we know that observational essays tend to have errors in the use of quotation marks, when writers quote the exact words of people they have interviewed. Check a writer's handbook for help with this problem.

REFLECTING ON WHAT YOU HAVE LEARNED

Observation

In this chapter, you have read critically several observational essays and have written one of your own. To better remember what you have learned, pause now to reflect on the reading and writing activities you completed in this chapter.

1. *Write* a page or so assessing what you have learned. *Begin* by describing what you are most pleased with in your essay. Then *explain* what you think contributed to your achievement. *Be specific* about this contribution.

   ▪ If it was something you learned from the readings, *indicate* which readings and specifically what you learned from them.

   ▪ If it came from your invention writing, interviews, or observations, *point out* the parts that helped you most.

   ▪ If you got good advice from a critical reader, *explain* exactly how the person helped you — perhaps by helping you understand a particular problem in your draft or by adding a new dimension to your writing.

   ▪ *Try to write* about your achievement in terms of what you have learned about the genre.

2. Now *reflect* more generally on the genre of observational writing. Observational essays may seem impartial and objective, but they inevitably reflect the writer's interests, values, and other characteristics, such as gender and ethnicity or cultural heritage. For example, readers would expect a vegetarian to write a very different profile of a cattle ranch from one a beef lover would write. *Identify* a reading in the chapter where the writer's attitudes or characteristics seemed to influence the choice of subject, the observations, and the essay as a whole. *Explain* briefly how this influence is apparent to you. Then *consider* the following questions about your own project: How did your interests, values, or other characteristics influence your choice of subject, your observations, and your interactions with the people you interviewed? In your essay itself, how do these influences show through? If you tried to keep them hidden, *explain* briefly why. How could these influences be made more visible in your essay, and do you wish you had made them more visible? *Explain* why briefly.

CHAPTER 4

Reflection

Like autobiographical and observational writing, reflective writing is based on the writer's personal experience. Reflective writers present something they did, saw, overheard, or read. They try to make their writing vivid so that the reader can imagine what they experienced. But unlike writers of autobiography and observation, their goal is not primarily to present their experience so that the reader can imagine it. Reflective writers, instead, present their experience in order to explore its possible meanings. They use events in their lives and people and places they have observed as the occasions or springboards for thinking about society — how people live and what people believe.

In this chapter, for example, one writer tells what happened one evening when he was taking a walk and he noticed a woman react to him with evident fear. This experience, and others like it, leads him to think about popular stereotypes concerning gender and race. Another writer, finding a stranded sea turtle on his beach, uses the occasion to reflect on the environment and our stewardship of the earth. Still another writer muses about the objects he has found on the sidewalks of his city and how they represent the signs of our times.

As you can see from these few examples, the subjects reflective essays explore are wide ranging. Reflective writers may think about social change with its many opportunities and challenges (changes in scientific knowledge, in the environment, and in ways to perfect the body). They may examine cultural customs in our culturally diverse society (such as those related to eating and dating). They may explore traditional virtues and vices (pride, jealousy, and compassion) or common hopes and fears (the desire for an ecologically balanced world).

These subjects may seem far reaching, but writers of reflection have relatively modest goals. They do not attempt to exhaust their subjects, nor do they set themselves up as experts. They simply try out their ideas. One early meaning of the word *essay*, in fact, was "to try out." Reflective essays are exercises, experiments, simply opportunities to explore ideas informally and tentatively.

Reflective writing is enjoyable to write and read precisely because it is exploratory and creative. Reflective writing can be as stimulating as a lively conversation. It often surprises us with its insights and unlikely connections and encourages us to look in new ways at even the most familiar things, examining with a critical eye what we usually take for granted.

The readings in this chapter will help you learn a good deal about reflective writing. From the readings and from the suggestions for writing that follow each reading, you will get ideas for your own reflective essay. As you read and write about the selections, keep in mind the following assignment, which sets out the goals for writing a reflective essay. To support your writing of this assignment, the chapter concludes with a Guide to Writing Reflective Essays.

THE WRITING ASSIGNMENT

Reflection

Write a reflective essay based on something you experienced or observed. Describe this occasion vividly so that readers can understand what happened and will care about what you have to say about it. In reflecting on the particular occasion, make some general statements exploring its possible meanings or cultural significance. Consider what the occasion might imply about how people in our society behave toward one another, what they value, and what assumptions or stereotypes they may hold consciously or unconsciously. Think of reflective writing as a stimulating conversation in which you seek to expose—and perhaps question—your readers' attitudes and beliefs as well as your own.

WRITING SITUATIONS FOR REFLECTIVE ESSAYS

Writers use a wide range of particular occasions to launch their reflections. These occasions nearly always lead them to reflect on some aspect of contemporary culture, as the following examples indicate:

- A former football player writes a reflective essay for his college alumni magazine about his experience playing professional sports. He recounts a specific occasion when he sustained a serious injury but continued to play because he knew that playing with pain was regarded as a sign of manliness. As he reflects on what happened, he recalls that he first learned the custom of playing with pain from his father but that the lesson was reinforced later by coaches and other players. He wonders why boys playing sports are taught not to show pain but encouraged to show other feelings like aggression and competitiveness. Taking an anthropological view, he sees contemporary sports as equivalent to the kind of training Native American boys traditionally went through to become warriors. This comparison leads him to question whether sports training today prepares boys (and perhaps girls, too) for the kinds of roles they need to play in contemporary society.

- Writing for a political science course, a student reflects on her first experience voting in a presidential election. She begins by describing a recent conversation with friends about how people decide to vote for one presidential candidate over another. They agreed that most people they know seem to base their decisions on trivial, even bizarre, reasons, rather than on a candidate's experience, voting record in previous offices, character, or even campaign promises. For example, one friend knew someone who voted for a presidential candidate who reminded her of her grandfather, while another friend knew someone who voted against a candidate because he did not like the way the candidate dressed. The writer then reflects on the humorous as well as the serious implications of such voting decisions.

- A first-year college student, in an essay for his composition course, reflects on a performance of his high-school chorus that far surpassed the members' expectations. He describes their trip to the statewide competition and their anxious rehearsals before the performance and, during the competition, their unexpected feelings of confidence, their precision and control, and the exuberance of the performance. He considers factors that led to their success, such as fear of embarrassment, affection for their teacher, the excitement of a trip to the state capital, and the fact that they had rehearsed especially attentively for weeks because the music was so challenging and the competition so fierce. After considering possible reasons for their success, the writer concludes with some ideas about the special pleasures of success where cooperation and individual creativity are essential.

THINKING ABOUT YOUR EXPERIENCE WITH REFLECTION

Before studying a type of writing, it is useful to spend some time thinking about what you already know about it. You may have written about your reflections as you explored your ideas and reactions to things you have seen, heard, or read by corresponding with friends or by writing for school.

To analyze your experience with reflections, you might recall a time when you communicated your reflections in writing or orally and then consider questions like these: What was the particular occasion that triggered your reflections? Was it something you observed firsthand, saw in a film, heard on the radio, or overheard on the street? Why did this particular occasion seem interesting or significant to you? Were you surprised by the ideas it stimulated?

Consider also reflections you have read, heard, or seen on television or online. If you recall someone else's reflections in some detail, try to identify what made them interesting to you. For example, were the ideas fascinating in themselves, were you intrigued by the person's take on things, or did something else account for your interest? What specific details do you recall? How did the specific details help you understand the more abstract ideas in the reflections?

Write at least a page about your experience with reflective writing.

■ A Guide to Reading Reflective Essays

This guide introduces you to reflective writing. By completing all the activities in it, you will prepare yourself to learn a great deal from the other readings in this chapter about how to read and write a reflective essay. The guide focuses on a brief but powerful piece of reflection by Brent Staples. You will read Staples's reflective essay twice. First, you will read it for meaning, seeking to understand Staples's experience, to follow his reflections, and to discover your own ideas about stereotyping and fear of others. Then you will read the essay like a writer, analyzing the parts to see how Staples crafts his essay and to learn the strategies he uses to make his reflective writing effective. These two activities — reading for meaning and reading like a writer — follow every reading in this chapter.

BRENT STAPLES
Black Men and Public Space

Brent Staples (b. 1951) earned his PhD in psychology from the University of Chicago and went on to become a journalist, writing for several magazines and newspapers, including the Chicago Sun-Times. *In 1985, he became assistant metropolitan editor of the* New York Times, *where he is now a member of the editorial board. His autobiography,* Parallel Time: Growing Up in Black and White *(1994), won the Anisfield Wolff Book Award.*

The following essay originally appeared in Ms. *magazine in 1986 under the title "Just Walk On By." Staples revised it slightly for publication in* Harper's *a year later under the present title. The particular occasion for Staples's reflections is an incident that occurred for the first time in the mid-1970s, when he discovered that his mere presence on the street late at night was enough to frighten a young white woman. Recalling this incident leads him to reflect on issues of race, gender, and class in the United States. The marginal annotations point to strategies that writers of reflective essays typically use. Add your own comments and questions, noting anything else you think is interesting.*

As you read, think about why Staples chose the new title, "Black Men and Public Space."

My first victim was a woman—white, well dressed, 1 probably in her early twenties. I came upon her late one evening on a deserted street in Hyde Park, a relatively affluent neighborhood in an otherwise mean, impoverished section of Chicago. As I swung onto the avenue behind her, there seemed to be a discreet, uninflammatory distance between us. Not so. She cast back a worried glance. To her, the youngish black man— a broad six feet two inches with a beard and billowing hair, both hands shoved into the pockets of a bulky military jacket—seemed menacingly close. After a few more quick glimpses, she picked up her pace and was soon running in earnest. Within seconds she disappeared into a cross street.

That was more than a decade ago, I was twenty-two 2 years old, a graduate student newly arrived at the University of Chicago. It was in the echo of that terrified woman's footfalls that I first began to know the unwieldy inheritance I'd come into—the ability to alter public space in ugly ways. It was clear that she thought herself the quarry of a mugger, a rapist, or worse. Suffering a bout of insomnia, however, I was stalking sleep, not defenseless wayfarers. As a softy who is scarcely able to take a knife to a raw chicken—let alone hold one to a person's throat—I was surprised, embarrassed, and dismayed all at once. Her flight made me feel like an accomplice in tyranny. It also made it clear that I was indistinguishable from the muggers who occasionally seeped into the area from the surrounding ghetto. That first encounter, and those that followed, signified that a vast, unnerving gulf lay between nighttime pedestrians—particularly women—and me. And I soon gathered that being perceived as dangerous is a hazard in itself. I only needed to turn a corner into a dicey situation, or crowd some frightened, armed person in a foyer somewhere, or make an errant move after being pulled over by a policeman. Where fear and weapons meet—and they often do in urban America—there is always the possibility of death.

In that first year, my first away from my hometown, 3 I was to become thoroughly familiar with the language of fear. At dark, shadowy intersections, I could cross in front of a car stopped at a traffic light and elicit the *thunk, thunk, thunk* of the driver—black, white, male, or female—hammering down the door locks. On less traveled streets after dark, I grew accustomed to but never comfortable with people crossing to the other side of the street rather than pass me. Then there were the standard unpleasantries with policemen, doormen, bouncers, cabdrivers, and others whose business it is to screen out troublesome individuals *before* there is any nastiness.

4   I moved to New York nearly two years ago and I have remained an avid night walker. In central Manhattan, the near-constant crowd cover minimizes tense one-on-one street encounters. Elsewhere—in SoHo, for example, where sidewalks are narrow and tightly spaced buildings shut out the sky—things can get very taut indeed.

5   After dark, on the warrenlike streets of Brooklyn where I live, I often see women who fear the worst from me. They seem to have set their faces on neutral, and with their purse straps strung across their chests bandolier-style, they forge ahead as though bracing themselves against being tackled. I understand, of course, that the danger they perceive is not a hallucination. Women are particularly vulnerable to street violence, and young black males are drastically overrepresented among the perpetrators of that violence. Yet these truths are no solace against the kind of alienation that comes of being ever the suspect, a fearsome entity with whom pedestrians avoid making eye contact.

Staples acknowledges the reasons that women are fearful.

6   It is not altogether clear to me how I reached the ripe old age of twenty-two without being conscious of the lethality nighttime pedestrians attributed to me. Perhaps it was because in Chester, Pennsylvania, the small, angry industrial town where I came of age in the 1960s, I was scarcely noticeable against a backdrop of gang warfare, street knifings, and murders. I grew up one of the good boys, had perhaps a half-dozen fist-fights. In retrospect, my shyness of combat has clear sources.

Staples repeats a time marker (highlighted) to maintain topical coherence.

7   As a boy, I saw countless tough guys locked away; I have since buried several, too. They were babies, really—a teenage cousin, a brother of twenty-two, a childhood friend in his mid-twenties—all gone down in episodes of bravado played out in the streets. I came to doubt the virtues of intimidation early on. I chose,

perhaps unconsciously, to remain a shadow—timid, but a survivor.

The fearsomeness mistakenly attributed to me in public places often has a perilous flavor. The most frightening of these confusions occurred in the late 1970s and early 1980s, when I worked as a journalist in Chicago. One day, rushing into the office of a magazine I was writing for with a deadline story in hand, I was mistaken for a burglar. The office manager called security and, with an ad hoc posse, pursued me through the labyrinthine halls, nearly to my editor's door. I had no way of proving who I was. I could only move briskly toward the company of someone who knew me.

Another time I was on assignment for a local paper and killing time before an interview. I entered a jewelry store on the city's affluent Near North Side. The proprietor excused herself and returned with an enormous red Doberman pinscher straining at the end of a leash. She stood, the dog extended toward me, silent to my questions, her eyes bulging nearly out of her head. I took a cursory look around, nodded, and bade her good night.

Relatively speaking, however, I never fared as badly as another black male journalist. He went to nearby Waukegan, Illinois, a couple of summers ago to work on a story about a murderer who was born there. Mistaking the reporter for the killer, police officers hauled him from his car at gunpoint and but for his press credentials would probably have tried to book him. Such episodes are not uncommon. Black men trade tales like this all the time.

Over the years, I learned to smother the rage I felt at so often being taken for a criminal. Not to do so would surely have led to madness. I now take precautions to make myself less threatening. I move about with care, particularly late in the evening. I give a wide berth to nervous people on subway platforms during the wee hours, particularly when I have exchanged business clothes for jeans. If I happen to be entering a building behind some people who appear skittish, I may walk by, letting them clear the lobby before I return, so as not to seem to be following them. I have been calm and extremely congenial on those rare occasions when I've been pulled over by the police.

Staples looks at racial stereotyping through two more examples of danger to himself and another example showing that this is a common experience among black men.

His persona so far has been even-tempered, but here he admits to rage.

12   And on late-evening constitutionals I employ what has proved to be an excellent tension-reducing measure: I whistle melodies from Beethoven and Vivaldi and the more popular classical composers. Even steely New Yorkers hunching toward nighttime destinations seem to relax, and occasionally they even join in the tune. Virtually everybody seems to sense that a mugger wouldn't be warbling bright, sunny selections from Vivaldi's *Four Seasons*. It is my equivalent of the cowbell that hikers wear when they know they are in bear country.

> Staples returns to his original occasion and concludes with a kind of barbed humor. How does this affect you?

READING FOR MEANING

This section presents three activities that will help you reread Staples's reflective essay with a critical eye. Done in sequence, these activities lead you from a basic understanding of the selection to a more personal response to it and finally to an analysis that deepens your understanding and critical thinking about what you are reading.

Read to Comprehend

Reread the selection, and write a few sentences explaining some of the ways Staples tries to alleviate people's fear of him and commenting on his feelings about these encounters. The following definitions may help you understand Staples's vocabulary:

discreet (paragraph 1): carefully chosen.

unwieldy (2): difficult to carry or manage because of size, shape, weight, or complexity.

avid (4): enthusiastic.

constitutionals (12): walks taken regularly to maintain good health.

Identify three or more additional words that you don't understand, and find the best definitions from the dictionary that work with their context.

To expand your understanding of this reading, you might use one or more of the following critical reading strategies that are explained and illustrated in Appendix 1: *summarizing* and *paraphrasing*.

Read to Respond

Write several paragraphs exploring your initial thoughts and feelings about Staples's reflective essay. Focus on anything that stands out for you, perhaps because it resonates with your own experience or because you find a statement puzzling.

You might consider writing about the following:

- your response as a reader to Staples's opening words: "My first victim was a woman";

- Staples's reactions to being seen as threatening, perhaps in relation to how you think you would react if you were in his position;

- an experience you have had in which racial, gender, age, or other differences caused tension, comparing your experience with that of Staples or one of the people he encountered; or

- whether in your experience the fear of strangers operates the same way in suburban or small-town public spaces as it does for Staples in an urban setting.

To develop your response to Staples's essay, you might use one or more of the following critical reading strategies that are explained and illustrated in Appendix 1: *reflecting on challenges to your beliefs and values*, *recognizing emotional manipulation*, and *judging the writer's credibility*.

Read to Analyze Assumptions

Reread Staples's reflective essay, and write a paragraph or two exploring one or more of the assumptions you find in the text. All writing contains assumptions—opinions, values, and beliefs that are taken for granted as commonly accepted truths by the writer or others. Personal or individual assumptions also tend to reflect the values and beliefs of a particular group or community, sometimes called *cultural ideology*, which shape the way those in the group think, act, and understand the world.

Analyzing assumptions is an important part of learning to read critically because assumptions tend to be unexamined and unquestioned (at least consciously) by those who hold them. When you read with a critical eye, you identify important assumptions in the text and ask questions about them. Sometimes assumptions are stated explicitly, but often they are only implied, so you may have to search for underlying assumptions in the word choices and examples. Here are some kinds of questions you should ask regarding the assumptions you find: How does the assumption support or oppose the status quo? Whose interests are served by it? What alternative ideas, beliefs, or values would challenge this assumption? If the writer uses the assumption to appeal to readers, how effective do you think this appeal is, and why?

To help you get started reading for assumptions in Staples's essay, note that even though he writes about his feelings and thoughts, they may be more complex or less obvious than they appear at first. For example, he mentions anger only once, in paragraph 11: "I learned to smother the rage I felt at so often being taken for a criminal. Not to do so would surely have led to madness." Notice that he acknowledges having felt angry (or enraged) but says that he has conquered the feeling. His use of the word "madness" is interesting because it can be taken in two ways—as insanity and as anger. To smother a feeling as strong as rage, particularly about an injustice such as the one Staples endures, surely could drive a person crazy as well as make him furious. Staples does not make the point, but the reader can infer that he thinks the fear with which black men are so often regarded reveals the insanity of a racist society. Staples may want readers to see him as a "softy" (2) who avoids conflict and tries to reduce "tension" in others as well as in himself (12). But his reflections may have the effect of enraging readers who share with him the sense of injustice.

You may want to examine Staples's assumptions about a racist society—or about racial profiling—and consider whether he assumes his readers will agree with him or whether his reflection is designed to reach readers who might be skeptical that we still have a racist society. You may also explore other assumptions in Staples's essay, assumptions you may touch on in one of the other Reading for Meaning or Reading Like a Writer activities, such as the following:

- **other assumptions about anger.** Staples seems to go out of his way to help readers see him *not* as an "angry Black" but as someone who "understand[s] . . . that the danger [women] perceive is not a hallucination. Women are particularly vulnerable to street violence, and young black males are drastically overrepresented among the perpetrators of that violence" (5). To think critically about cultural assumptions related to anger, reread the essay, trying to spot all the places where Staples tries to make himself sound like a person who would not resort to violence of any kind. Given his audience (*Harper's* is an upscale publication whose readers are well educated), why do you suppose Staples follows this strategy? How do Americans normally view outward signs of rage, in person or in writing? When an American feels angry, how does he or she behave, in your experience? What happens when anger goes unchecked? What do you think happens when a person has to "stuff" his anger over and over again? What assumptions do you have about anger— about how you feel you should deal with it and how you expect others to deal with it?

- **assumptions about music.** Staples concludes his essay by writing that to reduce tension on his late-night walks, he whistles Beethoven and Vivaldi along with works of other "classical" composers. He makes explicit the assumptions (both his own and those of people who hear him) that lie behind this strategy: "Virtually everybody seems to sense that a mugger wouldn't be warbling bright, sunny selections from Vivaldi's *Four Seasons*" (12). To think critically about assumptions related to music, ask yourself: Why is a classical piece more effective than rock, country music, or rap? Why is a "sunny selection" more effective than, say, blues? What would happen if he sang opera? Examine your and U.S. culture's assumptions about music and its effects in light of Staples's choices.

To probe assumptions more deeply, you might use one or more of the following critical reading strategies that are explained and illustrated in Appendix 1: *reflecting on challenges to your beliefs and values, exploring the significance of figurative language,* and *looking for patterns of opposition.*

READING LIKE A WRITER

This section guides you through an analysis of Staples's reflective writing strategies: *presenting the particular occasion, developing the reflections, maintaining topical coherence,* and *engaging readers.* For each strategy, you will be asked to reread and annotate part of Staples's essay to see how he uses the strategy in "Black Men and Public Space."

When you study the selections later in this chapter, you will see how different writers use these same strategies for different purposes. The Guide to Writing Reflective Essays near the end of the chapter suggests ways you can use these strategies in your own writing.

Presenting the Particular Occasion

Reflective writers present a particular occasion—something they experienced or observed—to introduce their general reflections. They may describe the occasion in detail, or they may sketch it out quickly. The key in either case is to present the occasion in a vivid and suggestive way that encourages readers to want to know more about the writer's thoughts. To succeed at presenting the occasion vividly, writers rely on the same narrating and describing strategies you practiced in Chapter 2 (Autobiography) and Chapter 3 (Observation).

Staples lets readers know from the word *first* in the introductory phrase ("My first victim") that what happened on this occasion happened again later. But he focuses in the opening paragraph on this first occasion, the one that started his reflections. Staples presents this first event in vivid detail, trying to give readers a sense of the surprise and anxiety he felt at the time. In addition to helping readers imagine what happened, Staples tries to present the event in a way that suggests the larger meanings he will develop in subsequent paragraphs. Looking closely at how he saw the woman and how she saw him helps readers understand his ideas about what happened.

Analyze

1. *Reread* the opening sentence of paragraph 1, where Staples describes the person he encountered. *Notice* that even before he identifies her by gender, he uses the word "victim" to name her. Then *underline* the details he gives to describe this person and the actions she takes.

2. Now *turn to* the places in paragraph 1 where Staples describes himself as the woman saw him. *Put brackets around* the names used to identify him, and

underline the details used to describe him physically as well as the actions he takes.

3. *Review* the details you have underlined. Then *choose* three or four details that you think help make this particular occasion especially vivid and dramatic.

Write

Write several sentences explaining what you have learned about how Staples uses this event to create a dramatic occasion that helps to introduce his reflections. *Support* your explanation with some of the details you singled out.

Developing the Reflections

While the particular occasion introduces the subject, the reflections explore the subject by developing the writer's ideas. For example, what occasions Staples's reflections is an event that occurred when his mere presence on the street frightened a woman into running away from him. He uses this particular event to introduce the general subject: fear resulting from racial stereotyping. As he explains, "It was in the echo of that terrified woman's footfalls that I first began to know the unwieldy inheritance I'd come into" (paragraph 2). Throughout the rest of the essay, Staples examines this "inheritance" from various angles, using a range of reflective writing strategies. He expresses his different feelings at being misperceived as a threat; he explains the effects of racial stereotyping, including the danger to himself; he gives examples of other occasions when people react to him with fear or hostility; and finally, he lists the "precautions" he takes to make himself appear "less threatening" (11). These are just some of the strategies writers use to develop their reflections. This activity will help you see how Staples uses examples to illustrate and explain his ideas.

Analyze

1. *Look at* the opening sentence of paragraph 3, where Staples introduces the idea that there is a "language of fear." *Reread* the rest of the paragraph to see how the writer uses examples to help readers understand what he means.

2. Now *look at* paragraphs 11 and 12, where Staples writes about the "precautions" he takes to make himself seem "less threatening." *Mark* the examples, and *choose* one or two that you think work especially well to help readers understand what he means.

Write

Write several sentences explaining what you have learned about Staples's use of examples, pointing to the examples you think are especially effective.

Maintaining Topical Coherence

Reflective essays explore ideas on a subject by turning them this way and that, examining them first from one perspective and then from another, and sometimes piling up examples to illustrate the ideas. Such essays may seem rambling, with one idea or example added to another in a casual way. It is not always clear where the writer is going, and the essay may not seem to end conclusively. This apparently casual organization is deceptive, however, because in fact the reflective writer has arranged the parts carefully to give the appearance of a mind at work.

While each new idea or example may seem to turn the essay in an unexpected new direction, reflective writers use what we call *topical coherence* to make the parts of a reflective essay connect to the central subject. An important way of achieving topical coherence is to refer to the subject at various points in the essay by repeating certain key words or phrases associated with the subject. In the opening anecdote that presents the particular occasion, Staples dramatizes the woman's fear of him. He does not use the word "fear," however, until the end of paragraph 2. He then repeats that word twice: at the beginning of paragraph 3, in the phrase "language of fear," and at the beginning of paragraph 5. He also concludes the latter paragraph with a phrase that indicates how others, particularly women, see him: as "a fearsome entity." In addition, Staples uses several related words, such as "terrified" and "frightened" (paragraph 2) as well as "nervous" and "skittish" (11). By repeating the word "fear" and words related to it, Staples highlights the subject of his reflections.

Another way reflective writers achieve topical coherence is through carefully placed transitions. Staples, as you will see in this activity, uses time and place markers to introduce a series of examples illustrating the fear he engenders in others simply because of his race and gender.

Analyze

1. *Skim* paragraphs 2 to 4, 7 to 9, and 11, and *put brackets around* the time and place markers. *Begin* by bracketing the time marker "more than a decade ago" and the place marker "at the University of Chicago" in the opening sentence of paragraph 2.

2. *Notice* how many different times and places Staples refers to with these markers.

Write

Write several sentences explaining how Staples uses time and place markers to help maintain topical coherence. *Support* your explanation with examples from the reading.

Engaging Readers

Readers of reflective essays, like readers of autobiographical and observational writing, expect writers to engage their interest. In fact, most readers have no pressing reason to read reflective writing. They choose to read an essay because something about it catches their eye—a familiar author's name, an intriguing title, an interesting graphic or drop quote. Journalists typically begin feature articles, ones that do not deal with "hard" news, with what they call a *hook*, designed to catch readers' attention. The particular occasion that opens many reflective essays often serves this purpose. Staples's opening phrase, "My first victim," certainly grabs attention.

But once "caught," readers have to be kept reading. One of the ways reflective writers keep readers engaged is by projecting an image of themselves—sometimes called the *writer's persona* or *voice*—that readers can identify with or at least find interesting. Staples, for example, uses the first-person pronouns *my* and *I* to present himself in his writing and to speak directly to readers. In paragraph 2, for example, he describes himself as "a softy" and explains how he felt when he realized that the woman was so frightened by him that she ran for her life. Like most reflective writers, Staples tries to make himself sympathetic to readers so that they will listen to what he has to say.

Analyze

1. *Reread* the essay looking for places where you get a sense of Staples as a person, and in the margin briefly *describe* the impression you get.

2. *Think about* what engages you or draws you into the essay.

Write

Write several sentences about the impressions you get of Staples from reading this essay, exploring how these impressions affect your interest in his ideas.

A SPECIAL READING STRATEGY

Comparing and Contrasting Related Readings: Brent Staples's "Black Men and Public Space" and an excerpt from his autobiography, Parallel Time

Comparing and contrasting related readings is a critical reading strategy useful both in reading for meaning and in reading like a writer. This strategy is particularly applicable when writers present similar subjects, as is the case in the two reflective readings by Brent Staples that are compared here. The first, "Black Men and Public Space," the essay you have just read, was first published in 1986. The second, the excerpt below from Staples's autobiography, *Parallel Time*, was published in 1994. Both readings deal with the same occasion—when Staples encountered his "first victim" (paragraph 1 in both). But you will notice that the details of this first encounter as well as Staples's reflections about it differ significantly in the two readings. As you read, notice what Staples keeps from the original and what he changes. To compare and contrast these two reflective readings, think about issues such as these:

- Compare these readings in terms of the way the particular occasion is described. What seems to you to be most significant about these two descriptions? Note, for example, the details about the location and the woman's appearance as well as how Staples describes his immediate reaction.

- Compare how Staples describes what he calls "the language of fear" in these readings (paragraph 3 in both). Highlight the places in each reading where the language of fear is described. In what ways is his description similar and different? How does he explain its causes?

- Compare these readings to see what Staples thinks and feels about the situation he finds himself in and what actions he decides to take. What are the main differences in his reactions? Speculate on why he decided to make so radical a revision of his earlier reflections in his autobiography published nearly a decade after his original essay was published. What do you think might have changed (in Staples's feelings, in the broader cultural climate, or in some other way) during that period that led Staples to share with readers his angry response rather than leaving readers with the image of himself he projects at the end of the original version?

See Appendix 1 for detailed guidelines on using the comparing and contrasting related readings strategy.

From *Parallel Time*

At night, I walked to the lakefront whenever the weather permitted. I was headed home from the lake when I took my first victim. It was late fall, and the wind was cutting. I was wearing my navy pea jacket, the collar turned up, my hands snug in the pockets. Dead leaves scuttled in shoals along the streets. I turned out of Blackstone Avenue and headed west on 57th Street, and there she was, a few yards ahead of me, dressed in business clothes and carrying a briefcase. She looked back at me once, then again, and picked up her pace. She looked back again and started to run. I stopped where I was and looked up at the surrounding windows. What did this look like to people peeking out through their blinds? I was out walking. But what if someone had thought they'd seen something they hadn't and called the police. I held back the urge to run. Instead, I walked south to The Midway, plunged into its darkness, and remained on The Midway until I reached the foot of my street.

I'd been a fool. I'd been walking the streets grinning good 2 evening at people who were frightened to death of me. I did violence to them by just being. How had I missed this? I kept walking at night, but from then on I paid attention.

I became expert in the language of fear. Couples locked arms or 3 reached for each other's hand when they saw me. Some crossed to the other side of the street. People who were carrying on conversations went mute and stared straight ahead, as though avoiding my eyes would save them. This reminded me of an old wives' tale: that rabid dogs didn't bite if you avoided their eyes. The determination to avoid my eyes made me invisible to classmates and professors whom I passed on the street.

It occurred to me for the first time that I was big. I was 6 feet 4 1½ inches tall, and my long hair made me look bigger. I weighed only 170 pounds. But the navy pea jacket that Brian had given me was broad at the shoulders, high at the collar, making me look bigger and more fearsome than I was.

I tried to be innocuous but didn't know how. The more I 5 thought about how I moved, the less my body belonged to me; I became a false character riding along inside it. I began to avoid people. I turned out of my way into side streets to spare them the sense that they were being stalked. I let them clear the lobbies of buildings before I entered, so they wouldn't feel trapped. Out of nervousness I began to whistle and discovered I was good at it. My whistle was pure and sweet—and also in tune. On the street at night I whistled popular tunes from the Beatles and Vivaldi's *Four Seasons*. The tension drained from people's bodies when they heard me. A few even smiled as they passed me in the dark.

Then I changed. I don't know why, but I remember when. I was 6 walking west on 57th Street, after dark, coming home from the lake. The man and the woman walking toward me were laughing and talking but clammed up when they saw me. The man touched the woman's elbow, guiding her toward the curb. Normally I'd have given way and begun to whistle, but not this time. This time I veered toward them and aimed myself so that they'd have to part to avoid walking into me. The man stiffened, threw back his head and assumed the stare: eyes dead ahead, mouth open. His face took on a bluish hue under the sodium vapor streetlamps. I suppressed the urge to scream into his face. Instead I glided between them, my shoulder nearly brushing his. A few steps beyond them I stopped and howled with laughter. I called this game Scatter the Pigeons.

Fifty-seventh Street was too well lit for the game to be much fun; people didn't feel quite vulnerable enough. Along The Midway were heart-stopping strips of dark sidewalk, but these were so frightening that few people traveled them. The stretch of Blackstone between 57th and 55th provided better hunting. The block was long and lined with young trees that blocked out the streetlight and obscured the heads of people coming toward you. 7

One night I stooped beneath the branches and came up on the other side, just as a couple was stepping from their car into their town house. The woman pulled her purse close with one hand and reached for her husband with the other. The two of them stood frozen as I bore down on them. I felt a surge of power: these people were mine; I could do with them as I wished. If I'd been younger with less to lose, I'd have robbed them, and it would have been easy. All I'd have to do was stand silently before them until they surrendered their money. I thundered, "Good evening!" into their bleached-out faces and cruised away laughing. 8

I held a special contempt for people who cowered in their cars as they waited for the light to change at 57th and Woodlawn. The intersection was always deserted at night, except for a car or two stuck at the red. *Thunk! Thunk! Thunk!* They hammered down the door locks when I came into view. Once I had hustled across the street, head down, trying to seem harmless. Now I turned brazenly into the headlights and laughed. Once across, I paced the sidewalk, glaring until the light changed. They'd made me terrifying. Now I'd show them how terrifying I could be. 9

▪ Readings

CARL SAFINA

Comes a Turtle, Comes the World

Carl Safina (b. 1955) earned his MS and PhD degrees at Rutgers University. Safina's books include Song for the Blue Ocean: Encounters along the World's Coasts and beneath the Seas *(1998),* Eye of the Albatross: Visions of Hope and Survival *(2002), and* Voyage of the Turtle: In Pursuit of the Earth's Last Dinosaur *(2006). He also cowrote (with Mercedes Lee and Suzanne Iudicello) the* Seafood Lover's Almanac: A Guide for Those Who Love to Eat Seafood but Are Concerned about Depleting Fish and Shellfish Populations *(2000). His conservation work has been profiled in the* New York Times, *on* Nightline, *and in the Bill Moyers television special* Earth on Edge. *A recipient of the Lannan Literary Award, the John Burroughs Writer's Medal, and fellowships from the Pew and MacArthur foundations and the World Wildlife Fund, he is founding president of Blue Ocean Institute (www.blueocean.org), which seeks to inspire a closer relationship between humans and the sea.*

"Comes a Turtle, Comes the World" was first published in 2006 as an "environmental activism" essay in the catalog of the Patagonia clothing company. In the words of the company's Web site, "the eminent author and ecologist, Dr. Carl Safina, reminds us, through the story of one Kemp's ridley turtle, of both the abundance and fragility of life in the sea."

As you read, think about your own experiences with the ocean, wildlife, or environmental issues. Note how Safina alternates narrative with explanation and how he uses vivid details to help you "see" the environment and its creatures. Annotate the text, noting the ways that Safina builds a case for human intervention and anything else interesting about his reflective writing strategies. (For help annotating, see the examples in this chapter on pages 153 and 196, as well as the advice on annotating on pages 597–603.)

The morning chill carried that clean-sheet crispness; that cleansing sort of air. Actually, for the tip of Long Island in early December, this weather was a little late in coming. But walking from our house to the shore of the bay, the new crystal air made me finally look ahead toward winter and turn my back to what had been a spectacular, lingering fall.

Every autumn here witnesses two great migrations: one axiomatic and one nearly unknown. Everybody knows birds fly south for the winter. Here, the marshes and barrier islands are interstate arteries for heavy traffic of songbirds, waterfowl, hawks and others. But except for people who fish, almost no one realizes the greater migration begins just beyond the beach.

This year, as usual, swarms of fish had arrived from New England in the last few weeks and departed down the coast in great migrating waves. They included millions and millions of anchovies and menhaden, pursued to the surface by armies of bluefish, striped bass, little tuna. Along the seafloor battalions of summer flounder, black sea bass, tautog, porgies and others moved to deeper grounds. Offshore, beyond sight of land on the rolling blue prairies of the sea, sharks and tunas passed like herds on the Serengeti (though now, like those herds, much diminished). Herring and mackerel had arrived mid-November with dolphins on their tails, and the remaining schools of striped bass, fattening for their long run to winter grounds, gobbled them greedily. Even now, into December, a few boats were still hunting bass. But we had caught enough, our freezer was stocked for winter and our smoker racks were busy, and we'd just hauled the boat.

Patricia and I put our footsteps to the gravelly beach and walked to the inlet to see who'd recently arrived. Bonaparte's gulls, a few long-tailed ducks, some black scoters and in the distance the feathered missiles called gannets were sending geysers skyward as a flock poured into a herring school. To me, this seasonal sense of place in the path of migrations, this finger on the pulse of the planet, is the purest joy.

We were just rounding the inlet entrance when, among the shells and tide-wrack, my gaze caught something so unexpected—here, and in this near-frost—it seemed improbable as a fallen angel: a sea turtle.

It was a baby, with a platter-sized shell. Species: Kemp's ridley, most endangered of all Atlantic turtles. Stunned by the boreal air and 49-degree water, the turtle's only sign of life was a mark in the wet sand suggesting a flipper had moved sometime since high tide had left it and withdrawn.

This nation that sees itself stretching from sea to shining sea conceals beneath her broad, waving skirts of bordering oceans some of the greatest wildlife in the world. And because it's so effectively hidden, it's some of the least understood.

Though the saltiness of our blood and tears speaks from within of our parent ocean, for most people oceans seem distant, out of sight and generally out of mind. Even many who love nature, who see our landscape and imagine herds of bison and skies darkened by passenger pigeons and clouds of waterfowl, who escape into the woods or mountains or even the shore, seem to get their vision stranded on the beach as though wildlife stops at the high-tide line, where our little stunned turtle reminded us that so much actually begins.

The water makes a perfect disguise that heightens the mystery, but in some ways that's a great pity, because the closest thing we have left to the thundering herds and great flocks is in the sea. Extending your vision into the grand swirl and suck of the many-fingered tides and beyond will grant you a renewed sense of both the abundance and fragility of life. 9

Whether or not we can see, hear, or feel the ocean from our own home territory, the ocean certainly feels all of us. Between a third and half the world's people now live within 50 miles of a coast (as any traveler can attest). In China, population density is three times higher in coastal areas than elsewhere. The collective weight of humanity may rest on land, but we levy heavy pressure on the sea. Most of us exert our most direct interaction with the sea through the seafood we buy. But even air quality affects water quality because what goes up alights elsewhere, and climate change is challenging ocean habitats by melting sea ice and cooking corals, undermining food supplies for penguins, polar bears and reef fishes. 10

People who think of themselves as conservationists carry a concern for wildlife, wildlands and habitat quality as part of their sense of right and wrong. It is time to take these concerns below high tide. Most people would not question a hawk's place in the sky, nor ask what good is a gazelle, nor wonder whether the world really needs wild orchids. Yet when told of the plight of, say, sharks, many still think it quite reasonable to inquire, "What good are they; why do we need them?" Fifty million buffalo once roamed the rolling green prairies of North America. Gunners reduced them to near-extinction. Now, hunters cut from the same cloth are at work on the rolling blue prairies of the sea and, already, the big fish—including miracles like thousand-pound, warm-blooded bluefin tuna—are 90 percent gone. What we regret happening on land may again happen in the sea. Those who care about wildlife should get to know about oceans. 11

We brought the turtle home and warmed it a bit in the sun. It began to shed tears, a sign of ongoing glandular function and, for us, heightened hope. Soon a flipper waved—a certain signal of persistent life. Shortly thereafter, the aquarium people arrived to bring our little patient into veterinary rehab. Slowly warmed, within a few hours it was conscious and swimming, safe until release next spring. 12

Whether we help one unlucky creature or wish to save the
world, for each of us the challenge and opportunity is to cherish all
life as the gift it is, envision it whole, seek to know it truly, and
undertake—with our minds, hearts and hands—to restore its
abundance. Where there's life there's hope, and so no place can
inspire more hopefulness than the great, life-making sea, home to
creatures of mystery and majesty, whose future now depends on
human compassion, and our next move.   13

Take the Next Step and Get Involved   14
For more information about our oceans and what you can do to
protect them from overfishing, habitat destruction and pollution,
visit these Web sites:

Blue Ocean Institute
The Ocean Conservancy
Oceana
Patagonia — Oceans as Wilderness

READING FOR MEANING

This section presents three activities that will help you reread Safina's reflective essay with a critical eye. Done in sequence, these activities lead you from a
basic understanding of the selection to a more personal response to it and finally
to an analysis that deepens your understanding and critical thinking about what
you are reading.

Read to Comprehend

Reread the selection, and write a few sentences briefly explaining the concerns of Carl Safina regarding our world. The following definitions may help you
understand Safina's vocabulary:

axiomatic (paragraph 2): evident without proof or argument.

battalions (3): large numbers of persons or things; force.

boreal (6): of or concerning the north wind.

levy (10): impose.

Find three or more additional words that you don't understand, and find the best
definitions from the dictionary that work with their context.

Read to Respond

Write several paragraphs exploring your initial thoughts and feelings about Safina's reflective essay. Focus on anything that stands out for you, perhaps because it resonates with your own experience or because you find a statement puzzling.

You might consider writing about the following:

- your own experiences with the ocean;

- your feelings about "global warming," to which Safina refers in the last sentence of paragraph 10; or

- what Safina means when he says "the ocean certainly feels all of us" (10).

To develop your response to Safina's essay, you might use one or more of the following critical reading strategies that are explained and illustrated in Appendix 1: *exploring the significance of figurative language* and *recognizing emotional manipulation*.

Read to Analyze Assumptions

Reread Safina's reflective essay, and write a paragraph or two exploring one or more of the assumptions you find in the text. The following suggestions may help:

- **assumptions about visibility.** At the end of paragraph 7, Safina discusses the ocean's wildlife and asserts that "because it's so effectively hidden, it's some of the least understood." People, he says, "seem to get their vision stranded on the beach as though wildlife stops at the high-tide line" (8). Throughout his essay, Safina compares wildlife on land to wildlife in the sea and gives examples to try to make the ocean become more *visible* to land dwellers like us. To think critically about the assumptions in this essay related to visibility, ask yourself: Why would Safina go to such efforts to make ocean creatures visible? What is it about visibility that matters in this context?

- **assumptions about human responsibility.** Throughout his essay, Safina uses figurative language to help readers get a sense both of nature's bounty and of the danger to its creatures. He seems to be sending a message to his readers: we humans are responsible for our world, and we have not been doing a good job. To think critically about the assumptions in this essay related to human responsibility, find five or six instances where what Safina writes seems to rest on the notion that humans bear responsibility for other creatures. Then ask yourself: Why does he hold this belief? What are *your* beliefs about who is responsible for the creatures of the earth, including the oceans? How is your view about oceans changed or reinforced as a result of reading this essay? What is the significance of the fact that Safina's narrative is about a *baby* turtle?

██ A SPECIAL READING STRATEGY

Exploring the Significance of Figurative Language

Figurative language adds color and richness to writing by taking words literally associated with one thing and applying them to something else, often in an unexpected or unconventional way, to create a vivid image or other sensory impression in readers' minds. For example, in this essay Safina conveys the look, feel, and smell of early-morning autumn air with the metaphors of "clean-sheet," "cleansing," and "crystal" (paragraph 1). To explore the significance of figurative language in this essay:

1. List and annotate all the figures of speech—metaphors, similes (metaphors that use "like" or "as") and symbols—that you find in "Comes a Turtle, Comes the World."

2. Look for patterns. Then, group the figures of speech according to similar feelings and attitudes and label them.

3. Write for ten minutes to explore the themes you discovered in step 2. What meanings emerge from the patterns and your writing?

Appendix 1 (pp. 617–20) provides detailed guidelines on exploring the significance of figurative language.

READING LIKE A WRITER
PRESENTING THE PARTICULAR OCCASION

Reflections are often triggered by a one-time event or observation. In the previous reading, for example, you saw how Brent Staples started thinking about his subject as a result of a particular event and how he uses the time marker "late one evening" (paragraph 1) to let readers know this was a one-time event. Later in his essay, however, Staples refers to other occasions to make the point that what he became aware of on that particular night became an unhappily frequent occurrence. Similarly, Safina begins his essay by referring to his event as occurring in "[t]he morning chill . . . in early December" (1), part of "two great migrations" every autumn (2). He then narrates how he and "Patricia" walk to the inlet to see what the latest migrations brought. Not until paragraph 5 does his particular event occur. The following activity will help you analyze the strategies Safina uses to present his particular occasion and his reflections that resulted from it.

Analyze

1. *Look closely* at Safina's narrative in paragraphs 5, 6, and 12.

2. *Next turn to* the paragraphs that follow the first part of the narrative (5, 6) and *note* the descriptive details that characterize Safina's reflections. Then *turn to* the paragraph that follows the second part of the narrative.

Write

Write several sentences explaining how Safina's descriptive details and narrative actions give the event its impact. *Support* your explanation with examples from your annotations.

CONSIDERING IDEAS FOR YOUR OWN WRITING

Safina's essay suggests many subjects for reflection. In his final paragraph, Safina invites us to ponder our role as caregivers or caretakers: "Whether we help one unlucky creature or wish to save the world, for each of us the challenge and opportunity is to cherish all life as the gift it is, envision it whole, seek to know it truly, and undertake — with our minds, hearts and hands — to restore its abundance" (13). Consider whether a particular occasion ever prompted you to think about how you could improve your world — whether your immediate family, your neighborhood, your school, your community, or the larger world. Safina also mentions that "[p]eople who think of themselves as conservationists carry a concern for wildlife, wildlands and habitat quality as part of their sense of right and wrong" (11). How did you form your own sense of right and wrong? Was there a particular occasion where your sense was challenged or reinforced? Your reflection could be about the environment (including the ocean), or it could be about your culture, your family, your job, or your schooling. Any occasion that spurs thinking deeply about a subject would work as a prompt for your reflective essay.

STEVEN DOLOFF

A Universe Lies on the Sidewalks of New York

> Steven Doloff is an associate professor of English and humanities
> and a lecturer in intensive English at the Pratt Institute in New York
> City, where he won a Distinguished Teacher Award in 2001. His writ-
> ing has been published in scholarly journals like the James Joyce
> Quarterly and the Shakespeare Quarterly as well as in the Washing-
> ton Post and the New York Times.
>
> "A Universe Lies on the Sidewalks of New York" was first published
> in 2002 in Newsday, a newspaper based on Long Island, New York, as
> part of a series called "City Life." As you read, think about any daily
> activity that might lead you to reflect on its meaning to your life as a
> whole. Annotate the text, noting the ways that Doloff conveys the tex-
> ture of city life with his examples and anything interesting about his
> reflective writing strategies. (For help annotating, see the examples in
> this chapter on pages 153 and 196, as well as the advice on annotating
> on pages 597–603.)

In an oversized brandy snifter on my kitchen counter I keep a   1
dozen bullets I have picked up off the sidewalks in my neighborhood. Along the northern edge of Greenwich Village, I have found,
over the last 10 years or so, mashed .45 caliber slugs, cute little
.22 caliber shells that look like they fell off a charm bracelet, and
inch-long snub-nosed other things that could smack down a
refrigerator.

With every one I have picked up, I've wondered the same things: 2
How did this get here? If it was a slug, did it miss someone? If it was
a shell, did it hit someone? Was it from a cop's gun or a felon's?
(I ruled out licensed animal hunters on 14th Street.) I haven't
found any loose ordnance lately, and homicide rates are currently
way down. I guess there's a connection.

Some urban sociologists study the contents of garbage cans, and   3
others mull over graffiti. As both a student and a member of the
passing parade, I look down to consider what we step on and over
as we march along to our various drummers. One could say that
New York's sidewalks make up a kind of endless concrete newspaper from which we can read, in the minute flotsam and jetsam at
our feet, news of the mass of people who walk them.

For instance, about 10 years ago, I noticed almost every day (but   4
did not pick up) dozens of party-colored crack vials scattered about
my neighborhood. They are now, I am happy to report, gone (at least
from my sidewalks), and crack abuse is also much diminished. Two

years ago, I actually found a crumpled hundred-dollar bill in the street. That, too, perhaps, was a sign of the times — wafted uptown from a stockbroker's window after the Dow Jones Industrial Average leapt to some record-breaking bullish height.

And how about those devalued pennies everywhere that almost nobody bothers to bend over for anymore? (I pick up the shiny ones.) I wonder if the fluctuating number of pennies to be found on some carefully selected stretch of sidewalk, say near Wall Street, might not be useful as a kind of economic indicator of imminent stock market movements (the "PDI-penny density index"). 5

Perhaps most intriguing are the gum spots — you know, those little black circles, ranging in size from nickels to drink coasters, that speckle the sidewalks and subway platforms from one end of our city to the other. While evenly distributed in most places, they tend to cluster like asteroid belts around phone booths, bus stops, litter baskets and building entrances. And they do not wear, fade or scrape away, ever. I once watched a building-maintenance worker with a steam hose trying to clear these chicle pox from a tiny patch of sidewalk near a doorway. I watched because I was amazed by his wonderfully futile gesture. It took him nearly 15 minutes to get rid of one stain. He was standing in a nest of hundreds. 6

We may not be able to see many stars in Manhattan, but there is this whole universe of gum spots before our eyes that most of us never even notice. If travelers from another planet ever visited New York City, I'm sure they would marvel at the trillions of spat, dropped and flicked lumps of flattened chewing gum that cover our metropolis, and wonder what kind of tree-sap chomping maniacs lived here. 7

Once in a while I come across spots in the making — small, pink baby circles, not yet stomped into wider, blackened, hardened spots. I almost feel sorry for these untrammeled innocents, these newly attached freckles to the concrete skin of our city. But then I remember they will outlive me and that the future belongs to them. 8

It's not all good news on the sidewalk, but it's the truth. 9

READING FOR MEANING

This section presents three activities that will help you reread Doloff's reflective essay with a critical eye. Done in sequence, these activities lead you from a basic understanding of the selection to a more personal response to it and finally to an analysis that deepens your understanding and critical thinking about what you are reading.

Read to Comprehend

Reread the selection, and write a few sentences briefly explaining what Doloff sees in the sidewalks of New York. The following definitions may help you understand Doloff's vocabulary:

felon (paragraph 2): a person who has committed a serious crime.

crack (4): pellet-size pieces of highly purified cocaine, prepared with other ingredients for smoking and known to be especially potent and addicting.

bullish (4): characterized by increases in the value of stocks and other securities.

chicle (6): a gumlike substance obtained from the latex of certain tropical American trees, as the sapodilla, used chiefly in the manufacture of chewing gum.

Identify three or more additional words that you don't understand, and find the best definitions from the dictionary that work with their context.

Read to Respond

Write several paragraphs exploring your initial thoughts and feelings about Doloff's reflective essay. Focus on anything that stands out for you, perhaps because it resonates with your own experience or because you find a statement puzzling.

You might consider writing about the following:

- sidewalks that you use (or whatever you walk on right outside where you live) and the things that you have found there;

- something that you have picked up from the ground in a public place and kept and its significance for you; or

- your response to Doloff's last sentence: "It's not all good news on the sidewalk, but it's the truth" (9).

To develop your response to Doloff's essay, you might use one or more of the following critical reading strategies that are explained and illustrated in Appendix 1: *exploring the significance of figurative language* and *judging the writer's credibility*.

Read to Analyze Assumptions

Reread Doloff's reflective essay, and write a paragraph or two exploring one or more of the assumptions you find in the text. The following suggestions may help:

- **assumptions about artifacts.** In each of his paragraphs, Doloff makes an assumption about the meaning of an artifact he has seen on the street, much as an archaeologist would make if discovering artifacts in a ruin. (An *artifact* is any object produced or shaped by human craft, especially a tool, weapon, or ornament of archaeological or historical interest.) What is your response to the conclusions he draws from his artifacts? Would you draw the same conclusions or perhaps different ones? Doloff also ponders what "travelers from another planet" would think if they saw all the gum splats on the sidewalks of New York. To think critically about the assumptions in this essay related to artifacts, ask yourself: What truths about humanity (or perhaps just New Yorkers) do you derive from Doloff's reflection?

- **assumptions about the future and immortality.** In paragraph 8, Doloff considers the new "small, pink baby circles, not yet stomped into wider, blackened, hardened spots." He almost feels "sorry" for them, until he remembers the "future belongs to them" (8). To think critically about the assumptions in this essay related to how we might be perceived by future generations, ask yourself: What larger concern is he hinting at by making gum spots and their immortality the last artifact he reflects on?

READING LIKE A WRITER
ENGAGING READERS

Reflective writers use an array of strategies early in an essay to engage readers' interest. They often craft an attention-grabbing title—"Diving into the Gene Pool," "Comes a Turtle, Comes the World," "A Universe Lies on the Sidewalks of New York"—and work to make their opening sentences intriguing. For example, Brent Staples opens his essay with a shocking confession ("My first victim was a woman"), and Wendy Lee begins with a mysterious statement ("When my friend told me that her father had once compared her to a banana, I stared at her blankly"). Reflective writers sometimes try to establish a tone or project a voice that will engage readers—by using humor or exaggeration, for instance.

Analyze

1. *Review* Doloff's title, and *recall* its initial impact on you. How well did it engage your interest? What did you expect?

2. *Reread* the first two paragraphs, and *notice* the strategies Doloff uses to interest readers, such as referring to bullet shells as "cute" and to "other things [bullet-sized] that could smack down a refrigerator." In the second paragraph, he makes a joke about ruling out "licensed animal hunters on 14th Street."

Write

Write several sentences explaining the strategies that Doloff uses to engage readers and their effectiveness for you as a reader.

CONSIDERING IDEAS FOR YOUR OWN WRITING

Steven Doloff's particular occasion was simply staring into a brandy snifter full of bullets he had collected over the years, which made him ponder where he got them and think about other things he had found on the sidewalks of New York. Reflective essays can be about almost anything, even something that is in front of you every day. Look around your room, your home, your school, and your neighborhood to see if any object or sight makes you think deeply or sends your mind into new places. How would you interpret your object? What does it symbolize for you? If you don't *see* anything that provokes thought, try *hearing*, *feeling*, or even *tasting*: our senses can often provide us with an entryway into intriguing topics. Think about how a song, a cooking smell, or a taste can trigger memories, and reflect on how and why those memories made a lasting impression on you. For some people, just the smell of chlorine can bring back a summer camp experience that changed their way of thinking, or the sweet taste of Halloween candy can remind them of a childhood experience worth reflection.

CAROLINA A. MIRANDA
Diving into the Gene Pool

Carolina A. Miranda teaches Spanish at the University of Hull in the United Kingdom. She previously taught in Argentina, also at the university level, and is pursuing a doctorate on the Argentinian writer Roberto Arlt. She is also the author of The Lonely Planet Guide to Costa Rica *and a reporter for* Time *magazine.*

"Diving into the Gene Pool" was first published in Time *in 2006. As you read, think about your own genetic history. Have you ever looked up any of your ancestors? Do you know your history further back than your parents or grandparents? Does your genetic history seem to shape who you are now? Note that Miranda is initially uninterested in her genetic history but that new discoveries have made her become interested.*

Annotate the text, noting places where Miranda explores her identity and anything else interesting about her reflective writing strategies. (For help annotating, see the examples in this chapter on pages 153 and 196, as well as the advice on annotating on pages 597–603.)

If they held a convention for racial purity, I would never make the guest list. Like most other Latin American families, mine is a multiethnic stew that has left me with the generic black-eyed and olive-skinned look typical of large swaths of the world's population. My father's family is from Peru, my mother's from Chile. Their parents were born and reared in South America. Beyond that, I know nothing about my ancestors. That was fine by me—until the new and growing industry of personal DNA analysis created a need I never knew I had. 1

Today at least half a dozen companies will, for about $200 a pop, take your spittle, analyze the heck out of it and tell you who and what you are. The tests are popular among adoptees, armchair genealogists and high school seniors praying that a link to some underrepresented ethnic group will help get them into the Ivies. Already a card-carrying minority, I thought a test might help me figure out a thing or two about my forebears—and my mixed-up identity. 2

So I hit the Internet and quickly found a couple of companies that looked promising. The first, DNA Tribes in Arlington, Va., filled its website with glossy shots of ethnic types. The next, DNAPrint in Sarasota, Fla., offered a cool Flash movie of a rotating double helix. I was doubly sold. I ordered a test from each and within a couple of days was scraping the inside of my cheek with swabs and depositing my cells into prepaid envelopes ready to be sent off to the labs. 3

Then I set about trying to predict the results. On my father's   4
side, I figured, high cheekbones and almond eyes probably showed
evidence of native-Andean blood. The aquiline profiles and curly
hair on my mother's side, on the other hand, are common on
Mediterranean shores. My best guess: I was mostly European, a bit
of native South American and perhaps a dash of Middle Eastern.
But like most other people who do this sort of thing, I also secretly
hoped I would be related to an American Indian tribe with a lucrative casino operation. Anything that would justify the tests on my
next expense account.

Within a few weeks, I received my first results, from DNA   5
Tribes. As I had guessed, the genetic indicators showed both Euro-
pean and American Indian roots. But No. 1 on the list of places
I was supposed to be from was—to my great surprise—sub-
Saharan Africa. What's more, No. 1 on the list of the top 10 regional
populations with which I was most likely to share a piece of genetic
code was Belorussia, followed closely by southeast Poland and
Mozambique.

That's when I began to wonder whether there had been some   6
kind of DNA mix-up. Fond as I am of stuffed cabbage, Poland
and Belorussia are not places I had ever identified with. The sub-
Saharan African connection was also puzzling. Any physical evidence of black Africa has apparently been diluted beyond
recognition in my murky gene pool. And while heavy traces of
African blood are not unusual in Latin America, they tend to be
linked to West Africa, where much of the slave trade to the Americas originated. Clearly, my ancestors got around.

My mother, when I finally told her about all this, thought I was joking. My father asked me to ring back during halftime. And none of us even want to think about how my more persnickety aunts—the ones convinced they're descendants of Spanish nobility—will react when they read about our Afro-Polish roots. 7

I was in for yet another surprise when, a few days later, the results from DNAPrint came in. The basic elements were similar, but the blend was different: 71% European, 26% Native American and 3% sub-Saharan African. Beyond a few inscrutable charts, there was little specific information. 8

In fact, there were a lot of things the tests didn't tell me. Unlike a pregnancy test, with its emphatic yes or no, ancestral-DNA testing gives you only a "statistical likelihood" of membership in a certain group. I don't know how many generations ago those ethnicities appeared in my family tree, nor (without further tests) on which side. Moreover, the gene test hasn't been invented that can unravel the improbable chain of events that connected Belorussians with Mozambicans, and American Indians with Poles—ultimately to produce me, a Latina living and working in New York City. 9

Did the tests change my view of myself? Not really. I'll still put my check in the Latino box, imperfect as it is. If the process proved anything, it's that we're all a messy amalgam of centuries of mixing and migration. True identity, it seems, resides not in our genes but in our mind. 10

READING FOR MEANING

This section presents three activities that will help you reread Miranda's reflective essay with a critical eye. Done in sequence, these activities lead you from a basic understanding of the selection to a more personal response to it and finally to an analysis that deepens your understanding and critical thinking about what you are reading.

Read to Comprehend

Reread the selection, and write a few sentences briefly explaining what the DNA test told Miranda—and what it didn't tell her. The following definitions may help you understand Miranda's vocabulary:

swath (paragraph 1): a wide path.

aquiline (4): curved or hooked like an eagle's beak.

lucrative (4): producing wealth; profitable.

Identify three or more additional words that you don't understand, and find the best definitions from the dictionary that work with their context.

Read to Respond

Write several paragraphs exploring your initial thoughts and feelings about Miranda's reflective essay. Focus on anything that stands out for you, perhaps because it resonates with your own experience or because you find a statement puzzling.

You might consider writing about the following:

- your own "gene pool," whether you are interested in your "roots," or whether you or anyone in your family has traced your genealogy;

- the reactions of Miranda's family to her findings;

- Miranda's possible meaning when she says "True identity, it seems, resides not in our genes but in our mind" (10); or

- how the drawing affects your understanding of and response to the essay.

To develop your response to Miranda's essay, you might use one or more of the following critical reading strategies that are explained and illustrated in Appendix 1: *annotating* and *contextualizing*.

Read to Analyze Assumptions

Reread Miranda's reflective essay, and write a paragraph or two exploring one or more of the assumptions you find in the text. The following suggestions may help:

- **assumptions about the value of "roots."** In paragraph 1, Miranda explains that she knows the geographical history of only her parents and her grand-parents and had not been interested in more until the "new and growing industry of personal DNA analysis created a need I never knew I had" (1). She then writes in paragraph 2 that "[t]oday at least half a dozen companies will . . . take your spittle, analyze the heck out of it and tell you who and what you are." Her assumption (even though it is not one she had beforehand) is that people *want* to know who and what they are, perhaps especially if they are a "card-carrying minority" with a "mixed-up identity" (2). How true is this assumption for you and people you know? To think critically about assumptions underlying the value of knowing one's "roots," ask yourself: Why does it matter "who and what" you are? How might knowing your own history affect your feelings about yourself?

- **assumptions about humor.** Humor often depends on specific circum-stances, and sometimes one person finds something funny that another does not. Probing the assumptions in material meant to be humorous can help you understand the author's beliefs and values and the ways that she is trying to tap into yours. For example, in paragraph 2, Miranda gently jokes about "affirmative action" admissions programs when she says that DNA tests are popular among "high school seniors praying that a link to some under-represented ethnic group will help get them into the Ivies" (members of the so-called Ivy League, some of the most prestigious colleges and universities). To think critically about assumptions underlying humor, look at the last two sentences of paragraph 4, the last sentence of paragraph 6, and all of paragraph 7, and ask yourself: Which sentences make you smile? *Why* did you smile? What assumptions do you share with Miranda?

READING LIKE A WRITER
MAINTAINING TOPICAL COHERENCE

Because reflective essays are exploratory, often trying out several ideas, they may appear to be only loosely organized, following a "first I had this idea and then I had another idea" principle of organization. Yet readers seldom become confused because writers are careful to maintain topical coherence and to provide cues to help readers follow the writer's train of thought. One of the main ways that writers establish logical coherence is by repeating a key word or phrase related to the essay's general subject. Recall that Brent Staples repeats the key word *fear* to help readers keep track of his reflections. Carl Safina also uses repetition in this way. As you reread Miranda's essay, you will see that the key word for the general subject of her essay is introduced in the title, *gene*, and is carried through in some form or other in several paragraphs: *generic* (1), *genealogists* (2), *genetic indicators* and *genetic code* (5), *murky gene pool* (6), *genes* (10). There are also several synonyms or words with related meanings, such as *multiethnic stew* (1), *ethnic group* (2), *ethnic types* (3), and many more. This repetition of an important word from one paragraph to the next serves as a chain that makes her paragraphs flow coherently from one to the next.

Analyze

1. *Skim* the essay, and *notice* the context for the repeated words that have "gene" as their base. *Examine* the instances in which you find additional words related to "gene."

2. *Note* the placement of these words in the paragraph and in the essay.

Write

Write several sentences explaining what you learned about Miranda's use of word repetition to maintain topical coherence and help readers follow her thinking.

CONSIDERING IDEAS FOR YOUR OWN WRITING

Miranda's essay suggests several ideas for writing your own reflection. Hers was prompted by the ability of science to find the truth (or make a good guess) about our ancestors. You could write an essay that explores what your ancestry means to you (and what particular occasion led you to know what it means), or you could write on families in general, especially since in American culture the makeup of families seems to be changing. What incidents have created the picture you have of your own families or of other families that you have observed? What occasions have led you to think about the dynamics of family relationships? The end of Miranda's essay also suggests likely topics for reflection: "If the process proved anything, it's that we're all a messy amalgam of centuries of mixing and migration. True identity, it seems, resides not in our genes but in our mind" (10). The question of identity is at the root of many reflections, since people wonder who they are and how they got that way. They also wonder where they are heading. Think of particular occasions that made you think about your own identity. Did they influence you to make any conclusions about your identity's influence on your behavior or on others' behavior toward you?

A SPECIAL READING STRATEGY

Comparing and Contrasting Related Readings: Miranda's "Diving into the Gene Pool" and Lee's "Peeling Bananas"

Comparing and contrasting related readings is a special critical reading strategy useful both in reading for meaning and in reading like a writer. This strategy is particularly applicable when writers present similar subjects, as in the reflective essays in this chapter by Carolina A. Miranda (p. 179) and Wendy Lee (p. 190). Both writers reflect about their ethnic heritage. To compare and contrast these two reflective essays, think about issues such as these:

- Compare these essays in terms of their authors' beliefs about identity. What aspects of identity do these two essays focus on? What do you learn about the influence of ethnic or racial background from reading them side by side?

- Compare how these two writers use material to develop their reflections. What material is external to them, and what is internal? What attitude or tone does each writer take toward the material? How do their different approaches affect you as a reader?

See Appendix 1 for detailed guidelines on using the comparing and contrasting related readings strategy.

Reflection Online

The Web provides many new kinds of spaces for writers to reflect on particular occasions that have been meaningful to them and for readers to find reflections of all kinds. These spaces include blogs, personal Web sites, networks in places like MySpace, online publications (such as Creative Nonfiction *online, a journal that can be reached through many college libraries), and other kinds of sites that are devoted to other kinds of writing but contain reflections.*

One such site, Global Voices Online, *is a nonprofit worldwide "citizens' media" project sponsored by the Berkman Center for Internet and Society at the Harvard Law School. It is a cooperative effort of contributors from dozens of countries, who explain themselves this way:*

Our Primary Goals

At a time when the international English-language media ignores many things that are important to large numbers of the world's citizens, Global Voices aims to redress some of the inequities in media attention by leveraging the power of citizens' media. We're using a wide variety of technologies—weblogs, wikis, podcasts, tags, aggregators and online chats—to call attention to conversations and points of view that we hope will help shed new light on the nature of our interconnected world. We aim to do the following:

1. To call attention to the most interesting conversations and perspectives emerging from citizens' media around the world by linking to text, audio, and video blogs and other forms of grassroots citizens' media being produced by people around the world.

2. To facilitate the emergence of new citizens' voices through training, online tutorials, and publicizing the ways in which open-source and free tools can be used safely by people around the world to express themselves.

3. To advocate for freedom of expression around the world and to protect the rights of citizen journalists to report on events and opinions without fear of censorship or persecution.

How Global Voices Works

A growing number of bloggers around the world are emerging as "bridge bloggers": people who are talking about their country or region to a global audience. Global Voices is your guide to the most interesting conversations, information, and ideas appearing around the world on various forms of participatory media such as blogs, podcasts, photo sharing sites, and videoblogs.

Our global team of regional blogger-editors is working to find, aggregate and track these conversations. Each day they link to 5–10 of the most interesting blog posts from their regions in the "daily roundups" section. A larger group of contributing bloggers is posting daily features in the left-hand Weblog section, shedding light on what blogging communities in their countries have been talking about recently.

The following reflection was written by the cofounder of Global Voices Online, *Rebecca MacKinnon, a former CNN bureau chief in Beijing and Tokyo who is now an assistant professor at the University of Hong Kong's Journalism and Media Studies Centre. It was posted on the* Global Voices *Web site and also on MacKinnon's blog, where this version appeared. MacKinnon's reflection was prompted by the particular occasion of the group's second "summit" meeting, held in New Delhi, India, in 2006, and the writer reflects on the differences between face-to-face and online conversation. The reflection was also prompted by* Time *magazine's decision to make its 2006 "person of the year" (usually a person who has made major news in that particular year) the people of the world—or, as* Time *put it, "you." The marginal annotations point out the writing strategies that readers expect to find in print versions of reflections. As you will see, online reflections share many of these strategies, but they also sometimes include other features that are characteristic of writing on the Web.*

« Global Voices Delhi Summit Slideshow | Main | Blogs and China correspondence - survey results »

December 19, 2006

Global Voices Delhi Summit: People of the Year

The opening sentence *presents the particular occasions* that prompt this reflection and *engages readers* by telling them that they are *Time*'s "person of the year."

As the Global Voices team held our second annual summit in Delhi this weekend, TIME magazine dedicated its "person of the year" to YOU: people around the world who are taking media creation into their own hands.

A reader can enlarge the photo by clicking on it, a feature distinctive to the Web.

(Photo by Jace. Click to enlarge.)

The TIME article praises the individual "for seizing the reins of the global media, for founding and framing the new digital democracy, for working for nothing and beating the pros at their own game," etc. The article concludes: "This is an opportunity to build a new kind of international understanding, not politician to politician, great man to great man, but citizen to citizen, person to person."

That, in a nutshell, is exactly what Global Voices is all about.

[...]

To illustrate camaraderie, the writer includes photos of people meeting face to face and details about how they socialized (highlighted).

This weekend's meeting also drove home the importance of face-to-face meetings even for a virtual organization like Global Voices. The Web has helped us find one another and has enabled us to work together in ways that would otherwise be completely impossible. But for the people who are devoting many hours every week to curating the global conversation on Global Voices, there is nothing like sitting down over curry and beers for building trust, camaraderie, commitment, and a feeling of shared ownership of the project.

People who are not very familiar with what we do often make snyde remarks about how strange it is that bloggers find it necessary to meet in physical space - as if the need for face-to-face meeting somehow proves the limitations or inadequacies of what we do. These remarks completely miss the point, of course. Global Voices may be a virtual organization with no physical headquarters (and no plans to create one), but what we do is ultimately about building understanding - and ideally dialogue - between real flesh-and-blood human beings and physical human communities.

We are not just generating chatter amongst avatars and usernames and online personas. We are not creating an alternative universe or online cyber-utopia into which our members escape from the realities of our daily lives and the problems within and between our countries. We are using the Internet's virtual space - and the creation of online citizens' media - as a means to a very physical end. The Web connects the physical human beings at the ends of it who are using it as a channel to express themselves and reach out to one another. When we as individuals can all create our own media, not only do we find each other and organize more easily around common causes. By taking control of our own narratives, our own stories, we gain greater control over how others perceive and define us. This in turn will make it more difficult (we believe) for outsiders to impose unwelcome, unsuitable, unjust or violent policies upon us - all of which are made much easier when mass media is used to stereotype, pigeonhole, and dehumanize us.

We use the Web *not* to escape our humanity, but to assert it.

09:37 PM in **Cyber-activism**, **Education**, **Freedom of Speech**, **Future of media**, **Global Voices**, **Weblogs** | **Permalink**

The author forecasts the topic of the reflection.

The author *develops a reflection* about how virtual, online communities can be used to achieve real, physical goals.

This one-sentence paragraph is boldfaced to emphasize the final point.

If you click on these lines, you can see the history of the Web site and also "feeds" (automatically generated updates) of the comments on these posts.

Readers are invited to join the conversation. You can guess that the site is monitored because it asks for information about posters.

TrackBack

TrackBack URL for this entry:
http://www.typepad.com/t/trackback/7216022

Listed below are links to weblogs that reference Global Voices Delhi Summit: People of the Year:

» And No, Heart of Darkness Is Not On The List from pf.org
Ethan Zuckerman, fresh off of the very successful Second Annual Global Voices Summit, is asking for suggestions for books about understanding Africa. I suggested Naipuls A Bend In The River, which is great look at an unnamed African country... [Read More]

Tracked on December 22, 2006 at 02:20 AM

Comments

Post a comment

Comments are moderated, and will not appear on this weblog until the author has approved them.

If you have a TypeKey or TypePad account, please Sign In

Name:

Email Address:

URL:

☐ Remember personal info?

Comments:

Preview   Post

Analyze

1. *Find* another example of an online reflection.

2. *Check to see* which basic features of reflective writing are displayed in the example that you found. These could include presenting or responding to a particular occasion, developing the reflection with illustration and examples, maintaining topical coherence with key phrases and transitions, and engaging readers.

3. Also *look for* any special online characteristics, such as links, informal language, or still or moving visuals.

4. In writing about the Global Voices summit, the author is reflecting not so much about her own life as about the life of her online community and the ways that it has added meaning now that many of its members have met face to face. In the example of reflection you find online, *note* whether the reflection is significant because of personal reasons or for more general reasons.

Write

Write several sentences explaining the features of the online reflection that you found, including its significance.

WENDY LEE

Peeling Bananas

> Wendy Lee wrote the following essay when she was a high-school student, and in 1993 it was published in Chinese American Forum, a quarterly journal of news and opinion. In the essay, Lee reflects on growing up in America as the child of parents born in China. While she focuses mainly on going to school, her interest is larger—to discover how she can be American without losing the knowledge and experience of her Chinese heritage.
>
> As you read, reflect on how you might hold on to the special qualities of your family or ethnic group while at the same time becoming part of a larger regional or national community.
>
> Annotate the text, noting places where Lee explores the meaning of her ancestry and anything else interesting about her reflective writing strategies. (For help annotating, see the examples in this chapter on pages 153 and 196, as well as the advice on annotating on pages 597–603.)

When my friend told me that her father had once compared her to a banana, I stared at her blankly. Then I realized that her father must have meant that outside she had the yellow skin of a Chinese, but inside she was white like an American. In other words, her appearance was Chinese, but her thoughts and values were American. Looking at my friend in her American clothes with her perfectly straight black hair and facial features so much like my own, I laughed. Her skin was no more yellow than mine.

In kindergarten, we colored paper dolls: red was for Indians, black for Afro-Americans, yellow was for Chinese. The dolls that we didn't color at all—the white ones—were left to be Americans. But the class wanted to know where were the green, blue or purple people? With the paper dolls, our well-meaning teacher intended to emphasize that everyone is basically the same, despite skin color. Secretly I wondered why the color of my skin wasn't the shade of my yellow Crayola. After we colored the dolls, we stamped each one with the same vacant, smiley face. The world, according to our teacher, is populated by happy, epidermically diverse people.

What does it mean to be a Chinese in an American school? One thing is to share a last name with a dozen other students, so that you invariably squirm when roll-call is taken. It means never believing that the fairy-tales the teacher read during story time could ever happen to you, because you don't have skin as white as snow or long golden hair. "You're Chinese?" I remember one classmate saying. "Oh, I *really* like Chinese food." In the depths of her overfriendly eyes I saw fried egg-rolls and chow mein. Once, for

show-and-tell, a girl proudly told the class that one of her ancestors was in the picture of George Washington crossing the Delaware. I promptly countered that by thinking to myself, "Well, my
grandfather was Sun Yat-sen's[1] physician, so THERE."

In my home, there is always a rather haphazard combination of   4
the past and present. Next to the scrolls of black ink calligraphy on
the dining room wall is a calendar depicting scenes from the midwest; underneath the stacked Chinese newspapers, the *L.A. Times*.
In the refrigerator, next to the milk and butter, are tofu and bok
choy from the weekly trips to the local Chinese supermarket. Spoons
are used for soup, forks for salad, but chopsticks are reserved for
the main course. I never noticed the disparity between my lifestyle
and that of white Americans — until I began school. There, I
became acquainted with children of strictly Caucasian heritage
and was invited to their homes. Mentally I always compared the
interiors of their homes to my own and to those of my mother's
Chinese friends. What struck me was that their homes seemed
to have no trace of their heritages at all. But nearly all Chinese-
American homes retain aspects of the Chinese culture; aspects that
reflect the yearning for returning home Chinese immigrants always
have.

Chinese immigrants like my parents have an unwavering faith   5
in China's potential to truly become the "middle kingdom," the
literal translation of the Chinese words for China. They don't want
their first-generation children to forget the way their ancestors
lived. They don't want their children to forget that China has a
heritage spanning thousands of years, while America has only a
paltry two hundred. My mother used to tape Chinese characters
over the words in our picture books. Ungratefully my sister and I
tore them off because we were more interested in seeing how the
story turned out. When she showed us her satin Chinese dresses,
we were more interested in playing dress-up than in the stories
behind the dresses; when she taught us how to use chopsticks, we
were more concentrated on eating the Chinese delicacies she had
prepared. (Incidentally, I still have to remind myself how to hold
my chopsticks properly, though this may merely be a personal
fault; I can't hold a pencil properly either.)

After those endless sessions with taped-over books and flash-   6
cards, my mother packed us off to Chinese School. There, we were
to benefit from interaction with other Chinese-American children
in the same predicament — unable to speak, read, or write Chinese

---

[1] *Sun Yat-sen* (1866–1925): Revolutionary leader of China and first president
of the Chinese Republic (1911–1912). [Ed.]

nicely. There, we were supposed to make the same progress we made in our American schools. But in its own way, Chinese School is as much of a banana as are Chinese-Americans. A Chinese School day starts and ends with a bow to the teacher to show proper reverence. In the intervening three hours, the students keep one eye on the mysterious symbols of Chinese characters on the blackboard and the other on the clock. Their voices may be obediently reciting a lesson, but silently they are urging the minute hand to go faster. Chinese is taught through the American way, with workbooks and homework and tests. Without distinctive methods to make the experience memorable and worthwhile for its students, Chinese School, too, is in danger of becoming completely Americanized. Chinese-American kids, especially those in their teens, have become bewitched by the American ideal of obtaining a career that makes lots and lots of money. Their Chinese heritage probably doesn't play a big part in their futures. Many Chinese-Americans are even willing to shed their skins in favor of becoming completely American. Certainly it is easier to go forward and become completely American than to regress and become completely Chinese in America.

Sometimes I imagine what it would be like to go back to Taiwan   7
or mainland China. Through eyes misty with romantic sentiment, I can look down a crooked, stone-paved street where a sea of black-haired and slanted-eyed people are bicycling in tandem. I see factories where people are hunch-backed over tables to manufacture plastic toys and American flags. I see fog-enshrouded mountains of Guilin, the yellow mud of the Yangtze River, and the Great Wall of China snaking across the landscape as it does in the pages of a *National Geographic* magazine. When I look up at the moon, I don't see the pale, impersonal sphere that I see here in America. Instead, I see the plaintive face of Chang-Oh, the moon goddess. When I look up at the moon, I may miss my homeland like the famous poet Li Bai did in the poem that every Chinese School student can recite. But will that homeland be America or China?

When the crooked street is empty with no bicycles, I see a girl   8
standing across from me on the other side of the street. I see mirrored in her the same perfectly straight black hair and facial features that my Chinese-American friend has, or the same that I have. We cannot communicate, for I only know pidgin Mandarin whereas she speaks fluent Cantonese, a dialect of southern China. Not only is the difference of language a barrier, but the differences in the way we were brought up and the way we live. Though we look the same, we actually are of different cultures, and I may cross

the street into her world but only as a visitor. However, I also realize that as a hybrid of two cultures, I am unique, and perhaps that
uniqueness should be preserved.

READING FOR MEANING

This section presents three activities that will help you reread Lee's reflective
essay with a critical eye. Done in sequence, these activities lead you from a basic
understanding of the selection to a more personal response to it and finally to an
analysis that deepens your understanding and critical thinking about what you
are reading.

Read to Comprehend

Reread the selection, and write a few sentences identifying the occasion for
Lee's reflections and listing two or three experiences by which Lee remains aware
of her Chinese ethnicity. The following definitions may help you understand
Lee's vocabulary:

haphazard (paragraph 4): lacking order or planning; determined by or
dependent on chance; aimless.

disparity (4): a lack of similarity or equality; inequality; difference.

paltry (5): ridiculously or insultingly small; utterly worthless.

reverence (6): a feeling or attitude of deep respect or worship.

Identify three or more additional words that you don't understand, and find the
best definitions from the dictionary that work with their context.

To expand your understanding of this reading, you might use one or more of
the following critical reading strategies that are explained and illustrated in
Appendix 1: *summarizing* and *questioning to understand and remember.*

Read to Respond

Write several paragraphs exploring your initial thoughts and feelings about
Lee's essay. Focus on anything that stands out for you, perhaps because it resonates with your own experience or because you find a statement puzzling.

You might consider writing about the following:

- the implications of calling someone a banana or an oreo;

- Lee's thoughts about her kindergarten teacher's decision to have students
  color paper dolls, perhaps in connection to your own experience of "well-
  meaning" but misguided teachers (paragraph 2);

- your response to Lee's observation that the homes of her Caucasian friends "seemed to have no trace of their heritages at all" (4), perhaps in relation to signs of your ethnic heritage evident in your home; or

- a comparison of Lee's experiences and your own personal experiences of feeling different ethnically or in some other way.

To develop your response to Lee's essay, you might use one or more of the following critical reading strategies that are explained and illustrated in Appendix 1: *contextualizing, reflecting on challenges to your beliefs and values, recognizing emotional manipulation,* and *judging the writer's credibility.*

Read to Analyze Assumptions

Reread Lee's reflective essay, and write a paragraph or two exploring one or more of the assumptions you find in the text. The following suggestions may help:

- **assumptions about school.** Lee writes that it was only when she began school that she "noticed the disparity between my lifestyle and that of white Americans" (paragraph 4). She has already referred to school experiences that awakened her to her "difference" — the colors of paper dolls and the stereotypes that other children had of Chinese people. What effect does school have on children that home does not? To think critically about the assumptions in this essay related to school and its functions in America — which seem to go beyond learning subjects in classes — ask yourself: How does school shape you, compared to how your family or home shapes you? When Lee goes to "Chinese School," she complains that "Chinese is taught through the American way, with workbooks and homework and tests" (6). What does she offer as an alternative to the American way, and what does she assume about how learning occurs?

- **assumptions about heritage.** Lee notes that American homes "seemed to have no trace of their heritages at all. But nearly all Chinese-American homes retain aspects of the Chinese culture" (4). She adds in the next paragraph that China has a "heritage spanning thousands of years, while America has only a paltry two hundred" (5). She seems to be assuming that the length of one's heritage may be more important than what that heritage is. To think critically about the assumptions in this essay related to heritage, ask yourself: Do you agree with this assumption? Why or why not? Does your home, or do the homes of your friends, reflect a distinctive heritage? Is that heritage long or short, and does it seem to make a difference? What positives and negatives about heritage is Lee perhaps not considering? What are your assumptions about the place of heritage in a person's home and, by implication, in his or her life? How do your assumptions affect your response to Lee's reflective essay?

To probe assumptions more deeply, you might use one or more of the following critical reading strategies explained and illustrated in Appendix 1: *reflecting on challenges to your beliefs and values* and *looking for patterns of opposition.*

READING LIKE A WRITER
DEVELOPING REFLECTIONS THROUGH
COMPARISON AND CONTRAST

In reflective writing, insights and ideas are central. Yet writers cannot merely list ideas, regardless of how fresh and daring their ideas might be. Instead, writers must work imaginatively to develop their ideas, to explain and elaborate them, and to view them from one angle and then another. One well-established way to develop ideas is through comparison and contrast.

Analyze

1. *Review* the comparisons and contrasts in paragraphs 4, 6, and 8 of Lee's essay.

2. *Choose one* of these paragraphs to analyze more closely. What exactly is being compared or contrasted? *Underline* details that highlight the comparisons and contrasts.

Write

Write several sentences describing how Lee uses comparisons and contrasts to develop her ideas. From the one paragraph you chose to analyze, *identify* the terms (the items being compared) of the comparison or contrast and the ideas they enable Lee to develop.

CONSIDERING IDEAS FOR
YOUR OWN WRITING

Consider reflecting on your own ethnicity, beginning your essay, as Lee does, with a concrete occasion. If you are among the "white Caucasians" Lee mentions, you may doubt that you have an ethnicity in the sense that Lee has one. Consider, however, that Asians do not comprise a single ethnicity. Among Asian Americans, there are many distinctly different ethnicities, as defined by their countries or regions of origin: Chinese, Japanese, Korean, Cambodian, Vietnamese, and Philippine, among others. "White Caucasians" also represent many national origins: German (still the single largest American immigrant group), Swedish, Russian, Polish, Irish, Italian, British, Greek, and French, to mention a few. In all of these immigrant groups, as well as others, intermarriage and acculturation to whatever is uniquely American have blurred many of the original ethnic distinctions. Nevertheless, Lee's reflections remind us of the likelihood that in nearly every American family there remain remnants of one or more national or regional ethnicities. This idea for writing invites you to reflect on whatever meanings remain for you personally in your ethnic identities.

KATHERINE HAINES

Whose Body Is This?

Katherine Haines wrote this essay for an assignment in her first-year college composition course. As the title suggests, the writer reflects on her dismay and anger about American society's obsession with the perfect body—especially the perfect female body. As you read, note the many kinds of details Haines uses to develop her reflections.

The other readings in this chapter are followed by reading and writing activities. Following this reading, however, you are on your own to decide how to read for meaning and read like a writer.

Haines *engages the reader's interest* by beginning with dialogue to *present the occasion* that led to her reflection.

"Hey Rox, what's up? Do you wanna go down to the 1 pool with me? It's a gorgeous day."

"No thanks, you go ahead without me."

"What? Why don't you want to go? You've got the day off work, and what else are you going to do?"

"Well, I've got a bunch of stuff to do around the house . . . pay the bills, clean the bathroom, you know. Besides, I don't want to have to see myself in a bathing suit—I'm so fat."

To maintain *topical coherence* throughout her essay, Haines poses questions and repeats words like *diet, body,* and *acceptable.*

Why do so many women seem obsessed with their 2 weight and body shape? Are they really that unhappy and dissatisfied with themselves? Or are these women continually hearing from other people that their bodies are not acceptable?

She illustrates the problem with examples—such as skimpy clothes. What are some current examples that illustrate her point?

In today's society, the expectations for women and 3 their bodies are all too evident. Fashion, magazines, talk shows, "lite" and fat-free food in stores and restaurants, and diet centers are all daily reminders of these expectations. For instance, the latest fashions for women reveal more and more skin: shorts have become shorter, to the point of being scarcely larger than a pair of underpants, and the bustier, which covers only a little more skin than a bra, is making a comeback. These styles are flattering on only the slimmest of bodies, and many women who were previously happy with their bodies may emerge from the dressing room after a run-in with these styles and decide that it must be diet time again. Instead of coming to the realization that these clothes are unflattering for most women, how many women will simply look for different and more flattering styles, and how many women will end up heading for the gym to burn off some more calories or to the bookstore to buy the latest diet book?

4   When I was in junior high, about two-thirds of the girls I knew were on diets. Everyone was obsessed with fitting into the smallest-size miniskirt possible. One of my friends would eat a carrot stick, a celery stick, and two rice cakes for lunch. Junior high (and the onset of adolescence) seemed to be the beginning of the pressure for most women. It is at this age that appearance suddenly becomes important, especially for those girls who want to be "popular" and those who are cheerleaders or on the drill team. The pressure is intense; some girls believe no one will like them or accept them if they are "overweight," even by a pound or two. The measures these girls will take to attain the body that they think will make them acceptable are often debilitating and life threatening.

> Haines shows how unhealthy fad diets are by examining the meals of the girls in her school and the pressures that they feel to be thin.

5   My sister was on the drill team in junior high. My sister wanted to fit in with the right crowd—and my sister drove herself to the edge of becoming anorexic. I watched as she came home from school, having eaten nothing for breakfast and at lunch only a bag of pretzels and an apple (and she didn't always finish that), and began pacing the Oriental carpet that was in our living room. Around and around and around, without a break, from four o'clock until dinnertime, which was usually at six or seven o'clock. And then at dinner, she would take minute portions and only pick at her food. After several months of this, she became much paler and thinner but not in any sort of attractive sense. Finally, after catching a cold and having to stay in bed for three days because she was so weak, she was forced to go to the doctor. The doctor said she was suffering from malnourishment and was to stay in bed until she regained some of her strength. He advised her to eat lots of fruits and vegetables until the bruises all over her body had healed (these were a result of vitamin deficiency). Although my sister did not develop anorexia, it was frightening to see what she had done to herself. She had little strength, and the bruises she had made her look like an abused child.

> Does this powerful example work for you, or is it too extreme to be a fair illustration? Have you or people you know taken similar unhealthy obsessive actions to reduce weight?

6   This mania to lose weight and have the "ideal" body is not easily avoided in our society. It is created by television and magazines as they flaunt their models and

> Haines probes at possible reasons for our diet mania, further developing answers to her questions. Can you think of other reasons?

latest diet crazes in front of our faces. And then there are the Nutri-System and Jenny Craig commercials, which show hideous "before" pictures and glamorous "after" pictures and have smiling, happy people dancing around and talking about how their lives have been transformed simply because they have lost weight. This propaganda that happiness is in large part based on having the "perfect" body shape is a message that the media constantly sends to the public. No one seems to be able to escape it.

My mother and father were even sucked in by this 7 idea. One evening, when I was in the fifth grade, I heard Mom and Dad calling me into the kitchen. Oh no, what had I done now? It was never good news when you got summoned into the kitchen alone. As I walked into the kitchen, Mom looked up at me with an anxious expression; Dad was sitting at the head of the table with a pen in hand and a yellow legal pad in front of him. They informed me that I was going on a diet. A diet!? I wanted to scream at them, "I'm only ten years old, why do I have to be on a diet?" I was so embarrassed, and I felt so guilty. Was I really fat? I guess so, I thought, otherwise why would my parents do this to me?

It seems that this obsession with the perfect body 8 and a woman's appearance has grown to monumental heights. It is ironic, however, that now many people feel that this problem is disappearing. People have begun to assume that women want to be thin because they just want to be "healthy." But what has happened is that the sickness slips in under the guise of wanting a "healthy" body. The demand for thin bodies is anything but "healthy." How many anorexics or bulimics have you seen that are healthy?

It is strange that women do not come out and object 9 to society's pressure to become thin. Or maybe women feel that they really do want to be thin and so go on dieting endlessly (they call it "eating sensibly"), thinking this is what they really want. I think if these women carefully examined their reasons for wanting to lose weight — and were not allowed to include reasons that relate to society's demands, such as a weight chart, a questionnaire in a magazine, a certain size in a pair of shorts, or even a scale — they would find that they are being ruled by what society wants, not what they want. So why do women not break free from these standards?

Another personal example. How do such examples engage readers?

Haines uses an extreme example in the last sentence of the paragraph. Does this help or hurt the effectiveness of her reflection?

Why do they not demand an end to being judged in such a demeaning and senseless way?

10   Self-esteem plays a large part in determining whether women succumb to the will of society or whether they are independent and self-assured enough to make their own decisions. Lack of self-esteem is one of the things the women's movement has had to fight the hardest against. If women didn't think they were worthy, then how could they even begin to fight for their own rights? The same is true with the issue of body size. If women do not feel their body is worthy, then how can they believe that it is okay to just let it stay that way? Without self-esteem, women will be swayed by society and will continue to make themselves unhappy by trying to maintain whatever weight or body shape society is dictating for them. It is ironic that many of the popular women's magazines (*Cosmopolitan, Mademoiselle, Glamour*) often feature articles on self-esteem, how essential it is, and how to improve it—and then in the same issue give the latest diet tips. This mixed message will never give women the power they deserve over their bodies and will never enable them to make their own decisions about what type of body they want.

11   *"Rox, why do you think you're fat? You work out all the time, and you just bought that new suit. Why don't you just come down to the pool for a little while?"*

"No, I really don't want to. I feel so self-conscious with all those people around. It makes me want to run and put on a big, baggy dress so no one can tell what size I am!"

"Ah, Rox, that's really sad. You have to learn to believe in yourself and your own judgment, not other people's."

> Haines questions whether we should behave according to society's demands. How do you feel about this assumption? How does her fuller explanation in this paragraph add to your understanding?

> Haines's conclusion maintains *topical coherence* and provides more details, followed by a return to the dialogue that opened her reflective essay. What is the effect of this kind of conclusion, especially in this kind of essay?

READING FOR MEANING

Reading for meaning involves three activities:

- reading to comprehend,
- reading to respond, and
- reading to analyze assumptions.

Reread Haines's essay, and then write a page or so explaining your understanding of its basic meaning or main point, a personal response you have to it, and what you see as one of its assumptions.

READING LIKE A WRITER

Writers of reflective essays

- present the particular occasion,

- develop the reflections,

- maintain topical coherence, and

- engage readers.

Focus on one of these strategies in Haines's essay, and analyze it carefully through close rereading and annotating. Then write several sentences explaining what you have learned, giving specific examples from the reading to support your explanation. Add a few sentences evaluating how successfully Haines uses the strategy to reflect on society's obsession with the perfect body.

REVIEWING WHAT MAKES REFLECTIVE ESSAYS EFFECTIVE

In this chapter, you have been learning how to read reflective essays for meaning and how to read them like a writer. Before going on to write a reflective essay, pause here to review and contemplate what you have learned about the elements of effective reflective essays.

Analyze

Choose one reading from this chapter that seems to you especially effective. Before rereading the selection, *jot down* one or two reasons you remember it as an example of good reflective writing.

Reread your chosen selection, adding further annotations about what makes it a particularly successful example of reflection. *Consider* the selection's purpose and how well it achieves that purpose for its intended readers. (You can make an informed guess about the intended readers and their expectations by noting the publication source of the essay.) Then *focus* on how well the essay

- presents the particular occasion,

- develops the reflections,

- maintains topical coherence, and

- engages readers.

You can review all of these basic features in the Guide to Reading Reflective Essays (p. 153).

Your instructor may ask you to complete this activity on your own or to work with a small group of other students who have chosen the same reading. If you work with others, allow enough time initially for all group members to reread the selection thoughtfully and to add their annotations. Then *discuss* as a group what makes the selection effective. *Take notes* on your discussion. One student in your group should then report to the class what the group has learned about the effectiveness of reflective writing. If you are working individually, write up what you have learned from your analysis.

Write

Write at least a page supporting your choice of this reading as an example of effective reflective writing. *Assume* that your readers — your instructor and classmates — have read the selection but will not remember many details about it. They also might not remember it as especially successful. Therefore, you will need to *refer* to details and specific parts of the essay as you explain how it works and as you justify your evaluation of its effectiveness. You need not argue that it is the best reading in the chapter or that it is flawless, only that it is, in your view, a strong example of the genre.

■ A Guide to Writing Reflective Essays

The readings in this chapter have helped you learn a great deal about reflective writing. At its best, the reflective essay is interesting, lively, insightful, and engaging—much like good conversation—and it avoids sounding pretentious or preachy in its focus on basic human and social issues that concern us all. Writers of reflection are not reluctant to say what they think or to express their most personal observations.

As you develop your reflective essay, you can review the readings to see how other writers use various strategies to solve problems you might also encounter. This Guide to Writing is designed to help you through the various decisions you will need to make as you plan, draft, and revise your reflective essay.

INVENTION AND RESEARCH

The following activities will help you find a particular occasion and a general subject, test your choices, present the particular occasion, and develop your reflections. Taking some time now to consider a wide range of possibilities will pay off later when you draft your essay, giving you confidence in your choice of subject and in your ability to develop it effectively.

Finding a Particular Occasion and a General Subject

As the readings in this chapter illustrate, writers of reflection usually center their essays on one (or more than one) event or occasion. They connect this occasion to a subject they want to reflect on. In the process of invention, however, the choice of a particular occasion does not always come before the choice of a general subject. Sometimes writers set out to reflect on a general subject (such as envy or friendship) and must search for the right occasion (an image or anecdote) with which to particularize it.

Start by listing several possible occasions and the general subjects they suggest in a two-column chart, as shown in the following example:

Particular Occasions	*General Subjects*
I met someone covered with tattoos.	Body art or self-mutilation
I am amazed by people's personal revelations on talk shows.	Desire for celebrity status
While shopping for clothes, I couldn't decide what to buy and let the sales person pressure me.	Indecisiveness and low self-esteem

RESEARCHING YOUR SUBJECT ONLINE

The Web offers a number of possible ways to help you write your reflective essay. A Web site might provide a particular occasion for your reflections, or you might see how other people use their experiences and observations as the occasion for their reflections. Reflective writing on various general subjects also can often be found on blogs. Once you have identified a general topic for your essay, you may be able to find sites with cultural and historical documents or photographs that stimulate your thinking or encourage you to create a multimedia text of your own. As you search the Web, here are some possibilities to consider:

- Find blog sites through google.com, blogsearchengine.com, blogarama.com, or other directories.

- Search for sites related to the general subject or particular occasion you are writing about.

Make notes of any ideas, memories, or insights suggested by your online research. Download any visuals you might consider using in your essay—such as pictures of people and places you may want to include. Also be sure to download or record the information necessary to cite any online sources you may want to refer to in your essay. See Appendix 2 for help in citing sources.

For particular occasions, consider conversations you have had or overheard; memorable scenes you observed, read about, or saw in a movie or on television; and other incidents in your own or someone else's life that might lead you to reflect more generally. Then consider the general subjects suggested by the particular occasions—human qualities such as compassion, vanity, jealousy, and faithfulness; social customs for dating, eating, and working; abstract notions such as fate, free will, and imagination.

In making your chart, you will find that a single occasion might suggest several subjects and that a subject might be particularized by a variety of occasions. Each entry will surely suggest other possibilities for you to consider. Do not be concerned if your chart starts to look messy. A full and rich exploration of possible topics will give you confidence in the subject you finally choose and in your ability to write about it. If you have trouble getting started, review the Considering Ideas for Your Own Writing activities following the readings in this chapter. As further occasions and subjects occur to you over the next two or three days, add them to your chart.

Testing Your Choices

Review your chart, and choose a particular occasion and a general subject you now think look promising. To test whether your choices will work, write for fifteen minutes or so, exploring your thoughts. Do not make any special demands on yourself to be profound or even coherent. Just write your ideas as they come to mind, letting one idea suggest another. Your aims are to determine whether you have enough to say about the occasion and subject and whether they hold your interest. If you discover that you do not have much to say about the occasion or that you quickly lose interest in the subject, choose another set of possibilities and try again. It might take a few preliminary explorations to find the right occasion and subject.

Presenting the Particular Occasion

The following activities will help you recall details about the particular occasion for your reflection. Depending on the occasion you have decided to write about, choose Narrating an Event or Describing What You Observed.

Narrating an Event.   *Write for five to ten minutes narrating what happened during the event.* Try to make your story vivid so that readers can imagine what it was like. Describe the people involved in the event — what they looked like, how they acted, what they said — and the place where it occurred.

Describing What You Observed.   *Write for five or ten minutes describing what you observed.* Include as many details as you can recall so that your readers can imagine what you experienced.

Developing Your Reflections

To explore your ideas about the subject, try an invention activity called *cubing*. Based on the six sides of a cube, this activity leads you to turn over your subject as you would a cube, looking at it in six different ways. Complete the following activities in any order, writing for five minutes on each one. Your goal is to invent new ways of considering your subject.

Generalizing.   *Consider what you have learned from the event or experience that will be the occasion for your reflections.* What ideas does it suggest to you? What does it suggest about people in general or about the society in which you live?

Giving Examples.   *Illustrate your ideas with specific examples.* What examples would best help your readers understand your ideas?

Comparing and Contrasting.   *Think of a subject that could be compared with yours, and explore the similarities and the differences.*

Extending. *Take your subject to its logical limits, and speculate about its implications.* Where does it lead?

Analyzing. *Take apart your subject.* What is it made of? How are the parts related to one another? Are they all of equal importance?

Applying. *Think about your subject in practical terms.* How can you use it or act on it? What difference would it make to you and to others?

Considering Your Purpose. *Write for several minutes about your purpose for writing this essay.* As you write, try to answer the question: What do I want my readers to think about the subject after reading my essay? Your answer to this question may change as you write, but thinking about your purpose now may help you decide which of your ideas to include in the essay. Use the following questions to help clarify your purpose:

- Which of your ideas are most important to you? Why?

- How do your ideas relate to one another? If your ideas seem contradictory, consider how you could use the contradictions to convey to readers the complexity of your ideas and feelings on the subject.

- Which of your ideas do you think will most surprise your readers? Which are most likely to be familiar?

- Is the particular occasion for your reflections likely to resonate with your readers' experience and observation? If not, consider how you can make the particular occasion vivid or dramatic for readers.

Formulating a Tentative Thesis Statement. *Review what you wrote for Considering Your Purpose and add another two or three sentences that will bring into focus your reflections.* What do they seem to be about? Try to write sentences that indicate what you think is most important or most interesting about the subject, what you want readers to understand from reading your essay.

Keep in mind that readers do not expect you to begin your reflective essay with the kind of thesis statement typical of an argumentative essay, which asserts an opinion the writer then goes on to support. None of the readings in this chapter begins with an explicit statement of the writer's main idea. They all begin with a particular occasion followed by ideas suggested by the occasion. Brent Staples, for example, follows the particular occasion with a general statement of his main idea: "It was in the echo of that terrified woman's footfalls that I first began to know the unwieldy inheritance I'd come into—the ability to alter public space in ugly ways" (paragraph 2). He then explores this rather abstract idea, indicating that his "unwieldy inheritance" is racial stereotyping and the fear it engenders in others. Similarly, Steven Doloff follows the particular occasion with the reflection that "New York's sidewalks make up a kind of endless concrete newspaper from which we can read, in the minute flotsam and jetsam at our feet, news of the mass of people who walk them" (paragraph 3). Katherine Haines also introduces her main idea after presenting the particular occasion: "In today's society, the expectations for women and their bodies are all too evident. Fashion, magazines, talk shows, 'lite' and fat-free food in stores and restaurants, and diet centers are all daily reminders of these expectations" (paragraph 3).

As you explore your ideas and think about the particular occasion for your reflections, you can expect your ideas to change. The fun of writing a reflective essay is that you can share with readers your thinking process, taking them along for the ride.

Considering Visuals.   *Consider whether visuals—cartoons, photographs, drawings—would help readers understand and appreciate your reflections.* If you submit your essay electronically to other students and your instructor, or if you post it on a Web site, consider including photographs and snippets of film or sound. You could construct your own visuals, scan materials from books and magazines, or download them from the Internet. Visual and audio materials are not at all a requirement of an effective reflective essay, as you can tell from the readings in this chapter, but they could add a new dimension to your writing. If you want to use photographs or recordings of people, though, be sure to obtain their permission.

DRAFTING

The following guidelines will help you set goals for your draft, plan its organization, and think about a useful sentence strategy.

Setting Goals

Establishing goals for your draft before you begin writing will enable you to make decisions and work more confidently. Consider the following questions now, and keep them in mind as you draft. They will help you set goals for drafting as well as recall how the writers you have read in this chapter tried to achieve similar goals.

- *How can I present the particular occasion vividly and in a way that anticipates my reflections?* Should I narrate the event, as Staples does? Refer to a surprising discovery, like Safina? Create an imaginary dialogue, like Haines?

- *How can I best develop my reflections?* Should I include brief and extended examples, as all of the writers in this chapter do? Should I use comparisons and contrasts, like Miranda and Lee? Refer to history, like Safina? Create an imaginary or conversational scene, like Lee and Haines?

- *How can I maintain topical coherence?* Like Miranda, can I use topic sentences to make clear the connections between my ideas or insights and the examples that develop them? Can I use word repetition, like Miranda and Haines, to keep my readers on track as they follow the course of my reflections?

- *How can I engage and hold my readers' interest?* Should I reveal the human interest and social significance of my subject by opening my essay with a dramatic event, as Staples does? Should I start with a personal observation, as Safina, Doloff, and Miranda do? A familiar dialogue, like Haines? An ethnic stereotype, like Staples and Lee? Like all the writers in this chapter, should I reveal my personal commitment to the subject, and should I attempt to inspire my readers to think deeply about their own lives?

Organizing Your Draft

You might find it paradoxical to plan a type of essay that does not aim to reach conclusions or that seeks to give readers the impression that it is finding its way as it goes. And yet you have seen in the readings in this chapter that reflective essays, at least after they have been carefully revised with readers in mind, are usually easy to follow. Part of what makes a reflective essay easy to read is its topical coherence, such as the repetition of key words and phrases that keep the reader's focus on the subject that is being explored in the essay. Writers often develop coherence as they draft and revise their essays, but there are some ways in which planning can also help.

For example, one approach to planning is to begin with the particular occasion, outlining the sequence of events in a way that emphasizes the main point you want the occasion to make. After figuring out how you will present the particular occasion, you could choose one idea you want to develop in detail or list several ideas you think your essay will touch on, possibly indicating how each idea relates to the one that follows. Sometimes when writers go this far in planning, they are actually drafting segments of the essay, discovering a tentative plan as they write.

Another approach to planning begins with the ideas you want to discuss. You could consider various ways of sequencing your ideas. For example, you could start with an obvious idea, one you expect most readers would think of. Then you could develop the idea in unexpected ways or build a train of ideas that leads in a surprising direction. Yet another approach is to pair ideas with examples and develop a sequence of pairs that explores different aspects of your subject or tries out different points of view on it.

Remember that the goal of planning is to discover what you want to say and a possible way of organizing your ideas. Planning a reflective essay can be especially challenging because the process of reflecting is itself a process of discovery: you won't really know what you want your essay to say until you've drafted and revised it. But if you think of planning simply as a way of getting started and remember that you will have a lot of opportunity to reorganize your ideas and develop them further, planning can become an extremely pleasurable and creative activity.

Using Time Cues to Orient Readers

In the essays that you will write in later chapters of this book, you will rely on interviews, observations, and print or visual sources to support your explanations or arguments. In writing a reflection, however, you will rely almost entirely on your memory, as you did with autobiography. As you complete the invention work, your memory will provide you with several pages of notes, and these notes will stimulate your memory further and lead to further notes. As you draft and revise, still more memories may flood in for you to incorporate in your essay.

Among these rich, varied mental and written sources are ones related to the particular occasion that prompted your reflection. Telling about this occasion will often require you to tell a story. As you develop your reflection, you will be exploring the consequences of that occasion, and you may need to continue the story. Your readers will expect you to keep them oriented to any story you tell by giving them explicit cues about time—cues about the decade, year, season, and time of day; about the pace at which events unfolded; and about the sequence in which the various events took place. Sometimes the occasion is not mentioned in the beginning but later (as with Carl Safina's discovery of the baby turtle), so it is especially important to keep your readers oriented.

When experienced writers of reflection use these cues, they nearly always place them at the beginnings of sentences (or main clauses), as Safina does in "Comes a Turtle, Comes the World":

The *morning* chill carried that clean-sheet crispness . . . (paragraph 1)

Every autumn here witnesses two great migrations . . . (2)

This year, as usual, swarms of fish had arrived . . . (3)

Placing these important time cues—time of day, time of year, and exact year—at the beginning of a sentence may not seem noteworthy, but the effect changes depending on where time cues are placed. Safina might have written

That clean-sheet crispness on the morning chill . . .

Two great migrations occur every autumn . . .

Swarms of fish had arrived as usual this year . . .

Why might Safina decide to locate these time cues at the beginning of the sentence, as he does with nearly all the time cues in his essay? The answer is that experienced writers of reflection give high priority to keeping readers oriented to time, including the overall time frame of the particular occasion as well as the sequence of consequences that result from the particular occasion. To do so, they can rely on words, phrases, or clauses:

> *Then* I set about trying to predict the results. . . . *Within a few weeks*, I received my first results, from DNA Tribes. . . . *That's when* I began to wonder whether there had been some kind of DNA mix-up. (Miranda, paragraphs 4, 5, and 6)

> For instance, *about 10 years ago*, I noticed almost every day (but did not pick up) dozens of party-colored crack vials scattered about my neighborhood. They are *now*, I am happy to report, gone (at least from my sidewalks), and crack abuse is also much diminished. *Two years ago*, I actually found a crumpled hundred-dollar bill in the street. (Doloff, paragraph 4)

As you draft and revise, look to locating your time cues at the beginnings of your sentences. It is easy to do, and your readers will follow you more easily.

Considering a Useful Sentence Strategy

In addition to planning the sequence of your ideas and repeating key words and phrases, you can enhance the topical coherence of your reflective essay by using parallel grammatical structures to connect related ideas or examples. In the three sentences that make up paragraph 3 of Safina's reflections on the ocean, for example, notice how each sentence (indicated in italics) uses not only similar language but also a similar structure:

> This year, as usual, *swarms of fish* had arrived from New England in the last few weeks and departed down the coast in great migrating waves. They included *millions and millions of anchovies and menhaden*, pursued to the surface by *armies of bluefish, striped bass, little tuna*. Along the seafloor *battalions of summer flounder, black sea bass, tautog, porgies and others* moved to deeper grounds.

Safina uses similar patterns that connote large numbers ("*swarms of . . . millions and millions of . . . armies of . . . battalions of*") to emphasize the plentiful extent of fish in the ocean. Now look at this sentence from his paragraph 10:

> Whether or not we can see, hear, or feel the ocean from our own home territory, the ocean certainly feels all of us.

This sentence uses a form of parallelism called reversed structure, where the subject and direct object of the first clause (*we . . . the ocean*) exchange places in the second clause (*the ocean . . . us*).

Here are some similar uses of parallel form to signal related ideas or examples from other essays in this chapter:

> The first, DNA Tribes in Arlington, Va., filled its website with glossy shots of ethnic types. The next, DNAPrint in Sarasota, Fla., offered a cool Flash movie of a rotating double helix. (Miranda, paragraph 3)

> If it was a slug, did it miss someone? If it was a shell, did it hit someone? (Doloff, paragraph 2)

> They don't want their first-generation children to forget. . . . They don't want their children to forget. . . . (Lee, paragraph 5)

While there are many ways to signal that a group of ideas is related, writers of reflective essays tend to rely on parallel form because it is highly visible; readers notice it at a glance. Parallel form also creates a pleasant rhythm that engages readers and keeps them reading. Moreover, it is very flexible; the variations are endless. Clearly, parallelism is not required for a successful reflective essay, yet it provides you with an effective sentence option to try out in your own essay.

READING A DRAFT CRITICALLY

Getting a critical reading of your draft will help you see how to improve it. Your instructor may schedule class time for reading drafts, or you may want to ask a classmate or a tutor in the writing center to read your draft. Ask your reader to use the following guidelines and to write out a response for you to consult during your revision.

Read for a First Impression

1. Read the draft without stopping to annotate or comment, and then write two or three sentences giving your general impression.

2. Identify one aspect of the draft that seems especially effective.

Read Again to Suggest Improvements

1. Suggest ways of presenting the occasion more effectively.

   - Read the paragraphs that present the occasion for the reflections, and tell the writer if the occasion dominates the essay, taking up an unjustified amount of space, or if it needs more development.

   - Note whether this occasion suggests the significance or importance of the subject, and consider how well it prepares readers for the reflections by providing a context for them.

   - Tell the writer what in the occasion works well and what needs improvement.

2. Help the writer develop the reflections.

- Look for two or three ideas that strike you as especially interesting, insightful, or surprising, and tell the writer what interests you about them. Then, most important, suggest ways these ideas might be developed further through examples, comparisons or contrasts, social implications, connections to other ideas, and so on.

- Identify any ideas you find uninteresting, explaining briefly why you find them so.

3. Recommend ways to strengthen topical coherence.

- Skim the essay, looking for gaps between sentences and paragraphs, those places where the meaning does not carry forward smoothly. Mark each gap with a double slash (//), and try to recommend a way to make the meaning clear.

- Skim the essay again, looking for irrelevant or unnecessary material that disrupts coherence and diverts the reader's attention. Put brackets around this material, and explain to the writer why it seems to you irrelevant or unnecessary.

- Consider the essay as a sequence of sections. Ask yourself whether some of the sections could be moved to make the essay easier to follow. Circle any section that seems out of place, and draw an arrow to where it might be better located.

4. Suggest ways to further engage readers.

- Point out parts of the essay that draw you in, hold your interest, inspire you to think, challenge your attitudes or values, or keep you wanting to read to the end.

- Try to suggest ways the writer might engage readers more fully. Consider the essay in light of what is most engaging for you in the essays you have read in this chapter.

5. Evaluate the effectiveness of visuals.

- Look at any visuals in the essay, and tell the writer what they contribute to your understanding of the writer's reflections.

- If any visuals do not seem relevant or if there seem to be too many visuals, identify the ones that the writer could consider dropping, explaining your thinking.

- If a visual does not seem to be appropriately placed, suggest a better place for it.

REVISING

This section offers suggestions for revising your draft. Revising means reenvisioning your draft, trying to see it in a new way, given your purpose and readers, in order to develop an engaging, coherent reflective essay.

The biggest mistake you can make while revising is to focus initially on words or sentences. Instead, first try to see your draft as a whole in order to assess its likely impact on your readers. Think imaginatively and boldly about cutting uninteresting material, adding new material, and moving material around. Your computer makes even drastic revisions physically easy, but you still need to make the mental effort and decisions that will improve your draft.

You may have received help with this challenge from a classmate or tutor who gave your draft a critical reading. If so, keep this feedback in mind as you decide which parts of your draft need revising and what specific changes you could make. The following suggestions will help you solve problems and strengthen your essay.

To Present the Particular Occasion More Effectively

- If the occasion for your reflections seems flat or too general and abstract, expand it with interesting details.

- If the occasion fails to illustrate the significance of your subject, revise it to do so.

- If the occasion seems not to anticipate the reflections that follow, revise it or come up with a new, more relevant occasion.

To Develop the Reflections More Fully

- If promising ideas are not yet fully developed, provide further examples, anecdotes, contrasts, and so on.

- If certain ideas now seem too predictable, drop them and try to come up with more insightful ideas.

- If your reflections do not move beyond personal associations, extend them into the social realm by commenting on their larger implications—what they mean for people in general.

To Strengthen Topical Coherence

- If there are distracting gaps between sentences or paragraphs, try to close them by revising sentences.

- If one section seems not to follow from the previous one, consider reordering the sequence of sections.

- If there are pairs or series of related ideas or examples, consider revising the items into parallel grammatical form.

To Better Engage Readers

- If your beginning—typically the presentation of the occasion—seems unlikely to draw readers in, make its event more dramatic, its comments less predictable, or its significance more pointed. If you cannot see how to make it more interesting, consider another beginning.

- If your reflections seem unlikely to lead readers to reflect on their own lives and their interactions with other people, try to carry your ideas further and to develop them in more varied ways.

EDITING AND PROOFREADING

After you have revised your essay, be sure to spend some time checking for errors in usage, punctuation, and mechanics and considering matters of style. If you keep a list of errors you typically make, begin by checking your draft against this list. Ask someone else to proofread your essay before you print out a copy for your instructor or send it electronically.

From our research on student writing, we know that essays reflecting on a particular occasion have a relatively high frequency of unnecessary shifts in verb tense and mood. Consult a writer's handbook for information on unnecessary verb shifts, and then edit your essay to correct any shifts that you find.

REFLECTING ON WHAT YOU HAVE LEARNED

Reflection

In this chapter, you have read critically several reflective essays and have written one of your own. To better remember what you have learned, pause now to reflect on the reading and writing activities you completed in this chapter.

1. *Write* a page or so reflecting on what you have learned. *Begin* by describing what you are most pleased with in your essay. Then *explain* what you think contributed to your achievement. *Be specific* about this contribution.

   - If it was something you learned from the readings, *indicate* which readings and specifically what you learned from them.

- If it came from your invention writing, *point out* the section or sections that helped you most.

- If you got good advice from a critical reader, *explain* exactly how the person helped you—perhaps by helping you understand a particular problem in your draft or by adding a new dimension to your writing.

- *Try to write* about your achievement in terms of what you have learned about the genre.

2. Now *reflect* more generally on reflective essays, a genre of writing that has been important for centuries and is still practiced in our society today. *Consider* some of the following questions: How comfortable do you feel relying on your own experiences or observations as a basis for developing ideas about general subjects or for developing ideas about the way people are and the ways they interact? How comfortable are you with merely trying out your own personal ideas on a subject rather than researching it or interviewing people to collect their ideas? How comfortable do you feel adopting a conversational rather than a formal tone? How would you explain your level of comfort? How might your gender, social class, or ethnic group have influenced the ideas you came up with for your essay? What contribution might reflective essays make to our society that other genres cannot make?

CHAPTER 5

Explaining Concepts

Essays explaining concepts feature a kind of explanatory writing that is especially important for college students to understand. Each of the essays you will analyze in this chapter explains a single concept, such as *parthenogenesis* in biology, *markedness* and *dating* in sociology, and *stickiness* in psychology. For your own explanatory essay, you will choose a concept from your current studies or special interests.

For you as a college student, a better understanding of how to read and write explanations of concepts is useful in several ways. It gives you strategies for critically reading the textbooks and other concept-centered material in your college courses. It helps give you confidence to write a common type of essay exam and paper assignment. And it acquaints you with the basic strategies or modes of development common to all types of explanatory writing—definition, classification or division, comparison and contrast, process narration, illustration, and causal explanation.

A *concept* is a major idea. Every field of study has its concepts: physics has quantum theory, subatomic particles, the Heisenberg principle; psychiatry has neurosis, schizophrenia, narcissism; composition has invention, heuristics, recursiveness; business management has corporate culture, micromanagement, and direct marketing; and music has harmony and counterpoint. Concepts include abstract ideas, phenomena, and processes. Concepts are central to the understanding of virtually every subject—we create concepts, name them, communicate them, and think with them.

As you work through this chapter, keep in mind that we learn a new concept by connecting it to what we have previously learned. Good explanatory writing, therefore, must be incremental, adding bit by bit to the reader's knowledge. Explanatory writing goes wrong when the flow of new information is either too fast or too slow for the intended readers, when the information is too difficult or too simple, or when the writing is digressive or just plain dull.

The readings in this chapter will help you see what makes explanatory writing interesting and informative. From the readings and from the ideas for writing

215

that follow each reading, you will get ideas for writing your own essay about a concept. As you read and write about the selections, keep in mind the following assignment, which sets out the goals for writing an essay explaining a concept. To support your writing of this assignment, the chapter concludes with a Guide to Writing Essays Explaining Concepts.

THE WRITING ASSIGNMENT

Explaining Concepts

Choose a concept that interests you enough to study further. Write an essay explaining the concept. Consider carefully what your readers already know about the concept and how your essay can add to their knowledge.

WRITING SITUATIONS FOR ESSAYS EXPLAINING CONCEPTS

Writing that explains concepts is familiar in college and professional life, as the following examples show:

- For a presentation at the annual convention of the American Medical Association, an anesthesiologist writes a report on the concept of *awareness during surgery*. He presents evidence that patients under anesthesia, as in hypnosis, can hear, and he reviews research demonstrating that they can perceive and carry out instructions that speed their recovery. He describes briefly how he applies the concept in his own work—how he prepares patients before surgery, what he tells them while they are under anesthesia, and what happens as they recover.

- A business reporter for a newspaper writes an article about *virtual reality*. She describes the lifelike, three-dimensional experience created by wearing gloves and video goggles wired to a computer. To help readers understand this new concept, she contrasts it with television. For investors, she describes which corporations have shown an interest in the commercial possibilities of virtual reality.

- As part of a group assignment, a college student at a summer biology camp in the Sierra Nevada mountains reads about the condition of mammals at birth. She discovers the distinction between infant mammals that are *altricial* (born nude and helpless within a protective nest) and those that are *precocial* (born well formed with eyes open and ears erect). In her part of a group report, she develops this contrast point by point, giving many examples of specific mammals but focusing in detail on altricial mice and precocial porcupines. Domestic cats, she points out, are an intermediate example—born with some fur but with eyes and ears closed.

THINKING ABOUT YOUR EXPERIENCE WITH EXPLANATORY WRITING

Before studying a type of writing, it is useful to spend some time thinking about what you already know about it. In school, you have undoubtedly written numerous explanations of concepts for exams and papers. In and out of school, you have probably also had extensive experience explaining concepts to friends and family.

To analyze your experience with explanations, you might recall an occasion when you tried to explain a concept to others. It may have been memorable because you were trying to explain something you cared about or because you had a hard time getting your audience to understand. Try to recall the situation, what you were trying to explain, why it was important, and what difficulties you were able to anticipate. What strategies did you use? For example, did you think of examples to make your explanation more understandable or compare your subject to something more familiar?

Consider also explanations you have heard or read in school, on the Internet, on television, or elsewhere. Think of one explanation that you thought was especially successful. Looking back on it, do you think this particular explanation worked well because it was so clear or well organized, because it used examples or images to make the information vivid, or for some other reason or combination of reasons?

Write at least a page about your experience with explanatory writing.

■ A Guide to Reading Essays Explaining Concepts

This guide introduces you to explanatory writing. By completing all of the activities in it, you will prepare yourself to learn a great deal from the other readings in this chapter about how to read and write an essay explaining a concept. The guide focuses on an engaging essay by the science writer David Quammen, "Is Sex Necessary? Virgin Birth and Opportunism in the Garden." You will read Quammen's essay twice. First, you will read it for meaning, looking closely at its content and ideas. Then you will reread the essay like a writer, analyzing the parts to see how Quammen crafts his essay and to learn the range of strategies he employs to make his concept explanation effective. These two activities—reading for meaning and reading like a writer—follow every reading in this chapter.

DAVID QUAMMEN
Is Sex Necessary? Virgin Birth and Opportunism in the Garden

David Quammen (b. 1948), a novelist and nature writer, writes a column and is editor-at-large for the magazine Outside *and has published articles in* Smithsonian Magazine, Audubon, Esquire, Rolling Stone, *and* Harper's. *His books include the novel* The Soul of Viktor Tronko *(1987) and an edited collection (with Burkhard Bilger) of outstanding writing in his specialties,* The Best American Science and Nature Writing 2000 *(2000). His most recent book is* The Reluctant Mr. Darwin: An Intimate Portrait of Charles Darwin and the Making of His Theory of Evolution *(2006). Several collections of his own writing have also been published, including* Natural Acts: A Sidelong View of Science and Nature *(1985),* Wild Thoughts from Wild Places *(1998),* Boilerplate Rhino: Nature in the Eye of the Beholder *(2000), and* Monster of God: The Man-Eating Predator in the Jungles of History and the Mind *(2003). He has been a Rhodes Scholar and twice has won the National Magazine Award, as well as other awards and prizes.*

The readers of Outside *have special interests in nature, outdoor recreation, and the environment, but few have advanced training in ecology or biology. In this essay, originally published as a column in* Outside *and reprinted in* Natural Acts, *Quammen gives us a nonscientist's introduction to parthenogenesis—not only to the facts of it but also to its significance in nature.*

As you read, annotate anything that helps you understand the concept of parthenogenesis. The marginal annotations below point to strategies typically used by writers who explain concepts. Add your own comments and questions, noting anything else you think is interesting.

To introduce his topic and engage readers, Quammen refers to a famous song and forecasts that he will talk about creatures who *"don't* do it."

Birds do it, bees do it, goes the tune. But the songsters, as usual, would mislead us with drastic oversimplifications. The full truth happens to be more eccentrically nonlibidinous: Sometimes they *don't* do it, those very creatures, and get the same results anyway. Bees of all species, for instance, are notable to geneticists precisely for their ability to produce offspring while doing *without.* Likewise at least one variety of bird—the Beltsville Small White turkey, a domestic dinnertable model out of Beltsville, Maryland—has achieved scientific renown for a similar feat. What we are talking about here is celibate motherhood, procreation without copulation, a phenomenon that goes by the technical name *parthenogenesis.* Translated from the Greek roots: virgin birth. 1

Quammen defines his topic in its simplest, dictionary terms (highlighted)—a strategy often used by explainers of concepts.

This one-sentence paragraph is meant to engage readers, but jokes about religion can backfire. Did you smile, or were you offended?

And you don't have to be Catholic to believe in this one. 2

Miraculous as it may seem, parthenogenesis is actually rather common throughout nature, practiced regularly or intermittently by at least some species within 3 almost every group of animals except (for reasons still unknown) dragonflies and mammals. Reproduction by virgin females has been discovered among reptiles, birds, fishes, amphibians, crustaceans, mollusks, ticks, the jellyfish clan, flatworms, roundworms, segmented worms; and among insects (notwithstanding those unrelentingly sexy dragonflies) it is especially favored. The order *Hymenoptera*, including all bees and wasps, is uniformly parthenogenetic in the manner by which males are produced: Every male honeybee is born without any genetic contribution from a father. Among the beetles, there are thirty-five different forms of parthenogenetic weevil. The African weaver ant employs parthenogenesis, as do twenty-three species of fruit fly and at least one kind of roach. The gall midge *Miastor* is notorious for the exceptionally bizarre and grisly scenario that allows its fatherless young to see daylight: *Miastor* daughters cannibalize the mother from inside, with ruthless impatience, until her hollowed out skin splits open like the door of an overcrowded nursery. But the foremost practitioners of virgin birth—their elaborate and versatile proficiency unmatched in the animal kingdom—are undoubtedly the aphids.

> Quammen cites many examples to illustrate how common parthenogenesis is.

4   Now no sensible reader of even this can be expected, I realize, to care faintly about aphid biology *qua* aphid biology. That's just asking too much. But there's a larger rationale for dragging you aphidward. The life cycle of these little nebbishy sap-sucking insects, the very same that infest rose bushes and house plants, not only exemplifies *how* parthenogenetic reproduction is done; it also very clearly shows *why*.

> Anticipating that ordinary readers might not care a lot about aphids, Quammen appeals to their curiosity by forecasting that his essay will explain not only the *how* but also the *why* of parthenogenesis.

5   First the biographical facts. A typical aphid, which feeds entirely on plant juices tapped off from the vascular system of young leaves, spends winter dormant and protected, as an egg. The egg is attached near a bud site on the new growth of a poplar tree. In March, when the tree sap has begun to rise and the buds have begun to burgeon, an aphid hatchling appears, plugging its sharp snout (like a mosquito's) into the tree's tenderest plumbing. This solitary individual aphid will be, necessarily, a wingless female. If she is lucky, she will become sole founder of a vast aphid population. Having sucked enough poplar sap to reach maturity, she produces— by *live birth* now, and without benefit of a mate—

> In paragraphs 5 and 6, Quammen uses metaphorical language (highlighted) to capture readers' interest and to help illustrate scientific terms and concepts. He also narrates the steps in the process—another explanatory strategy— of parthenogenesis and aphid procreation.

daughters identical to herself. These wingless daughters also plug into the tree's flow of sap, and they also produce further wingless daughters, until sometime in late May, when that particular branch of that particular tree can support no more thirsty aphids. Suddenly there is a change: The next generation of daughters are born with wings. They fly off in search of a better situation.

One such aviatrix lands on an herbaceous plant— 6 say a young climbing bean in some human's garden— and the pattern repeats. She plugs into the sap ducts on the underside of a new leaf, commences feasting destructively, and delivers by parthenogenesis a great brood of wingless daughters. The daughters beget more daughters, those daughters beget still more, and so on, until the poor bean plant is encrusted with a solid mob of these fat little elbowing greedy sisters. Then again, neatly triggered by the crowded conditions, a generation of daughters are born with wings. Away they fly, looking for prospects, and one of them lights on, say, a sugar beet. (The switch from bean to beet is fine, because our species of typical aphid is not inordinately choosy.) The sugar beet before long is covered, sucked upon mercilessly, victimized by a horde of mothers and nieces and granddaughters. Still not a single male aphid has appeared anywhere in the chain.

The lurching from one plant to another continues; 7 the alternation between wingless and winged daughters continues. But in September, with fresh tender plant growth increasingly hard to find, there is another change.

Flying daughters are born who have a different destiny: They wing back to the poplar tree, where they give 8 birth to a crop of wingless females that are unlike any so far. These latest girls know the meaning of sex! Meanwhile, at long last, the starving survivors back on that final bedraggled sugar beet have brought forth a generation of males. The males have wings. They take to the air in quest of poplar trees and first love. *Et voilà.* The mated females lay eggs that will wait out the winter near bud sites on that poplar tree, and the circle is thus completed. One single aphid hatching—call her the *fundatrix*—in this way can give rise in the course of a year, from her own ovaries exclusively, to roughly a zillion aphids.

Paragraph 7 serves to *summarize* the previous information and make a *transition* to an explanation of another.

Quammen continues to use humor (highlighted) to try to keep readers' interest.

9   Well and good, you say. A zillion aphids.

10   But what is the point of it? The point, for aphids as for most other parthenogenetic animals, is (1) exceptionally fast reproduction that allows (2) maximal exploitation of temporary resource abundance and unstable environmental conditions, while (3) facilitating the successful colonization of unfamiliar habitats. In other words the aphid, like the gall midge and the weaver ant and the rest of their fellow parthenogens, is by its evolved character a galloping opportunist.

> Paragraph 10 begins with a rhetorical question that readers expect Quammen to answer, which he does by *listing*, a forecasting and classifying strategy.

11   This is a term of science, not of abuse. Population ecologists make an illuminating distinction between what they label *equilibrium* and *opportunistic* species. According to William Birky and John Gilbert, from a paper in the journal *American Zoologist*: "Equilibrium species, exemplified by many vertebrates, maintain relatively constant population sizes, in part by being adapted to reproduce, at least slowly, in most of the environmental conditions which they meet. Opportunistic species, on the other hand, show extreme population fluctuations; they are adapted to reproduce only in a relatively narrow range of conditions, but make up for this by reproducing extremely rapidly in favorable circumstances. At least in some cases, opportunistic organisms can also be categorized as colonizing organisms." Birky and Gilbert also emphasize that "The potential for rapid reproduction is the essential evolutionary ticket for entry into the opportunistic lifestyle."

> "Opportunist" sounds negative, so Quammen explains that he is using a specific scientific meaning of the word. Here his strategy is to *classify* species into two categories and *define* each category. Note how he uses signal phrases (highlighted) to introduce the definitions and to integrate his sources smoothly.

12   And parthenogenesis, in turn, is the greatest time-saving gimmick in the history of animal reproduction. No hours or days are wasted while a female looks for a mate; no minutes lost to the act of mating itself. The female aphid attains sexual maturity and, bang, she becomes automatically pregnant. No waiting, no courtship, no fooling around. She delivers her brood of daughters, they grow to puberty and, zap, another generation immediately. . . . The time saved to parthenogenetic species may seem trivial, but it is not. It adds up dizzyingly: In the same time taken by a sexually reproducing insect to complete three generations for a total of 1,200 offspring, an aphid (assuming the *same* time required for each female to mature, and the *same* number of progeny in each litter), squandering no time on

> Quammen continues to use humor to engage readers, who are not likely to want to save time in the "act of mating." His language is informal here to diminish the effect of the scientific jargon he and his sources have used.

courtship or sex, will progress through six generations for an extended family of 318,000,000.

Even this isn't speedy enough for some restless opportunists. That matricidal gall midge *Miastor*, whose larvae feed on fleeting eruptions of fungus under the bark of trees, has developed a startling way to cut further time from the cycle of procreation. Far from waiting for a mate, *Miastor* does not even wait for maturity. When food is abundant, it is the *larva*, not the adult female fly, who is eaten alive from inside by her own daughters. And as those voracious daughters burst free of the husk that was their mother, each of them already contains further larval daughters taking shape ominously within its own ovaries. While the food lasts, while opportunity endures, no *Miastor* female can live to adulthood without dying of motherhood.

The implicit principle behind all this nonsexual reproduction, all this hurry, is simple: Don't argue with success. Don't tamper with a genetic blueprint that works. Unmated female aphids, and gall midges, pass on their own gene patterns virtually unaltered (except for the occasional mutation) to their daughters. Sexual reproduction, on the other hand, constitutes, by its essence, genetic tampering. The whole purpose of joining sperm with egg is to shuffle the genes of both parents and come up with a new combination that might perhaps be more advantageous. Give the kid something neither Mom nor Pop ever had. Parthenogenetic species, during their hurried phases at least, dispense with this genetic shuffle. They stick stubbornly to the gene pattern that seems to be working. They produce (with certain complicated exceptions) natural clones of themselves.

But what they gain thereby in reproductive rate, in great explosions of population, they give up in flexibility. They minimize their genetic options. They lessen their chances of adapting to unforeseen changes of circumstance.

Which is why more than one biologist has drawn the same conclusion as M. J. D. White: "Parthenogenetic forms seem to be frequently successful in the particular ecological niche which they occupy, but sooner or later the inherent disadvantages of their genetic system must be expected to lead to a lack of adaptability, followed by

13

14

15

16

In paragraph 13, Quammen uses yet another explanatory strategy, an additional example. Note the cleverness of the last sentence in light of his subject.

Finally, Quammen follows through on his promise in paragraph 4 to provide an explanation about *why* parthenogenesis exists.

Quammen again integrates a source smoothly (highlighted). In the quotation, he is also presenting the *effects* that the concept *causes*, an additional explanatory strategy.

eventual extinction, or perhaps in some cases by a return to sexuality."

17   So it *is* necessary, at least intermittently (once a year, for the aphids, whether they need it or not), this thing called sex. As of course you and I knew it must be. Otherwise surely, by now, we mammals and dragonflies would have come up with something more dignified.

Quammen's last sentence leaves his readers smiling as well as enlightened about parthenogenesis.

READING FOR MEANING

This section presents three activities that will help you reread Quammen's explanatory essay with a critical eye. Done in sequence, these activities lead you from a basic understanding of the selection to a more personal response to it and finally to an analysis that deepens your understanding and critical thinking about what you are reading.

Read to Comprehend

Reread the selection, and write a few sentences explaining the concept *parthenogenesis* and its significance. The following definitions may help you understand Quammen's vocabulary:

opportunism (in the title): taking advantage of any opportunity to achieve a goal, often in a way that is unfair or harmful to others.

celibate (paragraph 1): abstaining or refraining from sexual intercourse.

exploitation (10): making use of something to the greatest possible extent.

matricidal (13): related to the killing of one's mother.

Identify three or more additional words that you don't understand, and find the best definitions from the dictionary that work with their context.

To expand your understanding of this reading, you might use one or more of the following critical reading strategies that are explained and illustrated in Appendix 1: *outlining* and *questioning to understand and remember*.

Read to Respond

Write several paragraphs exploring your initial thoughts and feelings about Quammen's explanatory essay. Focus on anything that stands out for you, perhaps because it resonates with your own experience or because you find a statement puzzling.

You might consider writing about the following:

- the essay's title;

- your response to Quammen's assumption that his readers are uninterested in "aphid biology *qua* aphid biology" (paragraph 4);

- Quammen's joke about not having "to be Catholic to believe in this one" (2);

- the grisly description of the reproductive behavior of the gall midge *Miastor* (3); or

- the notion that parthenogenetic reproduction may be effective for opportunistic species but that even they need to reproduce sexually once in a while to refresh the gene pool (14–17).

To develop your response to Quammen's essay, you might use one or more of the following critical reading strategies that are explained and illustrated in Appendix 1: *contextualizing*, *recognizing emotional manipulation*, and *judging the writer's credibility*.

Read to Analyze Assumptions

Reread Quammen's essay explaining a concept, and write a paragraph or two exploring one or more of the assumptions you find in the text. All writing contains assumptions—opinions, values, and beliefs that are taken for granted as commonly accepted truths by the writer or others. Personal or individual assumptions also tend to reflect the values and beliefs of a particular group or community, sometimes called *cultural ideology*, which shape the way those in the group think, act, and understand the world.

Analyzing assumptions is an important part of learning to read critically because assumptions tend to be unexamined and unquestioned (at least consciously) by those who hold them. When you read with a critical eye, you identify important assumptions in the text and ask questions about them. Sometimes assumptions are stated explicitly, but often they are only implied, so you may have to search for underlying assumptions in the word choices and examples. Here are some kinds of questions you should ask regarding the assumptions you find: How does the assumption support or oppose the status quo? Whose interests are served by it? What alternative ideas, beliefs, or values would challenge this assumption? If the writer uses the assumption to appeal to readers, how effective do you think this appeal is, and why?

To help you get started reading for assumptions in Quammen's essay, note that he is helping us critique our own assumption that our own method of reproduction must be the best—the top of the evolutionary ladder. He starts with the opening lyrics "*Birds do it, bees do it,*" of Cole Porter's song "Let's Do It (Let's Fall in Love)," with their implied assumption that all other species, like ours, reproduce sexually. But then he challenges this assumption—as well as the related assumption of our own superior status—by noting that other species use different methods and also that their methods may be better than ours or at least enable them to adapt effectively to their habitats. He makes this comparison explicit in paragraph 12:

> And parthenogenesis, in turn, is the greatest time-saving gimmick in the history of animal reproduction. No hours or days are wasted while a

female looks for a mate; no minutes lost to the act of mating itself. . . .
No waiting, no courtship, no fooling around.

Here he is playing off the assumption that humans do not prize efficiency when
they are mating; they, and other species like them, dally over courtship. Note his
use of words that indicate there might be another way to look at the process: "no
hours or days are wasted," "no minutes lost," "no waiting, no courtship, no fooling
around." Once Quammen has aroused your curiosity (and sense of humor) about
how there might be other ways to view courtship, he is ready to explain the concept of parthenogenesis. Think about your own experience with scientific explanations, especially those about evolutionary behavior.

You may want to examine Quammen's assumptions about the value of evolutionary theory and also consider whether he assumes that his readers will agree
with him or whether his explanation of the concept of parthenogenesis is
designed to illustrate the value of this theory for skeptical readers. You may also
explore other assumptions in Quammen's essay, assumptions you may touch on
in one of the other Reading for Meaning or Reading Like a Writer activities, such
as the following:

- **assumptions about genetic tampering.** At the beginning of paragraph 14,
  Quammen makes explicit one of his assumptions about parthenogenesis:
  "The implicit principle behind all this nonsexual reproduction, all this hurry,
  is simple: Don't argue with success. Don't tamper with a genetic blueprint
  that works." Then he explains how sexual reproduction constitutes "genetic
  tampering" because sperm and egg "come up with a new combination that
  might perhaps be more advantageous." To think critically about the assumptions in this essay related to "genetic tampering," ask yourself: Is this what
  reproduction is all about—seizing the advantage? Does this assumption
  explain all sexual behavior, in your view? What does Quammen's essay make
  you think about the concept of evolution? Two of the more controversial
  issues in American society today are cloning and stem-cell research. Which
  assumptions might or might not be shared with Quammen by those who
  support either of these two activities?

- **assumptions about readers.** Quammen is quick to point out that "opportunist" (paragraph 10) is a "scientific" term (11). But he also could intend a
  double meaning because he includes "galloping," a slangy term that most
  readers will interpret as less than scientific. Look at the sentences that precede this phrase. To think critically about Quammen's assumptions about his
  readers, ask yourself: Why do you suppose Quammen combines slang and
  scientific terms in the same paragraph? Where else does he step away from a
  strictly scientific attitude to one that is more "everyday"? What does this pattern tell you about Quammen's assumptions about his readers? What is he
  assuming when he says that "no sensible reader of even this can be expected,
  I realize, to care faintly about aphid biology *qua* aphid biology" (4)?

To probe assumptions more deeply, you might use one or more of the following critical reading strategies that are explained and illustrated in Appendix 1: *reflecting on challenges to your beliefs and values* and *exploring the significance of figurative language*.

READING LIKE A WRITER

This section guides you through an analysis of Quammen's explanatory writing strategies: *devising a readable plan, using appropriate explanatory strategies, integrating sources smoothly*, and *engaging readers' interest*. For each strategy you will be asked to reread and annotate part of Quammen's essay to see how he uses the strategy in "Is Sex Necessary?"

When you study the selections later in this chapter, you will see how different writers use these same strategies. The Guide to Writing Essays Explaining Concepts near the end of the chapter suggests ways you can use these strategies in your own writing.

Devising a Readable Plan

Experienced writers of explanation know that readers often have a hard time making their way through new and difficult material and sometimes give up in frustration. Writers who want to avoid this scenario construct a reader-friendly plan by dividing the information into clearly distinguishable topics. They also give readers road signs—forecasting statements, topic sentences, transitions, and summaries—to guide them through the explanation.

Writers often provide a forecasting statement early in the essay to let readers know where they are heading. Forecasting statements can also appear at the beginnings of major sections of the essay. Topic sentences announce each segment of information as it comes up, transitions (such as *in contrast* and *another*) relate what is coming to what came before, and summaries remind readers what has been explained already. Quammen effectively deploys all of these strategies.

Analyze

Notice those sentences that forecast, announce topics, make transitions, and offer brief summaries. (These strategies are defined in the preceding paragraph.)

Write

Write several sentences, explaining how Quammen makes use of forecasting statements, transitions, brief summaries, and topic sentences to reveal his overall plan to readers. *Give examples* from the reading to support your explanation. Then, considering yourself among Quammen's intended readers, *write a few more sentences* evaluating how successful the writer's efforts are for you.

Using Appropriate Explanatory Strategies

When writers organize and present information, they rely on strategies we call the building blocks of explanatory essays—defining, classifying or dividing, comparing and contrasting, narrating a process, illustrating, and reporting causes or effects. The strategies a writer chooses are determined by the topics covered, the kinds of information available, and the writer's assessment of readers' knowledge about the concept. Following are brief descriptions of the writing strategies that are particularly useful in explaining concepts:

Defining: briefly stating the meaning of the concept or any other word likely to be unfamiliar to readers.

Classifying or dividing: grouping related information about a concept into two or more separate groups and labeling each group, or dividing a concept into parts to consider each part separately.

Comparing and contrasting: pointing out how the concept is similar to and different from a related concept.

Narrating a process: presenting procedures or a sequence of steps as they unfold over time to show the concept in practice.

Illustrating: giving examples, relating anecdotes, listing facts and details, and quoting sources to help readers understand a concept.

Reporting causes or effects: identifying the known causes or effects related to a concept.

Quammen makes good use of all these fundamentally important explanatory strategies—defining in paragraphs 1, 8, and 11; classifying in paragraphs 10 and 11; comparing and contrasting in paragraphs 11 to 14 (as well as establishing the analogy between insects and humans that runs through the essay); narrating a process in paragraphs 5 to 8; illustrating in paragraph 3; and reporting known effects in paragraphs 12 to 14.

Analyze

1. *Review* Quammen's use of each explanatory strategy described in the preceding paragraph, and *select one* to analyze more closely.

2. *Make notes* in the margin about how Quammen uses that one strategy and what special contribution it makes to your understanding of parthenogenesis within the context of the whole reading.

Write

Write several sentences explaining how the strategy you have analyzed works in this essay to help readers understand parthenogenesis.

Integrating Sources Smoothly

In addition to drawing on personal knowledge and fresh observations, writers often do additional research about the concepts they are trying to explain. Doing research in the library and on the Internet, writers immediately confront the ethical responsibility to their readers of locating relevant sources, evaluating them critically, and representing them without distortion. You will find advice on meeting this responsibility in Appendix 2 (pp. 670–79).

Developing an explanation sentence by sentence on the page or the screen, writers confront a different challenge in using sources. They need to know how to integrate source material smoothly into their own sentences and to cite the sources of those materials accurately, sometimes using formal citation styles that point readers to a full description of each source in a list of works cited at the end of the essay.

How writers cite or refer to research sources depends on the writing situation they find themselves in. Certain formal situations, such as college assignments or scholarly publications, have prescribed rules for citing sources. As a student, you may be expected to cite your sources formally because your writing will be judged in part by what you have read and how you have used your reading. For more informal writing occasions—newspaper and magazine articles, for example—readers do not expect writers to include page references or publication information, only to identify their sources. In this chapter's readings, all the writers except Quammen and Deborah Tannen cite their sources formally.

Writers may quote, summarize, or paraphrase their sources—quoting when they want to capture the exact wording of the original source; summarizing to convey only the gist or main points; and paraphrasing when they want to include most of the details in some part of the original. Whether they quote, summarize, or paraphrase, writers try to integrate source material smoothly into their writing. For example, they deliberately vary the way they introduce borrowed material, avoiding repetition of the same signal phrases (*X said, as Y put it*) or sentence pattern (a *that* clause, use of the colon).

Analyze

1. *Look closely* at paragraphs 11 and 16, where Quammen quotes sources directly.

2. *Put brackets* ([ ]) *around* the signal phrase or key part of a sentence pattern that he uses to introduce each quotation, noticing how he integrates the quotation into his sentence.

Write

Write a few sentences describing how Quammen introduces and integrates quotations into his writing. *Give examples* from your annotations in paragraphs 11 and 16.

Engaging Readers' Interest

Most people read explanations of concepts because they are helpful for work or school. Readers do not generally expect the writing to entertain but simply to inform. Nevertheless, explanations that keep readers engaged with lively writing are usually appreciated. Writers explaining concepts may engage readers' interest in a variety of ways. For example, they may remind readers of what they already know about the concept. They may show readers a new way of using a familiar concept or dramatize that the concept has greater importance than readers had realized. They can connect the concept, sometimes through metaphor or analogy, to common human experiences. They may present the concept in a humorous way to convince readers that learning about a concept can be painless or even pleasurable.

Quammen relies on many of these strategies to engage his readers' interest. Keep in mind that his original readers could either read or skip his column. Those who enjoyed and learned from his earlier columns would be more likely to try out the first few paragraphs of this one, but Quammen could not count on their having any special interest in parthenogenesis. He has to try to generate that interest—and rather quickly, in the first few sentences or paragraphs.

Analyze

Reread paragraphs 1 to 4, and *note in the margin* the various ways Quammen reaches out to interest readers in his subject.

Write

Write several sentences explaining how Quammen attempts to engage his readers' interest in parthenogenesis. To support your explanation, *give examples* from your annotations in paragraphs 1 to 4. What parts seem most effective to you? Least effective?

A SPECIAL READING STRATEGY

Comparing and Contrasting Related Readings: Quammen's "Is Sex Necessary?" and Curtis and Barnes's "Parthenogenesis"

Comparing and contrasting related readings is a critical reading strategy useful both in reading for meaning and in reading like a writer. This strategy is particularly applicable when writers present similar subjects, as is the case in the concept explanation by David Quammen (p. 218) and the following excerpt from a biology textbook by Helena Curtis and N. Sue Barnes. As you read the textbook explanation of parthenogenesis and compare it to Quammen's explanation, consider the following issues:

- Compare these two explanations in terms of how well they help you understand parthenogenesis—how it works, how widespread it is, and what its benefits are.

- Compare the use of technical terms and sources in the two explanations, considering the purpose and readers for each publication.

- Compare the use of examples, especially that of the gall midge (paragraph 3 in Quammen and paragraph 4 in Curtis and Barnes).

- Compare how the explanations attempt to engage readers' interest.

See Appendix 1 for detailed guidelines on using the comparing and contrasting related readings strategy.

HELENA CURTIS AND N. SUE BARNES

Parthenogenesis

Another form of asexual reproduction is parthenogenesis, the 1 development of an organism from an unfertilized egg. In species in which the male gamete determines the sex of the offspring, parthenogenesis always results in all female offspring. Hence, it is far more efficient than sexual reproduction. If . . . houseflies . . . reproduced parthenogenetically, each female would have . . . twice as many female young in every generation, and the population would [be] 358×10^{12} at the end of seven generations.

Parthenogenesis in plants lacks the advantage of the parental 2 support system supplied by vegetative growth, which is traded off for the possibilities of larger numbers and, usually, wider dispersal of the young. Dandelions reproduce parthenogenetically. They form conspicuous flowers and also some functionless pollen grains, which may be taken as evidence that the present asexual species of dandelions evolved from sexual ones. As a consequence of parthenogenetic reproduction, dandelions growing in a single locality often consist of several different populations, each composed of genetically identical individuals. Otto Solbrig compared two such populations of dandelions growing together in various localities near Ann Arbor, Michigan. One genotype, genotype D, outperformed the other under all environmental conditions, both in the number of plants that survived and in their total dry weight. On the other hand, genotype A always produced more seeds and produced them earlier, so it always got a head start whenever a newly disturbed area became available for occupation.

Completely asexual species are also found among small invertebrates—some rotifers, for example—as well as among plants. Recently, several species of fish, lizards, and frogs have been found that apparently reproduce only parthenogenetically. Many other organisms alternate sexual and asexual phases. Freshwater *Daphnia*, for instance, multiply by parthenogenesis when the plankton on which they feed is abundant. Then, in response to some environmental cue, they start producing both males and females. Typically, the asexual phase occurs when conditions are favorable for rapid local growth, and the sexual phase when the population is facing a less certain future and less homogeneous conditions. 3

Among the organisms that alternate sexual and asexual phases is the fungus-eating gall midge, which should perhaps be awarded the prize for precocious development among multicellular animals. These small flies, which are found on mushroom beds, can reproduce sexually. However, when abundant food is available, a female can produce parthenogenetic eggs, which are retained inside her body. The larvae develop inside the mother, devour her tissues, and, completely skipping the usual metamorphosis, emerge with eggs inside their own tissues. Within two days, larvae emerge from these eggs, devour their own mother, and are soon devoured in turn. Eventually, in response to some environmental signal, the parthenogenetic cycle is broken, and the females produce normal males and females that fly off in search of new mushrooms. 4

■ Readings

DEBORAH TANNEN

Marked Women

> *Deborah Tannen (b. 1945), who holds the title of University Pro-*
> *fessor in Linguistics at Georgetown University, has written more than*
> *twenty books and scores of articles. Although she does write technical*
> *works in linguistics, she also writes for a more general audience on the*
> *ways that language reflects the society in which it develops, particu-*
> *larly the society's attitudes about gender. Both her 1986 book,* That's
> Not What I Meant! How Conversational Style Makes or Breaks
> Your Relations with Others, *and her 1990 book,* You Just Don't
> Understand: Women and Men in Conversation, *were best-sellers.*
> *Her most recent books include* The Argument Culture: Moving from
> Debate to Dialogue *(1998),* I Only Say This Because I Love You:
> Talking to Your Parents, Partner, Sibs, and Kids When You're All
> Adults *(2002), and* You're Wearing THAT? Understanding Mothers
> and Daughters in Conversation *(2007). In addition, Tannen writes*
> *poetry, plays, and reflective essays.*
>
> *In the following selection, originally published in the* New York
> Times Magazine *in 1993, Tannen explains the concept of markedness,*
> *a "staple of linguistic theory." Linguistics—the study of language as a*
> *system for making meaning—has given birth to a new discipline*
> *called semiology, the study of any system for making meaning. Tan-*
> *nen's essay embodies this shift, as it starts with a verbal principle (the*
> *marking of words) and applies it to the visual world (the marking of*
> *hairstyle and clothing). As you read the opening paragraphs, annotate*
> *the text, noting places where Tannen unpacks the meaning of what*
> *various conference participants are wearing. (For help annotating, see*
> *the examples in this chapter on pages 218 and 278, as well as the*
> *advice on annotating on pages 597–603.)*

Some years ago I was at a small working conference of four 1
women and eight men. Instead of concentrating on the discussion I
found myself looking at the three other women at the table, thinking how each had a different style and how each style was coherent.

One woman had dark brown hair in a classic style, a cross 2
between Cleopatra and Plain Jane. The severity of her straight hair
was softened by wavy bangs and ends that turned under. Because
she was beautiful, the effect was more Cleopatra than plain.

The second woman was older, full of dignity and composure. 3
Her hair was cut in a fashionable style that left her with only one
eye, thanks to a side part that let a curtain of hair fall across half her

face. As she looked down to read her prepared paper, the hair robbed her of bifocal vision and created a barrier between her and the listeners.

The third woman's hair was wild, a frosted blond avalanche falling over and beyond her shoulders. When she spoke she frequently tossed her head, calling attention to her hair and away from her lecture.

Then there was makeup. The first woman wore facial cover that made her skin smooth and pale, a black line under each eye and mascara that darkened already dark lashes. The second wore only a light gloss on her lips and a hint of shadow on her eyes. The third had blue bands under her eyes, dark blue shadow, mascara, bright red lipstick and rouge; her fingernails flashed red.

I considered the clothes each woman had worn during the three days of the conference: In the first case, man-tailored suits in primary colors with solid-color blouses. In the second, casual but stylish black T-shirts, a floppy collarless jacket and baggy slacks or a skirt in neutral colors. The third wore a sexy jump suit; tight sleeveless jersey and tight yellow slacks; a dress with gaping armholes and an indulged tendency to fall off one shoulder.

Shoes? No. 1 wore string sandals with medium heels; No. 2, sensible, comfortable walking shoes; No. 3, pumps with spike heels. You can fill in the jewelry, scarves, shawls, sweaters—or lack of them.

As I amused myself finding coherence in these styles, I suddenly wondered why I was scrutinizing only the women. I scanned the eight men at the table. And then I knew why I wasn't studying them. The men's styles were unmarked.

The term "marked" is a staple of linguistic theory. It refers to the way language alters the base meaning of a word by adding a linguistic particle that has no meaning on its own. The unmarked form of a word carries the meaning that goes without saying— what you think of when you're not thinking anything special.

The unmarked tense of verbs in English is the present—for example, *visit*. To indicate past, you mark the verb by adding *ed* to yield *visited*. For future, you add a word: *will visit*. Nouns are presumed to be singular until marked for plural, typically by adding *s* or *es*, so *visit* becomes *visits* and *dish* becomes *dishes*.

The unmarked forms of most English words also convey "male." Being male is the unmarked case. Endings like *ess* and *ette* mark words as "female." Unfortunately, they also tend to mark them for frivolousness. Would you feel safe entrusting your life to a doctorette? Alfre Woodard, who was an Oscar nominee for best supporting actress, says she identifies herself as an actor because "actresses worry about eyelashes and cellulite, and women who are actors worry about the characters we are playing." Gender markers pick up extra meanings that reflect common association with the female gender: not quite serious, often sexual.

Each of the women at the conference had to make decisions about hair, clothing, makeup and accessories, and each decision carried meaning. Every style available to us was marked. The men in our group had made decisions, too, but the range from which they chose was incomparably narrower. Men can choose styles that are marked, but they don't have to, and in this group none did. Unlike the women, they had the option of being unmarked.   12

Take the men's hair styles. There was no marine crew cut or oily longish hair falling into eyes, no asymmetrical, two-tiered construction to swirl over a bald top. One man was unabashedly bald; the others had hair of standard length, parted on one side, in natural shades of brown or gray or graying. Their hair obstructed no views, left little to toss or push back or run fingers through and, consequently, needed and attracted no attention. A few men had beards. In a business setting, beards might be marked. In this academic gathering, they weren't.   13

There could have been a cowboy shirt with string tie or a three-piece suit or a necklaced hippie in jeans. But there wasn't. All eight men wore brown or blue slacks and nondescript shirts of light colors. No man wore sandals or boots; their shoes were dark, closed, comfortable, and flat. In short, unmarked.   14

Although no man wore makeup, you couldn't say the men didn't wear makeup in the sense that you could say a woman didn't wear makeup. For men, no makeup is unmarked.   15

I asked myself what style we women could have adopted that would have been unmarked, like the men's. The answer was none. There is no unmarked woman.   16

There is no woman's hair style that can be called standard, that says nothing about her. The range of women's hair styles is staggering, but a woman whose hair has no particular style is perceived as not caring about how she looks, which can disqualify her from many positions, and will subtly diminish her as a person in the eyes of some.   17

Women must choose between attractive shoes and comfortable shoes. When our group made an unexpected trek, the woman who wore flat, laced shoes arrived first. Last to arrive was the woman in spike heels, shoes in hand and a handful of men around her.   18

If a woman's clothing is tight or revealing (in other words, sexy), it sends a message—an intended one of wanting to be attractive, but also a possibly unintended one of availability. If her clothes are not sexy, that too sends a message, lent meaning by the knowledge   19 that they could have been. There are thousands of cosmetic products from which women can choose and myriad ways of applying them. Yet no makeup at all is anything but unmarked. Some men see it as a hostile refusal to please them.

Women can't even fill out a form without telling stories about themselves. Most forms give four titles to choose from. "Mr." carries no meaning other than that the respondent is male. But a woman who checks "Mrs." or "Miss" communicates not only whether she has been married but also whether she has conservative tastes in forms of address—and probably other conservative values as well. Checking "Ms." declines to let on about marriage (checking "Mr." declines nothing since nothing was asked), but it also marks her as either liberated or rebellious, depending on the observer's attitudes and assumptions.

I sometimes try to duck these variously marked choices by giving my title as "Dr."—and in so doing risk marking myself as either uppity (hence sarcastic responses like "Excuse *me!*") or an overachiever (hence reactions of congratulatory surprise like "Good for you!").

All married women's surnames are marked. If a woman takes her husband's name, she announces to the world that she is married and has traditional values. To some it will indicate that she is less herself, more identified by her husband's identity. If she does not take her husband's name, this too is marked, seen as worthy of comment: She has *done* something; she has "kept her own name." A man is never said to have "kept his own name" because it never occurs to anyone that he might have given it up. For him using his own name is unmarked.

A married woman who wants to have her cake and eat it too may use her surname plus his, with or without a hyphen. But this too announces her marital status and often results in a tongue-tying string. In a list (Harvey O'Donovan, Jonathan Feldman, Stephanie Woodbury McGillicutty), the woman's multiple name stands out. It is marked.

I have never been inclined toward biological explanations of gender differences in language, but I was intrigued to see Ralph Fasold bring biological phenomena to bear on the question of linguistic marking in his book *The Sociolinguistics of Language*. Fasold stresses that language and culture are particularly unfair in treating women as the marked case because biologically it is the male that is marked. While two X chromosomes make a female, two Y chromosomes make nothing. Like the linguistic markers *s*, *es*, or *ess*, the Y chromosome doesn't "mean" anything unless it is attached to a root form—an X chromosome.

Developing this idea elsewhere Fasold points out that girls are   25
born with full female bodies, while boys are born with modified
female bodies. He invites men who doubt this to lift up their shirts
and contemplate why they have nipples.

In his book, Fasold notes "a wide range of facts which demon-   26
strates that female is the unmarked sex." For example, he observes
that there are a few species that produce only females, like the
whiptail lizard. Thanks to parthenogenesis, they have no trouble
having as many daughters as they like. There are no species, however, that produce only males. This is no surprise, since any such
species would become extinct in its first generation.

Fasold is also intrigued by species that produce individuals not   27
involved in reproduction, like honeybees and leaf-cutter ants.
Reproduction is handled by the queen and a relatively few males;
the workers are sterile females. "Since they do not reproduce,"
Fasold said, "there is no reason for them to be one sex or the other,
so they default, so to speak, to female."

Fasold ends his discussion of these matters by pointing out that   28
if language reflected biology, grammar books would direct us to
use "she" to include males and females and "he" only for specifically male referents. But they don't. They tell us that "he" means
"he or she," and that "she" is used only if the referent is specifically
female. This use of "he" as the sex-indefinite pronoun is an innovation introduced into English by grammarians in the eighteenth
and nineteenth centuries, according to Peter Mühlhäusler and
Rom Harré in *Pronouns and People*. From at least about 1500, the
correct sex-indefinite pronoun was "they," as it still is in casual spoken English. In other words, the female was declared by grammarians to be the marked case.

Writing this article may mark me not as a writer, not as a lin-   29
guist, not as an analyst of human behavior, but as a feminist—
which will have positive or negative, but in any case powerful, connotations for readers. Yet I doubt that anyone reading Ralph
Fasold's book would put that label on him.

I discovered the markedness inherent in the very topic of gender   30
after writing a book on differences in conversational style based on
geographical region, ethnicity, class, age, and gender. When I was
interviewed, the vast majority of journalists wanted to talk about
the differences between women and men. While I thought I was
simply describing what I observed—something I had learned to
do as a researcher—merely mentioning women and men marked
me as a feminist for some.

When I wrote a book devoted to gender differences in ways of   31
speaking, I sent the manuscript to five male colleagues, asking
them to alert me to any interpretation, phrasing, or wording that

might seem unfairly negative toward men. Even so, when the book came out, I encountered responses like that of the television talk show host who, after interviewing me, turned to the audience and asked if they thought I was male-bashing.

Leaping upon a poor fellow who affably nodded in agreement, she made him stand and asked, "Did what she said accurately describe you?" "Oh, yes," he answered. "That's me exactly." "And what she said about women—does that sound like your wife?" "Oh, yes," he responded. "That's her exactly." "Then why do you think she's male-bashing?" He answered, with disarming honesty, "Because she's a woman and she's saying things about men."   32

To say anything about women and men without marking oneself as either feminist or anti-feminist, male-basher or apologist for men seems as impossible for a woman as trying to get dressed in the morning without inviting interpretations of her character.   33

Sitting at the conference table musing on these matters, I felt sad to think that we women didn't have the freedom to be unmarked that the men sitting next to us had. Some days you just want to get dressed and go about your business. But if you're a woman, you can't, because there is no unmarked woman.   34

READING FOR MEANING

This section presents three activities that will help you reread Tannen's explanatory essay with a critical eye. Done in sequence, these activities lead you from a basic understanding of the selection to a more personal response to it and finally to an analysis that deepens your understanding and critical thinking about what you are reading.

Read to Comprehend

Reread the selection, and write a few sentences explaining the linguistic concept of *marked* and its significance. The following definitions may help you understand Tannen's vocabulary:

referents (paragraph 28): things to which a linguistic expression refers or points.

inherent (30): existing in someone or something as a permanent and inseparable element or quality.

disarming (32): removing or capable of removing hostility or suspicion, such as by being charming.

Identify three or more additional words that you don't understand, and find the best definitions from the dictionary that work with their context.

To expand your understanding of this reading, you might use one or more of the following critical reading strategies that are explained and illustrated in Appendix 1: *outlining*, *summarizing*, and *paraphrasing*.

Read to Respond

Write several paragraphs exploring your initial thoughts and feelings about Tannen's explanatory essay. Focus on anything that stands out for you, perhaps because it resonates with your own experience or because you find a statement puzzling.

You might consider writing about the following:

- the idea that men have a choice of whether to be marked or unmarked but women are always marked no matter what they do, perhaps in relation to your own experience;

- the personal style that each of the three women described in paragraphs 1 to 8 created, perhaps in relation to your own efforts to create your own style;

- your response to the assertion that how a choice like checking "Ms." on a form is understood depends on the interpreter's "attitudes and assumptions" (paragraph 20), considering what might influence such attitudes and assumptions; or

- your view of Tannen in light of her assertion that "this article may mark me not as a writer, not as a linguist, not as an analyst of human behavior, but as a feminist — which will have positive or negative, but in any case powerful, connotations for readers" (29).

To develop your response to Tannen's essay, you might use one or more of the following critical reading strategies that are explained and illustrated in Appendix 1: *contextualizing*, *recognizing emotional manipulation*, and *judging the writer's credibility*.

Read to Analyze Assumptions

Reread Tannen's explanatory essay, and write a paragraph or two exploring one or more of the assumptions you find in the text. The following suggestions may help:

- **assumptions about biology and evidence.** Tannen is a linguist and therefore looks at "markers" through a linguist's eyes. For example, she provides a comparison to word forms that are "unmarked" and "marked" — such as the present and past forms of a verb and the plural form of a noun — to help her readers understand the concept of being "marked" (10). But near the end of her essay, she cites Ralph Fasold, who "bring[s] biological phenomena to bear on the question of linguistic marking" (24), and she explains that the "unmarked" gender should really be female rather than male. To think critically about the assumptions behind these decisions by Tannen, ask yourself: Why do you think she steps out of her field of expertise to support her thesis that women in our culture are marked and men are not? Does she assume that biologically based evidence will be particularly convincing to readers in our culture, or is there perhaps another reason she brings in Fasold's theories? If so, what might that reason be?

- **assumptions about the effects of being "marked."** In her final paragraph, Tannen says she feels "sad" that "women didn't have the freedom to be unmarked. . . . Some days you just want to get dressed and go about your business. But if you're a woman, you can't, because there is no unmarked woman" (34). Clearly she assumes that being "marked" is a burden. To think critically about this assumption, ask yourself: Do you share it, or can you think of ways in which being unmarked might be limiting or perhaps boring — or being marked could be liberating or creative? Examine Tannen's conclusions and your own in light of how your culture shapes your views of being marked or unmarked.

To probe assumptions more deeply, you might use one or more of the following critical reading strategies that are explained and illustrated in Appendix 1: *reflecting on challenges to your beliefs and values* and *looking for patterns of opposition.*

READING LIKE A WRITER
ENGAGING READERS' INTEREST

Explanatory writing aimed at nonspecialist readers usually makes an effort to engage those readers' interest in the information offered. David Quammen, for example, writing for a popular magazine, exerts himself to be engaging, even entertaining. Also writing for a magazine read by an educated but nonspecialist audience, Tannen likewise attempts to engage and hold her readers' interest. Like Quammen, she weaves these attempts to engage readers into the flow of information. While they are not separate from the information — for information itself, even dryly presented, can interest readers — direct attempts to engage are nevertheless a recognizable feature of Tannen's explanatory essay. For example, she opens the essay in an inviting way, with several intriguing descriptions, which later serve as examples of the concept. In addition, she adopts an informal conversational tone by using the first-person pronoun *I*, and she comments on her own thinking process.

Analyze

1. *Reread* paragraphs 1 to 8, and *look for* places where you are aware of Tannen's tone or voice.

2. *Skim* the rest of the essay, focusing on paragraphs 13 to 16, 21, 24, and 29 to 34, where Tannen uses the first-person *I* or other conversational devices, such as "Take the men's hair styles" as an opener for paragraph 13. *Make notes* about these devices and their effect on you as a reader.

Write

Write several sentences describing Tannen's tone and some of the strategies she uses to create it. *Give examples* from the reading to illustrate your analysis.

CONSIDERING IDEAS FOR YOUR OWN WRITING

If you are taking a course concerned with language and society, you might want to learn about and then explain another linguistic concept, such as semantics, language acquisition, connotation, or discourse community; or a semiotic concept, such as signification, code, iconography, ideology, or popular culture. Related fields with interesting concepts to learn and write about are gender studies and sociology. Gender studies is concerned with such concepts as gender, femininity, masculinity, identity formation, objectification, intersubjectivity, nonsexist language, androgyny, domesticity, patriarchy, and the construction of desire. Sociology studies group dynamics and social patterns using such concepts as socialization, the family, role model, community, cohort, social stratification, positivism, dysfunctional families, and status.

BETH L. BAILEY

Dating

Beth L. Bailey (b. 1957) is professor of history at Temple Univer-
sity. She has also taught at Barnard College, at the University of New
Mexico, and at the University of Indonesia. Bailey has written several
scholarly books on nineteenth- and twentieth-century American
culture, including Sex in the Heartland *(1999) and* A History of
Our Time *(2003). She has also edited, with David Farber,* The
Columbia Guide to America in the 1960s *(2001) and* America in
the Seventies *(2004). "Dating" comes from Bailey's first book,* From
Front Porch to Back Seat: Courtship in Twentieth-Century America *(1988).*

Bailey tells us that she first became interested in studying courtship
attitudes and behavior when, as a college senior, she appeared on a
television talk show to defend coed dorms, which were then relatively
new and controversial. She was surprised when many people in the
audience objected to coed dorms not on moral grounds but out of fear
that too much intimacy between young men and women would has-
ten "the dissolution of the dating system and the death of romance."

Before you read Bailey's historical explanation of dating, think
about the attitudes and behavior of people your own age in regard to
courtship and romance. Note how Bailey uses the features of explana-
tory writing, including integrating sources smoothly and using
appropriate explanatory strategies, such as defining, comparing
and contrasting, illustrating, and reporting causes or effects.

One day, the 1920s story goes, a young man asked a city girl if he   1
might call on her (Black, 1924, p. 340). We know nothing else
about the man or the girl—only that, when he arrived, she had her
hat on. Not much of a story to us, but any American born before
1910 would have gotten the punch line. "She had her hat on": those
five words were rich in meaning to early twentieth-century Americans. The hat signaled that she expected to leave the house. He
came on a "call," expecting to be received in her family's parlor, to
talk, to meet her mother, perhaps to have some refreshments or to
listen to her play the piano. She expected a "date," to be taken "out"
somewhere and entertained. He ended up spending four weeks'
savings fulfilling her expectations.

In the early twentieth century this new style of courtship, dat-   2
ing, had begun to supplant the old. Born primarily of the limits
and opportunities of urban life, dating had almost completely
replaced the old system of calling by the mid-1920s—and, in so
doing, had transformed American courtship. Dating moved
courtship into the public world, relocating it from family parlors

and community events to restaurants, theaters, and dance halls. At the same time, it removed couples from the implied supervision of the private sphere—from the watchful eyes of family and local community—to the anonymity of the public sphere. Courtship among strangers offered couples new freedom. But access to the public world of the city required money. One had to buy entertainment, or even access to a place to sit and talk. Money—men's money—became the basis of the dating system and, thus, of courtship. This new dating system, as it shifted courtship from the private to the public sphere and increasingly centered around money, fundamentally altered the balance of power between men and women in courtship.

The transition from calling to dating was as complete as it was   3
fundamental. By the 1950s and 1960s, social scientists who studied American courtship found it necessary to remind the American public that dating was a "recent American innovation and not a traditional or universal custom" (Cavin, as cited in "Some," 1961, p. 125). Some of the many commentators who wrote about courtship believed dating was the best thing that had ever happened to relations between the sexes; others blamed the dating system for all the problems of American youth and American marriage. But virtually everyone portrayed the system dating replaced as infinitely simpler, sweeter, more innocent, and more graceful. Hardheaded social scientists waxed sentimental about the "horse-and-buggy days," when a young man's offer of a ride home from church was tantamount to a proposal and when young men came calling in the evenings and courtship took place safely within the warm bosom of the family. "The courtship which grew out of the sturdy social roots [of the nineteenth century]," one author wrote, "comes through to us for what it was—a gracious ritual, with clearly defined roles for man and woman, in which everyone knew the measured music and the steps" (Moss, 1963, p. 151).

Certainly a less idealized version of this model of courtship had   4
existed in America, but it was not this model that dating was supplanting. Although only about 45 percent of Americans lived in urban areas by 1910, few of them were so untouched by the sweeping changes of the late nineteenth century that they could live that dream of rural simplicity. Conventions of courtship at that time were not set by simple yeoman farmers and their families but by the rising middle class, often in imitation of the ways of "society." . . .

The call itself was a complicated event. A myriad of rules gov-   5
erned everything: the proper amount of time between invitation and visit (a fortnight or less); whether or not refreshments should

be served (not if one belonged to a fashionable or semi-fashionable circle, but outside of "smart" groups in cities like New York and Boston, girls *might* serve iced drinks with little cakes or tiny cups of coffee or hot chocolate and sandwiches); chaperonage (the first call must be made on daughter and mother, but excessive chaperonage would indicate to the man that his attentions were unwelcome); appropriate topics of conversation (the man's interests, but never too personal); how leave should be taken (on no account should the woman "accompany [her caller] to the door nor stand talking while he struggles into his coat") ("Lady," 1904, p. 255).

Each of these "measured steps," as the mid-twentieth century author nostalgically called them, was a test of suitability, breeding, and background. Advice columns and etiquette books emphasized that these were the manners of any "well-bred" person — and conversely implied that deviations revealed a lack of breeding. However, around the turn of the century, many people who did lack this narrow "breeding" aspired to politeness. Advice columns in women's magazines regularly printed questions from "Country Girl" and "Ignoramus" on the fine points of calling etiquette. Young men must have felt the pressure of girls' expectations, for they wrote to the same advisers with questions about calling. In 1907, *Harper's Bazaar* ran a major article titled "Etiquette for Men," explaining the ins and outs of the calling system (Hall, 1907, pp. 1095–97). In the first decade of the twentieth century, this rigid system of calling was the convention not only of the "respectable" but also of those who aspired to respectability.

At the same time, however, the new system of dating was emerging. By the mid-1910s, the word *date* had entered the vocabulary of the middle-class public. In 1914, the *Ladies' Home Journal*, a bastion of middle-class respectability, used the term (safely enclosed in quotation marks but with no explanation of its meaning) several times. The word was always spoken by that exotica, the college sorority girl—a character marginal in her exoticness but nevertheless a solid product of the middle class. "One beautiful evening of the spring term," one such article begins, "when I was a college girl of eighteen, the boy whom, because of his popularity in every phase of college life, I had been proud gradually to allow the monopoly of my 'dates,' took me unexpectedly into his arms. As he kissed me impetuously I was glad, from the bottom of my heart, for the training of that mother who had taught me to hold myself aloof from all personal familiarities of boys and men" ("How," 1914, p. 9).

Sugarcoated with a tribute to motherhood and virtue, the dates—and the kiss—were unmistakably presented for a middle-class audience. By 1924, ten years later, when the story of the unfortunate young man who went to call on the city girl was current, dating had essentially replaced calling in middle-class culture. The knowing smiles of the story's listeners had probably started with the word *call*—and not every hearer would have been sympathetic to the man's plight. By 1924, he really should have known better. . . .

Dating, which to the privileged and protected would seem a system of increased freedom and possibility, stemmed originally from the lack of opportunities. Calling, or even just visiting, was not a practicable system for young people whose families lived crowded into one or two rooms. For even the more established or independent working-class girls, the parlor and the piano often simply didn't exist. Some "factory girls" struggled to find a way to receive callers. The *Ladies' Home Journal* approvingly reported the case of six girls, workers in a box factory, who had formed a club and pooled part of their wages to pay the "janitress of a tenement house" to let them use her front room two evenings a week. It had a piano. One of the girls explained their system: "We ask the boys to come when they like and spend the evening. We haven't any place at home to see them, and I hate seeing them on the street" (Preston, 1907, p. 31).

Many other working girls, however, couldn't have done this even had they wanted to. They had no extra wages to pool, or they had no notions of middle-class respectability. Some, especially girls of ethnic families, were kept secluded—chaperoned according to the customs of the old country. But many others fled the squalor, drabness, and crowdedness of their homes to seek amusement and intimacy elsewhere. And a "good time" increasingly became identified with public places and commercial amusements, making young women whose wages would not even cover the necessities of life dependent on men's "treats" (Peiss, 1986, pp. 51–52, 75). Still, many poor and working-class couples did not so much escape from the home as they were pushed from it.

These couples courted on the streets, sometimes at cheap dance halls or eventually at the movies. These were not respectable places, and women could enter them only so far as they, themselves, were not considered respectable. Respectable young women did, of course, enter the public world, but their excursions into the public were cushioned. Public courtship of middle-class and upper-class youth was at least *supposed* to be chaperoned; those with money and social position went to private dances with carefully controlled guest lists, to theater parties where they were a private group within the public. As rebels would soon complain, the supervision of society made the private parlor seem almost free by contrast. Women who were not respectable did have relative freedom of action—but the trade-off was not necessarily a happy one for them.

The negative factors were important, but dating rose equally   12
from the possibilities offered by urban life. Privileged youth, as Lewis Erenberg shows in his study of New York nightlife, came to see the possibility of privacy in the anonymous public, in the excitement and freedom the city offered (1981, pp. 60–87, 139–42). They looked to lower-class models of freedom—to those beyond the constraints of respectability. As a society girl informed the readers of the *Ladies' Home Journal* in 1914: "Nowadays it is considered 'smart' to go to the low order of dance halls, and not only be a looker-on, but also to dance among all sorts and conditions of men and women. . . . Nowadays when we enter a restaurant and dance place it is hard to know who is who" ("A Girl," 1914, p. 7). In 1907, the same magazine had warned unmarried women never to go alone to a "public restaurant" with any man, even a relative. There was no impropriety in the act, the adviser had conceded, but it still "lays [women] open to misunderstanding and to being classed with women of undesirable reputation by the strangers present" (Kingsland, May 1907, p. 48). Rebellious and adventurous young people sought that confusion, and the gradual loosening of proprieties they engendered helped to change courtship. Young men and women went out into the world *together*, enjoying a new kind of companionship and the intimacy of a new kind of freedom from adult supervision.

The new freedom that led to dating came from other sources as   13
well. Many more serious (and certainly respectable) young women were taking advantage of opportunities to enter the public world— going to college, taking jobs, entering and creating new urban professions. Women who belonged to the public world by day began to demand fuller access to the public world in general. . . .

Between 1890 and 1925, dating—in practice and in name—   14
had gradually, almost imperceptibly, become a universal custom in America. By the 1930s it had transcended its origins: Middle America associated dating with neither upper-class rebellion nor the urban lower classes. The rise of dating was usually explained, quite simply, by the invention of the automobile. Cars had given youth mobility and privacy, and so had brought about the system. This explanation—perhaps not consciously but definitely not coincidentally—revised history. The automobile certainly contributed to the rise of dating as a *national* practice, especially in rural and suburban areas, but it was simply accelerating and

extending a process already well under way. Once its origins were located firmly in Middle America, however, and not in the extremes of urban upper- and lower-class life, dating had become an American institution.

Dating not only transformed the outward modes and conventions of American courtship, it also changed the distribution of control and power in courtship. One change was generational: the dating system lessened parental control and gave young men and women more freedom. The dating system also shifted power from women to men. Calling, either as a simple visit or as the elaborate late nineteenth-century ritual, gave women a large portion of control. First of all, courtship took place within the girl's home—in women's "sphere," as it was called in the nineteenth century—or at entertainments largely devised and presided over by women. Dating moved courtship out of the home and into man's sphere—the world outside the home. Female controls and conventions lost much of their power outside women's sphere. And while many of the conventions of female propriety were restrictive and repressive, they had allowed women (young women and their mothers) a great deal of immediate control over courtship. The transfer of spheres thoroughly undercut that control. 15

Second, in the calling system, the woman took the initiative. Etiquette books and columns were adamant on that point: it was the "girl's privilege" to ask a young man to call. Furthermore, it was highly improper for the man to take the initiative. In 1909 a young man wrote to the *Ladies' Home Journal* adviser asking, "May I call upon a young woman whom I greatly admire, although she had not given me the permission? Would she be flattered at my eagerness, even to the setting aside of conventions, or would she think me impertinent?" Mrs. Kingsland replied: "I think that you would risk her just displeasure and frustrate your object of finding favor with her." Softening the prohibition, she then suggested an invitation might be secured through a mutual friend (Kingsland, 1909, p. 58). . . . 16

Contrast these strictures with advice on dating etiquette from the 1940s and 1950s: An advice book for men and women warns that "girls who [try] to usurp the right of boys to choose their own dates" will "ruin a good dating career. . . . Fair or not, it is the way of life. From the Stone Age, when men chased and captured their women, comes the yen of a boy to do the pursuing. You will control your impatience, therefore, and respect the time-honored custom of boys to take the first step" (Richmond, 1958, p. 11). . . . 17

This absolute reversal of roles almost necessarily accompanied courtship's move from woman's sphere to man's sphere. Although 18 the convention-setters commended the custom of woman's initiative because it allowed greater exclusivity (it might be "difficult for a girl to refuse the permission to call, no matter how unwelcome or unsuitable an acquaintance of the man might be"), the custom was based on a broader principle of etiquette (Hart and Brown, 1944, p. 89). The host or hostess issued any invitation; the guest did not invite himself or herself. An invitation to call was an invitation to visit in a woman's home.

An invitation to go out on a date, on the other hand, was an invitation into man's world—not simply because dating took place in the public sphere (commonly defined as belonging to men), though that was part of it, but because dating moved courtship into the world of the economy. Money—men's money—was at the center of the dating system. Thus, on two counts, men became the hosts and assumed the control that came with that position. 19

There was some confusion caused by this reversal of initiative, especially during the twenty years or so when going out and calling coexisted as systems. (The unfortunate young man in the apocryphal story, for example, had asked the city girl if he might call on her, so perhaps she was conventionally correct to assume he meant to play the host.) Confusions generally were sorted out around the issue of money. One young woman, "Henrietta L.," wrote to the *Ladies' Home Journal* to inquire whether a girl might "suggest to a friend going to any entertainment or place of amusement where there will be any expense to the young man." The reply: "Never, under any circumstances." The adviser explained that the invitation to go out must "always" come from the man, for he was the one "responsible for the expense" (Kingsland, Oct. 1907, p. 60). This same adviser insisted that the woman must "always" invite the man to call; clearly she realized that money was the central issue. 20

The centrality of money in dating had serious implications for courtship. Not only did money shift control and initiative to men by making them the "hosts," it led contemporaries to see dating as a system of exchange best understood through economic analogies or as an economic system pure and simple. Of course, people did recognize in marriage a similar economic dimension—the man undertakes to support his wife in exchange for her filling various roles important to him—but marriage was a permanent relationship. Dating was situational, with no long-term commitments implied, and when a man, in a highly visible ritual, spent money on a woman in public, it seemed much more clearly an economic act. 21

In fact, the term *date* was associated with the direct economic exchange of prostitution at an early time. A prostitute called 22

"Maimie," in letters written to a middle-class benefactor/friend in the late nineteenth century, described how men made "dates" with her (Peiss, 1986, p. 54). And a former waitress turned prostitute described the process to the Illinois Senate Committee on Vice this way: "You wait on a man and he smiles at you. You see a chance to get a tip and you smile back. Next day he returns and you try harder than ever to please him. Then right away he wants to make a date, and offer you money and presents if you'll be a good fellow and go out with him" (Rosen, 1982, p. 151). These men, quite clearly, were buying sexual favors—but the occasion of the exchange was called a "date."

Courtship in America had always turned somewhat on money 23 (or background). A poor clerk or stockyards worker would not have called upon the daughter of a well-off family, and men were expected to be economically secure before they married. But in the dating system money entered directly into the relationship between a man and a woman as the symbolic currency of exchange in even casual dating.

Dating, like prostitution, made access to women directly depen- 24 dent on money. . . . In dating, though, the exchange was less direct and less clear than in prostitution. One author, in 1924, made sense of it this way. In dating, he reasoned, a man is responsible for all expenses. The woman is responsible for nothing—she contributes only her company. Of course, the man contributes his company, too, but since he must "add money to balance the bargain" his company must be worth less than hers. Thus, according to this economic understanding, she is selling her company to him. In his eyes, dating didn't even involve an exchange; it was a direct purchase. The moral "subtleties" of a woman's position in dating, the author concluded, were complicated even further by the fact that young men, "discovering that she must be bought, [like] to buy her when [they happen] to have the money" (Black, 1924, p. 342).

Yet another young man, the same year, publicly called a halt to 25 such "promiscuous buying." Writing anonymously (for good reason) in *American Magazine*, the author declared a "one-man buyer's strike." This man estimated that, as a "buyer of feminine companionship" for the previous five years, he had "invested" about $20 a week—a grand total of over $5,000. Finally, he wrote, he had realized that "there is a point at which any commodity— even such a delightful commodity as feminine companionship— costs more than it is worth" ("Too-high," 1924, pp. 27, 145–50). The commodity he had bought with his $5,000 had been priced beyond its "real value" and he had had enough. This man said "enough" not out of principle, not because he rejected the implications of the economic model of courtship, but because he felt he wasn't receiving value for money.

In . . . these economic analyses, the men are complaining about the new dating system, lamenting the passing of the mythic good old days when "a man without a quarter in his pocket could call on a girl and not be embarrassed," the days before a woman had to be "bought" ("Too-high," 1924, pp. 145–50). In recognizing so clearly the economic model on which dating operated, they also clearly saw that the model was a bad one — in purely economic terms. The exchange was not equitable; the commodity was overpriced. Men were operating at a loss.

Here, however, they didn't understand their model completely. True, the equation (male companionship plus money equals female companionship) was imbalanced. But what men were buying in the dating system was not just female companionship, not just entertainment — but power. Money purchased obligation; money purchased inequality; money purchased control.

The conventions that grew up to govern dating codified women's inequality and ratified men's power. Men asked women out; women were condemned as "aggressive" if they expressed interest in a man too directly. Men paid for everything, but often with the implication that women "owed" sexual favors in return. The dating system required men always to assume control, and women to act as men's dependents.

Yet women were not without power in the system, and they were willing to contest men with their "feminine" power. Much of the public discourse on courtship in twentieth-century America was concerned with this contestation. Thousands of sources chronicled the struggles of, and between, men and women — struggles mediated by the "experts" and arbiters of convention — to create a balance of power, to gain or retain control of the dating system. These struggles, played out most clearly in the fields of sex, science, and etiquette, made ever more explicit the complicated relations between men and women in a changing society.

References

Black, A. (1924, August). Is the young person coming back? *Harper's*, 340, 342.

Erenberg, L. (1981). *Steppin' out*. Westport, Conn.: Greenwood Press.

A Girl. (1914, July). Believe me. *Ladies' Home Journal*, 7.

Hall, F. H. (1907, November). Etiquette for men. *Harper's Bazaar*, 1095–97.

Hart, S., & Brown, L. (1944). *How to get your man and hold him*. New York: New Power Publications.

How may a girl know? (1914, January). *Ladies' Home Journal*, 9.

Kingsland. (1907, May). *Ladies' Home Journal*, 48.

———. (1907, October). *Ladies' Home Journal*, 60.

———. (1909, May). *Ladies' Home Journal*, 58.

Lady from Philadelphia. (1904, February). *Ladies' Home Journal*, 255.

Moss, A. (1963, April). Whatever happened to courtship? *Mademoiselle*, 151.

Peiss, K. (1986). *Cheap amusements: Working women and leisure in turn-of-the-century New York*. Philadelphia: Temple University Press.

Preston, A. (1907, February). After business hours — what? *Ladies' Home Journal*, 31.

Richmond, C. (1958). *Handbook of dating*. Philadelphia: Westminster Press.

Rosen, R. (1982). *The lost sisterhood: Prostitution in America, 1900–1918*. Baltimore: Johns Hopkins University Press, 1982.

Some expert opinions on dating. (1961, August). *McCall's*, 125.

Too-high cost of courting. (1924, September). *American Magazine*, 27, 145–50.

READING FOR MEANING

This section presents three activities that will help you reread Bailey's explanatory essay with a critical eye. Done in sequence, these activities lead you from a basic understanding of the selection to a more personal response to it and finally to an analysis that deepens your understanding and critical thinking about what you are reading.

Read to Comprehend

Reread the selection, and write a few sentences about the differences between calling and dating as explained in Bailey's essay. The following definitions may help you understand Bailey's vocabulary:

supplant (paragraph 2): to replace (one thing) by something else.

chaperonage (5): an adult presence at an activity of young people.

propriety (15): behavior considered proper or respectable.

arbiters (29): those who have the power to judge or decide something.

Identify three or more additional words that you don't understand, and find the best definitions from the dictionary that work with their context.

To expand your understanding of this reading, you might use one or more of the following critical reading strategies that are explained and illustrated in Appendix 1: *outlining*, *summarizing*, and *questioning to understand and remember*.

Read to Respond

Write several paragraphs exploring your initial thoughts and feelings about Bailey's explanatory essay. Focus on anything that stands out for you, perhaps because it resonates with your own experience or because you find a statement puzzling.

You might consider writing about the following:

- the contrasts between the dating system in the early decades of the twentieth century (as described by Bailey) and the courtship system you know today, connecting your contrasts to specific features of the early system;

- the role of advice columns and etiquette books in the past compared to today;

- the identification of a "good time" with "public places and commercial amusements" (paragraph 10), perhaps in relation to your own view of what constitutes a good time; or

- the "centrality of money in dating" (21).

To develop your response to Bailey's essay, you might use one or more of the following critical reading strategies that are explained and illustrated in Appendix 1: *contextualizing*, *recognizing emotional manipulation*, and *judging the writer's credibility*.

Read to Analyze Assumptions

Reread Bailey's explanatory essay, and write a paragraph or two exploring one or more of the assumptions you find in the text. The following suggestions may help:

- **assumptions about control in courtship.** Bailey notes that the transformation from calling to dating in the twentieth century "changed the distribution of control and power in courtship" (15). Under calling, she argues, women had control; under dating, men had control. To think critically about the assumptions in this reading related to control in courtship, ask yourself: To what extent do you agree with Bailey on this issue? Are there other power dynamics involved in calling or dating that she is ignoring? What assumptions about and rituals of courtship do you see in play in our current society, and where does the power lie now? What are the rules? Or are there no cultural assumptions and rules that govern courtship today? If so, who decides how to initiate intimacy?

- **assumptions about the nature of courtship.** Bailey looks at courtship and intimacy between the sexes from the perspective of power and economic relationships. To think critically about the assumptions behind this perspective, ask yourself: Are these the only or even the main factors involved in this situation? How do love, affection, physical chemistry, or even simple pleasure in companionship complicate the picture—either in the period Bailey is writing about or today?

- **assumptions about the media.** Throughout her essay, Bailey uses examples from magazines, journals, and manuals to support her assertions about "calling" and "dating." She seems to assume that the information in these publications reflects accurately the customs of the time, but she also suggests that it may have helped to bring about the *changes* in these customs. To think critically about the assumptions in this essay related to the media, ask yourself: If someone were to write about the rituals of courtship in early twenty-first-century America, what would be the best sources of information? How accurately do you think they would represent what actually happens in American culture? To what extent do media (such as magazine articles, television shows, or Web sites like MySpace or FaceBook) *create* cultural assumptions—about courtship or anything else—as well as reflect them?

To probe assumptions more deeply, you might use one or more of the following critical reading strategies that are explained and illustrated in Appendix 1: *reflecting on challenges to your beliefs and values* and *looking for patterns of opposition*.

READING LIKE A WRITER
EXPLAINING THROUGH COMPARISON/CONTRAST

One of the best ways of explaining something new is to relate it, through comparison or contrast, to something that is familiar or well known. A *comparison* points out similarities between items; a *contrast* points out differences. Sometimes writers use both comparison and contrast; sometimes they use only one or the other. Bailey uses comparison and contrast a little differently. She is not explaining something new to readers by relating it to something already known to them. Instead, she is explaining something already known—dating—by relating it to something that is unknown to most readers—calling, an earlier type of courtship. Since she is studying dating as a sociologist, this historical perspective enables her to consider the changing relationship between men and women and the things that it tells us about changing social and cultural expectations and practices.

Analyze

1. *Reread* paragraphs 15 to 19, and *put a line* under the sentences that assert the points of the contrast Bailey develops in these paragraphs. To get started, *underline* the first and last sentences in paragraph 15. Except for paragraph 17, you will find one or two sentences in the other paragraphs that assert the points.

2. *Examine closely* the other sentences to discover how Bailey develops or illustrates each of the points of the contrast between calling and dating.

Write

Write several sentences reporting what you have learned about how Bailey develops the contrast between calling and dating. *Give examples* from paragraphs

15 to 19 to support your explanation. *Write a few more sentences* evaluating how informative you find Bailey's contrast given your own knowledge of dating. What parts are least and most informative? What makes the most informative part so successful?

CONSIDERING IDEAS FOR YOUR OWN WRITING

Like Bailey, you might choose a concept that tells something about current or historical social values, behaviors, or attitudes. To look at changing attitudes toward immigration and assimilation, for example, you could write about the concept of the melting pot and the alternatives that have been suggested. Some related concepts you might consider are multiculturalism, race, ethnicity, masculinity or femininity, heterosexuality or homosexuality, and affirmative action.

CHIP HEATH AND DAN HEATH

Made to Stick: Why Some Ideas Survive and Others Die

Chip Heath (b. 1963) received his BS in industrial engineering from Texas A&M University and his PhD in psychology from Stanford University and is now a professor at Stanford's Graduate School of Business. Much of his research examines why certain ideas — ranging from urban legends to folk medical cures — survive and prosper in the "social marketplace" and others do not. These "naturally sticky" ideas, Heath has found, spread without external help in the form of marketing dollars, public relations assistance, or the attention of leaders. His scholarly writing has appeared in the Journal of Organizational Behavior, Quarterly Journal of Economics, Cognitive Psychology, *and many other prestigious academic journals. He also writes for publications not intended for specialists, such as* Scientific American, *the* Washington Post, *and* Psychology Today.*

Dan Heath, Chip's brother (b. 1973), who received his BA from the University of Texas at Austin and his MBA from Harvard Business School, is a consultant at Duke Corporate Education. He designs and develops training programs, serves as teacher and facilitator, and manages client relationships with companies such as Microsoft, Wal-Mart, and Dow. Dan also cofounded a company called Thinkwell that produces innovative new-media college textbooks.

In the following selection, an excerpt from the introduction to their book Made to Stick: Why Some Ideas Survive and Others Die *(2007), the Heath brothers examine the concept of "stickiness," defining it with lively anecdotes and then listing their six principles to make things "stick" in people's minds.*

Before reading the essay, think about how you remember things. Do you have certain rituals or patterns to help your memories "stick"? What are they, and why do you think they work (or don't work, if you have trouble remembering things)?

A friend of a friend of ours is a frequent business traveler. Let's call him Dave. Dave was recently in Atlantic City for an important meeting with clients. Afterward, he had some time to kill before his flight, so he went to a local bar for a drink. He'd just finished one drink when an attractive woman approached and asked if she could buy him another. He was surprised but flattered. Sure, he said. The woman walked to the bar and brought back two more drinks — one for her and one for him. He thanked her and took a sip. And that was the last thing he remembered.

Rather, that was the last thing he remembered until he woke up, disoriented, lying in a hotel bathtub, his body submerged in ice. He looked around frantically, trying to figure out where he was and how he got there. Then he spotted the note: *don't move. call 911.*

A cell phone rested on a small table beside the bathtub. He picked it up and called 911, his fingers numb and clumsy from the ice. The operator seemed oddly familiar with his situation. She said, "Sir, I want you to reach behind you, slowly and carefully. Is there a tube protruding from your lower back?"

Anxious, he felt around behind him. Sure enough, there was a tube. The operator said, "Sir, don't panic, but one of your kidneys has been harvested. There's a ring of organ thieves operating in this city, and they got to you. Paramedics are on their way. Don't move until they arrive."

You've just read one of the most successful urban legends of the past fifteen years. The first clue is the classic urban-legend opening: "A friend of a friend . . ." Have you ever noticed that our friends' friends have much more interesting lives than our friends themselves?

You've probably heard the Kidney Heist tale before. There are hundreds of versions in circulation, and all of them share a core of three elements: (1) the drugged drink, (2) the ice-filled bathtub, and (3) the kidney-theft punch line. One version features a married man who receives the drugged drink from a prostitute he has invited to his room in Las Vegas. It's a morality play with kidneys.

Imagine that you closed the book right now, took an hourlong break, then called a friend and told the story, without rereading it. Chances are you could tell it almost perfectly. You might forget that the traveler was in Atlantic City for "an important meeting with clients"—who cares about that? But you'd remember all the important stuff.

The Kidney Heist is a story that sticks. We understand it, we remember it, and we can retell it later. And if we believe it's true, it might change our behavior permanently—at least in terms of accepting drinks from attractive strangers.

Contrast the Kidney Heist story with this passage, drawn from a paper distributed by a nonprofit organization. "Comprehensive community building naturally lends itself to a return-on-investment rationale that can be modeled, drawing on existing practice," it begins, going on to argue that "[a] factor constraining the flow of resources to CCIs is that funders must often resort to targeting or categorical requirements in grant making to ensure accountability."

Imagine that you closed the book right now and took an hour-long break. In fact, don't even take a break; just call up a friend and retell that passage without rereading it. Good luck.

Is this a fair comparison—an urban legend to a cherry-picked bad passage? Of course not. But here's where things get interesting: Think of our two examples as two poles on a spectrum of memorability. . . .

11

Good ideas often have a hard time succeeding in the world. Yet the ridiculous Kidney Heist tale keeps circulating, with no resources whatsoever to support it.

12

Why? Is it simply because hijacked kidneys sell better than other topics? Or is it possible to make a true, worthwhile idea circulate as effectively as this false idea?

13

THE TRUTH ABOUT MOVIE POPCORN

Art Silverman stared at a bag of movie popcorn. It looked out of place sitting on his desk. His office had long since filled up with fake-butter fumes. Silverman knew, because of his organization's research, that the popcorn on his desk was unhealthy. Shockingly unhealthy, in fact. His job was to figure out a way to communicate this message to the unsuspecting moviegoers of America.

14

Silverman worked for the Center for Science in the Public Interest (CSPI), a nonprofit group that educates the public about nutrition. The CSPI sent bags of movie popcorn from a dozen theaters in three major cities to a lab for nutritional analysis. The results surprised everyone.

15

The United States Department of Agriculture (USDA) recommends that a normal diet contain no more than 20 grams of saturated fat each day. According to the lab results, the typical bag of popcorn had 37 grams.

16

The culprit was coconut oil, which theaters used to pop their popcorn. Coconut oil had some big advantages over other oils. It gave the popcorn a nice, silky texture, and released a more pleasant and natural aroma than the alternative oils. Unfortunately, as the lab results showed, coconut oil was also brimming with saturated fat.

17

The single serving of popcorn on Silverman's desk—a snack someone might scarf down between meals—had nearly two days' worth of saturated fat. And those 37 grams of saturated fat were packed into a medium-sized serving of popcorn. No doubt a decent sized bucket could have cleared triple digits.

18

The challenge, Silverman realized, was that few people know what "37 grams of saturated fat" means. Most of us don't memorize the USDA's daily nutrition recommendations. Is 37 grams good or bad? And even if we have an intuition that it's bad, we'd wonder if it was "bad bad" (like cigarettes) or "normal bad" (like a cookie or a milk shake).

19

Even the phrase "37 grams of saturated fat" by itself was enough   20
to cause most people's eyes to glaze over. "Saturated fat has zero
appeal," Silverman says. "It's dry, it's academic, who cares?" Silverman could have created some kind of visual comparison —
perhaps an advertisement comparing the amount of saturated fat
in the popcorn with the USDA's recommended daily allowance.
Think of a bar graph, with one of the bars stretching twice as high
as the other.

But that was too scientific somehow. Too rational. The amount   21
of fat in this popcorn was, in some sense, not rational. It was ludicrous. The CSPI needed a way to shape the message in a way that
fully communicated this ludicrousness.

Silverman came up with a solution.   22

CSPI called a press conference on September 27, 1992. Here's   23
the message it presented: "A medium-sized 'butter' popcorn at a
typical neighborhood movie theater contains more artery-clogging
fat than a bacon-and-eggs breakfast, a Big Mac and fries for lunch,
and a steak dinner with all the trimmings — combined!"

The folks at CSPI didn't neglect the visuals — they laid out the   24
full buffet of greasy food for the television cameras. An entire day's
worth of unhealthy eating, displayed on a table. All that saturated
fat stuffed into a single bag of popcorn.

The story was an immediate sensation, featured on CBS, NBC,   25
ABC, and CNN. It made the front pages of *USA Today*, the *Los
Angeles Times*, and the *Washington Post*'s Style section. Leno and
Letterman cracked jokes about fat-soaked popcorn, and headline
writers trotted out some doozies: "Popcorn Gets an 'R' Rating,"
"Lights, Action, Cholesterol!" "Theater Popcorn Is Double Feature
of Fat."

The idea stuck. Moviegoers, repulsed by these findings, avoided   26
popcorn in droves. Sales plunged. The service staff at movie houses
grew accustomed to fielding questions about whether the popcorn
was popped in the "bad" oil. Soon after, most of the nation's biggest
theater chains — including United Artists, AMC, and Loews —
announced that they would stop using coconut oil.

ON STICKINESS

This is an idea success story. Even better, it's a truthful idea suc-   27
cess story. The people at CSPI knew something about the world
that they needed to share. They figured out a way to communicate the idea so that people would listen and care. And the idea
stuck. . . . The popcorn idea was a lot like the ideas that most of us
traffic in every day — ideas that are interesting but not sensational,
truthful but not mind-blowing, important but not "life-or-death."

Unless you're in advertising or public relations, you probably don't have many resources to back your ideas. You don't have a multimillion dollar ad budget or a team of professional spinners. Your ideas need to stand on their own merits.

We wrote this . . . to help you make your ideas stick. By "stick," we mean that your ideas are understood and remembered, and have a lasting impact—they change your audience's opinions or behavior.

28

At this point, it's worth asking why you'd need to make your ideas stick. After all, the vast majority of our daily communication doesn't require stickiness. "Pass the gravy" doesn't have to be memorable. When we tell our friends about our relationship problems, we're not trying to have a "lasting impact."

29

So not every idea is stick-worthy. When we ask people how often they need to make an idea stick, they tell us that the need arises between once a month and once a week, twelve to fifty-two times per year. For managers, these are "big ideas" about new strategic directions and guidelines for behavior. Teachers try to convey themes and conflicts and trends to their students—the kinds of themes and ways of thinking that will endure long after the individual factoids have faded. Columnists try to change readers' opinions on policy issues. Religious leaders try to share spiritual wisdom with their congregants. Nonprofit organizations try to persuade volunteers to contribute their time and donors to contribute their money to a worthy cause.

30

Given the importance of making ideas stick, it's surprising how little attention is paid to the subject. When we get advice on communicating, it often concerns our delivery: "Stand up straight, make eye contact, use appropriate hand gestures. Practice, practice, practice (but don't sound canned)." Sometimes we get advice about structure: "Tell 'em what you're going to tell 'em. Tell 'em, then tell 'em what you told 'em." Or "Start by getting their attention—tell a joke or a story."

31

Another genre concerns knowing your audience: "Know what your listeners care about, so you can tailor your communication to them." And, finally, there's the most common refrain in the realm of communication advice: Use repetition, repetition, repetition.

32

All of this advice has obvious merit, except, perhaps, for the emphasis on repetition. (If you have to tell someone the same thing ten times, the idea probably wasn't very well designed. No urban legend has to be repeated ten times.) But this set of advice has one glaring shortcoming: It doesn't help Art Silverman as he tries to figure out the best way to explain that movie popcorn is really unhealthful.

33

Silverman no doubt knows that he should make eye contact and practice. But what message is he supposed to practice? He knows

34

his audience—they're people who like popcorn and don't realize how unhealthy it is. So what message does he share with them? Complicating matters, Silverman knew that he wouldn't have the luxury of repetition—he had only one shot to make the media care about his story.

Or think about an elementary-school teacher. She knows her goal: to teach the material mandated by the state curriculum committee. She knows her audience: third graders with a range of knowledge and skills. She knows how to speak effectively—she's a virtuoso of posture and diction and eye contact. So the goal is clear, the audience is clear, and the format is clear. But the design of the message itself is far from clear. The biology students need to understand mitosis—okay, now what? There are an infinite number of ways to teach mitosis. Which way will stick? And how do you know in advance? . . .

In 2000, Malcolm Gladwell wrote a brilliant book called *The Tipping Point*, which examined the forces that cause social phenomena to "tip," or make the leap from small groups to big groups, the way contagious diseases spread rapidly once they infect a certain critical mass of people. Why did Hush Puppies experience a rebirth? Why did crime rates abruptly plummet in New York City? Why did the book *Divine Secrets of the Ya-Ya Sisterhood* catch on? *The Tipping Point* has three sections. The first addresses the need to get the right people, and the third addresses the need for the right context. The middle section of the book, "The Stickiness Factor," argues that innovations are more likely to tip when they're sticky. . . . We will identify the traits that make ideas sticky, a subject that was beyond the scope of Gladwell's book. Gladwell was interested in what makes social epidemics epidemic. Our interest is in how effective ideas are constructed—what makes some ideas stick and others disappear. . . .

WHO SPOILED HALLOWEEN?

In the 1960s and 1970s, the tradition of Halloween trick-or-treating came under attack. Rumors circulated about Halloween sadists who put razor blades in apples and booby-trapped pieces of candy. The rumors affected the Halloween tradition nationwide. Parents carefully examined their children's candy bags. Schools opened their doors at night so that kids could trick-or-treat in a safe environment. Hospitals volunteered to X-ray candy bags.

In 1985, an *ABC News* poll showed that 60 percent of parents worried that their children might be victimized. To this day, many parents warn their children not to eat any snacks that aren't prepackaged. This is a sad story: a family holiday sullied by bad people who, inexplicably, wish to harm children. But in 1985 the story took a strange twist. Researchers discovered something shocking about the candy-tampering epidemic: It was a myth.

The researchers, sociologists Joel Best and Gerald Horiuchi, studied every reported Halloween incident since 1958. They found no instances where strangers caused children life-threatening harm on Halloween by tampering with their candy.   39

Two children did die on Halloween, but their deaths weren't caused by strangers. A five-year-old boy found his uncle's heroin stash and overdosed. His relatives initially tried to cover their tracks by sprinkling heroin on his candy. In another case, a father, hoping to collect on an insurance settlement, caused the death of his own son by contaminating his candy with cyanide.   40

In other words, the best social science evidence reveals that taking candy from strangers is perfectly okay. It's your family you should worry about.   41

The candy-tampering story has changed the behavior of millions of parents over the past thirty years. Sadly, it has made neighbors suspicious of neighbors. It has even changed the laws of this country: Both California and New Jersey passed laws that carry special penalties for candy-tamperers. Why was this idea so successful?   42

SIX PRINCIPLES OF STICKY IDEAS

The Halloween-candy story is, in a sense, the evil twin of the CSPI story.   43

Both stories highlighted an unexpected danger in a common activity: eating Halloween candy and eating movie popcorn. Both stories called for simple action: examining your child's candy and avoiding movie popcorn. Both made use of vivid, concrete images that cling easily to memory: an apple with a buried razor blade and a table full of greasy foods. And both stories tapped into emotion: fear in the case of Halloween candy and disgust in the case of movie popcorn. The Kidney Heist, too, shares many of these traits. A highly unexpected outcome: a guy who stops for a drink and ends up one kidney short of a pair. A lot of concrete details: the ice-filled bathtub, the weird tube protruding from the lower back. Emotion: fear, disgust, suspicion.   44

We began to see the same themes, the same attributes, reflected in a wide range of successful ideas. What we found based on Chip's research—and by reviewing the research of dozens of folklorists, psychologists, educational researchers, political scientists, and proverb hunters—was that sticky ideas shared certain key traits. There is no "formula" for a sticky idea—we don't want to overstate   45 the case. But sticky ideas do draw from a common set of traits, which make them more likely to succeed.

It's like discussing the attributes of a great basketball player. You can be pretty sure that any great player has some subset of traits like height, speed, agility, power, and court sense. But you don't need all of these traits in order to be great: Some great guards are five feet ten and scrawny. And having all the traits doesn't guarantee greatness: No doubt there are plenty of slow, clumsy seven-footers. It's clear, though, that if you're on the neighborhood court, choosing your team from among strangers, you should probably take a gamble on the seven-foot dude.

Ideas work in much the same way. One skill we can learn is the ability to spot ideas that have "natural talent," like the seven-foot stranger. Later in the book, we'll discuss Subway's advertising campaign that focused on Jared, an obese college student who lost more than 200 pounds by eating Subway sandwiches every day. The campaign was a huge success. And it wasn't created by a Madison Avenue advertising agency; it started with a single store owner who had the good sense to spot an amazing story.

But here's where our basketball analogy breaks down: In the world of ideas, we can genetically engineer our players. We can create ideas with an eye to maximizing their stickiness.

As we pored over hundreds of sticky ideas, we saw, over and over, the same six principles at work.

Principle 1: Simplicity How do we find the essential core of our ideas? A successful defense lawyer says, "If you argue ten points, even if each is a good point, when they get back to the jury room they won't remember any." To strip an idea down to its core, we must be masters of exclusion. We must relentlessly prioritize. Saying something short is not the mission—sound bites are not the ideal. Proverbs are the ideal. We must create ideas that are both simple and profound. The Golden Rule is the ultimate model of simplicity: a one-sentence statement so profound that an individual could spend a lifetime learning to follow it.

Principle 2: Unexpectedness How do we get our audience to pay attention to our ideas, and how do we maintain their interest when we need time to get the ideas across? We need to violate people's expectations. We need to be counterintuitive. A bag of popcorn is as unhealthy as a whole day's worth of fatty foods! We can use surprise—an emotion whose function is to increase alertness and cause focus—to grab people's attention. But surprise doesn't last. For our idea to endure, we must generate interest and curiosity. How do you keep students engaged during the forty-eighth history class of the year? We can engage people's curiosity over a long period of time by systematically "opening gaps" in their knowledge — and then filling those gaps.

Principle 3: Concreteness How do we make our ideas clear? We must explain our ideas in terms of human actions, in terms of sensory information. This is where so much business communication goes awry. Mission statements, synergies, strategies, visions — they are often ambiguous to the point of being meaningless. Naturally sticky ideas are full of concrete images — ice-filled bathtubs, apples with razors — because our brains are wired to remember concrete data. In proverbs, abstract truths are often encoded in concrete language: "A bird in hand is worth two in the bush." Speaking concretely is the only way to ensure that our idea will mean the same thing to everyone in our audience.

52

Principle 4: Credibility How do we make people believe our ideas? When the former surgeon general C. Everett Koop talks about a public-health issue, most people accept his ideas without skepticism. But in most day-to-day situations we don't enjoy this authority. Sticky ideas have to carry their own credentials. We need ways to help people test our ideas for themselves — a "try before you buy" philosophy for the world of ideas. When we're trying to build a case for something, most of us instinctively grasp for hard numbers. But in many cases this is exactly the wrong approach. In the sole U.S. presidential debate in 1980 between Ronald Reagan and Jimmy Carter, Reagan could have cited innumerable statistics demonstrating the sluggishness of the economy. Instead, he asked a simple question that allowed voters to test for themselves: "Before you vote, ask yourself if you are better off today than you were four years ago."

53

Principle 5: Emotions How do we get people to care about our ideas? We make them feel something. In the case of movie popcorn, we make them feel disgusted by its unhealthiness. The statistic "37 grams" doesn't elicit any emotions. Research shows that people are more likely to make a charitable gift to a single needy individual than to an entire impoverished region. We are wired to feel things for people, not for abstractions. Sometimes the hard part is finding the right emotion to harness. For instance, it's difficult to get teenagers to quit smoking by instilling in them a fear of the consequences, but it's easier to get them to quit by tapping into their resentment of the duplicity of Big Tobacco.

54

Principle 6: Stories How do we get people to act on our ideas?   55
We tell stories. Firefighters naturally swap stories after every fire,
and by doing so they multiply their experience; after years of hearing stories, they have a richer, more complete mental catalog of
critical situations they might confront during a fire and the appropriate responses to those situations. Research shows that mentally
rehearsing a situation helps us perform better when we encounter
that situation in the physical environment. Similarly, hearing stories acts as a kind of mental flight simulator, preparing us to
respond more quickly and effectively.

Those are the six principles of successful ideas. To summarize,   56
here's our checklist for creating a successful idea: a Simple Unex-
pected Concrete Credentialed Emotional Story. A clever observer
will note that this sentence can be compacted into the acronym
SUCCESs. This is sheer coincidence, of course. (Okay, we admit,
SUCCESs is a little corny. We could have changed "Simple" to
"Core" and reordered a few letters. But, you have to admit,
CCUCES is less memorable.)

No special expertise is needed to apply these principles. There   57
are no licensed stickologists. Moreover, many of the principles
have a commonsense ring to them: Didn't most of us already have
the intuition that we should "be simple" and "use stories"? It's not
as though there's a powerful constituency for overcomplicated,
lifeless prose. But wait a minute. We claim that using these principles is easy. And most of them do seem relatively commonsensi-
cal. So why aren't we deluged with brilliantly designed sticky ideas?
Why is our life filled with more process memos than proverbs?

Sadly, there is a villain in our story. The villain is a natural psy-   58
chological tendency that consistently confounds our ability to
create ideas using these principles. It's called the Curse of Knowledge. . . . Once we know something, we find it hard to imagine
what it was like not to know it. Our knowledge has "cursed" us.
And it becomes difficult for us to share our knowledge with others,
because we can't readily re-create our listeners' state of mind. . . .
[T]o beat the Curse of Knowledge[, t]he six principles presented
earlier are your best weapons. They can be used as a kind of checklist. . . . But isn't the use of a template or a checklist confining?
Surely we're not arguing that a "color by numbers" approach will
yield more creative work than a blank-canvas approach?

Actually, yes, that's exactly what we're saying. If you want to   59
spread your ideas to other people, you should work within the
confines of the rules that have allowed other ideas to succeed over
time. You want to invent new ideas, not new rules.

READING FOR MEANING

This section presents three activities that will help you reread the Heaths' explanatory essay with a critical eye. Done in sequence, these activities lead you from a basic understanding of the selection to a more personal response to it and finally to an analysis that deepens your understanding and critical thinking about what you are reading.

Read to Comprehend

Reread the selection, and write a few sentences explaining the concept of *stickiness* and its significance. The following definitions may help you understand the Heaths' vocabulary:

ludicrous (paragraph 21): causing laughter by being ridiculous.

repulsed (26): driven back; rejected; refused.

proverb (45, 50): a short popular saying, usually of unknown and ancient origin, that expresses effectively some commonplace truth.

ambiguous (52): open to or having several possible meanings or interpretations.

Identify three or more additional words that you don't understand, and find the best definitions from the dictionary that work with their context.

Read to Respond

Write several paragraphs exploring your initial thoughts and feelings about the Heaths' explanatory essay. Focus on anything that stands out for you, perhaps because it resonates with your own experience or because you find a statement puzzling.

You might consider writing about the following:

- The way that you reacted when you first heard about any of these "sticky" ideas (before reading this essay)—the kidney heist, the tainted Halloween candy, the popcorn with saturated fat, or even the Reagan phrase about being better off now than four years ago—and why you think you had remembered or forgotten them;

- the common advice about memorable communication cited by the authors in paragraphs 31 and 32;

- your own experience in a situation where you wanted your ideas to be remembered and the ways in which it does or does not support the Heaths' advice;

- the effects on you of the headings in the essay;

- your response to the memory-aid device of SUCCESs (paragraph 56); or

- the authors' defense of their "template or checklist" approach to making ideas stick (paragraphs 58 and 59).

To develop your response to the Heaths' essay, you might use one or more of the following critical reading strategies that are explained and illustrated in Appendix 1: *contextualizing* and *recognizing emotional manipulation.*

Read to Analyze Assumptions

Reread the Heaths' explanatory essay, and write a paragraph or two exploring one or more of the assumptions you find in the text. The following suggestions may help:

- **assumptions about the value of ideas.** Throughout their essay, the Heaths mention the kinds of people who would benefit from having their ideas remembered, such as managers, teachers, columnists, religious leaders, non-profit organizations, folklorists, psychologists, educational researchers, political scientists, and proverb hunters. Yet the two "ideas" they talk about most are the kidney heist and the Halloween candy myths—ideas that are not particularly valuable to anyone (though they would be if they were true), but are remembered. To think critically about the assumptions in this essay related to the value of ideas, ask yourself: What assumptions are the authors making about which ideas are worth making "stick"? Why should you try to make *your* ideas "stick"? What effect do their assumptions about the value of your ideas have on you as a reader? To what extent do you share their assumptions?

- **assumptions about storytelling.** The final suggestion of the six offered by the authors to make an idea memorable is to "tell stories." Placing something last in a list often confers emphasis on it, but there are other indications throughout the essay that the Heaths assume storytelling is particularly effective as a memory aid. Note how often they tell a story to get their point across. To think critically about the assumptions in this essay related to storytelling, ask yourself: If you have ever used stories when you are writing, why did you use them? Was it for the same reasons the Heaths use them or for other purposes? How effective do you think storytelling is, and for what purposes would you urge people to tell stories?

READING LIKE A WRITER
DEVISING A READABLE PLAN

Think of a readable plan as a logical, interrelated sequence of topics. Each topic or main idea follows the preceding topic in a way that makes sense to readers. In addition, as you may have noticed in analyzing David Quammen's explanatory essay about parthenogenesis, readers appreciate a sequence of topics that is visibly cued by forecasting statements, topic sentences, transitions, and brief summaries. We see all of these cueing devices in the Heaths' essay. Note how they predict material by using the sequence "[t]he first . . . the third . . . [t]he middle" (paragraph 36) and also by providing headings for the six traits they have devised to make ideas stick (50–55). These important cueing strategies can do nothing to rescue an illogical sequence of topics, however. That is, they can only point out logical connections; they cannot *create* such connections. You can learn more about how writers devise readable plans by outlining their essays.

Analyze

1. *Skim* the essay, and *notice* how the headings and subheadings present the topics in a logical sequence. *Make an outline* of this system of heads and subheads.

2. *Examine* the authors' placement of headings, and *make notes* about where these headings are placed and the effects of them on the reader.

3. *Point* to any places where the writers forecast the topics that come next or summarize what came before.

Write

Write several sentences describing the main strategies that the Heaths use to construct a readable plan for their essay.

CONSIDERING IDEAS FOR YOUR OWN WRITING

The Heaths' explanation of "stickiness" mentions several kinds of professionals who have ideas that are worth remembering, and they point out that many people have between twelve and fifty-two significant ideas in any given year (paragraph 30). Think about what some of those ideas might be — such as "mitosis," which they say every third-grade biology student should know (35). Thumb through your college texts to get a sampling of ideas that have become important to various disciplines, and think about explaining one of those concepts — such as acculturation, ethnocentrism, or kinship in anthropology; social construction of identity, socialization, or stratification in sociology; torque, aerodynamics, or ergonomics in automotive design; and nanotechnology, stem-cell research, or genetic engineering in biology.

Explaining a Concept Online

The Web provides a space for writers to explain concepts using flexible, dynamic formats and for readers to find virtually any concept explained. Online dictionaries and encyclopedias join personal Web sites, blogs, corporate Web sites, and other places to provide explanations that may be intended for the general public or for specialized audiences. One public site is Wikipedia (www.wikipedia.com), an encyclopedia that is not refereed (judged by certified authorities in the field). Anyone can write or edit an entry, and contributors are not chosen on the basis of their credentials. Since the encyclopedia is available to anyone, though, errors and biases are usually quickly caught and corrected, and experts monitor the site for accuracy.

Because of Clayton Strothers's essay in this chapter, we looked up the term flow *on Wikipedia, where we found the following entry. You can see the history of the editing under the "history" tab on the top line.*

The marginal annotations point out the features and writing strategies that readers expect to find in any explanation of a concept. As you will see, online explanations share many of these features and strategies; they also sometimes include others that are unique to writing on the Web.

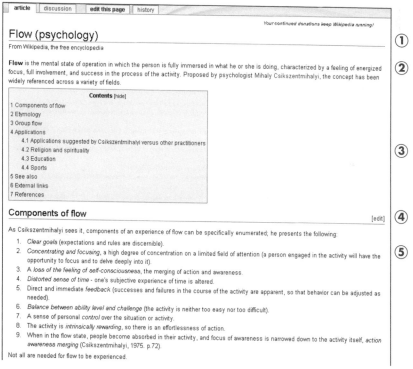

① Note that the concept is *categorized* into the field of psychology.

② The first explanatory strategy is a *definition* of *flow* that is attributed to the psychologist who first identified the concept.

③ This Contents box is a form of *devising a readable plan.* Each link takes readers to a part of the article's text.

④ Notice that each section of the entry has an "edit" link so that contributors can change the text if they want to.

⑤ This section provides a more detailed definition that divides flow into nine parts or components.

(6) Etymology   [edit]

Flow is so named because during Csikszentmihalyi's 1975 interviews several people described their 'flow' experiences using the metaphor of a current carrying them along. The psychological concept of *flow* as becoming absorbed in an activity is thus unrelated to the older phrase "to go with the flow" which means "to conform".

[. . .]

(7) Applications   [edit]

Applications suggested by Csikszentmihalyi versus other practitioners   [edit]

It is worth noting that only Csikszentmihalyi seems to have published suggestions for extrinsic applications of the Flow concept, such as design methods for playgrounds to elicit the Flow experience. Other practitioners of Csikszentmihalyi's Flow concept focus on intrinsic applications, such as spirituality, performance improvement or self-help. Reinterpretations of Csikszentmihalyi's Flow process exist to improve performance in areas as diverse as business [1] ⊞, sport psychology [2] ⊞, and standup comedy [3] ⊞.

[. . .]

(8) Sports   [edit]

The concept of "being in the zone" during an athletic performance fits within Csikszentmihalyi's description of the Flow experience, and theories and applications of "being in the zone" and its relationship with athletic competitive advantage are topics studied in the field of sport psychology.

The legendary soccer player Pele described his experience of being in the zone: "I felt a strange calmness. . . a kind of euphoria. I felt I could run all day without tiring, that I could dribble through any of their team or all of them, that I could almost pass through them physically. *[citation needed]*

(9) See also   [edit]

- Creativity
- Spirituality
- Imagination
- Hyperfocus
- Positive psychology

[. . .]

References   [edit]

- Csikszentmihalyi, Mihaly (1990). *Flow: The Psychology of Optimal Experience.* New York: Harper and Row. ISBN 0-06-092043-2
- Csikszentmihalyi, Mihaly (1996). *Creativity: Flow and the Psychology of Discovery and Invention.* New York: Harper Perennial. ISBN 0-06-092820-4
- Csikszentmihalyi, Mihaly (1998). *Finding Flow: The Psychology of Engagement With Everyday Life.* Basic Books. ISBN 0-465-02411-4 (a popular exposition emphasizing technique)
- Csikszentmihalyi, Mihaly (2003). *Good Business: Leadership, Flow, and the Making of Meaning.* New York: Penguin Books. ISBN 0-14-200409-X
- Langer, Ellen J. (1989). *Mindfulness.* Reading, Mass: Addison Wesley. ISBN 0-201-52341-8
- Nachmanovitch, Stephen (1990). *Free Play: Improvisation in Life and Art.* New York: Penguin-Putnam. ISBN 0-874-77631-7

Categories: Articles with unsourced statements since February 2007 | All articles with unsourced statements | Psychological theories | Educational psychology

(6) Apparently there was some controversy over whether the saying "go with the flow" came from Csikszentmihalyi's definition. You can see the controversy if you press the tab "discussion" at the top of the first page of the article.

(7) This section includes many links, an online-only form of *integrating sources smoothly.* These links take you to other Wikipedia entries that explain aspects of the concept or explain the linked terms. **(8)** These links are to other Wikipedia entries on topics related to flow. The next section, which is not shown, is a list of links to other online material about the topic, such as a personal narrative, a Google group, and a film.

(9) Wikipedia entries include a "References" section that lists works in which the contributors found the information they posted in the entry. **(10)** The date and time the entry was last changed help readers judge how up-to-date it is.

Analyze

1. *Find* an example of an online explanation of a concept.

2. *Check to see* which of the basic features of explanatory writing the example you found displays, such as laying out a readable plan, integrating sources smoothly, and engaging readers' interest. *Note* the writing strategies that are used in the explanation, such as defining, classifying, comparing and contrasting, narrating a process, illustrating, or reporting causes and effects.

3. Also *look for* any special online characteristics, such as links, informal language, or still or moving visuals.

Write

Write several sentences explaining the features of the online explanation of a concept that you found, including its significance.

A SPECIAL READING STRATEGY

Comparing and Contrasting Related Readings: Wikipedia's "Flow" and Clayton Strothers's "Flow"

Comparing and contrasting related readings is a special critical reading strategy useful both in reading for meaning and in reading like a writer. This strategy is particularly applicable when writers present similar subjects, as is the case in the explanatory readings in this chapter from Wikipedia (p. 267) and by Clayton Strothers (p. 278). Both readings seek to define the concept of flow. To compare and contrast these two readings, think about issues such as these:

- Compare these readings in terms of their explanatory strategies. What strategies do they share? How are their strategies different?

- Compare these readings in terms of their purposes and formats. Wikipedia is an online encyclopedia that seeks to provide information to the public, and its articles are organized according to standardized formats. Strothers, on the other hand, is defining flow for an assignment in college, which has to follow certain criteria but not a particular structure. How are the similarities and differences between these purposes and formats illustrated in the texts?

- Compare these readings in terms of how well they explain flow. Which one gives you the best sense of the concept, and why?

See Appendix 1 for detailed guidelines on using the comparing and contrasting related readings strategy.

LINH KIEU NGO

Cannibalism: It Still Exists

Linh Kieu Ngo wrote this essay when he was a first-year college student. In it, he explains a concept of importance in anthropology and of wide general interest — cannibalism, the eating of human flesh by other humans. Most Americans may know about survival cannibalism, but few may know about the importance historically of dietary and ritual cannibalism. Ngo explains all of these types in his essay.

Before you read, think about any examples of survival cannibalism you may have read about. Note also the strategies that Ngo employs for his explanation, such as classifying or dividing, comparing and contrasting, or others you find interesting.

Fifty-five Vietnamese refugees fled to Malaysia on a small fishing boat to escape communist rule in their country following the Vietnam War. During their escape attempt, the captain was shot by the coast guard. The boat and its passengers managed to outrun the coast guard to the open sea, but they had lost the only person who knew the way to Malaysia, the captain.

The men onboard tried to navigate the boat, but after a week fuel ran out and they drifted farther out to sea. Their supply of food and water was gone; people were starving, and some of the elderly were near death. The men managed to produce a small amount of drinking water by boiling salt water, using dispensable wood from the boat to create a small fire near the stern. They also tried to fish, but had little success.

A month went by, and the old and weak died. At first, the crew threw the dead overboard, but later, out of desperation, the crew turned to human flesh as a source of food. Some people vomited as they attempted to eat it, while others refused to resort to cannibalism and see the bodies of their loved ones sacrificed for food. Those who did not eat died of starvation, and their bodies in turn became food for others. Human flesh was cut out, washed in salt water, and hung to dry for preservation. The liquids inside the cranium were eaten to quench thirst. The livers, kidneys, heart, stomach, and intestines were boiled and eaten.

Five months passed before a whaling vessel discovered the drifting boat, looking like a graveyard of bones. There was only one survivor.

Cannibalism, the act of human beings eating human flesh (Sagan 2), has a long history and continues to hold interest and create controversy. Many books and research reports offer examples of cannibalism, but a few scholars have questioned whether cannibalism was ever practiced anywhere, except in cases of ensuring survival in times of famine or isolation (Askenasy 43–54). Recently, some scholars have tried to understand why people in the West have been so eager to attribute cannibalism to non-Westerners (Barker, Hulme, and Iversen). Cannibalism has long been a part of American popular culture. For example, Mark Twain's "Cannibalism in the Cars" tells a humorous story about cannibalism by well-to-do travelers on a train stranded in a snowstorm, and cannibalism is still a popular subject for jokes ("Cannibals").

If we assume there is some reality to the reports about cannibalism, how can we best understand this concept? Cannibalism can be broken down into two main categories: exocannibalism, the eating of outsiders or foreigners, and endocannibalism, the eating of members of one's own social group (Shipman 70). Within these categories are several functional types of cannibalism, three of the most common being survival cannibalism, dietary cannibalism, and religious and ritual cannibalism. 6

Survival cannibalism occurs when people trapped without food have to decide "whether to starve or eat fellow humans" (Shipman 70). In the case of the Vietnamese refugees, the crew and passengers on the boat ate human flesh to stay alive. They did not kill people to get human flesh for nourishment, but instead waited until the people had died. Even after human carcasses were sacrificed as food, the boat people ate only enough to survive. Another case of survival cannibalism occurred in 1945, when General Douglas MacArthur's forces cut supply lines to Japanese troops stationed in the Pacific Islands. In one incident, Japanese troops were reported to have sacrificed the Arapesh people of northeastern New Guinea for food in order to avoid death by starvation (Tuzin 63). The most famous example of survival cannibalism in American history comes from the diaries, letters, and interviews of survivors of the California-bound Donner Party, who in the winter of 1846 were snowbound in the Sierra Nevada Mountains for five months. Thirty-five of eighty-seven adults and children died, and some of them were eaten (Hart 116–17; Johnson). 7

Unlike survival cannibalism, in which human flesh is eaten as a last resort after a person has died, in dietary cannibalism, humans are purchased or trapped for food and then eaten as a part of a culture's traditions. In addition, survival cannibalism often involves people eating other people of the same origins, whereas dietary cannibalism usually involves people eating foreigners. 8

In the Miyanmin society of the west Sepik interior of Papua New Guinea, villagers do not value human flesh over that of pigs or marsupials because human flesh is part of their diet (Poole 17). 9

The Miyanmin people observe no differences in "gender, kinship, ritual status, and bodily substance"; they eat anyone, even their own dead. In this respect, then, they practice both endocannibalism and exocannibalism; and to ensure a constant supply of human flesh for food, they raid neighboring tribes and drag their victims back to their village to be eaten (Poole 11). Perhaps, in the history of this society, there was at one time a shortage of wild game to be hunted for food, and because people were more plentiful than fish, deer, rabbits, pigs, or cows, survival cannibalism was adopted as a last resort. Then, as their culture developed, the Miyanmin may have retained the practice of dietary cannibalism, which has endured as a part of their culture.

Similar to the Miyanmin, the people of the Leopard and Alligator societies in South America eat human flesh as part of their cultural tradition. Practicing dietary exocannibalism, the Leopard people hunt in groups, with one member wearing the skin of a leopard to conceal the face. They ambush their victims in the forest and carry their victims back to their village to be eaten. The Alligator people also hunt in groups, but they hide themselves under a canoelike submarine that resembles an alligator, then swim close to a fisherman's or trader's canoe to overturn it and catch their victims (MacCormack 54). 10

Religious or ritual cannibalism is different from survival and dietary cannibalism in that it has a ceremonial purpose rather than one of nourishment. Sometimes only a single victim is sacrificed in a ritual, while at other times many are sacrificed. For example, the Bangala tribe of the Congo River in central Africa honors a deceased chief or leader by purchasing, sacrificing, and feasting on slaves (Sagan 53). The number of slaves sacrificed is determined by how highly the tribe members revered the deceased leader. 11

Ritual cannibalism among South American Indians often serves as revenge for the dead. Like the Bangalas, some South American tribes kill their victims to be served as part of funeral rituals, with human sacrifices denoting that the deceased was held in high honor. Also like the Bangalas, these tribes use outsiders as victims. Unlike the Bangalas, however, the Indians sacrifice only one victim instead of many in a single ritual. For example, when a warrior of a tribe is killed in battle, the family of the warrior forces a victim to take the identity of the warrior. The family adorns the victim with the deceased warrior's belongings and may even force him to marry the deceased warrior's wives. But once the family believes the victim has assumed the spiritual identity of the deceased warrior, the family kills him. The children in the tribe soak their hands in the victim's blood to symbolize their revenge of the warrior's 12 death. Elderly women from the tribe drink the victim's blood and then cut up his body for roasting and eating (Sagan 53–54). By sacrificing a victim, the people of the tribe believe that the death of the warrior has been avenged and the soul of the deceased can rest in peace.

In the villages of certain African tribes, only a small part of a   13
dead body is used in ritual cannibalism. In these tribes, where the childbearing capacity of women is highly valued, women are obligated to eat small, raw fragments of genital parts during fertility rites. Elders of the tribe supervise this ritual to ensure that the women will be fertile. In the Bimin-Kuskusmin tribe, for instance, a widow eats a small, raw fragment of flesh from the penis of her deceased husband in order to enhance her future fertility and reproductive capacity. Similarly, a widower may eat a raw fragment of flesh from his deceased wife's vagina along with a piece of her bone marrow; by eating her flesh, he hopes to strengthen the fertility capacity of his daughters borne by his dead wife, and by eating her bone marrow, he honors her reproductive capacity. Also, when an elder woman of the village who has shown great reproductive capacity dies, her uterus and the interior parts of her vagina are eaten by other women who hope to further benefit from her reproductive power (Poole 16–17).

Members of developed societies in general practice none of these   14
forms of cannibalism, with the occasional exception of survival cannibalism when the only alternative is starvation. It is possible, however, that our distant-past ancestors were cannibals who through the eons turned away from the practice. We are, after all, descended from the same ancestors as the Miyanmin, the Alligator, and the Leopard people, and survival cannibalism shows that people are capable of eating human flesh when they have no other choice.

Works Cited

Askenasy, Hans. *Cannibalism: From Sacrifice to Survival.* Amherst, NY: Prometheus, 1994. Print.

Barker, Francis, Peter Hulme, and Margaret Iversen, eds. *Cannibalism and the New World.* Cambridge: Cambridge UP, 1998. Print.

Brown, Paula, and Donald Tuzin, eds. *The Ethnography of Cannibalism.* Washington: Society of Psychological Anthropology, 1983. Print.

"Cannibals." *Jokes and Funny Stories.* N.p., 2006. Web. 4 Apr. 2009.

Hart, James D. *A Companion to California.* Berkeley: U of California P, 1987. Print.

Johnson, Kristin. "New Light on the Donner Party." Kristin Johnson, 31 Jan. 2006. Web. 4 Apr. 2009.

MacCormack, Carol. "Human Leopard and Crocodile." Brown and Tuzin 54–55.

Poole, Fitz John Porter. "Cannibals, Tricksters, and Witches." Brown and Tuzin 11, 16–17.

Sagan, Eli. *Cannibalism*. New York: Harper, 1976. Print.

Shipman, Pat. "The Myths and Perturbing Realities of Cannibalism." *Discover* Mar. 1987: 70+. Print.

Tuzin, Donald. "Cannibalism and Arapesh Cosmology." Brown and Tuzin 61–63.

Twain, Mark. "Cannibalism in the Cars." *The Complete Short Stories of Mark Twain*. Ed. Charles Neider. New York: Doubleday, 1957. 9–16. Print.

READING FOR MEANING

This section presents three activities that will help you reread Ngo's explanatory essay with a critical eye. Done in sequence, these activities lead you from a basic understanding of the selection to a more personal response to it and finally to an analysis that deepens your understanding and critical thinking about what you are reading.

Read to Comprehend

Reread the selection, and write a few sentences briefly explaining the different types of cannibalism, according to Ngo. The following definitions may help you understand Ngo's vocabulary:

dispensable (paragraph 2): not essential.

kinship (9): connection by blood, marriage, or adoption; family relationship.

eons (14): indefinitely long periods of time; ages.

Find three or more additional words that you don't understand, and find the best definitions from the dictionary that work with their context.

To expand your understanding of this reading, you might use one or more of the following critical reading strategies that are explained and illustrated in Appendix 1: *paraphrasing* and *questioning to understand and remember*.

Read to Respond

Write several paragraphs exploring your initial thoughts and feelings about Ngo's explanatory essay. Focus on anything that stands out for you, perhaps because it resonates with your own experience or because you find a statement puzzling.

You might consider writing about the following:

- your response to the anecdotes about the Vietnamese refugees (paragraphs 1–4) and the Donner Party in California (7);

- your response to the idea that cannibalism may be performed for ceremonial or ritual purposes; or

- whether you think you would resort to cannibalism to survive.

To develop your response to Ngo's essay, you might use one or more of the following critical reading strategies that are explained and illustrated in Appendix 1: *recognizing emotional manipulation* and *judging the writer's credibility*.

Read to Analyze Assumptions

Reread Ngo's explanatory essay, and write a paragraph or two exploring one or more of the assumptions you find in the text. The following suggestions may help:

- **assumptions about origins of cultural practices.** Ngo speculates that the reason the Miyanmin practice both endo- and exocannibalism is that at one time they might have experienced shortages of wild game. They would have practiced cannibalism for survival then, and it may have remained in their culture as dietary cannibalism (paragraph 9). To think critically about such an assumption, ask yourself: Why do you think Ngo makes it? What other rituals do cultures practice based on needs that no longer exist?

- **assumptions about the dead.** Ngo discusses several tribes that practice cannibalism in some form to honor the dead or to take on the good traits of the dead (paragraphs 11–13). The people in these tribes believe that even a small portion of a human being can carry the meaning of the whole person. Many cultures and religions of the world practice a form of this belief, although they may substitute another substance to represent the human (bread as the body of Christ in communion, for example). Yet as Ngo reports, the practice of cannibalism, even of people who are already dead, is controversial (5). To think critically about the assumptions involved, ask yourself: Why does cannibalism create such controversy? What beliefs and values come into play among those who find cannibalism disgusting?

- **assumptions about "developed societies."** Ngo does not define "developed societies" (paragraph 14), so he must assume that readers know what he means. Many of the tribes he describes, though, might think our society is anything but "developed." To think critically about the assumptions in this essay related to "development," ask yourself: What might Western industrialized societies do that would make "undeveloped societies" uncomfortable? How do you feel about the assumptions behind the idea of societies' being "developed"?

To probe assumptions more deeply, you might use one or more of the following critical reading strategies that are explained and illustrated in Appendix 1: *reflecting on challenges to your beliefs and values*, and *looking for patterns of opposition*.

READING LIKE A WRITER
INTEGRATING SOURCES SMOOTHLY

When writers explain concepts to their readers, they nearly always rely in part on information gleaned from sources in a library or on the Internet. When they do so, they must acknowledge these sources. Within their essays, writers must find ways to integrate smoothly into their own sentences the information borrowed from each source and to acknowledge or cite each source. When you analyzed David Quammen's essay, you learned that writers rely on certain signal phrases and sentence structures to integrate quoted materials smoothly into their essays. Sometimes, however, writers do not quote a source but instead summarize or paraphrase it. (See Appendix 1, pp. 608–11, for examples of summarizing and paraphrasing.) When they do so, they may acknowledge the source of the summarized or paraphrased material through signal phrases or special sentence structures, or they may use a formal style of parenthetical citation. Ngo relies on both these strategies. (Ngo's parenthetical citations refer to sources in the works-cited list at the end of his essay.)

Analyze

1. In paragraphs 7 and 9, *notice* how Ngo sets up a sentence to integrate the quoted phrases.

2. *Put a check mark* in the margin by each instance of parenthetical citation in paragraphs 5, 6, and 9 to 13. *Notice* where these citations are located in Ngo's sentences and the different forms they take.

3. *Make notes* in the margin about similarities and differences you observe in Ngo's use of parenthetical citations.

Write

Write a few sentences explaining how Ngo integrates quoted phrases into his sentences and makes use of parenthetical citations. *Illustrate* your explanation with examples from the reading.

CONSIDERING IDEAS FOR YOUR OWN WRITING

Consider writing about some other well-established human taboo or practice, such as ostracism, incest, pedophilia, murder, circumcision, celibacy or virginity, caste systems, a particular religion's dietary restrictions, adultery, stealing, gourmandism, or divorce.

A SPECIAL READING STRATEGY

Summarizing

Summarizing, a potent reading-for-meaning strategy, is also a kind of writing you will encounter in your college classes and on the job. By rereading Ngo's essay on cannibalism with an eye toward finding its main ideas, you can do the groundwork for writing a summary of it. Taking the time to write a summary will help you remember what you have read and could help you explain to others the important ideas in Ngo's essay. For detailed guidelines on writing an extended summary, see Appendix 1 (pp. 608–10).

CLAYTON STROTHERS

Flow

Clayton Strothers wrote this essay for his freshman writing class at the University of California, Riverside. He explains the concept of flow, which he experienced and also researched.

As you read the essay, think about activities that give you pleasure, especially if they involve a form of work. Also think about whether Strothers explains the concept well enough for you to understand it even if you haven't experienced it. You may want to add your own annotations to the text, paying special attention to the features of explanatory writing, such as a readable plan, appropriate strategies, integrating sources smoothly, and engaging readers' interest.

To introduce his subject and *engage his readers,* Strothers uses two common strategies of writers explaining a concept—*narrating a story* and *explaining a process.* Notice how detailed he is, naming all the parts of the machine he is assembling.

It's Saturday morning. I stumble out of bed and put on the oldest and dirtiest clothes I can find. I walk into the garage, which I affectionately call the "garoffice," and sit in my lawn chair to survey the work ahead of me. I see a cylinder block on the stand, a pair of cylinder heads on the ground, an intake manifold, pistons, pushrods, rockers, a crankshaft, and all the other goodies that go along with a healthy new V8 engine. I begin work by prepping the bearings, checking clearances, and bolting pieces on. I fit the crank in place and begin bolting it in. I begin gapping and fitting the rings on all eight pistons, oiling the bearings as I go. It's a smooth process of picking up the part, checking the manual, bolting it into place, and checking the manual again to make sure it's correct. My fingers scrape against rough places on the block, but I don't notice. I get oil and dirt on my face, but I don't bother wiping it off.

Strothers gives these highlighted details to illustrate what flow does to us. He's so involved and focused that he doesn't notice pain, dirt, and hunger.

Once I'm finished, I take a sip from my soda and step back to look at what I have done. I am surprised at how fast the engine came together. I walk into the house to wash my hands for lunch. Once I step out of the garage and into the house, I suddenly become really hungry and have to go to the bathroom really badly. I look at the clock: it's almost 6 p.m.! Here I was thinking about lunch, and it's practically dinner time. I glance down at my hands, and it looks like I just had a fight with a cactus. My face probably looks like I was working in a coal mine all day. This type of thing always happens to me when I'm working on my car or doing anything that I like. Time flies, and nothing gets in my way. This phenomenon is known as *flow,* and it is experienced by everyone at one time or another.

In the last two sentences of this paragraph, Strothers names the concept he has been illustrating.

3   Mihaly Csikszentmihalyi has studied flow and has spent much of his time researching what makes people happiest and how flow affects their lives. Csikszentmihalyi is a professor of psychology at the University of Chicago and author of the book *Flow: The Psychology of Optimal Experience.* Flow can best be defined as "the state in which people are so involved in an activity that nothing else seems to matter; the experience itself is so enjoyable that people will do it even at great cost, for the sheer sake of doing it" (Csikszentmihalyi 4). When I was assembling my engine, it took so much of my concentration and focus that my hunger, the cuts on my hands, and my appearance didn't matter, and time seemed to pass at an incredible rate. Most athletes experience flow when they are performing well; this is often referred to as "being in the zone." Understanding the concept of flow is very easy; understanding when, where, and how flow happens takes a little more analysis.

4   Flow can occur during almost any activity and at any time of the day, but some activities are more likely to trigger flow than others. For example, sports are designed to trigger flow. They create challenges that require the competitors to focus completely on the task at hand. People are most likely to achieve flow when their skill level is equally matched with the level of challenge (Csikszentmihalyi 75). If we took Wayne Gretzky and matched him up against a ten-year-old, neither Gretzky nor the ten-year-old would achieve flow; Gretzky would probably be bored, and the boy would probably be frustrated. However, if we could put Gordie Howe and Gretzky on the ice together, they might both achieve flow. Just as Gretzky could be in flow during a championship hockey game, a little boy could be in flow at a Little League practice or a university student could be in flow while writing an essay. You may not be very skilled at an activity, but as long as your skill level is matched to the level of the challenge, you can achieve flow. But why do so many people strive to be in flow? Why do some people risk their lives to achieve flow, as ice climbers do when they scale sheer cliffs of ice? Can being in flow affect the way your body physically reacts to certain demands or even how your mind deals with problems?

Strothers begins the process of *integrating his sources smoothly.* He identifies the person who named the concept, provides information about him, and, with an informative signal phrase (highlighted), quotes his definition of *flow.*

To help readers understand his concept, Strothers compares flow to good athletic performance (highlighted), with which most people can identify. In the next sentence, he *devises a plan* for his essay: he will explain when, where, and how flow occurs.

Strothers illustrates with examples—in this case, sports—to show the optimum conditions for flow. Note that one example also shows when flow is *not* likely to occur. Such *contrasting* is another explanatory strategy.

Strothers poses three questions about flow that the reader might have been wondering about. This is a way to *devise a readable plan* and forecast what is coming.

Strothers uses a signal phrase (highlighted) to integrate his source smoothly.

In this section, Strothers employs *comparison and contrast* as an explanatory strategy, *engaging readers* by providing examples of situations that might have created flow for them and others that probably did not.

In paragraph 6, Strothers poses questions that interest him (highlighted). Had questions like these occurred to you as well?

Strothers devotes paragraphs 7 and 8 to his own experience of flow in a sport. Note how this personal example uses narration to *engage the reader.*

The first chapter in Csikszentmihalyi's book, "Happiness Revisited," helps answer the question of why people strive to be in flow. The simple but quite accurate answer is that flow makes people happy: "The best moments usually occur when a person's body or mind is stretched to its limits in a voluntary effort to accomplish something difficult and worthwhile" (Csikszentmihalyi 3). Think about the last time you watched TV because you had nothing else to do or when you relaxed from the time you woke up to the time you went to bed—how did you feel? Chances are you felt bored and tired, and you were thinking of something to do. Now think about the last time you scored a point in your favorite sport, broke a personal record, beat the twentieth level on your video game, or even the last time you spent hours writing an essay and received a good grade. How did you feel? You probably felt accomplished, energized, and happy. Even though at the time some of these experiences were painful, physically or mentally, in the long run it was worth it. Flow helps us overcome these great personal hurdles, and that is why so many people strive to achieve it.

Ever since I first heard of flow I have been interested in how it can affect the way your body and mind perform certain tasks. Does the simple fact of being in flow make you jump higher or run faster? Does being in flow make you smarter?

When I was ten years old, my hockey team was looking for a goalie. My coaches suited up all the players and shot the puck at each of them. Apparently, I was the best on my team at blocking those shots, so I became the team's goalie. I had no formal training, but I seemed to have a natural ability to stop the puck. Over the years, I honed my skills, and soon it became a personal obsession to stop the puck every time. Even though I concentrated while playing goalie, I didn't achieve flow until a few years into my hockey career. The first time I experienced flow wasn't during an important game but during a regular practice. We had been scrimmaging, and for the last play of the game my coach, who was a very skilled hockey player, joined the other team to try to score on me. I knew that my team's defense wasn't going to protect me well, and I needed to stop that puck.

8   Once the teams were established and the puck was dropped, I became extremely focused, almost as if someone had thrown a switch. I readjusted my armor and made the best blocking stance possible, focusing on where my glove and blocker were and trying to squat as low as I could. I was slightly in front of the goalie box, chewing on my mouth guard in anticipation. Once the coach got hold of the puck, I knew that was it. He charged down the ice, and sure enough it was a breakaway, one on one. I slowly backed up into my zone as he charged at me. Glaring through my face-mask I studied his movements, trying to anticipate how, when, and where he was going to fire the puck. He cranked his stick up and fired. The puck came fast and low, heading between my legs. I slammed my body onto my knees and laid my stick on the ground to block the puck, ricocheting it to the right of me. Before I could get back on my feet, he fired it again, and this time I threw myself to the right, where the puck hit my shoulder pad and bounced off. The coach had the puck again, but now I was laid out on the ground, leaving nearly the whole net open. He swung around in front of the net to shoot it over me, but at the same instant I spun myself around and stretched my glove-arm out to the center of the net. The coach raised his stick and launched the puck right into the safety of my glove. After the save, I completely collapsed, letting all of my muscles relax and slumping to the ground, and I started laughing. I had never made a save like that before, and even I was surprised. It felt like I was stronger and faster than ever, being able to throw my whole body from one side to another at any instant.

9   Did being in flow give me this super strength and speed? The answer is no. It's just that people don't use 100 percent of their physical abilities unless they are in fight-or-flight response or in flow. Flow isn't just an adrenaline rush but rather is a state in which the mind focuses all of its processing power on the challenge and nothing else.

Strothers again poses a question that his reader may have been wondering about, and then he answers it right away.

10   Flow is an important part of life for many people, whether they know it or not, and can many times be the key to happiness. There are some people who find happiness by visiting museums, reading books, writing, going to parties, or planning their next activities.

Strothers concludes with a summary and speculation about how flow leads to happiness.

Strothers ends with a paraphrase from the world's authority on the subject.

On the other hand, there are people who find true happiness sitting in their garages working on their favorite hobbies with nobody around. As Csikszentmihalyi said in his book, it doesn't matter *what* you spend your time doing but *how* you go about doing it.

READING FOR MEANING

Reading for meaning involves three activities:

- reading to comprehend,
- reading to respond, and
- reading to analyze assumptions.

Reread Strothers's essay, and then write a page or so explaining your understanding of its basic meaning or main point, a personal response you have to it, and one of its assumptions.

READING LIKE A WRITER

Writers of essays explaining concepts

- devise a readable plan,
- use appropriate explanatory strategies,
- integrate sources smoothly into the writing, and
- engage readers' interest.

Focus on one of these strategies in Strothers's essay, and analyze it carefully through close rereading and annotating. Then write several sentences explaining what you have learned, giving specific examples from the reading to illustrate your explanation. Add a few sentences evaluating how successfully Strothers uses the strategy to explain flow.

REVIEWING WHAT MAKES ESSAYS EXPLAINING CONCEPTS EFFECTIVE

In this chapter, you have been learning how to read essays explaining concepts for meaning and how to read them like a writer. Before going on to write an essay explaining a concept, pause here to review and contemplate what you have learned about the elements of effective concept explanations.

Analyze

  Choose one reading from this chapter that seems to you especially effective. Before rereading the selection, *jot down* one or two reasons you remember it as an example of good concept explanation.

  Reread your chosen selection, adding further annotations about what makes it a particularly successful example of concept explanation. *Consider* what the selection's purpose is and how well it achieves that purpose for its intended readers. (You can make an informed guess about the intended readers and their expectations by noting the publication source of the essay.) Then *focus* on how well the essay

- devises a readable plan,

- uses appropriate explanatory strategies,

- integrates sources smoothly into the writing, and

- engages readers' interest.

You can review all of these basic features in the Guide to Reading Essays Explaining Concepts (p. 217).

  Your instructor may ask you to complete this activity on your own or to work with a small group of other students who have chosen the same reading. If you work with others, allow enough time initially for all group members to reread the selection thoughtfully and to add their annotations. Then *discuss* as a group what makes the selection effective. *Take notes* on your discussion. One student in your group should then report to the class what the group has learned about the effectiveness of essays explaining concepts. If you are working individually, write up what you have learned from your analysis.

Write

  Write at least a page, justifying your choice of this reading as an example of effective concept explanation. *Assume* that your readers— your instructor and classmates—have read the selection but will not remember many details about it. They also might not remember it as especially successful. Therefore, you will need to *refer* to details and specific parts of the essay as you explain how it works and as you justify your evaluation of its effectiveness. You need not argue that it is the best reading in the chapter or that it is flawless, only that it is, in your view, a strong example of the genre.

■ A Guide to Writing Essays Explaining Concepts

The readings in this chapter have helped you learn a great deal about essays explaining concepts. The readings also have helped you understand new concepts and learn more about concepts with which you are already familiar. Now that you have seen how writers use explanatory strategies that are appropriate for their readers, anticipating what their readers are likely to know, you can approach this type of writing confidently. This Guide to Writing will help you at every stage in the process of composing an essay explaining a concept—from choosing a concept and organizing your explanatory strategies to evaluating and revising your draft.

INVENTION AND RESEARCH

The following activities will help you choose a concept, consider what your readers need to know, explore what you already know, and gather and sort through your information.

Choosing a Concept

List different concepts you could explain, and then choose the one that interests you and would be likely to interest your readers. To make the best choice and have alternatives in case the first choice does not work out, you should have a full list of possibilities. You might already have a concept in mind, possibly one suggested to you by the Considering Ideas for Your Own Writing activities following the readings in this chapter. Pause now to review the dozens of suggested concepts in those activities. Here are some other concepts from various fields of study for you to consider:

- *Literature:* representation, figurative language, canon, postcolonialism, modernism, irony, epic

- *Philosophy:* Platonic forms, causality, syllogism, existentialism, nihilism, logical positivism, determinism, phenomenology

- *Business management:* autonomous work group, quality circle, management by objectives, zero-based budgeting, benchmarking, focus group

- *Psychology:* phobia, narcissism, fetish, emotional intelligence, divergent and convergent thinking, behaviorism, Jungian archetype

- *Government:* one person/one vote, minority rights, federalism, communism, theocracy, popular consent, exclusionary rule, political machine, political action committee

- *Biology:* photosynthesis, ecosystem, plasmolysis, phagocytosis, DNA, species, punctuated evolution, homozygosity, diffusion

- *Art:* composition, cubism, iconography, pop art, conceptual art, performance art, graffiti, Dadaism, surrealism, expressionism

- *Math:* Mobius transformation, boundedness, null space, eigenvalue, complex numbers, integral, exponent, polynomial, factoring, Pythagorean theorem, continuity, derivative, infinity

- *Physical sciences:* gravity, mass, weight, energy, quantum theory, law of definite proportions, osmotic pressure, first law of thermodynamics, entropy, free energy, fusion

- *Public health:* alcoholism, epidemic, vaccination, drug abuse, contraception, prenatal care, AIDS education

- *Environmental studies:* acid rain, recycling, ozone depletion, sewage treatment, toxic waste, endangered species

- *Sports psychology:* Ringelman effect, leadership, cohesiveness, competitiveness, anxiety management, aggression, visualization, runner's high

- *Law:* arbitration, strike, minimum wage, liability, reasonable doubt, sexual harassment, nondisclosure agreement, assumption of evidence

- *Meteorology:* jet stream, hydrologic cycle, El Niño, Coriolis effect, Chinook or Santa Ana wind, standard time system, tsunami

- *Nutrition and health:* vegetarianism, bulimia, diabetes, food allergy, aerobic exercise, obesity, Maillard reaction

Choose a concept that interests you and that you think would interest your readers. You might not know very much about the concept now, but the guidelines that follow will help you learn more about it so that you can explain it to others.

Analyzing Your Readers

Write for a few minutes, analyzing your potential readers. Begin by identifying your readers and what you want them to know. Even if you are writing only for your instructor, you should consider what he or she knows about your concept. Ask yourself the following questions to stimulate your thinking: What might my potential readers already know about the concept or about the field of study to which it applies? What new, useful, or interesting information about the concept could I provide for them? What questions might they ask?

Researching the Concept

Even if you know quite a bit about the concept, you may want to do additional library or Internet research or consult an expert. Before you begin, check with your instructor for special requirements, such as submitting photocopies of your written sources or using a particular documentation style.

Exploring What You Already Know about the Concept.   *Write for a few minutes about the concept to discover what you know about it.* Pose any questions you now have about the concept, and try to answer questions you expect your readers would have.

Finding Information at the Library or on the Internet.   *Learn more about your concept by finding sources, taking notes on or making copies of relevant material, and keeping a working bibliography.* Before embarking on research, review any materials you already have at hand that explain your concept. If you are considering a concept from one of your courses, find explanatory material in your textbook and lecture notes. (See Appendix 2, Strategies for Research and Documentation, for detailed guidance on finding information at a library and on the Internet.)

RESEARCHING YOUR SUBJECT ONLINE

One way to get a quick initial overview of the information available on a concept is to conduct an online search. You can do this in several ways:

- Enter the name of your concept in a search tool such as Google <http://google.com> to discover possible sources of information about the concept.

- Check an online encyclopedia in the field to which the concept belongs. Here are a few specialized encyclopedias that may be helpful:

  Encyclopedia of Psychology <http://www.psychology.org>

  The Internet Encyclopedia of Philosophy <http://www.utm.edu/research/iep>

  Webopedia <http://webopedia.com>

Bookmark or keep a record of promising sites so that when you focus your search, you will know where to look. Download any materials, including visuals, that you might consider including in your essay.

Consulting Experts.   *Identify one or more people knowledgeable about the concept or the field of study in which it is used, and request information from them.* If you are writing about a concept from a course, consult the professor, teaching assistant, or other students. If the concept relates to your job, consider asking your supervisor. If it relates to a subject you have encountered on television, in the newspaper, or on the Internet, you might e-mail the author or post a query at a relevant Web site. Consulting experts can answer your questions as well as lead you to other sources — Web sites, chatrooms, articles, and books.

Focusing Your Explanation. *With your own knowledge of the concept and that of your readers in mind, consider how you might focus your explanation.* Determine how the information you have gathered so far could be divided. For example, if you were writing about the concept of schizophrenia, you might focus on the history of its diagnosis and treatment, its symptoms, its effects on families, the current debate about its causes, or the current preferred methods of treatment. If you were writing a book, you might want to cover all these aspects of the concept, but in a relatively brief essay you can focus on only one or two of them.

Confirming Your Focus. *Choose a focus for your explanation, and write several sentences justifying the focus you have chosen.* Why do you think this focus will appeal to your readers? What interests you about it? Do you have enough information to plan and draft your explanation? Do you know where you can find any additional information you need?

Formulating a Working Thesis. *Draft a thesis statement.* A working thesis — as opposed to a final, revised thesis — will help you begin drafting your essay purposefully. The thesis in an essay explaining a concept simply announces the concept and focus of the explanation. Here are three examples from the readings.

- "What we are talking about here is celibate motherhood, procreation without copulation, a phenomenon that goes by the technical name *parthenogenesis*. Translated from the Greek roots: virgin birth" (Quammen, paragraph 1).

- "Each of the women at the conference had to make decisions about hair, clothing, makeup and accessories, and each decision carried meaning. Every style available to us was marked. The men in our group had made decisions, too, but the range from which they chose was incomparably narrower. Men can choose styles that are marked, but they don't have to, and in this group none did. Unlike the women, they had the option of being unmarked" (Tannen, paragraph 12).

- "Cannibalism can be broken down into two main categories: exocannibalism, the eating of outsiders or foreigners, and endocannibalism, the eating of members of one's own social group (Shipman 70). Within these categories are several functional types of cannibalism, three of the most common being survival cannibalism, dietary cannibalism, and religious and ritual cannibalism" (Ngo, paragraph 6).

Notice that Ngo's thesis statement announces the concept and also forecasts the main topics he will take up in the essay. Forecasts, though not required, can be helpful to readers, especially when the concept is unfamiliar or the explanation is complicated.

Considering Visuals. *Consider whether visuals—tables, graphs, drawings, photographs—would make your explanation clearer.* You could construct your own visuals, download materials from the Internet, copy images from print sources (like books, magazines, and newspapers), or scan into your essay visuals from books and magazines. Visuals are not a requirement of an essay explaining a concept, as you can tell from the readings in this chapter, but they sometimes can add a new dimension to your writing.

DRAFTING

The following guidelines will help you set goals for your draft, plan its organization, and think about a useful sentence strategy.

Setting Goals

Establishing goals for your draft before you begin writing will enable you to make decisions and work more confidently. Consider the following questions now, and keep them in mind as you draft. They will help you set goals for drafting as well as recall how the writers you have read in this chapter tried to achieve similar goals.

- *How can I begin engagingly so as to capture my readers' attention?* Should I try to be amusing, like Quammen? Should I begin with an anecdote (as Tannen, Bailey, Ngo, and Strothers do), or with a scenario or "fabricated example" (as the Heaths do)? Should I begin by asking rhetorical questions?

- *How can I orient readers so they do not get confused?* Should I provide an explicit forecasting statement (as the Heaths and Ngo do)? Should I add transitions to help readers see how the parts of my essay relate to one another, as Ngo and Bailey do? Should I use rhetorical questions and summary statements, as Quammen and Strothers do? Or should I use all of these cueing devices, together with headings and subheadings, as the Heaths do?

- *How should I conclude my explanation?* Should I frame the essay by echoing the opening at the end, as Quammen and Tannen do? Should I summarize my explanation and discuss the implications, as the Heaths, Strothers, and Ngo do?

Organizing Your Draft

With goals in mind, make a tentative outline of the topics you now think you want to cover as you give readers information about the concept. You might want to make two or three different outlines before choosing the one that looks most promising. Try to introduce new material in stages, so that readers' understanding of the concept builds slowly but steadily. Keep in mind that an essay explaining a concept is made up of four basic parts:

1. an attempt to engage readers' interest in the explanation,

2. the thesis statement, announcing the concept and the way it will be focused and perhaps also forecasting the sequence of topics,

3. an orientation to the concept, which may include a description or definition of it, and

4. the information about the concept, organized around a series of topics that reflect how the information has been divided up.

An attempt to gain readers' interest could take as little space as two or three sentences or as much as four or five paragraphs. The thesis statement and orientation are usually quite brief, sometimes only a few sentences. One topic may require one or several paragraphs, and there can be few or many topics, depending on how the information has been divided up.

Consider tentative any outline you do before you begin drafting. Never be a slave to an outline. As you draft, you will usually see ways to improve on your original plan. Be ready to revise your outline, shift parts around, or drop or add parts as you draft.

WORKING WITH SOURCES

Introducing Sources Carefully and Precisely

When explaining concepts, writers usually need to present information from different sources, and they have many ways to introduce the information they quote or summarize. Here are a few examples from the concept essays in this chapter (the introductory words and phrases are in italics):

According to William Birky and John Gilbert, from a paper in the journal *American Zoologist*: "Equilibrium species, exemplified by many vertebrates, maintain relatively constant population sizes, in part by being adapted to reproduce, at least slowly, in most of the environmental conditions which they meet. . . ." (Quammen, paragraph 11)

In his book, Fasold *notes* "a wide range of facts which demonstrates that female is the unmarked sex." (Tannen, paragraph 26)

"The courtship which grew out of the sturdy social roots [of the nineteenth century]," one author *wrote*, "comes through to us for what it was—a gracious ritual, with clearly defined roles for man and woman, in which everyone knew the measured music and the steps". . . . (Bailey, paragraph 3)

By using the phrase *According to,* Quammen takes a neutral stance toward the information he got from Birky and Gilbert. Similarly, Tannen's *notes* and Bailey's *wrote* indicate that the authors are not characterizing or judging their sources but simply reporting them.

Often, however, writers are more descriptive — even opinionated — when they introduce information from sources, as these examples demonstrate:

> Birky and Gilbert also *emphasize* that "The potential for rapid reproduction is the essential evolutionary ticket for entry into the opportunistic lifestyle." (Quammen, paragraph 11)

> Which is why more than one biologist *has drawn the same conclusion* as M. J. D. White: "Parthenogenetic forms seem to be frequently successful in the particular ecological niche which they occupy. . . ." (Quammen, paragraph 16)

> Fasold *stresses* that language and culture are particularly unfair in treating women as the marked case because biologically it is the male that is marked. (Tannen, paragraph 24).

> Fasold ends his discussion of these matters by *pointing out* that if language reflected biology, grammar books would direct us to use "she" to include males and females and "he" only for specifically male referents. (Tannen, paragraph 28)

> By the 1950s and 1960s, social scientists who studied American courtship *found it necessary to remind* the American public that dating was a "recent American innovation and not a traditional or universal custom". . . . (Bailey, paragraph 3)

> The *Ladies' Home Journal approvingly reported* the case of six girls, workers in a box factory, who had formed a club and pooled part of their wages to pay the "janitress of a tenement house" to let them use her front room two evenings a week. (Bailey, paragraph 9).

> One of the girls *explained* their system: "We ask the boys to come when they like and spend the evening. . . ." (Bailey, paragraph 9)

> In . . . these economic analyses, the men *are complaining* about the new dating system, *lamenting* the passing of the mythic good old days when "a man without a quarter in his pocket could call on a girl and not be embarrassed," the days before a woman had to be "bought". . . . (Bailey, paragraph 26)

The verbs and verb phrases in these examples — *emphasize, has drawn the same conclusion, stresses, pointing out, found it necessary to remind, approvingly reported, explained, are complaining, lamenting*—do not neutrally report the source material but describe the particular role played by the source in explaining the concept. Verbs like *found, showed, discovered,* and *presented* are used to introduce information resulting from scientific research. When the Heaths report the findings of the Center for Science in the Public Interest, they introduce them this way: "Here's the message it *presented*" (paragraph 23). In contrast, verbs like *emphasize* and *stresses* may suggest that what is being reported is an interpretation that others may disagree with. Verbs like *approvingly report* and *complain* or *lament* suggest the state of mind of the person being quoted—or the writer's interpretation of it.

As you refer to sources in your concept explanation, you will want to choose carefully among a wide variety of precise verbs. When you are introducing sources in an argumentative essay, you also will want to draw from another set of verbs that suggest agreement or disagreement with a position, such as *argues, contends, asserts, claims, supports, refutes, repudiates, advocates, contradicts, rejects, corroborates,* and *acknowledges.*

Notice that Linh Kieu Ngo does not introduce his sources in the body of "Cannibalism: It Still Exists." Instead, he simply integrates the information from them into his sentences, and readers can see where he got it from the parenthetical citation and the Works Cited list. Here is an example from paragraph 9, in which Ngo includes a quotation together with information he paraphrases from his source:

> The Miyanmin people observe no differences in "gender, kinship, ritual status, and bodily substance"; they eat anyone, even their own dead. In this respect, then, they practice both endocannibalism and exocannibalism; and to ensure a constant supply of human flesh for food, they raid neighboring tribes and drag their victims back to their village to be eaten (Poole, paragraph 11).

This strategy of integrating but not introducing source material is useful when you want to emphasize the information and play down the source.

Considering a Useful Sentence Strategy

As you draft your essay, you will need to identify people, introduce terms, and present details to help readers understand the concept you are explaining. One way to accomplish these goals is to use sentences with appositives. An appositive is made up of a group of words, usually based on a noun or a pronoun, that identifies or gives more information about another noun or pronoun just preceding it. Appositives come in many forms and may be introduced by a comma, dash, parenthesis, or colon, as shown in these examples (the appositives appear in bold type):

this new style of courtship, **dating**, . . . (Bailey, paragraph 2)

The single serving of popcorn on Silverman's desk—**a snack someone might scarf down between meals**—had nearly two days' worth of saturated fat. (Heath and Heath, paragraph 18)

In proverbs, abstract truths are often encoded in concrete language: **"A bird in hand is worth two in the bush."** (Heath and Heath, paragraph 52)

One single aphid hatching—**call her the *fundatrix***—. . . (Quammen, paragraph 8)

True, the equation (**male companionship plus money equals female companionship**) was imbalanced. (Bailey, paragraph 27)

All of this chapter's readings use appositives. Writers explaining concepts rely on appositives because they serve many different purposes, as shown in the following examples.

- To identify a thing or person and establish a source's authority:

In 1914, the *Ladies' Home Journal*, **a bastion of middle-class respectability,** used . . . (Bailey, paragraph 7)

Silverman worked for the Center for Science in the Public Interest (CSPI), **a nonprofit group that educates the public about nutrition**. (Heath and Heath, paragraph 15)

- To introduce and define a new term:

What we are talking about here is celibate motherhood, procreation without copulation, **a phenomenon that goes by the technical name *parthenogenesis***. (Quammen, paragraph 1)

- To give examples or more specific information:

Naturally sticky ideas are full of concrete images—**ice-filled bathtubs, apples with razors**—because our brains are wired to remember concrete data. (Heath and Heath, paragraph 52)

The popcorn idea was a lot like the ideas that most of us traffic in every day—**ideas that are interesting but not sensational, truthful but not mind-blowing, important but not "life-or-death."** (Heath and Heath, paragraph 27)

The third woman's hair was wild, **a frosted blond avalanche falling over and beyond her shoulders.** (Tannen, paragraph 4)

Appositives accomplish these and other purposes efficiently by enabling the writer to put related bits of information next to each other in the same sentence, thereby merging two potential sentences into one or shrinking a potential clause to a phrase. For example, Ngo uses an appositive in this sentence:

> Cannibalism, **the act of human beings eating human flesh** . . . , has a long history and continues to hold interest and create controversy. (Ngo, paragraph 5)

But he could have conveyed the same information in either of the following sentences:

> Cannibalism can be defined as the act of human beings eating human flesh. It has a long history and continues to hold interest and create controversy.

> Cannibalism, which can be defined as the act of human beings eating human flesh, has a long history and continues to hold interest and create controversy.

Both of these versions are readable and clear. By using an appositive, however, Ngo saves four or five words, subordinates the definition of cannibalism to his main idea about history and controversy, and yet locates the definition exactly where readers need to see it, right after the word being defined.

In addition to using appositives, you can strengthen your concept explanation with other kinds of sentence strategies. For example, you may want to review the information in Chapter 6 on sentences that express comparison and contrast (pp. 365–66).

READING A DRAFT CRITICALLY

Getting a critical reading of your draft will help you see how to improve it. Your instructor may schedule class time for reading drafts, or you may want to ask a classmate or a tutor in the writing center to read your draft. Ask your reader to use the following guidelines and to write out a response for you to consult during your revision.

Read for a First Impression

1. Read the draft without stopping to annotate or comment, and then write two or three sentences giving your general impression.

2. Identify one aspect of the draft that seems particularly effective.

Read Again to Suggest Improvements

1. Consider whether the concept is clearly explained and focused.

   ▪ Restate briefly what you understand the concept to mean, indicating if you have any uncertainty or confusion about its meaning.

- Identify the focus of the explanation and assess whether the focus seems appropriate, too broad, or too narrow for the intended readers.

- If you can, suggest another, possibly more interesting, way to focus the explanation.

2. Recommend ways of making the organization clearer or more effective.

- Indicate whether a forecasting statement, topic sentences, or transitions could be added or improved.

- Point to any place where you become confused or do not know how something relates to what went before.

- Comment on whether the conclusion gives you a sense of closure or leaves you hanging.

3. Consider whether the content is appropriate for the intended readers.

- Point to any place where the information might seem obvious to readers or too elementary for them.

- Circle any terms that the writer should define or define more clearly, as well as any that the writer has defined but you do not think need to be defined.

- Think of unanswered questions readers might have about the concept. Try to suggest additional information that should be included.

- Recommend new strategies the writer could usefully adopt—comparing the concept to a concept more familiar to readers, dividing some of the information into smaller or larger topics, reporting known causes or effects of the concept, giving further facts or examples, or narrating how a part of the concept actually works. Explain how the writer could make use of the strategy.

4. Assess whether quotations are integrated smoothly and acknowledged properly.

- Point to any place where a quotation is not smoothly integrated into the writer's sentence and offer a revision.

- Indicate any quotations that would have been just as effective if put in the writer's own words.

- If sources are not acknowledged correctly, remind the writer to consult Appendix 2.

- If you can, suggest other sources that the writer might consult.

5. Evaluate the effectiveness of visuals.

- Look at any visuals in the essay, and tell the writer what they contribute to your understanding of the concept explanation.

- If any visuals do not seem relevant, or if there seem to be too many visuals, identify the ones that the writer could consider dropping, explaining your thinking.

- If a visual does not seem appropriately placed, suggest a better place for it.

REVISING

This section offers suggestions for revising your draft. Revising means reenvisioning your draft—trying to see it in a new way, given your purpose and readers, to develop a more lively, engaging, and informative essay explaining a concept.

The biggest mistake you can make while revising is to focus initially on words or sentences. Instead, first try to see your draft as a whole to assess its likely impact on your readers. Think imaginatively and boldly about cutting unconvincing material, adding new material, and moving material around. Your computer makes even drastic revisions physically easy, but you still need to make the mental effort and decisions that will improve your draft.

You may have received help with this challenge from a classmate or tutor who gave your draft a critical reading. If so, keep this feedback in mind as you decide which parts of your draft need revising and what specific changes you could make. The following suggestions will help you solve problems and strengthen your essay.

To Make the Concept Clearer and More Focused

- If readers are confused or uncertain about the concept's meaning, try defining it more precisely or giving concrete examples. Consider using an appositive to introduce and define new terms or give specific details.

- If the focus seems too broad, concentrate on one aspect of the concept and explain it in greater depth.

- If the concept seems too narrow, go back to your invention and research notes and look for a larger or more significant aspect of it to focus on.

To Improve the Organization

- If readers have difficulty following the essay, improve the forecasting at the beginning of the essay by listing the topics in the order they will appear.

- If there are places where the topic gets blurred from one sentence or paragraph to the next, make the connections between the sentences or paragraphs clearer.

- If the essay seems to lose steam before it comes to a conclusion, consider again what you want readers to learn from your essay.

- If the essay is long and complicated, consider using headings and subheadings to orient readers.

To Strengthen the Explanatory Strategies

- If the content seems thin, consider whether you could add any other explanatory strategies or develop more fully the ones you are using already.

- If some of the words you use are new to most readers, take the time to define them now, perhaps explaining how they relate to more familiar terms or adding analogies and examples to make them less abstract. Consider using an appositive for your definition.

- If the way you have divided or categorized the information is unusual or unclear, write a sentence or two making explicit what you are doing and why.

- If the concept seems vague to readers, try comparing it to something familiar or applying it to a real-world experience.

To Integrate Quotations Smoothly and Acknowledge Sources Properly

- If any quotations are not smoothly integrated into the text, add appropriate signal phrases or rewrite the sentences.

- If your critical reader has identified a quotation that could just as effectively be described in your own words, try paraphrasing or summarizing the quote.

- If your sources are not acknowledged properly, check Appendix 2 for the correct citation form. Consider using an appositive to identify your source and establish its authority.

EDITING AND PROOFREADING

After you have revised your essay, be sure to spend some time checking for errors in usage, punctuation, and mechanics and considering matters of style. If you keep a list of errors you typically make, begin by checking your draft against this list. Ask someone else to proofread your essay before you print out a copy for your instructor or send it electronically.

From our research on student writing, we know that essays explaining concepts tend to have errors in essential or nonessential clauses beginning with *who*, *which*, or *that*, as well as errors in the use of commas to set off phrases that interrupt the flow of the sentence. Check a writer's handbook for help with these potential problems.

REFLECTING ON WHAT YOU HAVE LEARNED

Explaining Concepts

In this chapter, you have read critically several essays explaining concepts and have written one of your own. To better remember what you have learned, pause now to reflect on the reading and writing activities you completed in this chapter.

1. *Write* a page or so reflecting on what you have learned. *Begin* by describing what you are most pleased with in your essay. Then *explain* what you think contributed to your achievement. *Be specific* about this contribution.

   ▪ If it was something you learned from the readings, *indicate* which readings and specifically what you learned from them.

   ▪ If it came from your invention writing, *point out* the section or sections that helped you most.

   ▪ If you got good advice from a critical reader, *explain* exactly how the person helped you—perhaps by helping you understand a particular problem in your draft or by adding a new dimension to your writing.

   ▪ *Try to write* about your achievement in terms of what you have learned about the genre.

2. Now *reflect* more generally on explaining concepts, a genre of writing that plays an important role in education and in our society. *Consider* that concept explanations attempt to present their information as uncontested truths. *Reflect* on your own essay, and *write* answers to the following questions: When you were doing research on the concept, did you discover that some of the information was being challenged by experts? If so, what were the grounds for this challenge? Did you at any point think that your readers might question any of the information you were presenting? How did you decide what information might seem new or surprising to readers? Did you feel comfortable in your roles as the selector and giver of knowledge? *Describe* how you felt in these roles.

Evaluation

We make evaluations every day, stating judgments about such things as food, clothes, books, classes, teachers, political candidates, television programs, performers, and films. Most of our everyday judgments simply express our personal preference: "I liked it" or "I didn't like it." But as soon as someone asks "Why?," we realize that evaluation goes beyond individual taste and needs to present an argument to support our judgment.

If you want others to take your judgment seriously, you have to give reasons for it, and your reasons must be based on shared criteria that readers recognize as appropriate for evaluating a particular type of subject. For example, in writing a review of an action film like *Mission Impossible III*, you would want to show that you are judging the film according to standards most people would use to evaluate other action films, including the first two films in the *Mission Impossible* series. In his ReelViews.com review, James Berardinelli places the film in a general category ("if you're yearning for a flashy, leave-your-brain-at-the-door summer movie"). Then he goes on to argue that even though it has all the characteristics of a summer blockbuster ("It's loud, raucous, frenetic, and blows things up real good"), he found the film disappointing because "it's testosterone without adrenaline, danger without suspense." Berardinelli shows readers that he understands that they expect him to judge the film as an example of its genre, so he bases his judgment on qualities such as the film's special effects, its action sequences, and, most important, its ability to generate excitement — to be a thrilling cinematic roller-coaster ride. He even makes a point of saying that he is not criticizing the film's "plot contrivances" because "they go with the territory."

Readers would think Berardinelli is suffering shell shock from seeing too many action films if the reasons he gave for his judgment were that the seats in the theater were uncomfortable or that the popcorn was stale. These reasons are inappropriate for judging the quality of a film, but they are excellent criteria for judging the quality of a movie theater. For reasons to be considered appropriate, they must reflect the values or standards typically used in evaluating the kind of thing under consideration, such as a film or a car. The criteria you would use for evaluating a film obviously differ from those you would use for evaluating a car. Acting, musical score, and story are common standards for judging films. Handling, safety, and styling are some of the standards used for judging cars.

Readers expect writers of evaluations both to offer appropriate reasons and to support their reasons. If one of your reasons for liking the BMW 330i sports sedan is its quick acceleration, you could cite the *Consumer Reports* road-test results (0 to 60mph in 6.6 seconds) as evidence. (Statistical support like this makes sense only when BMW's rate is compared with the acceleration rates of other comparable cars.) Similarly, if one of your reasons for liking a particular song is the wit and insight of the lyrics, you could quote lines as examples to show readers how witty and insightful the lyrics are. Support is important because it deals in specifics, showing exactly what value terms like *witty* and *insightful* mean to you.

As you can see, evaluation of the kind you will read and write in this chapter is intellectually rigorous. In college, you will have many opportunities to write evaluations. You may be asked to critique a book or a journal article, judge a scientific hypothesis against the results of an experiment, assess the value of conflicting interpretations of a historical event or a short story, or evaluate a class you have taken. You will also undoubtedly read evaluative writing in your courses and be tested on what you have read.

Written evaluations will almost certainly play an important part in your work life as well. On the job, you will probably be evaluated periodically and may have to evaluate people whom you supervise. It is also likely that you will be asked your opinion of various plans or proposals under consideration, and your ability to make reasonable, well-supported evaluations will affect your chances for promotion.

As the word *evaluation* suggests, evaluative arguments are basically about values, about what each of us thinks is important. Reading and writing evaluations will help you understand your own values as well as those of others. You will learn that when your basic values conflict with your readers' values, you may not be able to convince readers to accept a judgment different from their own. In such cases, you will usually want to try to bridge the difference by showing respect for their concerns despite your disagreement with them or to clarify the areas of agreement and disagreement.

The readings in this chapter will help you learn a good deal about evaluative writing. From the readings and from the ideas for writing that follow each reading, you will get ideas for your own evaluative essay. As you read and write about the selections, keep in mind the following assignment, which sets out the goals for writing an evaluative essay. To support your writing of this assignment, the chapter concludes with a Guide to Writing Evaluations.

Evaluation

Choose a subject that you can both evaluate and make a confident judgment about. Write an essay evaluating this subject. State your judgment clearly, and back it up with reasons and support. Describe the subject for readers unfamiliar with it, and give them a context for understanding it. Your purpose is to convince readers that your judgment is informed and based on generally accepted standards for this kind of subject.

WRITING SITUATIONS FOR EVALUATIONS

Following are a few examples to suggest the range of situations that may call for evaluative writing, including academic and work-related situations:

- For a conference on innovation in education, an elementary schoolteacher evaluates *Schoolhouse Rock*, an animated television series developed in the 1970s and reinvented in several new formats: books, CD-ROM learning games, and DVDs. She praises the original series as an entertaining way of presenting information, giving two reasons the series remains an effective teaching tool. Witty lyrics and catchy tunes make the information memorable, and cartoonlike visuals make the lessons pleasurable. She supports each reason by showing and discussing examples of popular *Schoolhouse Rock* segments, such as "Conjunction Junction," "We the People," and "Three Is a Magic Number." She ends by expressing her hope that teachers and developers of educational multimedia will learn from the example of *Schoolhouse Rock*.

- A supervisor reviews the work of a probationary employee. She judges the employee's performance as being adequate overall but still needing improvement in several key areas, particularly completing projects on time and communicating clearly with others. To support her judgment, she describes several problems that the employee has had over the six-month probationary period.

- An older brother, a college junior, sends an e-mail message to his younger brother, a high-school senior who is trying to decide which college to attend. Because the older brother attends one of the colleges being considered and has friends at another, he feels competent to offer advice. He centers his message on the question of what standards to use in evaluating colleges. He argues that if playing football is the primary goal, then college number one is the clear choice. But if having the opportunity to work in an award-winning scientist's genetics lab is more important, then the second college is the better choice.

THINKING ABOUT YOUR EXPERIENCE WITH EVALUATIONS

Before studying a type of writing, it is useful to spend some time thinking about what you already know about it. You may have discussed with friends or family why a particular movie or diet is good or bad, successful or unsuccessful. You might have written evaluative essays for school about a literary text, a theatrical performance, or a scientific report.

To analyze your experience with evaluations, try to recall a time when you were evaluating — orally or in writing — something you had seen, heard, read, or tried, such as a movie, performance, CD, book, magazine, restaurant, television show, video game, computer software, or concept. What were your criteria for evaluation — the standards on which you based your judgments? Who was your audience for your argument? What did you hope to achieve with your evaluation? What interested you about your topic or made you think it was significant? Was your judgment all positive or all negative, or a mixture?

Also consider the evaluations you have read, heard, or seen on television. If you recall one of them in some detail, try to identify what made it interesting. Was it the subject, or did the author perhaps present ideas new to you? How did the author make the evaluation convincing? Did it contain illuminating details or an unusual point of view?

Write at least a page about your experience with evaluations.

■ A Guide to Reading Evaluations

This guide introduces you to evaluative writing. By completing all the activities in it, you will prepare yourself to learn a great deal from the other readings in this chapter about how to read and write an evaluative essay. The guide focuses on "Working at McDonald's," a well-known essay by Amitai Etzioni, a sociologist and one of the founders of the communitarian movement, which promotes the spirit of community and fosters civic responsibility. You will read Etzioni's evaluative essay twice. First, you will read it for meaning, looking closely at its content and ideas. Then you will reread the essay like a writer, analyzing the parts to see how Etzioni crafts his essay and to learn the strategies he uses to make the evaluation informative and convincing. These two activities — reading for meaning and reading like a writer — follow every reading in this chapter.

AMITAI ETZIONI
Working at McDonald's

Amitai Etzioni (b. 1929) is a sociologist who has taught at Columbia, Harvard, and George Washington Universities, and he currently directs GWU's Institute for Communitarian Policy Studies. Etzioni is respected as a scholar—he served as president of the American Sociological Association as well as founding president of the Society for the Advancement of Socio-Economics—and he is a highly visible public intellectual whose writing is read by many people outside of academia. Etzioni has written numerous articles and twenty-four books, including The Moral Dimension: Toward a New Economics *(1988),* The Spirit of Community *(1993),* My Brother's Keeper: A Memoir and a Message *(2003), and* From Empire to Community: A New Approach to International Relations *(2004). Among his many awards are the Simon Wiesenthal Center's 1997 Tolerance Book Award and the Conference on Value Inquiry's award for Extraordinary Contributions to the Appreciation and Advancement of Human Values.*

The following essay was originally published in 1986 in the Miami Herald, *a major newspaper that circulates in South Florida. The original headnote identifies Etzioni as the father of five sons, including three teenagers, and points out that his son Dari helped Etzioni write this essay—although it does not say what Dari contributed.*

Before you read, think about the paying jobs you held during high school or hold now in college—not just summer jobs but those you worked during the months when school was in session. Think about what you learned that might have made you a better student and prepared you for college or for the kind of work you hope to do in the future.

As you read, think about how the standards or criteria that Etzioni uses to evaluate jobs at fast-food restaurants would apply to the kinds of jobs you have held. The marginal annotations point to strategies writers of evaluation typically use. Add your own comments and questions, noting anything else you think is interesting.

Asserting this judgment grabs readers' attention. Etzioni then presents the subject *and establishes its importance.*

McDonald's is bad for your kids. I do not mean the flat patties and the white-flour buns; I refer to the jobs teen-agers undertake, mass-producing these choice items. 1

As many as two-thirds of America's high school juniors and seniors now hold down part-time paying jobs, according to studies. Many of these are in fast-food chains, of which McDonald's is the pioneer, trend-setter, and symbol. 2

At first, such jobs may seem right out of the Founding Fathers' educational manual for how to bring up self-reliant, work-ethic-driven, productive youngsters. 3

Here Etzioni forecasts the three reasons he develops in the essay.

But in fact, these jobs undermine school attendance and involvement, impart few skills that will be useful in later life, and simultaneously skew the values of teen-agers—especially their ideas about the worth of a dollar.

4   It has been a longstanding American tradition that youngsters ought to get paying jobs. In folklore, few pursuits are more deeply revered than the newspaper route and the sidewalk lemonade stand. Here the youngsters are to learn how sweet are the fruits of labor and self-discipline (papers are delivered early in the morning, rain or shine), and the ways of trade (if you price your lemonade too high or too low . . .).

Etzioni shows he shares traditional values and criteria for evaluating teen jobs.

5   Roy Rogers, Baskin Robbins, Kentucky Fried Chicken, et al. may at first seem nothing but a vast extension of the lemonade stand. They provide very large numbers of teen jobs, provide regular employment, pay quite well compared to many other teen jobs, and, in the modern equivalent of toiling over a hot stove, test one's stamina.

6   Closer examination, however, finds the McDonald's kind of job highly uneducational in several ways. Far from providing opportunities for entrepreneurship (the lemonade stand) or self-discipline, self-supervision, and self-scheduling (the paper route), most teen jobs these days are highly structured—what social scientists call "highly routinized."

After acknowledging in paragraph 5 the reasons that readers are likely to favor teen jobs, Etzioni gives the primary reason for his negative judgment.

7   True, you still have to have the gumption to get yourself over to the hamburger stand, but once you don the prescribed uniform, your task is spelled out in minute detail. The franchise prescribes the shape of the coffee cups; the weight, size, shape, and color of the patties; and the texture of the napkins (if any). Fresh coffee is to be made every eight minutes. And so on. There is no room for initiative, creativity, or even elementary rearrangements. These are breeding grounds for robots working for yesterday's assembly lines, not tomorrow's high-tech posts.

Here he supports his reason that teens' jobs are "uneducational" with details describing such jobs.

8   There are very few studies of the matter. One of the few is a 1984 study by Ivan Charper and Bryan Shore Fraser. The study relies mainly on what teen-agers write in response to questionnaires rather than actual observations of fast-food jobs. The authors argue that the employees develop many skills such as how to operate a food-preparation machine and a cash register. However, little attention is paid to how long it takes to acquire such a skill, or what its significance is.

Etzioni cites research studies to support his reason. He does not document sources formally for this newspaper article, but you must for college papers.

9   What does it matter if you spend 20 minutes to learn to use a cash register, and then—"operate" it? What

skill have you acquired? It is a long way from learning to work with a lathe or carpenter tools in the olden days or to program computers in the modern age.

He uses research to argue that long-term losses outweigh short-term gains from teen jobs.

A 1980 study by A. V. Harrell and P. W. Wirtz found 10 that, among those students who worked at least 25 hours per week while in school, their unemployment rate four years later was half of that of seniors who did not work. This is an impressive statistic. It must be seen, though, together with the finding that many who begin as part-time employees in fast-food chains drop out of high school and are gobbled up in the world of low-skill jobs.

Etzioni *refutes an alternative judgment,* counterarguing that fast-food jobs are worse, not better, for "disadvantaged" students.

Some say that while these jobs are rather unsuited 11 for college-bound, white, middle-class youngsters, they are "ideal" for lower-class, "non-academic," minority youngsters. Indeed, minorities are "over-represented" in these jobs (21 percent of fast-food employees). While it is true that these places provide income, work, and even some training to such youngsters, they also tend to perpetuate their disadvantaged status. They provide no career ladders, few marketable skills, and undermine school attendance and involvement.

The hours are often long. Among those 14 to 17, a 12 third of fast-food employees (including some school dropouts) labor more than 30 hours per week, according to the Charper-Fraser study. Only 20 percent work 15 hours or less. The rest: between 15 and 30 hours.

Etzioni uses these statistics to *support his second reason*: teen jobs interfere with school work.

Often the stores close late, and after closing one 13 must clean up and tally up. In affluent Montgomery County, Md., where child labor would not seem to be a widespread economic necessity, 24 percent of the seniors at one high school in 1985 worked as much as five to seven days a week; 27 percent, three to five. There is just no way such amounts of work will not interfere with school work, especially homework. In an informal survey published in the most recent yearbook of the high school, 58 percent of the seniors acknowledged that their jobs interfere with their school work.

He *concedes some value in an alternative judgment* but then calls it into question.

The Charper-Fraser study sees merit in learning 14 teamwork and working under supervision. The authors have a point here. However, it must be noted that such learning is not automatically educational or wholesome. For example, much of the supervision in fast-food places leans toward teaching one the wrong kinds of compliance: blind obedience, or shared alienation with the "boss."

15   Supervision is often both tight and woefully inappropriate. Today, fast-food chains and other such places of work (record shops, bowling alleys) keep costs down by having teens supervise teens with often no adult on the premises.

16   There is no father or mother figure with which to identify, to emulate, to provide a role model and guidance. The work-culture varies from one place to another: Sometimes it is a tightly run shop (must keep the cash registers ringing); sometimes a rather loose pot party interrupted by customers. However, only rarely is there a master to learn from, or much worth learning. Indeed, far from being places where solid adult work values are being transmitted, these are places where all too often delinquent teen values dominate. Typically, when my son Oren was dishing out ice cream for Baskin Robbins in upper Manhattan, his fellow teen-workers considered him a sucker for not helping himself to the till. Most youngsters felt they were entitled to $50 severance "pay" on their last day on the job.

> He *returns to his first reason* (teens learn the wrong lessons at such jobs) *to make a transition to his third reason* (about values).

17   The pay, oddly, is the part of the teen work-world that is most difficult to evaluate. The lemonade stand or paper route money was for your allowance. In the old days, apprentices learning a trade from a master contributed most, if not all of their income to their parents' household. Today, the teen pay may be low by adult standards, but it is often, especially in the middle class, spent largely or wholly by the teens. That is, the youngsters live free at home ("after all, they are high school kids") and are left with very substantial sums of money.

> Etzioni admits that one aspect of his subject is hard to evaluate and that some teens need their earnings.

18   Where this money goes is not quite clear. Some use it to support themselves, especially among the poor. More middle-class kids set some money aside to help pay for college, or save it for a major purchase — often a car. But large amounts seem to flow to pay for an early introduction into the most trite aspects of American consumerism: flimsy punk clothes, trinkets, and whatever else is the last fast-moving teen craze.

> He brings up "American consumerism" to *develop his reason about values.* What does he seem to be assuming here?

19   One may say that this is only fair and square; they are being good American consumers and spend their money on what turns them on. At least, a cynic might

add, these funds do not go into illicit drugs and booze. On the other hand, an educator might bemoan that these young, yet unformed individuals, so early in life driven to buy objects of no intrinsic educational, cultural, or social merit, learn so quickly the dubious merit of keeping up with the Joneses in ever-changing fads, promoted by mass merchandising.

Etzioni restates his argument by summarizing the reasons he has supported.

Many teens find the instant reward of money, and 20 the youth status symbols it buys, much more alluring than credits in calculus courses, European history, or foreign languages. No wonder quite a few would rather skip school—and certainly homework—and instead work longer at a Burger King. Thus, most teen work these days is not providing early lessons in work ethic; it fosters escape from school and responsibilities, quick gratification, and a short cut to the consumeristic aspects of adult life.

Etzioni ends by addressing both parents and teens. How convincing is his argument likely to be for these two groups?

Thus, parents should look at teen employment not 21 as automatically educational. It is an activity—like sports—that can be turned into an educational opportunity. But it can also easily be abused. Youngsters must learn to balance the quest for income with the needs to keep growing and pursue other endeavors that do not pay off instantly—above all education.

Go back to school.

READING FOR MEANING

This section presents three activities that will help you reread with a critical eye the article "Working at McDonald's" by Amitai Etzioni. All three activities add up to between one and two pages of writing, but they lead you from basic comprehension to a response and analysis that deepens your understanding and critical thinking about what you are reading. Your instructor may ask you to do one or more of these activities in class or as homework.

Read to Comprehend

Reread the article, and write a few sentences briefly summarizing Etzioni's argument about the value of part-time jobs for teenagers. The following definitions may help you understand Etzioni's vocabulary:

skew (paragraph 3): to distort or have a bad influence on.

entrepreneurship (6): the skills involved in organizing and managing a business.

dubious (19): questionable or doubtful.

Identify three or more additional words that you don't understand, and find the best definitions from the dictionary that work with their context.

To expand your understanding of this reading, you might use one or more of the following critical reading strategies that are explained and illustrated in Appendix 1: *outlining* and *summarizing*.

Read to Respond

Write several paragraphs exploring your initial thoughts and feelings about Etzioni's evaluation. Focus on anything that stands out for you, perhaps because it resonates with your own experience or because you find a statement puzzling. You might consider writing about the following:

- Etzioni's assertion that McDonald's-type jobs "skew the values of teen-agers—especially their ideas about the worth of a dollar" (paragraph 3);

- the "longstanding American tradition that youngsters ought to get paying jobs" (4)—considering the reasons for this tradition or whether it is a tradition that other cultures with which you are familiar share;

- Etzioni's argument that working while attending school interferes with school work (13), perhaps in relation to your own work and school experience; or

- how Etzioni's description of McDonald's-type jobs reminds you of the kind of work you have done as a teenager. What would Etzioni have thought of your job? What do you think of it, having read this evaluation?

To develop your response to Etzioni's essay, you might use one or more of the following critical reading strategies that are explained and illustrated in Appendix 1: *contextualizing, recognizing emotional manipulation,* and *judging the writer's credibility.*

Read to Analyze Assumptions

Reread Etzioni's evaluation essay, and write a paragraph or two exploring one or more of the assumptions you find in the text. All writing contains assumptions—opinions, values, and beliefs that are taken for granted as commonly accepted truths by the writer or others. Personal or individual assumptions also tend to reflect the values and beliefs of a particular group or community, some-times called *cultural ideology*, which shape the way those in the group think, act, and understand the world.

Analyzing assumptions is an important part of learning to read critically because assumptions tend to be unexamined and unquestioned (at least con-sciously) by those who hold them. When you read with a critical eye, you identify important assumptions in the text and ask questions about them. Sometimes assumptions are stated explicitly, but often they are only implied, so you may have to search for underlying assumptions in the word choices and examples.

Here are some kinds of questions you should ask regarding the assumptions you find: Who holds this assumption? How does the assumption reinforce or critique the status quo? What alternative ideas, beliefs, or values would challenge this assumption? If the writer uses the assumption to appeal to readers, how effective do you think this appeal is, and why?

To help you get started reading for assumptions in Etzioni's essay, notice that when he writes that "jobs undermine school attendance and involvement," Etzioni is expressing explicitly an assumption that the "work" of school is more important than the "work" that makes money (paragraph 3). To think critically about this assumption, you might ask yourself: What is Etzioni assuming about the socioeconomics of teens who work at McDonald's-type jobs? Note that he takes issue with the assumption that fast-food jobs are "unsuited" for "white, middle-class youngsters" but " 'ideal' for lower class, 'non-academic,' minority youngsters" (11). Nevertheless, is there any evidence in the essay to suggest that Etzioni assumes teens have a choice to work or not to work? And does he assume teens work to buy luxuries or necessities? Finally, a critique could be made that Etzioni misses the opportunity to challenge businesses to provide apprenticeships for teens that would teach them more useful skills or to pay teens better salaries and benefits for the work they do.

Here are some other possibilities you might consider writing about:

- **assumptions about useful skills.** Etzioni asserts that fast-food jobs "impart few skills that will be useful in later life" (paragraph 3). For example, he claims they do not provide "opportunities for entrepreneurship . . . or self-discipline, self-supervision, and self-scheduling" (6) and "[t]here is no room for initiative, creativity" (7). To think critically about the assumptions in this essay related to what skills are learned at fast-food jobs and how useful they are, examine the opposition Etzioni sets up between the kinds of jobs teens held in "olden days"—the lemonade stand, the paper route—and the jobs available to them today. Ask yourself: How different, really, is delivering newspapers from working at McDonald's in terms of the skills learned about discipline, scheduling, and so on? Similarly, what more is a young person likely to learn about entrepreneurship by operating a lemonade stand than by working in a fast-food restaurant (4)? What other kinds of skills do teens learn when working at fast-food restaurants, and what potential use do you think these skills have in future life?

- **assumptions about consumerism.** Toward the end of the essay, Etzioni complains that the things teenagers choose to buy with the money they earn from fast-food jobs represent "the most trite aspects of American consumerism: flimsy punk clothes, trinkets, and whatever else is the last fast-moving teen craze" (18). By referring to consumerism—enthusiastic spending on material possessions such as clothes, entertainment, and other consumer goods—as something "American," Etzioni makes clear he is referring to a cultural ideology that is not limited to teenagers. Nevertheless, his focus on teens — what they buy and why they buy it — reveals Etzioni's ideas about teenagers' indoctrination into a consumerist ideology. To think critically about the assumptions in this essay related to American consumerism, note that Etzioni uses the words *trite, flimsy*, and *trinkets* to criticize the things teens buy. Ask yourself: If teens purchased items that were original, well-made, and valuable, to what extent, if any, would he still object? What might he be criticizing other than teenagers' taste? In referring to "fads" and "mass merchandising," Etzioni seems to assume teens are especially vulnerable to the influence of advertising (19). Why do you suppose he makes judgments about teens' vulnerability rather than about advertisers' responsibility or about the underlying ideology itself?

To probe assumptions more deeply, you might use one or more of the following critical reading strategies that are explained and illustrated in Appendix 1: *reflecting on challenges to your beliefs and values, evaluating the logic of an argument*, and *judging the writer's credibility*.

READING LIKE A WRITER

This section leads you through an analysis of Etzioni's evaluative writing strategies: *presenting the subject, asserting an overall judgment, giving reasons and support*, and *anticipating objections and alternative judgments*. For each strategy, you will be asked to reread and annotate part of Etzioni's essay to see how he uses the strategy in "Working at McDonald's."

When you study the selections later in this chapter, you will see how different writers use these same strategies. The Guide to Writing Evaluations near the end of the chapter suggests ways you can use these strategies in your own writing.

Presenting the Subject

Writers must present the subject so readers know what is being judged. Writers can simply name the subject, but usually they describe it in some detail. A film reviewer, for example, might identify the actors, describe the characters they play, and tell some of the plot. As a critical reader, you may notice that the language used to present the subject also may serve to evaluate it. Therefore, you should look closely at how the subject is presented. Note where the writer's information about the subject comes from, whether the information is reliable, and whether anything important seems to have been left out.

Analyze

1. *Reread* paragraphs 5–7, 9, 12, 15, and 16, and *underline* the factual details that describe the people who work at fast-food restaurants and what they do. *Ask* yourself the following question as you analyze how Etzioni presents the

subject: Where does the writer seem to get his information—from firsthand observation, from conversation with others, or from published research?

2. Based on your own knowledge of fast-food jobs, *point to* the details in these paragraphs that you accept as valid as well as to details you think are inaccurate or only partially true. Finally, *consider* whether any information you know about fast-food jobs is missing from Etzioni's presentation of work at fast-food places.

Write

Write several sentences discussing how Etzioni presents the subject to his intended audience—education-minded adults, particularly parents of high-school students—and *give examples* from the reading. Then *write a few more sentences* evaluating Etzioni's presentation of the subject in terms of accuracy and completeness.

Asserting an Overall Judgment

A writer's overall judgment of the subject is the main point of an evaluative essay, asserting that the subject is good or bad, or better or worse, than something comparable. Although readers expect a definitive judgment, they also appreciate a balanced one that acknowledges, for example, some good qualities of a subject judged overall to be bad. Evaluations usually explicitly state the judgment up front in the form of a thesis and may restate it in different ways throughout the essay.

Analyze

1. *Reread* paragraphs 3, 20, and 21, where Etzioni states his overall judgment, and *consider* whether you find his statements clear.

2. *Decide* whether Etzioni changes his initial judgment in any way when he restates it in somewhat different language at the end of the essay. *Consider* why he restates his judgment.

Write

Write a few sentences describing and evaluating Etzioni's assertion of his overall judgment.

Giving Reasons and Support

Any evaluative argument must explain and justify the writer's judgment. To be convincing, the reasons given must be recognized by readers as appropriate for evaluating the type of subject under consideration. That is, the reasons must reflect the values or standards of judgment that people typically use in similar situations. The reasons also must be supported by relevant examples, quotations, facts, statistics, or personal anecdotes. This support may come from the writer's own knowledge or experience, from that of other people, and from published materials.

Analyze

1. Etzioni names three principal reasons for his judgment in the final sentence of paragraph 3. *Underline* these reasons, and then *consider* the appropriateness of each one given Etzioni's intended readers—the largely middle-class adult subscribers to the *Miami Herald*. Why do you think they would or would not likely accept each reason as appropriate for evaluating part-time jobs for teenagers? What objections, if any, might a critical reader have to Etzioni's reasoning?

2. One reason Etzioni gives to clarify his view that working at McDonald's is "bad" for students is that the jobs "impart few skills that will be useful in later life" (paragraph 3). Etzioni then attempts to support (to argue for) this reason in paragraphs 4 to 9. *Reread* these paragraphs noticing the kinds of support Etzioni relies on.

3. *Evaluate* how well Etzioni supports his argument in paragraphs 4 to 9. Why do you think his readers will or will not find the argument convincing? Which supporting details might they find most convincing? Least convincing?

Write

Write several sentences reporting what you have learned about how Etzioni uses reasons and support as an evaluative writing strategy in his essay. *Give examples* (from paragraphs 4 to 9) of the type of support he provides for the "impart few skills" reason. *Write a few more sentences* explaining how convincing you think his readers will find this support.

Anticipating Objections and Alternative Judgments

Sometimes reviewers try to anticipate and respond to readers' possible objections and alternative judgments, but counterarguing is not as crucial for evaluation as is arguing directly for a judgment by giving reasons and support. When they do counterargue, reviewers may simply acknowledge that others perhaps disagree, may accommodate into their argument points others have made, or may try to refute objections and alternative judgments. For example, some parents with children in high school may question Etzioni's reasons for damning an easily available source of income. A relatively poor family, for instance, might firmly oppose his judgment, seeing part-time work at McDonald's as good for high-school students who must buy their own clothes and pay for their entertainment. Other parents may object to Etzioni's comparing a fast-food job unfavorably to a job selling lemonade or delivering newspapers.

Etzioni certainly is aware that some readers have questions and objections in mind. These objections do not cause him to waver in his own judgment, as you have seen, but they do persuade him to anticipate readers' likely questions and objections and to respond to them by counterarguing. There are two basic ways to counterargue. A writer can *refute* readers' objections, arguing that they are simply wrong, or *accommodate* objections, acknowledging that they are justified but do not irreparably damage the writer's reasoning. Etzioni uses both refutation and accommodation in his counterarguments.

Analyze

1. *Reread* paragraphs 8 to 11, 14, and 19, where Etzioni brings up either a reader's likely objection or an alternative judgment about the worth of part-time work. (Some alternative judgments are attributed to researchers rather than readers, though it is likely some readers would have similar ideas.) *Underline* the alternative judgment or objection in each of these paragraphs.

2. *Choose* any two of these counterarguments, and then *look closely* at Etzioni's strategy. *Decide* first whether he refutes or accommodates the objection or alternative judgment. Then *note* how he goes about doing so.

3. *Evaluate* whether Etzioni's counterarguments are likely to convince skeptical readers to accept his views.

Write

Write several sentences identifying the objections and alternative judgments against which Etzioni counterargues. *Describe* his counterarguments, and *evaluate* how persuasive they are likely to be with his intended audience.

■ Readings

ELLA TAYLOR

Hooverville: Little Miss Sunshine *Lights into the American Family*

> *Ella Taylor is a film critic for the* LA Weekly, *the Los Angeles–based newspaper in which this evaluation essay originally appeared in 2006. Her reviews also appear regularly in the* Village Voice *and* Seattle Weekly *as well as the arts and entertainment supplement of the* Atlantic Monthly. *One anonymous reader commented on the Metacritic Web site that "[u]nlike the other critics . . . who take great pride in regurgitating the entire plot as if they wrote it, Ms. Taylor can let me get a feel for a movie w/o ruining it." Most people read film reviews to decide whether to see a particular film. As you read this review of* Little Miss Sunshine, *annotate the passages where Taylor gives plot detail or other kinds of information about the film. Consider whether she tells too much or just enough about the plot and whether the other information would help you decide whether to see the film.*

    Little Miss Sunshine, a raucously entertaining slice of slapstick dressed up as domestic satire, is probably best seen under the conditions in which I saw it first time around at this year's Sundance Film Festival, in a theater full of critics so exhausted by a grueling diet of movie misery, we were ready to take to our jaded bosoms almost anything that announced itself as comedy. As far as my eye could see, the audience was laughing its head off, and though the movie doesn't hold up quite as well in the lonely confines of a studio screening room with two others present, it's still a pretty good night out for those who find the real world close to unbearable right now.   1

    Not that you could call this movie about domestic infrastructure cracking beneath the weight of depression, therapeutic mumbo jumbo and rotting notions of what counts as success in America an escape vehicle. A first foray into feature films by the music-video- and commercial-making team of Jonathan Dayton and Valerie Faris, this tale of an ordinary (i.e., barking mad) family on the road across America to a kiddie pageant in Redondo Beach is more alive than competent. The cheerfully cheesy filmmaking is glued together, more or less, by joie de vivre, a few inspired moments and an outstanding cast playing their cartoon roles absolutely straight. "Dysfunctional" must be the most overused word in America but, by any definition except that of novice screenwriter Michael Arndt,   2 who bestows on this tattered bunch a ruined heroism, the Hoovers are a bunch of unraveling lower-middle-class losers straight out of Jules Feiffer,[1] and beset by every topical social ill on Dr. Laura's[2] shitlist. Greg Kinnear, a mounting panic poking through his pretty-boy politician's looks, is funny and unnerving as Richard Hoover, an aspiring motivational speaker trying in vain to peddle his 9-step Refuse to Lose program.

Any sane person would see through this recipe for successful 3 living, let alone Richard's heroin-snorting, porn-obsessed father (Alan Arkin, hamming over the top like the star attraction at a summer-camp talent show); his pimply teenage son (Paul Dano), a Nietzsche[3] freak who refuses to speak until he gets accepted into the Air Force Academy; and his suicidal brother-in-law (Steve Carell, all wounded eyes and rodent nose), a Proust[4] scholar fresh out of the funny farm after being dumped by his boyfriend for a far more successful Proust scholar. Even Richard's chubby, be-spectacled little daughter Olive (the unflappable Abigail Breslin), an unlikely but grimly determined contender in the Little Miss Sunshine beauty pageant, is only briefly taken in by her father's shopworn rhetoric, and the tipping point comes when he stops believing it himself. Trapped together in an ailing minivan, the Hoovers bicker and curse their way westward in search of a tacky American Dream under the ball-breaking stare and matter-of-fact hardiness of matriarch Sheryl (the ever-versatile Toni Collette). The only character to escape caricature, she's the lynchpin who gathers the movie's energy to her, even as her warm common sense and unwavering commitment to her brood sacrifice Little Miss Sunshine's candidacy for true satire.

Critics who damn the movie for trashing ordinary Joes miss the 4 point. If anything, the filmmakers' lapse into squishy redemption guarantees that the Hoovers will end up too lovable for biting social critique. For myself, I couldn't help but admire, in a slack-jawed way, the effrontery with which Dayton and Faris shamelessly

---

[1] *Jules Feiffer* (b. 1929): A satirical cartoonist and author whose works are distinguished by their neurotic characters. [Ed.]

[2] *Dr. Laura Schlessinger* (b. 1947): Host of a nationally syndicated radio call-in show, known for her socially conservative opinions. [Ed.]

[3] *Friedrich Nietzsche* (1844–1900): An influential German philosopher and one of the founders of existentialism. [Ed.]

[4] *Marcel Proust* (1871–1922): A French novelist whose major work, *Remembrance of Things Past*, is considered one of the masterpieces of world literature. [Ed.]

Too close for comfort: Sunshine's dysfunctional clan (Photo by Eric Lee)

milk every cobwebbed trick in the book of farce—the adenoidal whine of a jammed car horn, Carell's idiotic gait as he chases after the runaway bus, an inconveniently dead body flopping around as it's hauled hither and yon. Kick yourself for laughing if you like, but if *Little Miss Sunshine* is, finally, too sentimental for satire, it's precisely the farce that saves it. The climax, an unhinged horror show of JonBenét Ramsey–inspired vulgarity ineffably enhanced by Matt Winston's uproarious turn as the salon-tanned greaseball of an MC, is spring-loaded with a nimble twist I promise you won't see coming. And it says everything there is to say about the hyper-sexualization of childhood and the primal solidarity of families, however crippled, without a finger-wagging moment. For that, in this age of unctuous movie pedagogy, I'm willing to forgive it everything.

READING FOR MEANING

This section presents three activities that will help you reread Taylor's evaluation essay with a critical eye. Done in sequence, these activities lead you from a basic understanding of the selection to a more personal response to it and finally to an analysis that deepens your understanding and critical thinking about what you are reading.

Read to Comprehend

Reread the selection, and write a few sentences briefly explaining Taylor's overall judgment of the film *Little Miss Sunshine* and listing the aspects of the film she judges to be good and bad. The following definitions may help you understand Taylor's vocabulary:

raucously (paragraph 1): in a noisy, rowdy way.

grueling (1): exhausting, physically or mentally demanding.

joie de vivre (2): enjoyment of life.

Identify three or more additional words that you don't understand, and find the best definitions from the dictionary that work with their context.

To expand your understanding of this reading, you might use one or more of the following critical reading strategies that are explained and illustrated in Appendix 1: *annotating* and *paraphrasing*.

Read to Respond

Write several paragraphs exploring your initial thoughts and feelings about Taylor's evaluation of *Little Miss Sunshine*. Focus on anything that stands out for you, perhaps because it resonates with your own experience or because you find a statement puzzling.

You might consider writing about the following:

- Taylor's suggestions that mood may affect receptiveness to a film and that seeing a comedy in a crowded theater may be more fun than seeing it alone or with only a few people, perhaps in relation to your own experience;

- what the still photograph from the film adds to your understanding of and response to the essay;

- the effectiveness in comedy of combining predictability (milking "every cobwebbed trick in the book of farce") with surprise ("a nimble twist I promise you won't see coming"), perhaps in relation to another film or television program with which you are familiar (4); or

- the idea that "however crippled" or dysfunctional a family may be, it may still share a "primal solidarity," perhaps even love (4).

To develop your response to Taylor's evaluation, you might use one or more of the following critical reading strategies that are explained and illustrated in Appendix 1: *contextualizing*, *looking for patterns of opposition*, and *evaluating the logic of an argument*.

Read to Analyze Assumptions

Reread Taylor's evaluation essay, and write a paragraph or two exploring one or more of the assumptions you find in the text. The following suggestions may help:

- **assumptions about humor.** Taylor argues that even though she and her fellow critics found *Little Miss Sunshine* very funny, its serious themes—"depression, therapeutic mumbo jumbo and rotting notions of what counts as success in America" (paragraph 2) as well as "the hypersexualization of childhood" (4)—keep the film from being "an escape vehicle" (2). To think critically about the assumptions in this essay related to humor, ask yourself: Are there films that are pure escapist humor, or does comedy necessarily have a serious undercurrent? For something to be funny, must it reveal human weaknesses and faults, undercut pretension and arrogance, or satirize hypocrisy? Think of comedies you know well, and examine their humor.

- **assumptions about the American Dream.** Taylor calls the Hoover family's search for wealth and celebrity in the Little Miss Sunshine beauty pageant "a tacky American Dream" (paragraph 3), and she describes the Hoovers in socioeconomic terms as "lower-middle-class losers" who hold "rotting notions of what counts as success in America" (2). To think critically about the essay's—and the Hoovers'—assumptions about the American Dream, ask yourself: What has the idea of the American Dream traditionally motivated people to do to improve their socioeconomic status? How does the Hoover family's desire for their young daughter to win a beauty pageant fit in with or ironically undercut the American Dream ideology, as you understand it? How does Richard Hoover's Refuse to Lose program relate to this idea?

To probe assumptions more deeply, you might use one or both of the following critical reading strategies that are explained and illustrated in Appendix 1: *judging the writer's credibility* and *performing a Toulmin analysis.*

READING LIKE A WRITER
PRESENTING THE SUBJECT

Writers of evaluative essays usually begin by naming and describing their subject, but they usually provide only enough information to give readers a context for the judgment. However, certain kinds of evaluations—such as book, musical performance, television, and film reviews—may require more information because readers are trying to decide whether to buy the book, attend the performance, or see the film or television program. Reviewers of these kinds of subjects carefully choose details that help readers make a decision. Film reviews, for example, typically identify the actors and director, describe the setting, tell a little about the plot without giving too much away, and identify the film by genre or type. Informing readers about the genre is especially important because different genres have different criteria to meet. All films may be evaluated on the basis of the acting, directing, screenwriting, and so on. But comedies have to be funny, and action films have to be exciting. Therefore, as a critical reader, you will want to see how Taylor attempts to classify *Little Miss Sunshine.*

Analyze

1. *Circle* the words Taylor uses to describe the genre of the film. To get started, notice that she calls it "slapstick" and "satire" in paragraph 1. These words indicate different comedic qualities. For example, slapstick is associated with exaggerated physical humor, whereas satire suggests that the humor makes what Taylor later calls "biting social critique" (4). Note the other terms that she uses to describe the kind of film she thinks *Little Miss Sunshine* is and their implications about the film's genre.

2. Think about how the terms Taylor uses to describe the film's genre help you understand the kind of film she thinks *Little Miss Sunshine* is and why she judges it as she does.

Write

Write a few sentences discussing Taylor's view of the film's genre. What kind of film does she think *Little Miss Sunshine* is? *Add a sentence or two* discussing how classifying the film in the way she does affects her judgment of it.

CONSIDERING IDEAS FOR YOUR OWN WRITING

Consider writing an evaluation of a film, a television show, or another visual or media event. You could review another film in this genre (comedy) or one in any other genre that you find appealing (such as action, drama, adventure, fantasy, thriller, docudrama, and so on). Try to choose a genre with which you are already familiar; your evaluation will be richer because of your greater knowledge. Remember that you do not have to write an all-positive or all-negative evaluation. A mixed review can be just as valuable to readers.

FARHAD MANJOO

iPod: I Love You, You're Perfect, Now Change

> *Farhad Manjoo (b. 1978) was the editor of his college newspaper before embarking on a career in journalism. He has written about new media for* Wired News *and is currently a staff writer for* Salon.com, *where he also writes about politics. This essay evaluating the iPod originally appeared in* Salon *in 2006 and was occasioned by the fifth anniversary of the iPod and the publication of Steven Levy's book about it entitled* The Perfect Thing. *Among the articles Manjoo has written about music is a review of neuroscience research, "This Is Your Brain on Music," in which he explains how different parts of the brain are excited by music and produce pleasure-giving neurotransmitters. He concludes that essay with a statement that sheds light on his evaluation of the iPod: "This is obvious — that music elicits emotion better than speech is something we all understand. It's why movies have soundtracks, and it's why couples have favorite songs." Before reading Manjoo's essay, think about how you listen to music and whether music serves as a kind of soundtrack to enhance your experiences.*
>
> *As you read, annotate the essay, noting in the margin where Manjoo identifies aspects of the iPod that he judges to be either worthy of praise or deserving of criticism.*

The tech journalist Steven Levy calls his new book about the iPod *The Perfect Thing*, a title that seems to skip past the boundaries of mere affection and into a land of wild-eyed cultish idolatry. Nobody's perfect, you know, and if there's perfection to be found in some earthly thing, the thing is not a six-ounce digital music player made by Apple.

Every honest iPod owner keeps a playlist of Pod-related pet peeves; mine begins much like yours, I bet, with a mournful dirge on its feeble battery, which weakens exponentially with age. The damn thing gets scratched too easily, too. What good is a beautiful white-plastic-and-steel skin if you've got to hide it in a thick slab of plexiglass armor? The iPod can't carry songs from one computer to another (unless you elicit outside help), and the music Apple sells on its online store won't play on any other company's devices. How perfect is that? Worst of all is that the iPod inflames my ADD and encourages my OCD — it has me worrying, just about every time I'm playing a song, that there's something else somewhere on the enormous hard disk that would better fit the mood. In the age of iPod, listening to music is too often an anxious affair.

"The iPod is not perfect, of course," Levy writes, and proceeds to list many of the flaws I put down above. He suggests that the "perfect" in his title isn't supposed to mean "flawless," but something more like (I'm paraphrasing for concision) incredibly interesting and unbelievably awesome in ways you've probably never even thought of. What's perfect about the iPod is the "seemingly uncanny alignment of technology, design, culture, and media" that made it the biggest thing in the world, "the center of just about every controversy in the digital age," Levy says. . . .

[T]he iPod, which turns five years old today . . . got so big, so 4 fast, so unexpectedly, penetrating so deep into the culture (both the pope and Dick Cheney have one!), its success begs for probing analysis. . . . At the moment, though, let's focus on the most important question occasioned by Levy's book and by iPod's fifth birthday: What's it done to the music? I mean to take a wider view here, because the iPod isn't just the iPod—it's a stand-in for the more general phenomenon of media going digital, leaving the physical realm and coming under the dominion of computers. I wouldn't want to shortchange the transistor radio and the Walkman, but you can make a good case that digitization has altered how we experience music more fundamentally than any technology since the advent of audio recording. First Napster, then iPod: Music is now on-demand, instant, portable—fast, cheap and out of control. Apple's current top-of-the-line model sells for $350, weighs five ounces, and holds 20,000 songs (it plays videos, too). It won't let you listen to anything you want wherever you want, at the exact moment you desire it—but it comes damn close. And a device that will allow you infinite choice on demand is surely coming; we'll see it within the decade, from Apple or from someone else, and most of us will have one.

There's undeniable joy in this new situation. Levy writes that 5 "just about anyone who owns an iPod will at one point—usually when a favorite tune appears spontaneously and the music throbs through the ear buds, making a dull day suddenly come alive—say or think the following: 'Perfect.'" What he's describing is the euphoria of free music—unconstrained music, not stolen music. It's this freedom—the freedom to boogie, let's call it—that iPod's marketers are getting at in those ubiquitous dancing silhouette ads. Freedom is iPod's biggest selling point.

And yet. Am I the only one who worries that for all its wonders, 6 the iPod has also tremendously complicated our relationship to music—has made us more mindlessly consumptive of songs, less attentive to the context and the quality of music, and concerned, constantly, with just always getting more, more, more? If you've spent enough time with the iPod—over the years, I've had four, and there is a new Shuffle in Shanghai with my name on it—you must recognize the vague worry of which I speak. The iPod is so good. But I can't be the only one who sometimes wishes it hadn't been invented at all. . . .

There are probably millions of people for whom the iPod has turned a dark day bright. Because here's the thing about the iPod, its transcendent reason for success, more important than its design, its interface, Apple's marketing, or Jobs' charisma: Sometimes, it can just stop you cold. This is more a function of the music than the device, perhaps, and if you think about it the chill really has to do with your mood, and where you are, and what you're doing, and who you're thinking about, and probably the weather. . . . But sometimes, things align just right, and a song comes on, and the music and the world around you seem to sync up in a kind of cosmic way.

Levy writes that when this happens, the music becomes a "soundtrack" for the scenery, which is a good way to put it. The iPod turns ordinary life — riding the bus, waiting in line at the post office, staring at a spreadsheet for 12 hours a day — into cinema. Levy describes the work of sociologist Michael Bull, who, when studying the habits of fans of the iPod's great ancestor the Sony Walkman, found that people liked to think of themselves "as imaginary movie stars" playing out scenes dictated by the music in their ears. One subject who listened to music from spaghetti westerns said that the Walkman turned him into a "verbal bounty hunter" bent on firing "short cool blasts of verbal abuse" at his co-workers. The science fiction writer William Gibson once described the Walkman as having done "more to change human perception than any virtual reality gadget. I can't remember any technological experience that was quite so wonderful as being able to take music and move it through landscape and architecture." The iPod, with its greater capacity, alters perception even more profoundly; when the right song comes on, the world actually feels different.

There's a strain of oldster, Luddite criticism out there that goes after iPod listeners for cutting themselves off from the sounds of the everyday world. But, as Levy points out, "escaping" the real world is only part of the reason that people insert their earbuds in public places. The main jag isn't escape, but, instead, enhancement. There are moments when you're out in the world and circumstances seem to demand a certain particular song — nothing else will do. You've just had a fight with your girlfriend, and as you're sitting on the bus you realize the only thing that will console you is putting on that devastating Postal Service duet "Nothing Better." This is what Levy means when he describes the iPod as enhancing your world: It lets you use music to polish up an otherwise inadequate existence. When it works, the iPod seems to confirm

Arthur C. Clarke's third law of prediction: Any sufficiently advanced technology is indistinguishable from magic. The iPod puts a spell on you.

There is, however, a problem with the way the iPod encourages   10
you to listen to music — on the move, as you're out and about in the noisy world. Music portability has changed — for the worse — the way engineers record music. To ensure that people can hear new songs in noisy settings, record labels now use a very low dynamic range when they're mastering new albums. This means they set everything in a track — the vocals, the various instruments — to be at more or less the same volume, making for few interesting variations during a song between quiet moments and loud moments. To be sure, this is chiefly an audiophile's complaint, one that doesn't bother even most ardent music fans. It goes along with that other common snooty-sounding complaint about the iPod — that the digital compression required to make the thing work ruins music, especially classical and jazz.

Neither of these problems frustrate the iPod-loving hordes very   11
much, and Levy doesn't address them in his book. I suspect a more widespread issue, though, has to do with the way the iPod seems to work against listening to new music, which has become my chief complaint about the machine. Like many others in the so-called iPod generation, years of surfing the Web have reduced my attention span to not much more time than the length of a typical YouTube clip; consequently, my iPod, stocked with 4,124 songs, routinely turns me into a hyperactive freak show. If you have an iPod, I'm sure you know what I mean. You put on something that you've been wanting to listen to all day. Lucinda Williams' *Car Wheels on a Gravel Road* album, say. But you're three-quarters of the way through the first track, and even though you're really digging it, something about the scratchiness of Williams' voice reminds [you] of something else entirely — the Carter Family. And, hey, don't you have a copy of *Wildwood Flower* on here? Why, yes, you do. So you switch. But of course, putting on the Carter Family is going to remind you of Johnny Cash. And you have the feeling that you must, just this minute, play Cash's version of "In My Life" now. So you switch again. But you're a minute into Johnny and you start to wonder about the Beatles' original version of the track. . . .

The plethora of choice makes taking in something completely   12
new particularly difficult. Listening to an album you've never heard before is work; it requires time, patience, and attention. You can't do it half-assed. But when you play your new album on your iPod, there's always the lure of all those other tracks, and your mind drifts to all that familiar music, all that stuff you know and don't need to work to appreciate. So you inevitably start playing

the same stuff over and over. The numbers seem to bear this out—though iPods can store thousands of songs, the average iPod user's library numbers just about 500 well-worn tracks.

The irony here is that digitization has made acquiring new   13
music particularly easy—file-sharing networks still work really well, friend, and Apple's one-click purchasing system encourages many impulse purchases. Levy points out, too, that the iPod has eliminated the gap between rock-snob music collectors and the rest of us poseurs. If you've got a friend whose iPod always has the latest, coolest songs on it, all you have to do is plug it in to your machine to acquire the fruits of his taste. (As the *New Republic*'s resident rock aficionado Michael Crowley has noted, this situation greatly concerns the tribe of snobs: "We are being ruined by the iPod.") Thus it's possible, these days, to sort of mindlessly collect music without ever coming to appreciate it.

I remember what I did the first time I heard "Lua," that dreamy   14
Bright Eyes single of a couple years ago. I went to a BitTorrent site and downloaded Conor Oberst's entire oeuvre, more than a giga-byte of music that I've never since played. My iPod's got a whole lot of unplayed Ryan Adams, too, a plunder inspired by the time *The West Wing* featured "Desire" in an episode. A month ago I bought a Dan Reeder album that I've only played one time. I also bought the new Yo La Tengo album—but every time I try to listen to it, my fingers start to switch to their older stuff. In the past week, I got at least three new albums from various sources; I can listen to them whenever I want, but I don't know if I ever will. More and more, I'm pretty much always playing *OK Computer*—an album that, not coincidentally, I first came to love when the main thing I used for music was a Discman, and, despite my attention-deficit prob-lems, played constantly for weeks on end. . . .

It's possible that bitching about the way the iPod has changed   15
the way I listen to music isn't a legitimate gripe about the iPod at all. The iPod is a large portable hard drive that plays music—it is a logical end-point to decades of technological trends. It arises from the modern condition, and it's the modern condition, more than the iPod itself, that I'm really complaining about. And there is, of course, no going back.

Indeed, we ought to be thankful that if we have to live with   16
something like the iPod, the thing we got is as good as it is. The iPod's not perfect. But for all its flaws, the iPod is just about alone in our world of things in at least striving for perfection. Think about the millions of objects you interact with every day: the computers, the cars, the cookware, the books, the bedding, the furniture, all those clothes. Unless you own a Mercedes or regularly totter about in Manolos, the iPod surely stands out amid your

dreary workaday existence: for its beauty; for its sublime function; for the obvious thoughtfulness with which it was made—the way every detail, from the earbuds to the interface font to the packaging in which it arrives, seems to have been fussed over. "If there was ever a product that catalyzed what's Apple's reason for being, it's this," Jobs told Levy. "Because it combines Apple's incredible technology base with Apple's legendary ease of use with Apple's awesome design. . . . So if anybody was ever wondering why is Apple on earth, I would hold this up as a good example."

Jobs is right. His machine is amazing. I just hope he comes up with something better.   17

READING FOR MEANING

This section presents three activities that will help you reread Manjoo's evaluation essay with a critical eye. Done in sequence, these activities lead you from a basic understanding of the selection to a more personal response to it and finally to an analysis that deepens your understanding and critical thinking about what you are reading.

To expand your understanding of this reading, you might use one or more of the following critical reading strategies that are explained and illustrated in Appendix 1: *outlining, questioning to understand and remember,* and *summarizing.*

Read to Comprehend

Reread the selection, and write a few sentences briefly explaining Manjoo's overall judgment of the iPod and listing the aspects of the iPod he judges to be good and bad. The following definitions may help you understand Manjoo's vocabulary:

dirge (paragraph 2): a song of mourning or sorrow.

dominion (4): rule or power.

Luddite (9): a person who opposes new technology.

Identify three or more additional words that you don't understand, and find the best definitions from the dictionary that work with their context.

To expand your understanding of this reading, you might use one or more of the following critical reading strategies that are explained and illustrated in Appendix 1: *outlining, questioning to understand and remember,* and *summarizing.*

Read to Respond

Write several paragraphs exploring your initial thoughts and feelings about Manjoo's evaluation of the iPod. Focus on anything that stands out for you, perhaps because it resonates with your own experience or because you find a statement puzzling.

You might consider writing about the following:

- the assertion that "[e]very honest iPod owner keeps a playlist of Pod-related pet peeves," perhaps in relation to your own feelings about the shortcomings of your iPod or other music player (paragraph 2);

- Manjoo's concern that "the iPod has also tremendously complicated our relationship to music — has made us more mindlessly consumptive of songs, less attentive to the context and the quality of music, and concerned, constantly, with just always getting more, more, more" (6);

- Manjoo's idea that "[l]istening to an album you've never heard before is work; it requires time, patience, and attention," perhaps in relation to your own experience (12); or

- the irony Manjoo points out that "it's possible, these days, to sort of mindlessly collect music without ever coming to appreciate it" (13).

To develop your response to Manjoo's evaluation, you might use one or more of the following critical reading strategies that are explained and illustrated in Appendix 1: *contextualizing, reflecting on challenges to your beliefs and values*, and *judging the writer's credibility*.

Read to Analyze Assumptions

Reread Manjoo's evaluation essay, and write a paragraph or two exploring one or more of the assumptions you find in the text. The following suggestions may help:

- **assumptions about freedom.** Manjoo points out that the "iPod's biggest selling point" is "[f]reedom" (paragraph 5) and that music is now "on-demand, instant, portable — fast, cheap and out of control" (4) — meaning, presumably, out of control of the music production and distribution industry. To think critically about the assumptions in this essay related to freedom, ask yourself: How does digitalizing give consumers more freedom to control what music they listen to and when and where they do so? Consider also that individual songs have been liberated from the packaging of the album and that artists can produce their own music without needing contracts from record companies. What has been gained through this freeing of music from traditional modes of production and distribution? What may have been lost as well? For example, Manjoo suggests that the iPod has increased our desire to have more and more music, possibly lowering our standards.

- **assumptions about mediated experience.** Having music on demand 24/7 everywhere we go has the potential to change the way we experience the world. As Manjoo argues, "[T]he iPod turns ordinary life . . . into cinema" (8).

Cultural theorists calls this experiencing of the world through music *mediated*. Instead of being bombarded by random sounds we encounter, we use our iPods to provide a filter through which we experience reality, adding a musical score to our everyday lives. As Manjoo points out, "when the right song comes on, the world actually *feels* different" (8). He acknowledges that some people think listening to music all the time is an "escape," but Manjoo argues that it is really an "enhancement" (9). This argument seems to be based both on his personal experience and on the neuroscience research on how music affects the brain, which is mentioned in the headnote to this essay.

To think critically about the assumptions in this essay related to how the iPod changes the way we experience the world, ask yourself: How apt is the comparison between the effect the soundtrack has on your experience of a film and the effect listening to music has on your ordinary experience? Think of a particular song or artist whose music you use to make the world feel different, to borrow Manjoo's words. Assuming that music does change the way we experience reality, is such a change a good thing, or does it insulate us in unhealthy ways from reality and divert our attention from addressing real-world problems? In addition, are we so immersed in sound that we cannot hear ourselves think? Or worse, is music so prepackaged and generic that it prevents us from thinking our own original, perhaps even revolutionary thoughts?

To probe assumptions more deeply, you might use one or both of the following critical reading strategies that are explained and illustrated in Appendix 1: *evaluating the logic of an argument* or *performing a Toulmin analysis*.

READING LIKE A WRITER
ASSERTING AN OVERALL JUDGMENT

Readers expect an evaluative essay to make a definitive overall judgment of the subject—an assertion that the subject is good or bad or that it is better or worse than something else of the same kind. But since few subjects are perfect, readers appreciate a balanced evaluation in which the weaknesses as well as the strengths are pointed out. In this essay, Farhad Manjoo is evaluating two things at once—the Apple iPod music player and the iPod as "a stand-in for the more general phenomenon of media going digital" (paragraph 4). Although he makes clear that the iPod is not "perfect" in the sense of being "flawless," he agrees with Steven Levy's judgment that "[w]hat's perfect about the iPod is the 'seemingly uncanny alignment of technology, design, culture, and media' that made it the biggest thing in the world" (3). This is Manjoo's overall judgment and thesis statement. This activity will help you separate Manjoo's judgments of the iPod as a machine and as a phenomenon.

Analyze

1. *Reread the essay, marking in the margin* with an *M* for machine where Manjoo is talking about the iPod specifically as a machine and with a *P* for phenomenon where he is talking about what the iPod represents. (Instead of writing *M* and *P* in the margin, you can highlight the passages in different colors.)

2. Review the places where Manjoo evaluates the iPod as a machine, and list what he thinks are its strengths and weaknesses.

3. Also review the places where Manjoo evaluates the iPod as a phenomenon, and list what he thinks are its benefits and shortcomings.

Write

Write a sentence or two summarizing Manjoo's judgment of the iPod as a machine, listing its strengths and weaknesses. Add another few sentences summarizing Manjoo's judgment of the iPod as a phenomenon, listing its benefits and shortcomings.

CONSIDERING IDEAS FOR YOUR OWN WRITING

Consider evaluating something that involves new technology or innovations in a field, as Manjoo has done with the iPod. Recent innovations in automobiles include hybrid and electric cars; in media, high-definition television, digital video recorders, and flat screen LCDs; in architecture, houses where interior walls have been replaced with electronic fields that can shield a room from view or, with a flick of a switch, allow the room to be seen. You could also write about innovations in landscaping, in museum displays, in music, in art, in computers, or in theaters or other performance spaces. For such an evaluation, you could choose something that is completely accessible to you and with which you are familiar, or you could do some research to educate yourself.

STACY SCHIFF

Know It All: Can Wikipedia Conquer Expertise?

Stacy Schiff (b. 1961) is the author of several biographies, includ-
ing Vera *(Mrs. Vladimir Nabokov), which won the Pulitzer Prize,*
and Saint-Exupéry, *which was a Pulitzer finalist. Her most recent*
book is A Great Improvisation: Franklin, France, and the Birth of
America *(2004). Schiff has received fellowships from the Guggenheim*
Foundation and the National Endowment for the Humanities and
was a Director's Fellow at the Center for Scholars and Writers at the
New York Public Library. This evaluation of the popular online ency-
clopedia, Wikipedia, first appeared in the New Yorker *in 2006.*

Wikipedia is controversial in academia because it is not considered
authoritative, meaning that the information in its articles cannot
always be counted on as accurate or reliable. For this reason, several
colleges and universities have banned the use of Wikipedia as a source
in student writing. As you read Schiff's evaluation, think about how
she judges the site's authoritativeness. Also annotate in the margin
where she brings up other criteria. Consider whether she has left out
any criterion you think is important.

On March 1st, Wikipedia, the online interactive encyclopedia, 1
hit the million-articles mark, with an entry on Jordanhill, a railway
station in suburban Glasgow. Its author, Ewan MacDonald, posted
a single sentence about the station at 11 p.m., local time; over the
next twenty-four hours, the entry was edited more than four hundred times, by dozens of people. (Jordanhill happens to be the
"1029th busiest station in the United Kingdom"; it "no longer has a
staffed ticket counter.") The *Encyclopædia Britannica*, which for
more than two centuries has been considered the gold standard for
reference works, has only a hundred and twenty thousand entries
in its most comprehensive edition. . . . Wikipedia includes fine
entries on Kafka and the War of the Spanish Succession, and also a
complete guide to the ships of the U.S. Navy, a definition of Philadelphia cheesesteak, a masterly page on Scrabble, a list of historical
cats (celebrity cats, a cat millionaire, the first feline to circum-
navigate Australia), a survey of invented expletives in fiction ("bip-
pie," "cakesniffer," "furgle"), instructions for curing hiccups, and
an article that describes, with schematic diagrams, how to build a
stove from a discarded soda can. The how-to entries represent territory that the encyclopedia has not claimed since the eighteenth
century. You could cure a toothache or make snowshoes using the
original *Britannica*, of 1768–71. (You could also imbibe a lot of

prejudice and superstition. The entry on Woman was just six words: "The female of man. See *Homo*.") If you look up "coffee preparation" on Wikipedia, you will find your way, via the entry on Espresso, to a piece on types of espresso machines, which you will want to consult before buying. There is also a page on the site dedicated to "Errors in the *Encyclopædia Britannica* that have been corrected in Wikipedia" (Stalin's birth date, the true inventor of the safety razor).

Because there are no physical limits on its size, Wikipedia can aspire to be all-inclusive. It is also perfectly configured to be current: there are detailed entries for each of the twelve finalists on this season's *American Idol*, and the article on the "2006 Israel-Lebanon Conflict" has been edited more than four thousand times since it was created, on July 12th, six hours after Hezbollah militants ignited the hostilities by kidnapping two Israeli soldiers. Wikipedia, which was launched in 2001, is now the seventeenth-most-popular site on the Internet, generating more traffic daily than MSNBC.com and the online versions of the *Times* and the *Wall Street Journal* combined. The number of visitors has been doubling every four months; the site receives as many as fourteen thousand hits per second. . . .

The site has achieved this prominence largely without paid staff or revenue. It has five employees in addition to Jimmy Wales, Wikipedia's thirty-nine-year-old founder, and it carries no advertising. In 2003, Wikipedia became a nonprofit organization; it meets most of its budget, of seven hundred and fifty thousand dollars, with donations, the bulk of them contributions of twenty dollars or less. Wales says that he is on a mission to "distribute a free encyclopedia to every single person on the planet in their own language," and to an astonishing degree he is succeeding. Anyone with

Anyone with Internet access can create a Wikipedia entry or edit one. The site has hundreds of thousands of contributors.

Internet access can create a Wikipedia entry or edit an existing one. The site currently exists in more than two hundred languages and has hundreds of thousands of contributors around the world. Wales is at the forefront of a revolution in knowledge gathering: he has marshalled an army of volunteers who believe that, working collaboratively, they can produce an encyclopedia that is as good as any written by experts, and with an unprecedented range.

Wikipedia is an online community devoted not to last night's party or to next season's iPod but to a higher good. It is also no more immune to human nature than any other utopian project. Pettiness, idiocy, and vulgarity are regular features of the site. Nothing about high-minded collaboration guarantees accuracy, and open editing invites abuse. Senators and congressmen have been caught tampering with their entries; the entire House of Representatives has been banned from Wikipedia several times. . . . Curiously, though, mob rule has not led to chaos. Wikipedia, which began as an experiment in unfettered democracy, has sprouted policies and procedures. At the same time, the site embodies our newly casual relationship to truth. When confronted with evidence of errors or bias, Wikipedians invoke a favorite excuse: look how often the mainstream media, and the traditional encyclopedia, are wrong! . . .

Wales's most radical contribution may be not to have made information free but . . . to have invented a system that does not favor the Ph.D. over the well-read fifteen-year-old. "To me, the key thing is getting it right," Wales has said of Wikipedia's contributors. "I don't care if they're a high-school kid or a Harvard professor." At the beginning, there were no formal rules, though Sanger[1] eventually posted a set of guidelines on the site. The first was "Ignore all the rules." Two of the others have become central tenets: articles must reflect a neutral point of view (N.P.O.V., in Wikipedia lingo), and their content must be both verifiable and previously published. Among other things, the prohibition against original research heads off a great deal of material about people's pets. . . .

Perhaps Wikipedia's greatest achievement—one that Wales did not fully anticipate—was the creation of a community. Wikipedians are officially anonymous, contributing to unsigned entries under screen names. They are also predominantly male—about eighty percent, Wales says—and compulsively social, conversing with each other not only on the talk pages attached to each entry but on Wikipedia-dedicated I.R.C. channels and on user pages, which regular contributors often create and which serve as a sort of

[1] *Sanger:* Larry Sanger, whom Jimmy Wales hired to start the online encyclopedia that eventually became Wikipedia. [Ed.]

personalized office cooler. . . . According to a page on the site, an avid interest in Wikipedia has been known to afflict "computer programmers, academics, graduate students, game-show contestants, news junkies, the unemployed, the soon-to-be unemployed and, in general, people with multiple interests and good memories." You may travel in more exalted circles, but this covers pretty much everyone I know. . . .

Wikipedia has become a regulatory thicket, complete with an elaborate hierarchy of users and policies about policies. . . . For all its protocol, Wikipedia's bureaucracy doesn't necessarily favor truth. In March 2005, William Connolley, a climate modeller at the British Antarctic Survey, in Cambridge, was briefly a victim of an edit war over the entry on global warming, to which he had contributed. After a particularly nasty confrontation with a skeptic, who had repeatedly watered down language pertaining to the greenhouse effect, the case went into arbitration. "User William M. Connolley strongly pushes his POV with systematic removal of any POV which does not match his own," his accuser charged in a written deposition. "His views on climate science are singular and narrow." A decision from the arbitration committee was three months in coming, after which Connolley was placed on a humiliating one-revert-a-day parole.[2] The punishment was later revoked, and Connolley is now an admin,[3] with two thousand pages on his watchlist—a feature that enables users to compile a list of entries and to be notified when changes are made to them. He says that Wikipedia's entry on global warming may be the best page on the subject anywhere on the Web. Nevertheless, Wales admits that in this case the system failed. It can still seem as though the user who spends the most time on the site—or who yells the loudest—wins.

Connolley believes that Wikipedia "gives no privilege to those who know what they're talking about," a view that is echoed by many academics and former contributors, including Larry Sanger, who argues that too many Wikipedians are fundamentally suspicious of experts and unjustly confident of their own opinions. He left Wikipedia in March 2002, after Wales ran out of money to support the site during the dot-com bust. Sanger concluded that he had become a symbol of authority in an anti-authoritarian community. "Wikipedia has gone from a nearly perfect anarchy to an anarchy with gang rule," he told me. (Sanger is now the director of collaborative projects at the online foundation Digital Universe,

[2] *revert:* The deletion of edited text. [Ed.]

[3] *admin:* An administrator who polices the site for abuse, reverts or deletes text, and blocks certain users from editing text. [Ed.]

where he is helping to develop a Web-based encyclopedia, a hybrid between a wiki[4] and a traditional reference work. He promises that it will have "the lowest error rate in history.") Even Eric Raymond, the open-source pioneer whose work inspired Wales, argues that "'disaster' is not too strong a word" for Wikipedia. In his view, the site is "infested with moonbats." (Think hobgoblins of little minds, varsity division.) He has found his corrections to entries on science fiction dismantled by users who evidently felt that he was trespassing on their terrain. "The more you look at what some of the Wikipedia contributors have done, the better *Britannica* looks," Raymond said. He believes that the open-source model is simply inapplicable to an encyclopedia. For software, there is an objective standard: either it works or it doesn't. There is no such test for truth. . . .

Is Wikipedia accurate? Last year, *Nature* published a survey comparing forty-two entries on scientific topics on Wikipedia with their counterparts in *Encyclopædia Britannica*. According to the survey, Wikipedia had four errors for every three of *Britannica*'s, a result that, oddly, was hailed as a triumph for the upstart. Such exercises in nitpicking are relatively meaningless, as no reference work is infallible. *Britannica* issued a public statement refuting the survey's findings, and took out a half-page advertisement in the *Times*, which said, in part, "*Britannica* has never claimed to be error-free. We have a reputation not for unattainable perfection but for strong scholarship, sound judgment, and disciplined editorial review." Later, Jorge Cauz, *Britannica*'s president, told me in an e-mail that if Wikipedia continued without some kind of editorial oversight it would "decline into a hulking mediocre mass of uneven, unreliable, and, many times, unreadable articles." Wales has said that he would consider *Britannica* a competitor, "except that I think they will be crushed out of existence within five years."

Larry Sanger proposes a fine distinction between knowledge that is useful and knowledge that is reliable, and there is no question that Wikipedia beats every other source when it comes to breadth, efficiency, and accessibility. Yet the site's virtues are also liabilities. Cauz scoffed at the notion of "good enough knowledge." "I hate that," he said, pointing out that there is no way to know which facts in an entry to trust. Or, as Robert McHenry, a veteran editor at *Britannica*, put it, "We can get the wrong answer to a question quicker than our fathers and mothers could find a pencil." . . .

Wikipedia remains a lumpy work in progress. The entries can read as though they had been written by a seventh grader: clarity and concision are lacking; the facts may be sturdy, but the

9

10

11

[4] *wiki:* A kind of computer software that enables users to collaborate in writing and editing text. [Ed.]

connective tissue is either anemic or absent; and citation is hit or miss. Wattenberg and Viégas, of I.B.M.,[5] note that the vast majority of Wikipedia edits consist of deletions and additions rather than of attempts to reorder paragraphs or to shape an entry as a whole, and they believe that Wikipedia's twenty-five-line editing window deserves some of the blame. It is difficult to craft an article in its entirety when reading it piecemeal, and, given Wikipedians' obsession with racking up edits, simple fixes often take priority over more complex edits. Wattenberg and Viégas have also identified a "first-mover advantage": the initial contributor to an article often sets the tone, and that person is rarely a Macaulay[6] or a Johnson.[7] The overall effect is jittery, the textual equivalent of a film shot with a handheld camera.

What can be said for an encyclopedia that is sometimes right,   12 sometimes wrong, and sometimes illiterate? When I showed the Harvard philosopher Hilary Putnam his entry, he was surprised to find it as good as the one in the *Stanford Encyclopedia of Philosophy*. He was flabbergasted when he learned how Wikipedia worked. "Obviously, this was the work of experts," he said. In the nineteen-sixties, William F. Buckley, Jr.,[8] said that he would sooner "live in a society governed by the first two thousand names in the Boston telephone directory than in a society governed by the two thousand faculty members of Harvard University." On Wikipedia, he might finally have his wish. How was his page? Essentially on target, he said. All the same, Buckley added, he would prefer that those anonymous two thousand souls govern, and leave the encyclopedia writing to the experts.

Over breakfast in early May, I asked Cauz for an analogy with   13 which to compare *Britannica* and Wikipedia. "Wikipedia is to *Britannica* as *American Idol* is to the Juilliard School,"[9] he e-mailed me the next day. A few days later, Wales also chose a musical metaphor. "Wikipedia is to *Britannica* as rock and roll is to easy listening," he suggested. "It may not be as smooth, but it scares the parents and is a lot smarter in the end." He is right to emphasize the fright factor

---

[5] *Wattenberg and Viégas:* Martin Wattenberg and Fernanda B. Viégas, who have studied patterns of contributions and editing on Wikipedia. [Ed.]

[6] *Thomas Babington Macaulay:* A nineteenth-century British historian who is known for his prose style. [Ed.]

[7] *Dr. Samuel Johnson:* An eighteenth-century British writer who is known for his prose style. [Ed.]

[8] *William F. Buckley, Jr.:* A conservative writer and commentator. [Ed.]

[9] *Juilliard School:* A prestigious New York City school for drama, music, and dance. [Ed.]

over accuracy. . . . Not only are we impatient with the authorities but we are in a mood to talk back. Wikipedia offers endless opportunities for self-expression. It is the love child of reading groups and chat rooms, a second home for anyone who has written an Amazon review. This is not the first time that encyclopedia-makers have snatched control from an élite, or cast a harsh light on certitude. Jimmy Wales may or may not be the new Henry Ford, yet he has sent us tooling down the interstate, with but a squint back at the railroad. We're on the open road now, without conductors and timetables. We're free to chart our own course, also free to get gloriously, recklessly lost. Your truth or mine?

READING FOR MEANING

This section presents three activities that will help you reread Schiff's evaluation essay with a critical eye. Done in sequence, these activities lead you from a basic understanding of the selection to a more personal response to it and finally to an analysis that deepens your understanding and critical thinking about what you are reading.

Read to Comprehend

Reread the selection, and write a few sentences briefly explaining Schiff's overall judgment of Wikipedia and listing the aspects of Wikipedia she judges to be good and bad. The following definitions may help you understand Schiff's vocabulary:

the gold standard (paragraph 1): a model of excellence.

unprecedented (3): never existing before.

lingo (5): specialized vocabulary, jargon.

Identify three or more additional words that you don't understand, and find the best definitions from the dictionary that work with their context.

To expand your understanding of this reading, you might use one or more of the following critical reading strategies that are explained and illustrated in Appendix 1: *outlining, questioning to understand and remember,* and *summarizing.*

Read to Respond

Write several paragraphs exploring your initial thoughts and feelings about Schiff's evaluation of Wikipedia. Focus on anything that stands out for you, perhaps because it resonates with your own experience or because you find a statement puzzling.

You might consider writing about the following:

- the comparison between Wikipedia and the *Encyclopædia Britannica* or any other print encyclopedia with which you are familiar;

- what the drawings add to your understanding of and response to the essay;

- the idea that the founder's "utopian" mission for the site is to "distribute a free encyclopedia to every single person on the planet in their own language" (4); or

- the widespread ban on the use of Wikipedia as a source in academic essays, perhaps in relation to your own college and to your opinion about the use-fulness of the site.

To develop your response to Schiff's evaluation, you might use one or more of the following critical reading strategies that are explained and illustrated in Appendix 1: *contextualizing, looking for patterns of opposition*, and *reflecting on challenges to your beliefs and values.*

Read to Analyze Assumptions

Reread Schiff's evaluation essay, and write a paragraph or two exploring one or more of the assumptions you find in the text. The following suggestions may help:

- **assumptions about neutrality.** Schiff explains that the "central tenets" of the Web site are that the "articles must reflect a neutral point of view (N.P.O.V., in Wikipedia lingo), and their content must be both verifiable and previously published" (paragraph 5). But she demonstrates with the example of the "edit war over the entry on global warming" that these criteria are not easy to apply when people differ, even in the seemingly objective realm of science (7). To think critically about the assumptions in this essay—and your own assumptions—related to neutrality, ask yourself: What, if anything, in the essay suggests Schiff's opinion about the way Wikipedia treated William M. Connolley and about the site's decision not to distinguish between experts and other contributors? How do you think an encyclopedia should handle contentious subjects like global warming? How would having only experts serve as contributors or having experts in each field serve on an editorial review committee (as occurs in print encyclopedias) solve or fail to solve this problem? Should differences of opinion be pointed out so that readers can understand the debate and decide for themselves what to believe, or are certain kinds of knowledge not a matter of belief or individual choice?

- **assumptions about utopia.** Schiff explains that Wikipedia is utopian in that it seeks to "distribute a free encyclopedia to every single person on the planet in their own language" (paragraph 3). She also places the site "at the forefront of a revolution in knowledge gathering"(3), explaining that it "began as an experiment in unfettered democracy" (4). To think critically about the assumptions in this essay related to this "utopian project" (4), ask yourself: Where in the essay do you get a sense of Schiff's own view of these utopian goals of knowledge sharing and gathering or of how well she thinks the site has succeeded in achieving these goals? Is it really likely that sharing knowledge with everyone in the world could change the world for the better? Schiff does not break down the nationalities or economic status of the contributors, but she does point out that 80 percent are male (6). If the contributors come from mostly one gender or only certain parts of the world's population, then how likely is it that the knowledge included will be comprehensive and unbiased?

To probe assumptions more deeply, you might use one or both of the following critical reading strategies that are explained and illustrated in Appendix 1: *judging the writer's credibility* and *performing a Toulmin analysis.*

READING LIKE A WRITER
GIVING REASONS AND SUPPORT

At the center of every evaluation are the writer's reasons for making a judgment and the support for those reasons. The reasons should be appropriate for evaluating the subject, and they should be convincing to readers. Furthermore, the reasons should be visible: you do not want readers to miss them. As a writer, you make reasons visible by cueing them strongly—for example, by putting them at the beginnings of paragraphs. Schiff offers several reasons to support the high opinion she has of Wikipedia, and she attempts to support each reason.

Analyze

1. *Reread* the first two paragraphs, where Schiff gives two reasons for reviewing Wikipedia so positively (its inclusiveness and its currency).

2. *Mark* where Schiff uses examples to support these reasons.

3. Also mark where she uses comparisons to support these reasons.

Write

Write several sentences explaining what you have learned about how Schiff uses reasons and support to justify her evaluation of Wikipedia. *Give examples* from the reading.

CONSIDERING IDEAS FOR YOUR OWN WRITING

You might consider evaluating another example of new media that replaces old technology, such as online newspapers or audiobooks. Also consider other Web sites you might be interested in evaluating, such as social networking, sports, entertainment, and consumer product sites. If you evaluate one of these sites, what could you compare it to, and how do you think this comparison would help you support your evaluation?

A SPECIAL READING STRATEGY

Judging the Writer's Credibility

Establishing credibility is especially important for writers of evaluation because they want readers to accept their judgments as being well founded and authoritative. Writers need to demonstrate that they are knowledgable about the subject, that their evaluation is based on values readers share (or at least recognize as legitimate), and that they are fair in handling objections and opposing arguments. Follow the detailed guidelines for judging the writer's credibility in Appendix 1, and write a few sentences about how Stacy Schiff establishes credibility in this essay.

Evaluation Online

The Internet provides lots of sites where you can both read and post evaluations of films, performances, consumer products, and other subjects. Most evaluation sites provide relatively brief reviews, but Steve's Digicams (http://www.steves-digicams.com) offers an in-depth evaluation and analysis of the latest digital cameras. This site was created in 1997 by a person using the name Steve, who is described only as having "over 30 years' experience in photography." The "About Us" page explains that the site is designed to appeal to readers with little knowledge of computers or photography as well as to those with a great deal of expertise. By selecting what parts of a review to read, readers can easily control the amount and kind of information they get. The review illustrated here is of the Nikon Coolpix S9 camera. The marginal annotations point out the writing strategies that readers expect in print evaluations and some of the features that are characteristic of writing on the Web.

Clicking on the camera's name brings you to the "Introduction & Physical Views" page, which includes the date the review was posted and a pull-down menu headed "Select Review Page." The menu lists the following pages you can click on to access:

Introduction & Physical Views

Specifications

Features & Controls

Record Modes & Screens

Playback Modes & Screens

Steve's Conclusion

Sample Pictures

360-degree Quick Time VR Tour

Steve's Reviews Index

Clicking on the camera image gives you a 360-degree animated view.

Introduction & Physical Views

Click on the Coolpix S9 to take a QuickTime VR tour

The COOLPIX S9 is an affordable, easy-to-use digital camera that's housed in a slim and stylish body and features 6.1 megapixel image resolution, a 3x Zoom-Nikkor ED glass lens and a large 2.5 inch color LCD screen. It's loaded with Nikon's advanced imaging technology that allows anyone in your family to easily take great pictures.

The COOLPIX S9 is equipped with a One-Touch Portrait Button, which activates Nikon's In- Camera Image Innovations to fix common photo problems. This system includes Face-priority AF, which automatically finds and focuses on a subject's face, In-Camera Red-Eye Fix, which automatically corrects red-eye, and D-Lighting, an innovation that automatically corrects images with insufficient light. The S9 is equipped with Blur Warning, which alerts the user when an image is blurred and Best Shot Selector, a feature that automatically identifies and saves the sharpest image from a series.

Available for the first time in a COOLPIX camera, the S9 offers a Stop-Motion feature for creating fun, stop-motion animated video shorts. To use the feature, the consumer simply needs to pose an object they want to animate, take a picture, re-position the object and photograph again. Opaque versions of previous shots are shown on the camera's LCD to assist users when positioning and repositioning their object. Once shooting is completed, the S9 automatically creates a Quicktime™ video of the object's movement in-camera.

Similar to other COOLPIX cameras, the S9 has 15 scene modes, 4 with scene assist that automatically program cameras settings such as flash and focus for great pictures in a variety of locations and situations.

The COOLPIX S9 successfully packs all of these features into an ultra-slim, compact metal body. The camera's wave surface body is pleasing to the hand as well as to the eyes as it is comfortable to hold and ultra-portable.

For transferring pictures to computers and other peripherals, the S9 is USB compatible. The camera utilizes a rechargeable EN-EL8 Li-on battery and can take up to 190 shots on a single charge. For storage, the S9 has 24MB of internal memory and is SD/SDHC memory card- compatible. The S9 comes with Nikon's PictureProject Software for the importing, editing and organization of images.

Steve begins by presenting the subject, summarizing the camera's features, and offering his initial judgment.

He puts the S9 in its class (COOLPIX) and describes a new feature.

He points out other criteria appropriate for evaluating cameras of this type— settings, shape, and compatibility.

Steve goes on to list the camera's features and specifications. He ends the page with more pictures and with links to retailers that sell the S9, to a review of a larger, "swiveling" S10 model, and to the next "Features & Controls" page, an excerpt of which follows.

The large 2.5-inch color LCD with 153,600 pixels of resolution serves as the viewfinder as well as for reviewing your images and movies and accessing the menu screens. In lower light conditions the LCD will "gain up" for better framing and provides 100% coverage.

Controls on the back: The Record / Playback mode button. The "M"ode button calls up the onscreen mode dial to select the desired recording mode. The 4-way selector is for navigating menus and selecting pictures. In record mode pressing it "Up" selects flash mode, "Left" activates the selftimer and "Down" enables macro focus mode. The center OK button accepts menu selections and enables Auto Transfer of images. The MENU button calls up and dismisses menu screens. The "trashcan" button is for deleting images.

Steve continues to describe the camera's features and evaluate them.

If you click on the link "onscreen mode dial" in the previous paragraph, you get animated images showing the mode button and the Record Mode Menu, as well as other layers of menuing. Let's skip now to the page called "Steve's Conclusion," where Steve presents his evaluative argument.

Steve begins his conclusion by discussing how the camera fits into its class and comparing it to other S cameras and to last year's model.

Yet another "ultra-compact" model to add to Nikon's "S" series ranks, the Coolpix S9 is among the most compact point-n-shoot digicams that Nikon has to offer (as of March 2007). This new model is almost identical to the ____ from last year. While being very compact (weighing in at just 4 oz. without battery or memory card, and measuring just .08-inches thick), the S9 boasts a 6-megapixel imager, internal Zoom-Nikkor 3x optical zoom lens, QuickTime 2.5-inch LCD does not feature a anti-reflective coating, I found it a pleasure to use outdoors, even in the bright sunlight. The display was also effective indoors, VGA movie mode, 2.5-inch LCD as well as Nikon's exclusive Face Priority AF, D-lighting, and Red-eye Fix technologies. The only real difference in these models is the S9 does not feature an Underwater scene mode, but does include the new Stop-Motion movie mode. Aimed more towards beginner to novice users, this point-n-shoot offers the usual Auto exposure mode with limited adjustments for ISO, white balance, Color modes, etc. There's also 15 pre-programmed scene modes that help users capture great photos in various shooting environments.

He begins giving reasons for his overall judgment.

The S9's ergonomics are somewhat difficult. This is a very small camera, and I found unless you use the "pinch" technique (using your left thumb and forefinger to pinch the left side of the camera), it can be hard to use. The controls on the back of the model are well placed, however, I did not like how the buttons were arranged on the top of the camera. The Zoom controls are where the shutter release should be. This made it uncomfortable to use, and because these controls are so "touchy" I found myself changing the zoom position when trying to capture a framed shot. The menu system is logically organized, which allowed for quick navigation. You can even choose the style (Text or Icons) in which menu options are displayed via the Menu's option in the setup menu. While the 2.5-inch LCD does not feature a anti-reflective coating, I found it a pleasure to use outdoors, even in the bright sunlight. The display was also effective indoors, intensifying the live image in marginal lighting to aid in shot composition.

Steve supports his judgment with technical details that may not be understood by readers who did not read the earlier pages, but they can easily go back.

Shooting performance is a bit sluggish. Power up to first image captured measured about 3 seconds. Shutter lag, the delay between pressing the shutter release and capturing an image, averaged 1/10 of a second when pre-focused, but slowed to a leisurely 8/10 of a second including autofocus time. The shot to shot delay averaged about 2.5 seconds between frames without the use of the flash and between 3 and 5 seconds with the flash, depending on subject distance and battery life. When using red eye reduction flash mode, the LCD blanks during the pre-flash, a critical period of about one second. The LCD also goes blank and the camera freezes while the flash is recharging.

Steve continues giving his reasons and pointing out the camera's strengths and weaknesses for a few more paragraphs, ending with the following.

The label "Bottom line" announces Steve's overall judgment. He summarizes his main reasons and recommends other cameras that readers could look at for comparison.

Bottom line - The Nikon Coolpix S9 is a mixed bag. While offering good image quality, loads of user-friendly exposure modes, and a stylish "ultra-compact" body, the sluggish shooting performance dwindles a lot of its appeal. So, if you're in the market for an extremely pocketable camera, then we suggest also looking at other cameras, like the Canon PowerShot SD620, Casio Exilim EX-Z600 or Sony Cyber-shot DSC-W35 just to name a few.

Compare this "bottom line" judgment to what Steve said at the beginning of his review: "The COOLPIX S9 is an affordable, easy-to-use digital camera that's housed in a slim and stylish body. . . . It's loaded with Nikon's advanced imaging technology that allows anyone in your family to easily take great pictures." His opening praise for the "slim and stylish body" is echoed in his concluding reference to "a stylish 'ultra-compact' body," and his introductory claim that the camera takes "great pictures" is repeated in his final assertion that it offers "good image quality." But by the end of this multipage review, Steve has provided readers with an understanding of the S9's weaknesses as well as its strengths. Consequently, he gives it "a mixed bag" review that enables readers to decide whether the camera would meet their needs.

Analyze

1. *Find* another example of an online evaluation.

2. *Check* to see which of the evaluative writing strategies it displays, such as presenting the subject, asserting a clear overall judgment, giving appropriate reasons and convincing support, and anticipating objections and alternative judgments.

3. Also *note* any special online characteristics such as links, audio, and still or moving images.

Write

Write a paragraph or two describing what you have learned from this example of online evaluation writing.

CHRISTINE ROMANO

Jessica Statsky's "Children Need to Play, Not Compete": An Evaluation

> *Christine Romano wrote the following essay when she was a first-year college student. In it, she evaluates a position paper written by another student, Jessica Statsky's "Children Need to Play, Not Compete," which appears in Chapter 9 of this book (pp. 574–79). Romano focuses not on the writing strategies or basic features of this position paper but rather on its logic — on whether the argument is likely to convince the intended readers. She evaluates the logic of the argument according to the standards presented in Appendix 1 (pp. 624–27). You might want to review these standards before you read Romano's evaluation. Also, if you have not read Statsky's essay, you might want to do so now, thinking about what seems most and least convincing to you about her argument that competitive sports can be harmful to young children.*

Parents of young children have a lot to worry about and to hope for. In "Children Need to Play, Not Compete," Jessica Statsky appeals to their worries and hopes in order to convince them that organized competitive sports may harm their children physically and psychologically. Statsky states her thesis clearly and fully forecasts the reasons she will offer to justify her position: Besides causing physical and psychological harm, competitive sports discourage young people from becoming players and fans when they are older and inevitably put parents' needs and fantasies ahead of children's welfare. Statsky also carefully defines her key terms. By *sports*, for example, she means to include both contact and noncontact sports that emphasize competition. The sports may be organized locally at schools or summer sports camps or nationally, as in the examples of Peewee Football and Little League Baseball. She is concerned only with children six to twelve years of age.

In this essay, I will evaluate the logic of Statsky's argument, considering whether the support for her thesis is appropriate, believable, consistent, and complete. While her logic *is* appropriate, believable, and consistent, her argument also has weaknesses. It seems incomplete because it neglects to anticipate parents' predictable questions and objections and because it fails to support certain parts fully.

Statsky provides appropriate support for her thesis. Throughout her essay, she relies for support on different kinds of information (she cites twelve separate sources, including books, newspapers, and Web sites). Her quotations, examples, and statistics all support the reasons she believes competitive sports are bad for children. For example, in paragraph 3, Statsky offers the reason that "overly competitive sports" may damage children's growing bodies and that contact sports, in particular, may be especially hazardous. She supports this reason by paraphrasing Koppett that muscle strain or even lifelong injury may result when a twelve-year-old throws curve balls. She then quotes Tutko on the dangers of tackle football. The opinions of both experts are obviously appropriate. They are relevant to her reason, and we can easily imagine that they would worry many parents.

Not only is Statsky's support appropriate but it is also believable. Statsky quotes or summarizes authorities to support her argument in paragraphs 3–6, 8, 9, and 11. The question is whether readers would find these authorities believable or credible. Since Statsky relies almost entirely on authorities to support her argument, readers must believe these authorities for her argument to succeed. I have not read Statsky's sources, but I think there are good reasons to consider them authoritative. First of all, the newspaper authors she quotes write for two of America's most respected newspapers, the *New York Times* and the *Los Angeles Times*. These newspapers are read across the country by political leaders and financial experts and by people interested in the arts and popular culture. Both have sports reporters who not only report on sports events but also take a critical look at sports issues. In addition, both newspapers have reporters who specialize in children's health and education. Second, Statsky gives background information about the authorities she quotes, information intended to increase the person's believability in the eyes of parents of young children. In paragraph 3, she tells readers that Thomas Tutko is "a psychology professor at San Jose State University and coauthor of the book *Winning Is Everything and Other American Myths*." In paragraph 5, she announces that Martin Rablovsky is "a former sports editor for the *New York Times*," and she notes that he has watched children play organized sports for many years. Third, she quotes from three Web sites—the official Little League site, the site of the National Association of Sports Officials, and the Parentsknow.com database. Parents are likely to accept the authority of the Little League site and be interested in what other parents and sports officials have to say.

In addition to quoting authorities, Statsky relies on examples and anecdotes to support the reasons for her position. If examples and anecdotes are to be believable, they must seem representative to readers, not bizarre or highly unusual or completely unpredictable. Readers can imagine a similar event happening elsewhere. For anecdotes to be believable, they should, in addition, be specific and true to life. All of Statsky's examples and anecdotes fulfill these requirements, and her readers would find them believable. For example, early in her argument, in paragraph 4, Statsky reasons that fear of being hurt greatly reduces children's enjoyment of contact sports. The anecdote comes from Tosches's investigative report on Peewee Football as does the quotation by the mother of an eight-year-old player who says that the children become frightened and pretend to be injured in order to stay out of the game. In the anecdote, a seven-year-old makes himself vomit to avoid playing. Because these echo the familiar "I feel bad" or "I'm sick" excuse children give when they do not want to go somewhere (especially school) or do something, most parents would find them believable. They could easily imagine their own children pretending to be hurt or ill if they were fearful or depressed. The anecdote is also specific. Tosches reports what the boy said and did and what the coach said and did.

Other examples provide support for all the major reasons   6
Statsky gives for her position:

- That competitive sports pose psychological dangers — children becoming serious and unplayful when the game starts (paragraph 5)

- That adults' desire to win puts children at risk — parents fighting each other at a Peewee Football game, a coach setting fire to an opposing team's jersey, and the fatal beating of a man supervising a hockey game by the unhappy parent of a player (paragraph 8)

- That organized sports should emphasize cooperation and individual performance instead of winning — a coach banning scoring but finding that parents would not support him and a New York City basketball league in which all children play an equal amount of time and scoring is easier (paragraph 11)

All of these examples are appropriate to the reasons they support. They are also believable. Together, they help Statsky achieve her purpose of convincing parents that organized, competitive sports may be bad for their children and that there are alternatives.

If readers are to find an argument logical and convincing, it   7
must be consistent and complete. While there are no inconsistencies or contradictions in Statsky's argument, it is seriously incomplete because it neglects to support fully one of its reasons, it fails to anticipate many predictable questions parents would have, and it pays too little attention to noncontact competitive team sports. The most obvious example of thin support comes in paragraph 11, where Statsky asserts that many parents are ready for children's

team sports that emphasize cooperation and individual performance. Yet the example of a Little League official who failed to win parents' approval to ban scores raises serious questions about just how many parents are ready to embrace noncompetitive sports teams. The other support, a brief description of City Sports for Kids in New York City, is very convincing but will only be logically compelling to those parents who are already inclined to agree with Statsky's position. Parents inclined to disagree with Statsky would need additional evidence. Most parents know that big cities receive special federal funding for evening, weekend, and summer recreation. Brief descriptions of six or eight noncompetitive teams in a variety of sports in cities, rural areas, suburban neighborhoods— some funded publicly, some funded privately—would be more likely to convince skeptics. Statsky is guilty here of failing to accept the burden of proof, a logical fallacy.

Statsky's argument is also incomplete in that it fails to anticipate   8
certain objections and questions that some parents, especially those she most wants to convince, are almost sure to raise. In the first sentences of paragraphs 6, 9, and 10, Statsky does show that she is thinking about her readers' questions. She does not go nearly far enough, however, to have a chance of influencing two types of readers: those who themselves are or were fans of and participants in competitive sports and those who want their six- to twelve-year-old children involved in mainstream sports programs despite the risks, especially the national programs that have a certain prestige. Such parents might feel that competitive team sports for young children create a sense of community with a shared purpose, build character through self-sacrifice and commitment to the group, teach children to face their fears early and learn how to deal with them through the support of coaches and team members, and introduce children to the principles of social cooperation and collaboration. Some parents are likely to believe and to know from personal experience that coaches who burn opposing teams' jerseys on the pitching mound before the game starts are the exception, not the rule. Some young children idolize teachers and coaches, and team practice and games are the brightest moments in their lives. Statsky seems not to have considered these reasonable possibilities, and as a result her argument lacks a compelling logic it might have had. By acknowledging that she was aware of many of these objections—and perhaps even accommodating more of them in her own argument, as she does in paragraph 10, while refuting other objections—she would have strengthened her argument.

Finally, Statsky's argument is incomplete because she overlooks   9
examples of noncontact team sports. Track, swimming, and tennis are good examples that some readers would certainly think of. Some

elementary schools compete in track meets. Public and private clubs and recreational programs organize competitive swimming and tennis competitions. In these sports, individual performance is the focus. No one gets trampled. Children exert themselves only as much as they are able to. Yet individual performances are scored, and a team score is derived. Because Statsky fails to mention any of these obvious possibilities, her argument is weakened.

The logic of Statsky's argument, then, has both strengths and   10
weaknesses. The support she offers is appropriate, believable, and consistent. The major weakness is incompleteness—she fails to anticipate more fully the likely objections of a wide range of readers. Her logic would prevent parents who enjoy and advocate competitive sports from taking her argument seriously. Such parents and their children have probably had positive experiences with team sports, and these experiences would lead them to believe that the gains are worth whatever risks may be involved. Many probably think that the risks Statsky points out can be avoided by careful monitoring. For those parents inclined to agree with her, Statsky's logic is likely to seem sound and complete. An argument that successfully confirms readers' beliefs is certainly valid, and Statsky succeeds admirably at this kind of argument. Because she does not offer compelling counterarguments to the legitimate objections of those inclined not to agree with her, however, her success is limited.

READING FOR MEANING

This section presents three activities that will help you reread Romano's evaluation with a critical eye. Done in sequence, these activities lead you from a basic understanding of the selection to a more personal response to it and finally to an analysis that deepens your understanding and critical thinking about what you are reading.

Read to Comprehend

Reread the selection, and write a few sentences briefly explaining the strengths and weaknesses of Statsky's argument, according to Romano. The following definitions may help you understand Romano's vocabulary:

hazardous (paragraph 3): risky, dangerous.

bizarre (5): odd, very strange, weird.

skeptics (7): people who doubt or question the truth of something they are told.

Identify three or more additional words that you don't understand, and find the best definitions from the dictionary that work with their context.

To expand your understanding of this reading, you might use one or more of the following critical reading strategies that are explained and illustrated in Appendix 1: *annotating, paraphrasing,* and *synthesizing.*

Read to Respond

Write several paragraphs exploring your initial thoughts and feelings about Romano's evaluation. Focus on anything that stands out for you, perhaps because it resonates with your own experience or because you find a statement puzzling.

You might consider writing about the following:

- reasons that Romano finds Statsky's argument believable (paragraphs 4–6);

- reasons that Romano finds Statsky's argument incomplete;

- further reasons that parents of six- to twelve-year-old children might find Statsky's argument incomplete; or

- your own experience as a member of an organized sports team for children of the same age group, comparing or contrasting it with what Romano finds believable or incomplete in Statsky's argument.

To develop your response to Romano's evaluation, you might use one or more of the following critical reading strategies that are explained and illustrated in Appendix 1: *contextualizing, looking for patterns of opposition,* and *evaluating the logic of an argument.*

Read to Analyze Assumptions

Reread Romano's evaluation essay, and write a paragraph or two exploring one or more of the assumptions you find in the text. The following suggestions may help:

- **assumptions about competition and cooperation.** Statsky assumes that team sports for young children "should emphasize cooperation and individual performance over winning" (paragraph 6). In paragraph 8, however, Romano suggests that some parents assume that team sports may teach cooperation together with competition and that the two skills and attitudes may be more closely related than Statsky acknowledges. To think critically about the assumptions in this essay related to competition and cooperation, ask yourself: What do you think leads Romano to claim that children learn both competition and cooperation when they participate in team sports? Do you think that competition is highly valued in our society and, if so, why? Do you think that cooperation is valued as highly as competition? How is learning to cooperate and collaborate beneficial for us as individuals and as a society?

- **assumptions about facing fear.** Statsky assumes that "fear of being hurt greatly reduces children's enjoyment of contact sports," and as support she cites Tosches's anecdote about the child who "makes himself vomit to avoid playing" (5). Nevertheless, Romano suggests that some parents assume that facing fear is a good thing—that "competitive team sports for young children . . . teach children to face their fears early and learn how to deal with them" (8). To think critically about the assumptions in this essay related to facing fear, ask yourself: In what contexts, other than sports, do people typically experience physical or psychological fear? Why might some people think that learning "how to deal" with fear (presumably by doing something even though it causes us to be fearful) is a good thing? How do the stories we read and watch on television and film reinforce this assumption that fear should be faced and dealt with, if not overcome?

To probe assumptions more deeply, you might use one or more of the following critical reading strategies that are explained and illustrated in Appendix 1: *reflecting on challenges to your beliefs and values, evaluating the logic of an argument,* and *judging the writer's credibility.*

READING LIKE A WRITER
ANTICIPATING OBJECTIONS AND ALTERNATIVE JUDGMENTS

Writers of evaluation usually try to anticipate and respond to readers' possible objections and alternative judgments. In anticipating readers, writers may simply acknowledge that others disagree, may accommodate into their argument some points that others have made, or may try to refute objections and alternative judgments. Romano's first draft of her evaluation of Statsky's essay was totally positive. It did not anticipate objections that readers might make to her evaluation or alternative judgments that they might have of Statsky's essay. Two classmates who read Romano's draft helped her understand that readers might disagree with her evaluation and see flaws in Statsky's argument. This constructive criticism led Romano to modify her essay to accommodate other views. The revised essay above offers a balanced evaluation of Statsky's essay by both arguing for its apparent strengths and anticipating readers' objections and alternative judgments.

Analyze

1. *Reread* paragraphs 7 to 10, noting where Romano anticipates readers' possible alternative judgments of Statsky's argument.

2. *Make notes* in the margin about how Romano accommodates or refutes readers' criticisms of Statsky's argument.

Write

Write several sentences reporting on what you have learned about how Romano anticipates readers' objections and alternative judgments. Give examples to show how she accommodates or refutes readers' criticism.

CONSIDERING IDEAS FOR YOUR OWN WRITING

List several texts you would consider evaluating. For example, you might include in your list an essay from one of the chapters in this book. If you choose an argument from Chapters 6 through 9, you could evaluate its logic (as Romano does), emotional appeals, or credibility, relying on the guidelines in Appendix 1. You might prefer to evaluate a children's book you read when you were younger or one you now read to your own children, a magazine for people interested in computers or cars (or another topic), or a scholarly article you read for a research paper. You need not limit yourself to texts written on paper; also consider a Web site or an article from the online magazine *Slate* or *Salon*. Choose one possibility from your list, and see whether you can come up with three or four reasons for why you find it a strong or weak text.

A SPECIAL READING STRATEGY

Comparing and Contrasting Related Readings: Romano's and Kim's Reviews of Print and Online Texts

Comparing and contrasting related readings is a critical reading strategy that is useful both in reading for meaning and in reading like a writer. This strategy is particularly applicable when writers present similar subjects, as is the case in the essays by Christine Romano (p. 342) and Wendy Kim (p. 350). Both writers are evaluating texts they have read: Romano reviews another essay in this book, and Wendy Kim reviews a Web site. To compare and contrast these two reviews, think about issues such as these:

- Compare how the two writers refer to the texts they are evaluating. Highlight the places in each essay where the text is referred to. Which strategies for citing textual evidence—quoting the exact language, paraphrasing, summarizing, or describing the appearance of the text—does each writer rely on?

- Compare the reasons and the standards or criteria on which they are based that the two writers use to evaluate the texts. Romano and Kim are evaluating texts in different genres as well as in different media. Consider how the genre and medium influences the reasons and criteria for evaluating texts.

See Appendix 1 for detailed guidelines on using the comparing and contrasting related readings strategy.

WENDY KIM

Grading Professors

Wendy Kim immigrated to the United States from South Korea when she was eight years old. A business administration major, Kim plans to go to graduate school in business. For a composition course, she decided to research a Web site she uses regularly to decide which classes to take — RateMyProfessors.com. You may already be familiar with this site or with comparable online or campus publications evaluating professors. If you look at RateMy Professors.com, you will see that it has been redesigned since Kim wrote this essay, but it retains the same features.

The other readings in this chapter are followed by reading and writing activities. Following this reading, however, you are on you own to decide how to read for meaning and read like a writer.

Kim attracts readers with the title and opening quotation. She piles up statistics to show the site's popularity.

"Where the students do the grading" is the tagline 1 for the Web site <www.RateMyProfessors.com> (RMP). Users just choose their state and find their school among the 5,962 (and counting) campuses listed, and they're ready to start grading their professors. The home page proudly displays the numbers: last I looked, there were 5,537,682 ratings, covering 753,577 professors in the United States and Canada. In fact, RMP has been so successful that it has expanded to Australia, Ireland, and the United Kingdom, and its sister site for high-school students, *RateMyTeachers.com,* already has a user base of 3 million students (RateMyProfessors). While not everyone agrees that these ratings provide an entirely accurate assessment, many students, like me,

Kim's thesis *states her overall judgment* and forecasts her reasons.

routinely consult RMP at the beginning of every term to decide which classes to take. Overall, the Web site is well designed, amusing, and extremely helpful.

Kim *states her first reason:* the site is well designed.

The design of *RateMyProfessors.com* makes the site 2 attractive and easy to browse. In my senior year of high school, I took a class that taught me how to make a good Web site and learned that Web site design requires care in picking colors and in organizing the layout. The layout of RMP's home page is smart, with information grouped in clearly defined rectangular boxes. Across the top is a blue banner with the name in

Kim *supports this reason* by showing how the site's information is easily visible and accessible.

easy to read letters. At the bottom of the banner, three links ("help," "about," and "create a free account") are printed in small but easy-to-see white lettering. Below the banner, the page is divided into boxes, three across and two down, with plenty of white space along the left and right borders and bottom so that the page looks neatly organized and uncluttered. The top box on the left has the main menu in blue lettering against a white background with links to "Most-Rated Colleges," "Funny Ratings," "Forums," and so forth. The placement of the menu is smart because readers of English are used to reading from left to right as well as top to bottom. Below the menu, a box titled "Statistics" (many of which I cited in the first paragraph) reveals how many students use the ratings.

3   The viewer's eye is drawn to the center box, which is three times as wide as the boxes on the sides and includes the all-important member log-in box (in white lettering against the same blue background as the top banner). The boxes on the right are ads, which pick up the same colors as the rest of the page and are not too distracting. The placement of information seems just right and the log-in box is not buried on the page but easy to see and use.

4   The navigation system is smooth and fast. When you log in, you get the main member page; from there, you easily link to your school's page. On the member page, you can edit your ratings, go to the message board, or manage your account. Your school's page is the destination for checking out professors whose classes you are considering, entering your own rating of a professor, and adding a professor not already listed. Finding a particular professor is quick and easy because professors' names are listed in alphabetical order. The list is easy to skim and contains lots of valuable information. To the left of each name is a face icon (which I will explain in a minute) followed by a check icon that you can click on to add your own rating. To the right of the name is the professor's department, the date he or she was last rated, the number of ratings, and the vital average ratings for overall quality and ease. Clicking on a name takes you to the professor's page, which presents even more information—a box with averages in each rating category and a list of individual users' ratings starting with the most recent. These ratings identify the class, give the student's rating in each category, and often include a comment. You can add your own rating of the professor or respond to

Kim continues to support her first reason by showing how well the navigation system works.

other users' ratings. Every page displays the information clearly, without distractions. Even though there are ads, they do not flicker or get in the way. This is not the kind of Web site that takes minutes just to find what you need. Not only is it easy to browse, but it also doesn't lag because there are no large files or images to slow it down. For me, the longest it took to get to another page was two seconds using a cable modem.

Here Kim introduces her second reason: the site's information is useful.

Most important, *RateMyProfessors.com* is full of 5 useful information that helps students make informed decisions when it comes to choosing teachers and preparing for a class they are about to take. A student debating whether to take a history or a sociology class, for example, can go to the Web site, look at the overall ratings of each professor, and then find user ratings for the classes being considered. Assuming that the professor has been graded by other students, a great deal can be learned about the professor and possibly also about the specific class.

Professors are rated in several categories on a scale 6 of 1 (worst) to 5 (best). The scores on clarity and helpfulness are averaged for the "Overall Quality" rating that determines which icon is placed next to the professor's name. A yellow smiley face indicates "good quality," a bluish-gray sad face "poor quality," and an indifferent-looking green face "average quality." The numerical rating in each category is displayed along with the face so that students and professors can see the breakdown. In addition to evaluating the professor's clarity and helpfulness, students also rate the difficulty of the course. This rating, however, has no effect on assigning the face icon because, as the site explains, "an Easiness rating of 5 may actually mean the teacher is TOO easy." Although RMP acknowledges that easiness is "definitely the most controversial" reason for judging a class, they still present it because "many students decide what class to take based on the difficulty of the teacher." Another category that is not included in the overall rating is "Rater Interest." To explain this category, the Web site quotes from a study that found student "motivation correlated with the overall evaluation," meaning that the more motivated a student was to succeed in a course, the higher the professor's overall quality score. "Instructors," however, as RMP acknowl-

Here Kim anticipates readers' concern about the Easiness rating.

edges, "usually have little control over student motivation" (RateMyProfessors).

7 The faces and numbers are informative, but I think the comments help the most because they are so detailed. Not surprisingly, the comments on *RateMy Professors.com* tend to address many of the same issues that my college's course evaluation forms do. For example, one question on my campus evaluation asks if the instructor presented the material in "an organized, understandable manner." Many of the RMP comments answer this question—from high praise ("lectures are interesting, and he's happy to answer whatever questions you could ask") to severe criticism ("lectures are BORING and POINTLESS" or "totally disorganized!! boring and reads off the power point!!"). Another question on my campus form asks if the instructor was "concerned about students learning and understanding the course material." This issue also draws many comments on RMP, from highly positive comments ("he wrote a personal whole-page response to each of my papers. So I knew exactly what he liked and how to improve on my writing") to slams ("Kinda scary and intimidating" or "He does not care if the students are learning the basic concepts. He teaches as if he were teaching a Graduate level class. This is an INTRO class, let us learn the basics 1st"). In addition to these kinds of comments, RMP also posts information that course evaluations do not include—advice on how to pass the course ("If you keep up w/ your notes and the reading, you should be fine. Pop quizzes every week." or "Has notes available online. Test are extremely difficult and require a lot of reading from the book to be successful as well as attending class. Gives surprise quizzes"). The site also gives students warnings ("He's ****in' hard. Fails half his class." or "OMG, one of the worst teachers I've ever had. . . . Does not know how to teach and wears the tightest pants ever . . . gross").

The many comments Kim quotes help readers appreciate how informative the site is.

8 And as this last comment suggests, we can't forget the last rating category: Is your professor hot or not? The answer to this question makes the Web site amusing. "Hot" professors are marked with a red chili pepper beside their names. Some students also comment in this area: "good lookin guy, nice body" and "this chick [the professor] totally blew my mind. She was

Here Kim *introduces her third reason:* RMP is amusing.

sooo hot. I'm serious take this class just to check her out. SEXY!!!!" In fact, this issue may not be just a sideline to ones that supposedly are more serious. Students give professors higher overall ratings if they are hot, according to a *New York Times* article, "The Hunk Differential," which the RMP site provides as the answer to its FAQ question "Why do you have the 'hot' category?" The article, written by a professor of business, economics, and information management, reports a study that found "good-looking professors got significantly higher teaching scores" than those who did not rate as high on a beauty scale (Varian). So it may be that a professor who is considered "hot" on the site may be judged on a more lenient scale of teaching effectiveness.

This question about the possible effect of the teacher's appearance on student response and learning leads to a more basic question about the credibility of the evaluations on *RateMyProfessors.com*: Are the ratings statistically valid? The simple answer, the Web site itself admits, is "Not really. They are a listing of opinions and should be judged as such" (RateMy Professors). The results are statistically invalid, as one psychology professor explained, because the users are self-selected and not selected randomly (Harmon). And the fewer student ratings an instructor has been given, the less reliable the overall evaluation. Nevertheless, RMP claims "we often receive emails stating that the ratings are uncannily accurate, especially for schools with over 1000 ratings" (RateMyProfessors). RMP also refers readers to an article reporting a study at the University of Waterloo, Canada (UW), that found fifteen of the sixteen Distinguished Teacher Award winners also had yellow smiley faces on *RateMyProfessors.com* ("RateMyProfessors.ca"). While this correlation is reassuring, students should not approach the ratings uncritically. And evidence suggests most don't. As one college newspaper reporter put it, "[S]tudents claim they do not blindly follow the comments" (Espach). A recent study of RMP published in the *Journal of Computer-Mediated Communication* found that students "are aware that ratings and comments on the site could reflect students exacting revenge or venting" (Kindred and Mohammed). As one student explained:

Kim anticipates a concern—refuting possible criticism with support from published research.

Kim concedes a third possible criticism: the ratings are statistically invalid. Nevertheless, she defends her positive overall judgment with support from researchers and students.

"If half the ratings are bad, I will ask around about the professor. If every rating is poor, I won't take the teacher" (Espach).

10   There are other Internet professor evaluation sites, but none is as widely used or as easy to use as Rate MyProfessors.com. I compared RMP with three competitors: *Professor Performance, Reviewum.com,* and *RatingsOnline.* The user base of the first two sites looks too small to provide reliable information. *Professor Performance* has 73,040 evaluations at 1,742 colleges and universities, and *Reviewum.com* claims to have 20,098 records for 137 campuses. In addition, for the limited number of professors who are listed, there are only a small number of evaluations—not enough to enable students to make informed judgments.

Kim compares RMP to competing Web sites. Using statistics, she argues for BMP's greater reliability.

11   Although *RatingsOnline* does not appear to display its statistics, it claims to have ratings for "thousands of professors." However, there are only nineteen professors from my campus listed compared to 1,252 on RMP. Still, *RatingsOnline* is better designed and includes more helpful information than the other two competitors, and it may even be better than RMP in terms of helpfulness. Students not only identify the class and term it was taken but also are asked to list the grade they received. Of course, this information about the grade is no more reliable than any other information a user gives, but it could help students judge the user's credibility. The ratings categories on *RatingsOnline* also seem more specific than on RMP—prepared, enthusiastic, focused, available, material, exam prep, quality. In addition, students are prompted to indicate the percentage given to homework, quizzes, and exams in determining the final grade. This information could be useful in helping students decide which classes to take but only if there are enough reviews posted. In its design and potential helpfulness, *RatingsOnline* is a very good site but not likely to be as good as RMP because its user base appears to be smaller.

Kim points out the relative strengths and weaknesses of *RatingsOnline* compared to *RateMyProfessors.*

12   When you have the option of choosing a teacher, wouldn't you really like some information? *RateMy Professors.com* allows you to see what other students have to say about professors and courses you may be considering as well as to voice your opinion. As a Web site, it is helpful, easy to use, and amusing to read.

Kim concludes by reminding readers of her reasons.

Works Cited

Kim uses MLA style to document her sources.

Espach, Alison. "RateMyProfessors.com—Blessing or Bluffing?" *The Cowl.* Providence College, 27 Apr. 2006. Web. 15 May 2006.

Harmon, Christine. "Professors Rate Reliability of RateMyProfessors.com." *Online Forty-Niner.* California State U Long Beach, 2 May 2006. Web. 15 May 2006.

Kindred, Jeannette, and Shaheed N. Mohammed. "'He Will Crush You Like an Academic Ninja!' Exploring Teacher Ratings on RateMyProfessors.com." *Journal of Computer-Mediated Communication.* Journal of Computer-Mediated Communication, Apr. 2005. Web. 15 May 2006.

ProfessorPerformance. Professor Performance, 2006. Web. 19 May 2006.

RateMyProfessors. Rate My Professors, 2006. Web. 13 May 2006.

"RateMyProfessors.ca." *Teaching Matters Newsletter.* U of Waterloo Teaching Resources Office, Sept. 2001. Web. 13 May 2005.

RatingsOnline. N.p., 2006. Web. 19 May 2006.

Reviewum.com. Reviewum.com, 2006. Web. 19 May 2006.

Varian, Hal R. "The Hunk Differential." *New York Times.* New York Times, 28 Aug. 2003. Web. 14 May 2006.

READING FOR MEANING

Reading for meaning involves three activities:

- reading to comprehend,

- reading to respond, and

- reading to analyze assumptions.

Reread Kim's essay, and then write a page or so explaining your understanding of its basic meaning or main point, a personal response you have to it, and what you see as one of its assumptions.

READING LIKE A WRITER

Writers of evaluative essays

- present the subject,

- assert an overall judgment,

- give reasons and support, and

- anticipate objections and alternative judgments.

Focus on one of these strategies in Kim's essay, and analyze it carefully through close rereading and annotating. Then write several sentences explaining what you have learned, giving specific examples from the reading to support your explanation. Add a few sentences evaluating how successfully Kim uses the strategy to evaluate RateMyProfessors.com.

REVIEWING WHAT MAKES EVALUATIONS EFFECTIVE

In this chapter, you have been learning how to read evaluative essays for meaning and how to read them like a writer. Before going on to write an evaluation of your own, pause here to review and contemplate what you have learned about the elements of effective evaluations.

Analyze

Choose one reading from this chapter that seems to you especially effective. Before rereading the selection, *jot down* one or two reasons you remember it as an example of good evaluative writing.

Reread your chosen selection, adding further annotations about what makes it a particularly successful example of evaluation. *Consider* the selection's purpose and how well it achieves that purpose for its intended readers. (You can make an informed guess about the intended readers and their expectations by noting the publication source of the essay.) Then *focus* on how well the essay

- presents the subject,

- asserts an overall judgment,

- gives reasons and support, and

- anticipates objections and alternative judgments.

You can review all of these basic features in the Guide to Reading Evaluations (p. 301).

Your instructor may ask you to complete this activity on your own or to work with a small group of other students who have chosen the same reading. If you work with others, allow enough time initially for all group members to reread the selection thoughtfully and to add their annotations. Then *discuss* as a group what makes the essay effective. *Take notes* on your discussion. One student in your group should then report to the class what the group has learned about the effectiveness of evaluative writing. If you are working individually, write up what you have learned from your analysis.

Write

Write at least a page supporting your choice of this reading as an example of effective evaluative writing. *Assume* that your readers—your instructor and classmates—have read the selection but will not remember many details about it. They also might not remember it as especially successful. Therefore, you will need to *refer* to details and specific parts of the reading as you explain how it works and as you justify your evaluation of its effectiveness. You need not argue that it is the best essay in the chapter or that it is flawless, only that it is, in your view, a strong example of the genre.

■ A Guide to Writing Evaluations

The readings in this chapter have helped you learn a great deal about evaluative writing. Now that you have seen how writers of evaluations argue to support their assertions, you are in a good position to approach this type of writing confidently. As you develop your essay, you can review the readings to see how other writers use various strategies to solve the problems you face in your own writing.

This Guide to Writing is designed to assist you in writing an evaluation. Here you will find activities to help you choose a subject and discover what to say about it, organize your ideas and draft the essay, read the draft critically, revise the draft to strengthen your argument, and edit and proofread the essay to improve its readability.

INVENTION AND RESEARCH

Invention is a process of discovery and planning by which you generate something to say. The following activities will help you choose a subject and develop your evaluation of it. A few minutes spent on each writing activity will improve your chances of producing a detailed and convincing first draft.

Choosing a Subject

Begin by looking over the subjects suggested in the Considering Ideas for Your Own Writing activities in this chapter. The selections suggest several different subjects you could write about. Arts and entertainment products are popular subjects for review—fashion, sports, television programs, films, magazines, books, restaurants, and video games. Technology, since it changes so quickly, is also a source of many possible subjects: new hardware and software, new procedures, and laws. There are countless other possibilities, such as public figures, businesses, educational programs, and types of equipment (cars, sporting gear).

To find a subject, list specific examples in several of the following categories. Although you may be inclined to pick the first idea that comes to mind, try to make your list of possible subjects as long as you can. This will ensure that you have a variety of subjects from which to choose and will encourage you to think of unique subjects:

- A film or group of films by a single director or actor
- A hit song or music CD
- A live or videotaped concert or theatrical performance
- A magazine or newspaper
- A book (perhaps one—either fiction or nonfiction—that you have recently read for one of your classes)

- A club or organized activity—dance instruction, camping or hiking trip, college sports programs, debate group—or a subject (like Etzioni's) that is generally viewed positively but that your experience leads you to evaluate more negatively (or, alternatively, a subject generally viewed negatively that your experience leads you to evaluate more positively)

- A contemporary political movement (perhaps evaluating the movement's methods as well as its goals and achievements)

- A proposed or existing law

- A noteworthy person—someone in the news or a local professional, such as a teacher, doctor, social worker, auto mechanic, or minister (perhaps using your personal experience with the local figure to strengthen your evaluation)

- An artist, a writer, or his or her works

- A local business or businessperson

- Particular brands of machines or equipment with which you are familiar (perhaps comparing a "superior" to an "inferior" brand to make your evaluation more authoritative)

- One of the essays in this book (evaluating it as a strong or weak example of its type) or two essays (arguing that one is better than the other)

After you have a list of possible subjects, consider the following questions as you make your final selection:

- *Do I already know enough about this subject, or can I get the information I need in time?* If, for instance, you decide to review a film, you should be able to see it soon. If you choose to evaluate a brand of machine or equipment, you should already be somewhat familiar with it or have time to learn enough about it to be able to write with some authority.

- *Do I already have a settled judgment about this subject?* It is always easier to write about a subject that you think you can judge confidently, although it is conceivable that you could change your mind as you write. If you choose a subject about which you feel indifferent, you may experience difficulty devising an argument to support your judgment. The more sure you are of your judgment, the more persuasive your evaluation is likely to be.

Developing Your Argument

The writing and research activities that follow will enable you to explore your subject, analyze your readers, and begin developing your evaluation.

Exploring Your Subject.   *To find out what you already know about the subject, list the main things you now know about it and then make notes about how you will go* *about becoming familiar enough with your subject to write about it like an expert or insider.* You may know little or much about your subject, and you may feel uncertain how to learn more about it. For now, discover what you do know.

Analyzing Your Readers. *Make notes about your readers.* Who exactly are your readers? They may be your classmates, or you may want—or be asked by your instructor—to write for another audience. You could write for the general public, as most of the writers in this chapter seem to be doing. Or you could write for a more narrow audience—parents ready to purchase a new child's learning game, advanced users of e-mail or some other technology, or viewers who have seen (or who have never seen) several other films by the director of the film you are reviewing. How much will your readers know about your subject and others of its type? How can you describe your readers' attitudes and opinions about the subject? What standards might they use to judge a subject like yours?

Considering Your Judgment. *Make a list of the good and bad qualities of your subject.* Then decide whether your judgment will be positive or negative. You can certainly acknowledge both the good and the bad qualities in your essay, but your judgment should not be ambivalent throughout. In a movie review, for example, you must ultimately decide whether or not you recommend that your readers try to see the film. If your list leaves you feeling genuinely ambivalent, you might want to trust the processes of learning and writing about your subject to help you decide whether you want to praise or criticize it. Another option, of course, is to choose a different subject to evaluate.

If you can judge your subject now, *write a sentence or two asserting your judgment.* At the end of these activities, you will have an opportunity to revise this assertion.

Testing Your Choice. *Pause now to decide whether you have chosen a subject about which you may be able to make a convincing evaluative argument.* At this point, you should be very familiar with your subject—you have viewed the movie again, reread the essay, listened to the music CD, attended another concert, reexamined a machine or piece of equipment, or consumed another meal at the restaurant. It is important that you be able to continue studying your subject as you complete these invention activities and, later, as you draft and revise your essay: The more intimate your knowledge of the subject, the more details you can bring to bear to support your evaluation. If your interest in the subject is growing and you feel increasingly confident about your judgment of it, you have probably made a good choice. If you have not made progress in experiencing and understanding your subject and do not see how you can do so right away, it is probably wise for you to choose another subject.

Listing Reasons. *List all the reasons you might give to persuade your readers of your judgment of the subject.* Reasons answer the question "Everything considered, why do you evaluate this subject positively [or negatively]?" Write down all the reasons you can think of.

Then look over your list to consider which reasons you feel are the most important and which would be most convincing to your readers, given the generally accepted standards for evaluating this type of subject. *Put an asterisk by these convincing reasons.*

Consider this list only a starting point. Continue to revise it as you learn more about your subject. A preliminary list of reasons gives you a head start on planning your essay.

Finding Support for Your Reasons.   *Make notes about how to support your most promising reasons.* For support, most evaluations rely largely on details and examples from the subject itself. For that reason, you will have to reexamine the subject closely even if you know it quite well. Depending on the subject, evaluations may also make use of facts, quotations from experts, statistics, or the writer's personal experience.

Work back and forth between your list of reasons and notes for support. The reasons list will remind you of the support you need and help you discover which reasons have substance. The credibility of your argument will depend to a large extent on the amount of specific, relevant support you can bring to your argument.

Anticipating Readers' Alternative Judgments, Questions, and Objections.   *List a few questions your particular readers would likely want to ask you or objections they might have to your argument. Write for a few minutes responding to at least two of these questions or objections.* Now that you can begin to see how your argument might shape up, assume that some of your particular readers would judge your subject differently from the way you do. Remember that your responses — your counterargument — could simply acknowledge the disagreements, accommodate readers' views by conceding certain points, or refute readers' arguments as uninformed or mistaken.

RESEARCHING YOUR SUBJECT ONLINE

One way to learn more about judgments of your subject that differ from your own judgment is to search for reviews or evaluations of your subject online. You may even decide to incorporate quotations from or references to alternative judgments as part of your counterargument, although you need not do so to write a successful evaluation. Enter the name of your subject — movie title, restaurant name, compact disc title, title of a proposed law, name of a candidate for public office — in a search engine such as Google <www.google.com> or Yahoo! Directory

<http://dir.yahoo.com>. (Sometimes you can narrow the search usefully by including the keyword *review* as well.) Not all subjects are conveniently searchable online, and some subjects—a local concert, a college sports event, a campus student service, a neighborhood program—will likely not have been reviewed by anyone but you.

Bookmark or keep a record of promising sites. Download any materials you might wish to cite in your evaluation, making sure you have all the information necessary to document the source.

Considering Visuals. *Consider whether visuals—screen shots, photographs, or drawings—would help you present your subject more effectively to readers or strengthen your evaluation of it.* If you submit your essay electronically to other students and your instructor, or if you post it on a Web site, consider including photographs as well as snippets of film or sound or other memorabilia that might give readers a more vivid sense of your subject. Visual and audio materials are not at all a requirement of an effective evaluative argument, as you can tell from the readings in this chapter, but they could add a new dimension to your writing. If you want to use photographs or recordings of people, though, be sure to obtain their permission.

Considering Your Purpose. *Write for a few minutes exploring your purpose for writing an evaluative essay.* The following questions may help you think about your purpose:

- What do I want my readers to believe or do after they read my essay?

- How can I connect to their experience with my subject (or subjects like it)? How can I interest them in a subject that is outside their experience?

- Can I assume that readers will share my standards for judging the subject, or must I explain and justify the standards?

- How can I offer a balanced evaluation that will enhance my credibility with readers?

Formulating a Working Thesis. *Draft a thesis statement.* A working thesis—as opposed to a final, revised thesis—will help you begin drafting your essay purposefully. The thesis statement in an evaluative essay is simply a concise assertion of your overall judgment. Here are two examples from the readings:

- "McDonald's is bad for your kids." (Etzioni, paragraph 1)

- "While her logic *is* appropriate, believable, and consistent, her argument also has weaknesses. It seems incomplete because it neglects to anticipate parents' predictable questions and objections and because it fails to support certain parts fully." (Romano, paragraph 2)

Both of these thesis statements are clear and assertive. But whereas Etzioni's thesis is unmistakably negative in its overall judgment, Romano's is mixed. Another difference between these two thesis statements is that whereas Romano forecasts the reasons she will develop in the essay, Etzioni does not forecast his reasons. Forecasts are not required, but readers often find them helpful.

DRAFTING

The following guidelines will help you set goals for your draft, plan its organization, and think about a useful sentence strategy.

Setting Goals

Establishing goals for your draft before you begin writing will enable you to make decisions and work more confidently. Consider the following questions now, and keep them in mind as you draft. They will help you set goals for drafting as well as recall how the writers you have read in this chapter tried to achieve similar goals.

- *What is my primary purpose in writing this evaluation?* What do I want to accomplish with my evaluation? Is my primary purpose to make a recommendation, as Etzioni and Taylor do? Do I want to celebrate my subject, as Manjoo does, or expose its flaws, as Etzioni does? Do I want to strive for a carefully balanced evaluation, as Steve, Schiff, and Romano do?

- *How can I present the subject so that I can inform and interest my readers in it?* How much experience evaluating a subject of this kind can I expect my readers to have? Must I provide a full context for my subject, as Steve and Schiff do, or describe it in a general way, as Taylor does? Can I assume familiarity with it, as does Etzioni? Will readers share my standards, as Taylor seems to assume her readers do, or will I need to explain or defend some of my standards, as Etzioni, Manjoo, and Schiff do?

- *How can I assert my judgment effectively?* How can I construct a clear, unambiguous thesis statement like those in all of the readings in this chapter? Should I assert my judgment in the first sentence and reassert it at the end of my evaluation, as Etzioni does? Or should I first describe my subject or provide a context for evaluating it, as the other writers do?

- *How can I give convincing reasons and adequate support for my reasons?* How can I ensure that the reasons I offer to justify my judgment will seem appropriate and convincing to my readers? Should I forecast my reasons, as Etzioni, Romano, and Kim do? For my subject, will I offer a wide range of types of support, as Etzioni does? How can I gather an adequate amount of support for my reasons, as do all of the writers in this chapter? Should I rely on comparisons to support my reasoning, as Etzioni, Manjoo, Schiff, and Kim do?

- *How can I anticipate readers' questions and alternative judgments?* Should I pointedly anticipate my readers' likely reservations, objections, and questions, as Etzioni, Schiff, and Romano do?

WORKING WITH SOURCES

Using Summary to Support Your Evaluative Argument

Writers of evaluation often use summary to support their argument. As the following examples show, evaluations may summarize an expert source (as Kim does in her Web site evaluation), the plot of a film or video game (as Taylor does in her film review), or an aspect of an essay or story (as Romano does in her evaluation of another essay in this book), to name just a few of the more common uses of summary. Here are examples of these various uses of summary:

> The results are statistically invalid, as one psychology professor explained, because the users are self-selected and not selected randomly (Harmon). (Kim, paragraph 9)

> . . . this tale of an ordinary (i.e., barking mad) family on the road across America to a kiddie pageant in Redondo Beach. . . . (Taylor, paragraph 2)

> In the anecdote, a seven-year-old makes himself vomit to avoid playing. (Romano, paragraph 5)

All of these examples are brief summaries, but writers sometimes summarize extended passages, as in the following example from Romano's essay:

> For example, in paragraph 3, Statsky offers the reason that "overly competitive sports" may damage children's growing bodies and that contact sports, in particular, may be especially hazardous. She supports this reason by paraphrasing Koppett that muscle strain or even lifelong injury may result when a twelve-year-old throws curve balls. She then quotes Tutko on the dangers of tackle football. (Romano, paragraph 3).

To understand how this summary works, it helps to compare Romano's summary to the original passage in Statsky's essay (paragraph 3):

> One readily understandable danger of overly competitive sports is that they entice children into physical actions that are bad for growing

bodies. Although the official Little League Web site acknowledges that children do risk injury playing baseball, they insist that severe injuries are infrequent, "far less than the risk of riding a skateboard, a bicycle, or even the school bus" ("What about My Child?"). Nevertheless, Leonard Koppett in *Sports Illusion, Sports Reality* claims that a twelve-year-old trying to throw a curve ball, for example, may put abnormal strain on developing arm and shoulder muscles, sometimes resulting in lifelong injuries (294). Contact sports like football can be even more hazardous. Thomas Tutko, a psychology professor at San Jose State University and coauthor of the book *Winning Is Everything and Other American Myths*, writes:

> I am strongly opposed to young kids playing tackle football. It is not the right stage of development for them to be taught to crash into other kids. Kids under the age of fourteen are not by nature physical. Their main concern is self-preservation. They don't want to meet head on and slam into each other. But tackle football absolutely requires that they try to hit each other as hard as they can. And it is too traumatic for young kids. (qtd. in Tosches A1)

What is most significant about this summary is that Romano not only repeats Statsky's main ideas in a condensed form (reducing 214 words to 55), but also describes Statsky's moves as a writer:

Statsky offers the reason. . . .

She supports this reason by paraphrasing Koppett. . . .

She then quotes Tutko. . . .

This description of each step in Statsky's argument shows readers exactly how Statsky uses paraphrase and quotation to support her argument about the potential for "overly competitive sports" to endanger children. Note that in summarizing, Romano here refers directly to the writer (*Statsky, She*). By naming Statsky and describing what Statsky is doing in this passage (*offers, supports, quotes*), Romano does not focus on the content of the original passage (as she does in our first example of her summarizing an anecdote in Statsky's essay). Instead, Romano focuses here on Statsky's argumentative strategy of providing support for her reasons. Not every summary needs to include this kind of play-by-play description of the writer's strategic moves, but when you are evaluating an argument, it does help readers see how the writer constructs the argument.

Notice also that in this summary, Romano puts quotation marks around only one of the phrases she borrows from Statsky ("overly competitive sports"). Perhaps the reason she uses quotation marks around this particular phrase is that Statsky uses it twice in her essay (paragraphs 3 and 11). It is a key phrase for Statsky and captures the essence of her argument that organized sports may be too competitive for children. Romano may have decided not to use quotation marks around other borrowed phrases such as *contact sports* and *tackle football* because they are common expressions and not specific to Statsky. Readers of summaries expect to see some words from the original. If writers, like Romano, make it perfectly clear when they are re-presenting a source's language and ideas and also include careful citations to indicate where in the original text the material comes from, there is little concern about plagiarizing. Remember, however, that putting quotation marks around quoted words and phrases would avoid any misunderstanding. If you are unsure about whether you need quotation marks, consult your instructor.

Organizing Your Draft

With goals in mind and invention notes at hand, you are ready to make a first outline of your draft. Review the list of reasons you have developed. Tentatively select from that list the reasons you think will most effectively convince your readers of the plausibility of your judgment. Then decide how you will sequence these reasons. Some writers prefer to save their most telling reason or reasons for the end, whereas others try to group the reasons logically (for example, the technical reasons in a movie review). Still other writers like to begin with reasons based on standards of judgment familiar to their readers. Whatever sequence you decide on for your reasons, make sure it will strike your readers as a logical or step-by-step sequence.

Considering a Useful Sentence Strategy

As you draft your evaluative essay, you may want to compare or contrast your subject with similar subjects to establish your authority with readers. In addition, you are likely to want to balance your evaluation by criticizing one or more aspects of the subject if you generally praise it or by praising one or more aspects of it if you generally criticize it. To do so, you will need to use sentences that express comparisons or contrasts, including ones that contrast criticism with praise and vice versa.

Use sentences comparing or contrasting your subject with similar subjects to help convince readers that you are knowledgeable about the kind of subject you are evaluating. These sentences often make use of key comparative terms, such as *more, less, most, least, as, than, like, unlike, similar,* and *dissimilar,* as the readings in this chapter illustrate.

> . . . the iPod has also tremendously complicated our relationship to music — has made us **more** mindlessly consumptive of songs, **less** attentive to the context and the quality of music. . . . (Manjoo, paragraph 6)

> . . . you can make a good case that digitization has altered how we experience music **more** fundamentally **than** any technology since the advent of audio recording. (Manjoo, paragraph 4)

> Still, RatingsOnline is **better** designed and includes **more** helpful information **than** the other two competitors, and it may even be **better than** RMP in terms of helpfulness. . . . The ratings categories on RatingsOnline also seem **more** specific **than** on RMP. . . . RatingsOnline is a very good site but **not** likely to be **as good** because its user base appears to be **smaller**. (Kim, paragraph 11).

Sometimes writers do not use comparative terms but simply put compared or contrasted information side-by-side, as in these examples:

> According to the survey, Wikipedia had four errors for every three of *Britannica's*. . . . (Schiff, paragraph 9)

> Roy Rogers, Baskin Robbins, Kentucky Fried Chicken, et al., may at first seem nothing but a vast extension of the lemonade stand. (Etzioni, paragraph 5)

Yet another interesting comparing strategy is to make an analogy (or quote one, as in this example):

> "Wikipedia is to *Britannica* as rock and roll is to easy listening. . . ." (Schiff, paragraph 13)

You can also increase your authority with readers by using sentences expressing comparison or contrast to balance criticism and praise. In general, these sentences rely on words expressing contrast — *but, although, however, while,* and *yet* — to set up the shift between the two responses.

- Praise followed by criticism:

> **True**, you still have to have the gumption to get yourself over to the hamburger stand, **but** once you don the prescribed uniform, your task is spelled out in minute detail. (Etzioni, paragraph 7)

> **While** it is true that these places provide income, work, and even some training to such youngsters, they also tend to perpetuate their disadvantaged status. (Etzioni, paragraph 11)

> Statsky does show that she is thinking about her readers' questions. She does not go nearly far enough, **however**, to have a chance of influencing two types of readers. . . . (Romano, paragraph 8)

- Criticism followed by praise:

  As far as my eye could see, the audience was laughing its head off, and **though** the movie doesn't hold up quite as well in the lonely confines of a studio screening room with two others present, it's **still** a pretty good night out for those who find the real world close to unbearable right now. (Taylor, paragraph 1)

In addition to using sentences that make comparisons or contrasts with other subjects and sentences that balance criticism and praise, you can strengthen your evaluation with other kinds of sentences as well. You may want to look at the information about using appositives (pp. 291–93) and sentences that combine concession and refutation (pp. 588–90).

READING A DRAFT CRITICALLY

Getting a critical reading of your draft will help you see how to improve it. Your instructor may schedule class time for reading drafts, or you may want to ask a classmate or a tutor in the writing center to read your draft. Ask your reader to use the following guidelines and to write out a response for you to consult during your revision.

Read for a First Impression

1. Read the draft without stopping to annotate or comment, and then write two or three sentences giving your general impression.

2. Identify one aspect of the draft that seems especially effective.

Read Again to Suggest Improvements

1. Recommend ways to strengthen the presentation of the subject.

   - Locate the places in the draft where the subject is described. The description might be spread out over several paragraphs, serving both to identify the subject and to provide support for the argument. Point to any areas where you do not understand what is being said or where you need more detail or explanation.

   - If you are surprised by the way the writer has presented the subject, briefly explain your expectations for reading about this particular subject or subjects of this kind.

   - Indicate whether any of the information given about the subject seems unnecessary.

   - Finally and most important, raise questions wherever information about the subject seems unconvincing, inaccurate, or only partially true.

2. Suggest ways to strengthen the thesis statement.

- Find and underline the statement of the writer's overall judgment in the draft. If you cannot find a clear thesis, let the writer know.

- If you find several restatements of the thesis, examine them closely for consistency. Look specifically at the value terms the writer uses to see whether they are unclear or waffling.

3. Recommend ways to strengthen the supporting reasons.

- Highlight the reasons you find in the essay. The reasons in an evaluation may take the form of judgments of the subject's qualities, judgments that in turn need to be explained and supported. Look closely at any reasons that seem problematic, and briefly explain what bothers you. Be as specific and constructive as you can, suggesting what the writer might do to solve the problem. For example, if a reason seems inappropriate, indicate what other kind of reason you would expect a writer to use when evaluating this subject.

- Look for instances of faulty logic. Note whether the writer's argument is based on personal tastes rather than on generally accepted standards of judgment. Point out any areas where you detect *either/or* reasoning (that is, seeing only the good or only the bad qualities) and weak or misleading comparisons.

4. Suggest ways to extend and improve anticipation of objections and alternative judgments.

- Locate places where the writer anticipates readers' questions, objections, and reservations about the reasons and support. Consider whether these anticipations seem cursory or adequate, logical or questionable, considerate or dismissive. Point to specific problems you see, and suggest possible revisions.

- Look for areas where the writer anticipates readers' alternative judgments of the subject (that is, where readers may value the subject for different reasons or judge the subject in a different way). Note whether the writer addresses readers' alternative judgments responsibly and accurately and responds to them fairly.

- If the writer does not anticipate readers' concerns, consider where doing so might be appropriate. Help the writer anticipate any objections and alternative judgments that have been overlooked, providing advice on how to respond to them. Keep in mind that the writer may choose to accommodate *or* refute readers' reservations or alternative judgments.

5. Suggest how the organizational plan might be improved.

- Consider the overall plan of the draft, perhaps by making a scratch outline. (Scratch outlining is illustrated in Appendix 1, p. 607.) Decide whether the sequence of reasons and counterarguments is logical or whether you can suggest rearrangements to improve it.

- Indicate where new or better transitions might help identify different steps in the argument and keep readers on track.

6. Evaluate the effectiveness of visuals.

- Look at any visuals in the essay, and tell the writer what they contribute to your understanding of the evaluation.

- If any visuals do not seem relevant, or if there seem to be too many visuals, identify the ones that the writer could consider dropping, explaining your thinking.

- If a visual does not seem appropriately placed, suggest a better place for it.

REVISING

This section offers suggestions for revising your draft. Revising means reenvisioning your draft, trying to see it in a new way, given your purpose and readers, in order to develop a better-argued evaluation.

The biggest mistake you can make while revising is to focus initially on words or sentences. Instead, first try to see your draft as a whole to assess its likely impact on your readers. To improve readability and strengthen your argument, think imaginatively and boldly about cutting unconvincing material, adding new material, and moving material around. Your computer makes even drastic revisions physically easy, but you still need to make the mental effort and decisions that will improve your draft.

You may have received help with this challenge from a classmate or tutor who gave your draft a critical reading. If so, keep this feedback in mind as you decide which parts of your draft need revising and what specific changes you could make. The following suggestions will help you solve problems and strengthen your essay.

To Present the Subject More Effectively

- If more specific information about the subject is needed, review your invention writing to see whether you have forgotten details you could now add to the draft. Or do some further invention work to generate and add new information.

- If critical readers have asked specific questions, consider whether you need to answer those questions in your revision.

- If you have included information that readers regard as unnecessary or redundant, consider cutting it.

- If any of the information strikes readers as inaccurate or only partially true, reconsider its accuracy and completeness and then make any necessary changes to reassure readers.

- Consider comparing or contrasting your subject with similar subjects to highlight its features.

To Clarify the Overall Judgment

- If your overall judgment is not stated explicitly or clearly, state it more obviously.

- If readers think your restatements of the judgment are contradictory, reread them with a critical eye and, if you agree, make them more consistent.

- If readers think your judgment is unemphatic or waffling, reconsider the value terms you use.

- If your essay discusses both the good and the bad qualities of the subject, be sure that your thesis statement is compatible with what you say about the subject in the essay.

To Strengthen the Reasons and Support

- If a reason seems inappropriate to readers, consider how you might better convince them that the reason is appropriate (for example, that it is used often by others or that it is based on widely shared and valid standards of judgment).

- If readers do not fully understand how a particular reason applies to the subject, make your thinking more explicit.

- If the connection between a reason and its support seems vague or weak, explain why you think the support is relevant.

- Most important, if you have not fully supported your reasons with many examples from your subject, collect further examples by revisiting your subject (revisit the Web site, see the movie again, reread the text, play the computer game again, and so forth).

To Strengthen the Anticipation of Objections and Alternative Judgments

- If you have not anticipated readers' likely questions, objections, or reservations, revise to accommodate or refute them.

- If you have not anticipated alternative judgments that are likely for your particular audience, revise to respond to them.

- If any counterargument seems to attack your readers rather than their ideas, revise it to focus on the ideas.

To Make the Organizational Plan More Effective

- If readers express confusion over your plan, consider a different sequence for your reasons, or forecast your plan more explicitly by giving clear signals like transitions and topic sentences to distinguish the stages of your argument.

- If readers point to gaps in your argument, close the gaps by making connections explicit.

- If readers find your conclusion abrupt or less than helpful, try restating your judgment or summarizing your argument.

EDITING AND PROOFREADING

After you have revised your essay, be sure to spend some time checking for errors in usage, punctuation, and mechanics and considering matters of style. If you keep a list of errors you typically make, begin by checking your draft against this list. Ask someone else to proofread your essay before you print out a copy for your instructor or send it electronically.

From our research on student writing, we know that evaluative essays have frequent problems in sentences that set up comparisons. The comparisons can be incomplete, illogical, or unclear. Edit carefully any sentences that set up comparisons between your subject and others. Check a writer's handbook for help with making all comparisons complete, logical, and clear.

REFLECTING ON WHAT YOU HAVE LEARNED

Evaluation

In this chapter, you have read critically several evaluative essays and have written one of your own. To better remember what you have learned, pause now to reflect on the reading and writing activities you completed in this chapter.

1. *Write* a page or so reflecting on what you have learned. *Begin* by describing what you are most pleased with in your essay. Then *explain* what you think contributed to your achievement. *Be specific* about this contribution.

   - If it was something you learned from the readings, *indicate* which readings and specifically what you learned from them.

- If it came from your invention writing, *point out* the section or sections that helped you most.

- If you got good advice from a critical reader, *explain* exactly how the person helped you—perhaps by helping you understand a particular problem in your draft or by adding a new dimension to your writing.

- *Try to write* about your achievement in terms of what you have learned about the genre.

2. Now *reflect* more generally on evaluative essays, a genre of writing that plays an important role in education and in many other areas of life and work in the United States. *Consider* some of the following questions: How confident do you feel about asserting a judgment and supporting it? How comfortable are you playing the role of judge and jury on the subject? How do your personal preferences and values influence your judgment? How might your gender, ethnicity, religious beliefs, age, or social class influence your ideas about the subject? What contribution might evaluative essays make to our society that other genres cannot make?

CHAPTER **7**

Speculating about Causes or Effects

When a surprising event occurs, we automatically look to the past and ask, "Why did that happen?" Whether we want to understand the event, prevent its recurrence, or make it happen again, we need to speculate about what *caused* it.

Sometimes our focus may shift from "Why did that happen?" to "What is going to happen?" Anticipating the possible *effects* of an event can be useful in planning and decision making.

In many cases, questions about causes and effects are relatively easy to answer. Through personal experience or scientific experimentation, we know what causes some things to happen and what the effects will be. For example, scientists have discovered that the HIV virus causes AIDS, and we all know its potential deadly effects. We cannot be completely certain, however, what causes the virus to develop into AIDS in particular individuals or what long-term effects AIDS will have on society. In these situations, the best we can do is to *speculate*—to make educated guesses. In this chapter, you will read and write speculative essays about causes and effects that cannot be known for certain.

This kind of speculative cause-and-effect writing is published every day. A political analyst conjectures about the cause of the outcome of the most recent presidential election. An economist suggests some likely effects of the Iraq war on the U.S. economy. A sportswriter speculates about why the Pacific Ten nearly always defeats the Big Ten in the Rose Bowl.

Speculation about causes or effects also plays an important role in government, business, and education. To give credit where it is due, a mayor asks the police commission to report on why complaints by African Americans and Latinos against the police have decreased recently. A salesperson writes a memo to the district sales manager explaining why a local advertising campaign may have failed to increase sales of hybrid cars. Before proposing changes in the math curriculum, a school principal appoints a committee to investigate the causes of falling math test scores at the school.

Cause-and-effect speculation is equally important in college study. For example, you might read a history essay in which a noted scholar first evaluates other scholars' proposed causes of the Civil War and then argues for a never-before-considered cause. (If the essay merely summarizes other scholars' proposed causes, the historian would be reporting established information, not speculating about new possibilities.) Or you might encounter a sociological report conjecturing about a recent increase in marriages among the elderly. The writer may not know for certain why this trend exists but could conjecture about its possible causes — and then argue with relevant facts, statistics, or anecdotes to support the conjectures.

Writing an essay in which you speculate about causes or effects involves some of the most challenging problem-solving and decision-making situations a writer can experience. You will test your powers of reasoning and creativity as you search out hidden, underlying causes or speculate about effects that are surprising yet plausible. You will continue to develop a sensitivity to your readers' knowledge and attitudes, anticipating their objections and discovering ways to convince them to take your speculations seriously.

The readings in this chapter will help you see what makes arguments about causes or effects convincing. From the readings and from the ideas for writing that follow each reading, you will get ideas for your own essay speculating about causes or effects. As you read and write about the selections, keep in mind the following assignment, which sets out the goals for writing an essay speculating about causes or effects. To support your writing of this assignment, the chapter concludes with a Guide to Writing Essays Speculating about Causes or Effects.

THE WRITING ASSIGNMENT

Speculating about Causes or Effects

Choose a subject — an event, a phenomenon, or a trend — that invites you to speculate about its causes or effects: why it may have happened or what its effects may be. Write an essay arguing for your proposed causes or effects. Essays about causes look to the past to ponder why something happened, whereas essays about effects guess what is likely to happen in the future. Whether you choose to write about causes or effects, you need to do two things: (1) establish the existence and significance of the subject, and (2) convince readers that the causes or effects you propose are plausible.

WRITING SITUATIONS FOR ESSAYS SPECULATING ABOUT CAUSES OR EFFECTS

The following examples suggest further the kinds of causal arguments writers typically make:

- A science writer notes that relatively few women get advanced degrees in science and speculates that social conditioning may be the major cause. To support her causal argument, she cites research on the way boys and girls are treated differently in early childhood. She also gives examples to attempt to show that the social pressure to conform to female role expectations may discourage middle-school girls from doing well in math and science. She acknowledges that other as-yet-unrecognized causes may contribute as well.

- A student writes in the school newspaper about the rising number of pregnancies among high-school students. Interviews with pregnant students lead her to speculate that the chief cause of the trend is a new requirement that parents must give written consent for minors to get birth-control devices at the local clinic. She explains that many students fail to get birth-control information, let alone devices, because of this regulation. She reports that her interviews do not support alternative explanations—that young women have babies to give meaning to their lives, gain status among their peers, or live on their own supported by public assistance.

- A psychology student writes about the effects—positive and negative—of extensive video-game playing among preteens. Based on his own experience and observation, he suggests that video games may improve children's hand-eye coordination, as well as their ability to concentrate on a single task. He speculates that, on the negative side, some children's grades may suffer as a result of spending too much time playing video games.

THINKING ABOUT YOUR EXPERIENCE WITH CAUSE-AND-EFFECT ARGUMENTS

Before studying a type of writing, it is useful to spend some time thinking about what you already know about it. You may have discussed with friends or family members why a certain phenomenon, event, or trend occurred, in which case you were trying to figure out the causes. Or you may have discussed what a phenomenon, event, or trend might lead to or result in, in which case you were speculating about effects. In school, you may have written essays examining the causes, say, of a scientific phenomenon such as the extinction of the dinosaurs or the effects of a social trend such as an increase in interracial marriage.

To analyze your experience with cause-and-effect arguments, try to recall times when you were arguing—orally or in writing—for the reasons you think something happened or the effects that would result from some event, phenomenon, or trend that concerned you. What triggered your speculations? Who was your audience for your argument? What did you hope to achieve with your speculations? What interested you about this issue or made you think it was significant? Did you choose to address the causes, the effects, or both?

Consider also the cause-and-effect arguments you have read, heard, or seen on television. If you recall someone else's argument in some detail, try to identify what made it interesting to you. Was it the subject, or did the author perhaps present ideas new to you? How did the author make the argument for causes or effects convincing? Were you intrigued by illuminating details or an unusual point of view?

Write at least a page about your experience with cause-and-effect arguments.

■ A Guide to Reading Essays Speculating about Causes or Effects

This guide introduces you to written texts that speculate about causes or effects. By completing all of the activities in it, you will prepare yourself to learn a great deal from the other readings in this chapter about how to read and write a speculative essay. The guide makes use of "Why We Crave Horror Movies," a well-known essay by the novelist and screenwriter Stephen King. You will read King's essay twice. First, you will read it for meaning, looking closely at the content and ideas. Then you will read the essay like a writer, analyzing the parts to see how King crafts his essay and to learn the strategies he uses to make his speculative writing convincing. These two activities—reading for meaning and reading like a writer—follow every reading in this chapter.

STEPHEN KING

Why We Crave Horror Movies

Stephen King (b. 1947) is internationally known for his best-selling horror novels, such as Carrie *(1974),* The Shining *(1977),* Misery *(1987),* Bag of Bones *(1998), and* Dreamcatcher *(2001). His most recent novels are* Cell *(2006) and* Lisey's Story *(2006). He also has published a number of short-story collections, the serial novels* The Green Mile *(1996–2000)* and The Dark Tower *(1982–2004), and* On Writing: A Memoir of the Craft *(2001). Many of his novels have been made into movies, and recently some of his works have been dramatized on television* (Salem's Lot, Riding the Bullet). *He has received numerous awards, among them the Lifetime Achievement Award from the Horror Writers Association (2003) and the Medal for Distinguished Contribution to American Letters (2003).*

The following selection originally appeared in Playboy *magazine in 1981. As King's title indicates, the essay attempts to explain the causes for a common phenomenon: most people's liking—even craving—for horror movies. Before you read, think about the horror movie that you remember best and consider why it appeals to you. How old were you when you first saw it? What was most terrifying about it? How did you talk about it at the time, and how do you remember it now?*

As you read, test King's argument about the appeal of horror movies against your own experience. On first reading, how convincing do you find his causal speculations? The marginal annotations below point to strategies typically used by writers who speculate about causes. Add your own comments and questions, noting anything else you think is interesting.

1   I think that we're all mentally ill; those of us outside the asylums only hide it a little better—and maybe not all that much better, after all. We've all known people who talk to themselves, people who sometimes squinch their faces into horrible grimaces when they believe no one is watching, people who have some hysterical fear— of snakes, the dark, the tight place, the long drop . . . and, of course, those final worms and grubs that are waiting so patiently underground.

King creates interest with a shocking statement and gives examples of mental illness as he defines it.

2   When we pay our four or five bucks and seat ourselves at tenth-row center in a theater showing a horror movie, we are daring the nightmare.

3   Why? Some of the reasons are simple and obvious. To show that we can, that we are not afraid, that we can ride this roller coaster. Which is not to say that a really good horror movie may not surprise a scream out of us at some point, the way we may scream when the roller coaster twists through a complete 360 or plows through a lake at the bottom of the drop. And horror movies, like roller coasters, have always been the special province of the young; by the time one turns 40 or 50, one's appetite for double twists or 360-degree loops may be considerably depleted.

"Why?" is a key causal question. After he briefly presents the subject in paragraph 2, King argues for cause 1 (highlighted). How does his analogy to roller coasters support this cause?

4   We also go to re-establish our feelings of essential normality; the horror movie is innately conservative, even reactionary. Freda Jackson as the horrible melting woman in *Die, Monster, Die!* confirms for us that no matter how far we may be removed from the beauty of

King argues for cause 2. How is it related to his idea about mental illness?

a Robert Redford or a Diana Ross, we are still light-years from true ugliness.

And we go to have fun. 5

Cause 3. Fun may be an obvious reason, but King uses the rest of the essay to explain and support it. Another analogy helps readers understand this kind of fun: a horror film is to lynching as pro football is to combat.

Ah, but this is where the ground starts to slope away, 6
isn't it? Because this is a very peculiar sort of fun, indeed. The fun comes from seeing others menaced—sometimes killed. One critic has suggested that if pro football has become the voyeur's version of combat, then the horror film has become the modern version of the public lynching.

It is true that the mythic, "fairy tale" horror film 7
intends to take away the shades of gray. . . . It urges us to put away our more civilized and adult penchant for analysis and to become children again, seeing things in pure blacks and whites. It may be that horror movies provide psychic relief on this level because this invitation to lapse into simplicity, irrationality, and even outright madness is extended so rarely. We are told we may allow our emotions a free rein . . . or no rein at all.

King returns to his opening premise that we are all mentally ill.

If we are all insane, then sanity becomes a matter of 8
degree. If your insanity leads you to carve up women like Jack the Ripper or the Cleveland Torso Murderer, we clap you away in the funny farm (but neither of those two amateur-night surgeons was ever caught, heh-heh-heh); if, on the other hand, your insanity leads you only to talk to yourself when you're under stress or to pick your nose on your morning bus, then you are left alone to go about your business . . . though it is doubtful that you will ever be invited to the best parties.

The potential lyncher is in almost all of us (exclud- 9
ing saints, past and present; but then, most saints have been crazy in their own ways), and every now and then, he has to be let loose to scream and roll around in the grass. Our emotions and our fears form their own body, and we recognize that it demands its own exercise to maintain proper muscle tone. Certain of these emotional muscles are accepted—even exalted—in civilized society; they are, of course, the emotions that tend to maintain the status quo of civilization itself. Love, friendship, loyalty, kindness—these are all the emotions that we applaud, emotions that have been immortalized in the couplets of Hallmark cards and

This analogy (repeated in paragraph 11) supports the entire essay: our emotions are like our muscles and need exercise.

in the verses (I don't dare call it poetry) of Leonard Nimoy.

10   When we exhibit these emotions, society showers us with positive reinforcement; we learn this even before we get out of diapers. When, as children, we hug our rotten little puke of a sister and give her a kiss, all the aunts and uncles smile and twit and cry, "Isn't he the sweetest little thing?" Such coveted treats as chocolate-covered graham crackers often follow. But if we deliberately slam the rotten little puke of a sister's fingers in the door, sanctions follow—angry remonstrance from parents, aunts, and uncles; instead of a chocolate-covered graham cracker, a spanking.

> King provides examples of behavior inspired by good emotions (those that are rewarded) and bad emotions (those that are punished).

11   But anticivilization emotions don't go away, and they demand periodic exercise. We have such "sick" jokes as "What's the difference between a truckload of bowling balls and a truckload of dead babies?" (You can't unload a truckload of bowling balls with a pitchfork . . . a joke, by the way, that I heard originally from a ten-year-old.) Such a joke may surprise a laugh or a grin out of us even as we recoil, a possibility that confirms the thesis: If we share a brotherhood of man, then we also share an insanity of man. None of which is intended as a defense of either the sick joke or insanity but merely as an explanation of why the best horror films, like the best fairy tales, manage to be reactionary, anarchistic, and revolutionary all at the same time.

> More analogies compare horror movies to "sick" jokes and (in the last sentence of the paragraph) fairy tales.

> King once again asserts that we are all insane.

12   The mythic horror movie, like the sick joke, has a dirty job to do. It deliberately appeals to all that is worst in us. It is morbidity unchained, our most base instincts let free, our nastiest fantasies realized . . . and it all happens, fittingly enough, in the dark. For those reasons, good liberals often shy away from horror films. For myself, I like to see the most aggressive of them—*Dawn of the Dead*, for instance—as lifting a trap door in the civilized forebrain and throwing a basket of raw meat to the hungry alligators swimming around in that subterranean river beneath.

> King *establishes credibility* (gains readers' trust) by showing his knowledge that "good liberals often shy away from horror films" and that *Dawn of the Dead* is "the most aggressive of them." A final analogy compares horror movies to raw meat and our emotions to hungry alligators.

13   Why bother? Because it keeps them from getting out, man. It keeps them down there and me up here. It was Lennon and McCartney who said that all you need is love, and I would agree with that.

14   As long as you keep the gators fed.

> The highlighted question *anticipates a possible objection*, and King *counterargues* that horror movies provide an important social outlet.

READING FOR MEANING

This section presents three activities that will help you reread King's causal argument with a critical eye. Done in sequence, these activities lead you from a basic understanding of the selection to a more personal response to it and finally to an analysis that deepens your understanding and critical thinking about what you are reading.

Read to Comprehend

Reread the selection, and write a few sentences briefly explaining why King thinks we watch horror movies. The following definitions may help you understand King's vocabulary:

innately (paragraph 4): naturally; by its nature.

menaced (6): threatened by harm or injury.

anarchistic (11): seeking to destroy all forms and institutions of society and government, with nothing to take their place.

Identify three or more additional words that you don't understand, and find the best definitions from the dictionary that work with their context.

To expand your understanding of this reading, you might use one or more of the following critical reading strategies that are explained and illustrated in Appendix 1: *outlining* and *questioning to understand and remember*.

Read to Respond

Write several paragraphs exploring your initial thoughts and feelings about King's causal argument essay. Focus on anything that stands out for you, perhaps because it resonates with your own experience or because you find a statement puzzling.

You might consider writing about the following:

- the reasons that King writes "[i]f we are all insane, then sanity becomes a matter of degree" (paragraph 8);

- the difference between procivilization and "anticivilization" emotions as King presents them in paragraphs 10 to 13, indicating what you think about his distinction between these two kinds of emotions; or

- your own experiences and feelings about horror novels or films.

To develop your response to King's essay, you might use one or more of the following critical reading strategies that are explained and illustrated in Appendix 1: *recognizing emotional manipulation* and *judging the writer's credibility*.

Read to Analyze Assumptions

Reread King's essay speculating about causes, and write a paragraph or two exploring one or more of the assumptions you find in the text. All writing contains assumptions—opinions, values, and beliefs that are taken for granted as commonly accepted truths by the writer or others. Personal or individual assumptions also tend to reflect the values and beliefs of a particular group or community, sometimes called *cultural ideology*, which shape the way those in the group think, act, and understand the world.

Analyzing assumptions is an important part of learning to read critically because assumptions tend to be unexamined and unquestioned (at least consciously) by those who hold them. When you read with a critical eye, you identify important assumptions in the text and ask questions about them. Sometimes assumptions are stated explicitly, but often they are only implied, so you may have to search for underlying assumptions in the word choices and examples. Here are some kinds of questions you should ask regarding the assumptions you find: How does the assumption support or oppose the status quo? Whose interests are served by it? What alternative ideas, beliefs, or values would challenge this assumption? If the writer uses the assumption to appeal to readers, how effective do you think this appeal is, and why?

To help you get started reading for assumptions in King's essay, notice his use of the idea of the *subconscious*. He never uses the word, but he refers to something that lies under our "civilized forebrain . . . in that subterranean river beneath" (paragraph 12) to help explain why we crave horror movies. Even if we know little about Sigmund Freud's theories about the subconscious, we share the cultural ideology that there is a part of our minds over which we do not have conscious control and that this part of our minds can sometimes govern our behavior. Notice that King also assumes that "[o]ur emotions and our fears" (9) need exercise, just as our bodies do. He uses analogies, or comparisons, to make these abstract ideas vivid.

But these comparisons often carry their own emotional and cultural associations, reflecting beliefs and values that are not as obvious. For example, is the subconscious mind really like the physical body in that it requires "exercise to maintain proper muscle tone"? Or are the two things really not very similar at all, and are we readers being swept along by the power of the writer's metaphor? If a reader does not share King's cultural ideology (is not familiar with theories of divided minds, perhaps, or hates exercise), what might that reader say to King? How persuasive would his analogies be for such a reader? What could some alternative beliefs be?

You may want to examine King's assumptions about the subconscious mind and the value of exercising it. Also consider whether he seems to assume that his readers will agree with him about horror movies or whether his essay is intended to demonstrate their value for skeptical readers. Or you may consider writing about other assumptions you find in the essay, such as the two listed below:

- **assumptions about human emotions.** King asserts that "[t]he mythic horror movie . . . has a dirty job to do. It deliberately appeals to all that is worst in us" (12). He adds that "[i]t is morbidity unchained, our most base instincts let free, our nastiest fantasies realized" (12). To think critically about the assumptions in this essay related to human emotions, ask yourself: What if we don't watch horror movies, don't like them, or don't believe they represent our "nastiest fantasies"? If you don't share King's assumption about universal human nastiness, how do you respond to his essay? What alternatives to his thinking occur to you? In a culture that has a different view of the human mind, what other causes of horror movies' popularity might be just as believable?

- **assumptions about the young.** King asserts that "horror movies . . . have always been the special province of the young" (3) and that we go to see them "to put away our more civilized and adult penchant for analysis and to become children again" (7). To think critically about assumptions in this essay about children and young people, ask yourself: What viewpoints do they have that adults do not have or have outgrown? What does King assume distinguishes them in, say, their attitude toward scary situations (3) or complex ones (7)? Why would adults want to become children again?

To probe assumptions more deeply, you might use one or more of the following critical reading strategies that are explained and illustrated in Appendix 1: *reflecting on challenges to your beliefs and values* and *exploring the significance of figurative language.*

READING LIKE A WRITER

This section guides you through an analysis of King's argumentative strategies: *presenting the subject, making a cause-and-effect argument, counterarguing,* and *establishing credibility.* For each strategy you will be asked to reread and annotate part of King's essay to see how King uses the strategy in "Why We Crave Horror Movies."

When you study the selections later in this chapter, you will see how different writers use the same strategies to make causal arguments or speculate about effects. The Guide to Writing Essays Speculating about Causes or Effects near the end of the chapter suggests ways you can use these strategies in your own writing.

Presenting the Subject

In presenting the subject of an essay speculating about causes or effects, the writer must be sure that readers will recognize and understand the subject. In some writing situations, the writer can safely assume that readers will already know a great deal about a familiar subject. In this case, the writer can simply identify the subject and immediately begin the speculations about its causes or effects.

In many other cases, however, writers must present an unfamiliar subject in enough detail for readers to understand it fully. On occasion, writers may even need to convince readers that their subject is important and worth speculating about.

When writers decide they need to prove that the trend or phenomenon they are writing about exists, they may describe it in great detail, give examples, offer factual evidence, cite statistics, or quote statements by authorities. To establish the importance of the trend or phenomenon, writers may show that it involves a large number of people or has great importance to certain people.

Analyze

1. How does King present horror movies as a particular movie genre? *Skim* the essay to see which horror movies he mentions by title. Are the few examples he cites sufficient? Do you think readers need to have seen the movies he mentions to get the point? What does King seem to assume about his readers' experiences with horror films?

2. *Consider* how King establishes the importance of his subject. *Underline* one or two comments King makes about the subject that are likely to increase his readers' curiosity about why people crave horror movies.

Write

Write several sentences explaining how King presents his subject.

Making a Cause-and-Effect Argument

At the heart of an essay speculating about causes or effects is an argument. The argument is made up of at least two parts—(1) the proposed causes or effects and (2) the reasoning and support for each cause or effect. In addition, the writer may anticipate readers' objections or questions, a strategy we take up in the next section on counterargument. In analyzing King's argument, we will look at some of the causes he proposes and how he supports them.

Writers speculating about causes or effects rarely consider only one possibility. They know that most puzzling phenomena (like people's attraction to horror movies) have multiple possible causes. However, they also know that it would be foolish to try to identify every possible cause. Writers must therefore be selective if they hope to make a convincing argument. The best arguments avoid the obvious. They offer new and imaginative ways of thinking—either proposing causes or effects that will surprise readers or arguing for familiar causes or effects in new ways.

Writers support their arguments with various kinds of evidence—facts, statistical correlations, personal anecdotes, testimony of authorities, examples, and analogies. In this activity, we focus on King's use of analogies.

Analyze

1. *Reread* paragraphs 3 and 12, and *identify* the analogy in each paragraph. An analogy is a special form of comparison in which one part of the comparison is used to explain the other. In arguing by analogy, the writer reasons that if two situations are alike, their causes will also be similar.

2. *Think about* how well the comparisons in paragraphs 3 and 12 hold up. For example, you may be able to use your personal experience to test whether watching a horror movie is much like riding a roller coaster. *Ask yourself* in what ways the two are alike—and different. Are they more alike than different? Also *consider* how you are or are not like a hungry alligator when you watch a horror movie.

Write

Describe and *evaluate* King's support by analogy in paragraphs 3 and 12. *Explain* the parts of each analogy—the two separate things being compared. *Evaluate* how well each analogy works logically. In what ways are the two things being compared actually alike? Also *evaluate* what the two analogies contribute to King's causal argument. How is the essay strengthened by them?

Counterarguing

When causes or effects cannot be known for certain, there is bound to be disagreement. Consequently, writers try to anticipate possible objections and alternative causes or effects readers might put forward. Writers bring these objections and alternatives directly into their essays and then either refute (argue against) them or find a way to accommodate them in the argument.

Analyze

1. King anticipates a possible objection from readers when he poses the question "Why bother?" in paragraph 13. *Reread* paragraphs 11 and 12 to understand the context in which King anticipates the need to pose that question. *Notice* his direct answer to the question in paragraph 13.

2. *Think about* the effectiveness of King's counterargument. *Consider* whether it satisfactorily answers the objection.

Write

Write a few sentences explaining why you think King asks the question at this point in his argument. *Consider* whether some of King's readers would ask themselves this question. *Evaluate* how satisfied they would be with King's response.

Establishing Credibility

Because cause-and-effect writing is highly speculative, its effectiveness depends in large part on whether readers trust the writer. Readers sometimes use information about the writer's professional and personal accomplishments in forming their judgments about the writer's credibility. The most important information, however, comes from the writing itself, specifically how writers argue for their own proposed causes or effects, as well as how they handle readers' objections.

Writers seek to establish their credibility with readers by making their reasoning clear and logical, their evidence relevant and trustworthy, and their handling of objections fair and balanced. They try to be authoritative (knowledgeable) without appearing authoritarian (opinionated and dogmatic).

Analyze

1. *Reread* the headnote that precedes King's essay, and *reflect on* what his *Playboy* readers might have already known about him. King is more widely known now than he was when "Why We Crave Horror Movies" was published in 1981, but his readers at that time would likely have heard of him.

2. With King's readers in mind, *skim* the essay to decide whether the reasoning is clear and logical and the examples and analogies relevant and trustworthy. *Notice* that King's reasoning is psychological. He argues that mental and emotional needs explain why some people crave horror films. Therefore, you, along with King's intended readers, can evaluate King's credibility in light of your own personal experience — your understanding of the role horror novels and films play in your own life. On the basis of your own experience and your evaluation of the logic and consistency of King's argument, *decide* whether you think most readers would consider him a credible writer on the subject of horror films.

Write

Write several sentences describing the impression readers might get of King from reading both the headnote and his essay on horror films. What might make them trust or distrust what he says about his subject?

■ Readings

NATALIE ANGIER
Intolerance of Boyish Behavior

> *One of America's preeminent science writers, Natalie Angier (b. 1958) won a Pulitzer Prize in 1991 for her reports on various scientific topics published in the* New York Times, *where she has worked as a reporter since 1990, specializing in biology and medicine. Angier has also published articles in magazines, including* Discovery, Time, *and the* Atlantic, *and has taught in New York University's Graduate Program in Science and Environmental Reporting. Her 1988 book,* Natural Obsessions: The Search for the Oncogene, *won the Lewis Thomas Award for excellence in writing about the life sciences. Her most recent books are* Natural Obsessions: Striving to Unlock the Deepest Secrets of the Cancer Cell *(1999),* Woman, an Intimate Geography *(2000), and* The Canon: A Whirligig Tour of the Beautiful Basics of Science *(2007). She also edited* The Best American Science and Nature Writing *(2002).*
>
> *The following selection appeared in the* New York Times *in 1994. The* Times *is a major newspaper in the New York City region, but it has wide national influence because people living throughout the United States read it daily. Politicians, academics, and other journalists give it special attention. Journalists such as Angier who write about scientific topics for newspapers and magazines do not assume that readers have a high level of scientific training. They write for a broad audience, including college students interested in ideas and issues.*
>
> *In this reading, Angier seeks to explain the increasing intolerance by teachers, parents, counselors, and therapists of certain kinds of behavior that she labels "boyish." Angier speculates about the causes of a trend — an increase or decrease in something over time. Unexpected or alarming social trends — such as the increasing use of medication with boys for behavior that was previously tolerated or overlooked — especially invite causal speculation. You will notice that Angier is careful to demonstrate that there is in fact an increasing intolerance of what she calls "boyish behavior."*
>
> *As you read, think about your own experience as a sibling, as a friend of other young children, as a student in elementary school, or perhaps even as a parent of a boy with "boyish behavior." Does Angier convince you that most boys are more rambunctious than most girls? Do you believe that many teachers and parents now see this as a big problem? Note where Angier surprises you or supports her causal argument with evidence — facts, statistics, personal anecdotes, testimony of authorities, examples, or analogies. Consider also how plausible you find Angier's proposed causes for the growing intolerance of "boyish behavior."*

Until quite recently, the plain-spun tautology "boys will be boys" summed up everything parents needed to know about their Y-chromosome bundles. Boys will be very noisy and obnoxious. Boys will tear around the house and break heirlooms. They will transform any object longer than it is wide into a laser weapon with eight settings from stun to vaporize. They will swagger and brag and fib and not do their homework and leave their dirty underwear on the bathroom floor.

But they will also be . . . boys. They will be adventurous and brave. When they fall down, they'll get up, give a cavalier spit to the side, and try again. Tom Sawyer may have been a slob, a truant and a hedonist; he may have picked fights with strangers for no apparent reason; but he was also resourceful, spirited and deliciously clever. Huckleberry Finn was an illiterate outcast, but as a long-term rafting companion he had no peer.

Today, the world is no longer safe for boys. A boy being a shade too boyish risks finding himself under the scrutiny of parents, teachers, guidance counselors, child therapists—all of them on watch for the early glimmerings of a medical syndrome, a bona fide behavioral disorder. Does the boy disregard authority, make snide comments in class, push other kids around and play hooky? Maybe he has a conduct disorder. Is he fidgety, impulsive, disruptive, easily bored? Perhaps he is suffering from attention-deficit hyperactivity disorder, or ADHD, the disease of the hour and the most frequently diagnosed behavioral disorder of childhood. Does he prefer computer games and goofing off to homework? He might have dyslexia or another learning disorder.

"There is now an attempt to pathologize what was once considered the normal range of behavior of boys," said Melvin Konner of the departments of anthropology and psychiatry at Emory University in Atlanta. "Today, Tom Sawyer and Huckleberry Finn surely would have been diagnosed with both conduct disorder and ADHD." And both, perhaps, would have been put on Ritalin, the drug of choice for treating attention-deficit disorder.

To be fair, many children do have genuine medical problems like ADHD, and they benefit enormously from the proper treatment. Psychiatrists insist that they work very carefully to distinguish between the merely rambunctious child, and the kid who has a serious, organic disorder that is disrupting his life and putting him at risk for all the demons of adulthood: drug addiction, shiftlessness, underemployment, criminality and the like.

At the same time, some doctors and social critics cannot help but notice that so many of the childhood syndromes now being diagnosed in record numbers affect far more boys than girls.

Attention-deficit disorder, said to afflict 5 percent of all children, is thought to be about three to four times more common in boys than girls. Dyslexia is thought to be about four times more prevalent in boys than girls; and boys practically have the patent on conduct disorders. What is more, most of the traits that brand a child as a potential syndromeur just happen to be traits associated with young males: aggression, rowdiness, restlessness, loud-mouthedness, rebelliousness. None of these characteristics is exclusive to the male sex, of course — for the ultimate display of aggressive intensity, try watching a group of city girls engaged in a serious game of jump-rope — but boys more often will make a spectacle of themselves. And these days, the audience isn't smiling at the show.

"People are more sensitized to certain extremes of boyishness,"   7
said Dr. John Ratey, a psychiatrist at Harvard Medical School. "It's not as acceptable to be the class clown. You can't cut up. You won't be given slack anymore." Woe to the boy who combines misconduct with rotten grades; he is the likeliest of all to fall under professional observation. "If rowdiness and lack of performance go together, you see the button being pushed much quicker than ever before," he said, particularly in schools where high academic performance is demanded.

Lest males of all ages feel unfairly picked upon, researchers   8
point out that boys may be diagnosed with behavioral syndromes and disorders more often than girls for a very good reason: their brains may be more vulnerable. As a boy is developing in the womb, the male hormones released by his tiny testes accelerate the maturation of his brain, locking a lot of the wiring in place early on; a girl's hormonal bath keeps her brain supple far longer. The result is that the infant male brain is a bit less flexible, less able to repair itself after slight injury that might come, for example, during the arduous trek down the birth canal. Hence, boys may well suffer disproportionately from behavioral disorders for reasons unrelated to cultural expectations.

However, biological insights can only go so far in explaining why   9
American boyhood is coming to be seen as a state of protodisease. After all, the brains of boys in other countries also were exposed to testosterone in utero, yet non-American doctors are highly unlikely to diagnose a wild boy as having a conduct disorder or ADHD.

"British psychiatrists require a very severe form of hyperactivity   10
before they'll see it as a problem," said Dr. Paul R. McHugh, chairman and director of psychiatry at the Johns Hopkins School of Medicine in Baltimore. "Unless a child is so clearly disturbed that he goes at it until he falls asleep in an inappropriate place like a wastebasket or a drawer, and then wakes up and starts it all over

again, he won't be put on medication." Partly as a result of this sharp difference in attitudes, the use of Ritalin-like medications has remained fairly stable in Britain, while pharmaceutical companies here have bumped up production by 250 percent since 1991.

Perhaps part of the reason why boyish behavior is suspect these days is Americans' obsessive fear of crime. "We're all really terrified of violence," said Dr. Edward Hallowell, a child psychiatrist at Harvard. "Groups of people who have trouble containing aggression come under suspicion." And what group has more trouble containing aggression than males under the age of 21? Such suspiciousness is not helped by the fact that the rate of violent crime has climbed most steeply among the young, and that everybody seems to own a gun or know where to steal one. Sure, it's perfectly natural for boys to roll around in the dirt fighting and punching and kicking; but toss a firearm into the equation, and suddenly no level of aggression looks healthy.

Another cause for the intolerance of boyish behavior is the current school system. It is more group-oriented than ever before, leaving little room for the jokester, the tough, the tortured individualist. American children are said to be excessively coddled and undisciplined, yet in fact they spend less time than their European or Japanese counterparts at recess, where kids can burn off the manic energy they've stored up while trapped in the classroom. Because boys have a somewhat higher average metabolism than do girls, they are likely to become more fidgety when forced to sit still and study.

The climate is not likely to improve for the world's Sawyers or Finns or James Deans or any other excessively colorful and unruly specimens of boyhood. Charlotte Tomaino, a clinical neuropsychologist in White Plains, notes that the road to success in this life has gotten increasingly narrow in recent years. "The person who used to have greater latitude in doing one thing and moving onto another suddenly is the person who can't hold a job," she said. "We define success as what you produce, how well you compete, how well you keep up with the tremendous cognitive and technical demands put upon you." The person who will thrive is not the restless version of a human tectonic plate, but the one who can sit still, concentrate and do his job for the 10, 12, 14 hours a day required.

A generation or two ago, a guy with a learning disability—or an ornery temperament—could drop out of school, pick up a trade and become, say, the best bridge builder in town. Now, if a guy cannot at the very least manage to finish college, the surging, roaring, indifferent Mississippi of the world's economy is likely to take his little raft, and break it into bits.

READING FOR MEANING

This section presents three activities that will help you reread Angier's causal argument with a critical eye. Done in sequence, these activities lead you from a basic understanding of the selection to a more personal response to it and finally to an analysis that deepens your understanding and critical thinking about what you are reading.

Read to Comprehend

Reread the selection, and write a few sentences explaining the causes that Angier gives for the rise in intolerance of "boyish behavior." The following definitions may help you understand Angier's vocabulary:

hedonist (paragraph 2): a person devoted to pleasure, especially to the pleasures of the senses.

pathologize (4): to characterize as medically or psychologically abnormal.

syndromes (8): abnormal conditions or diseases identified by an established group of symptoms.

obsessive (11): absorbing too much attention; preoccupying.

Identify three or more additional words that you don't understand, and find the best definitions from the dictionary that work with their context.

To expand your understanding of this reading, you might use one or both of the following critical reading strategies that are explained and illustrated in Appendix 1: *outlining* and *contextualizing*.

Read to Respond

Write several paragraphs exploring your initial thoughts and feelings about Angier's causal argument. Focus on anything that stands out for you, perhaps because it resonates with your own experience or because you find a statement puzzling.

You might consider writing about the following:

- why Angier uses examples from Mark Twain's novels *The Adventures of Tom Sawyer* and *The Adventures of Huckleberry Finn* and how her use of them contributes to your understanding of the essay;

- Angier's assertion that "it's perfectly natural for boys to roll around in the dirt fighting and punching and kicking" (paragraph 11);

- a time when you experienced, expressed, or observed intolerance of boyish behavior, connecting your experience to ideas or examples in Angier's essay;

- the extent to which your own experience and observation supports Angier's proposed causes in paragraphs 11 to 14; or

- how the World Wide Web and other information technologies that have come into wide use since Angier's article was published might affect her argument.

To develop your response to Angier's essay, you might use one or more of the following critical reading strategies that are explained and illustrated in Appendix 1: *contextualizing* and *recognizing emotional manipulation*.

Read to Analyze Assumptions

Reread Angier's causal essay, and write a paragraph or two exploring one or more of the assumptions you find in the text. The following suggestions may help:

- **assumptions about U.S. culture.** In paragraph 9, Angier says that growing intolerance of what she calls "boyish behavior" is a trend particular to the United States. She then speculates that the causes of this intolerance include Americans' "fear of crime" (paragraph 11), a school system that is group-oriented and does not allow adequate recess time (12), and sedentary jobs that require great concentration (13). To think critically about the assumptions in this essay related to American culture, ask yourself: To what extent, if any, do you connect a fear of crime to a concern about boys' rambunctious behavior? If Angier is right that U.S. school activities are "more group-oriented than ever before" (12), does a preference for group work necessarily deny the value that more unconventional individuals might bring to the group? Why? If you share Angier's belief that modern jobs are constricting, consider the national trends toward jobs in the service and technology sectors. These currently are the largest-growing job markets, and technology in particular employs far more people today than when Angier was writing. How could growth in service and technology jobs affect people's tolerance or intolerance of those who have trouble containing their aggression?

- **assumptions about the power of words.** Look at some of the words that Angier uses in her first two paragraphs to describe boys: "Noisy and obnoxious . . . swagger and brag and fib (1); adventurous and brave . . . cavalier . . . slob, a truant and a hedonist . . . resourceful, spirited and deliciously clever" (2). Midway through the essay, she characterizes "traits associated with young males: aggression, rowdiness, restlessness, loud-mouthedness, rebelliousness" (6) as problematic for people these days. To think critically about assumptions regarding the power of words, ask yourself: What kind of response is called up by these words? Do their emotional associations help the reader understand Angier's attitude toward boys and toward those whom she perceives as overdiagnosing them with behavior disorders? How? What effect do these words have on you as you form your opinions from reading this essay? As you read further, make a note of additional words that Angier uses to influence the reader, either about boys or about our responses to them. How do these word choices affect you?

To probe assumptions more deeply, you might use one or more of the following critical reading strategies that are explained and illustrated in Appendix 1: *reflecting on challenges to your beliefs and values* and *recognizing emotional manipulation*.

READING LIKE A WRITER
COUNTERARGUING

Writers speculating about causes must work imaginatively and persistently to support their proposed causes, using all the relevant resources available to them—quoting authorities, citing statistics and research findings, comparing and contrasting, posing rhetorical questions, offering literary allusions, and crafting metaphors, among others. (Angier uses all of the resources in this list.) In addition to supporting their proposed causes, writers usually do more. Because they aim to convince particular readers of the plausibility of their causal argument, writers try to be keenly aware that at every point in the argument their readers will have questions, objections, and other causes in mind. Anticipating and responding to these questions, objections, and alternative causes is known as *counterarguing*.

As readers work their way through a causal argument, nearly all of them will think of questions they would like to ask the writer. They also might resist or object to certain aspects of the support, such as the way the writer uses facts or statistics, relies on an authority, sets up an analogy, or presents an example or personal experience. Readers may doubt whether the support is appropriate, believable, or consistent with the other support provided by the writer. They may come to believe that the writer relies too much on emotional appeals and too little on reason. Readers may also resist or reject the writer's proposed causes, or they may believe that other causes better explain the trend. Experienced writers anticipate all of these predictable concerns. Just as imaginatively as they argue for their proposed causes, writers attempt to answer readers' questions, react to their objections, and evaluate their preferred causes. When you write your essay about causes or effects, anticipating and responding to your readers' concerns will be one of the most challenging and interesting parts of constructing your argument.

Analyze

1. Angier counterargues in at least three places in her causal argument—paragraphs 5, 6, and 8. *Reread* these paragraphs, and *identify* and *underline* the three main objections that Angier anticipates her readers will have to her argument. For example, in the first sentence of paragraph 5, she anticipates readers' likely objection that some boys do have medical problems requiring treatment.

2. *Examine closely* how Angier counterargues readers' objections and questions. For the three objections or questions you identified in paragraphs 5, 6, and 8, *notice* the kinds of support she relies on to argue against each objection. *Decide* whether the support is similar or different among the three cases.

Write

Write several sentences reporting what you have learned about how Angier anticipates her readers' objections. Specifically, in each case, how does she support her counterargument? How appropriate do you, as one of her intended readers, find her support? How believable do you find it?

A SPECIAL READING STRATEGY

Evaluating the Logic of an Argument

To evaluate the logic of an argument speculating about causes, ask yourself three basic questions:

- How appropriate is the support for each cause being speculated about?
- How believable is the support?
- How consistent and complete is the overall argument?

Such an evaluation requires a comprehensive and thoughtful critical reading, but your efforts will help you understand more fully what makes a causal argument successful. To evaluate the logic of Angier's argument, follow the guidelines in Appendix 1 (pp. 624–27). There you will find definitions and explanations as well as an illustration based on an excerpt from a famous essay by Martin Luther King Jr. (the excerpt appears on pp. 598–602).

CONSIDERING IDEAS FOR YOUR OWN WRITING

Think about other groups or categories of people you have the opportunity to observe, and try to identify trends or changes in aspects of their behavior. For example, does it seem to you that girls or women are increasingly interested in math and science or in participating in team sports? If you have been working for a few years, have you noticed that employees have become more docile and more eager to please management? If you have young children, does it seem to you that day-care workers have become increasingly professional?

Select one group whose behavior is changing, and consider how you would convince readers that the behavior is in fact changing—increasing or decreasing over time. What kind of evidence would you need to gather in the library or on the Internet to corroborate your personal impressions? As a writer speculating about a behavioral change, consider how you would come up with some possible causes for the trend.

JOHN DUTTON
Toxic Soup

> John Dutton (b. 1961) received his B.A. in environmental studies
> from the University of California at Santa Cruz. He has worked as a
> rafting guide and as an Outward Bound lead instructor and assistant
> program director and says that he spends as much time on the
> water—surfing, paddling, sailing, and fishing—as possible. He has
> published articles in Surfer, Longboard Magazine, Paddler, Sea
> Kayaker, and other magazines as well as in the Patagonia clothing
> company's catalog and its anthology Notes from the Field (1999). He
> currently works as a managing editor for Patagonia.
>
> The following essay first appeared in the Patagonia winter 2006–
> 2007 catalog and on the company's Oceans as Wilderness Campaign
> Web site as part of an effort to raise public awareness of the need for
> environmental protection of oceans. In this essay, Dutton explores how
> various forms of pollution in the oceans are affecting many fish and
> other animals—including humans. At the end, he points to action
> that readers can take to minimize the damage. As you read the essay,
> think about your own experience with the ocean or other bodies of
> water that might be suffering from some of the effects that Dutton
> worries about.
>
> Annotate the text, noting places where Dutton presents his subject
> and establishes his credibility and anything else interesting about his
> writing strategies. (For help annotating, see the examples in this chap-
> ter on pages 378 and 422, as well as the advice on annotating on pages
> 597–98.)

As a kid I surfed almost every day—rain or shine, surf or no   1
surf. I progressed from mat surfing (there were no boogie boards
back then) to body surfing and ultimately board surfing. Just being
in the ocean was a joy: I mat surfed beachbreaks on summer south
swells, tucked into Black's barrels with only fins and a wetsuit, and
surfed Pleasure Point at speeds that made the surfboard's fin hum.

Forty years later I surf much less, but not because I'm more dis-   2
criminating or jaded. No, it's a matter of knowing too much in an
increasingly polluted world. Where I used to surf 12 months a year,
rain or shine, today I make the most of the fall days with glassy
head-high surf. When the rains come in January, my surfing stops
until the rains stop. We've all seen the water-quality reports and the
off-the-charts fecal coliform counts and known friends who got a
stomach or sinus bug when they surfed too soon after a storm.

But if you think it's bad in the lineup for you, consider the ani-   3
mals. You might suffer a sore throat and a stuffed-up nose or a case
of the runs after surfing your home break, but it's far worse for the
organisms that live there 24/7.

Surfers on the central California coast might not notice it, but   4
sea otters are taking a hit. After a high in 1995, the otter population
dipped 10 percent to a low in 2002 and then slowly rebounded. But
of the otters washed up dead on the beach, a higher percentage are
dying from disease rather than other causes. In a 2002 study conducted by a team at UC Davis, researchers think they found the
main culprit: the *Toxoplasma gondii* that plagues cats. "We think
that the eggs from the parasites in cat waste may get transported to
the ocean from fields and yards by surface runoff after storms. . . ,"
concludes Melissa Miller, the study's lead author. The parasite kills
otters by causing brain infections that result in seizures and paralysis and interferes with the otters' feeding—a far cry from an ear
infection, a common cold or the runs.

In Kaneohe Bay, O'ahu, where turtles and surfers coexist in pol-   5
luted waters, the green turtles have been developing fibropapillo-
matosis (FP). FP is a disease that riddles turtles with multiple fibrous
tumors, both internally and externally. What is unusual about FP is
that it is the first recorded pandemic in a species other than humans.
The disease is associated with human viruses, heavily polluted
coastal waters, agricultural runoff, biotoxin-producing algae and
areas of high human density. It was first reported in the late '30s in
Florida but now has reached epidemic proportions around the
world. Like sea otters, sea turtles are already at risk of going extinct.
FP is also reported in loggerhead, olive ridley, Kemp's ridley and flat-
back turtles. If left untreated (read surgically removed), the tumors
result in death by hindering the turtle's ability to see, swim and feed.
Once the tumors become internal, there is no treatment.

Surfers on the Outer Banks know all about the danger in the   6
estuaries of North Carolina. *Pfiesteria piscicida*, a dinoflagellate, is
killing fish and causing more than sore throats and colds in
humans. It can rapidly change itself, acting like a mild-mannered
dinoflagellate feeding on algae and other tiny organisms one
moment, and then transforming into an "ambush predator" when
a school of fish swims by. It gives chase, stuns the fish with a neurotoxin, and secretes a compound that causes hemorrhaging lesions
to form on the skin. It then turns into a carnivore and starts
devouring the fish's deeper tissues. *P. piscicida* was responsible for
the massive fish kills in the 1990s in North Carolina and Maryland
estuaries. The dinoflagellate has been linked to untreated sewage
from hog farms. And this is where it gets personal for surfers: *P.
piscicida* has been implicated in lesions, respiratory distress and
neurological symptoms (like memory loss) in humans.

The outbreaks in North Carolina are just the tip of the iceberg   7
in "an apparent global epidemic of novel phytoplankton blooms,"
according to Theodore Smayda, a leading expert on the subject.

Most of these algal blooms—called red tides—are naturally occurring, but humans are exacerbating the rate and severity of the blooms. Nutrient enrichment from pollution and agricultural runoff, changes in sea temperature from global warming, and the transport of invasive algae in the ballast water of ships all contribute to the problem.

No one knows this better than Southern California surfers who witnessed a summer of epic red tides in 2005. They have also seen the dead and rotting, or seizure-ridden and dying, seals and dolphins on the beach caused by domoic acid, a naturally occurring toxin produced by a particular form of red tide that has been intensified by nutrient enrichment. The neurotoxin concentrates up the food chain from baitfish all the way to marine mammals and seabirds. Once the neurotoxin reaches high-enough concentrations, it ultimately results in death.

8

I might surf less these days because I know more than when I was a kid, but I also know what to do about the problem. Although it might seem too big to tackle, the solutions are there; all it takes is the right choices in our day-to-day lives. Buy organic food and fibers to help eliminate chemical fertilizers that contribute to nutrient enrichment of coastal waters. Pick up after your pet and don't let leaves, yard waste, motor oil or cleaners get in the street gutter—everything that goes in the gutters ends up in the ocean. Fight developers who want to fill in wetlands that act as natural water filters. Write your representatives to beef up sewage treatment facilities and strengthen the Clean Water Act. We can clean up our oceans; it's just a matter of knowledge and action.

9

READING FOR MEANING

This section presents three activities that will help you reread Dutton's essay with a critical eye. Done in sequence, these activities lead you from a basic understanding of the selection to a more personal response to it and finally to an analysis that deepens your understanding and critical thinking about what you are reading.

Read to Comprehend

Reread the selection, and write a few sentences explaining the effects that Dutton sees as resulting from toxic waste in the oceans. The following definitions may help you understand Dutton's vocabulary:

discriminating (paragraph 2): having good taste or judgment; choosy or particular.

pandemic (5): present throughout an entire country or continent or the whole world; epidemic over a large area.

implicated in (6): identified as the cause of.

Identify three or more additional words that you don't understand, and find the best definitions from the dictionary that work with their context.

Read to Respond

Write several paragraphs exploring your initial thoughts and feelings about Dutton's essay. Focus on anything that stands out for you, perhaps because it resonates with your own experience or because you find a statement puzzling.

You might consider writing about the following:

- whether you think Dutton is being too alarmist or not alarmist enough;

- activities of your own that, like Dutton's surfing, have been affected by pollution or other environmental considerations;

- your own experiences with bodies of water and how they might affect your response to this essay;

- steps you have taken or would like to take to help the environment; or

- your response to the last paragraph and whether you think Dutton's suggestions are appropriate and will make a big enough difference.

To develop your response to Dutton's essay, you might use one or both of the following critical reading strategies that are explained and illustrated in Appendix 1: *questioning to understand and remember* and *recognizing emotional manipulation*.

Read to Analyze Assumptions

Reread Dutton's effects essay, and write a paragraph or two exploring one or more of the assumptions you find in the text. The following suggestions may help:

- **assumptions about humans' relationship to the environment.** In this essay, John Dutton weaves together his personal experiences as a surfer and ocean lover with his knowledge of the medical effects of water pollution on humans and animals. Most readers will readily grant that the pollution of oceans, lakes, and rivers has become a problem for humans, but many may not have thought much about pollution's effects on the wildlife that lives in the water. To think critically about assumptions in this essay related to humans' relationship with the environment, ask yourself: How are your feelings or behavior affected by knowledge about the physical suffering or reduced fertility of certain ocean animals or fish from human carelessness about waste products on the land? What beliefs about human responsibility shape your attitude toward Dutton's essay? Dutton seems to think that if he can educate readers about the effects of pollution, they will want to take action. To what extent do you share his assumption that one essay could create a significant change in a reader's outlook? Why? See if you can discover your own assumptions about the relationship of humans to the environment in your responses.

- **assumptions about the personal and the scientific.** Dutton could have written this essay without any personal narrative. Yet he chooses to start with how as a kid he surfed almost every day, and he refers to surfing in every paragraph but one. Interspersed with his surfing narrative is an explanatory argument about the toxic effects of water pollution, and he supports this argument with medical information, statistics, many examples, vivid descriptions, and references to the effects on surfers. To think critically about Dutton's assumptions in this essay related to mixing the personal with the objective or scientific, ask yourself: What difference does it make to this essay to have these two approaches to the topic combined in this way? If Dutton had omitted either the personal examples or the scientific evidence and examples, what would the effect have been on readers, and why? What was Dutton assuming about his readers?

READING LIKE A WRITER
PRESENTING THE SUBJECT

When writers speculate about the effects of a phenomenon or trend, they must define or describe the trend for readers. Readers must be assured that the trend actually exists. Furthermore, readers are more likely to be engaged by the speculations if they can recognize or be convinced that the trend is important to them personally or has a larger significance. In some writing situations, writers may safely assume that readers are thoroughly familiar with the trend and therefore need little more than a mention of it. In most situations, however, writers know that readers will require a relatively full presentation of the subject. Dutton knows that his readers are familiar with the *idea* of water pollution but probably have little knowledge of pollution's actual effects on both wildlife and humans. He therefore describes the effects in detail, gives many examples, cites statistics, and quotes authorities, all to help the reader see how "toxic" are the effects of pollution.

Analyze

1. *Reread* paragraphs 4 to 8. *Underline* all of the forms of marine life affected by ocean pollution.

2. Now *underline* the diseases that afflict the wildlife and humans who live in or near the ocean.

Write

Write several sentences explaining how Dutton presents his subject. Then *add a few more sentences* evaluating how successfully he does so. What effects are most significant, in your view? What strategies seem most helpful to readers? What, if anything, seems to be missing from his presentation? Where is he most successful in declaring or suggesting the importance of his subject?

A SPECIAL READING STRATEGY

Comparing and Contrasting Related Readings: Dutton's "Toxic Soup" and Ripplinger's "Declining Coral Reefs: A Real Problem"

Comparing and contrasting related readings is a critical-reading strategy that is useful both in reading for meaning and in reading like a writer. This strategy is particularly applicable when writers present similar subjects, as is the case in the *effects* essay by John Dutton (p. 396) and the *causal* essay by Amber Ripplinger (p. 416). Both writers are concerned with the degradation of the environment in the ocean. To compare and contrast these two essays, think about issues such as these:

- Compare the authors' beliefs about who is responsible for the decline in the health of marine animals.

- Compare the strategies each author uses to cite sources, and speculate about why in specific cases their approaches are different or similar.

- Compare the two authors' attitudes toward marine life.

CONSIDERING IDEAS FOR YOUR OWN WRITING

Dutton wrote his *effects* essay because he is concerned about the growing trend of pollution of the ocean. You may know of an environmental trend or phenomenon that you find alarming and could write about, or you might have experienced an event, such as the eruption of a volcano, that made you concerned about a long-range environmental impact, such as changes in the temperature of the earth (global warming). Many scientific topics lend themselves to speculation about causes or effects; you may find several in your college textbooks or in your community. Any time you are puzzled by *why* something happened or how something *triggered* something else, you have a potential cause or effect essay topic.

JONATHAN KOZOL

The Human Cost of an Illiterate Society

A well-known critic of American schools, Jonathan Kozol (b. 1936) was in the forefront of educational reformers during the 1970s and 1980s. He has taught in the Boston and Newton, Massachusetts, public schools, as well as at Yale University and the University of Massachusetts at Amherst. Kozol's books include Death at an Early Age *(1967), for which he won the National Book Award;* On Being a Teacher *(1981);* Illiterate America *(1985);* Amazing Grace: The Lives of Children and the Conscience of a Nation *(1985);* Savage Inequalities: Children in America's Schools *(1991);* Blueprint for a Democratic Education *(1992);* Ordinary Resurrections: Children in the Years of Hope *(2000); and* The Shame of the Nation: The Restoration of Apartheid Schooling in America *(2005).*

The following selection is from Illiterate America, *a comprehensive study of the nature, causes, and effects of illiteracy. The book is intended for a broad readership. Certainly, you are among Kozol's intended readers. In this chapter from the book, Kozol speculates about the human consequences of illiteracy, outlining the limitations and dangers in the lives of adults who cannot read or write. Elsewhere in the book, Kozol conjectures about the causes of illiteracy, but here he concentrates on the effects of the phenomenon, speculating about what life is like for illiterates. He adopts this strategy to argue that the human costs of the problem pose a moral dilemma for our country.*

As you read, note how Kozol presents his subject by giving many vivid examples to illustrate the effects of illiteracy, and decide whether he convinces you that illiteracy is not just a social problem but also a special danger to democracy.

PRECAUTIONS. READ BEFORE USING.
Poison: Contains sodium hydroxide (caustic soda-lye).
Corrosive: Causes severe eye and skin damage, may cause blindness.
Harmful or fatal if swallowed.
If swallowed, give large quantities of milk or water.
Do not induce vomiting.
Important: Keep water out of can at all times to prevent contents from violently erupting. . . .

— WARNING ON A CAN OF DRANO

Questions of literacy, in Socrates' belief, must at length be judged as matters of morality. Socrates could not have had in mind the moral compromise peculiar to a nation like our own. Some of our Founding Fathers did, however, have this question in their minds. One of the wisest of those Founding Fathers [James Madison] recognized the special dangers that illiteracy would pose to basic equity in the political construction that he helped to shape:

A people who mean to be their own governors must arm themselves with the power knowledge gives. A popular government without popular information or the means of acquiring it, is but a prologue to a farce or a tragedy, or perhaps both.

2

Tragedy looms larger than farce in the United States today. Illiterate citizens seldom vote. Those who do are forced to cast a vote of questionable worth. They cannot make informed decisions based on serious print information. Sometimes they can be alerted to their interests by aggressive voter education. More frequently, they vote for a face, a smile, or a style, not for a mind or character or body of beliefs.

3

The number of illiterate adults exceeds by 16 million the entire vote cast for the winner in the 1980 presidential contest. If even one third of all illiterates could vote, and read enough and do sufficient math to vote in their self-interest, Ronald Reagan would not likely have been chosen president. There is, of course, no way to know for sure. We do know this: Democracy is a mendacious term when used by those who are prepared to countenance the forced exclusion of one third of our electorate. So long as 60 million people are denied significant participation, the government is neither of, nor for, nor by, the people. It is a government, at best, of those two thirds whose wealth, skin color, or parental privilege allows them opportunity to profit from the provocation and instruction of the written word.

4

The undermining of democracy in the United States is one "expense" that sensitive Americans can easily deplore because it represents a contradiction that endangers citizens of all political positions. The human price is not so obvious at first.

5

Illiterates cannot read the menu in a restaurant.

6

They cannot read the cost of items on the menu in the *window* of the restaurant before they enter.

7

Illiterates cannot read the letters that their children bring home from their teachers. They cannot study school department circulars that tell them of the courses that their children must be taking if they hope to pass the SAT exams. They cannot help with homework. They cannot write a letter to the teacher. They are afraid to visit in the classroom. They do not want to humiliate their child or themselves.

8

Illiterates cannot read instructions on a bottle of prescription medicine. They cannot find out when a medicine is past the year of safe consumption; nor can they read of allergenic risks, warnings to diabetics, or the potential sedative effect of certain kinds of nonprescription pills. They cannot observe preventive health care

9

admonitions. They cannot read about "the seven warning signs of cancer" or the indications of blood-sugar fluctuations or the risks of eating certain foods that aggravate the likelihood of cardiac arrest.

Illiterates live, in more than literal ways, an uninsured existence. They cannot understand the written details on a health insurance form. They cannot read the waivers that they sign preceding surgical procedures. Several women I have known in Boston have entered a slum hospital with the intention of obtaining a tubal ligation and have emerged a few days later after having been subjected to a hysterectomy. Unaware of their rights, incognizant of jargon, intimidated by the unfamiliar air of fear and atmosphere of ether that so many of us find oppressive in the confines even of the most attractive and expensive medical facilities, they have signed their names to documents they could not read and which nobody, in the hectic situation that prevails so often in those overcrowded hospitals that serve the urban poor, had even bothered to explain.   10

Even the roof above one's head, the gas or other fuel for heating that protects the residents of northern city slums against the threat of illness in the winter months become uncertain guarantees. Illiterates cannot read the lease that they must sign to live in an apartment which, too often, they cannot afford. They cannot manage check accounts and therefore seldom pay for anything by mail. Hours and entire days of difficult travel (and the cost of bus or other public transit) must be added to the real cost of whatever they consume. Loss of interest on the check accounts they do not have, and could not manage if they did, must be regarded as another of the excess costs paid by the citizen who is excluded from the common instruments of commerce in a numerate society.   11

"I couldn't understand the bills," a woman in Washington, D.C., reports, "and then I couldn't write the checks to pay them. We signed things we didn't know what they were."   12

Illiterates cannot read the notices that they receive from welfare offices or from the IRS. They must depend on word-of-mouth instruction from the welfare worker—or from other persons whom they have good reason to mistrust. They do not know what rights they have, what deadlines and requirements they face, what options they might choose to exercise. They are half-citizens. Their rights exist in print but not in fact.   13

Illiterates cannot look up numbers in a telephone directory. Even if they can find the names of friends, few possess the sorting skills to make use of the yellow pages; categories are bewildering and trade names are beyond decoding capabilities for millions of nonreaders. Even the emergency numbers listed on the first page of   14 the phone book — "Ambulance," "Police," and "Fire" — are too frequently beyond the recognition of nonreaders.

Many illiterates cannot read the admonition on a pack of ciga-   15
rettes. Neither the Surgeon General's warning nor its reproduction on the package can alert them to the risks. Although most people learn by word of mouth that smoking is related to a number of grave physical disorders, they do not get the chance to read the detailed stories which can document this danger with the vividness that turns concern into determination to resist. They can see the handsome cowboy or the slim Virginia lady lighting up a filter cigarette; they cannot heed the words that tell them that this product is (not "may be") dangerous to their health. Sixty million men and women are condemned to be the unalerted, high-risk candidates for cancer.

Illiterates do not buy "no-name" products in the supermarkets.   16
They must depend on photographs or the familiar logos that are printed on the packages of brand-name groceries. The poorest people, therefore, are denied the benefits of the least costly products.

Illiterates depend almost entirely upon label recognition. Many   17
labels, however, are not easy to distinguish. Dozens of different kinds of Campbell's soup appear identical to the nonreader. The purchaser who cannot read and does not dare to ask for help, out of the fear of being stigmatized (a fear which is unfortunately realistic), frequently comes home with something which she never wanted and her family never tasted.

Illiterates cannot read instructions on a pack of frozen food.   18
Packages sometimes provide an illustration to explain the cooking preparations; but illustrations are of little help to someone who must "boil water, drop the food — *within* its plastic wrapper — in the boiling water, wait for it to simmer, instantly remove."

Even when labels are seemingly clear, they may be easily mis-   19
taken. A woman in Detroit brought home a gallon of Crisco for her children's dinner. She thought that she had bought the chicken that was pictured on the label. She had enough Crisco now to last a year — but no more money to go back and buy the food for dinner.

Illiterates cannot travel freely. When they attempt to do so, they   20
encounter risks that few of us can dream of. They cannot read traffic signs and, while they often learn to recognize and to decipher symbols, they cannot manage street names which they haven't seen before. The same is true for bus and subway stops. While ingenuity can sometimes help a man or woman to discern directions from familiar landmarks, buildings, cemeteries, churches, and the like, most illiterates are virtually immobilized. They seldom wander past the streets and neighborhoods they know. Geographical

paralysis becomes a bitter metaphor for their entire existence. They are immobilized in almost every sense we can imagine. They can't move up. They can't move out. They cannot see beyond. Illiterates may take an oral test for drivers' permits in most sections of America. It is a questionable concession. Where will they go? How will they get there? How will they get home? Could it be that some of us might like it better if they stayed where they belong?

Travel is only one of many instances of circumscribed existence. Choice, in almost all its facets, is diminished in the life of an illiterate adult. Even the printed TV schedule, which provides most people with the luxury of preselection, does not belong within the arsenal of options in illiterate existence. One consequence is that the viewer watches only what appears at moments when he happens to have time to turn the switch. Another consequence, a lot more common, is that the TV set remains in operation night and day. Whatever the program offered at the hour when he walks into the room will be the nutriment that he accepts and swallows. Thus, to passivity, is added frequency—indeed, almost uninterrupted continuity. Freedom to select is no more possible here than in the choice of home or surgery or food.

"You don't choose," said one illiterate woman. "You take your wishes from somebody else." Whether in perusal of a menu, selection of highways, purchase of groceries, or determination of affordable enjoyment, illiterate Americans must trust somebody else: a friend, a relative, a stranger on the street, a grocery clerk, a TV copywriter.

Billing agencies harass poor people for the payment of the bills for purchases that might have taken place six months before. Utility companies offer an agreement for a staggered payment schedule on a bill past due. "You have to trust them," one man said. Precisely for this reason, you end up by trusting no one and suspecting everyone of possible deceit. A submerged sense of distrust becomes the corollary to a constant need to trust. "They are cheating me . . . I have been tricked . . . I do not know. . . ."

Not knowing: This is a familiar theme. Not knowing the right word for the right thing at the right time is one form of subjugation. Not knowing the world that lies concealed behind those words is a more terrifying feeling. The longitude and latitude of one's existence are beyond all easy apprehension. Even the hard, cold stars within the firmament above one's head begin to mock the possibilities for self-location. Where am I? Where did I come from? Where will I go?

"I've lost a lot of jobs," one man explains. "Today, even if you're a janitor, there's still reading and writing. . . . They leave a note saying, 'Go to room so-and-so. . . .' You can't do it. You can't read it. You don't know."

"Reading directions, I suffer with. I work with chemicals. . . . That's scary to begin with. . . ."

26

"You sit down. They throw the menu in front of you. Where do you go from there? Nine times out of ten you say, 'Go ahead. Pick out something for the both of us.' I've eaten some weird things, let me tell you!"

27

A landlord tells a woman that her lease allows him to evict her if her baby cries and causes inconvenience to her neighbors. The consequence of challenging his words conveys a danger which appears, unlikely as it seems, even more alarming than the danger of eviction. Once she admits that she can't read, in the desire to maneuver for the time in which to call a friend, she will have defined herself in terms of an explicit importance that she cannot endure. Capitulation in this case is preferable to self-humiliation. Resisting the definition of oneself in terms of what one cannot do, what others take for granted, represents a need so great that other imperatives (even one so urgent as the need to keep one's home in winter's cold) evaporate and fall away in face of fear. Even the loss of home and shelter, in this case, is not so terrifying as the loss of self.

28

Another illiterate, looking back, believes she was not worthy of her teacher's time. She believes that it was wrong of her to take up space within her school. She believes that it was right to leave in order that somebody more deserving could receive her place.

29

People eat what others order, know what others tell them, struggle not to see themselves as they believe the world perceives them. A man in California spoke about his own loss of identity, self-location, definition:

30

"I stood at the bottom of the ramp. My car had broke down on the freeway. There was a phone. I asked for the police. They was nice. They said to tell them where I was. I looked up at the signs. There was one that I had seen before. I read it to them: ONE WAY STREET. They thought it was a joke. I told them I couldn't read. There was other signs above the ramp. They told me to try. I looked around for somebody to help. All the cars was going by real fast. I couldn't make them understand that I was lost. The cop was nice. He told me: 'Try once more.' I did my best. I couldn't read. I only knew the sign above my head. The cop was trying to be nice. He knew that I was trapped. 'I can't send out a car to you if you can't tell me where you are.' I felt afraid. I nearly cried. I'm forty-eight years old. I only said: 'I'm on a one-way street. . . .'"

31

Perhaps we might slow down a moment here and look at the realities described above. This is the nation that we live in. This is a

32

society that most of us did not create but which our President and other leaders have been willing to sustain by virtue of malign neglect. Do we possess the character and courage to address a problem which so many nations, poorer than our own, have found it natural to correct?

The answers to these questions represent a reasonable test of   33
our belief in the democracy to which we have been asked in public school to swear allegiance.

READING FOR MEANING

This section presents three activities that will help you reread Kozol's essay with a critical eye. Done in sequence, these activities lead you from a basic understanding of the selection to a more personal response to it and finally to an analysis that deepens your understanding and critical thinking about what you are reading.

Read to Comprehend

Reread the selection, and write a few sentences identifying the most serious effects of illiteracy and explaining Kozol's purpose for writing. Does he seem to be simply describing a hopeless situation, hoping for reform, or aiming for a specific response from readers? What in the text leads you to your answer? The following definitions may help you understand Kozol's vocabulary:

mendacious (paragraph 4): false, untrue, lying.

subjugation (24): the condition of being conquered or under total control.

malign (32): bad or harmful.

Identify three or more additional words that you don't understand, and find the best definitions from the dictionary that work with their context.

To expand your understanding of this reading, you might use one or more of the following critical reading strategies that are explained and illustrated in Appendix 1: *outlining*, *paraphrasing*, and *questioning to understand and remember*.

Read to Respond

Write several paragraphs exploring your initial thoughts and feelings about "The Human Cost of an Illiterate Society." Focus on anything that stands out for you, perhaps because it resonates with your own experience or because you find a statement puzzling.

You might consider writing about the following:

- Kozol's claim that illiteracy undermines democracy, summarizing his main ideas (from paragraphs 2–4) and adding any ideas of your own;

- the connection made between morality and literacy in paragraph 1, explaining possible connections you see and speculating about whom Kozol seems to be accusing of immoral actions;

- "the power [that] knowledge gives" (2), using firsthand examples of how the knowledge you have gained from reading has contributed to your achievements, sense of identity, or privileges;

- your own experience with someone who is illiterate; or

- the effect on you of Kozol's use of many examples to illustrate his point.

To develop your response to Kozol's essay, you might use the following critical reading strategy that is explained and illustrated in Appendix 1: *evaluating the logic of an argument.*

Read to Analyze Assumptions

Reread Kozol's "effects" essay, and write a paragraph or two exploring one or more of the assumptions you find in the text. The following suggestions may help:

- **assumptions about literacy.** When you think about literacy, what is the first definition that comes to mind? Kozol focuses mostly on the ability to read. But literacy includes the ability to write and is also used to mean knowledge in a particular field (such as "computer literacy"). To think critically about the assumptions in this essay related to the nature of literacy, ask yourself: Why do you think Kozol, when contemplating the "human price" (paragraph 5) of illiteracy, focuses mostly on reading? For instance, he worries that illiterates cannot read the messages from school that their children bring home (8). Kozol believes that communications from schools to parents are critical to children's education. What do his other examples reveal about his assumptions about the value of literacy? Which of his assumptions do you share?

- **assumptions about democracy.** Kozol begins his essay by quoting James Madison that for people to be self-governing in a democracy, they "must arm themselves with the power knowledge gives" (paragraph 2). To think critically about assumptions in this essay related to voting and literacy, look closely at his argument in paragraphs 1 to 3. Then ask yourself: Even though Kozol was writing about an earlier period in American history (the early 1980s), how well do you think his argument applies today? How does literacy—what you read and how well you understand it—contribute to your voting decisions?

To probe assumptions more deeply, you might use one or both of the following critical reading strategies that are explained and illustrated in Appendix 1: *reflecting on challenges to your beliefs and values* and *recognizing emotional manipulation.*

READING LIKE A WRITER
SUPPORTING PROPOSED EFFECTS

Kozol proposes many effects of illiteracy. A mere list of possible effects would be interesting, but to convince readers to take all of these effects seriously, Kozol must argue for — or support — them in ways that enhance their plausibility. To do so, all writers speculating about effects have many resources available to them to support their proposed effects — examples, statistics, quotations from authorities, personal anecdotes, analogies, scenarios, quotes from interviews, and more. As a writer speculating about causes or effects, you will need to support your speculations in these ways to make them plausible. You can learn more about supporting speculations by analyzing how Kozol does it.

Analyze

1. *Choose* one of Kozol's proposed effects of illiteracy: helplessness in financial affairs (paragraphs 11 and 12), confusion about supermarket purchases (16–19), limited travel (20), or loss of self (28–31).

2. *Examine* the support carefully. What kind of support do you find? More than one kind? Does the support seem to come from many or few sources?

3. *Evaluate* the support. Does it seem appropriate for the proposed effect? Does it seem believable and trustworthy? Does it seem consistent with the other support for the effect? If so, how does it complement the other support?

Write

Write several sentences explaining how Kozol supports the effect you have chosen. Also *evaluate* the plausibility of the support he offers. *Give details* from the paragraphs you have analyzed. As one of Kozol's intended readers, *explain* how convincing you find the support.

CONSIDERING IDEAS FOR YOUR OWN WRITING

Consider speculating, as Kozol does, about the effects of a significant social problem. List several major social problems (local or national) that concern you. Your list might include, for example, the high pregnancy rate among unmarried teenagers, high-school dropout rates, high costs of a college education, unsafe working conditions at your job, shortages of adequate day-care facilities for working parents, growth in the number of people without health insurance, or uncontrolled development in your community. Choose one problem, and consider how you can speculate about its effects. What effects can you argue for? As a writer, how could you convince readers that your proposed effects are plausible? Will you need to research the problem to write about it authoritatively? Remember, your purpose is not to propose a solution to the problem but to speculate about its possible effects.

Alternatively, you could recall a recent controversial decision by college or community leaders that concerns you, such as a decision about campus life (safety, recreation, tutoring, or other special services) or about the future of your community (growth, transportation, safety). List several such decisions, and then choose one you would like to write about. Consider how you would write a letter to your college or community newspaper speculating about the effects or consequences of the decision. What short-term and long-term consequences would you propose? How would you convince readers to take your ideas seriously?

Speculating about Causes or Effects Online

The Internet provides many sites where you can find speculative arguments about causes or effects on just about any subject, and on some of them you can post your own causal speculations as well. Among these spaces is About.com, a site that provides information about a large variety of topics. As do most reputable Web sites, About.com includes a page that introduces the site and provides background on the sponsors and contributors. Here is an excerpt from this page (http://ourstory.about.com):

> About.com was founded in 1996 (as The Mining Company) by Scott Kurnit and a dedicated group of entrepreneurs. It was re-named About.com in 1999 to reflect its growing breadth of content, services and ease of use. In 2001, About, Inc. was acquired by PRIMEDIA Inc. In 2005 About, Inc. was acquired by the New York Times Company (NYSE: NYT).

The background page also provides information about the "Guides," the authors of the site's articles, mentioning that the "selection process is rigorous—only 10% of those that apply graduate to the live service." Information about the site's popularity includes statistics that might resonate with the site's audience: About.com claims to reach "more women than iVillage.com, more men than ESPN.com and more teens than MTV.com."

The home page offers a list of categories (such as "Business and Finance," "Education," "Sports and Recreation," "Style," and "Teens") where articles can be found. The article reproduced here appeared under "People and Relationships" (you can see the chain of links at the top of the page) and deals with the causes of homosexuality. Notice how the article uses the common online format of frequently asked questions (FAQs) to structure a causal speculation. The marginal annotations point out features and writing strategies that readers expect to find in any causal speculation, as well as ones that are distinctive to writing on the Web.

 About: Lesbian Life

What Causes Homosexuality?

① From Kathy Belge,
Your Guide to Lesbian Life.
FREE Newsletter. Sign Up Now!

What Makes someone Gay or Lesbian?

② What causes homosexuality? There has been much debate about what causes homosexuality. Is there a gay gene? Is homosexuality caused by environmental factors, such as upbringing, child molestation, an absent mother or affectionate father? Or is it something we're born with, an inherited trait, like skin or hair color?

---

① Readers can click on the author's name to find more information about her background and qualifications—an important consideration in *establishing credibility.* Know-

ing that Kathy Belge is herself a lesbian may influence how some readers react to her causal argument.

② As in most offline causal arguments, the author starts by *presenting the subject.* Headings, mostly in the form of questions, guide readers through the article.

Although there have been few studies on the cause of homosexuality, the debate seems to be divided, with scientists in one corner and religious fundamentalists in another.

What is Sexual Orientation?

The American Psychological Association defines sexual orientation as such: *Sexual orientation is an enduring emotional, romantic, sexual, or affectional attraction that a person feels toward another person. Sexual orientation falls along a continuum. In other words, someone does not have to be exclusively homosexual or heterosexual, but can feel varying degrees of attraction for both genders. Sexual orientation develops across a person's lifetime—different people realize at different points in their lives that they are heterosexual, gay, lesbian, or bisexual.*

③

They go on to say that sexual behavior is not the same as sexual orientation. Certainly gay individuals can engage in heterosexual sex, in fact many do before they come out. One needs to look no further than the prison population to see evidence of homosexual behavior in otherwise heterosexual individuals. (And I'm not including incidents of prison rape in this analysis.)

Also, the work of Alfred Kinsey in the 1950s determined that most individuals are not exclusively homosexual or heterosexual, but most fall somewhere in the between the two.

④

Why does it matter?

Does it matter if homosexuality is a choice or if it's something one is born with? Shouldn't gay people be afforded the same rights as heterosexuals whether being gay is a choice or not? Not all people think that way.

If homosexuality is caused by genetic or inborn traits, then gay and lesbian people would be unable to change their sexual orientation, even if they wanted to. But if homosexuality is caused by some environmental factor, then gays and lesbians could change and become straight with therapy. Or so some religious fundamentalists and other anti-gay crusaders would have you believe.

⑤

Is being gay a choice?

If you ask most gay people they will tell you that being gay is not something they chose. Why would anyone choose to be something that could cause them to be scorned by society, rejected by their families, deny them rights and subject them to possible violent hate crimes? That is not to say that all of being gay or lesbian is negative. In fact, most lesbians, once they come out, say they've never been happier or more fulfilled.

⑥

Some lesbians will contend that being gay is a choice, especially those who were once married or came out later in life. Others are angered to hear someone say that. Sheryl Swoopes received some scorn from the gay and lesbian community when she said she thought being gay was her choice. "I think there are a lot of people -- gays and lesbians -- who believe you are born that way. I think there also a lot of people who believe it's a choice. And, for me, I believe it was a choice. I was at a point in my life where I had gone through a divorce and was not in a relationship, and the choice I made happened to be that I fell in love with another woman" she said in an interview on Gay.com

Many gays and lesbians would argue that being gay is not a choice, but whether to act on it is. We don't choose our sexual orientation, but we do choose whether or not to come out of the closet.

Most scientific organizations also believe that homosexuality is not a choice, that biology plays some role. The National Mental Health Association says, "Most researchers believe sexual orientation is complex, and that biology plays an important role. This means that many people are born with their sexual orientation, or that it's established at an early age."

③ The author uses a respected professional authority, the American Psychological Association, to define a central term, *sexual orientation.*
④ A link to Alfred Kinsey, a pioneer in studying human sexuality, adds credibility.

⑤ The author continues *presenting the subject,* explaining why the cause of homosexuality is important to some people. Showing readers the importance of the argument is often crucial to engaging their interest in it.
⑥ This section begins to *make the causal argument through counterargument.* It brings up

a cause favored by some readers (that being gay is a choice by individuals) and points out that "most gay people" and "[m]ost scientific organizations," one of which is quoted, disagree with this view. But it also acknowledges a kind of counterargument to the counterargument, including a quotation from a celebrity athlete.

What Twin Studies Tell us about Homosexuality

Scientists have studied twins to try and learn if being gay is biologically determined. Studies of identical and fraternal twins suggest that there is a genetic influence on sexual orientation. If being gay were strictly genetic, then in identical twins, there would be a 100% concordance rate for sexual orientation. But one study in 1995 found a 52% correlation for male identical twins and 22% for male fraternal twins. A study on females came up with similar results. If one identical twin was a lesbian, in 48% of cases, the other twin was also a lesbian. For fraternal twins, the concordance was 16%. (source Simon LeVay

These studies show that people with the same genetic make up (identical twins) are more likely to share sexual orientation than those with different genetic make up (fraternal twins.) Genetics alone cannot cause sexual orientation, but they do play a part.

Is there a gay gene?

Scientists have not been able to conclude that there is any gene or combination of genes that will make someone gay. Genetics is very complex and scientists continue to study both humans and animals chromosomes for linkage to sexual orientation.

What about the gay brain study?

A widely publicized study in 1999 found that a certain part of the hypothalamus was smaller in gay men then in heterosexual men. This study was widely touted at the time as "proof" that one's sexual orientation is biological and not chosen. But it is not known whether these differences in brain are present at birth or if they occur over a lifetime.

In conclusion

Despite social science and biological research, it is still not known what causes someone to be gay, lesbian, bisexual or straight. Scientists and social scientists will no doubt continue to study the **causes of homosexuality** in both animals and humans.
No matter what they find, gays, lesbians and their supporters will continue the fight for fair and equal treatment.

Join the Discussion
- Why Are U Gay?

More Lesbian Questions
- Am I Bisexual?
- Can people Tell I'm Gay?
- Am I a Lesbian?

Related Articles
- Weird Science – Could Invisible Turn Ons Lead to a...
- Charles S. Peirce on Reason, Belief, and Logic: Why Don...
- What Causes Sexual Orientation - Biology or Socializati...
- Louis Schwartzberg Interview - America's Heart and...
- Loyalty in Judaism

⑦ The author uses statistics from research studies, with a link to the source, to *argue for genetics as a cause*. The last sentence summarizes her argument and serves as a kind of thesis statement for the article. Note that it is carefully qualified to say that genetics is not the *only* cause.

⑧ These sections address two of readers' likely questions about specific aspects of the biological argument, pointing out that these issues remain unsettled.

⑨ The author acknowledges that the causes of sexual orientation remain largely unknown, but concludes with what she sees as the significance of this argument: whatever the causes, homosexuals deserve "fair and equal treatment."

⑩ Gay and lesbian readers are invited to contribute their own views about the origins of homosexuality.

⑪ More links take readers to other parts of the Web site and to other online articles on related subjects.

Analyze

1. *Find* another example of an online speculation about causes or effects.

2. *Check* to see which writing strategies that are typical of this genre are displayed. These strategies might include presenting the subject, making a logical cause or effect argument, arguing for each cause or effect, counterarguing, and establishing credibility.

3. Also *note* any special online characteristics—such as links, audio, or still or moving images.

Write

Write a paragraph or two describing what you have learned from this example of online speculation about causes or effects.

AMBER RIPPLINGER

Declining Coral Reefs: A Real Problem

> *Amber Ripplinger wrote this essay for an assignment in her first-year writing course at Western Wyoming Community College. Like Natalie Angier, Ripplinger speculates about a trend—a decrease in the number of healthy coral reefs in recent years. She begins by establishing that the trend exists, and then she explains that most of the causes of the decline are human activities. She acknowledges that there are natural reasons for the decline as well but explains that when reefs are hurt by natural events, they can grow back stronger than before, somewhat as a pruned fruit tree will put out new growth and more fruit. Because the decline that she is examining is caused by humans, humans could presumably reverse it. But Ripplinger does not make a proposal here; she limits herself to speculation about causes.*
>
> *As you read, bear in mind that one of the responsibilities of a writer is to establish the significance of the topic—in this case, the degradation of coral reefs. Think about where you begin, as a reader, to understand why you should care about this issue.*

What is coral? An underwater plant? Stone? In fact, corals are minute animals called *polyps* living together in colonies and coexisting in a symbiotic relationship with algae. The algae provide the polyps with the oxygen and other nutrients they need to survive and in return, the polyps provide the algae with needed shelter and food (Tangley 26).

Rivaled only by tropical rainforests, coral reefs host the widest assortment of life on earth (Hirsch), including mollusks, urchins, and tropical fish. Corals are the "animals that helped make the world," and whether we know it or not, coral reefs and the life they support are important to us (Chadwick 29). Unfortunately, these living environments are as fragile as they are remarkable. Coral reefs have begun, undeniably, to decline due to problems that can be directly linked to humans.

One of the most pressing and enigmatic problems facing coral reefs is the global phenomenon of coral bleaching. Corals "bleach" or turn white when they lose the algae that give them their characteristic brilliant coloring. It was originally thought that the polyps were expelling the algae, perhaps as a result of hurricanes or local diseases among the coral. Researchers now know enough to conclude that this may not be true. In her article "White Plague," Laura Tangley suggests that "the algae could actually be leaving on their own in response to inhospitable conditions" (28).

At first, scientists had little, if any, idea what was causing corals to bleach on such a massive scale; however, it is now generally accepted that major causes of coral bleaching include agricultural runoff, overfishing, and natural disasters such as hurricanes.

Agricultural and logging runoff brings tremendous amounts of soil to the seas via rivers and streams. This obscures sunlight, inhibiting the photosynthesis process of the algae and weakening the coral that derives nourishment from it (Chadwick 31).

Far more disturbing than the problem of agricultural runoff, however, is the damage done by overfishing. For years fishermen in the tropics have been using cyanide and homemade explosives to fish in the coral reefs. Cyanide fishing involves squirting cyanide into the coral, prying it apart with a crowbar, and extracting the stunned fish. With explosives, one lobs a grenade into the coral and gathers the fish (Chadwick 31). Fishing with cyanide and explosives makes the fisherman's job infinitely easier, but at what cost to such a fragile ecosystem? It is no exaggeration to say that if the coral reefs of this world are destroyed, all the life they support would become extinct. Multitudes of fish depend on corals as a source of shelter, safety, and food, and millions of people depend on these fish as a major food source, particularly in developing countries.

Along with the environmental stress placed on coral reefs by overfishing, natural causes such as El Niño and hurricanes also play a role in coral bleaching. El Niño, a warm current that appears every three to seven years in the eastern Pacific Ocean, can cause the water temperatures to rise above the corals' tolerance level, and hurricanes can cause physical damage to the coral colony. Some researchers, however, believe that corals are resilient enough to handle this abuse and will be made hardier because of it. They even suggest that the corals need periodic stresses like these to start anew. The process can be compared to that of a forest fire, which wipes out the old, unhealthy vegetation in forests, giving new life a chance to grow. As David Kobluk, a geologist at the University of Toronto, puts it, "reefs are robust and can take a lot of punishment. They rebound like an elastic band" (qtd. in Tangley 30). Researchers feel, however, that the majority of the damage done to the coral reefs around the world is caused by humans. Studies have shown that bleaching is a recent problem: corals show no evidence of bleaching before the past fifteen years, when the interaction with humans began in earnest.

Reefs are immeasurably important to humans for more reasons than that they are a major tourist attraction. Used in houses and institutes, cement and art, coral has also provided us with medicinal advances in "compounds active against inflammations, asthma, heart disease, leukemia, tumors, bacterial and fungal infections, and viruses, including HIV" (Chadwick 30). To put the crisis into perspective, coral reefs deposit calcium carbonate at a rate of about three millimeters a year. Time is not on their side; reefs grow infinitely more slowly than the destructive forces surging behind them, and at the rate we're tearing them down, they can never catch up. So how to balance humanity's dependence on reefs for our pressing needs and the reefs' dependence on us for survival? The answer may not be as complicated as some think. The key lies in understanding that the fragile balances of nature must not be upset, and that humanity can coexist in harmony with those balances.

Works Cited

Chadwick, Douglas H., and David Doubilet. "Coral in Peril." *National Geographic* Jan. 1999: 30–38. *Academic Search Premier.* Web. 17 Sept. 2002.

Hirsch, Jerry. "Damage to Coral Reef Mounts, Study Says." *Los Angeles Times* 26 Aug. 2002: A14. *Academic Search Premier.* Web. 17 Sept. 2002.

Tangley, Laura. "White Plague." *Earthwatch* Apr. 1991: 25–31. *Academic Search Premier.* Web. 17 Sept. 2002.

READING FOR MEANING

This section presents three activities that will help you reread Ripplinger's causal essay with a critical eye. Done in sequence, these activities lead you from a basic understanding of the selection to a more personal response to it and finally to an analysis that deepens your understanding and critical thinking about what you are reading.

Read to Comprehend

Reread the selection, and write a few sentences briefly explaining the causes Ripplinger offers to explain the decline in coral reefs. The following definitions may help you understand Ripplinger's vocabulary:

symbiotic (paragraph 1): An interdependent or mutually beneficial relationship between two persons or groups.

enigmatic (3): puzzling or mysterious.

photosynthesis (5): the process by which green plants, algae, and certain forms of bacteria use energy captured from sunlight by chlorophyll to make carbohydrates from carbon dioxide and water and release oxygen as a byproduct.

Identify three or more additional words that you don't understand, and find the best definitions from the dictionary that work with their context.

Read to Respond

Write several paragraphs exploring your initial thoughts and feelings about Ripplinger's causal argument. Focus on anything that stands out for you, perhaps because it resonates with your own experience or because you find a statement puzzling.

You might consider writing about the following:

- the absence of statistics in the essay to demonstrate the decline of coral reefs;

- another fragile ecosystem that you know about that might be in as much jeopardy as coral reefs;

- what steps you think humans could take to begin rolling back the problem with coral reefs; or

- whether you found the essay successful in its purpose, and why.

Read to Analyze Assumptions

Reread Ripplinger's causal essay, and write a paragraph or two exploring one or more of the assumptions you find in the text. The following suggestions may help:

- **assumptions about human responsibility.** At the end of paragraph 2, Ripplinger asserts her thesis: "Coral reefs have begun, undeniably, to decline due to problems that can be directly linked to humans." To think critically about assumptions in this essay related to the responsibility of humans to the earth, ask yourself: If the main causes of the decline in coral reefs are human ones, what assumption is Ripplinger making about how humans should respond? Even if coral-reef damage were not linked to humans, should we be expected to do something about it? Or should we do something only if we are directly responsible? What are your assumptions about human responsibility for the earth? Do you think humans could or should be trying to influence the environment in any way? If you don't, why not? If you do, in what ways?

- **assumptions about sources.** After Ripplinger finished her research about coral reefs, she could have written her essay without any references to sources. She knew, though, that her credibility would be lost were she to do so, since readers could just dismiss her as talking through her hat or, even worse, as passing off ideas and information from other people as her own. Instead, she uses three sources, starting with one in her first paragraph and using at least one in every subsequent paragraph. She assumes that her readers will find her argument more credible because of these sources. To think critically about the assumptions in this essay related to sources, ask yourself: What kinds of sources does Ripplinger use? How credible are the sources themselves? How does Ripplinger use her sources? To support her argument? To support a differing argument? What can the reader assume about Ripplinger from her choice of sources and from how she uses them?

READING LIKE A WRITER
ESTABLISHING CREDIBILITY

To be credible is to be believable. When you write an essay speculating about the causes or effects of something, readers will tend to find your argument believable when you are able to show the various complexities of your subject. Therefore, you will establish your credibility with readers if you do not oversimplify, trivialize, or stereotype your subject; if you do not overlook possible alternative causes or effects that will occur to readers; and if you convey more than casual knowledge of your subject and show that you have thought about it deeply and seriously.

Before you attempt your own essay speculating about causes or effects, consider how Ripplinger establishes her credibility to speculate about the reasons for the decline in coral reefs.

Analyze

1. *Reread* this brief essay, and *annotate* it for evidence of credibility or lack of it. (Because you cannot know Ripplinger personally, you must look closely at the words, evidence, and arguments of her essay to decide whether she constructs a credible argument.) *Examine closely* how knowledgeable she seems about the subject. Where does her knowledge assure or even impress you as one of her intended readers? Where does her knowledge seem thin? *Consider* especially how she presents the subject and trend (paragraphs 1 and 2). *Assess* also the sources she relies on and how effectively she uses them.

2. *Look for* evidence that Ripplinger has not trivialized a complex subject. Keeping in mind that she appropriately limits herself to speculating about possible causes, *note* how her argument reflects the complexity of her subject or fails to do so.

3. *Consider* how Ripplinger's counterargument (paragraphs 3 and 7) influences your judgment of her credibility.

4. *Examine* her approach to readers. What assumptions does she make about their knowledge and beliefs? What attitude does she have toward her readers? *Note* evidence of her assumptions and attitude.

Write

Write several sentences presenting evidence of Ripplinger's attempts to establish her credibility. Then *add a few more sentences* evaluating how credible her essay is to you as one of her intended readers. To explain your judgment, *point to* parts of the essay, and *comment* on the influence of your own attitudes about and knowledge of coral reefs.

CONSIDERING IDEAS FOR YOUR OWN WRITING

Ecology is the branch of biology dealing with the interactions between organisms and their environment, including other organisms. Following Ripplinger's lead, you could speculate about the causes of a trend or phenomenon in the earth's ecology that you have noticed or that has been pointed out to you and you want to investigate. Some examples include the decline of the rainforest (which Ripplinger mentions), a species that is on the brink of extinction, a species that has returned to healthy numbers after being on the brink of extinction, changes in zookeeping or in attitudes toward zoos, a specific topic within the global warming debate, and a local ecological change that has occurred where you live.

JOSHUA SLICK
Not Just for Nerds Anymore

Joshua Slick was a student at Hawkeye Community College in Iowa when he wrote this essay speculating about the causes of the increase in online dating. Like Natalie Angier and Amber Ripplinger, Slick relies in large part on speculations from a wide range of published research to put together his argument. He is in control of the argument because he selects certain speculations (and not others) and weaves them into his own design.

As you read, notice how Slick discusses his causes in the same order as he presented them in his first paragraph and that he intersperses his speculations with references to reasons that people object to online dating, addressing those concerns as he writes.

The other readings in this chapter are followed by reading and writing activities. Following this reading, however, you are on your own to decide how to read for meaning and read like a writer.

Slick begins with a common scenario—searching out social contact on Friday night—and acknowledges critics of online dating.

It's Friday night, and instead of going out to a bar to 1 look for Mr. or Ms. Right, you are sitting at home in front of your computer, talking in a chat room with a couple dozen other people your age or perusing a list of people in your area. Some would call you lazy or antisocial, but that number is dwindling. Online dating is becoming more mainstream. The increase in the use of the Internet as a dating tool in the last ten years is due to the increase in homes with computers, the increase in Web sites and chat rooms whose purpose it is to bring people together, and the ease with which daters can now research potential mates.

Note how clearly Slick *presents his subject* in the last sentence of this paragraph.

According to a U.S. Census Bureau report from Sep- 2 tember 2001, the number of homes with computers dramatically increased from 1993 to 2000: "In August 2000, 54 million households, or 51 percent, had one or more computers," up from 22.8 percent in 1993 (U.S. Department of Commerce, 2001, p. 1). Internet use has also increased: "In 1997, less than half of households with computers had someone using the Internet. In 2000, more than 4 in 5 households with a computer had at least one member using the Internet at home" (U.S. Department of Commerce, 2001, p. 2). These changes are due largely to the increased power and decreased cost of computers. David D. Thornburg (2005) makes this comparison:

Slick *enhances his credibility* and *supports his first cause*—an increase in home computers—by using statistics and other information from government agencies and other reliable sources, as well as from his own experience.

> A 1980 model Cray supercomputer was the fastest machine of its day. It cost $12 million, weighed 10,000 pounds, consumed 150 kilowatts of electric-

ity—and had only 8 megabytes of RAM and operated at a speed of 80 MHz. You can't find personal computers that poorly equipped on the market now. A typical personal computer today has about twice the raw power of that $12 million Cray and can be purchased for $2,500.

Even these figures—from 1998—are laughably out of date. My computer has a gigabyte of RAM and runs at 1.9 gigahertz, and it cost me less than a thousand dollars. More and more people have access to the Internet in their homes; it's only logical that they would use it to find other people to converse with and date.

3   The online dating industry has also grown by leaps and bounds in the last few years. *CNNMoney* staff writer Shaheen Pasha writes that although the growth of the industry has slowed, it is still growing: by 77 percent in 2003 and 19 percent in 2004. There are currently nearly a thousand dating Web sites, and one in a hundred Internet users visits such sites (Pasha, 2005). Chat rooms are also plentiful, and singles visit them to interact with other singles. The newest kind of chat room is the niche site, which focuses on some specific quality, belief, or interest such as religion or ethnicity (Pasha). Another development is the introduction of social networking sites such as MySpace and Friendster, which don't try to match singles but rather link users with friends of friends. Of course, socializing—whether online or off—often leads to dating (Pasha, 2005).

4   The inherent danger of dealing with strangers is one of the major reasons that online dating has been looked down on. That is all changing, however. Michael Bazeley (2005) mentions the online ratings and review systems that have been around since the Internet got started; eBay's user feedback system is a perfect example. Bazeley refers to these as "reputation-management systems." This model has been applied to the Internet dating scene on sites like TrueDater, which let users give feedback on others to warn and inform. Sites like Opinity also allow users to list their user names from other sites, making it easier to track them down (Bazeley, 2005). Because the Web can now be used to research everything from pictures to credit reports, Rebecca Heslin (2005) of Gannett News Services states in a USA Today.com article that "technology has made anonymity

Slick *supports his second cause* by showing the growth in dating Web sites and other kinds of social sites, such as the well-known MySpace.

Here Slick *addresses a concern* of many critics of dating Web sites—that meeting strangers online leads to meeting dangerous strangers in person. Does his information seem likely to reassure such critics?

largely a thing of the past." With online background check sites, Google, and specific Web sites for singles doing searches such as TrueDater and Facebook, you can find out virtually anything about anyone without ever leaving your home. By increasing knowledge of the person on the other computer, these tools have led to more comfort about potentially dating him or her.

Comparing online dating to meeting people in churches and bars is another way to reassure readers that online dating does not have to be dangerous. Slick points out that online dating is just as successful as traditional dating.

The world of conventional dating isn't going to 5 go away. Technological advancements have just given singles another option to explore the possibilities and find meaningful relationships. At some point, there must be some real-life interaction, and only then will daters be able to judge the effectiveness of the online arena. Even so, more and more people are finding that online dating is just as viable for meeting people as going to church or bars. In a recent study released by the University of Bath, England, Dr. Jeff Gavin and associates found that Internet dating can be just as successful as more traditional dating. Of those surveyed, 94 percent who had established a significant relationship online and then met their "e-partner" face to face went on to see him or her more than once. Of those relationships, 18 percent continued for more than a year ("Internet Dating," 2005). With the combination of increased ownership and usage of home computers, the saturation of Web sites that cater to singles, and the ready availability of tools to research people and ensure safety, online dating has definitely shaken off its stigma to become a mainstream tool to help singles meet their potential partners.

Works Cited

Following APA style, Slick documents the sources he cited parenthetically in his essay.

Bazeley, Michael. (2005). Web of anonymity. *San Jose Mercury News*, *23*, E1. Retrieved September 23, 2005, from http://infoweb.newsbank.com

Heslin, Rebecca. (2005, August 21). With the Internet, the blind date is vanishing. *USA Today.com*. Retrieved from http://www.usatoday.com

Internet dating is much more successful than previously thought, study shows. (2005, February 14). *University of Bath News*. Retrieved from http://www.bath.ac.uk/pr/releases/internet-dating.htm

Pasha, Shaheen. (2005, August 18). Online dating feeling less attractive. *CNNMoney*. Retrieved from http://money.

cnn.com/2005/08/18/technology/online_dating/
index.htm

Thornburg, David D. (1998). Reading the future: Here's
what's on hand for technology and education. *Electronic
School*. Retrieved from http://www.electronicschool.com/
0698f1.html

U.S. Department of Commerce, Economics and Statistics
Administration. (2001). *Home computers and Internet
use in the United States: August 2000*. U.S. Census Bureau,
Washington, DC. Retrieved from http://www.census.gov/
prod/2001pubs/p23-207.pdf

READING FOR MEANING

Reading for meaning involves three activities:

- reading to comprehend,

- reading to respond, and

- reading to analyze assumptions.

Reread Slick's essay, and then write a page or so explaining your understanding of its basic meaning or main point, a personal response you have to it, and what you see as one of its assumptions.

READING LIKE A WRITER

Writers of essays speculating about causes or effects

- present the subject,

- make a logical, step-by-step cause-and-effect argument,

- support—or argue for—each cause or effect,

- take into account readers' likely objections to the proposed causes or effects as well as readers' alternative or preferred causes or effects, and

- establish their credibility.

Focus on one of these strategies in Slick's essay, and analyze it carefully through close rereading and annotating. Then write several sentences explaining what you have learned, giving specific examples from the reading to support your explanation. Add a few sentences evaluating how successfully Slick uses the strategy to argue convincingly for what has caused the increase in online dating.

REVIEWING WHAT MAKES ESSAYS SPECULATING ABOUT CAUSES OR EFFECTS EFFECTIVE

In this chapter, you have been learning how to read cause-and-effect arguments for meaning and how to read them like a writer. Pause here to review and contemplate what you have learned about the elements of effective cause-and-effect essays.

Analyze

Choose one reading from this chapter that seems to you especially effective. Before rereading the selection, *jot down* one or two reasons you remember it as an example of effective cause-and-effect writing.

Reread the selection, adding annotations about what makes it particularly effective. *Consider* its purpose and how well it achieves that purpose for its readers. (You can make an informed guess about the intended readers and their expectations by noting the publication source.) Then *focus* on how well the essay does the following:

- Presents the subject,

- Makes a logical, step-by-step cause-and-effect argument and supports — or argues for — each cause or effect,

- Handles readers' likely objections to the proposed causes or effects,

- Evaluates readers' alternative or preferred causes or effects and establishes the writer's credibility.

You can review all of these basic features in the Guide to Reading Essays Speculating about Causes or Effects (p. 378).

Your instructor may ask you to complete this activity on your own or with other students who have chosen the same reading. If you work with others, after all group members have reread the selection and added their annotations, *discuss* as a group what makes the essay effective. *Take notes* on your discussion. One student in your group should then report to the class what the group has learned about the effectiveness of cause-and-effect argument. If you are working individually, write up what you have learned from your analysis.

Write

Write at least a page, justifying your choice of this essay. *Assume* that your readers — your instructor and classmates — have read it but will not remember many details about it. They also might not remember it as especially successful. Therefore, you will need to *refer* to details of the essay as you explain how it works and justify your evaluation of its effectiveness. You need not argue that it is the best essay in the chapter or that it is flawless, only that it is a strong example of the genre.

■ A Guide to Writing Essays Speculating about Causes or Effects

The readings in this chapter have helped you learn a great deal about writing that speculates about causes or effects. Now that you have seen how writers present their subjects to particular readers, propose causes or effects that readers may not think of, support those causes or effects to make them plausible to readers, and anticipate readers' questions and objections, you can approach this type of writing confidently. The readings remain an important resource for you as you develop your own essay. Use them to review how other writers have solved the problems you face and to rethink the strategies that help writers achieve their purposes.

This Guide to Writing is designed to assist you in writing your essay. Here you will find activities to help you identify a subject and discover what to say about it, organize your ideas and draft the essay, read the draft critically, revise the draft to strengthen your argument, and edit and proofread the essay to improve its readability.

INVENTION AND RESEARCH

The following activities will help you find a subject and begin developing your argument. A few minutes spent completing each writing activity will improve your chances of producing a detailed and convincing first draft. You can decide on a subject for your essay, explore what you presently know about it and gather additional information, think about possible causes or effects, and develop a plausible argument.

Choosing a Subject

The subject of an essay speculating about causes or effects may be a trend, an event, or a phenomenon, as the readings in this chapter illustrate. List the most promising subjects you can think of, beginning with any you listed for the Considering Ideas for Your Own Writing activities following the readings in this chapter. These varied possibilities for analyzing causes or effects may suggest a subject you would like to explore, or you may still need to find an appropriate subject for your essay. Continue listing possible topics. Making such a list often generates ideas: as you list subjects, you will think of new ideas you cannot imagine now.

Even if you feel confident about a subject you have selected, continue listing other possibilities to test your choice. Try to list specific subjects, and make separate lists for trends, events, and phenomena. Here are some other ideas to consider:

Trends

- Increasing reliance on the Internet for research, entertainment, shopping, and conversation
- Changes in men's or women's roles and opportunities in marriage, education, or work
- Changing patterns in leisure, entertainment, lifestyle, religious life, health, or technology
- Completed artistic or historical trends (art movements or historical changes)
- Long-term changes in economic conditions or political behavior or attitudes

Events

- A recent national or international event that is surrounded by confusion or controversy
- A recent surprising or controversial event at your college, such as the closing of a tutorial or health service, the cancellation of popular classes, a change in library hours or dormitory regulations, the loss of a game by a favored team, or some hateful or violent act by one student against another
- A recent puzzling or controversial event in your community, such as the abrupt resignation of a public official, a public protest by an activist group, a change in traffic laws, a zoning decision, or the banning of a book from school libraries
- A historical event about which there is still some dispute as to its causes or effects

Phenomena

- A social problem, such as discrimination, homelessness, child abuse, illiteracy, high-school dropout rates, youth suicides, or teenage pregnancy
- One or more aspects of college life, such as libraries too noisy to study in, large classes, lack of financial aid, difficulties in scheduling classes, shortcomings in student health services, or insufficient availability of housing (in this essay you would not need to solve the problems, only to speculate about their causes or effects)
- A human trait, such as anxiety, selfishness, fear of success or failure, leadership, jealousy, insecurity, envy, opportunism, curiosity, or restlessness

After you have completed your lists, reflect on the possible topics you have compiled. Because an authoritative essay analyzing causes or effects requires sustained thinking, drafting, revising, and possibly even research, you will want to choose a subject to which you can commit yourself enthusiastically for a week or two. Above all, choose a topic that interests you, even if you feel uncertain about how to approach it. Then consider carefully whether you are more interested in the causes or the effects of the event, trend, or phenomenon. Consider, as well, whether the subject in which you are interested invites speculation about its causes or effects or perhaps even precludes speculation about one or the other. For example, you could speculate about the causes for increasing membership in your church, whereas the effects (the results or consequences) of the increase might for now be so uncertain as to discourage plausible speculation. Some subjects invite speculation about both their causes and their effects. For this assignment, however, you need not do both.

Developing Your Subject

The writing and research activities that follow will enable you to test your subject choice and to discover what you have to say about it. These activities, most of which take only a few minutes to complete, will help you produce a fuller, more focused draft.

Exploring Your Subject.   *You may discover that you know more about your subject than you suspect if you write about it for a few minutes without stopping.* This brief sustained writing will stimulate your memory, help you probe your interest in the subject, and enable you to test your subject choice. As you write, consider the following questions:

- What interests me in this subject? What about it will interest my readers?

- What do I already know about the subject?

- Why does the trend, event, or phenomenon not already have an accepted explanation for its causes or effects? What causes or effects have others already suggested for this subject?

- How can I learn more about the subject?

Considering Causes or Effects.   *Before you research your subject (should you need to), you want to discover which causes or effects you can already imagine. Make a list of possible causes or effects.* For *causes* consider underlying or background causes, immediate or instigating causes, and ongoing causes. For example, if you lost your job delivering pizzas,

- An underlying cause could be that years ago a plant closing in your town devastated the local economy, which has never recovered;

- An immediate cause could be that the pizza-chain outlet you worked for has been hit hard by the recent arrival of a new pizza-chain outlet;

- An ongoing cause could be that for several years some health-conscious residents regularly eat salad, rather than pizza, for dinner.

For *effects*, consider both short-term and long-term consequences, as well as how one effect may lead to another in a kind of chain reaction. Try to think of obvious causes or effects and also of those that are likely to be overlooked in a superficial analysis of your subject.

Identify the most convincing causes or effects in your list. Do you have enough to make a strong argument? Imagine how you might convince readers of the plausibility of some of these causes or effects.

Researching Your Subject.   *When developing an essay analyzing causes or effects, you can often gain great advantage by researching your subject.* (See Appendix 2, Strategies for Research and Documentation.) You can gain a greater understanding of the event, trend, or phenomenon, and you can review and evaluate others' proposed causes or effects in case you want to present any of these alternatives in your own essay. Reviewing others' causes or effects may suggest to you plausible causes or effects you have overlooked. You may also find support for your own counterarguments to readers' objections.

If you are speculating about the causes of a trend, you will also need to do some research to confirm that it actually is a trend and not just a short-term fluctuation or a fad. To do so, you will need to find examples and probably statistics that show an increase or a decrease in the trend over time and that indicate the date when this change began. (For example, recall that Natalie Angier cites authorities and statistics to demonstrate that intolerance for what she calls "boyish behavior" has actually increased.) If you are unable to find evidence to confirm that a trend exists, you will have to choose a different subject for your essay.

RESEARCHING YOUR SUBJECT ONLINE

Searching the Web may help you establish the existence of the phenomenon or trend and provide information you can use in presenting it to your readers. Enter a key term describing your subject in a search engine such as Google (google.com) or Yahoo! (yahoo.com). Adding the word *trend* to your key term may help—for example, *religion trends* or *dieting trends*.

If you are interested in trends in education, you might find information at the National Center for Education Statistics Web site at http://nces.ed.gov/ssbr/pages/trends.asp. For other national trends, look for the relevant statistics link on the U.S. government Web site at http://firstgov.gov.

Bookmark or keep a record of promising sites. Download any materials you might wish to cite in your evaluation, remembering to record the source information required to document them.

Analyzing Your Readers.   *Write for a few minutes, identifying who your readers are, what they know about your subject, and how they can be convinced by your proposed causes or effects.* Describe your readers briefly. Mention anything you know about them as a group that might influence the way they would read your essay. Estimate how much they know about your subject, how extensively you will have to present it to them, and what is required to demonstrate to them the importance of the subject. Speculate about how they will respond to your argument.

Rehearsing Part of Your Argument.   *Select one of your causes or effects and write several sentences about it, trying out an argument for your readers.* The heart of your essay will be the argument you make for the plausibility of your proposed causes or effects. Like a ballet dancer or baseball pitcher warming up for a performance, you can prepare for your first draft by rehearsing part of the argument you will make. How will you convince readers to take this cause or effect seriously? This writing activity will focus your thinking and encourage you to keep discovering new arguments until you start drafting. It may also lead you to search for additional support for your speculations.

Testing Your Choice.   *Pause now to decide whether you have chosen a subject about which you will be able to make a convincing argument.* At this point you have probed your subject in several ways and have some insights into how you would attempt to present and argue for it with particular readers. If your interest in the subject is growing and you are gaining confidence in the argument you want to make, you have probably made a good choice. However, if your interest in the subject is waning or you have been unable to come up with several plausible causes or effects beyond the simply obvious ones, you may want to consider choosing another subject. If your subject does not seem promising, return to your list of possible subjects to select another.

Considering Visuals.   *Consider whether visuals — drawings, photographs, tables, or graphs — would strengthen your argument.* You could construct your own visuals, scan materials from books and magazines, or download them from the Internet. If you submit your essay electronically to other students and your instructor, or if you post it on a Web site, consider including photographs as well as snippets of film or sound. Visual and audio materials are not at all a requirement of an effective speculative essay, as you can tell from the readings in this chapter, but they could add a new dimension to your writing. If you want to use photographs or recordings of people, be sure to obtain their permission. If you want to post a visual on the Web, ask permission from the source. Also, be sure to document the sources of visuals just as you would for written texts.

Considering Your Purpose.   *Write for several minutes about your purpose for writing this essay.* The following questions will help you think about your purpose:

- What do I hope to accomplish with my readers? What one big idea do I want them to grasp and remember?

- How can I interest them in my subject? How can I help them see its importance or significance? How can I convince them to take my speculations seriously?

- How much resistance should I expect from readers to each of the causes or effects I propose? Will my readers be largely receptive? Skeptical but convinceable? Resistant and perhaps even antagonistic?

Formulating a Working Thesis.   *Draft a thesis statement.* A *working*—as opposed to final—*thesis* enables you to bring your invention work into focus and begin your draft with a clearer purpose. At some point during the drafting of your essay, however, you will likely decide to revise your working thesis or even try out a new one. A thesis for an essay speculating about causes or effects nearly always announces the subject; it may also mention the proposed causes or effects and suggest the direction the argument will take. Here are two sample thesis statements from the readings in this chapter:

- "Today, the world is no longer safe for boys. A boy being a shade too boyish risks finding himself under the scrutiny of parents, teachers, guidance counselors, child therapists—all of them on watch for the early glimmerings of a medical syndrome, a bone fide behavioral disorder" (Angier, paragraph 3).

- "Online dating is becoming more mainstream. The increase in the use of the Internet as a dating tool in the last ten years is due to the increase in homes with computers, the increase in Web sites and chat rooms whose purpose it is to bring people together, and the ease with which daters can now research potential mates" (Slick, paragraph 1).

Notice, for instance, that Slick's thesis clearly announces his subject—an increase in online dating—as well as how he will approach the subject: by speculating about the causes of the dating increase. His thesis also forecasts his speculations, identifying the causes and the order in which he will argue for them in the essay.

DRAFTING

The following guidelines will help you set goals for your draft, plan its organization, and think about a useful sentence strategy.

Setting Goals

Establishing goals for your draft before you begin writing will enable you to make decisions and work more confidently. Consider the following questions now, and keep them in mind as you draft. They will help you set goals for drafting as well as recall how the writers you have read in this chapter tried to achieve similar goals.

- *How can I convince my readers that my proposed causes or effects are plausible?* Should I give many examples, as Kozol does, or quote authorities and published research, as Angier, Dutton, Ripplinger, and Slick all do? Can I, like Kozol, include personal anecdotes and cases or, like King and Angier, introduce analogies?

- *How should I anticipate readers' objections to my argument?* What should I do about alternative causes or effects? Should I anticipate readers' objections and questions, as Angier does, or answer readers' likely questions, like Slick? Can I refute alternative causes, as Ripplinger does? How can I find common ground—shared attitudes, values, and beliefs—with my readers, even with those whose objections or alternative causes I must refute?

- *How much do my readers need to know about my subject?* Do I need to describe my subject in some detail, in the way that Dutton describes ocean pollution or in the way that Ripplinger describes overfishing? Or can I assume that my readers have personal experience with my subject, as King seems to assume? If my subject is a trend, how can I demonstrate that the trend exists?

- *How can I begin engagingly and end conclusively?* Should I begin, as Angier and Dutton do, by emphasizing the importance or timeliness of my subject? Might I begin with an anecdote like Slick, or with an unusual statement like King's? Can I conclude by returning to an idea in the opening paragraph (as Kozol does), or restating the urgency of the problem (Dutton and Ripplinger)?

- *How can I establish my authority and credibility to argue the causes or effects of my subject?* Can I do this by showing a comprehensive understanding of the likely effects of the phenomenon, as Kozol does, or by showing a willingness to consider a wide range of causes, like Angier and Dutton? Or can I do this by displaying my research (Slick), by counterarguing responsibly (Ripplinger), or by relying on what I have learned through research and interviews (Angier)?

Organizing Your Draft

With goals in mind and invention notes at hand, you are ready to make a tentative outline of your draft. The sequence of proposed causes or effects will be at the center of your outline, but you may also want to plan where you will consider alternatives or counterargue objections. Notice that some writers who conjecture about causes consider alternative causes—evaluating, refuting, or accepting them—before they present their own. Much of an essay analyzing causes may be devoted to considering alternatives. Both writers who conjecture about causes and writers who speculate about effects usually consider readers' possible objections to their causes or effects along with the argument for each cause or effect. If you must provide readers with a great deal of information about your subject as context for your argument, you may want to outline this information carefully. For your essay, this part of the outline may be a major consideration. Your plan should make the information readily accessible to your readers. This outline is tentative; you may decide to change it after you start drafting.

WORKING WITH SOURCES

Citing a Variety of Sources

Writers of essays that speculate about the causes or effects of a phenomenon or trend must establish that the causes or effects they offer are plausible. To do so, they often rely on evidence from experts or others who have researched and thought about the topic. But using too few sources or using sources that are too narrow in scope can undercut the effectiveness of the argument because readers may feel they are being provided with only a limited vision of the evidence. Consequently, offering information from a number of sources and from sources that reflect a variety of areas of expertise can be useful.

Look, for example, at the sources that Joshua Slick refers to in speculating about the causes for the growing trend of Internet dating in his essay "Not Just for Nerds Anymore," which appears on page 422. He cites the U.S. Census Bureau and the U.S. Department of Commerce to report how the number of homes with computers has risen and how Internet use also has increased. He then cites a technology magazine for K–12 educators, *Electronic School*, which is published as a supplement to *American School Board Journal* in cooperation with a program of the National School Boards Association. All of these sources carry a great deal of weight. To indicate how the online dating industry has grown, Slick uses a less scholarly source, *CNNMoney*, a popular special-interest magazine. As he gets deeper into his essay, Slick adds to his own credibility by using varied sources, such as the newspapers *San Jose Mercury News* and *USA Today*, to support his argument that potential dates can be evaluated through online ratings and reviews. He makes his final point — that online dating is as viable an option for social contacts as bars or churches — by citing a study released by the University of Bath. All together, the number of expert and popular sources he cites is impressive, and the variety of his sources adds to his credibility.

In her essay "Declining Coral Reefs: A Real Problem" (p. 416), Amber Ripplinger cites only three sources, including one from which she uses both the author's own words and ideas and a quotation from someone else. (The quotation, by a geologist at the University of Toronto, is included as a way to acknowledge and deal with an opposing view—that damage to coral reefs may be caused only by weather or El Niño rather than mainly by humans.) All of her sources—*National Geographic* and *Earthwatch* magazines and the *Los Angeles Times* newspaper—are reputable ones, though *Earthwatch*, published by an environmental organization, might be biased toward Ripplinger's view of humanity's role in the decline that she is investigating. It is up to the reader to determine whether these sources are sufficient to trust Ripplinger's argument or whether she needed to show a fuller range of support.

As you determine how many and what kinds of sources to cite in your essay, keep in mind that readers of essays speculating about causes or effects are more likely to be persuaded if the sources you rely on are neither too few nor too narrowly focused. When you begin to draft, if you find that your research seems skimpy, you may need to return to your source and to new sources to cast a wider net.

Considering a Useful Sentence Strategy

As you draft your essay, you will want to help your readers recognize the stages of your argument and the support you offer for each proposed cause or effect. One effective way to do so is to use clear topic sentences, especially ones that are grammatically parallel. Topic sentences usually open the paragraph or are placed early in the paragraph.

They can announce a new cause or effect, introduce counterargument (the writer's response to readers' likely questions or alternative causes or effects), or identify different parts of the support for a cause, an effect, or a counterargument. Topic sentences may also include key terms that the writer introduced in a thesis statement at the beginning of the essay, and they may take identical or similar sentence forms so that readers can recognize them more easily. The following topic sentences from King's essay identify what King believes to be the three main causes for many moviegoers' attraction to horror movies:

> Why? Some of the reasons are simple and obvious. To show that we can, that we are not afraid, that we can ride this roller coaster. (paragraph 3)

> We also go to re-establish our feelings of essential normality. (4)

> And we go to have fun. . . . The fun comes from seeing others menaced—sometimes killed. (5–6)

King assists readers in identifying each new stage of his argument by introducing the grammatical subject *we* in the first topic sentence and then repeating it to signal the next two stages: "we can," "We also go," "And we go."

While King relies on topic sentences within paragraphs to signal the stages in his argument, as do all the writers in this chapter, Kozol signals his topic sentences of support for his argument by writing them in parallel grammatical form, reinforcing his point about the harmful effects of illiteracy on people:

> **Illiterates cannot** read the menu in a restaurant. (paragraph 6)
>
> **Illiterates cannot** read the letters that their children bring home from their teachers. (8)
>
> **Illiterates cannot** read instructions on a bottle of prescription medicine. (9)
>
> **Illiterates cannot** read instructions on a pack of frozen food. (18)
>
> **Illiterates cannot** travel freely. (20)

Although Angier does not use exact parallel structure, she does signal the causes of intolerance of what she calls "boyish behavior" with clear topic sentences that use common terminology for a causal essay — *reason* and *causes*:

> Perhaps part of the **reason** why boyish behavior is suspect these days is Americans' obsessive fear of crime. (paragraph 11)
>
> Another **cause** for the intolerance of boyish behavior is the current school system. (12)

In addition to using topic sentences that help readers follow the stages of your argument and using parallel grammatical form to present related examples, you can strengthen your causal argument by using other sentence strategies as well. You may want to look at the information about using appositives (pp. 291–93) and sentences that combine concession and refutation (pp. 588–90).

READING A DRAFT CRITICALLY

Getting a critical reading of your draft will help you see how to improve it. Your instructor may schedule class time for reading drafts, or you may want to ask a classmate or a tutor in the writing center to read your draft. Ask your reader to use the following guidelines and to write out a response for you to consult during your revision.

Read for a First Impression

1. Read the draft without stopping to annotate or comment, and then write two or three sentences giving your general impression.

2. Identify one aspect of the draft that seems particularly effective.

Read Again to Suggest Improvements

1. Recommend ways to make the presentation of the subject more effective.

   - Read the opening paragraphs that present the subject to be speculated about, and then tell the writer what you find most interesting and useful.

   - Point out one or two places where a reader unfamiliar with the subject might need more information.

   - Suggest ways the writer could make the subject seem more interesting or significant.

   - If the subject is a trend, explain what you understand to be the increase or decrease and let the writer know whether you think further evidence is required to demonstrate conclusively that the subject is indeed a trend.

   - If the beginning seems unlikely to engage readers, suggest at least one other way of beginning.

2. Suggest ways to strengthen the cause or effect argument.

   - List the causes or effects. Tell the writer whether there seem to be too many, too few, or just about the right number. Point to one cause or effect that seems especially imaginative or surprising and to one that seems too obvious. Make suggestions for dropping or adding causes or effects.

   - Evaluate the support for each cause or effect separately. To help the writer make every cause or effect plausible to the intended readers, point out where the support seems thin or inadequate. Point to any support that seems irrelevant to the argument, hard to believe, or inconsistent with other support. Consider whether the writer has overlooked important resources of support: anecdotes, examples, statistics, analogies, or quotations from publications or interviews.

3. Suggest ways to strengthen the counterargument.

   - Locate every instance of counterargument—places where the writer anticipates readers' objections or questions or evaluates readers' preferred alternative causes or effects. Mark these in the margin of the draft. Review these as a set, and then suggest objections, questions, and alternative causes or effects the writer seems to have overlooked.

   - Identify counterarguments that seem weakly supported, and suggest ways the writer might strengthen the support.

   - If any of the refutations attack or ridicule readers, suggest ways the writer could refute without insulting or unduly irritating readers.

4. Suggest how credibility can be enhanced.

- Tell the writer whether the intended readers are likely to find the essay knowledgeable and authoritative. Point to places where it seems most and least authoritative.

- Identify places where the writer seeks common ground—shared values, beliefs, and attitudes—with readers. Try to identify other places where the writer might do so.

5. Suggest how the organizational plan could be improved.

- Consider the overall plan, perhaps by making a scratch outline (see Appendix 1). Analyze closely the progression of the causes or effects. Decide whether the causes or effects follow a logical step-by-step sequence.

- Suggest ways the causes or effects might be more logically sequenced.

- Review the places where counterarguments appear and consider whether they are smoothly woven into the argument. Give advice on the best places for the counterarguments.

- Indicate where new or better transitions might cue the steps in the argument and keep readers on track.

6. Evaluate the effectiveness of visuals.

- Look at any visuals in the essay, and tell the writer what they contribute to your understanding of the writer's speculations.

- If any visuals do not seem relevant, or if there seem to be too many visuals, identify the ones that the writer could consider dropping, explaining your thinking.

- If a visual does not seem appropriately placed, suggest a better place for it.

REVISING

This section offers suggestions for revising your draft. Revising means reenvisioning your draft, trying to see it in a new way, given your purpose and readers, in order to strengthen your cause or effect argument.

The biggest mistake you can make while revising is to focus initially on words or sentences. Instead, first try to see your draft as a whole to assess its likely impact on your readers. Think imaginatively and boldly about cutting unconvincing material, adding new material, and moving material around. Your computer makes even drastic revisions physically easy, but you still need to make the mental effort and decisions that will improve your draft.

You may have received help with this challenge from a classmate or tutor who gave your draft a critical reading. If so, keep this valuable feedback in mind as you decide which parts of your draft need revising and what specific changes you could make. The following suggestions will help you solve problems and strengthen your essay.

To Present the Subject More Effectively

- If readers unfamiliar with the subject may not understand it readily, provide more information.

- If the importance or significance of the subject is not clear, dramatize it with an anecdote or highlight its social or cultural implications.

- If the subject is a trend, show evidence of a significant increase or decrease over an extended period of time.

To Strengthen the Cause-and-Effect Argument

- If you propose what seem like too many causes or effects, clarify the role of each one or drop one or more that seem too obvious, obscure, or minor.

- If a cause or an effect lacks adequate support, come up with further examples, anecdotes, statistics, or quotes from authorities.

To Strengthen the Counterargument

- If you do not anticipate readers' likely questions about your argument and objections to it, do so now. Remember that you can either accommodate these objections and questions in your argument, conceding their value by making them part of your own argument, or refute them, arguing that they need not be taken seriously.

- If you do not anticipate readers' likely alternative causes or effects, do so now, conceding or refuting each one.

- If you attack or ridicule readers in your refutations, seek ways to refute their ideas decisively while showing respect for them as people.

- If you neglect to establish common ground with your readers, especially those who may think about your subject quite differently from the way you do, attempt to show them that you share some common values, attitudes, and beliefs.

To Enhance Credibility

- If readers of your draft question your credibility as a writer of cause-and-effect argument, learn more about your subject, support your argument more fully, anticipate a wider range of readers' likely objections, or talk with others who can help you think more imaginatively about your speculations.

- If your choice of words or your approach to readers weakens your credibility, consider your word choices throughout the essay and look for ways to show readers respect and to establish common ground with them.

To Organize More Logically and Coherently

- If readers question the logical sequence of your causes or effects, consider strengthening your plan by adding or dropping causes or effects or changing their sequence. Ensure that one cause or effect leads to the next in a logically linked chain of reasoning.

- If your logic seems sound but the links are not clear to your readers, provide clearer transitions from one step in the argument to the next. Use clear topic sentences to signal the stages of your argument and the support you provide for each cause or effect.

- If your various counterarguments are not smoothly integrated into your argument, move them around to make the connections clearer.

EDITING AND PROOFREADING

After you have revised your essay, be sure to spend some time checking for errors in usage, punctuation, and mechanics and considering matters of style. If you keep a list of errors you typically make, begin by checking your draft against this list. Ask someone else to proofread your essay before you print out a copy for your instructor or send it electronically.

From our research on student writing, we know that essays speculating about causes or effects have a high percentage of errors in the use of numbers and "reason is because" sentences. Because you must usually rely on numbers to present statistics when you support your argument or demonstrate the existence of a trend, you will need to learn and follow the conventions for presenting different kinds of numbers. Because you are usually drawn into "reason is because" sentences when you make a causal argument, you will need to know options for revising such sentences. Refer to a writer's handbook for help with these potential problems.

REFLECTING ON WHAT YOU HAVE LEARNED

Speculating about Causes or Effects

In this chapter, you have read critically several essays that speculate about causes or effects and have written one of your own. To better remember what you have learned, pause now to reflect on the reading and writing activities you completed in this chapter.

1. *Write* a page or so reflecting on what you have learned. *Begin* by describing what you are most pleased with in your essay. Then *explain* what you think contributed to your achievement. *Be specific* about this contribution.

   - If it was something you learned from the readings, *indicate* which readings and specifically what you learned from them.

   - If it came from your invention writing, *point out* the section or sections that helped you most.

   - If you got good advice from a critical reader, *explain* exactly how the person helped you—perhaps by helping you understand a particular problem in your draft or by adding a new dimension to your writing.

   - *Try to write* about your achievement in terms of what you have learned about the genre.

2. Now *reflect* more generally on speculation about causes or effects, a genre of writing that plays an important role in social life and public policy in the United States. *Consider* some of the following questions: Do you tend to adopt a tentative or an assertive stance when making speculations? Why do you think you generally adopt this stance over the other? How might your personal preferences and values influence your speculations? How might your gender, ethnicity, religious beliefs, age, or social class influence your ideas about a subject? What contribution might essays speculating about causes or effects make to our society that other genres cannot make?

CHAPTER 8

Proposal to Solve a Problem

Proposals are vital to democratic institutions. By reading and writing proposals, citizens and colleagues learn about problems affecting their well-being and explore possible actions that could be taken to remedy these problems. People read and write proposals every day in government, business, education, and other professions.

Many proposals address social problems and attempt to influence the direction of public policy. For example, a student activist group writes a proposal advocating that all campus food services be restricted from using genetically manufactured foods until the potential health hazards of such foods have been fully researched. A special United Nations task force recommends ways to eliminate acid rain worldwide. The College Entrance Examination Board commissions a report proposing strategies for reversing the decline in Scholastic Assessment Test (SAT) scores. A specialist in children's television writes a book suggesting that the federal government fund the development of new educational programming for preschool and elementary school students.

Proposals are also a basic ingredient of the world's work. A team of engineers and technical writers in a transportation firm, for example, might write a proposal to compete for a contract to build a new subway system. The manager of a fashion outlet might write a memo to a company executive proposing an upgrading of the computer system to include networking within the chain of stores. Seeking funding to support her research on a new cancer treatment, a university professor might write a proposal to the National Institutes of Health.

Still other proposals are written by individuals who want to solve problems involving groups or communities to which they belong. A college student irritated by long waits to see a nurse at the campus health clinic writes the clinic director, proposing a more efficient way to schedule and accommodate students. After funding for dance classes has been cut by their school board, students and parents interested in dance write a proposal to the school principal, asking her help in arranging after-school classes taught by a popular high-school teacher who would be paid with community funds. The board of directors of a historical society in a small ranching community proposes to the county board of supervisors that it donate an unused county building to the society so it can display historical records, photographs, and artifacts.

Proposal writing requires a critical questioning attitude—wondering about alternative approaches to bringing about change, puzzling over how a goal might be achieved, questioning why a process unfolds in a particular way, posing challenges to the status quo. In addition, it demands imagination and creativity. To solve a problem, you need to see it anew, to look at it from new perspectives and in new contexts.

Because a proposal tries to convince readers that its way of analyzing and creatively solving the problem makes sense, proposal writers must be sensitive to readers' needs and different perspectives. Readers need to know details of the solution and to be convinced that it will solve the problem and can be implemented. If readers initially favor a different solution, knowing why the writer rejects it will help them decide whether to support or reject the writer's proposed solution. Readers may be wary of costs, demands on their time, superficial changes, and grand schemes.

As you plan and draft a proposal, you will want to determine whether your readers know about the problem and whether they recognize its seriousness. In addition, you will want to consider how your readers might rate other possible solutions. Knowing what your readers know, what their assumptions and biases are, and what kinds of arguments appeal to them is crucial to proposal writing, as it is to all good argumentative writing.

Reading the proposal essays in this chapter will help you discover why the genre is so important and how it works. From the readings and from the suggestions for writing that follow each reading, you will get ideas for your own proposal essay. As you read and write about the selections, keep in mind the following assignment, which sets out the goals for writing a proposal. To support your writing of this assignment, the chapter concludes with a Guide to Writing Proposals.

THE WRITING ASSIGNMENT

Proposal

Write an essay proposing a solution to a problem affecting a community or group to which you belong. Your tasks are to analyze the problem and establish that it is serious enough to need solving, to offer a solution that will remedy the problem or at least help solve it, and to lay out the particulars by which your proposed solution would be put into effect. Address your proposal to one or more members of the group or to outsiders who could help solve the problem, being sure to take into account readers' likely objections to your proposed solution as well as their preferred alternative solutions.

WRITING SITUATIONS FOR PROPOSALS

Writing that proposes solutions to problems plays a significant role in college and professional life, as the following examples indicate:

- Frustrated by what they see as the failure of high schools to prepare students for the workplace, managers of a pharmaceuticals company decide to develop a proposal to move vocational and technical training out of an ill-equipped high-school system and onto the plant's floor. Seven divisional managers plus the firm's technical writers meet weekly to plan the proposal. They read about other on-the-job training programs and interview selected high-school teachers and current employees who attended the high-school program they want to replace. After several weeks' research, they present to the company CEO and to the school board a proposal that includes a timetable for implementing their solution and a detailed budget.

- For a political science class, a college student analyzes the question of presidential term limits. Citing examples from recent history, she argues that U.S. presidents spend the first year of each term getting organized and the fourth year either running for reelection or weakened by their status as a lame duck. Consequently, they are fully productive for only half of their four-year terms. She proposes limiting presidents to one six-year term, claiming that this change would remedy the problem by giving presidents four or five years to put their programs into effect. She acknowledges that it could make presidents less responsive to the public will but insists that the system of legislative checks and balances would make that problem unlikely.

- For an economics class, a student looks into the many problems arising from *maquiladoras*—industries in Mexico near the border with the United States that provide foreign exchange for the Mexican government, low-paying jobs for Mexican workers, and profits for American manufacturers. Among the problems are inadequate housing and health care for workers, frequent injuries on the job, and environmental damage. His instructor encourages him to select one of the problems, research it more thoroughly, and propose a solution. Taking injuries on the job as the problem most immediately within the control of American manufacturers, he proposes that they observe standards established by the U.S. Occupational Safety and Health Administration.

THINKING ABOUT YOUR EXPERIENCE WITH PROPOSALS

Before studying a type of writing, it is useful to spend some time thinking about what you already know about it. You may have discussed with friends an idea of yours or theirs that you hoped would solve a problem or make changes for the better. You might have written essays for classes examining the proposals of experts in a field such as sociology or political science, or you might have written a proposal of your own to solve a social or political problem. Mathematicians, astronomers, anthropologists, physicists, philosophers—people in these and other disciplines are called upon to make proposals to solve problems in their fields.

To analyze your experience with proposal arguments, try to recall a time when you argued—orally or in writing—for a plan or an action that interested or concerned you. What problem existed that made you think of a proposal to solve it? Who was the audience for your argument? What did you hope to achieve with your proposal? What interested you about it or made you think it was significant? Did you need to explain in detail the problem that prompted your solution, or was the problem already understood by your audience?

Consider also the proposal arguments you have read, heard, or seen on television. If you recall someone else's argument in detail, try to identify what made it interesting to you. Was it the problem itself, or did the author's solution seem uniquely imaginative or practical to you? Did the author make the argument for the proposal convincing? If so, how? Were there illuminating details or unusual points of view?

Write at least a page about your experience with proposal arguments.

■ A Guide to Reading Proposals

This guide introduces you to proposal writing. By completing all the activities in it, you will prepare yourself to learn a great deal from the other readings in this chapter about how to read and write a proposal. The guide focuses on a proposal by Michael Pollan, a well-known writer on environmental issues. You will read Pollan's essay twice. First, you will read it for meaning, seeking to understand Pollan's argument and the meaning it holds for you. Then you will reread the essay like a writer, analyzing the parts to see how Pollan constructs his argument and to learn the strategies he uses to make his proposal effective. These two activities—reading for meaning and reading like a writer—follow every reading in this chapter.

MICHAEL POLLAN

The Vegetable-Industrial Complex

Michael Pollan is the director of the Knight Program in Science and Environmental Journalism at the University of California, Berkeley. He has received the Reuters World Conservation Union Global Award in environmental journalism and the Genesis Award from the

American Humane Association. The author of four books, most recently The Omnivore's Dilemma: A Natural History of Four Meals *(2006), Pollan is also the former editor of* Harper's Magazine, *and his essays have been reprinted in* Best American Science Writing *(2004) and* Best American Essays *(2003). This proposal originally appeared in October 2006 in the* New York Times, *for which Pollan is a contributing writer. The title, "The Vegetable-Industrial Complex," is a play on the phrase "military-industrial complex," which President Dwight D. Eisenhower coined in his January 1961 farewell address to the nation as he warned Americans about the troubling relationships of mutual support among the military, defense contractors, and the civilian government.*[1]

In an interview, Pollan commented, "I don't know how far you can go in solving problems by changing patterns of consumer behavior, though I think you can go pretty far." As you read this essay, think about where you and your family shop for food and whether buying locally raised vegetables and meat is even possible.

Pollan begins by giving an example of the problem.

He *introduces an alternative solution that he will argue against* — irradiation.

Soon after the news broke last month that nearly 1 200 Americans in 26 states had been sickened by eating packaged spinach contaminated with *E. coli,* I received a rather coldblooded e-mail message from a friend in the food business. "I have instructed my broker to purchase a million shares of RadSafe," he wrote, explaining that RadSafe is a leading manufacturer of food-irradiation technology. It turned out my friend was joking, but even so, his reasoning was impeccable. If bagged salad greens are vulnerable to bacterial contamination on such a scale, industry and government would very soon come looking for a technological fix; any day now, calls to irradiate the entire food supply will be on a great many official lips. That's exactly what happened a few years ago when we learned that *E. coli* from cattle feces was winding up in American hamburgers. Rather than clean up the kill floor and the feedlot diet, some meat processors simply started nuking the meat — sterilizing the manure, in other words, rather than removing it from our food. Why? Because it's easier to find a technological fix than to address the

---

[1] Dwight D. Eisenhower, who served as supreme commander of the U.S.-backed military force in Europe during World War II and as president of the United States from 1953 to 1961, warned in his farewell address to the nation: "We must never let the weight of this combination [of "an immense military establishment and a large arms industry" asserting undue influence on Congress and the executive branch of government] endanger our liberties or democratic processes."

root cause of such a problem. This has always been the genius of industrial capitalism—to take its failings and turn them into exciting new business opportunities.

2   We can also expect to hear calls for more regulation and inspection of the produce industry. Already, watchdogs like the Center for Science in the Public Interest have proposed that the government impose the sort of regulatory regime it imposes on the meat industry— something along the lines of the Hazard Analysis and Critical Control Point system (HACCP, pronounced HASS-ip) developed in response to the *E. coli* contamination of beef. At the moment, vegetable growers and packers are virtually unregulated. "Farmers can do pretty much as they please," Carol Tucker Foreman, director of the Food Policy Institute at the Consumer Federation of America, said recently, "as long as they don't make anyone sick."

Pollan mentions another alternative solution—more regulation.

3   This sounds like an alarming lapse in governmental oversight until you realize there has never before been much reason to worry about food safety on farms. But these days, the way we farm and the way we process our food, both of which have been industrialized and centralized over the last few decades, are endangering our health. The Centers for Disease Control and Prevention estimate that our food supply now sickens 76 million Americans every year, putting more than 300,000 of them in the hospital, and killing 5,000. The lethal strain of *E. coli* known as 0157:H7, responsible for this latest outbreak of food poisoning, was unknown before 1982; it is believed to have evolved in the gut of feedlot cattle. These are animals that stand around in their manure all day long, eating a diet of grain that happens to turn a cow's rumen into an ideal habitat for *E. coli* 0157:H7. (The bug can't survive long in cattle living on grass.) Industrial animal agriculture produces more than a billion tons of manure every year, manure that, besides being full of nasty microbes like *E. coli* 0157:H7 (not to mention high concentrations of the pharmaceuticals animals must receive so they can tolerate the feedlot lifestyle), often ends up in places it shouldn't be, rather than in pastures, where it would not only be harmless but also actually do some good. To think of animal manure as pollution rather than fertility is a relatively new (and industrial) idea.

He argues that the root of the problem is industrialization and centralization of farming and food processing.

Pollan *presents his pre-ferred "old solution,"* arguing that the alternative solutions actually cause or worsen the problem of unsafe food.

Wendell Berry[2] once wrote that when we took animals off farms and put them onto feedlots, we had, in effect, taken an old solution—the one where crops feed animals and animals' waste feeds crops—and neatly divided it into two new problems: a fertility problem on the farm, and a pollution problem on the feedlot. Rather than return to that elegant solution, however, industrial agriculture came up with a technological fix for the first problem—chemical fertilizers on the farm. As yet, there is no good fix for the second problem, unless you count irradiation and HACCP plans and overcooking your burgers and, now, staying away from spinach. All of these solutions treat *E. coli* 0157:H7 as an unavoidable fact of life rather than what it is: a fact of industrial agriculture.

But if industrial farming gave us this bug, it is industrial eating that has spread it far and wide. We don't yet know exactly what happened in the case of the spinach washed and packed by Natural Selection Foods, whether it was contaminated in the field or in the processing plant or if perhaps the sealed bags made a trivial contamination worse. But we do know that a great deal of spinach from a great many fields gets mixed together in the water at that plant, giving microbes from a single field an opportunity to contaminate a vast amount of food. The plant in question washes 26 million servings of salad every week. In effect, we're washing the whole nation's salad in one big sink.

It's conceivable the same problem could occur in your own kitchen sink or on a single farm. Food poisoning has always been with us, but not until we started processing all our food in such a small number of "kitchens" did the potential for nationwide outbreaks exist.

He evaluates the efficiency of his own versus the alternative solutions.

Surely this points to one of the great advantages of a decentralized food system: when things go wrong, as they sooner or later will, fewer people are affected and, just as important, the problem can be more easily traced to its source and contained. A long and complicated food chain, in which food from all over the coun-

4

5

6

7

---

[2] Wendell Berry is a cultural and economic critic as well as a farmer and prolific writer. He advocates sustainable agriculture, local economies, appropriate use of technology, and recognition of the interconnectedness of all living things.

tryside is gathered together in one place to be processed and then distributed all over the country to be eaten, can be impressively efficient, but by its very nature it is a food chain devilishly hard to follow and to fix.

8   Fortunately, this is not the only food chain we have. The week of the *E. coli* outbreak, washed spinach was on sale at my local farmers' market, and at the Blue Heron Farms stand, where I usually buy my greens, the spinach appeared to be moving briskly. I tasted a leaf and wondered why I didn't think twice about it. I guess it's because I've just always trusted these guys; I buy from them every week. The spinach was probably cut and washed that morning or the night before—it hasn't been sitting around in a bag on a truck for a week. And if there ever is any sort of problem, I know exactly who is responsible. Whatever the risk, and I'm sure there is some, it seems manageable.

Pollan uses personal experience to *support his argument.*

9   These days, when people make the case for buying local food, they often talk about things like keeping farmers in our communities and eating fresh food in season, at the peak of its flavor. We like what's going on at the farmers' market—how country meets city, how children learn that a carrot is not a glossy orange bullet that comes in a bag but is actually a root; how we get to taste unfamiliar flavors and even, in some sense, reconnect through these foods and their growers to the natural world. Stack all this up against the convenience and price of supermarket food, though, and it can sound a little . . . sentimental.

In paragraphs 9 and 10, he *anticipates an objection*—that the advantages of locally produced food are largely sentimental—*and refutes it.*

10   But there's nothing sentimental about local food— indeed, the reasons to support local food economies could not be any more hardheaded or pragmatic. Our highly centralized food economy is a dangerously precarious system, vulnerable to accidental—and deliberate—contamination. This is something the government understands better than most of us eaters. When Tommy Thompson retired from the Department of Health and Human Services in 2004, he said something chilling at his farewell news conference: "For the life of me, I cannot understand why the terrorists have not attacked our food supply, because it is so easy to do." The reason it is so easy to do was laid out in a 2003 G.A.O. report to Congress on bioterrorism. "The high concentration of our livestock industry and the

He cites authorities and statistics to *support his argument.*

centralized nature of our food-processing industry" make them "vulnerable to terrorist attack." Today 80 percent of America's beef is slaughtered by four companies, 75 percent of the precut salads are processed by two and 30 percent of the milk by just one company. Keeping local food economies healthy—and at the moment they are thriving—is a matter not of sentiment but of critical importance to the national security and the public health, as well as to reducing our dependence on foreign sources of energy.

Yet perhaps the gravest threat now to local food 11 economies—to the farmer selling me my spinach, to the rancher who sells me my grass-fed beef—is, of all things, the government's own well-intentioned efforts to clean up the industrial food supply. Already, hundreds of regional meat-processing plants—the ones that local meat producers depend on—are closing because they can't afford to comply with the regulatory requirements the U.S.D.A. rightly imposes on giant slaughterhouses that process 400 head of cattle an hour. The industry insists that all regulations be "scale neutral," so if the U.S.D.A. demands that huge plants have, say, a bathroom, a shower and an office for the exclusive use of its inspectors, then a small processing plant that slaughters local farmers' livestock will have to install these facilities, too. This is one of the principal reasons that meat at the farmers' market is more expensive than meat at the supermarket: farmers are seldom allowed to process their own meat, and small processing plants have become very expensive to operate, when the U.S.D.A. is willing to let them operate at all. From the U.S.D.A.'s perspective, it is much more efficient to put their inspectors in a plant where they can inspect 400 cows an hour rather than in a local plant where they can inspect maybe one.

So what happens to the spinach grower at my farm- 12 ers' market when the F.D.A. starts demanding a HACCP plan—daily testing of the irrigation water, say, or some newfangled veggie-irradiation technology? When we start requiring that all farms be federally inspected? Heavy burdens of regulation always fall heaviest on the smallest operations and invariably wind up benefiting the biggest players in an industry, the ones who can spread the costs over a larger output of goods. A result is that regulating food safety tends to accelerate the sort of industrialization that made food safety a problem in

Pollan emphasizes the importance of solving the problem for a reason that may surprise readers—national security.

He *argues against the alternative solution* to regulate food production more strictly, pointing out that it makes the problem worse by encouraging even more centralization and industrialization.

the first place. We end up putting our faith in RadSafe rather than in Blue Heron Farms—in technologies rather than relationships.

13   It's easy to imagine the F.D.A. announcing a new rule banning animals from farms that produce plant crops. In light of the threat from *E. coli*, such a rule would make a certain kind of sense. But it is an industrial, not an ecological, sense. For the practice of keeping animals on farms used to be, as Wendell Berry pointed out, a solution; only when cows moved onto feedlots did it become a problem. Local farmers and local food economies represent much the same sort of pre-problem solution—elegant, low-tech and redundant. But the logic of industry, apparently ineluctable, has other ideas, ideas that not only leave our centralized food system undisturbed but also imperil its most promising, and safer, alternatives.

Pollan concludes by summarizing his argument and reemphasizing the importance of solving the problem.

READING FOR MEANING

This section presents three activities that will help you reread Pollan's proposal with a critical eye. Done in sequence, these activities lead you from a basic understanding of the selection to a more personal response to it and finally to an analysis that deepens your understanding and critical thinking about what you are reading.

Read to Comprehend

Reread the selection, and write a few sentences briefly explaining in your own words Pollan's proposed solution.

The following definitions may help you understand Pollan's vocabulary:

E. coli (paragraph 1): *Escherichia coli*, one of the bacteria that are found in the lower intestines of mammals and can cause diarrhea and sometimes death in humans.

feedlot (1): an enclosed area where cattle are raised before being slaughtered.

regime (2): a system.

Identify three or more additional words that you don't understand, and find the best definitions from the dictionary that work with their context.

To expand your understanding of this reading, you might use one or more of the following critical reading strategies that are explained and illustrated in Appendix 1: *annotating, previewing,* and *summarizing.*

Read to Respond

Write several paragraphs exploring your initial thoughts and feelings about Pollan's proposal. Focus on anything that stands out for you, perhaps because it resonates with your own experience or because you find a statement puzzling.

You might consider writing about the following:

- your feelings about food safety, perhaps in relation to a recent food scare such as the spinach *E. coli* contamination that Pollan writes about;

- Pollan's title, "The Vegetable-Industrial Complex," and its relation to the "military-industrial complex"; or

- how convincing you find Pollan's argument for his proposed solution.

To develop your response to Pollan's proposal, you might use one or both of the following critical reading strategies that are explained and illustrated in Appendix 1: *contextualizing* and *reflecting on challenges to your beliefs and values.*

Read to Analyze Assumptions

Reread Pollan's proposal essay, and write a paragraph or two exploring one or more of the assumptions that you find in the text. All writing contains assumptions—opinions, values, and beliefs that are taken for granted as commonly accepted truths by the writer or others. Personal or individual assumptions also tend to reflect the values and beliefs of a particular group or community, sometimes called *cultural ideology*, which shape the way those in the group think, act, and understand the world.

Analyzing assumptions is an important part of learning to read critically because assumptions tend to be unexamined and unquestioned (at least consciously) by those who hold them. When you read with a critical eye, you identify important assumptions in the text and ask questions about them. Sometimes assumptions are stated explicitly, but often they are only implied, so you may have to search for underlying assumptions in the word choices and examples. Here are some kinds of questions you should ask regarding the assumptions you find: Who holds this assumption? How does the assumption reinforce or critique the status quo? What alternative ideas, beliefs, or values would challenge this assumption? If the writer uses the assumption to appeal to readers, how effective do you think this appeal is, and why?

To help you get started reading for assumptions in Pollan's essay, notice his assumptions about buying spinach from his "local farmer's market" during the "*E. coli* outbreak" (paragraph 8). He claims that he "didn't think twice" about the danger. But then he goes on to mention several assumptions he was making—(1) that he has "just always trusted these guys," (2) that they "probably cut and washed" the spinach very recently and therefore "it hasn't been sitting around in a bag on a truck for a week," and (3) that "if there ever is any sort of problem, I know exactly who is responsible." To think critically about assumptions in this essay related to the safety of local farmer's markets, ask yourself: Why does Pollan trust Blue Heron Farms? His use of the phrase *these guys* suggests that Pollan trusts them because he knows them personally, but you might wonder whether being friends with farmers assures that their food is not contaminated. In fact, doesn't Pollan's third assumption acknowledge that food could be contaminated at local farms? How about Pollan's second assumption about the freshness of Blue Heron's produce? Given that we now know that the spinach was contaminated in the fields by pigs' feces, getting the food to market quickly would not affect safety. To what extent do you think that Pollan's assumptions reflect an unrealistic nostalgia for the small, local, and personal?

You may want to examine cultural assumptions about local food markets, or you may choose to explore other assumptions in "The Vegetable-Industrial Complex," such as the following:

- **assumptions about technology.** Pollan asserts in the opening paragraph that industry and government prefer "a technological fix" to solving problems by removing their causes. He assumes also that this preference for technology "has always been the genius of industrial capitalism—to take its failings and turn them into exciting new business opportunities." To think critically about the assumptions in this essay related to technology, ask yourself: What do Pollan's use of the words *fix* and *genius* suggest about his attitude? The technological solution that Pollan mentions is irradiating food. Is there anything in the essay to suggest that this solution would be less effective or more costly than the kind of nontech solution he proposes? Pollan seems to assume that technology is bad and that food grown organically is better. But historically, vegetables and fruit as well as meat, eggs, and dairy products have often been cultivated through selective breeding, which might be considered an early version of genetic engineering. How might Pollan's assumptions oversimplify the issue?

- **assumptions about government regulation.** Pollan assumes that "the government's own well-intentioned efforts to clean up the industrial food supply" constitute "the gravest threat" to local farmers and ranchers (11), and he predicts that "regulating food safety" would put small farmers out of business and benefit the "biggest players" (12). To think critically about the assumptions in this essay related to government regulation, ask yourself: Pollan assumes that big business would gain more than independent small farmers from regulating the food industry, but what about the consumer? Would the consumer benefit from inspections and regulations? In addition, isn't it likely that business—large and small—will pass on to consumers the cost of meeting regulations? How high a safety standard are consumers willing to pay for in the form of government regulation?

READING LIKE A WRITER

This section guides you through an analysis of Pollan's argumentative strategies: *introducing the problem; presenting the proposed solution; arguing directly for the proposed solution;* and *counterarguing readers' objections, questions, and alternative solutions.* For each strategy you will be asked to reread and annotate part of Pollan's essay to see how he uses the strategy in "The Vegetable-Industrial Complex."

When you study the selections later in this chapter, you will see how different writers use these same strategies. The Guide to Writing Proposals near the end of the chapter suggests ways you can use these strategies in writing your own proposal.

Introducing the Problem

Every proposal begins with a problem. Depending on what their readers know about the problem, writers may explain how it came to be or what attempts have been made to solve it. Sometimes, readers are already aware of a problem, especially if it affects them directly. In such cases, the writer can merely identify the problem and move directly to presenting a solution. At other times, readers will be unaware that the problem exists or have difficulty imagining it. In these situations, the writer may have to describe the problem in detail, helping readers recognize its importance and the consequences of failing to solve it.

Writers may also believe that readers misunderstand the problem, failing to recognize it for what it really is or to understand how serious it is. They may then decide that their first task is to redefine the problem in a way that helps readers see it in a different way. Pollan does precisely that. He introduces the problem in the first sentence, and it is a problem his readers would already have known about because the *E. coli* contamination of spinach was the lead story in the news at the time. Then he goes on to redefine the problem by speculating about its root cause because he believes that efforts to secure the food supply are doomed if they fail to recognize what he believes is the real problem.

Analyze

1. *Reread* paragraphs 3 to 7, noting in the margin the strategies that Pollan uses to help readers understand the seriousness of the problem and see that it is a deep-rooted structural problem caused by the food production and distribution system.

2. *Consider* how effectively Pollan redefines the problem. As one of his intended readers, *explain* why you are or are not convinced of his redefinition. In what ways might he have made his argument more convincing?

Write

Write several sentences explaining Pollan's strategy for introducing the problem and evaluating how convincing you find his argument. *Give details* from the reading to illustrate your analysis.

Presenting the Proposed Solution

The proposal writer's primary purposes are to convince readers of the wisdom of the proposed solution and to convince them to take action on its implementation. To achieve these purposes, the writer must ensure that readers understand what is being proposed and can imagine how the solution could be implemented.

For proposed solutions likely to be familiar to readers because they already exist elsewhere, the writer may need only to give the solution a recognizable name, identify where it is being applied successfully, and perhaps also compare it to less successful alternative solutions that have been suggested or tried. In cases where the proposed solution is likely to be unfamiliar to readers or where readers might have difficulty imagining how it could be put into effect, writers usually opt to explain how it would work. Explaining in detail how to implement the solution, however, might take too much space and require too much technical knowledge. Therefore, writers must gauge how much detail their readers need to grasp the idea and accept it as feasible or able to be carried out.

Before he introduces his own solution, Pollan brings up the likely alternative solutions: "a technological fix . . . to irradiate the entire food supply" (paragraph 1) and "more regulation and inspection of the produce industry" (2). In this way, he sets the stage for his nontechnological, nonregulatory solution that he hints at in the last two sentences of paragraph 3. This activity will help you analyze and evaluate how Pollan presents his proposed solution.

Analyze

1. *Reread* paragraph 4 where Pollan introduces his preferred solution—what he calls both "an old solution" and an "elegant solution." *Notice* also that Pollan does not claim this solution as his own idea but attributes it to Wendell Berry, a prolific writer, cultural critic, philosopher, and farmer whom readers familiar with environmentalism would be likely to recognize as a kind of guru. *Consider* how effective the reference to Berry is for readers unfamiliar with him and whether Pollan gives readers enough information to get the point even if they don't know Berry.

2. *Reread* paragraphs 7 to 10 where Pollan elaborates on his proposed solution. *Notice* that here he labels it with the rather abstract phrase "decentralized food system" (paragraph 7) as well as the more concrete phrase "local food" (9, 10). *Mark in the margin* where Pollan uses an example to help readers grasp what he means by these terms.

Write

Write several sentences describing the strategies that Pollan uses to present his proposed solution, explaining the purpose of each strategy and evaluating its effectiveness. For instance, why do you think he refers to Wendell Berry, and how well does this reference work for you as one reader? Why do you think he gives an example, and how effectively does it accomplish its purpose?

Arguing Directly for the Proposed Solution

In arguing for solutions, writers rely on two interrelated strategies: arguing directly for the proposed solution and counterarguing readers' likely objections, questions, and alternative solutions. (We take up the second strategy, counterargument, in the next section.)

Whatever else proposal writers do, they must argue energetically, imaginatively, and sensitively for their proposed solutions. A proposal may describe a problem well or complain with great feeling about it; if it goes no further, however, it is not a proposal. Writers must try to convince readers that the solution presented will actually alleviate the problem. The solution should also appear feasible, cost-effective, and more promising than alternative solutions.

In thinking about how to support their argument, proposal writers should ask themselves why their solution would work. Such support may include personal experience, hypothetical cases and scenarios, statistics, facts, assertions, examples, speculations about causes or consequences, and quotations from authorities. The most convincing support surprises readers. They see it and think, "I never thought of it that way."

Analyze

1. *Reread* paragraphs 5 to 8 to see how Pollan develops his main reason for proposing the decentralization of the food production and distribution system. *Annotate* the kinds of support Pollan uses in these paragraphs. *Also make notes* about what you see as the strengths and weaknesses of the kinds of support he uses in these paragraphs.

2. Then *reread* paragraph 10 to see how Pollan extends his argument to apply not only to contamination that is "accidental" but to a "deliberate" act of "bioterrorism" as well. *Make notes* about the kinds of support Pollan uses in this part of his argument. *Consider* how effective this part of his argument is likely to be with his readers.

Write

Write several sentences summarizing Pollan's argument in the paragraphs you analyzed. What kinds of support does he use? *Give examples* from the reading. *Conclude with a few more sentences* that evaluate the effectiveness of Pollan's argument.

Counterarguing Readers' Objections, Questions, and Alternative Solutions

As they argue for their solutions, experienced writers are continually aware of readers' objections to the argument or questions about it. Writers may *accommodate* readers' likely objections and questions by modifying their own arguments, perhaps even pointing out how they have done so. What better way to disarm a skeptical or antagonistic reader? Or writers may *refute* readers' objections; that is, try to show them to be wrong. Experienced arguers bring their readers' questions and objections right into their arguments. They do not ignore their readers' concerns or conveniently assume that readers are on their side.

Experienced proposal writers may also acknowledge other solutions that have been proposed or tried. When a writer knows or suspects readers may have alternative solutions in mind, it is best to discuss them directly in the argument. If Pollan had failed to acknowledge obvious alternative solutions, readers would have regarded him as ill-informed about the problem. As with questions and objections, a writer can either accommodate an alternative solution by integrating all or part of it into his or her own solution, or refute the alternative as unworkable.

Analyze

1. *Reread* paragraphs 9 and 10, where Pollan anticipates a likely objection to his argument in favor of buying local food. *Underline* the specific objection against which Pollan seems to be counterarguing. Then *note in the margin* whether he accommodates or refutes the objection and the strategies he uses to do so.

2. *Reread* paragraphs 11 and 12, where Pollan opposes the alternative solution to apply "scale neutral" regulations to all facilities. Then *consider* whether Pollan accommodates or refutes the alternative and how he goes about doing so.

Write

Write a few sentences explaining how Pollan counterargues. *Give examples* of how he handles an objection and an alternative solution. Then *write a few more sentences* evaluating Pollan's counterarguments.

■ Readings

WILLIAM F. SHUGHART II

Why Not a Football Degree?

> *William F. Shughart II (b. 1947) is the Frederick A. P. Barnard
> Distinguished Professor of Economics at the University of Mississippi,
> known to football fans as Ole Miss. He is the senior editor of the schol-
> arly journal* Public Choice *and the associate editor of the* Southern
> Economic Journal. *His honors include the University of Mississippi
> Outstanding Researcher Award, the Sir Anthony Fisher International
> Memorial Award, and the* Business Week *Award. Shughart has writ-
> ten numerous articles and ten books, most recently* Policy Challenges
> and Political Responses: Public Choice Perspectives on the Post-
> 9/11 World *(2005) and* The Economics of Budget Deficits *(2002).*
>
> > *This essay originally appeared in the* Wall Street Journal *in 1990
> > and was updated by Shughart in 2007. As you read his proposal,
> > notice that Shughart dismisses as "half-measures" (paragraph 3) the
> > efforts by the National Collegiate Athletic Association (NCAA) to
> > solve the problem of "loss of amateurism in college sports" (2). In their
> > place, he offers a three-pronged solution designed to help student ath-
> > letes succeed in their academic studies as well as in their collegiate
> > sports careers and also to eliminate what he calls "illegal financial
> > inducements" (11) while at the same time removing the "built-in
> > advantages" (14) of the most successful college sports programs. Con-
> > sider how well Shughart's three "suggestions" (3) would work together
> > to offer a complete solution to the problem.*

The college football career of 2006's Heisman Trophy winner,   1
Ohio State University quarterback Troy Smith, nearly was cut
short at the end of his sophomore year following allegations that
he had accepted $500 from a Buckeye booster. He was barred from
playing in the 2005 Alamo Bowl and the next season's opener
against Miami (Ohio). Quarterback Rhett Bomar was dismissed
from the University of Oklahoma's football team after it was disclosed that he had earned substantially more than justified by the
number of hours worked during the summer of 2006 at a job
arranged for him by a patron of OU athletics. As a result of charges
that, from 1993 to 1998, Coach Clem Haskins paid to have more
than 400 term papers ghost-written for 18 of his players, the postseason tournament victories credited to the University of Minnesota's basketball team were erased from the NCAA's record
books and the program was placed on a four-year probation from
which it has not yet recovered. In recent years, gambling and point-

shaving scandals have rocked the basketball programs at Arizona State, Northwestern, and Florida; player suspensions and other penalties have been handed out for illegal betting on games by members of the Boston University, Florida State, and University of Maryland football teams.

Each of these events, which are only the latest revelations in a long series of NCAA rule violations, has generated the usual hand-wringing about the apparent loss of amateurism in college sports. Nostalgia for supposedly simpler times when love of the game and not money was the driving force in intercollegiate athletics has led to all sorts of reform proposals. The NCAA's decision in the late 1980s to require its member institutions to make public athletes' graduation rates is perhaps the least controversial example. Proposition 48's mandate that freshman athletes must meet more stringent test score and grade point requirements to participate in NCAA-sanctioned contests than is demanded of entering non-student-athletes has been criticized as a naked attempt to discriminate against disadvantaged (and mostly minority) high-school graduates who see college sports as a way out of poverty.

But whether or not one supports any particular reform proposal, there seems to be a general consensus that something must be done. If so, why stop at half-measures? I hereby offer three suggestions for solving the crisis in college athletics.

1. *Create four-year degree programs in football and basketball.* Many colleges and universities grant bachelors' degrees in vocational subjects. Art, drama, and music are a few examples, but there are others. Undergraduates who major in these areas typically are required to spend only about one of their four years in introductory English, math, history and science courses; the remainder of their time is spent in the studio, the theater or the practice hall honing the creative talents they will later sell as professionals.

Although a college education is no more necessary for success in the art world than it is in the world of sports, no similar option is available for students whose talents lie on the athletic field or in the gym. Majoring in physical education is a possibility, of course, but while PE is hardly a rigorous, demanding discipline, undergraduates pursuing a degree in that major normally must spend many more hours in the classroom than their counterparts who are preparing for careers on the stage. While the music major is receiving academic credit for practice sessions and recitals, the PE major is studying and taking exams in kinesiology, exercise physiology and nutrition. Why should academic credit be given for practicing the violin, but not for practicing a three-point shot?

2. *Extend the time limit on athletic scholarships by two years.* In   6
addition to practicing and playing during the regular football or
basketball season, college athletes must continue to work to
improve their skills and keep in shape during the off-season. For
football players, these off-season activities include several weeks of
organized spring practice as well as year-round exercise programs
in the weight room and on the running track. Basketball players
participate in summer leagues and practice with their teams during the fall. In effect, college athletes are required to work at their
sports for as much as 10 months a year.

These time-consuming extracurricular activities make it ex-   7
tremely difficult for college athletes to devote more than minimal
effort to the studies required for maintaining their academic eligibility. They miss lectures and exams when their teams travel, and
the extra tutoring they receive at athletic department expense often
fails to make up the difference.

If the NCAA and its member schools are truly concerned about   8
the academic side of the college athletic experience, let them put
their money where their collective mouth is. The period of an athlete's eligibility to participate in intercollegiate sports would
remain at four years, but the two additional years of scholarship
support could be exercised at any time during the athlete's lifetime.
Athletes who use up their college eligibility and do not choose
careers in professional sports would be guaranteed financial back-
ing to remain in school and finish their undergraduate degrees.
Athletes who have the talent to turn pro could complete their
degrees when their playing days are over.

3. *Allow a competitive marketplace to determine the compensa-*   9
tion of college athletes. Football and basketball players at the top
NCAA institutions produce millions of dollars in benefits for their
respective schools. Successful college athletic programs draw more
fans to the football stadium and to the basketball arena. They generate revenues for the school from regular season television
appearances and from invitations to participate in postseason play.
There is evidence that schools attract greater financial support
from public and private sources—both for their athletic and academic programs—if their teams achieve national ranking. There
even is evidence that the quality of students who apply for admission to institutions of higher learning improves following a successful football or basketball season.

Despite the considerable contributions made to the wealth and   10
welfare of his or her school, however, the compensation payable to
a college athlete is limited by the NCAA to a scholarship that
includes tuition, books, room and board, and a nominal expense

allowance. Any payment above and beyond this amount subjects the offending athletic program to NCAA sanctions. In-kind payments to players and recruits in the form of free tickets to athletic contests, T-shirts, transportation and accommodations likewise are limited. These restrictions apply to alumni and fans as well as to the institutions themselves. The NCAA also limits the amount of money athletes can earn outside of school by curtailing the use of summer jobs as a means by which coaches and boosters can pay athletes more than authorized.

The illegal financial inducements reported to be widespread in collegiate football and basketball supply conclusive evidence that many college athletes are now underpaid. The relevant question is whether the current system of compensation ought to remain in place. Allowing it to do so will preserve the illusion of amateurism in college sports and permit coaches, athletic departments and college administrators to continue to benefit financially at the expense of the players. On the other hand, shifting to a market-based system of compensation would transfer some of the wealth created by big-time athletic programs to the individuals whose talents are key ingredients in the success of those programs.

It would also cause a sea change in the distribution of power among the top NCAA institutions. Under the present NCAA rules, some of the major college athletic programs, such as Southern Cal, LSU and Florida in football, and Duke, North Carolina and Florida in basketball, have developed such strong winning traditions over the years that they can maintain their dominant positions without cheating.

These schools are able to attract superior high-school athletes season after season by offering packages of non-monetary benefits (well-equipped training facilities, quality coaching staffs, talented teammates, national exposure and so on) that increases the present value of an amateur athlete's future professional income relative to the value added by historically weaker athletic programs. Given this factor, along with NCAA rules that mandate uniform compensation across the board, the top institutions have a built-in competitive advantage in recruiting the best and brightest athletes.

It follows that under the current system, the weaker programs are virtually compelled to offer illegal financial inducements to players and recruits if they wish to compete successfully with the traditional powers. It also follows that shifting to a market-based system of compensation would remove some of the built-in advantages now enjoyed by the top college athletic programs. It is surely this effect, along with the reductions in the incomes of coaches and the "fat" in athletic department budgets to be expected once a competitive marketplace is permitted to work, that is the cause of the objection to paying student-athletes a market-determined wage, not the rhetoric about the repugnance of professionalism.

It is a fight over the distribution of the college sports revenue pie that lies at the bottom of the debate about reforming NCAA rules. And notwithstanding the high moral principles and concern for players usually expressed by debaters on all sides of the issue, the interests of the athlete are in fact often the last to be considered.   15

READING FOR MEANING

This section presents three activities that will help you reread Shughart's essay with a critical eye. Done in sequence, these activities lead you from a basic understanding of the selection to a more personal response to it and finally to an analysis that deepens your understanding and critical thinking about what you are reading.

Read to Comprehend

Reread the selection, and write a few sentences briefly explaining Shughart's proposed solution. The following definitions may help you understand his vocabulary:

ghost-written (paragraph 1): written by someone other than the person who claims to be the author.

point-shaving (1): an illegal gambling practice by which players deliberately limit the number of points scored by their team, usually to try to ensure that it wins by fewer points than predicted.

sanctions (10): penalties, punishments.

Identify three or more additional words that you don't understand, and find the best definitions from the dictionary that work with their context.

To expand your understanding of this reading, you might use one or more of the following critical reading strategies that are explained and illustrated in Appendix 1: *summarizing* and *questioning to understand and remember.*

Read to Respond

Write several paragraphs exploring your initial thoughts and feelings about Shughart's proposal. Focus on anything that stands out for you, perhaps because it resonates with your own experiences or because you find a statement puzzling.

You might consider writing about the following:

- the rule violations that Shughart lists in the first paragraph, perhaps adding other, more recent violations with which you are familiar;

- Shughart's idea that academic credit should be given to "practicing a three-point shot" (paragraph 5); or

- Shughart's observation that playing and practicing sports "make it extremely difficult for college athletes to devote more than minimal effort" to their studies (7), perhaps in relation to your own experience as an athlete in college or high school.

To develop your response to Shughart's proposal, you might use one or more of the following critical reading strategies that are explained and illustrated in Appendix 1: *contextualizing, reflecting on challenges to your beliefs and values,* and *judging the writer's credibility.*

Read to Analyze Assumptions

Reread Shughart's proposal essay, and write a paragraph or two exploring one or more of the assumptions you find in the text. The following suggestions may help:

- **assumptions about amateurism.** Shughart argues that amateurism in college sports is an "illusion" (paragraph 11). The NCAA rules require that to play college sports, athletes must retain amateur status, meaning that they cannot be paid by recruiters and that their scholarships can cover only such things as tuition and housing. To think critically about the assumptions in this essay related to amateurism, ask yourself: Who, according to Shughart, benefits from keeping college athletes amateurs, and who would benefit if they were allowed to become professionals? If you assume that the NCAA intended amateur status to protect college athletes and perhaps also college sports, what was it supposed to protect them from and how effective has it been?

- **assumptions about majoring in sports.** Shughart compares football to "vocational subjects" such as art, drama, and music (paragraph 4). He argues that football should be a major in its own right, like music where students receive "academic credit for practice sessions and recitals" (5). To think critically about the assumptions in this essay related to majoring in sports, ask yourself: What cultural assumptions does Shughart's choice of the word *vocational* suggest? Traditionally, an undergraduate degree has sought to give students a broad or liberal education and to leave vocational training to specialized programs or graduate school. What do you and other students at your college assume that the purpose of college should be—vocational training? a liberal education? something else?

To probe assumptions more deeply, you might use one or both of the following critical reading strategies that are explained and illustrated in Appendix 1: *reflecting on challenges to your beliefs and values* and *looking for patterns of opposition.*

READING LIKE A WRITER
INTRODUCING THE PROBLEM

In introducing the problem, proposal writers may define or describe it as well as argue that it exists and is serious. Depending on their purpose and readers, writers must decide whether they need to identify the problem briefly, as Michael Pollan does in the first essay in this chapter because he could safely assume that contemporary readers were aware of the much reported contamination of packaged spinach, or describe it at some length, as Karen Kornbluh does in her essay because she assumes that few readers would be aware of the extent and seriousness of the problem that she is introducing. To establish the problem, writers have an array of strategies they can use. Pollan cites one example that is currently in the news, and Kornbluh provides a historical context and statistics. This activity will help you analyze Shughart's method of introducing the problem to his readers.

Analyze

1. *Reread* paragraphs 1 and 2, where Shughart introduces the problem. *Underline* the specific details he provides about each example—such as dates, names, schools, and violations. Consider how the sheer number of examples plus the details about each example contribute to establishing that the problem exists and is serious.

2. *Notice* also Shughart's word choices. For example, why do you think Shughart describes the problem at the beginning of paragraph 2 as "the apparent loss of amateurism in college sports"? And why does he use the expression "[n]ostalgia for supposedly simpler times"? Consider what words like *apparent* and *supposedly* convey to readers in this context.

Write

Write several sentences describing how Shughart uses examples to introduce the problem and emphasize its importance in paragraphs 1 and 2. *Cite specifics* from the reading to support your answer. *Conclude with a sentence or two* about Shughart's word choices and how they affect the tone of his proposal in the opening paragraphs.

CONSIDERING IDEAS FOR YOUR OWN WRITING

Consider proposing a way to improve a popular sport. Your idea need not revolutionize the sport, though it might. It could offer only a small refinement such as changing a rule or adding a feature to the game. (Recent developments such as the designated hitter in baseball and instant replays to resolve disputed official calls in football were originally subjects of proposals.) Your proposal could seek to improve the safety of the game for participants, the way records are kept, the way athletes are recruited into the sport, the way athletes are treated, or the entertainment value of the game to spectators. You could focus on either a professional or amateur sport, a team sport or individual competition, high school or college teams, or the National Hockey League. You could address your proposal to players, officials, fans, or the general public.

GARY BECK
Not Your Everyday Homeless Proposal

> *Gary Beck has spent most of his adult life as a theater director and worked as an art dealer when he couldn't earn a living in the theater. He has also been a tennis pro, a ditch digger, and a salvage diver. His own plays and translations of Molière, Aristophanes, and Sophocles have been produced off Broadway and toured colleges and outdoor performance venues. Beck also writes fiction, and his short stories have appeared in numerous literary magazines. He currently lives in New York City.*
>
> *This essay, "Not Your Everyday Homeless Proposal," was first published in 2006 in* OUTCRY Magazine, *an online publication that describes itself as "the voice of the voiceless." Beck acknowledges that there are "no simple solutions" to the problem of homelessness and cites a pressing need for "innovative" solutions (paragraph 4). As you read, consider how innovative Beck's proposed solution is and how practical it would be to implement.*

Homelessness has become a persistent problem in urban environments and multiplies rapidly in the periods of economic downturn that follow cycles of prosperity. In New York City, for example, recognized by some as the homeless capital of the world, the dim economic forecast through at least the year 2007 makes it exceedingly improbable that there will be additional funds to alleviate the resurgent homeless situation. Families with children are entering the homeless system in record numbers that have surpassed even the dreadful surge of homelessness during the Koch administration in the 1980s.[1] Regardless of the reasons that homeless families enter the shelter system, they should be accorded the highest priority of attention, because children are the group most vulnerable to the pernicious effects of homelessness. There is a moral and constitutional duty to insure that homeless children, who are the victims rather than the cause of their family's plight, will have a chance for education, happiness and an opportunity to obtain a piece of the mythical American dream.

Too often in New York City there is an ongoing struggle between not-for-profit advocacy groups and the Department of Homeless Services, regarding issues related to intake, shelter and services for the homeless. Without the efforts of the non-government organizations the shelter system would be in even more dismal shape. Not every city has a staunch defender of the rights of the homeless like Justice Helen E. Freedman of the New

[1] Edward Koch was the mayor of New York City from 1978 to 1989.

York State Supreme Court. She has played a major role in shaping the city's policies for the homeless, with particular concern for the treatment of families with children. Despite all efforts by government and the private sector, the situation of the homeless remains perilous. Successive New York City administrations have continued to house homeless families in deteriorated and dangerous welfare hotels and motels, rife with drugs, prostitution and violence, that are the children's learning curricula in these unchartered crime academies.

Since it is an acknowledged fact that cities cannot afford to build a sufficiency of low-income housing with concomitant support services for the homeless, other options should be explored. A New York City proposal to house the homeless in an abandoned prison showed a typical government insensitivity to this population group. . . . it appeared that the government was going to put the homeless in jail. When the homeless problem became a major embarrassment to the Koch administration in the mid-eighties, homeless families were placed in decrepit midtown Manhattan hotels, where no tourists in their right minds would have conceived of spending even one night. These hotels could not previously rent rooms for $29.00 per night. Suddenly they were billing the city $100.00 per night. . . . The Bloomberg administration continues to house the homeless in tawdry hotels and motels at the cost of $3,500.00 to $4,500.00 per month, for rooms that most people would deem uninhabitable.[2] . . . It was beyond the capacity of the Giuliani administration to address the needs of the working poor.[3] Therefore, a convoluted mechanism to avoid the issue was contrived: emergency funds for temporary housing only, however extravagant the cost of the rentals. We are confronted with a peculiar dysfunction when the government pays upper-middle-class rental rates for accommodations below slum standards.

There are no simple solutions for this desperate situation that devours the futures of hundreds of youth annually. The real problem is society's lack of will to urgently address an issue that should have been resolved in the 19th century: cooperation between the government and the private sector to provide solutions for the problems of the needy. There is an overwhelming need to develop innovative plans that will concentrate efforts on alleviating the burdens of homelessness on the most fragile group, families with children. One possible plan would target economically depressed communities, using upstate New York as an example, that are struggling to remain solvent and functional. This could be a model

[2] Michael Bloomberg became mayor in 2002.

[3] Rudolph Giuliani was mayor from 1994 to 2001.

for other areas of the country. Depressed communities face a grim future, with little hope of the arrival of new industries that will replace lost blue collar and farm jobs. Certain qualifying communities could be offered a partnership with select pioneer homeless families, in a venture that could benefit both groups.

Appropriate towns that have an infrastructure of schools, transportation, medical services, grocery stores, laundromats and most important, a civic system capable of problem solving would be identified. They would be approached by designated personnel who would present a proposal that would demonstrate the economic benefits to the towns for providing residential sites and a supportive environment for designated homeless families. Abandoned property would be leased, reactivating the tax base for the towns. Renovation of the properties would stimulate local employment and generate earnings for businesses that sell construction materials and supplies. Support services for the families would develop new jobs that would infuse cash in the towns. Some jobs, after negotiations with the towns, would be reserved for the new residents. Living expenses of the families would directly contribute cash to the local economies.

Suitable families would be recruited for "small town pioneering" after a careful selection and preparation process. The first requirement would be functionality. The mentally ill homeless would not be an appropriate target group. But at least 25% to 30% of homeless families are functional, many having fallen into the system because of economic disaster like loss of job, or a fire that destroyed home or apartment, etc. The benefits of small town life would be presented as a positive alternative to the stress of urban shelters and poverty communities. The families would have to be prepared to adapt to a new and unaccustomed environment. The towns would also need preparation to receive a new population group as welcome neighbors. Job development for both town residents and the newcomer families would be a priority.

The small town pioneering program would start as a pilot project. Appropriate personnel would be assigned to contact potentially qualified towns. Ten towns would be chosen to house ten families each, for a total of one hundred families. Questionnaires should be developed in cooperation with NGOs[4] and the Departments of Homeless Services to identify qualified families, willing to undergo a major change in their way of life. Funds required for the initial phase of the project, outreach to the designated towns and families, are minimal. If funds are not available from the Department

5

6

7

---

[4] NGOs are nongovernmental organizations, or private nonprofit groups.

of Homeless Services, or other concerned government agencies, they would be solicited from private foundations. Once towns and families have been selected, project activities would commence simultaneously in the towns and the homeless shelters.

The towns should identify suitable residential space, preferably one- or two-family homes that have been underutilized or abandoned, that would then be renovated for habitation. Assisted living services would be identified and organized. Social workers, one per town, each to manage a caseload of ten families, would be recruited, with incentives offered to induce them to live in the community. Budgets for living expenses would be prepared. Training for the families in small town living skills would be followed by orientation tours of the intended communities. There would be introductions to the local residents: shopkeepers, teachers, town officials, neighbors, etc. The families and towns respectively should be prepared to fulfill their obligations to each other. The nearest colleges should be invited to participate in the project and provide educational services, as well as job or career training.

Funding for this demonstration program would be requested from the New York State legislature, various federal agencies, the New York City Department of Homeless Services, the office of the Mayor of New York City, private foundations and corporations. Small town pioneering should be developed as a model program that would be replicable, after an appropriate demonstration period. The relatively low start-up cost per family, as well as proportionately low operating costs, would be far less than the cost of housing a family in a temporary shelter. This would make it possible to run the program for far less than the cost to maintain a family in a shelter, which is approximately $45,000 annually for a family of three. The savings to the taxpayer would be considerable and the benefits to both towns and families would be immense.

Concerned officials, agencies and NGOs should consider this program as a possible amelioration to the problem of homelessness for a substantial number of families capable of rebuilding their future. This proposal is presented as only one possible solution to a major problem for which many new initiatives are needed. Other programs that could be explored might include: the development of co-operative apartment houses; an urban pioneering initiative utilizing abandoned buildings in poverty neighborhoods, for reclamation as housing stock; perhaps a more daring venture in commune/kibbutz experiments. Hopefully, these suggestions will stimulate consideration by those concerned with the future well-being of neglected members of our society, of the urgent need for new, practical solutions for the problems of homeless families with children.

READING FOR MEANING

This section presents three activities that will help you reread Beck's essay with a critical eye. Done in sequence, these activities lead you from a basic understanding of the selection to a more personal response to it and finally to an analysis that deepens your understanding and critical thinking about what you are reading.

Read to Comprehend

Reread the selection, and write a few sentences briefly explaining Beck's proposed solution. The following definitions may help you understand his vocabulary:

resurgent (paragraph 1): rising again.

pernicious (1): harmful, damaging.

concomitant (3): existing alongside and at the same time.

Identify three or more additional words that you don't understand, and find the best definitions from the dictionary that work with their context.

To expand your understanding of this reading, you might use one or more of the following critical reading strategies that are explained and illustrated in Appendix 1: *summarizing* and *questioning to understand and remember*.

Read to Respond

Write several paragraphs exploring your initial thoughts and feelings about Beck's proposal. Focus on anything that stands out for you, perhaps because it resonates with your own experience or because you find a statement puzzling.

You might consider writing about the following:

- the fact that New York City has paid to "house the homeless in tawdry hotels and motels at the cost of $3,500.00 to $4,500.00 per month, for rooms that most people would deem uninhabitable" (paragraph 3);

- the ways that the "pioneer homeless families" and residents of small towns might react to Beck's proposed solution or the ways that you might react if you were in their place (4); or

- your feelings, as a college student, about Beck's suggestion that local colleges "provide," presumably for free, "educational services, as well as job or career training" to the pioneer homeless families (8).

To develop your response to Beck's proposal, you might use one or more of the following critical reading strategies that are explained and illustrated in Appendix 1: *contextualizing* and *reflecting on challenges to your beliefs and values*.

Read to Analyze Assumptions

Reread Beck's proposal essay, and write a paragraph or two exploring one or more of the assumptions you find in the text. The following suggestions may help:

- **assumptions about society's responsibility.** In paragraph 1, Beck asserts that society has "a moral and constitutional duty to insure that homeless children . . . will have a chance for education, happiness and an opportunity to obtain a piece of the mythical American dream." To think critically about the assumptions in this essay related to society's responsibility to children, homeless or not, ask yourself: In referring to "a moral and constitutional duty," what does Beck assume is the basis for society's responsibility? Do you think that most Americans, and do you individually, agree that we share a *moral* as well as a *constitutional* responsibility? Why do you think Beck assumes the American dream is *mythical*?

- **assumptions about causes of homelessness.** In defining the problem of homelessness, Beck suggests that it is part of a larger issue: "the needs of the working poor" (3) and "the problems of the needy" (4). He also makes a distinction between "mentally ill" and "functional" homeless people (6) and points out that "at least 25% to 30% of homeless families are functional, many having fallen into the system because of economic disaster like loss of job, or a fire that destroyed home or apartment" (6). To think critically about the assumptions in this essay related to the causes of homelessness, ask yourself: Why do you think Beck makes this distinction and puts homelessness in a broader economic context? What does he seem to assume about the reasons people become homeless, and whom does he hold responsible? How does the knowledge that some homeless people have jobs affect Beck's—and possibly your own—attitude toward the homeless? Why do you think Beck does not bring up the other economic causes of homelessness, such as the lack of affordable health care or the many jobs that pay only minimum wage or less?

To probe assumptions more deeply, you might use one or both of the following critical reading strategies that are explained and illustrated in Appendix 1: *evaluating the logic of an argument* and *judging the writer's credibility*.

READING LIKE A WRITER
PRESENTING THE PROPOSED SOLUTION

In some cases, the solution can simply be named and briefly described, as Michael Pollan does in his proposal to return to local small farms and farmer's markets in place of the highly centralized, technological, and regulated system that aggravates rather than solves the problem of contaminated food. Unlike

Pollan, Beck cannot point to an example of his solution that has already been put into practice. Therefore, Beck calls his proposed solution "innovative" (paragraph 4) and sets out a detailed plan to show how it could be implemented. Explaining how the solution could be put into effect not only introduces the solution but also serves as part of the argument for it because if readers are not convinced that the solution is feasible, they are unlikely to consider it. The need to show how it could be implemented is especially crucial in Beck's case because his proposal is unusual and would require the enthusiastic cooperation of the homeless families who would be relocated, the government officials who would administer the program, the voters who would have to fund it, and the small-town residents and officials who would have to accommodate strangers into their communities. As you analyze Beck's proposal, you will see how he tries to convince all of these groups that his solution is workable and advantageous for everyone.

Analyze

1. *Reread* paragraphs 4 to 9, where Beck provides many details about how his "small town pioneering program" could be set up. *Annotate* the information he presents on how the solution could be implemented—how small towns would be chosen and convinced to participate, how homeless families would be chosen and prepared for small-town life, and how the program would be funded.

2. *Note in the margin* where Beck argues the advantages of his proposal, indicating which group he is addressing specifically—the homeless families, government officials, small-town residents. *Consider* how effective you think his arguments are likely to be for each of these groups.

Write

Write several sentences explaining how Beck presents the solution in paragraphs 4 to 9. *Include specific examples* from these paragraphs. Also briefly *evaluate* the success of Beck's presentation for each group of potential readers.

CONSIDERING IDEAS FOR YOUR OWN WRITING

Beck's topic suggests a type of proposal that you might want to consider for your essay—a proposal to improve the living or working conditions of one or more groups of people. You could focus on a particular category of people and a problem they face. For example, you might think of ways to help elderly and infirm people in your community who need transportation, or you might want to help elementary school kids who have no after-school music or sports programs. If you were to write about developing a job-training and referral program for your campus to help college students find work to pay for their education, you could begin by finding out what resources are already available on your campus and check the Internet to discover if other campuses provide any services that might be useful. You might also interview students as well as employers in the community to see whether a new campus job-referral service could be developed or an existing one could be improved.

KAREN KORNBLUH

Win-Win Flexibility

Karen Kornbluh earned a BA in economics and English and an MA from Harvard University's Kennedy School of Government. She worked in the private sector as an economist and management consultant and in the public sector as director of the office of legislative and intergovernmental affairs at the Federal Communications Commission before becoming the deputy chief of staff at the Treasury Department in the Clinton administration. Kornbluh serves currently as the policy director for Senator Barack Obama of Illinois.

As director of the Work and Family Program of the New America Foundation, a nonprofit, nonpartisan institute that sponsors research and conferences on public policy issues, Kornbluh led an effort to change the American workplace to accommodate what she calls the new "juggler family," in which parents have to juggle their time for parenting and work. Her book Running Harder to Stay in Place: The Growth of Family Work Hours and Incomes *was published in 2005 by the New America Foundation, and Kornbluh's articles have appeared in such venues as the* New York Times, *the* Washington Post, *and the* Atlantic Monthly. *The following proposal was published in 2005 by the Work and Family Program.*

As you read, think about your own experiences as a child or a parent and the ways that they affect your response to Kornbluh's proposal. Have you or your parents had to juggle time for parenting and work — and if so, how did you or they manage it?

INTRODUCTION

Today fully 70 percent of families with children are headed by two working parents or by an unmarried working parent. The "traditional family" of the breadwinner and homemaker has been replaced by the "juggler family," in which no one is home full-time. Two-parent families are working 10 more hours a week than in 1979 (Bernstein and Kornbluh).

To be decent parents, caregivers, and members of their communities, workers now need greater flexibility than they once did. Yet good part-time or flex-time jobs remain rare. Whereas companies have embraced flexibility in virtually every other aspect of their businesses (inventory control, production schedules, financing), full-time workers' schedules remain largely inflexible. Employers often demand workers be available around the clock. Moreover, many employees have no right to a minimum number of sick or vacation days; almost two-thirds of all workers — and an even larger percentage of low-income parents—lack the ability to take a day off to care for a family member (Lovell). The Family and Medical Leave Act (FMLA) of 1993 finally guaranteed that workers at large companies could take a leave of absence for the birth or adoption of a baby, or for the illness of a family member. Yet that guaranteed leave is unpaid.

Many businesses are finding ways to give their most valued   3
employees flexibility but, all too often, workers who need flexibility find themselves shunted into part-time, temporary, on-call, or contract jobs with reduced wages and career opportunities—and, often, no benefits. A full quarter of American workers are in these jobs. Only 15 percent of women and 12 percent of men in such jobs receive health insurance from their employers (Wenger). A number of European countries provide workers the right to a part-time schedule and all have enacted legislation to implement a European Union directive to prohibit discrimination against part-time workers.

In America, employers are required to accommodate the needs   4
of employees with disabilities—even if that means providing a part-time or flexible schedule. Employers may also provide religious accommodations for employees by offering a part-time or flexible schedule. At the same time, employers have no obligation to allow parents or employees caring for sick relatives to work part-time or flexible schedules, even if the cost to the employer would be inconsequential.

In the twenty-first-century global economy, America needs a new   5
approach that allows businesses to gain flexibility in staffing without sacrificing their competitiveness and enables workers to gain control over their work lives without sacrificing their economic security. This win-win flexibility arrangement will not be the same in every company, nor even for each employee working within the same organization. Each case will be different. But flexibility will not come for all employees without some education, prodding, and leadership. So employers and employees must be required to come to the table to work out a solution that benefits everyone. American businesses must be educated on strategies for giving employees flexibility without sacrificing productivity or morale. And businesses should be recognized and rewarded when they do so.

America is a nation that continually rises to the occasion. At the   6
dawn of a new century, we face many challenges. One of these is helping families to raise our next generation in an increasingly demanding global economy. This is a challenge America must meet with imagination and determination.

BACKGROUND: THE NEED FOR WORKPLACE FLEXIBILITY

Between 1970 and 2000, the percentage of mothers in the work-   7
force rose from 38 to 67 percent (Smolensky and Gootman).
Moreover, the number of hours worked by dual-income families
has increased dramatically. Couples with children worked a full 60
hours a week in 1979. By 2000 they were working 70 hours a week
(Bernstein and Kornbluh). And more parents than ever are working long hours. In 2000, nearly 1 out of every 8 couples with children was putting in 100 hours a week or more on the job, compared
to only 1 out of 12 families in 1970 (Jacobs and Gerson).

In addition to working parents, there are over 44.4 million   8
Americans who provide care to another adult, often an older relative. Fifty-nine percent of these caregivers either work or have
worked while providing care ("Caregiving").

In a 2002 report by the Families and Work Institute, 45 percent   9
of employees reported that work and family responsibilities inter-
fered with each other "a lot" or "some" and 67 percent of employed
parents report that they do not have enough time with their children (Galinksy, Bond, and Hill).

Over half of workers today have no control over scheduling   10
alternative start and end times at work (Galinksy, Bond, and Hill).
According to a recent study by the Institute for Women's Policy
Research, 49 percent of workers—over 59 million Americans—
lack basic paid sick days for themselves. And almost two-thirds of
all workers—and an even larger percentage of low-income parents—lack the ability to take a day off to care for a family member
(Lovell). Thirteen percent of non-poor workers with caregiving
responsibilities lack paid vacation leave, while 28 percent of poor
caregivers lack any paid vacation time (Heymann). Research has
shown that flexible arrangements and benefits tend to be more
accessible in larger and more profitable firms, and then to the most
valued professional and managerial workers in those firms
(Golden). Parents with young children and working welfare recipients—the workers who need access to paid leave the most—are
the least likely to have these benefits, according to research from
the Urban Institute (Ross Phillips).

In the U.S., only 5 percent of workers have access to a job that   11
provides paid parental leave. The Family and Medical Leave Act
grants the right to 12 weeks of unpaid leave for the birth or adoption of a child or for the serious illness of the worker or a worker's
family member. But the law does not apply to employees who work
in companies with fewer than 50 people, employees who have
worked for less than a year at their place of employment, or

employees who work fewer than 1,250 hours a year. Consequently, only 45 percent of parents working in the private sector are eligible to take even this unpaid time off (Smolensky and Gootman).

Workers often buy flexibility by sacrificing job security, benefits, and pay. Part-time workers are less likely to have employer-provided health insurance or pensions and their hourly wages are lower. One study in 2002 found that 43 percent of employed parents said that using flexibility would jeopardize their advancement (Galinksy, Bond, and Hill).

Children, in particular, pay a heavy price for workplace inflexibility (Waters Boots 2004). Almost 60 percent of child care arrangements are of poor or mediocre quality (Smolensky and Gootman). Children in low-income families are even less likely to be in good or excellent care settings. Full-day child care easily costs $4,000 to $10,000 per year — approaching the price of college tuition at a public university. As a result of the unaffordable and low-quality nature of child care in this country, a disturbing number of today's children are left home alone: Over 3.3 million children age 6–12 are home alone after school each day (Vandivere et al.).

Many enlightened businesses are showing the way forward to a twenty-first-century flexible workplace. Currently, however, businesses have little incentive to provide families with the flexibility they need. We need to level the playing field and remove the competitive disadvantages for all businesses that do provide workplace flexibility.

This should be a popular priority. A recent poll found that 77 percent of likely voters feel that it is difficult for families to earn enough and still have time to be with their families. Eighty-four percent of voters agree that children are being short-changed when their parents have to work long hours. . . .

PROPOSAL: WIN-WIN FLEXIBILITY

A win-win approach in the U.S. to flexibility . . . might function as follows. It would be "soft touch" at first — requiring a process and giving business an out if it would be costly to implement — with a high-profile public education campaign on the importance of workplace flexibility to American business, American families, and American society. A survey at the end of the second year would determine whether a stricter approach is needed.

Employees would have the right to make a formal request to their employers for flexibility in the number of hours worked, the times worked, and/or the ability to work from home. Examples of such flexibility would include part-time, annualized hours,[1] compressed hours,[2] flex-time,[3] job-sharing, shift working, staggered hours, and telecommuting.

The employee would be required to make a written application providing details on the change in work, the effect on the employer, and solutions to any problems caused to the employer. The employer would be required to meet with the employee and give the employee a decision on the request within two weeks, as well as provide an opportunity for an internal appeal within one month from the initial request.

18

The employee request would be granted unless the employer demonstrated it would require significant difficulty or expense entailing more than ordinary costs, decreased job efficiency, impairment of worker safety, infringement of other employees' rights, or conflict with another law or regulation.

19

The employer would be required to provide an employee working a flexible schedule with the same hourly pay and proportionate health, pension, vacation, holiday, and FMLA benefits that the employee received before working flexibly and would be required thereafter to advance the employee at the same rate as full-time employees.

20

Who would be covered: Parents (including parents, legal guardians, foster parents) and other caregivers at first. Eventually all workers should be eligible in our flexible, 24x7 economy. During the initial period, it will be necessary to define non-parental "caregivers." One proposal is to define them as immediate relatives or other caregivers of "certified care recipients" (defined as those whom a doctor certifies as having three or more limitations that impede daily functioning—using diagnostic criteria such as Activities of Daily Living (ADL)/Instrumental Activities of Daily Living (IADL)—for at least 180 consecutive days). . . .

21

Public Education: Critical to the success of the proposal will be public education along the lines of the education that the government and business schools conducted in the 1980s about the need for American business to adopt higher quality standards to com-

22

---

[1] *Annualized hours* means working different numbers of hours a week but a fixed annual total.

[2] *Compressed hours* means working more hours a day in exchange for working fewer days a week.

[3] *Flex-time* means working on an adjustable daily schedule.

pete against Japanese business. A Malcolm Baldridge-like award[4] should be created for companies that make flexibility win-win. A public education campaign conducted by the Department of Labor should encourage small businesses to adopt best practices of win-win flexibility. Tax credits could be used in the first year to reward early adopters.

Works Cited

Bernstein, Jared, and Karen Kornbluh. *Running Harder to Stay in Place: The Growth of Family Work Hours and Incomes.* Washington, DC: New America Foundation, 2005. Print.

Galinksy, Ellen, James Bond, and Jeffrey E. Hill. *Workplace Flexibility: What Is It? Who Has It? Who Wants It? Does It Make a Difference?* New York: Families and Work Institute, 2004. Print.

Golden, Lonnie. *The Time Bandit: What U.S. Workers Surrender to Get Greater Flexibility in Work Schedules.* Washington, DC: Economic Policy Institute, 2000. Print.

Heymann, Jody. *The Widening Gap: Why America's Working Families Are in Jeopardy — and What Can Be Done about It.* New York: Basic, 2000. Print.

Jacobs, Jerry, and Kathleen Gerson. *The Time Divide: Work, Family and Gender Inequality.* Cambridge, MA: Harvard UP, 2004. Print.

Lovell, Vicky. *No Time to Be Sick: Why Everyone Suffers When Workers Don't Have Paid Sick Leave.* Washington, DC: Institute for Women's Policy Research, 2004. Print.

The National Alliance for Caregiving and AARP. *Caregiving in the U.S.* Bethesda: NAC, 2004. National Alliance for Caregiving. Web. 20 May 2008.

Ross Phillips, Katherine. *Getting Time Off: Access to Leave Among Working Parents.* Assessing the New Federalism. Washington, DC: Urban Institute, April 2004. Print.

Smolensky, Eugene, and Jennifer A. Gootman, eds. *Working Families and Growing Kids: Caring for Children and Adolescents.* Washington, DC: The National Academies P, 2003. Print.

Vandivere, Sharon, et al. *Unsupervised Time: Family and Child Factors Associated with Self-Care.* Washington, DC, Urban Institute, Nov. 2003. Print. Assessing the New Federalism Occasional Paper No. 71.

Waters Boots, Shelley. *The Way We Work: How Children and Their Families Fare in a Twenty-first-Century Workplace.* Washington, DC: New America Foundation, 2004. Print.

Wenger, Jeffrey. *Share of Workers in "Nonstandard" Jobs Declines.* Washington, DC: Economic Policy Institute, 2003. Print.

[4] The Malcolm Baldridge National Quality Award is given by the U.S. president to outstanding businesses.

READING FOR MEANING

This section presents three activities that will help you reread Kornbluh's essay with a critical eye. Done in sequence, these activities lead you from a basic understanding of the selection to a more personal response to it and finally to an analysis that deepens your understanding and critical thinking about what you are reading.

Read to Comprehend

Reread the selection, and write a few sentences briefly explaining Kornbluh's proposed solution. The following definitions may help you understand her vocabulary:

shunted (paragraph 3): turned aside.

inconsequential (4): too small to have any effect.

morale (5): positive attitude.

Identify three or more additional words that you don't understand, and find the best definitions from the dictionary that work with their context.

To expand your understanding of this reading, you might use one or more of the following critical reading strategies that are explained and illustrated in Appendix 1: *summarizing* and *questioning to understand and remember*.

Read to Respond

Write several paragraphs exploring your initial thoughts and feelings about Kornbluh's proposal. Focus on anything that stands out for you, perhaps because it resonates with your own experience or because you find a statement puzzling.

You might consider writing about the following:

- Kornbluh's assertion that the "traditional family" of the breadwinner and homemaker has been replaced by the "'juggler family,' in which no one is home full-time" (paragraph 1);

- the fact that "[p]arents with young children and working welfare recipients—the workers who need access to paid leave the most—are the least likely to have" flexible arrangements at work (10);

- the idea that "[c]hildren, in particular, pay a heavy price for workplace inflexibility," perhaps related to your own experience as a child or a parent (13).

To develop your response to Kornbluh's proposal, you might use one or more of the following critical reading strategies that are explained and illustrated in Appendix 1: *contextualizing* and *reflecting on challenges to your beliefs and values*.

Read to Analyze Assumptions

Reread Kornbluh's proposal essay, and write a paragraph or two exploring one or more of the assumptions you find in the text. The following suggestions may help:

- **assumptions about childcare.** In paragraph 13, Kornbluh cites research that finds that "[a]lmost 60 percent of child care arrangements are of poor or mediocre quality." She concludes that "[a]s a result of the unaffordable and low-quality nature of child care in this country, a disturbing number of today's children are left home alone: Over 3.3 million children age 6–12 are home alone after school each day (Vandivere et al.)." Note that she seems to assume that readers will accept the research she cites and yet she gives us no information about the standards used to evaluate different child-care arrangements. To think critically about assumptions in this essay related to child care, ask yourself: What criteria would you apply? What assumptions do you make about the quality of different child-care arrangements—such as a relative's or a teenager's babysitting or various kinds of private or public day-care facilities? Kornbluh also assumes that being "home alone after school" is bad for children age six to twelve. At what age do you think that it is safe to leave children home alone? What age do other people you know (including, perhaps, your parents) consider appropriate?

- **assumptions about American business.** Kornbluh asserts that companies have been "largely inflexible" regarding "full-time workers' schedules" (2). But she seems to assume that if business were educated and prodded as well as "rewarded," companies would give "employees flexibility without sacrificing productivity or morale" (5). To think critically about the assumptions in this essay related to American business, ask yourself: Why do you think Kornbluh assumes companies would respond to government leadership, including education and prodding? Also, why would business need to be recognized and rewarded for doing something that does not sacrifice worker productivity or morale but actually might improve them?

To probe assumptions more deeply, you might use one or both of the following critical reading strategies that are explained and illustrated in Appendix 1: *looking for patterns of opposition* and *judging the writer's credibility*.

READING LIKE A WRITER
COUNTERARGUING READERS' OBJECTIONS AND ALTERNATIVE SOLUTIONS

Because proposal writers want their readers to accept their proposed solution and even to take action to help implement it, they must make an effort to anticipate objections to their argument as well as alternative solutions with which readers may be familiar. This task is a major part of what is known as *counterargument*. Kornbluh knows she faces tough opposition because changing the way businesses treat workers with family obligations calls for a significant change in thinking. Her proposal also involves money, and employers don't usually like to spend money on benefits for workers if they do not see how doing so would benefit their business. Kornbluh therefore devotes part of her proposal to counterargument. The following activity will guide you in analyzing her approach. It will also prepare you to anticipate and effectively counterargue readers' likely objections and popular alternative solutions in your own proposal.

Analyze

1. *Reread* paragraphs 2 to 3 and 10 to 12, *annotating* references to the alternative solutions that Kornbluh anticipates her readers could claim are already in place to solve the problem of the "juggler family." *Identify* these alternative solutions, and *make notes* about the way that Kornbluh counterargues.

2. *Reread* paragraph 21 where Kornbluh anticipates an objection to her proposal—that people (other than parents) could cheat by claiming to be caregivers. *Make notes* on how she handles this objection and whether her counterargument is likely to allay readers' concerns.

Write

Write several sentences explaining how Kornbluh anticipates and counterargues alternative solutions and objections. *Cite examples* from the reading. Then *add a few sentences* evaluating her counterarguments.

CONSIDERING IDEAS FOR YOUR OWN WRITING

Consider writing about a problem that seems to be national but might be solvable on a local scale for your community or college. For example, you might have your own ideas to add to Kornbluh's about how to solve the problem of getting adequate local child care for working parents. Or you might want to investigate whether local companies have policies about flex time for working parents. Other national problems are binge drinking and hazing in college fraternities or other social groups that sometimes lead to serious injury or even death. Perhaps you could propose a solution for groups in your college that are experiencing problems. Or you might consider the growing problem of lack of health insurance and how it affects children, thinking of proposals to ease the crisis in your local community that no one else has yet thought of. "Suburban sprawl" is another national issue that might be affecting your area; do some research on planned growth to see if you could make a proposal to solve this or a similar problem.

Proposing a Solution Online

Elayne Boosler is a writer, a comedian, and an activist, especially on behalf of the humane treatment of animals, for which she formed the rescue and advocacy organization Elayne Boosler's Tails of Joy. Her writing has appeared in newspapers and magazines such as the New York Times, *the* Los Angeles Times, Barron's, *and* Esquire. *She frequently posts tongue-in-cheek and serious commentaries on her own Web site <www.elayneboosler.com> as well as on* The Huffington Post *blog, where the following proposal, "When (and How) the Shooting Stops," first appeared in April 2007, shortly after Seung-Hui Cho's shooting rampage at Virginia Tech. Also included are six comments by readers of the blog. As you read, notice how Boosler combines her special brand of humor with serious argument.*

ELAYNE BOOSLER | BIO

When (And How) The Shooting Stops

49 Comments | Posted April 26, 2007 | 05:10 PM (EST)

Read More: Brian Williams, Jim Lehrer, Roger Ailes, Mark David Chapman, John Lennon, Hideki Irabu   ①

Murderer Seung-Hui Cho - 24,000,000 Google listings.

Email ▶   Murderer Mark David Chapman - 2,460,000 Google listings.   ②

Print ▶   Outlaw Jesse James - 16,600,000 Google listings.

Polio Vaccine Developer Dr. Jonas Salk - 491,000 Google listings.

All right, so there's a big part of our problem right there; the glorification of the criminal. Ever since Roger Ailes destroyed television news by merging it with the entertainment division, polluting the public's right to know by making the news subject to ratings and profits ("The World Will End At Ten P.M. Tonight!!! Details At 11"), we have had to live with the gratuitous, dramatic sludge ("Plastic Surgery For Dogs!") that is now the evening news (not you Jim Lehrer).   ③

STEP ONE IN SOLVING OUR PROBLEM: YOU DON'T "GOT A NAME"   ④

Why should Mark David Chapman get to be John Lennon's posterity buddy because in one sick second he destroyed fifty years of beauty and goodness? The Nazis knew how to erase people; give them a number. I propose NO MORE GLORY FOR MURDERERS. In the way

① These are links to other postings on *The Huffington Post* and other sites that deal with people that Boosler mentions.
② Beginning with this list arouses readers' curiosity.

③ Boosler *introduces the problem* in the opening sentence. Note that she claims to address only "part" of it.

④ The heading *presents her proposed solution,* which she then explains. Note that Boosler uses all capital letters to emphasize the main points and puts examples in parentheses; she even labels one of them *example.*

that felons lose the right to vote, murderers should lose their public identities, their NAMES. All we'll hear on the news that night is, Murderer X left a note saying he didn't like rich people. For record keeping purposes, the government can number the X's, starting anew each year (example: X-1, 2007, X-20, 2008). People planning killing sprees (and that murderer last week carefully planned his - They'll remember MY name!) need to know in advance that they will gain NO FAME by killing. They'll be just another X. No guy wants to be just a number, especially if another guy is going to have his number next year (think Hideki Irabu). As an added bonus it will publicly spare their innocent families and their ethnic groups shame and retaliation.

⑤   **IT WON'T WORK!**

⑥   It will work. It works already. Over forty thousand people a night (unless you're the Devil Rays) sit mere feet from the baseball players they love, hate, would like to hug, or slug. There are no fences keeping the fans away, and the games are televised. Why then, do the same guys who "Wooo!!!" and holler into any available camera, and who are often sloshed on beer, why do these people not constantly run onto the field and disrupt the games? One reason only; baseball does not show them on camera when they do. Hear that Brian Williams? It is not worth the arrest (and possible loose fist from a cop whose team you just disrupted while they were about to tie it up, unless you're the Devil Rays), to do something that no one is going to see or hear about. The news needs to stop covering the murderers who run onto the field.

And while we're on sports, stop making murder an Olympic event: "The biggest school shooting EVER! Thirty two, thirty three counting the gunman!" Do I hear thirty five?

BUT THE PUBLIC HAS A RIGHT TO KNOW! THEY PRINTED THE UNABOMBERS MANIFESTO AND IT HELPED CATCH HIM!

There's a big difference between putting a guys picture up at the post office, and putting it on the cover of *Entertainment Weekly*. Brian Williams: "It's newsworthy. We want the public to see inside the mind of a killer." Newsworthy? When a guy goes on a rampage because Liza can't work Vegas anymore, that will be news. Nothing new here.

⑦   **THE NRA HAS MADE FIVE GROUPS RICH: ITSELF. GUN MANUFACTURERS. SLEAZY POLITICIANS. MAKERS OF TEDDY BEARS. AND THE FLOWER INDUSTRY.**

Last weeks murderer should not have been allowed to have a gun under Virginia law (found to be a danger to himself) but the information never made it into a database because "there isn't enough money to put all of the already known names of people who should never be allowed to own a gun into a national database". Sorry, your child was

---

⑤ Boosler uses this heading and the next one to introduce her *counterarguments* refuting likely objections. What effect do the exclamation points have?

⑥ This *argument for the solution* is based on an analogy to the way disruptive baseball fans are handled. How well does the comparison hold up? In the next paragraph, analogies comparing murder to sports and media headlines to an auctioneer's call provide further support.

⑦ Boosler raises another part of the problem here—the easy availability of guns.

killed due to clerical backlog. The NRA, with its hundred million dollars, has the money to buy politicians and sway elections. While they claim to champion the public, they don't care enough about your children, or you, to use some of that money to insure the safe distribution of their product. And why should they? Their members are immune from prosecution, thanks to President Earp.

Comments

💬 3. OhioRuthie

I think you are right...I bet not giving them an identity would cut down on these glory killers.

You need your own show Elayne...this blog is great but I could see you with your own radio show. Hey now that Imus is out..they should hire you...a radio/tv show would be awesome.

You might have to go back to your natural nappy hair..a nappy headed girl taking his place would be sweet...notice I didn't say Ho..but hey if the money is right maybe you'd negotiateLOL

Seriously...awesome awesome blog...but waiting patiently for your radio show.
April 26, 2007 at 06:44pm PM EDT | ⚠ *Flag as abusive*

💬 14. peterg76

I like the idea in principle, but a murderer is innocent until proven guilty, and you can't take away their identity with anything less than a conviction in a court of law. By then the name is public knowledge.

But once it ceases to be news, the name does not need to come up again unless there is a public safety issue.

Now, if the media were to return to, you know, journalism, instead of vacuous sensationalism, that would help a lot.
April 26, 2007 at 11:37pm PM EDT | ⚠ *Flag as abusive*

💬 16. Transrational

Exactly right!
I've sad but true; it is easier to be infamous
than famous.
To be "famous" (in a non celebrity way) you must be very intelligent or work very hard. To be infamous all you have to do is pull a trigger.
(the more you pull it the more infamous you become)
Go figure....
April 26, 2007 at 11:50pm PM EDT | ⚠ *Flag as abusive*

⑧

💬 23. vurz

Thank you, Ms. Boosler;

Another thing we need to do is start using the proper language to describe murderers. I'm a bit of a true crime addict, mainly watch forensic shows because I find the advances in the field fascinating. I get very upset at the way they describe the killers though.

⑧ Note the typo "I've" for "It's." Errors are common on blogs.

Police are always 'hunting the dangerous predator' while he 'stalks his next victim' after "terrorizing the town" with his "monstrous crimes". The murderer always ends up sounding cool and powerful.

It would be much better to take control of the language. Say things like:

Police hunted the pathetic loser responsible for the crime. They wanted to catch them before the worthless tool hurt another person.

April 27, 2007 at 02:26am AM EDT | ▲ Flag as abusive

⑨

💬 **26. lenzorizzo**
John Lennon was only 40 when he was murdered.

ELAYNE RESPONDS:
Oh dear. Thanks.

April 27, 2007 at 04:35am AM EDT | ▲ Flag as abusive

💬 **32. anotherbozo**
Another bull's-eye, Ms Boozler! (Sorry. A poor choice of metaphor. But maybe I was referring to archery.)

You may be too good for HuffPo, but I will enjoy you while I can. (I always hated the cover + 2 drink minimum for live standup, and buying a NY Times just for the occasional good, witty column seems extravagant)

Here there's the satisfaction that someone is expressing what I couldn't nearly as well, and doing it with high entertainment value. "President Earp." "President Dillinger." "Albertoville." Love it.

P.S. Several apostrophes are missing from this post. I'll be your copy editor gratis. Email address on request.

ELAYNE RESPONDS:

⑩

Dang! I swear we're going to solve the gun problem before we solve the apostrophe problem. I NEVER get it right. No apostrophe to show possession? But then it looks wrong, sigh..

April 27, 2007 at 11:17am AM EDT | ▲ Flag as abusive

⑨ Boosler expresses her appreciation for a commenter's pointing out a factual error.

⑩ Boosler expresses her frustration in understanding when to use apostrophes.

Analyze

1. *Find* another example of an online proposal.

2. *Check* to see which of the typical proposal-writing strategies it displays, such as introducing the problem, presenting the proposed solution, arguing directly for the proposed solution, and counterarguing readers' objections, questions, and alternative solutions.

3. Also *note* any special online characteristics such as links, comments, and audio.

Write

Write a paragraph or two describing what you have learned from this example of online proposal writing.

A SPECIAL READING STRATEGY

Recognizing Emotional Manipulation

Proposals sometimes try to arouse emotion in readers to fuel their desire to solve the problem or to urge readers to take a particular action. Because of the conversational tone of blogging, writers tend to use more emotional language than they would in a more formal or academic proposal. Following the guidelines for recognizing emotional manipulation in Appendix 1, analyze Elayne Boosler's use of emotion in this proposal, and write a few sentences exploring what you have learned.

PATRICK O'MALLEY

More Testing, More Learning

> *Patrick O'Malley wrote the following proposal while he was a first-year college student. He proposes that college professors give students frequent brief examinations in addition to the usual midterm and final exams. After discussing his unusual rhetorical situation—a student advising teachers on how to plan their courses—with his instructor, O'Malley decided to revise the essay into the form of an open letter to professors on his campus, a letter that might appear in the campus newspaper.*
>
> *O'Malley's essay may strike you as unusually authoritative. This air of authority is due in large part to what O'Malley learned from interviewing two professors (his writing instructor and the writing program director) and several students in his classes. As you read, notice particularly how O'Malley responds to the objections to his proposal that he expects many professors to raise as well as their preferred solutions to the problem he identifies.*

It's late at night. The final's tomorrow. You got a C on the midterm, so this one will make or break you. Will it be like the midterm? Did you study enough? Did you study the right things? It's too late to drop the course. So what happens if you fail? No time to worry about that now—you've got a ton of notes to go over. 1

Although this last-minute anxiety about midterm and final exams is only too familiar to most college students, many professors may not realize how such major, infrequent, high-stakes exams work against the best interests of students both psychologically and intellectually. They cause unnecessary amounts of stress, placing too much importance on one or two days in the students' entire term and judging ability on a single or dual performance. They don't encourage frequent study, and they fail to inspire students' best performance. If professors gave additional brief exams at frequent intervals, students would learn more, study more regularly, worry less, and perform better on midterms, finals, and other papers and projects. 2

Ideally, a professor would give an in-class test or quiz after each unit, chapter, or focus of study, depending on the type of class and course material. A physics class might require a test on concepts after every chapter covered, while a history class could necessitate quizzes covering certain time periods or major events. These exams should be given weekly or at least twice monthly. Whenever possible, they should consist of two or three essay questions rather than many multiple-choice or short-answer questions. To preserve class time for lecture and discussion, exams should take no more than 15 or 20 minutes. 3

The main reason that professors should give frequent exams is   4
that when they do and when they provide feedback to students on
how well they are doing, students learn more in the course and
perform better on major exams, projects, and papers. It makes
sense that in a challenging course containing a great deal of material, students will learn more of it and put it to better use if they
have to apply or "practice" it frequently on exams, which also helps
them find out how much they are learning and what they need to
go over again. A recent Harvard study notes students' "strong preference for frequent evaluation in a course." Harvard students feel
they learn least in courses that have "only a midterm and a final
exam, with no other personal evaluation." They believe they learn
most in courses with "many opportunities to see how they are
doing" (Light, 1990, p. 32). In a review of a number of studies of
student learning, Frederiksen (1984) reports that students who
take weekly quizzes achieve higher scores on final exams than students who take only a midterm exam and that testing increases
retention of material tested.

Another, closely related argument in favor of multiple exams is   5
that they encourage students to improve their study habits. Greater
frequency in test taking means greater frequency in studying for
tests. Students prone to cramming will be required—or at least
strongly motivated—to open their textbooks and notebooks more
often, making them less likely to resort to long, kamikaze nights of
studying for major exams. Since there is so much to be learned in
the typical course, it makes sense that frequent, careful study and
review are highly beneficial. But students need motivation to study
regularly, and nothing works like an exam. If students had frequent
exams in all their courses, they would have to schedule study time
each week and gradually would develop a habit of frequent study.
It might be argued that students are adults who have to learn how
to manage their own lives, but learning history or physics is more
complicated than learning to drive a car or balance a checkbook.
Students need coaching and practice in learning. The right way to
learn new material needs to become a habit, and I believe that frequent exams are key to developing good habits of study and learning. The Harvard study concludes that "tying regular evaluations
to good course organization enables students to plan their work
more than a few days in advance. If quizzes and homework are
scheduled on specific days, students plan their work to capitalize
on them" (Light, 1990, p. 33).

By encouraging regular study habits, frequent exams would also   6
decrease anxiety by reducing the procrastination that produces
anxiety. Students would benefit psychologically if they were not
subjected to the emotional ups and downs caused by major exams,

when after being virtually worry-free for weeks they are suddenly ready to check into the psychiatric ward. Researchers at the University of Vermont found a strong relationship among procrastination, anxiety, and achievement. Students who regularly put off studying for exams had continuing high anxiety and lower grades than students who procrastinated less. The researchers found that even "low" procrastinators did not study regularly and recommended that professors give frequent assignments and exams to reduce procrastination and increase achievement (Rothblum, Solomon, & Murakami, 1986, pp. 393, 394).

Research supports my proposed solution to the problems I have described. Common sense as well as my experience and that of many of my friends support it. Why, then, do so few professors give frequent brief exams? Some believe that such exams take up too much of the limited class time available to cover the material in the course. Most courses meet 150 minutes a week—three times a week for 50 minutes each time. A 20-minute weekly exam might take 30 minutes to administer, and that is one-fifth of each week's class time. From the student's perspective, however, this time is well spent. Better learning and greater confidence about the course seem a good trade-off for another 30 minutes of lecture. Moreover, time lost to lecturing or discussion could easily be made up in students' learning on their own through careful regular study for the weekly exams. If weekly exams still seem too time-consuming to some professors, their frequency could be reduced to every other week or their length to 5 or 10 minutes. In courses where multiple-choice exams are appropriate, several questions could be designed to take only a few minutes to answer.

Another objection professors have to frequent exams is that they take too much time to read and grade. In a 20-minute essay exam, a well-prepared student can easily write two pages. A relatively small class of 30 students might then produce 60 pages, no small amount of material to read each week. A large class of 100 or more students would produce an insurmountable pile of material. There are a number of responses to this objection. Again, professors could give exams every other week or make them very short. Instead of reading them closely they could skim them quickly to see whether students understand an idea or can apply it to an unfamiliar problem; and instead of numerical or letter grades they could give a plus, check, or minus. Exams could be collected and responded to only every third or fourth week. Professors who have readers or teaching assistants could rely on them to grade or check exams. And the Scantron machine is always available for instant grading of multiple-choice exams. Finally, frequent exams could be given *in place of* a midterm exam or out-of-class essay assignment.

Since frequent exams seem to some professors to create many problems, however, it is reasonable to consider alternative ways to achieve the same goals. One alternative solution is to implement a program that would improve study skills. While such a program might teach students to study for exams, it cannot prevent procrastination or reduce "large test anxiety" by a substantial amount. One research team studying anxiety and test performance found that study skills training was "not effective in reducing anxiety or improving performance" (Dendato & Diener, 1986, p. 134). This team, which also reviewed other research that reached the same conclusion, did find that a combination of "cognitive/relaxation therapy" and study skills training was effective. This possible solution seems complicated, however, not to mention time-consuming and expensive. It seems much easier and more effective to change the cause of the bad habit than treat the habit itself. That is, it would make more sense to solve the problem at its root: the method of learning and evaluation.

Still another solution might be to provide frequent study questions for students to answer. These would no doubt be helpful in focusing students' time studying, but students would probably not actually write out the answers unless they were required to. To get students to complete the questions in a timely way, professors would have to collect and check the answers. In that case, however, they might as well devote the time to grading an exam. Even if it asks the same questions, a scheduled exam is preferable to a set of study questions because it takes far less time to write in class, compared to the time students would devote to responding to questions at home. In-class exams also ensure that each student produces his or her own work.

Another possible solution would be to help students prepare for midterm and final exams by providing sets of questions from which the exam questions will be selected or announcing possible exam topics at the beginning of the course. This solution would have the advantage of reducing students' anxiety about learning every fact in the textbook, and it would clarify the course goals, but it would not motivate students to study carefully each new unit, concept, or text chapter in the course. I see this as a way of complementing frequent exams, not as substituting for them.

From the evidence and from my talks with professors and students, I see frequent, brief in-class exams as the only way to improve students' study habits and learning, reduce their anxiety and procrastination, and increase their satisfaction with college.

These exams are not a panacea, but only more parking spaces and a winning football team would do as much to improve college life. Professors can't do much about parking or football, but they can give more frequent exams. Campus administrators should get behind this effort, and professors should get together to consider giving exams more frequently. It would make a difference.

References

Dendato, K. M., & Diener, D. (1986). Effectiveness of cognitive/relaxation therapy and study-skills training in reducing self-reported anxiety and improving the academic performance of test-anxious students. *Journal of Counseling Psychology, 33*, 131–135.

Frederiksen, N. (1984). The real test bias: Influences of testing on teaching and learning. *American Psychologist, 39*, 193–202.

Light, R. J. (1990). *Explorations with students and faculty about teaching, learning, and student life.* Cambridge, MA: Harvard University Graduate School of Education and Kennedy School of Government.

Rothblum, E. D., Solomon, L., & Murakami, J. (1986). Affective, cognitive, and behavioral differences between high and low procrastinators. *Journal of Counseling Psychology, 33*, 387–394.

READING FOR MEANING

This section presents three activities that will help you reread O'Malley's proposal with a critical eye. Done in sequence, these activities lead you from a basic understanding of the selection to a more personal response to it and finally to an analysis that deepens your understanding and critical thinking about what you are reading.

Read to Comprehend

Reread the selection, and write a few sentences briefly explaining the problem O'Malley sees and the solution he proposes. Then list the alternative solutions that O'Malley counterargues. The following definitions may help you understand his vocabulary:

retention (paragraph 4): remembering.

kamikaze (5): reckless or suicidal.

cognitive (9): using mental processes of reasoning and judgment.

Identify three or more additional words that you don't understand, and find the best definitions from the dictionary that work with their context.

To expand your understanding of this reading, you might use one or more of the following critical reading strategies that are explained and illustrated in Appendix 1: *annotating* and *contextualizing*.

Read to Respond

Write several paragraphs exploring your initial thoughts and feelings about "More Testing, More Learning." Focus on anything that stands out for you, perhaps because it resonates with your own experience or because you find a statement puzzling.

You might consider writing about the following:

- whether O'Malley's proposal, if it were adopted by professors, would make a difference in your own study habits or address any problems that you have with studying;

- the relation O'Malley attempts to establish between high-pressure exams and poor performance (paragraph 2), testing it against your own experience; or

- kinds of classes, in your experience, that are and are not suited to frequent brief exams.

To develop your response to O'Malley's proposal, you might use one or both of the following critical reading strategies that are explained and illustrated in Appendix 1: *looking for patterns of opposition* and *judging the writer's credibility*.

Read to Analyze Assumptions

Reread O'Malley's proposal essay, and write a paragraph or two exploring one or more of the assumptions you find in the text. The following suggestions may help:

- **assumptions about motivation and procrastination.** In paragraph 5, O'Malley argues that college students would be "strongly motivated . . . to open their textbooks and notebooks more often" if they had to take exams frequently. He explains that the assumption underlying this argument is that "students need motivation to study regularly." In the next paragraph, however, he reviews research on procrastination that "found that even 'low' procrastinators did not study regularly." To think critically about the assumptions in this essay related to motivation and procrastination, ask yourself: What seems to be the relationship, if any, between motivation and procrastination? If even students categorized as "low" procrastinators "did not study regularly," does it make sense to assume, as O'Malley does, that frequent tests would motivate most students to do so? Given your own experiences and observations of other students, what would be likely to motivate most students and overcome their tendency to procrastinate?

- **assumptions about "the right way to learn."** O'Malley claims, "Students need coaching and practice in learning. The right way to learn new material needs to become a habit" (paragraph 5). He seems to assume that studying regularly is "the right way to learn" and that cramming the night before the exam is the wrong way. To think critically about the assumptions in this essay related to "the right way to learn," ask yourself: Why does O'Malley assume that cramming is inferior to studying regularly? In your experiences and observations of other students, to what extent, if any, does cramming result in poorer performance on exams? If students studied regularly, wouldn't they need to cram the night before the exam anyway to remind themselves of what they had studied days and weeks earlier? Is there a single "right way" for everyone, a single way that works for all subjects and for every occasion?

To probe assumptions more deeply, you might use one or both of the following critical reading strategies that are explained and illustrated in Appendix 1: *reflecting on challenges to your beliefs and values* and *using a Toulmin analysis*.

READING LIKE A WRITER
ARGUING DIRECTLY FOR THE PROPOSED SOLUTION

Arguing directly for the proposed solution, like counterarguing readers' likely questions and alternative solutions, is especially important in proposals. Writers argue directly for a proposed solution by explaining the reasons it should be implemented and then supporting those reasons with evidence or examples. Many types of support are available — personal experience, assertions, research, reviews of research, quotes from authorities, effects or consequences, benefits, contrasts, analogies, and causes. O'Malley makes use of all of these types of support.

Analyze

1. *Skim* paragraphs 4 to 6. In each paragraph, *underline* the sentence that announces the reason for the solution.

2. *Note in the margin* the kinds of support O'Malley relies on. *Categorize* all of his support.

3. *Evaluate* how effectively O'Malley argues to support his solution. Do the reasons seem plausible? Is one reason more convincing to you than the others? How believable do you find the support?

Write

Write several sentences explaining what you have learned about O'Malley's attempt to convince readers to take his proposed solution seriously. *Give examples* from the reading. Then *add a few sentences* evaluating how convincing you find his argument. Which parts do you find most convincing? Least convincing? *Explain* your choices.

CONSIDERING IDEAS FOR
YOUR OWN WRITING

Much of what happens in high school and college is predictable and conventional. Examples of conventional practices that have changed very little over the years are exams, classroom lectures, graduation ceremonies, required courses, and lower admission requirements for athletes. Think of additional examples of established practices in high school or college. Then select one that you believe needs to be improved or refined in some way. What changes would you propose? What individual or group might be convinced to take action on your proposal for improvement? What questions or objections should you anticipate? How could you discover whether others have previously proposed improvements in the practice you are concerned with? Whom might you interview to learn more about the practice and the likelihood of changing it?

A SPECIAL READING STRATEGY

Comparing and Contrasting Related Readings:
O'Malley's and Varley's Proposals to Improve Education

Comparing and contrasting related readings is a critical-reading strategy that is useful both in reading for meaning and in reading like a writer. This strategy is particularly applicable when writers present similar subjects, as is the case in the essays by Patrick O'Malley (p. 488) and Jeff Varley (p. 496). These writers have identified problems that affect the quality of education at the high-school and college levels. To compare and contrast these two proposals, think about issues such as these:

- Compare how the two writers describe the problems they are trying to solve. Highlight the places in each essay where the problem is presented. What strategies—such as narrating an anecdote, presenting a scenario, citing statistics, and quoting authorities—does each of the writers use to help readers understand the problem and appreciate its significance?

- Compare how the two writers support their proposed solutions and how they counterargue objections or questions that readers might raise as well as alternative solutions that readers might prefer. How effectively do you think each writer addresses readers' likely concerns?

See Appendix 1 for detailed guidelines on using the comparing and contrasting related readings strategy.

JEFF VARLEY

High-School Starting Time

Jeff Varley wrote this essay for a first-year college composition course. As you read, think about your own experiences waking up early to attend class. How well do you think that Varley supports his proposed solution?

The other readings in this chapter are followed by reading and writing activities. Following this reading, however, you are on your own to decide how to read for meaning and read like a writer.

Varley's ironic statement and realistic scenario catch readers' attention.

Ah, sweet memories of high school: waking up at 6:30 in the morning, stumbling into the bathroom to get ready for the day, dressing while still half asleep, munching a piece of toast while listening to our parents tell us that if we just went to bed earlier we wouldn't be so sleepy in the morning (or worse, listening to our parents call us lazy), catching the bus as the sun began to top the trees, and wandering into our first period classes merely to lay our head down on our desks to doze off for the next fifty-five minutes.

We never could seem to catch up on our sleep, especially during the week. And even if we followed our parents' advice and tried going to bed earlier, the earlier bed time did not make much, if any, difference in how awake we were the next morning. In fact, for those of us who tried going to bed earlier, we generally just lay there until 10:30 or 11:00 before finally going to sleep. The next school morning we were still as tired as when we had gone to bed later.

To lend authority to his introduction of the problem, Varley cites research findings.

But recent studies have provided evidence that the sleep patterns for adolescents are significantly different from those of both young children and adults. Studies by Mary Carskadon, a professor of psychiatry and human behavior at the Brown University School of Medicine and Director of Sleep and Chronobiology Research at E. P. Bradley Hospital in East Providence, Rhode Island, on sleep patterns in people revealed that adolescents, as opposed to younger children or adults, actually function better when they go to bed later and awake later. Professor Carskadon's research demonstrates that most adolescents' biological clocks are naturally set to a different pattern than the clocks of most children and adults.

4   The timing of the need for sleep also shows biological changes as children reach puberty. Melatonin, a hormone produced in the pineal gland, is an indicator for the biological clock that influences wake/sleep cycles. Carefully controlled studies found that "more mature adolescents had a later timing of the termination of melatonin secretion" (Carskadon 351). This indicates that postpubescent teens have a biological need to sleep later in the morning. The impact of forcing people to try to be alert when every nerve in their body is begging for more sleep can only be negative. This discovery has a major impact on high-school students who are required to awaken early in order to arrive at school early, for asking teens to learn a complex subject, such as math, science, or English, before the brain is awake is futile.

Note the use of MLA parenthetical citation keyed to the Works Cited list at the end of the essay.

5   Tardiness, poor grades, depression, automobile accidents, after-school-on-the-job accidents, and general lethargy have all been identified as the consequences of insufficient sleep among high-school students. Yet school districts persist in retaining high-school starting times that begin early in the morning, usually around 7:30 a.m. But such an early starting time does not benefit the students for whom the educational system is supposedly structured. How do we resolve the conflict of early high-school starting times versus sleepy students?

Varley lists the negative effects to emphasize the problem's seriousness.

6   One obvious solution would be to start high-school classes later in the morning. A later starting time for high schools can be a controversial proposal if all of the affected parties are not consulted and kept informed. Kyla Wahlstrom of the Center for Applied Research and Educational Improvement at the University of Minnesota pointed out that "changing a school's starting time provokes the same kind of emotional reaction from stakeholders as closing a school or changing a school's attendance area" (Wahlstrom 346). Presumably, if parents and other interested parties knew about Carskadon's research, they would be more willing to consider changing the start time for high school.

This rhetorical question makes a transition to his presentation of the solution. Note that he immediately anticipates objections and counterargues them.

7   Some schools have recognized the benefits of later starting time and have implemented a new schedule. One such school is located in eastern Minnesota. In

Varley *argues for his solution* by referring to a place where it has been successfully implemented. In paragraphs 7 and 8, he cites more research showing its positive effects.

1996 the Edina School District pushed back the start time for 1,400 high-school students from 7:25 to 8:30 a.m. Edina Public School District Superintendent Kenneth Dragseth reported that the later schedule has led to better grades, fewer behavioral problems, and a better-rested student body (Dragseth). Dragseth's anecdotal evidence that better-rested students perform better is supported by research performed by psychologists at the College of the Holy Cross in Worcester, Massachusetts. Working with Carskadon, the psychologists "surveyed more than 3,120 Providence [Rhode Island] area high-school students and found students who got A's and B's averaged about 35 minutes more sleep on both weeknights and weekends than students who received D's and F's" (Bettelheim 557).

In addition to better grades, other positive effects 8 cited by researchers include better attendance, fewer tardies, far fewer students falling asleep at their desks, more alert students more engaged in the learning process, less depression, fewer problems at home and among friends, enhanced school atmosphere, and fewer illnesses (Lawton; Wahlstrom and Taylor). With so many benefits to starting high-school classes later, why haven't more districts done so?

He *anticipates a likely concern of readers and counterargues* by suggesting ways of handling it.

One of the most common concerns comes from 9 participants in extracurricular activities. If practices currently often run until 8 or 9 p.m. with a school day that begins at 7:30 a.m., what will happen if school starts an hour later? This is a legitimate concern that would need to be addressed on a team-by-team or group-by-group basis. Some practice sessions could be held immediately after class in the early afternoon. Some activities could convene after a short dinner break. If these activities began earlier in the evening, they could be finished sooner in the evening. The one factor every coach or sponsor would have to consider is how important any extracurricular activity is in relation to the primary mission of the school, which, of course, is learning and education, not sports or clubs.

Availability of buses is another concern for many 10 school districts when any discussion of changing schedules begins. School officials in Montgomery

County, Maryland, estimate it would cost $31 million to buy enough buses to accommodate later start times for high school without inconveniencing elementary and middle-school students (Bettelheim 557). Minneapolis, which buses 90 percent of the 50,000 students in the school district, solved the transportation problems caused by starting high-school classes later by starting the grade school classes earlier (Lawton). This has the added benefits of bringing younger children to school at a time when many of them are most alert and decreasing the need for before-school child care for these students (Reiss; Lawton). With careful planning and scheduling, the transportation tribulations can be addressed in cost-effective ways.

He *counterargues* another concern by showing how it is handled in one school district.

11   As the world we live in becomes ever more complex, education becomes ever more important. It is important that the time spent on education be spent as effectively as possible. It is time to look at school schedules that provide the best education at times that are most appropriate to the students. James Maas, a psychologist at Cornell University, points out that "people are beginning to realize it doesn't make sense to pay heavy school taxes when the audience you're teaching is asleep" (qtd. in Bettelheim 556).

Varley concludes by stressing why solving the problem is "important" not just to students but to society in general.

Works Cited

Bettelheim, Adriel. "Sleep Deprivation." *CQ Researcher* 8 (1998): 555–62. Print.

Carskadon, Mary A. "When Worlds Collide: Adolescent Need for Sleep Versus Societal Demands." *Phi Delta Kappan* 80.5 (1999): 348–53. Print.

Dragseth, Kenneth A. "A Minneapolis Suburb Reaps Early Benefits from a Late Start." *School Administrator* 56.3 (Mar. 1999): n. pag. *General OneFile*. Web. 22 Mar. 2003.

Lawton, Millicent. "For Whom the School Bell Tolls." *School Administrator* 56.3 (Mar. 1999): 6+. *General OneFile*. Web. 22 Mar. 2003.

Reiss, Tammy. "Wake-up Call on Kids' Biological Clocks." *NEA Today* 6.6 (1998): 19. Print.

Wahlstrom, Kyla L. "The Prickly Politics of School Starting Times." *Phi Delta Kappan* 80.5 (1999): 345–47. Print.

Wahlstrom, Kyla L. "Sleep Research Warns: Don't Start High School without the Kids." *Education Digest* 66.1 (2000): 15–20. *MasterFILE Premier*. Web. 22 Mar. 2003.

The Works Cited list follows MLA style.

READING FOR MEANING

Reading for meaning involves three activities:

- reading to comprehend,
- reading to respond, and
- reading to analyze assumptions.

Reread Varley's essay, and then write a page or so explaining your under-standing of its basic meaning or main point, a personal response you have to it, and what you see as one of its assumptions.

READING LIKE A WRITER

Writers of proposals

- introduce the problem,
- present the solution,
- argue directly for the proposed solution, and
- counterargue readers' objections, questions, and alternative solutions.

Focus on one of these strategies in Varley's essay, and analyze it carefully through close rereading and annotating. Then write several sentences explaining what you have learned about the strategy, giving specific examples from the read-ing to support your explanation. Add a few sentences evaluating how successfully Varley uses the strategy to construct a persuasive argument.

REVIEWING WHAT MAKES PROPOSALS EFFECTIVE

In this chapter, you have been learning how to read proposals for meaning and how to read them like a writer. Before going on to write a proposal of your own, pause here to review and contemplate what you have learned about the elements of effective proposal writing.

Analyze
Choose one reading from this chapter that seems to you especially effective. Before rereading the selection, *jot down* one or two reasons you remember it as an example of good proposal writing.
Reread your chosen selection, adding further annotations about what makes it a particularly successful example of proposal writing. *Consider* the selection's purpose and how well it achieves that purpose for its intended readers. (You can make an informed guess about the

intended readers and their expectations by noting the publication source of the essay.) Then *focus* on how well the essay

- introduces the problem,

- presents the solution,

- argues directly for the proposed solution, and

- counterargues readers' objections, questions, and alternative solutions.

You can review all of these basic features in the Guide to Reading Proposals (p. 445).

Your instructor may ask you to complete this activity on your own or to work with a small group of other students who have chosen the same reading. If you work with others, allow enough time initially for all group members to reread the selection thoughtfully and to add their annotations. Then *discuss* as a group what makes the essay effective. *Take notes* on your discussion. One student in your group should then report to the class what the group has learned about the effectiveness of proposal writing. If you are working individually, write up what you have learned from your analysis.

Write

Write at least a page explaining your choice of this reading as an example of effective proposal writing. *Assume* that your readers—your instructor and classmates—have read the selection but will not remember many details about it. They also may not remember it as especially successful. Therefore, you will need to *refer* to details and specific parts of the reading as you explain how it works and as you justify your evaluation of its effectiveness. You need not argue that it is the best essay in the chapter or that it is flawless, only that it is, in your view, a strong example of the genre.

■ A Guide to Writing Proposals

The readings in this chapter have helped you learn a great deal about proposal writing. A proposal has two basic features—the problem and the solution. Now that you have seen how writers establish that the problem exists and is serious, offer a detailed analysis of the problem, attempt to convince readers to accept the solution offered, and demonstrate how the proposed solution can be implemented, you can approach this type of writing confidently. Using these strategies will help you develop a convincing proposal of your own.

This Guide to Writing is designed to assist you in writing your essay. Here you will find activities to help you identify a subject and discover what to say about it, organize your ideas and draft the essay, read the draft critically, revise the draft to strengthen your argument, and edit and proofread the essay to improve readability.

INVENTION AND RESEARCH

Invention is a process of discovery and planning by which you generate something to say. The following activities will help you choose a problem for study, analyze the problem and identify a solution, consider your readers, develop an argument for your proposed solution, and research your proposal. A few minutes spent completing each writing activity will improve your chances of producing a detailed and convincing first draft.

Choosing a Problem

Begin the selection process by reviewing what you wrote for the Considering Ideas for Your Own Writing activities following the readings in this chapter. Then try listing several groups or organizations to which you currently belong—for instance, a neighborhood or town, film society, dormitory, sports team, biology class. For each group, list as many problems facing it as you can. If you cannot think of any problems for a particular organization, consult with other members. Reflect on your list of problems, and choose the one for which you would most like to find a solution. It can be a problem that everyone already knows about or one about which only you are aware.

Proposing to solve a problem in a group or community to which you belong gives you an important advantage: you can write as an expert, an insider. You know about the history of the problem, have felt the urgency to solve it, and perhaps have already thought of possible solutions. Equally important, you know precisely where to send the proposal and who would most benefit from it. You have the access needed to interview others in the group, who can contribute different, even dissenting viewpoints about the problem and solution. You are in a position of knowledge and authority—from which comes confident, convincing writing. If you choose a problem that affects a wider group, concentrate on one with which you have direct experience and for which you can suggest a detailed plan of action.

Developing Your Proposal

The writing and research activities that follow will enable you to test your problem and proposal and develop an argument that your readers will take seriously.

Analyzing the Problem. Write a few sentences in response to each of these questions:

- Does the problem really exist? How can you tell?
- What caused this problem? Consider immediate and deeper causes.
- What is the history of the problem?
- What are the negative consequences of the problem?
- Who in the community or group is affected by the problem?
- Does anyone benefit from the existence of the problem?

Considering Your Readers. *With your understanding of the problem in mind, write for a few minutes about your intended readers.* Will you be writing to all members of your group or to only some of them? To an outside committee that might supervise or evaluate the group or to an individual in a position of authority inside or outside the group? Briefly justify your choice of readers. Then gauge how much they already know about the problem and what solutions they might prefer. Consider the problem's direct or indirect impact on them. Comment on what values and attitudes you share with your readers and how they have responded to similar problems in the past.

Finding a Tentative Solution. *List at least three possible solutions to the problem.* Think about solutions that have already been tried as well as solutions that have been proposed for related problems. Find, if you can, solutions that eliminate causes of the problem. Also consider solutions that reduce the symptoms of the problem. If the problem seems too complex to be solved all at once, list solutions for one or more parts of the problem. Maybe a series of solutions is required and a key solution should be proposed first. From your list, choose the solution that seems to you most timely and practicable and write two or three sentences describing it.

Anticipating Readers' Objections. *Write a few sentences defending your solution against each of the following predictable objections* (listed on the next page). For your proposal to succeed, readers must be convinced to take the solution seriously. Try to imagine how your prospective readers will respond.

- It won't really solve the problem.

- I'm comfortable with things as they are.

- We can't afford it.

- It will take too long.

- People won't do it.

- Too few people will benefit.

- I don't see how to get started on your solution.

- It's already been tried, with unsatisfactory results.

- You're making this proposal because it will benefit you personally.

Counterarguing Alternative Solutions. *Identify two or three likely solutions to the problem that your readers may prefer, solutions different from your own.* Choose the one that poses the most serious challenge to your solution. Then write a few sentences comparing your solution with the alternative solution, weighing the strengths and weaknesses of each. Explain how you might demonstrate to readers that your solution has more advantages and fewer disadvantages than the alternative solution.

RESEARCHING YOUR SUBJECT ONLINE

Searching the Web can be a productive way of learning about solutions other people have proposed or tried out. Here are some specific suggestions for finding information about solutions:

- Enter keywords—words or brief phrases related to the problem or a solution—into a search tool such as Google <www.google.com> or Yahoo! <www.yahoo.com>. For example, if you are concerned that many children in your neighborhood have no adult supervision after school, you could try keywords associated with the problem such as *latchkey kids* or keywords associated with possible solutions such as *after-school programs*.

- If you think solutions to your problem may have been proposed by a government agency, you could try adding the word *government* to your keywords or searching on <FirstGov.gov>, the U.S. government's official Web portal. For example, you might explore the problem of latchkey children by following links at the Web site of the U.S. Department of Health and Human Services <www.hhs.gov>. If you want to see whether the problem has been addressed by your state or local government, you can go to the Library of Congress Internet Resource Page on State and Local Governments <www.loc.gov/global/state> and follow the links.

Bookmark or keep a record of promising sites. You may want to download or copy information you could use in your essay, including visuals; if so, remember to record documentation information.

Supporting Your Solution. *Write down every plausible reason your solution should be heard or tried.* Then review your list and highlight the strongest reasons, the ones most likely to persuade your readers. Write for a few minutes about the single most convincing reason for your solution. Support this reason in any way you can. You want to build an argument that readers will take seriously.

Researching Your Proposal. *Try out your proposal on members of the group, or go to the library to research a larger social or political problem.* If you are writing about a problem affecting a group to which you belong, talk with other members of the group to learn more about their understanding of the problem. Try out your solution on one or two people; their objections and questions will help you counterargue and support your argument more successfully.

If you are writing about a larger social or political problem, you should do research to confirm what you remember and to learn more about the problem. You can probably locate all the information you need in a good research library or on the Internet; you could also interview an expert on the problem. Readers will not take you seriously unless you are well informed.

Formulating a Working Thesis. *Draft a working thesis statement.* A working thesis helps you begin drafting your essay purposefully. The thesis statement in a proposal is simply a statement of the solution you propose. Keep in mind that you may need to revise your working thesis as you learn more about your subject and as you draft your essay.

Review the readings in this chapter to see how other writers construct their thesis statements. For example, recall that Patrick O'Malley states his thesis in paragraph 2:

> If professors gave additional brief exams at frequent intervals, students would learn more, study more regularly, worry less, and perform better on midterms, finals, and other papers and projects.

O'Malley's thesis announces his solution — brief, frequent exams — to the problems that students experience in courses where testing is limited to anxiety-producing, high-stakes midterms and finals. The thesis lists the reasons that students will benefit from the solution in the order in which the benefits appear in the essay. A forecast is not a requirement of a thesis statement, but it does enable readers to predict the stages of the argument and thereby increases their understanding.

As you draft your own thesis statement, pay attention to the language you use. It should be clear and unambiguous, emphatic but appropriately qualified. Although you will probably refine your thesis statement as you draft and revise your essay, trying now to articulate it will help give your planning and drafting direction and impetus.

Considering Visuals. *Consider whether visuals — drawings, photographs, tables, or graphs — would strengthen your proposal.* You could construct your own visuals, scan materials from books and magazines, or download them from the Internet. If you submit your essay electronically to other students and your instructor or if you post it on a Web site, consider including photographs as well as snippets of film or sound. Visual and auditory materials are not at all a requirement of a successful proposal, as you can tell from the readings in this chapter, but they could add a new dimension to your writing. If you want to use photographs or recordings of people, though, be sure to obtain their permission.

DRAFTING

The following guidelines will help you set goals for your draft, plan its organization, and consider a useful sentence strategy for it.

Setting Goals

Establishing goals for your draft before you begin writing will enable you to make decisions and work more confidently. Consider the following questions now, and keep them in mind as you draft. They will help you set goals for drafting as well as recall how the writers you have read in this chapter tried to achieve similar goals.

- *How can I introduce the problem in a way that interests my readers and convinces them that it needs to be solved?* Do I have to convince my readers that the problem is not as simple as it appears to be, as Pollan does, or that there really is a problem, as Kornbluh does? Can I demonstrate that the problem exists with examples, as Shughart, Boosler, O'Malley, and Varley do, or with statistics, as Kornbluh does? Should I cite research to stress the problem's importance, as Kornbluh, O'Malley, and Varley do?

- *How should I present my proposed solution?* Should I describe in detail how the solution might be implemented, as do Kornbluh and Beck? Or need I describe the solution only briefly, as the other writers do, letting other interested parties work out the details and take action?

- *How can I argue convincingly for my proposed solution?* Should I give examples of my solution that have proven successful, as Pollan does? Describe the benefits of my solution, as Varley, Beck, and O'Malley do? Offer statistics, like Kornbluh, or refer to research, like Varley, O'Malley, and Kornbluh?

- *How should I counterargue readers' objections?* Should I refute readers' likely objections to the argument for my solution, as O'Malley and Pollan do? Should I attempt to answer readers' concerns, as Varley does? Should I accommodate objections by modifying my proposal, as O'Malley does?

- *How should I counterargue alternative solutions?* Can I argue that they are too expensive and time-consuming, as O'Malley does; that they will not really solve the problem, as Kornbluh does; or that they make the problem worse, as Pollan does? In rejecting these other solutions, should I criticize their proponents, as Beck and Boosler do; simply provide my reasons, as O'Malley does; or marshal statistics, as Kornbluh does?

Organizing Your Draft

With goals in mind and invention notes at hand, you are ready to make a first outline of your draft. The basic parts are quite simple — the problem, the solution, and the reasons in support of the solution. This simple plan is nearly always complicated by other factors, however. In outlining your material, you must take into consideration many other details, such as whether readers already recognize the problem, how much agreement exists on the need to solve the problem, how much attention should be given to alternative solutions, and how many objections and questions by readers should be expected.

Your outline should reflect your own writing situation. You should not hesitate to change this outline after you start drafting. For example, you might discover a more convincing way to order the reasons for adopting your proposal, or you might realize that counterargument must play a larger role than you first imagined. The purpose of an outline is to identify the basic features of your proposal, not to lock you in to a particular structure.

WORKING WITH SOURCES

Citing Statistics to Establish the Problem's Existence and Seriousness

Statistics can be helpful in establishing that the problem exists and is serious. For example, Patrick O'Malley cites research to support his assertion that students prefer frequent exams to fewer high-stakes exams: "A recent Harvard study notes students' 'strong preference for frequent evaluation in a course'" (paragraph 4). But his argument would have been stronger and possibly more convincing if he had cited statistics to support the study's conclusion. Karen Kornbluh, in contrast, bombards readers with statistics. Let us look at some of the ways that Kornbluh uses statistics to define the problem.

The success of Kornbluh's proposal depends on her ability to persuade readers that the problem really exists and that it is serious and widespread enough to require a solution. Therefore, she cites statistics to demonstrate that the "juggler family," as she calls it, has taken the place of the "traditional family" that had a homemaker capable of taking care of children and dependent parents:

> Today fully 70 percent of families with children are headed by two working parents or by an unmarried working parent. The "traditional family" of the breadwinner and homemaker has been replaced by the "juggler family," in which no one is home full-time. (paragraph 1)

Kornbluh begins with an impressive statistic: "fully 70 percent of families with children." But how many people is this? She does not answer this question with a number, but at other points in the essay Kornbluh does provide the raw numbers along with the statistics. Here are a couple of examples:

> In addition to working parents, there are over 44.4 million Americans who provide care to another adult, often an older relative. Fifty-nine percent of these caregivers either work or have worked while providing care ("Caregiving"). (paragraph 8)

> Over half of workers today have no control over scheduling alternative start and end times at work (Galinksy, Bond, and Hill). According to a recent study by the Institute for Women's Policy Research, 49 percent of workers—over 59 million Americans—lack basic paid sick days for themselves. (paragraph 10)

Because of the raw numbers, readers can see at a glance that the percentages that Kornbluh cites are truly significant: 59 percent of 44.4 million people have worked while providing care to another adult, and 59 million people lack paid sick leave. Her use of statistics here is especially convincing because of the large numbers of people affected by the problem. Note that Kornbluh spells out some of the numbers she provides and uses numerals for others, depending on whether the number begins a sentence.

Kornbluh also compares different time periods to show that the problem has worsened over the last thirty years. Here are several examples from paragraph 7. Note that Kornbluh represents statistics in three different ways—percentages, numbers, and proportions:

Between 1970 and 2000, the percentage of mothers in the workforce rose from 38 to 67 percent (Smolensky and Gootman). Moreover, the number of hours worked by dual-income families has increased dramatically. Couples with children worked a full 60 hours a week in 1979. By 2000 they were working 70 hours a week (Bernstein and Kornbluh). And more parents than ever are working long hours. In 2000, nearly 1 out of every 8 couples with children was putting in 100 hours a week or more on the job, compared to only 1 out of 12 families in 1970 (Jacobs and Gerson).

To establish that there is a widespread perception among working parents that the problem is serious, Kornbluh cites survey results:

> In a 2002 report by the Families and Work Institute, 45 percent of employees reported that work and family responsibilities interfered with each other "a lot" or "some" and 67 percent of employed parents report that they do not have enough time with their children (Galinksy, Bond, and Hill).

This example, from paragraph 9, shows that a large percentage, nearly half of all employees surveyed, are aware of interference between work and family responsibilities. The actual amount of interference is vague, however, because "some" and "a lot" may mean different things to different survey respondents. Nevertheless, the readers that Kornbluh is addressing—employers—are likely to find this statistic important because it suggests that their employees are spending work time worrying about family instead of focusing on work.

For statistics to be considered credible, they must be from sources that readers consider reliable. Readers need to know who did the study so they can determine whether its researchers can be trusted. Researchers' trustworthiness depends, in turn, on their credentials as experts in the field they are investigating and also on the degree to which they are disinterested, or free from bias.

Kornbluh provides a Works Cited list of sources that readers can check to determine whether the sources are indeed reliable. Some of her sources are books published by major publishers (Harvard University Press and Basic Books, for example), which helps establish their credibility. Other sources she cites are research institutes (such as New America Foundation, Economic Policy Institute, and Families and Work Institute) that readers can easily check on the Internet. Another factor that adds to the appearance of reliability at least is that Kornbluh cites statistics from a range of sources instead of relying on only one or two sources. Moreover, the statistics are current and clearly relevant to her argument.

Considering a Useful Sentence Strategy

As you draft your essay proposing a solution to a problem, you will want to connect with your readers. You will also want readers to become concerned with the seriousness of the problem and thoughtful about the challenge of solving it. Sentences that take the form of rhetorical questions can help you achieve these goals. A *rhetorical question* is conventionally defined as a sentence posing a question that the writer does not expect the reader to answer. (In most cases, a reader could not possibly answer it.) In proposals, however, rhetorical questions do important rhetorical work—that is, they assist writers in realizing a particular purpose and they influence readers in certain ways. In particular, you can use rhetorical questions to engage and orient your readers, introduce and emphasize parts of your argument, and appeal readers' emotions.

O'Malley, for example, begins his proposal with a series of rhetorical questions designed to engage readers:

> Will it be like the midterm? Did you study enough? Did you study the right things? It's too late to drop the course. So what happens if you fail? (O'Malley, paragraph 1)

O'Malley uses these rhetorical questions to dramatize the plight of students studying for a high-risk exam to put his primary readers—professors who are capable of implementing his solution—in a receptive frame of mind.

Other writers in this chapter use different kinds of rhetorical questions for various purposes:

- to make a transition from establishing the problem to presenting the solution:

    If so, why stop at half-measures? (Shughart, paragraph 3)

    How do we resolve the conflict of early high-school starting times versus sleepy students? (Varley, paragraph 5)

- to provide transitions to other aspects of the proposal:

    Who would be covered (Kornbluh, paragraph 21)

    Why, then, do so few professors give frequent brief exams? (O'Malley, paragraph 7)

    With so many benefits to starting high-school classes later, why haven't more districts done so? (Varley, paragraph 8)

    If practices currently often run until 8 or 9 p.m. with a school day that begins at 7:30 a.m., what will happen if school starts an hour later? (Varley, paragraph 9)

Kornbluh puts her question in italics but she replaces the question mark with a colon to indicate that what follows is the answer. Thus, her rhetorical question functions as a heading introducing an important part of the argument: who would be affected by the solution? O'Malley and Varley use their rhetorical questions as transitions to counterarguing readers' likely concerns about and objections to their proposed solutions.

- to emphasize particular points in the argument:

  So what happens to the spinach grower at my farmers' market when the F.D.A. starts demanding a HACCP plan—daily testing of the irrigation water, say, or some newfangled veggie-irradiation technology? When we start requiring that all farms be federally inspected? (Pollan, paragraph 12)

  Why should academic credit be given for practicing the violin, but not for practicing a three-point shot? (Shughart, paragraph 5)

  Why should Mark David Chapman get to be John Lennon's posterity buddy because in one sick second he destroyed fifty years of beauty and goodness? (Boosler, paragraph 2)

  Why then, do the same guys who "Wooo!!!" and holler into any available camera, and who are often sloshed on beer, why do these people not constantly run onto the field and disrupt the games? (Boosler, paragraph 3)

  Hear that Brian Williams? (Boosler, paragraph 3)

  Do I hear thirty five? (Boosler, paragraph 4)

This last rhetorical question shows how writers sometimes use rhetorical questions not only to introduce or emphasize a point but also to appeal to readers' emotions. Boosler's rhetorical questions fit well in the conversational atmosphere of blogging, where emotion, often in the form of sarcasm and righteous indignation, is commonly used by writers to get a reaction from readers. Because rhetorical questions appeal directly to readers, they tend to be used sparingly in academic writing and by professional writers. It is interesting to note that the writers in this chapter who use a lot of them—O'Malley uses five (most of which are bunched together in the opening paragraph), Boosler four, and Varley three—are students and a blogger. Even though rhetorical questions are useful, they are not a requirement for a successful proposal and should be used only for a specific purpose. They should not be overused because readers may find them annoying and unnecessary.

READING A DRAFT CRITICALLY

Getting a critical reading of your draft will help you see how to improve it. Your instructor may schedule class time for reading drafts, or you may want to ask a classmate or a tutor in the writing center to read your draft. Ask your reader to use the following guidelines and to write out a response for you to consult during your revision.

Read for a First Impression

1. Read the draft without stopping to annotate or comment, and then write two or three sentences giving your general impression.

2. Identify one aspect of the draft that seems to you particularly effective.

Read Again to Suggest Improvements

1. Recommend ways to present the problem more effectively.

   - Locate places in the draft where the problem is defined and described. Point to places where you believe the intended readers will need more explanation or where the presentation seems unclear or confusing.

   - Consider whether readers might want to know more about the causes or effects of the problem. Suggest ways the writer might do more to establish the seriousness of the problem, creating a sense of urgency to gain readers' support and to excite their curiosity about solutions.

2. Suggest ways to present the solution more effectively.

   - Find the solution, and notice whether it is immediately clear and readable. Point to places where it could be made clearer and more readable.

   - Advise the writer whether it would help to lay out steps for implementation.

   - Tell the writer how to make the solution seem more practical, workable, and cost-effective.

3. Recommend ways to strengthen the argument for the solution.

   - List the reasons the writer gives for adopting the solution or considering it seriously. Point out the reasons most and least likely to be convincing. Let the writer know whether there are too many or too few reasons. If the reasons are not sequenced in a logical, step-by-step order, suggest a new order.

   - Evaluate the support for each reason. Point out any passages where the support seems insufficient, and recommend further kinds of support.

4. Suggest ways to extend and improve the counterargument.

   - Locate places where the writer anticipates readers' objections to and questions about the proposal. Keeping in mind that the writer can accommodate or refute each objection or question, evaluate how successfully the writer does so. Recommend ways to make the response to each question or objection more convincing.

   - Suggest any likely objections and questions the writer has overlooked.

- Identify any alternative solutions the writer mentions. Give advice on how the writer can present these alternative solutions more clearly and responsibly, and suggest ways to accommodate or refute them more convincingly.

5. Suggest how the organization might be improved.

- Consider the overall plan, perhaps by making a scratch outline (see Appendix 1 for advice on scratch outlining). Decide whether the reasons and counterarguments follow a logical, step-by-step sequence. Suggest a more logical sequence, if necessary.

- Indicate where new or better transitions might help identify steps in the argument and keep readers on track.

6. Evaluate the effectiveness of visuals.

- Look at any visuals in the essay, and tell the writer what they contribute to your understanding of the writer's argument.

- If any visuals do not seem relevant, or if there seem to be too many visuals, identify the ones that the writer could consider dropping, explaining your thinking.

- If a visual does not seem to be appropriately placed, suggest a better place for it.

REVISING

This section offers suggestions for revising your draft. Revising means reenvisioning your draft, trying to see it in a new way, given your purpose and readers, in order to develop a convincing proposal.

The biggest mistake you can make while revising is to focus initially on words or sentences. Instead, first try to see your draft as a whole in order to assess its likely impact on readers. Think imaginatively and boldly about cutting unconvincing material, adding new material, and moving material around to improve readability and strengthen your argument. Your computer makes even drastic revisions physically easy, but you still need to make the mental effort and decisions that will improve your draft.

You may have received help with this challenge from a classmate or tutor who gave your draft a critical reading. If so, keep this valuable feedback in mind as you decide which parts of your draft need revising and what specific changes you could make. The following suggestions will help you solve problems and strengthen your essay.

To Introduce the Problem More Effectively

- If readers are unfamiliar with the problem or doubt that it exists, briefly address its history or describe it in some detail to make its impact seem real.

- If readers know about the problem but believe it is insignificant, argue for its seriousness, perhaps by dramatizing its current and long-term effects or by adding a dramatic rhetorical question. Or speculate about the complications that might arise in the future if the problem is not solved.

To Present the Solution More Effectively

- If readers cannot see how to implement your proposed solution, outline the steps of its implementation. Lead them through it chronologically, perhaps with the help of rhetorical questions. Demonstrate that the first step is easy to take; or, if it is unavoidably challenging, propose ways to ease the difficulty.

- If a solution is beyond your expertise, explain where the experts can be found and how they can be put to use.

- If all readers can readily imagine how the solution would be implemented and how it would look once in place, reduce the amount of space you give to presenting the solution.

To Strengthen the Argument for the Proposed Solution

- If you have not given adequate reasons for proposing the solution, give more reasons.

- If your reasons are hidden among other material, move them to the foreground. Consider announcing them explicitly at the beginnings of paragraphs (the first reason why, the second, the third; the main reason why; the chief reason for; and so on).

- If your argument seems unconvincing, support your reasoning and argument with examples, anecdotes, statistics, quotes from authorities or members of the group, or any other appropriate support.

To Strengthen the Counterarguments

- If you have not anticipated all of your readers' weighty objections and questions, do so now. (You may want to use a rhetorical question or two for this purpose.) Consider carefully whether you can accommodate some objections by either granting their wisdom or adapting your solution in response to them. If you refute objections or dismiss questions, do so in a spirit of continuing collaboration with members of your group; there is no need to be adversarial. You want readers to support your solution and perhaps even to join with you in implementing it.

- If you have neglected to mention alternative solutions that are popular with readers, do so now. (You may want to use a rhetorical question or two for this purpose.) You may accommodate or reject these alternatives, or — a compromise—incorporate some of their better points. If you must reject all aspects of an alternative, do so through reasoned argument, without questioning the character or intelligence of those who prefer the alternative. You may be able to convince some of them that your solution is the better one.

To Organize More Logically and Coherently

- If your argument lacks logical progression, reorganize the reasons supporting your proposed solution.

- If your various counterarguments are not smoothly integrated into your argument, try another sequence or add better transitions.

- If your critical reader had trouble following the logical progression of your proposal, consider adding one or two rhetorical questions to forecast your plan of argument or introduce parts of it.

EDITING AND PROOFREADING

After you have revised the essay, be sure to spend some time checking for errors in usage, punctuation, and mechanics and considering matters of style. If you keep a list of errors you typically make, begin by checking your draft against this list. Ask someone else to proofread your essay before you print out a copy for your instructor or send it electronically.

From our research on student writing, we know that proposal writers tend to refer to the problem or solution by using the pronoun *this* or *that* ambiguously. Edit carefully any sentences with *this* or *that* to ensure that a noun immediately follows the pronoun to make the reference clear. Check a writer's handbook for help with avoiding ambiguous pronoun reference.

REFLECTING ON WHAT YOU HAVE LEARNED

Proposal to Solve a Problem

In this chapter, you have read critically several proposals and have written one of your own. To better remember what you have learned, pause now to reflect on the reading and writing activities you completed in this chapter.

1. *Write* a page or so reflecting on what you have learned. *Begin* by describing what you are most pleased with in your essay. Then *explain* what you think contributed to your achievement. *Be specific* about this contribution.

- If it was something you learned from the readings, *indicate* which readings and specifically what you learned from them.

- If it came from your invention writing, *point out* the section or sections that helped you most.

- If you got good advice from a critical reader, *explain* exactly how the person helped you—perhaps by helping you understand a particular problem in your draft or by adding a new dimension to your writing.

- *Try to write* about your achievement in terms of what you have learned about the genre.

2. Now *reflect* more generally on proposals, a genre of writing that plays an important role in our society. *Consider* some of the following questions: How confident do you feel about making a proposal that might lead to improvements in the functioning of an entire group or community? Does your proposal attempt fundamental or minor change in the group? How necessary is your proposed change in the scheme of things? Whose interest would be served by the solution you propose? Who else might be affected? In what ways does your proposal challenge the status quo in the group? What contribution might essays proposing solutions to problems make to our society that other genres of writing cannot make?

Position Paper

You may associate arguing with quarreling or with the in-your-face debating we often hear on radio and television talk shows. These ways of arguing may let us vent strong feelings, but they seldom lead us to consider seriously other points of view, let alone to look critically at our own thinking or learn anything new.

This chapter presents a more deliberative way of arguing that we call *reasoned argument* because it depends on giving reasons rather than raising voices. It demands that positions be supported rather than merely asserted. It also commands respect for the right of others to disagree with you as you may disagree with them. Reasoned argument requires more thought than quarreling but no less passion or commitment, as you will see when you read the position papers in this chapter.

Controversial issues are, by definition, issues about which people have strong feelings and sometimes disagree vehemently. The issue may involve a practice that has been accepted for some time, such as coeducational public schooling, or it may concern a newly proposed policy or recently controversial issue, such as whether biofuels will solve our energy crisis. People may agree about goals but disagree about the best way to achieve them, as in the perennial debate over how to guarantee adequate health care for all citizens. Or they may disagree about fundamental values and beliefs, as in the debate over affirmative action in college admissions.

As these examples suggest, position papers take on controversial issues that have no obvious "right" answer, no truth everyone accepts, no single authority everyone trusts. Consequently, simply gathering information — finding the facts or learning from experts — will not settle these disputes because ultimately they are matters of opinion and judgment.

Although it is not possible to prove that a position on a controversial issue is right or wrong, it is possible through argument to convince others to consider a particular position seriously or to accept or reject a position. To be convincing, a position paper must argue for its position by giving readers strong reasons and solid support. It also must anticipate opposing arguments.

As you read and discuss the selections in this chapter, you will discover why position papers play such an important role in college, the workplace, and civic life. You will also learn how position papers work. From the essays and from the ideas for writing that follow each selection, you will get many ideas for taking a position on an issue that you care about. As you read and write about the selections, keep in mind the following assignment, which sets out the goals for writing a position paper. The Guide to Writing Position Papers, which follows the readings, supports your writing of this assignment.

THE WRITING ASSIGNMENT

Arguing a Position on an Issue

Choose an issue that you have strong feelings about, and write an essay arguing your position on this issue. Your purpose is to convince your readers to take your argument seriously. Therefore, you will need to acknowledge readers' opposing views as well as any objections or questions they might have.

WRITING SITUATIONS FOR POSITION PAPERS

Writing that takes a position on a controversial issue plays a significant role in college work and professional life, as the following examples indicate:

- A committee made up of business and community leaders investigates the issue of regulating urban growth. After reviewing the arguments for and against government regulation, committee members argue against it on the grounds that supply and demand alone will regulate development, that landowners should be permitted to sell their property to the highest bidder, and that developers are guided by the needs of the market and thus serve the people.

- For a sociology class, a student writes a term paper on surrogate mothering. She first learns about the subject from television news, but she knows that she needs more information to write a paper on the topic. In the library, she finds several newspaper and magazine articles that help her understand better the debate over the issue. In her paper, she presents the strongest arguments on each side but concludes that, from a sociological perspective, surrogate mothering should not be allowed because it exploits poor women by creating a class of professional breeders.

- For a political science class, a student is assigned to write an essay on public employees' right to strike. Having no well-defined position herself, she discusses the issue with her mother, a nurse in a county hospital, and her uncle, a firefighter. Her mother believes that public employees like hospital workers and teachers should have the right to strike but that police officers and firefighters should not because public safety would be endangered. The uncle disagrees, arguing that allowing hospital workers to strike would jeopardize public safety as much as allowing firefighters to strike. He insists that the central issue is not public safety but individual rights. In her essay, the student supports the right of public employees to strike, but she argues that the timing of a strike should be arbitrated whenever a strike might jeopardize public safety.

THINKING ABOUT YOUR EXPERIENCE WITH POSITION ARGUMENTS

Before studying a type of writing, it is useful to spend some time thinking about what you already know about it. You may have discussed with friends or family your position on a controversial issue, trying to help them see why you think the way you do. You also may have written essays for classes examining the positions of experts in fields where controversial issues abound, such as in science, social science, business, education, and even your writing class. People in all fields, ranging from medicine and government to corporations and small businesses, deal with controversial issues every day and take positions based on their knowledge at the time.

To analyze your experience with position arguments, you might recall a time when you argued orally or in writing about a controversial issue that captured your interest. What did you already know about the issue when you took your position? What was at stake for you? What prompted your original interest in the issue, and what made you care strongly enough about it to take a position to begin with? Who was your audience for your argument? What did you hope to achieve by taking your position? What made you think it was significant? Did you need to present the issue in detail, or was your audience already familiar with it?

Consider also the position arguments you have read, heard, or seen in the media. If you recall someone's argument in detail, try to identify what made it interesting and memorable. Was it the issue itself, or did the person's position seem powerful and well supported? How did the person make the argument convincing? Were there illuminating details or unusual points of view?

Write at least a page about your experiences with position arguments.

■ A Guide to Reading Position Papers

This guide introduces you to essays that take a position on controversial issues. By completing all the activities in it, you will prepare yourself to learn a great deal from the other readings in this chapter about how to read and write a position paper. The guide focuses on a forceful argument by Vinod Khosla in favor of developing biofuels—especially ethanol—to address our energy crisis and dependence on oil. You will read Khosla's essay twice. First, you will read it for meaning, seeking to understand and respond to Khosla's argument. Then you will read the essay like a writer, analyzing the parts to see how Khosla crafts his essay and to learn the strategies he uses to make his argument convincing. These two activities—reading for meaning and reading like a writer—follow every reading in this chapter.

VINOD KHOSLA

My Big Biofuels Bet

Vinod Khosla (b. 1955), a native of Poona, India, received his bachelor of technology degree in electrical engineering from the Indian Institute of Technology, an MS in biomedical engineering from Carnegie Mellon University, and an MBA from Stanford Graduate School of Business. A cofounder of Sun Microsystems, he also founded Daisy Systems and Khosla Ventures (www.khoslaventures.com), a venture-capital firm.

Khosla has written a three-part series of papers on ethanol and related "biohol" fuels. He also gave a presentation on alternative fuels to the United States Senate Committee on Foreign Relations in 2006 and was featured in the August 2006 issue of Bloomberg Markets, *a venture-capital magazine. In the article below, published in* Wired *magazine in 2006, Khosla argues that by developing ethanol and taking other steps to convert plant matter into engine-running fuel, the United States could almost eliminate its dependence on oil.*

Before you read this essay, think about what you've heard or read about U.S. dependence on oil. Do you or does anyone you know use alternative fuels, such as solar or wind power? Think about why the dependence of the United States on foreign oil is problematic. Think also about all the things you have that use electricity. Do you know where your electricity comes from? As you read, think about the strategies that Khosla uses to persuade readers that his position argument about the possibilities for biofuels is valid. The marginal annotations point to strategies that writers of position essays typically use. Add your own comments and questions, noting anything else you think is interesting.

It may surprise you to learn that the most promising solution to our nation's energy crisis begins in the bowels of a waste trough, under the slotted concrete floor of a giant pen that holds 28,000 Angus, Hereford, and Charolais beef cattle. But for some time now, I've been searching for a renewable fuel that could realistically replace the 140 billion gallons of gasoline consumed in the U.S. each year. And now I believe the key to producing this fuel starts with cow manure—because this waste powers a facility that turns corn into ethanol.

2   I'm standing on a grassy hill in the middle of an 880-acre commercial feedlot just outside Mead, Nebraska, which is a long way from my home turf of clean labs and wood-paneled conference rooms in Silicon Valley. In front of me are four open-air cattle sheds. Each is the width of a giant barn and a full half-mile in length. From up here, they look more like jumbo-jet landing strips than animal pens. Beyond the sheds are several hundred acres of cornfields, from which much of the animals' feed is harvested.

3   It may look like a typical, if huge, cattle feedlot—but for the glittering white four-story structure below that resembles the Centre Pompidou in Paris. Indeed, until recently this operation just off Mead's County Road 10 was not unlike any other finishing ground for Nebraska's beef cattle: a last stop before the abattoir. But starting in November, Oscar Mayer will no longer be the marquee product here. A company called E3 Biofuels is about to fire up the most energy-efficient corn ethanol facility in the country: a $75 million state-of-the-art biorefinery and feedlot capable of producing 25 million gallons of ethanol a year. What's more, it will run on methane gas produced from cow manure. The super-efficient operation capitalizes on a closed loop of resources available here on the prairie—cattle (fed on corn), manure (from the cows), and corn (fed into the ethanol distiller). The output: a potential gusher of renewable, energy-efficient transportation fuel.

4   Of course, 25 million gallons of ethanol is a drop in the tanker when it comes to our 140 billion-a-year oil habit. And ethanol itself is a subject of controversy for all sorts of reasons. Many of the criticisms, while true in some small ways, are aggressively promoted by the oil lobby and other interested parties in an effort to forestall change. Most are myths. Challenges certainly exist with ethanol, but none are insurmountable, and—with apologies to Al Gore—the convenient truth is that corn ethanol is a crucial first step toward kicking our oil addiction. I believe we can replace most of our gasoline needs in 25 years with biomass from our

Khosla grabs the reader with a surprising opening: cow manure could solve our energy crisis.

He provides context and *establishes his credibility* by pointing out that he is a scientist accustomed to working in the computer capital of the world. Also, he's willing to travel for his science.

He *anticipates likely objections* to his claim but refutes them by saying that oil companies are the main objectors.

He *asserts a clear, unequivocal position* about the usefulness of biofuels.

farmlands and municipal waste, while creating a huge economic boom cycle and a cheaper, cleaner fuel for consumers.

Which is why this Mead, Nebraska, farm is so excit- 5 ing to me: The ethanol made here is not only clean but also cheap—this is perhaps the first ethanol plant to achieve both. More important, it is an early demonstration of the great potential of biohols—liquid fuels derived from biomass for internal combustion engines. The facility is the first data point in what I call the biohol trajectory. (See "March of the Biohols.") Like Moore's law, this trajectory tracks a steady increase in performance, affordability, and, importantly, yield per acre of farmland. A number of biohols appear along this performance curve, among them corn ethanol, cellulosic ethanol, higher-energy-content butanol, and other biomass-derived fuels that are even more energy-rich than butanol. We'll see fuels with higher energy density and better environmental characteristics, and we'll develop engines better optimized for biohols. Ethanol and the newer fuels will yield better fuel efficiency as innovations like higher compression-ratio engines make their way into vehicles. In addition, we can count on the emergence of complementary technologies like cheaper hybrid vehicles, better batteries, plug-in hybrids, and more efficient, lighter-weight cars.

Khosla defines important terms—"biohols" and "biohol trajectory."

He explains the relationship between biohols and the internal combustion engine in cars and predicts that other technologies will complement the new fuels.

March of the Biohols With the right combination of technological breakthroughs and investment, the US transportation fuel economy could make the transition to biofuels by 2030. Here's how Vinod Khosla sees it playing out.

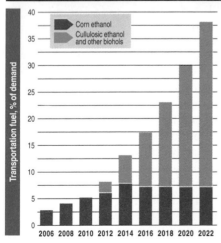

Transportation fuel, % of demand

Corn ethanol
Cullulosic ethanol and other biohols

2006 → E6 and E10 are widely available as high-octane fuel. E85 is available primarily in the Midwest.

2008 → Investor focus shifts to lowering production costs of E85, now in early distribution nationwide.

2010 → Investors roll out special pumps and pipelines to broadly deliver E85. Cellulosic ethanol production starts scaling.

2012 → Cellulosic ethanol production explodes with large-scale farming of miscanthus and switchgrass.

2014 → Automakers begin designing cars especially for E85, advancing "flex-fuel" engines. Hybrids become E85-compatible.

2016 → Butanol is introduced at commercial scale, and plug-in hybrids become biofuel-compatible.

2018 → Biofuels made from human and animal waste products achieve large scale, lowering production costs.

2020 → Genetic engineering, plant breeding, and "grass cocktails" are used to amplify energy yields of biofuels, decrease environmental impact, and lower costs further.

2022 → Chemists introduce biofuels that go beyond butanol.

6   But the single most critical variable in the biohol trajectory is the coming rise in the number of gallons of fuel produced per acre. As we migrate from biomass derived from corn to biomass from so-called energy crops like switchgrass and miscanthus, I estimate that biomass yield will reach 20 to 24 tons per acre, a four-fold increase. At the same time, new technologies will enable us to extract more biohols from every ton of biomass, potentially to 110 gallons per ton. The result: We'll be extracting 2,000 to 2,700 gallons of fuel per acre (as opposed to about 400 gallons with today's technology). With better fuels and more-efficient engines improving mileage by about 50 percent, we can safely predict a seven- to tenfold gain in miles driven per acre of land over the next 25 years. Given this biohol trajectory, a future of independence from gasoline becomes not only possible but probable. And the trajectory begins with garden-variety corn ethanol.

Arguing directly for the position, Khosla uses statistics to make an important point: fuel produced per acre will increase and cause a significant gain in miles driven per acre.

7   We learned to formulate corn ethanol way back—it's nothing more than moonshine. What makes the E3 Biofuels facility so novel isn't its spectacular equipment but the way the equipment is fueled. The most important structures here happen also to be the least beautiful: a pair of four-story, 4 million-gallon fuel tanks, each filled to the brim with cow manure. Historically, ethanol plants were fired by coal or natural gas. But methane, produced from manure, powers this operation. Not only do no fossil fuels go into the plant, very little pollution comes out. It's nearly a closed energy loop (some corn has to be bought from other farms).

He explains that the new E3 Biofuels facility is run by methane, which is produced by manure—not fossil fuels.

8   E3 Biofuels achieves what's known as a positive energy balance. For every BTU of energy used to run the ethanol plant, five BTUs are produced. A typical corn ethanol plant produces 1.3 to 1.8 BTUs for every BTU of fossil fuel input, including the energy required to grow the corn. (Gasoline has half the efficiency of corn ethanol, producing 0.8 BTUs for every BTU input.)

9   Here in Mead, almost nothing goes to waste: Components of the corn kernel that aren't good for ethanol—the protein—are valuable additions to the cattle feed. The biodigestor waste left after methane production from cow manure is processed to produce ammonia fertilizer for the cornfields. The system is also environmentally friendly. Normally, groundwater pollution from cattle feedlots is a serious problem. But the

He demonstrates the "closed circle" in Mead, giving examples of how efficient and clean the system is.

process of producing fertilizer from the cattle manure keeps the phosphates out of the groundwater. Significantly, the energy system also prevents the venting of methane into the atmosphere, which is notable because methane is 23 times worse than carbon dioxide as a greenhouse gas. Another benefit: Even under a blazing mid-August sun, I can barely smell the cattle. . . .

When it comes to technology, the best way to change 10 the world is not by revolution but by evolutionary steps. Change must follow from step to step, from innovation to innovation, as technology matures, each step justifying its economic viability and attracting investment. So while ethanol may not be ideal, I'm convinced it's the best first step on the biohol trajectory. Ethanol offers one thing no other oil substitute can: a clear path from where we are to where we hope to be.

There are other scenarios we can imagine — say, 11 wind-driven hydrogen generators powering our cars — but they are just that: blue-sky flights of imagination from academics and dreamers with no notion of reality. Then there are those tunnel-vision skeptics who refuse to believe that there is a trajectory to energy independence. I invite those folks to sit on the sidelines and watch the show or to go work on a better solution. Twenty-five years ago such doubters were dismissive of personal computing, the Internet, and biotechnology.

Ethanol is the first step on the biohol trajectory for 12 three reasons. The first is economic: Ethanol can be produced and sold cheaper than gasoline. Most ethanol facilities can produce their fuel for about $1 a gallon — almost half the production cost of gasoline. And innovative producers like E3 Biofuels claim to make it for 75 cents a gallon. It's true that American ethanol today benefits from agricultural subsidies for corn farmers. I would like to eliminate ethanol subsidies gradually in conjunction with the removal of tariffs on imported ethanol. For kicks, we might consider removing the substantial direct subsidies to oil, too. Free markets demand level playing fields. The switch to cars and trucks that can run on E85 would be relatively economical, too. There are already 6 million such flex-fuel vehicles on the road in the U.S. It costs a paltry $35 to make a new car capable of handling both ethanol and gasoline.

The second reason is scientific: New breakthroughs 13 make it eminently feasible to scale up ethanol to na-

Khosla imagines an argument that calls for revolutionary technological change and counterargues *that technology evolves through small steps. In the next paragraph, he implies that his position is a practical middle ground between "dreamers" and "doubters."*

In the next few paragraphs, he argues that for economic, scientific, and pragmatic reasons, ethanol is the best way to start using biohols. He supports each reason with evidence in the form of examples and statistics.

tional and even global proportions. Today, corn yields about 400 gallons of ethanol per acre of cropland. While corn yields will increase over time thanks to genetic modification (a new variety from Monsanto may yield 750 gallons per acre), corn can get us only so far. The real promise for ethanol lies in cellulose, which can be derived from plants like switchgrass and miscanthus, a tropical grass native to southeast Asia. Cellulosic ethanol technology promises to deliver as much as 2,700 gallons per acre by 2030. This is the key to achieving scale, substantially lower costs, and manageable land-use scenarios. Biotechnology, plant breeding, chemical process technologies, synthetic biology, energy crop engineering, systems biology, computational modeling, and new fuel chemistries will all offer tools, approaches, and possibilities for improvement. Failure to use them will be a failure of imagination.

Khosla's knowledge about all these alternative technologies enhances his credibility.

14   The third reason is pragmatic: Ethanol is already here—and in use! We know how to produce it, we know how to distribute it, and we already have cars that can use it. So why reinvent the wheel? Today in the U.S., there are 925 stations that dispense E85. Expanding that number to just 20,000 would be sufficient to make E85 broadly available—an investment I estimate at much less than a billion dollars. Just the subsidy decrease I have proposed would more than pay for this infrastructure. The sooner E85 corn ethanol primes the alternative-energy pump, the sooner we can progress to the next steps on the biohol trajectory. Several entrepreneurs are already working on cheaper, more energy-efficient biofuels that will ultimately replace corn ethanol. Mascoma, one of my investments, is developing new cellulosic ethanol technology. Richard Branson's Virgin Group is engineering an ethanol-like fuel robust enough for jet engines. Greenfuel Technologies is harnessing algae farming for ethanol and biodiesel production. Human genome pioneer J. Craig Venter is busy developing a synthetic chromosome that may be able to produce ethanol. Another Khosla Ventures company called LS9 is applying synthetic biology to produce a new biofuel.

Arguing directly for his position, Khosla asserts that ethanol will "prime the pump" for even cheaper, more efficient biofuels.

His investments in ethanol technology and knowledge about other companies establish his credibility.

15   All of these fuels will be derived from biomass, share similar manufacturing and distribution processes, and power improved internal combustion engines, so all of them will benefit from the trailblazing, market acceptance, and established infrastructure of corn ethanol.

There is a problem, however. There are folks who 16
don't want us to have cheaper alternatives, at least not
quickly. With the oil companies and their nearly un-
limited financial and political resources fighting the
development of new fuels, and in the absence of any
sort of national Manhattan Project for energy, a new
Silicon Valley of energy development has yet to get off
the ground. . . . At every turn in the history of our oil
dependence, the oil companies have spent their considerable fortune to make sure that we as a nation remained dependent on oil. They did this in large part
by lobbying Congress, by providing congressmembers
with large amounts of campaign cash, and by trying to
suppress cleaner, cheaper alternatives to oil. I hope they
realize soon that alternative energy is a major business
opportunity for them. . . .

Ethanol—and soon cellulosic ethanol and its suc- 17
cessors—offers not only a cleaner, cheaper alternative
to gasoline but one that's made in America. The environment can no longer sustain fossil-fuel emissions,
and the U.S. economy and foreign policy would be far
better off without our dependence on foreign oil.

We don't need far-off technologies like hydrogen 18
fuel cells to achieve a future that is more environmentally and economically secure. And we don't have to pay
more for cleaner transportation energy. We have the
fuel in ethanol, and we have the technology to produce
it, the distribution systems to move it, the pumps to
dispense it, and the cars to run on it—all in place and
ready to go today. The doorway to a future with fewer
economic and environmental risks is before us. All we
need do is step through it.

> Khosla *counterargues* by urging oil companies to think of alternatives to oil as a business opportunity. He builds credibility with American readers by pointing out that all of these new fuels will be made in America.

> Khosla concludes with a summary of his points and an invitation to readers to act. In the following "sidebar," he lists six objections to ethanol (what he calls "myths") and *counterargues* each one, labeling the counterarguments "Reality."

Six Ethanol Myths

by Vinod Khosla

The most promising alternative fuel has been dogged by misinforma-
tion. Here's a look at the reality behind the ethanol myths.

1) It takes more energy to make ethanol than the fuel itself produces.
Reality: Not so. Critics like to cite a 2005 study that shows a negative
energy balance for ethanol, but that study was coauthored by a former

oil company employee. It is contradicted by five others showing that corn ethanol delivers 20 to 50 percent more energy output than it takes to produce, and cellulosic up to 600 percent more. The National Resources Defense Council calls corn ethanol "energy well spent."

2) Ethanol is expensive to produce.
Reality: Ethanol costs about $1 a gallon to produce at typical facilities, which explains why E85 was selling for $1.95 at pumps in South Dakota this summer. In 2004, it was selling for $1.40 a gallon wholesale. Prices spiked higher recently because oil companies mismanaged the switch to ethanol as a replacement for the environmentally disastrous additive MBTE. Once demand and supply reach equilibrium, it can profitably sell for $1.40 a gallon without subsidies.

3) There's not enough land to grow crops for ethanol.
Reality: Former secretary of state George Schultz and ex-CIA director R. James Woolsey estimate that 30 million acres can replace half our gasoline. I estimate that 40 million to 60 million acres can replace our gasoline needs. By taking land now used to grow export crops and instead planting energy crops, it's feasible to eliminate our need to import oil for gasoline.

4) Switching to ethanol is expensive.
Reality: It didn't cost much in Brazil. Automakers already produce 10 flex-fuel models. There are almost as many flex-fuel vehicles in California as there are diesel cars and light trucks. A new car can be made flex-fuel-capable for about $35. And the cost to adapt a retail gas pump for E85 is a bargain—as little as $10,000.

5) Ethanol is unfairly subsidized.
Reality: Yes, ethanol producers and blenders share in a 51-cent-a-gallon federal credit that costs taxpayers about $2 billion a year. The majority of that accrues to oil companies, not farmers. But not mentioned by critics is the 54-cent-a-gallon tariff on imported ethanol, which hampers global competition. Meanwhile, the U.S. also directly subsidizes Big Oil. The General Accounting Office reports that the industry has netted $82 billion from just one line item alone, something called "excess of percentage over cost depletion," and there are many other such clauses.

6) Cars that run on ethanol get lower mileage.
Reality: Ethanol gets 25 percent lower mileage compared to gasoline. But that difference is likely to shrink dramatically as engines are optimized. The Saab 9-5 gets only 18 percent less mileage and can be further optimized easily. Significantly, the cost per mile driven should be lower using E85.

READING FOR MEANING

This section presents three activities that will help you reread with a critical eye the article "My Big Biofuels Bet" by Vinod Khosla. All three activities add up to between one and two pages of writing, but they lead you from basic comprehension to a response and an analysis that deepen your understanding and critical thinking about what you are reading. Your instructor may ask you to do one or more of these activities in class or as homework.

Read to Comprehend

Reread the selection, and write a few sentences briefly explaining why Khosla thinks biofuels are the solution to our fuel crisis. The following definitions may help you understand Khosla's vocabulary:

abbatoir (paragraph 3): a slaughterhouse.

forestall (4): to prevent by action in advance.

trajectory (5): the path of something moving through space and/or time.

pragmatic (14): practical.

Identify three or more additional words that you don't understand, and find the best definitions from the dictionary that work with their context.

To expand your understanding of this reading, you might use one or more of the following critical reading strategies that are explained and illustrated in Appendix 1 — *outlining* and *evaluating the logic of an argument*.

Read to Respond

Write several paragraphs exploring your initial thoughts and feelings about Khosla's position argument. Focus on anything that stands out for you, perhaps because it resonates with your own experiences or because you find a statement puzzling. You might consider writing about the following:

- Khosla's list of technologies in paragraph 13 and his assertion that "[f]ailure to use them will be a failure of imagination" (13).

- Khosla's view of oil companies (4, 12, 16, 17, sidebar).

- how Khosla's own investment in ethanol development affects your response to his argument.

- the effect on you of the sidebar about ethanol "myths."

- how energy issues affect the way you live.

Read to Analyze Assumptions

Reread Khosla's position essay, and write a paragraph or two exploring one or more of the assumptions you find in the text. All writing contains assumptions—opinions, values, and beliefs that are taken for granted as commonly accepted truths by the writer or others. Personal or individual assumptions also tend to reflect the values and beliefs of a particular group or community, sometimes called *cultural ideology*, which shape the way those in the group think, act, and understand the world.

Analyzing assumptions is an important part of learning to read critically because assumptions tend to be unexamined and unquestioned (at least consciously) by those who hold them. When you read with a critical eye, you identify important assumptions in the text and ask questions about them. Sometimes assumptions are stated explicitly, but often they are only implied, so you may have to search for underlying assumptions in the word choices and examples. Here are some kinds of questions you should ask regarding the assumptions you find: Who holds this assumption? How does the assumption support or oppose the status quo? What alternative ideas, beliefs, or values would challenge this assumption? If the writer uses the assumption to appeal to readers, how effective do you think this appeal is, and why?

To help you get started reading for assumptions in Khosla's essay, notice the attitudes he expresses in the following sentences: "Many of the criticisms [of ethanol], while true in some small ways, are aggressively promoted by the oil lobby and other interested parties in an effort to forestall change. Most are myths. Challenges certainly exist with ethanol, but none are insurmountable, and—with apologies to Al Gore—the convenient truth is that corn ethanol is a crucial first step toward kicking our oil addiction" (paragraph 4). Khosla believes that oil companies are trying to prevent change, presumably to keep their hold on the worldwide market for fuel. He himself favors change, and he probably assumes that, with oil prices climbing, his audience will also favor change. He also feels that using ethanol is the first step toward significant change, and he devotes a large portion of his argument to trying to prove that such a start is correct. Note also that in the same passage he assumes that Americans are "addicted" to oil. To think critically about these assumptions, you might ask yourself whether you share the belief that Americans are addicted to oil and whether you think alternative fuels are our only salvation. If you do not share these assumptions, then what do you believe about how the United States should meet its future energy needs, and how does your belief shape your behavior? What kind of response do you have to Khosla's argument if you do not believe we have an oil crisis?

You may want to examine Khosla's assumptions about oil companies and their motives and to consider whether he assumes his readers will agree with him about an energy crisis and possible solutions. Or you may consider writing about other assumptions you find in the essay, such as the two listed below:

- **assumptions about trajectories.** Khosla claims that "[w]hen it comes to technology, the best way to change the world is not by revolution but by evolutionary steps" (paragraph 10). He asserts that ethanol is the "first data point in what I call the biohol trajectory" (5) and that it "offers one thing no other oil substitute can: a clear path from where we are to where we hope to be" (10). He feels so strongly about this point that he writes a self-contained "essay" to support it, giving economic, scientific, and pragmatic reasons (12–14). To think critically about the assumptions in this essay related to trajectories, examine these three paragraphs, and ask yourself: Does Khosla succeed in persuading you that a step-by-step approach is the only feasible one for a solution to our dependence on oil? Does he provide enough statistics and define enough specialized terms to make clear the need for a trajectory? Aside from the kind of sudden, radical technological innovation that Khosla considers unrealistic, what might be some other possibilities to lessen our dependence on oil that do not rely on assumptions about trajectories?

- **assumptions about the format of an argument.** In paragraph 4, Khosla acknowledges that ethanol is "a subject of controversy," although he points out that "[m]any of the criticisms . . . are aggressively promoted by the oil lobby" and asserts that "[m]ost are myths." Khosla knows that in arguing his point, he will lose credibility with his audience if he does not respond to these myths. Look at the sidebar "Six Ethanol Myths." Why would Khosla give this much space and an eye-catching sidebar to people who disagree with him? What is the effect on you as a reader to have an author highlight opposing views and deal with them one by one? Now look at the graph "The March of the Biohols." What purpose does such a graph serve for an audience? Why do you think Khosla decides to present information in the format of a graph? What assumptions does he make about the effects of the sidebar and the graph on his readers?

READING LIKE A WRITER

This section guides you through an analysis of Khosla's argumentative writing strategies: *presenting the issue*; *asserting a clear, unequivocal position*; *arguing directly for the position*; *counterarguing objections and opposing positions*; and *establishing credibility*. For each strategy, you will be asked to reread and annotate part of Khosla's essay to see how he uses the strategy in "My Big Biofuels Bet."

When you study the selections later in this chapter, you will see how different writers use the same strategies to develop a position paper. The Guide to Writing Position Papers near the end of this chapter suggests ways you can use these strategies in your own writing.

Presenting the Issue

For position papers published during an ongoing public debate, writers may need only to mention the issue. In most cases, however, writers need to identify the issue as well as explain it to readers. To present the issue, writers may provide several kinds of information. They may, for example, place the issue in its historical or cultural context, cite specific instances to make the issue seem less abstract, show their personal interest in the debate, or establish or redefine the terms of the debate.

Analyze

1. *Reread* paragraphs 1 to 3, where Khosla introduces the issue, and *make notes* about the approach he takes.

2. Then *reread* paragraph 5, where Khosla provides background and context for the issue. *Look closely* at his description of the "biohol trajectory," and *underline* any words that might lead readers to take his argument seriously.

Write

Write several sentences describing how Khosla presents the issue. How does he introduce the issue and connect it to his readers' experiences and interests? Then *add a few sentences* evaluating how successfully Khosla presents the issue and prepares readers for his argument.

Asserting a Clear, Unequivocal Position

Writers of position papers always take sides. Their primary purposes are to assert a position of their own and to influence readers' thinking. The assertion is the main point of the essay—its thesis. Writers try to state the thesis simply and directly, although they may limit the scope of it. For example, a thesis in favor of the death penalty might limit capital punishment to certain kinds of crimes. The thesis statement often forecasts the stages of the argument as well, identifying the main reason or reasons that will be developed and supported in the essay.

Where the thesis is placed depends on various factors. Most likely, you will want to place the thesis early in the essay to let readers know right away where you stand. But when you need to spend more time presenting the issue or defining the terms of the debate, you might postpone introducing your own position. Restating the thesis at various points in the body of the essay and at the end can also help keep readers oriented.

Analyze

1. *Find* the first place where Khosla explicitly asserts his position (at the end of paragraph 4), and *underline* the sentence that states the thesis.

2. *Skim* paragraphs 6, 7, 10, 12, 15, 17, and 18, and *put brackets around* the sentences in these paragraphs that restate the thesis.

3. *Examine* the context for each of these restatements. *Look closely* at the language Khosla uses to see whether he repeats key words, uses synonyms for them, or adds new phrasing.

Write

Write a few sentences explaining what you have learned about how Khosla states and restates his position. *Describe* the different contexts in which he restates the thesis and how the wording changes. *Cite examples* from the reading. Then *add a few sentences* speculating about the possible reasons for reasserting a thesis so often in a brief essay like this one.

Arguing Directly for the Position

Not only do writers of position papers explicitly assert their positions, but they also give reasons for them. Moreover, they usually support their reasons with facts, statistics, examples, anecdotes, quotes from authorities, and analogies:

- *Facts* are statements that can be proven objectively to be true, but readers may need to be reassured that the facts come from trustworthy sources.

- Although *statistics* may be mistaken for facts, they often are only interpretations or correlations of numerical data. Their reliability depends on how and by whom the information was collected and interpreted.

- *Examples* and *anecdotes* are not usually claimed to be proof of the writer's position or to be evidence that the position applies in every case. Instead, they present particular stories and vivid images that work by appealing to readers' emotions.

- Somewhere in between these two extremes are *expert opinions* and *analogies*. Readers must decide whether to regard quotations from experts as credible and authoritative. They must also decide how much weight to give analogies — comparisons that encourage readers to assume that what is true about one thing is also true about something to which it is compared.

Analyze

1. *Reread* paragraphs 6 and 13, where Khosla develops his reason that the number of gallons of fuel produced per acre is about to increase enough to cause a "seven- to tenfold gain in miles driven per acre of land over the next 25 years." *Find* the first place in each paragraph where Khosla explicitly asserts his reason, and *put brackets around* the sentence or sentences in each paragraph that state this part of his argument.

2. *Look closely* at how Khosla supports this reason with statistics. *Underline* the statistics throughout both paragraphs, and then *compare* them to each other.

3. *Consider* how persuasive his statistics are in paragraphs 6 and 13.

Write

Write several sentences briefly describing Khosla's strategy of argument by statistics. *Cite examples* of his statistics. Then *add a few sentences* speculating about the persuasiveness of his strategy. Why do you think that some readers would find the argument in this part of the essay compelling and other readers would not?

Counterarguing Objections and Opposing Positions

Writers of position papers often try to anticipate the likely objections, questions, and opposing positions that readers might raise. Writers may concede points with which they agree and may even modify a thesis to accommodate valid objections. But when they think that the criticism is groundless or opposing arguments are flawed, writers counterargue aggressively. They refute the challenges to their argument by poking holes in their opponents' reasoning and support.

Analyze

1. *Reread* paragraphs 4, 11, and 16 and the sidebar on six ethanol myths, where Khosla introduces opposing arguments to his position. *Underline* the sentence in each paragraph that best states an opposing position.

2. *Examine* these paragraphs and the sidebar to see how Khosla counterargues these opposing arguments. For example, *notice* that he both concedes and refutes, and *consider* why he would attempt to do both. What seems to be his attitude toward those who disagree with him or who object to parts of his argument?

3. *Consider* how the comparisons to the Manhattan Project and Silicon Valley support his counterargument, particularly for readers who might remember or have studied the significance of the nuclear arms race and the telecommunications revolution.

Write

Write several sentences briefly explaining Khosla's counterarguments. Then *add a few sentences* evaluating the probable success of these strategies with his readers.

Establishing Credibility

Readers judge the credibility of a position paper about a controversial issue by the way it presents the issue, argues for the position, and counterargues objections and opposing positions. Critical readers expect writers to advocate forcefully for their position, but at the same time they expect writers to avoid misrepresenting other points of view, attacking opponents personally, or manipulating readers' emotions. To establish credibility, writers thus aim instead to support their position responsibly with the help of authoritative sources and a well-reasoned, well-supported argument.

Another factor that can influence readers' judgment of an argument's credibility is whether the writer seems to share at least some of their values, beliefs, attitudes, and ideals. Readers often are more willing to trust a writer who expresses concerns that they also have about an issue. Many readers respect arguments based on strong values even if they do not share those particular values or hold to them as strictly. Yet readers also tend to dislike moralizing and resent a condescending or belittling tone as much as a shrill or lecturing one. Instead, readers usually appreciate a tone that acknowledges legitimate differences of opinion, while seeking to establish common ground where possible.

Analyze

1. Quickly *reread* Khosla's entire essay. As you read, *put a question mark* in the margin next to any passages where you doubt Khosla's credibility, and *put a check mark* next to any passages where he seems especially trustworthy.

2. *Review* the passages you marked. Where possible, *note in the margin* a word or phrase that describes the dominant tone of each marked passage.

3. Then *consider* what language, information, or other element in the marked passages contributes to your judgment of Khosla's credibility.

Write

Write several sentences describing your impression of Khosla's credibility. *Cite examples* from the reading to support your view.

■ Readings

KAREN STABINER

Boys Here, Girls There: Sure, If Equality's the Goal

Karen Stabiner received her BA from the University of Michigan. A contributing editor for Mother Jones *and a columnist for* New West, *she has also written for magazines and newspapers such as the* Los Angeles Times, O: The Oprah Magazine, Vogue, *the* New York Times, Los Angeles Magazine, *and the* New Yorker. *Stabiner has written several books on relationships and single-sex education. Her most recent are* My Girl: Adventures with a Teen in Training *(2005) and* The Empty Nest: Thirty-one Parents Tell the Truth about Relationships, Love, and Freedom after the Kids Fly the Coop *(2007).*

"Boys Here, Girls There: Sure, If Equality's the Goal" was first published in the Washington Post *Sunday Outlook section on May 12, 2002. The occasion was the George W. Bush administration's endorsement of single-sex schools as part of the No Child Left Behind Act. Before you read, think about the role that gender played in your high-school education. Do you feel that boys and girls were treated differently, and if so, how? If they were treated the same, do you think it would have been better had they been treated differently? Why? As you read, annotate the text, noting especially Stabiner's strategies for responding to those who disagree with her.*

Many parents may be wondering what the fuss was about this past week, when the Bush administration endorsed single-sex public schools and classes. Separating the sexes was something we did in the days of auto shop and home ec, before Betty Friedan, Gloria Steinem and Title IX.[1] How, then, did an apparent return to the Fifties come to symbolize educational reform? 1

Here's how: By creating an alternate, parallel universe where smart matters more than anything, good looks hold little currency and a strong sense of self trumps a date on Saturday night—a place where "class clown" is a label that young boys dread and "math whiz" is a term of endearment for young girls. 2

[1] Betty Friedan (1921–2006) and Gloria Steinem (b. 1934) were pioneers in the Second Wave feminist movement that began in the 1960s. Title IX of the Education Amendments of 1972 is the federal legislation that bans sexual discrimination in public schools, whether in academics or athletics.

I have just spent three years working on a book about two all-girls schools, the private Marlborough School in Los Angeles, and The Young Women's Leadership School of East Harlem (TYWLS), a six-year-old public school in New York City. I went to class, I went home with the girls, I went to dances and basketball games and faculty meetings, and what I learned is this: Single-sex education matters, and it matters most to the students who historically have been denied access to it.

Having said that, I do not intend to proselytize. Single-sex education is not the answer to everyone's prayers. Some children want no part of it and some parents question its relevance. The rest of us should not stop wondering what to do with our coeducational public schools just because of this one new option.

But single-sex education can be a valuable tool—if we target those students who stand to benefit most. For years, in the name of upholding gender equity, we have practiced a kind of harsh economic discrimination. Sociologist Cornelius Riordan says that poor students, minorities and girls stand to profit most from a single-sex environment. Until now, though, the only students who could attend a single-sex school were the wealthy ones who could afford private tuition, the relatively few lucky students who received financial aid or those in less-expensive parochial schools. We denied access to the almost 90 percent of American students who attend public schools.

For the fortunate ones—like the girls at Marlborough—the difference is one of attitude, more than any quantifiable measure; their grades and scores may be similar to the graduates of coed prep schools, but they perceive themselves as more competent, more willing to pursue advanced work in fields such as math and science.

At TYWLS, though, the difference is more profound. Students there are predominantly Latina and African American, survivors of a hostile public system. Half of New York's high school students fail to graduate on time, and almost a third never graduate. Throughout the nation, one in six Latina and one in five African American teens become pregnant every year. But most of the members of TYWLS's two graduating classes have gone on to four-year colleges, often the first members of their families to do so, and pregnancy is the stark exception.

There are now 11 single-sex public schools in the United States, all of which serve urban students, many of them in lower-income neighborhoods. Most are side-by-side schools that offer comparable programs for boys and girls in the same facility. The stand-alone girls' schools say that they are compensating for years of gender discrimination; several attempts at similar schools for boys have failed, however, casualties of legal challenges.

Now, thanks to a bipartisan amendment to President Bush's education reform bill, sponsored by Sens. Kay Bailey Hutchison (R-Tex.) and Hillary Rodham Clinton (D-N.Y.), the administration is about to revise the way it enforces Title IX, to allow for single-sex schools and classes.

The first objections last week came from the National Organization for Women and the New York Civil Liberties Union, both of which opposed the opening of TYWLS in the fall of 1996. The two groups continue to insist—as though it were 1896 and they were arguing *Plessy v. Ferguson*[2]—that separate can never be equal. I appreciate NOW's wariness of the Bush administration's endorsement of single-sex public schools, since I am of the generation that still considers the label "feminist" to be a compliment—and many feminists still fear that any public acknowledgment of differences between the sexes will hinder their fight for equality.

But brain research has shown us that girls and boys develop and process information in different ways; they do not even use the same region of the brain to do their math homework. We cannot pretend that such information does not exist just because it conflicts with our ideology. If we hang on to old, quantifiable measurements of equality, we will fail our children. If we take what we learn and use it, we have the chance to do better.

Educators at single-sex schools already get it: Equality is the goal, not the process. There may be more than one path to the destination—but it is the arrival, not the itinerary, that counts.

Some researchers complain that we lack definitive evidence that single-sex education works. There are so many intertwined variables; the students at TYWLS might do well because of smaller class size, passionate teachers and an aggressively supportive atmosphere. Given that, the absence of boys might be beside the point.

The American Association of University Women called for more research even after publishing a 1998 report that showed some girls continued to suffer in the coed classroom. But it is probably impossible to design a study that would retire the question permanently, and, as TYWLS's first principal, Celenia Chevere, liked to say, "What am I supposed to do with these girls in the meantime?"

[2] In *Plessy v. Ferguson* (1896), the U.S. Supreme Court upheld racial segregation by stating that separate facilities for blacks and whites in public accommodations were constitutional as long as they were equal. The ruling was reversed by the Supreme Court in *Brown v. Board of Education* (1954).

What is this misplaced reverence for the coed school? Do not think that it was designed with the best interests of all children at heart. As education professors David and Myra Sadker explained in their 1994 book, *Failing at Fairness: How America's Schools Cheat Girls*, our schools were originally created to educate boys. In the late 1700s, girls went to class early in the morning and late in the day—and unlike the boys, they had to pay for the privilege. When families demanded that the public schools do more for their girls, school districts grudgingly allowed the girls into existing classrooms—not because it was the best way to teach children but because no one had the money to build new schools just for girls. Coed classrooms are not necessarily better. They just are.

For those who like hard data, here is a number: 1,200 girls on the waiting list for a handful of spaces in the ninth grade at TYWLS. There is a growing desire for public school alternatives, for an answer more meaningful than a vague if optimistic call for systemwide reform. The demand for single-sex education exists— and now the Bush administration must figure out how to supply it.

Implementation will not be easy. Girls may learn better without boys, but research and experience show that some boys seem to need the socializing influence of girls: Will there be a group of educational handmaidens, girls who are consigned to coed schools to keep the boys from acting out? Who will select the chosen few who get to go to single-sex schools, and how will they make that choice? Will they take students who already show promise or those who most need help? Or perhaps the philosophy of a new pair of boys' and girls' schools in Albany, N.Y., provides the answer: Take the poorest kids first.

Whatever the approach, no one is calling for a wholesale shift to segregation by gender, and that means someone will be left out. Single-sex public schools perpetuate the kind of two-tiered system that used to be based solely on family income, even if they widen the net. But that has always been true of innovative public schools, and it is no reason to hesitate.

The most troubling question about single-sex public education—Why now?—has nothing to do with school. When support comes so readily from opposite ends of the political spectrum, it is reasonable to ask why everyone is so excited, particularly given the political debate about vouchers and school choice.

If the intention is to strengthen the public school system by responding to new information about how our children learn, then these classes can serve as a model of innovative teaching techniques, some of which can be transported back into existing coed classrooms. Single-sex public schools and classes, as odd as it may sound, are about inclusion; any school district that wants one can have one and everyone can learn from the experience.

But if this is about siphoning off the best and potentially bright-   21
est, and ignoring the rest, then it is a cruel joke, a warm and fuzzy set-up for measures like vouchers. If single-sex becomes a satisfy-ing distraction from existing schools that desperately need help, then it only serves to further erode the system. The new educa-tional reform law is called the No Child Left Behind Act, an irre-sistible sentiment with a chilling edge to it—did we ever actually intend to leave certain children behind? The challenge, in develop-ing these new schools and programs, is to make them part of a dynamic, ongoing reform, and not an escape hatch from a troubled system.

READING FOR MEANING

This section presents three activities that will help you reread Stabiner's arti-cle with a critical eye. All three activities add up to between one and two pages of writing, but they lead you from basic comprehension to a response and an analy-sis that deepen your understanding and critical thinking about what you are reading. Your instructor may ask you to do one or more of these activities in class or as homework.

Read to Comprehend

Reread the selection, and write a few sentences briefly explaining why Stabiner favors single-sex public schools for girls. The following definitions may help you understand Stabiner's vocabulary:

proselytize (paragraph 4): to try to convert from one belief to another.

implementation (17): the process of putting a plan into effect.

perpetuate (18): to keep in existence; continue.

Identify three or more additional words that you don't understand, and find the best definitions from the dictionary that work with their context.

Read to Respond

Write several paragraphs exploring your initial thoughts and feelings about Stabiner's position argument. Focus on anything that stands out for you, perhaps because it resonates with your own experience or because you find a statement puzzling. You might consider writing about the following:

- any experience you have had with single-sex schools;

- your response to Stabiner's assertion that "[f]or years, in the name of upholding gender equity, we have practiced a kind of harsh economic discrimination" (paragraph 5);

- whether you think a difference in *attitude* (6) can make the kind of difference Stabiner explores in her essay; or

- other school reforms that you think would improve public education in the United States.

To develop your response to Stabiner's position, you might use the following critical reading strategy that is explained and illustrated in Appendix 1: *looking for patterns of opposition.*

Read to Analyze Assumptions

Reread Stabiner's position essay, and write a paragraph or two exploring one or more of the assumptions you find in the text. The following suggestions may help:

- **assumptions about innovations in education.** In paragraph 20, speaking about single-sex classrooms, Stabiner notes that "[i]f the intention is to strengthen the public school system by responding to new information about how our children learn, then these classes can serve as a model of innovative teaching." What kinds of innovative teaching might Stabiner mean? To think critically about the assumptions in this essay related to innovations, ask yourself: What is your response to the principal of TYWLS, who asks, referring to the American Association of University Women's call for more research on coed versus single-sex schools, "What am I supposed to do with these girls in the meantime?" What would happen to schools if innovations were encouraged (rather than being seen as a threat to the status quo) or if students—both boys and girls—were treated as "experiments" to see how they would turn out under single-sex circumstances? What kinds of circumstances could lead to disastrous innovations? To wondrous innovations? Why would teaching innovations for girls necessarily be transferable to boys?

- **assumptions about poverty.** When Stabiner speculates about the consequences of single-sex schools, she notes that "some boys seem to need the socializing influence of girls" (17), leading her to the assumption that *some* girls would—and perhaps should—be placed in coed schools. She asks a series of questions about how girls would be chosen for either kind of school, and at the end of the paragraph she opts for an answer given by single-sex schools in Albany: "Take the poorest kids first." Stabiner asserts that "Single-sex education . . . matters most to the students who historically have been denied access to it" (3), by whom she means "poor students, minorities and girls" (5). To think critically about the assumptions in this essay related to poverty, ask yourself: What would be the consequences if single-sex public schools took "poorest kids first"? Why does a difference in "attitude" (6) among students in single-sex schools lead them to pursue advanced degrees? How are attitude and economics linked?

READING LIKE A WRITER
COUNTERARGUING OBJECTIONS AND OPPOSING POSITIONS

One of the challenges — and pleasures — of writing position papers is that in nearly every writing situation writers recognize that some, many, or even all of their readers will hold opposing positions or, if they have no position, will question or object to some part of the argument. Therefore, one of the special challenges of the position paper is to counterargue readers' positions, objections, or questions. To do so convincingly, writers must succeed with two basic moves — (1) demonstrate that they understand their readers' opposing positions and recognize their readers' objections or questions and (2) concede or refute those positions, objections, or questions without exasperating, insulting, or harassing readers. To *concede* is to admit the usefulness or wisdom of readers' views. To *refute* is to attempt to argue that readers' views are limited or flawed. (For more on counterarguing, turn to the Reading like a Writer section following the Khosla selection, p. 530, and to Considering a Useful Sentence Strategy on p. 588.)

Stabiner counterargues extensively. In fact, she organizes her argument around particular objections she anticipates her readers will raise.

Analyze

1. In paragraph 4, *underline* the last three sentences, which acknowledge the objections that single-sex schools cannot solve all of the problems of education and that many parents and students don't find them an answer.

2. *Reread* paragraphs 10 and 13 and the first sentences of 15 and 21, where Stabiner acknowledges objections to single-sex schools. Then *reread* paragraphs 11, 12, and 14 and the rest of 15 and 21. *Make notes* in the margins about what strategies Stabiner uses, noticing where she refutes, where she concedes, and what her attitude seems to be toward those who oppose single-sex schools.

Write

Write several sentences explaining what you have learned about how Stabiner counterargues. *Give examples* from the reading. Then *add a few sentences* evaluating how convincingly Stabiner counterargues. What do you find most or least convincing in her counterargument — and why?

CONSIDERING IDEAS FOR YOUR OWN WRITING

Consider the many issues in contemporary culture that involve gender. Many issues concern reproductive rights, such as abortion and fetal selection (where parents choose to abort a fetus because it has genetic disorders or, in some cultures, is female) and requirements for parental notification if a teenager seeks advice for birth control. The subject of education also yields many issues: Is the current structure of high schools best for educating teenagers? Are college admissions fair? Is testing a solution to our national educational crisis? Is there a national educational crisis? Should we change our notion of the right of every citizen to a public education? Does the profession of teaching need to change, and if so, how? Should everyone have a right to a college education? Since you have already reached college, you may want to take a position on one of these topics.

A SPECIAL READING STRATEGY

Comparing and Contrasting Related Readings: Orenstein's "The Daily Grind: Lessons in the Hidden Curriculum" and Stabiner's "Boys Here, Girls There: Sure, If Equality's the Goal"

Comparing and contrasting related readings is a special critical reading strategy useful both in reading for meaning and in reading like a writer. This strategy is particularly applicable when writers present similar subjects, as in the observational essay in Chapter 3 by Peggy Orenstein (p. 111) and the position paper in this chapter by Karen Stabiner (p. 535). Both essays focus on gender in the classroom. To compare and contrast these two essays, think about issues such as these:

- Compare these essays in terms of their cultural contexts. How do you think Orenstein or her subject Amy Wilkinson would react to Stabiner's argument in favor of single-sex education? If Wilkinson's school were single sex instead of coed, what do you think she would gain and/or lose?

- Compare these essays in terms of their purpose and genre. Orenstein's essay describing her observations of a coed classroom may lead readers to question coed education, but she does not argue, at least not directly, either for or against it. Stabiner, on the other hand, makes an explicit argument in favor of giving public-school students the opportunity to attend single-sex schools. Compare the way these two essays try to influence readers.

See Appendix 1 for detailed guidelines on using the comparing and contrasting related readings strategy.

DAVID BROOKS

A Nation of Grinders

> David Brooks (b. 1961) graduated with a degree in history from the University of Chicago and now is a contributing editor at Newsweek and the Atlantic Monthly, a senior editor at the Weekly Standard, and a columnist for the New York Times. He has written two books, Bobos in Paradise: The New Upper Class and How They Got There (2000) and On Paradise Drive: How We Live Now (and Always Have) in the Future Tense (2004), and has edited the anthology Backward and Upward: The New Conservative Writing (1996). A widely respected spokesperson for politically conservative views, Brooks also regularly appears on The NewsHour with Jim Lehrer on PBS, Late Edition on CNN, and National Public Radio.
>
> In "A Nation of Grinders," which first appeared in the New York Times Magazine in 2003, Brooks uses Abraham Lincoln as a model for the worker of our time. Lincoln was a man whose work ethic enabled him to transcend his class and achieve greatness—though Brooks does not think that "greatness" is what most people need to achieve to be successful. Before you read, think about your model for success: do you think of a person, a particular job, or a way of life?
>
> As you read, annotate the text, noting where Brooks argues directly for his position; what kinds of evidence does he use to support his argument?

We're at an odd cultural moment. There's no dominant image of business success. Neither dot-com millionaires nor the Wall Street whizzes seem alluring. The risk-taking, push-the-envelope executives no longer inspire confidence. The charismatic CEOs just seem like overplayed blowhards. And yet nobody gets inspired at the thought of being the safe, secure, highly anal Organization Man. 1

So how about Abraham Lincoln as the defining capitalist figure for our age? As the Yuppie was to the 80s, as the dot-commer was to the 90s, maybe Abraham Lincoln could be for the coming decade. Not the great statesman Lincoln—the president Lincoln—but rather the middle-aged corporate-lawyer Lincoln, the guy who in the 1850s represented railroads and banks, the guy who traveled relentlessly around the legal circuit handling cases big and small, the guy who, when he made some money, added a second floor to his house so his family could have more space, the guy whose ambition, as his law partner famously said, knew no rest. That middle-aged Lincoln represents all the sometimes homely but invariably dreamy pushers who are what American striving is really all about. 2

Lincoln began life with high anticipations of glorious success. 3
When he was young, he had a little boat, which he kept on the
Ohio River. One day a pair of travelers asked him if he would row
them to the middle of the river, where they could intercept a
steamboat. Lincoln took them out, and as the men boarded the
steamboat, they each threw a silver half-dollar into the bottom of
his boat. "You may think it was a very little thing," Lincoln later
recalled, "but it was a most important incident in my life. I could
scarcely credit that I, a poor boy, had earned a dollar in less than a
day. . . . The world seemed wider and fairer before me."

He became a fervent believer in social mobility and came to 4
see, as the historian Allen C. Guelzo has pointed out, that self-
transformation is almost a moral responsibility for the aspiring
American.

Many people start out like Lincoln, fervently convinced that 5
easy and quick riches lie just over the horizon. Four-fifths of American college students, according to a Jobtrak.com study, believe it
will take them 10 years or less to achieve their career goals. Three-
quarters of U.S. college students expect to become millionaires,
and 52 percent expect to have achieved this stratospheric status by
the time they are 50.

But success didn't come quickly for Lincoln, just as it doesn't 6
come quickly for most people. Recent research has indicated that
the United States is, and always has been, a less mobile society than
we think. Americans do move upward as we age. Only 5 percent of
the individuals who were in the bottom income quintile in 1975
were still there in 1991. But an individual's mobility is likely to be
measured in decades, not years. We rise as we age and as we get
gradual promotions, not because we strike it rich. That's what happened through most of Lincoln's life. The Lincoln of the 1850s was
prosperous and apparently a brilliant lawyer, but he felt that his
greatest dreams were not realized. And that, too, is not atypical. For
every Bill Gates and Jack Welch, there are millions of men and
women doing well but not spectacularly, somehow not fulfilling
the media image of corporate heroism.

They shouldn't worry. There is now a pile of books and articles 7
correcting the distorted image of American capitalism that
emerged during the Nasdaq bubble years, when instant fortunes
did seem like some normal part of life, and when success seemed to
be based on the ability to have a great visionary breakthrough in
identifying the next big thing.

Now things have calmed down. A book called *Execution* recently 8
hit the top of the *Wall Street Journal* best-seller list, about the need
to actually execute and finish your strategies, rather than just

develop grand visions and capitalize in earth-shaking revolutions. *Leading Quietly* hit the *New York Times* best-seller list, celebrating executives who avoid headlines and do not follow the leadership secrets of George S. Patton or Attila the Hun. When they find themselves with no good options, these businesspeople stall, play for time and muddle through. The most successful book along these lines is Jim Collins's *Good to Great.* Collins and his research team investigated companies that outperformed the overall stock market from the 1970s through 1990s by anywhere from 300 to 1,800 percent, crushing the performance of the Nasdaq superstars. It is hard to imagine a less fabulous list—Walgreens, Kroger, Pitney Bowes.

The culture at these companies encourages the Lincolnian virtues of simplicity and humility. In these places it would be socially unacceptable for an executive to portray himself as an intellectual pioneer. "Throughout our research," Collins says, "we were struck by the continual use of words like 'disciplined,' 'rigorous,' 'dogged,' 'determined,' 'diligent,' 'precise,' 'fastidious,' 'systematic,' 'methodical,' 'workmanlike,' 'demanding,' 'consistent,' 'focused,' 'accountable' and 'responsible.'" These are the classic, staid but unexciting bourgeois virtues. One executive at Wells Fargo described Carl Reichardt, then the CEO, this way: "If Carl were an Olympic diver, he would not do a five-flip twisting thing. He would do the best swan dive in the world, and do it perfectly over and over again." Success, for most Americans, really is built upon the slow, steady, boring accumulation of accomplishments and money.

Most successful people, like Lincoln, also have a core faith in the moral power of hard work. "I hold the value of life is to improve one's condition," Lincoln once told an audience of immigrants. "Labor is the great source from which nearly all, if not all, human comforts and necessities are drawn," he declared during one of his debates with Stephen Douglas.

This work ethic is different from what you might call the creativity ethic or the lifestyle ethic. It emphasizes neatness, regularity and order. Sometimes you'll walk into a grocery store in rural America and you will notice that every can on the shelves is aligned to almost millimeter-width precision, and the floors are clean and stain free. Here is some stocker, in a supposedly dead-end job, committed to work done precisely and well. Here is some Horatio Alger hero for our day.

We think of the Horatio Alger stories as rags-to-riches tales. In fact they are not. The Alger heroes are almost never plucky young boys who become millionaires or moguls. Instead, most Alger stories are about plucky young boys who become middle-class clerks or midlevel executives. They achieve respectability, not riches. Alger would have insulted the democratic sensibilities of his readers if he had concluded his books with his heroes sitting around in grand palaces, employing servants. In most parts of the country, this suspicion of aristocracy still lingers. Lincolnesque plow horses are suspicious of quick wealth just as they are suspicious of great wealth. The goal is respectability and the self-esteem that comes with being seen as a winner in the game of life.

The sad thing for those of us who write about these people is   13
that many of the hard-working people who make up the ranks of the gradually successful are flamboyance vacuums. Often they are far more interested in working and making money than in consuming and spending money. According to research that Thomas J. Stanley did for his book *The Millionaire Next Door*, written with William D. Danko, 70 percent of millionaires have their shoes resoled and repaired rather than replaced, and the average millionaire spends about $140 on a pair of shoes, which doesn't get you Guccis. After Visa and MasterCard, the most common credit cards in the millionaire's wallets are charge cards for Sears and J. C. Penney. In that 1996 study, Stanley and Danko reported that the typical millionaire paid $399 for his most expensive suit and $24,800 for his or her most recent car or truck, which is only $3,800 more than what the average American spent.

In other words, they shop the way most Americans shop, in that   14
confused hierarchy-busting manner the market researchers now call *rocketing*. They spend lots of money on a few items they really care about—their barbecue grills or their lawnmowers—and then they go downmarket to Wal-Mart to buy most of the other stuff they don't care about. This isn't upper-class consumption or even relentlessly middle-class consumption. It's mixed-up no-class consumption.

In this, as in so many respects, people who live in Manhattan or   15
Los Angeles or San Francisco or even Dallas have to keep reminding themselves that their experience is not typical. In most places in America, there are no massive concentrations of rich people and hence no Madison Avenue boutiques, no fine art galleries, no personal shoppers. There is just the country club, and certain social pressures to be just this affluent, to prove you are a success, and no more so.

In the land of the plow horses, wealth is acceptable because it is   16
legitimized by the creed of social mobility, which in many ways originated with Lincoln and the Whig Party, of which he was a member for most of his career. According to this creed, affluence is admired because it is the product of hard work, and it does not

corrupt because you continue to work even when you don't have to anymore. According to this creed, social mobility is the saving fire that redeems society. Social mobility opens up horizons because people can see wider opportunities and live transformed lives. Social mobility reduces class conflict because each person can build his own fortune, rather than taking from the fortunes of others. Social mobility unleashes creative energies and keeps everything new and dynamic. It compensates for inequality, because the family that is poor today may become richer tomorrow. It is the very essence of justice, because each person's destiny is somehow related to the amount of talent and effort he or she pours into life. The purpose of government is to ensure that there is, to use Lincoln's words, "an open field and a fair chance" so that everyone can compete in the race of life.

This is the sensible, steady and admirable ethic of American life. 17
And people who hew to this ethic are still rewarded. If you get an education, get married and stay married, the odds are overwhelming that you will rise. If you migrate here from a developing country, and if you work hard, the odds are pretty good that you and your children will enjoy brighter and more open futures.

But, of course, in our own lives few of us are entirely sensible. 18
And neither was Lincoln. While he was plodding upward, he still harbored dreams of greatness, and suddenly in the late 1850s fate plucked him up and sent him suddenly to the pinnacle. In the meantime, he was building the spiritual and moral resources that enabled him to face the greatest crisis any American has ever faced.

As many studies have by now documented, success is surpris- 19
ingly loosely correlated with happiness. The most delicious moments in life are often not the ones experienced in the big houses or at the vacation resorts. They are experienced in the modern-day equivalent of Lincoln's boyhood boat on the Ohio River, with the two silver half-dollars floating toward you, opening up visions of a future life that is limitless and fair.

READING FOR MEANING

This section presents three activities that will help you reread Brooks's article with a critical eye. All three activities add up to between one and two pages of writing, but they lead you from basic comprehension to a response and an analysis that deepen your understanding and critical thinking about what you are reading. Your instructor may ask you to do one or more of these activities in class or as homework.

Read to Comprehend

Reread the selection, and write a few sentences briefly explaining why Brooks thinks Abraham Lincoln is "the defining capitalist figure for our age" (paragraph 2). The following definitions may help you understand Brooks's vocabulary:

social mobility (paragraph 4): the ability of individuals or groups to move upward in status within a society.

distorted (7): mentally or morally twisted.

aristocracy (12): a class of people considered superior to others because of their ancestry, wealth, or leisure.

Identify three or more additional words that you don't understand, and find the best definitions from the dictionary that work with their context.

Read to Respond

Write several paragraphs exploring your initial thoughts and feelings about Brooks's position argument. Focus on anything that stands out for you, perhaps because it resonates with your own experience or because you find a statement puzzling. You might consider writing about the following:

- your own definition of the American dream;

- your response to Brooks's notion that Abraham Lincoln best represents the business hero of the early twenty-first century;

- your feelings about Brooks's statement that the successful hard-working people he writes about "are far more interested in working and making money than in consuming and spending money" (13);

- your or your family's experiences with "social mobility" and the forms it took; or

- your response to the title "A Nation of Grinders."

To develop your response to Brooks's position, you might use one of the following critical reading strategies that are explained and illustrated in Appendix 1: *contextualizing* and *using a Toulmin analysis*.

Read to Analyze Assumptions

Reread Brooks's position essay, and write a paragraph or two exploring one or more of the assumptions you find in the text. The following suggestions may help:

- **assumptions about hard work.** "Most successful people, like Lincoln," writes Brooks, "also have a core faith in the moral power of hard work" (paragraph

10). Brooks examines how this ethic of hard work drives Americans who are pursuing the American dream toward upward social mobility. To think critically about the assumptions in this essay related to the value of hard work, ask yourself: What does someone have to believe about hard work to think that it can change social status? To what extent is this faith in hard work believed and practiced in the United States? To what extent is it justified — that is, actually rewarded by upward mobility? What about the belief that "hard work is its own reward"—how much do you share that belief or do you think Brooks does? How much do Americans in general share it?

- **assumptions about fairness.** At the end of paragraph 16, Brooks writes that "[t]he purpose of government is to ensure that there is, to use Lincoln's words, 'an open field and a fair chance' so that everyone can compete in the race of life." To think critically about the assumptions in this essay related to fairness, ask yourself: How does Brooks support the notion that social mobility and the American dream are based on fairness? How is American political life (as well as working life) based on the assumption that everyone in America is treated with fairness? If fairness is not at the root of the American dream, what *is* at the root of it? Are there situations in which fairness is trumped by other conditions that take precedence or that are more fundamental?

READING LIKE A WRITER
ARGUING DIRECTLY FOR THE POSITION

Central to creating a successful position paper is the development of a strong argument in support of the writer's position on the issue. The writer may effectively counterargue readers' or opponents' questions, objections, and opposing positions, but doing so does not complete the argument. Readers also want to know in positive terms why the writer holds his or her particular position and what sort of reasoned argument the writer can devise. In brief, readers expect reasons and support.

Brooks's essay shows how writers of position papers make use of several strategies to support their reasons. Although he is professing to use Lincoln as the "defining capitalist figure for our age" (2), at the same time he presents his argument for the characteristics possessed by a capitalist for our age.

Analyze

1. *Reread* the following groups of paragraphs, looking for examples of the strategies Brooks uses to support his reasons: defining key terms (paragraphs 4, 9–11, and 16), reporting on or speculating about results (6, 8–12, 14, and 17), citing statistics (5, 6, 8, and 13), citing authorities (3, 4, 8–10, and 13), giving examples (2, 6, 8–15, and 19), setting up comparisons or contrasts (2, 5–8, 10–15, 18, and 19), and creating analogies (3, 9, 13, 16, 18, 19).

2. *Select two* of these strategies to analyze and evaluate, and *look closely* at the relevant paragraphs to see how Brooks uses each strategy.

3. *Make notes* in the margin about how he develops the strategy. What kinds of details does he include, and what sorts of sentences does he rely on?

4. *Evaluate* how effectively Brooks uses each strategy to support his reasons. What is most and least convincing about the support? What does it contribute to the overall argument?

Write

Write several sentences explaining Brooks's use of the two strategies you analyzed. *Support* your explanation with details from the paragraphs. Then *add a few sentences* evaluating how successfully Brooks uses the strategies.

CONSIDERING IDEAS FOR YOUR OWN WRITING

Consider imitating Brooks's approach by taking a position on an issue that you see being transformed in modern society, such as the "dominant image of business success" he examines. Perhaps in your academic major you see changes that would bear a closer look. Similarly, you could examine a hero from another time and show how his or her qualities are now valued in an arena different from the original one. Or you could disagree with Brooks and show that major heroes from our time—such as sports heroes or business heroes like Bill Gates—show different qualities from those Brooks believes are valued now.

A SPECIAL READING STRATEGY

Comparing and Contrasting Related Readings: Brooks's "A Nation of Grinders" and Moberg's "Class Consciousness Matters"

Comparing and contrasting related readings is a special critical reading strategy useful both in reading for meaning and in reading like a writer. This strategy is particularly applicable when writers deal with similar subjects, as is the case in the position papers written by David Brooks (p. 543) and David Moberg (p. 552) on class and social mobility. As you compare and contrast the positions of Brooks and Moberg, think about issues such as these:

- Compare and contrast the general rhetorical approach and tone each writer takes. In considering tone, you might look at the way each writer deploys the sentence strategies for counterarguing discussed on page 541. Highlight these strategies to see whether they are effective in making the writer appear fair and reasonable. Also, think about how your opinion of the credibility of the authors is affected by these strategies.

- Compare and contrast the fundamental beliefs about social mobility explored by Brooks and Moberg. How do their beliefs help you understand the positions they take on this issue?

- Compare and contrast any differences you may find between Brooks's and Moberg's views of how class affects one's chances of success in the United States and how class might affect one's *definition* of what constitutes success.

- Compare and contrast the authors' different points of view on democracy. Brooks is politically conservative, and Moberg is politically liberal. How do these different stances appear in their essays? How do these beliefs affect their presentations?

See Appendix 1 for detailed guidelines on using the comparing and contrasting related readings strategy.

DAVID MOBERG
Class Consciousness Matters

> *David Moberg received a PhD in anthropology from the University of Chicago in 1978. He is a senior editor for* In These Times, *an independent magazine of news, culture, and opinion. One of the country's leading journalists covering the labor movement, Moberg has written for the* Nation, Salon, *the* New York Times, *the* Chicago Tribune, *the* Chicago Sun-Times, *the* New Republic, World Policy Journal, *the* Boston Globe, Utne Reader, Mother Jones, *and others. He has also contributed to several books and has taught sociology and anthropology at DePaul University, Roosevelt University, Loyola University, the Illinois Institute of Technology, and Northeastern Illinois University. He has received a number of awards, including the Max Steinbock Award from the International Labor Communications Association in 2003, and has also received fellowships from organizations such as The Nation Institute and the John D. and Catherine T. MacArthur Foundation.*
>
> *"Class Consciousness Matters" was posted on the Web site AlterNet in 2005 in response to two series of newspaper articles—one on class in the* New York Times *and one on social mobility in the* Wall Street Journal. *Before you read, think about what* class *means to you. Do you consider yourself a member of any particular class, either economic or social? Do you feel bound to this class, or could you move out of it if you wished? As you read, annotate the text, noting where Moberg is responding to the two newspaper series and where he is arguing directly for his position.*

The myth of the self-made man is American culture's own special heart of darkness, helping to explain both its infectious optimism and ruthless greed. The idea holds enough truth and seductiveness to make it easy to forget its delusional dangers. To reprise Marx's famous formulation, individuals, like humankind, do make their own personal history, but not under conditions they choose. But in America, we choose to ignore the caveat about conditions at our peril.

The myth, or belief, that people are solely what they make of themselves is useful to keep in mind while reading two ongoing series: the *New York Times'* on class and the *Wall Street Journal's* on social mobility. Both focus attention on a truth about American society that runs counter to most people's deep-seated beliefs: There is less social mobility in the United States now than in the '80s (and less then than in the '70s) and less mobility than in many other industrial countries, including Canada, Finland, Sweden and Germany. Yet 40 percent of respondents to a *Times* poll said that there was a greater chance to move up from one class to another now than 30 years ago, and 46 percent said it was easier to do so in the United States than in Europe.

Although the news about social mobility has not been widely reported, it is generally recognized that inequality has grown over the past thirty years. The *Times* series highlights how much the super-rich have made out like, well, bandits. While the real income of the bottom 90 percent of Americans fell from 1980 to 2002, the income of the top 0.1 percent — making $1.6 million or more — went up two and a half times in real terms before taxes. With the help of the Bush tax cuts, the gap between the super-rich and everyone else grew even larger.

The American people accept this, it is argued, because they think not only that there's more social mobility than there is, but also that they'll personally get rich. Indeed, a poll in 2000 indicated that 39 percent of Americans thought they were either in the wealthiest one percent or would be "soon." The *Times* poll was slightly less exuberant: 11 percent thought it was very likely they would become wealthy, another 34 percent somewhat likely.

"It is OK to have ever-greater differences between rich and poor, [Americans] seem to believe," David Wessel wrote in the *Wall Street Journal*, "as long as their children have a good chance of grasping the brass ring."

This view is problematic. First, the greater the inequality, the less likely the possibility of mobility. Increased inequality worsens the large disparities in resources that families can devote to education — resources that are increasingly important for both entering many careers and for social mobility. A college degree, it should be stressed, is important not just because of the knowledge acquired, but because college serves as a class-biased sorting mechanism for entry to certain jobs. In contrast, the record suggests that countries with greater equality also have greater mobility. Substantive equality creates more equality of opportunity.

But even if there were mobility, such inequality would be problematic. Is it fair that society's wealth be divided so unevenly? Isn't there a decent standard of living — rising as economies become wealthier — to which everyone who "works hard and plays by the rules," in the Clintonian formulation, should be entitled? Great social disparity means that the financially well-off use their money and greater political leverage to protect their privilege rather than to design policies for the common good.

In defense of the rich getting richer, former Bush economic advisor Gregory Mankiw wrote in response to the *Times* series that the richest increased their share when the economy boomed; so if we want prosperity, let the plutocrats prosper. But the economy grew faster in the first three decades after World War II when equality was increasing than in the next three decades when equality was decreasing. In any case if the income from growth is captured by the very rich, as it largely has been for a couple decades, this path to prosperity offers little to most people. Also, with high inequality, even the pretense of community declines, social conflict increases and society functions more poorly. Individual mobility is not the only way to improve one's lot. Social solidarity and working together can improve everyone's lot.

This brings us back to the self-made man. It becomes clear, as the *Times* series is titled, that "class matters," just as race, gender and other accidents of history matter. The social class into which someone is born largely defines one's class as an adult, and both make a difference in how healthy or how long-lived the person will be, especially in the absence of universal health insurance. It influences access to education and to jobs.

9

The myth of the self-made person, however, encourages the person who succeeds to think his good fortune is due entirely to his work and genius. For this reason businessmen in the United States have historically been more anti-union and hostile to government than their counterparts in Europe. And the myth makes those who fail blame themselves.

10

According to recent polls, American workers—worried more about job insecurity, rising costs of education, health care expenses, the availability of insurance, pension failures and social security privatization—are increasingly looking for stronger social action to provide security. They are deeply skeptical about the globalization that has increased inequality and insecurity. Like the French vote on the European Union constitution, a U.S. referendum on globalization might well divide along class lines. The irony is that taking responsibility as a society to guarantee more stability and equality—by regulating the global economy and establishing universal guarantees of health care, education, and retirement security—can provide citizens with more individual freedom.

11

For now, the realm of freedom for most Americans remains constricted to the shopping mall, where they can buy their identities. Both the *Journal* and *Times* point to the rapid growth of personal credit as one way that Americans have continued to buy while earnings have stagnated. Former United Auto Workers official Frank Joyce even sees the rise of credit cards as undermining workers' interest in unions. Income, earned or borrowed, obviously greatly differentiates people's lives, even if a working class consumer can only indulge in a box of luxury chocolates or sub-luxury car. And the growing differences in income are exacerbated

12

by growing but unmeasured differences in health insurance, as well as various business perks such as free cars or expense accounts.

But the focus on income ignores the even greater inequalities of wealth. Wealth provides security. As the *Times* series points out, the better-off consistently talk of making choices while working class individuals talk about feeling trapped. Kids from wealthy families can take unpaid internships, spend a year abroad or experiment with careers; kids from working class families are likely to stick with a summer job that pays the bills and provides health insurance, thus failing to finish college. 13

More important, wealth and class are issues of power. Aaron Kemp, who lost his job when Maytag shifted production from Illinois to Mexico and Korea . . . , remarked, "I never remember even thinking about what class I was in until after the plant closing announcement and layoff. And then you begin to think about what class you're in." Rather than manners or fashion, class ultimately has more to do with who has the power to make such decisions and the powerlessness of the majority. These crucial aspects of class — social, political and economic power — have been missing from the series. 14

It might have been good for the *Times* to run an excerpt of Michael Graetz and Ian Shapiro's new book, *Death by a Thousand Cuts*. It recounts how the super-rich worked with ultra-conservatives to demonize and possibly eliminate the estate tax, which they renamed the "death tax." As William Gates, Sr., father of Microsoft Bill, often argued on behalf of the tax, the very rich accumulate their wealth not simply because of what they did but because of the society in which they lived, and they have a debt to that society. And the heirs of such wealth are the antithesis of self-made men. 15

The rich used their political power, their money and the right's shameless, mendacious hucksters to protect their riches, at the expense of society. But belief in the myth of the self-made man — abetted by the feckless incompetence of Democratic opposition — made many ordinary people suckers for the right-wing pitch. Class matters, but so does consciousness of class. That's another, longer story. 16

READING FOR MEANING

This section presents three activities that will help you reread Moberg's article with a critical eye. All three activities add up to between one and two pages of writing, but they lead you from basic comprehension to a response and an analysis that deepen your understanding and critical thinking about what you are reading. Your instructor may ask you to do one or more of these activities in class or as homework.

Read to Comprehend

Reread the selection, and write a few sentences briefly explaining what Moberg means by "class." The following definitions may help you understand Moberg's vocabulary:

delusional (paragraph 1): based on a false belief or opinion.

reprise (1): to repeat.

globalization (11): the tendency of businesses to extend their operations beyond national borders.

feckless (16): ineffective or incompetent.

Identify three or more additional words that you don't understand, and find the best definitions from the dictionary that work with their context.

Read to Respond

Write several paragraphs exploring your initial thoughts and feelings about Moberg's position argument. Focus on anything that stands out for you, perhaps because it resonates with your own experience or because you find a statement puzzling. You might consider writing about the following:

- your own beliefs about class and social mobility in America;
- the question Moberg poses in paragraph 7: "Is it fair that society's wealth be divided so unevenly?";
- your worries, or those of your parents or other people you know, about job insecurity, rising costs of education, health-care expenses, the availability of medical insurance, pension failures, and social security privatization; or
- Moberg's assertion that "[f]or now, the realm of freedom for most Americans remains constricted to the shopping mall, where they can buy their identities" (paragraph 12).

To develop your response to Moberg's position, you might use one of the following critical reading strategies that are explained and illustrated in Appendix 1: *summarizing* and *reflecting on challenges to your beliefs and values.*

Read to Analyze Assumptions

Reread Moberg's position essay, and write a paragraph or two exploring one or more of the assumptions you find in the text. The following suggestions may help:

- **assumptions about social mobility.** Moberg claims that there is less social mobility in the United States than thirty years ago and less than in many countries in the European Union. Yet individual Americans think they themselves have a good chance to be upwardly mobile. Moberg links this belief to what he calls "the myth of the self-made man" (paragraph 1)—the belief that "people are solely what they make of themselves" (2). To think critically about the assumptions in this essay related to social mobility, ask yourself: What role does Moberg assume education plays in social mobility? What happens if you are born into a class that does not value education or cannot afford it? When Moberg says that "[t]he social class into which someone is born largely defines one's class as an adult" (9), what is he saying about social mobility?

- **assumptions about security.** In paragraph 11, Moberg writes that "[a]ccording to recent polls, American workers—worried more about job insecurity, rising costs of education, health care expenses, the availability of insurance, pension failures and social security privatization—are increasingly looking for stronger social action to provide security." Moberg's assumption is that citizens of a democracy deserve security in the areas he mentions. To think critically about the assumptions in this essay related to social programs and security, ask yourself: Why has "globalization . . . increased inequality and insecurity" (11)? If, as Moberg says, a "self-made person" believes that one's wealth comes from one's own hard work and ability (10), then who is responsible if a person is laid off or lacks funds for health care, education, or retirement? To what extent, if any, is society responsible for a person's security?

READING LIKE A WRITER
PRESENTING THE ISSUE

Every position paper begins with an issue. Consequently, in planning and drafting a position paper, one of the first questions that a writer must answer is how much readers know about the issue. If readers are familiar with the issue, the writer may need to tell them very little about it. If they are unfamiliar with it, however, the writer may need to present it in great detail. Whether they are familiar or unfamiliar with it, readers may benefit from knowing about its history. They may also appreciate the writer's speculations about the larger social significance of the issue and even its likely immediate personal importance to themselves. Writers generally should not assume that readers will find an issue immediately engaging and worth their reading time. Therefore, they will often want to open a position paper with an interesting anecdote, arresting quotation, troubling fact, doomsday scenario, rhetorical question, or something else that is likely to engage readers' interest.

In addition, writers must address another important question—how to define the issue. Often, writers seek to redefine an issue to convince readers to look at it in a new way. If they succeed, then they can argue about the issue in their own terms, as they have redefined it. Moberg offers an example of this strategy. He begins by pointing out that both the *New York Times* and *Wall Street Journal* series demonstrate the growing inequality among social classes in the United States but that Americans don't believe they personally will be affected by the widening gap. To the contrary, many Americans (including, presumably, some of his readers) think they will become rich or move up in social class. "This view is problematic" (paragraph 6), Moberg says, and he goes on to argue that growing inequality produces a number of effects that challenge the "myth of the self-made man" (1).

Analyze

1. *Reread* paragraphs 1 and 2, and *underline* key words connected to "myth" and "social mobility."

2. Then *skim* the essay, noting ways Moberg develops the argument that class matters.

Write

Write several sentences describing how Moberg defines the problem of Americans' "delusion" about social mobility. Then *add a few sentences* explaining how, in subsequent paragraphs, Moberg develops his argument about both social mobility and economic inequality. How are these issues connected?

A SPECIAL READING STRATEGY

Evaluating the Logic of an Argument

To evaluate the logic of an argument, apply the ABC test by asking yourself three basic questions:

A. How *appropriate* is the support for each reason offered?

B. How *believable* is the support?

C. How *consistent and complete* is the overall argument?

Such an evaluation requires a comprehensive and thoughtful critical reading, but your efforts will help you understand more fully what makes a position paper successful. To evaluate the logic of Moberg's argument, follow the guidelines in Appendix 1. There you will find definitions and explanations (pp. 624–27) as well as an illustration based on an excerpt from a famous essay by Martin Luther King Jr. (p. 598).

CONSIDERING IDEAS FOR YOUR OWN WRITING

Consider writing about an issue related to Moberg's concern about security. Should communities provide homeless people with free food and shelter? Should we have a national health-care program? Should outsourcing be banned or limited? Should the social security system be changed? Or you could write on a more general topic that is not necessarily connected to Moberg's issue of social mobility, the self-made man, or economic inequality but that has local resonance. Should community growth be limited? Should height and design restrictions be placed on new commercial buildings? Should there be a police review board to handle complaints against the police? Should skateboarding be banned from all sidewalks? Should parents be held responsible legally and financially for crimes committed by their children under age eighteen? One major advantage of writing a position paper on a local civic issue is that you can gather information by researching the issue in local newspapers and talking with community leaders and residents.

Taking a Position Online

The Internet has made it easier than ever before for people to express their opinions in writing and find an audience for them. Blogs, chatrooms, personal and professional Web sites, and many other online venues are filled with "position papers" of one kind or another. These online arguments, reflecting the speed and quick-response capacity of the electronic medium, tend not to be as long or as detailed as position papers in print. But the Web also includes many spaces for writers to take a position in a more extended way. One of these is Salon, *an online-only general-interest magazine (available at salon.com).*

The following essay appeared in Salon's *"Opinion" section in May 2007 in response to Michelle Obama's decision to cut back on her professional life to help her husband, Barack Obama, campaign for president. It was written by Debra Dickerson (b. 1959), a freelance writer who a few months earlier had argued in another* Salon *opinion piece that because Barack Obama was not descended from Africans who had been slaves in the United States, he was not really "black" in the context of American culture. A former linguist and intelligence officer in the U.S. Air Force, where she rose to the rank of captain, Dickerson (like Barack Obama) attended Harvard Law School. Her work has appeared in the* Washington Post, *the* New York Times Magazine, Essence, VIBE, Talk, Good Housekeeping, *and many other publications. She has written two books—a memoir,* An American Story *(2000), and* The End of Blackness *(2004).*

As you read, think about women—or men—you know (including, possibly, yourself) who have had to make difficult decisions about how much time and energy to spend on their careers, families, and other social obligations. Add your own annotations to the text, paying attention to the strategies of the writers of position papers.

① As in many articles in print, this online essay provides a one-sentence opening summary of the writer's position.

② Dickerson grabs the reader's attention with a frustrated exclamation and then *presents the issue.* In the next paragraph, she develops the issue with *examples* of other women who have changed for the cameras.

political version of that process: Any day now, Michelle Obama's handlers will have her glued into one of those Sunday-go-to-meeting Baptist grandma crown hats while smiling vapidly for hours at a time. When, of course, she's not staring moonstruck, à la Nancy Reagan, at her moon doggie god-husband who's not one bit smarter than she is.

My heart breaks for her just thinking about it. Being president will be hard. So will being first lady for the brilliant Michelle -- imagine, having to begin all your sentences with "My husband and I..."

I'm in a feminist fury about Michelle (I'll use her first name to avoid confusion with her husband) feeling forced to quit, but make no mistake: I'm not blaming her. Few could stand up to the pressure she's facing, especially from blacks, to sacrifice herself on the altar of her husband's ambition. He could be the first black president, you know! Also, she must be beside herself trying to hold things together for her daughters. I'm blaming the world and every man, woman, child and border collie in it who helps send the message that women's lives must be subordinate to everyone else's. ③

No doubt her modern, progressive husband assured her she didn't have to quit -- probably even tried to dissuade her. It's also quite likely she's making this sacrifice so her children will have at least one parent available. But the result is the same. Our daughters grow up knowing that their freedom to work at hard-won, beloved careers hinges on the doings of their husbands.

Still, there's an opportunity in this setback. Now is the time for feminism to reach out to black women via the contingent of Obama-esque overachievers out there who ought to be chilled to the bone by Michelle's retirement from work of her own. Given Secretary Rice's, not to mention Oprah's, persistent singleness, black women who have earned high status may well wonder why they should bother trying to both date and develop successful careers if one's going to cancel out the other. No other group is less likely to marry. Given the innate conservatism of the black community, the burden to tend to hearth and home falls disproportionately on its women, sending the message to ambitious black girls that they can't have both fulfilling careers and families. ④

It would be one thing if Michelle had tired of working, but she's clearly ambivalent about leaving paid employment, as the Washington Post's recent coverage made clear:

> "Every other month [since] I've had children I've struggled with the notion of 'Am I being a good parent? Can I stay home? Should I stay home? How do I balance it all?'" she said. "I have gone back and forth every year about whether I should work." When she finally winds down her duties as vice president of community and external affairs at the University of Chicago Hospitals in the days ahead..., she said, it "will be the first time that I haven't gotten up and gone to a job." "It's a bit disconcerting," she said. "But it's not like I'll be bored."

No, you'll have your well-manicured hands full being your husband's hostess in chief. Funny how she didn't mention her husband's parental angst; there have been whispers that he's been pretty busy, too, what with being the great black hope and all. Wonder what finally made her decide to quit.

While I'm not blaming Michelle, I am issuing a challenge: This political and professional sutee won't end until women refuse to step into the fire, disapproval be damned. Sen. Clinton can't do everything: The rest of us women must stand our ground. Whatever else you think of Clinton, you can't deny that she blazed a trail for women's right to work and, like, be smart in public. And, man, what a beatdown she got. Since it was bringing about the end of the civilization as we know it, she caved, took her husband's name and gave up a public policy role; she had to wait, like a good girl, until her husband couldn't run for anything else. Valuable years of productivity, wasted. But at least giving up her career wasn't Hillary Clinton's first choice, as it is for most of the elite women who are abandoning their careers. ⑤

Linda Hirshman was an early observer of the phenomenon of top-tier women leading the retreat back to the kitchen. Following up a controversial article, "Homeward Bound," with an equally controversial book, "Get to Work," she harshly chastised elite, well-educated women for choosing not to work once they married high earners. Using census data and interviews, she argues that:

③ After assuring readers that she does not blame Obama for her decision to reduce her workload, Dickerson *asserts a clear, unequivocal position* in the last sentence of this paragraph. She then *counterargues objections and opposing positions* by acknowledging them but saying that whatever the reasons the result is the same.

④ The underlining indicates the first of eight links to online sources that help readers understand the context and content of this essay. (This one is to a *Washington Post* article on unmarried black professional women.) Links are often used in online position papers to provide additional support for reasons and to *establish credibility*.

⑤ Dickerson uses an analogy to suttee—the (now outlawed) Hindu custom of a widow throwing herself onto her husband's cremation fire— to *argue directly for the position.*

As a result of feminist efforts -- and larger economic trends -- the percentage of [working] women ... rose robustly through the 1980s and early '90s. But then the pace slowed. The census numbers for all working mothers leveled off around 1990 and have fallen modestly since 1998. In interviews, women with enough money to quit work say they are choosing to opt out. Their words conceal a crucial reality: the belief that women are responsible for child-rearing and homemaking was largely untouched by decades of workplace feminism ... Among the affluent-educated-married population, women are letting their careers slide to tend the home fires. If my interviewees are working, they work largely part time, and their part-time careers are not putting them in the executive suite.

I am not saying Michelle Obama is just another member of the so-called opt-out revolution; clearly, her reasons for leaving her job are historic -- and even so, she clearly seems pained to do it. And I hate to add to Michelle's load, but even though she's made the choice to leave work, I hope she'll keep her role in women's history in mind and increase the tiny inroad political wives have made in something approaching women's freedom of choice. With her personal wealth (albeit obtained by marriage) Theresa Heinz laid some groundwork, speaking her mind on the campaign trail and generally refusing to be mealy-mouthed and dull. Kudos to Dr. Judith Steinberg Dean, too, for refusing to give up saving lives to chat up reporters on her husband's tour bus. But until more women who want to work feel free to do just that, they'll continue to be mere appendages of their men, and the American workplace will remain just as family-unfriendly as it is now.

Next page: Shouldn't such an accomplished woman do more than organize white-tie dinners?

What can Michelle do? If Obama wins, she should go for it and take on a meaningful public policy role, à la Hillary Clinton's healthcare work. Just a lot more carefully. Why on earth should such an accomplished woman just arrange white-tie dinners? Until then, she should become more outspoken, building on her husband's willingness to confront dysfunction in the black community -- a black mother can get away with what no one else could. Obama has chastised blacks for apathy, for crime, for equating achievement with "acting white," for allowing their neighborhoods to deteriorate; Michelle's street cred as a churchgoing, "round the way" sister who made good makes her "ghetto pass" (her ability to operate as an insider) irrevocable. There will be no discussion of whether or not she's "black."

Since the Obamas are liberals, Michelle is bullet proof. Anyone who dares to insult her with the same level of vitriol as has been visited on Hillary Clinton and leading white Democrats like Nancy Pelosi or Dianne Feinstein will be trampled by a herd of black ministers, civil rights leaders and church ladies in big hats. (Condoleezza Rice doesn't get the same protection.) In a post-Imus world, any critiques of Michelle had best be worded very carefully. She could also build on her husband's interfaith pioneering with mainstream organizations to bring the resources of those well-endowed communities to bear on black problems.

Of course, "black" problems are really American problems; having the golden couple spearheading the fight will make it sexy to help blacks with their systemic problems (education and entrepreneurship, to name two). The two Obamas can de-race these issues (here is where she can use her fancy education) and help America understand that black progress is American progress.

Most important, though, I hope Michelle will bring feminism to black women.

Feminism is rightfully criticized for being irrelevant to black women and ignoring their issues. When it's not plain arrogant, that is. An excellent example of mainstream feminism's high-handedness is Maureen Dowd's recent petty bitching about Michelle's jabs at her husband on the campaign trail. She sounded like a 1940s white woman reprimanding a "sassy" black maid. But feminism's failure to engage with black women is only partly its own fault; black men have worked hard to reinforce the image of feminism as not just "white," not

---

6 She *establishes credibility* by quoting and linking to reliable sources to *argue directly for the position.*

7 Dickerson *counterargues* the idea that Obama might prefer to cut back on work and compares her with other wives of politicians (John Kerry and Howard Dean) who have resisted becoming "mere appendages of their men."

8 A "Next page" preview at the end of the first Web page encourages readers to continue.

9 Dickerson shows the complexity of the issues she has presented, providing context about Obama's unique position in the black community. Note that she defines "ghetto pass" and links to her own article about whether Barack Obama is "black."

10 Anticipating the objection that Obama would be attacked for being outspoken, Dickerson *counterargues* that her "street cred" makes her "bulletproof."

11 This dramatic one-sentence paragraph highlights what Dickerson sees as the connections between Obama, feminism, and black culture—an important aspect of *arguing directly for her position.*

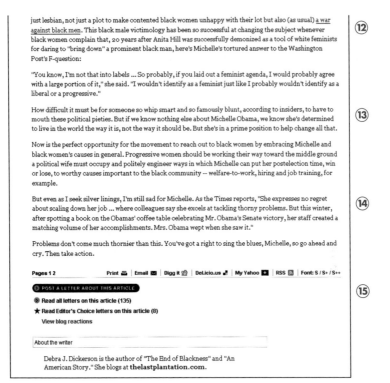

just lesbian, not just a plot to make contented black women unhappy with their lot but also (as usual) a war against black men. This black male victimology has been so successful at changing the subject whenever black women complain that, 20 years after Anita Hill was successfully demonized as a tool of white feminists for daring to "bring down" a prominent black man, here's Michelle's tortured answer to the Washington Post's F-question:

"You know, I'm not that into labels ... So probably, if you laid out a feminist agenda, I would probably agree with a large portion of it," she said. "I wouldn't identify as a feminist just like I probably wouldn't identify as a liberal or a progressive."

How difficult it must be for someone so whip smart and so famously blunt, according to insiders, to have to mouth these political pieties. But if we know nothing else about Michelle Obama, we know she's determined to live in the world the way it is, not the way it should be. But she's in a prime position to help change all that.

Now is the perfect opportunity for the movement to reach out to black women by embracing Michelle and black women's causes in general. Progressive women should be working their way toward the middle ground a political wife must occupy and politely engineer ways in which Michelle can put her postelection time, win or lose, to worthy causes important to the black community -- welfare-to-work, hiring and job training, for example.

But even as I seek silver linings, I'm still sad for Michelle. As the Times reports, "She expresses no regret about scaling down her job ... where colleagues say she excels at tackling thorny problems. But this winter, after spotting a book on the Obamas' coffee table celebrating Mr. Obama's Senate victory, her staff created a matching volume of her accomplishments. Mrs. Obama wept when she saw it."

Problems don't come much thornier than this. You've got a right to sing the blues, Michelle, so go ahead and cry. Then take action.

| Pages 1 2 | Print 🖨 | Email ✉ | Digg it 🔖 | Del.icio.us 🔖 | My Yahoo ★ | RSS 📶 | Font: S / S+ / S++ |

⊙ **POST A LETTER ABOUT THIS ARTICLE**
◉ **Read all letters on this article (135)**
★ **Read Editor's Choice letters on this article (8)**
   View blog reactions

About the writer

Debra J. Dickerson is the author of "The End of Blackness" and "An American Story." She blogs at **thelastplantation.com**.

⑫ Dickerson provides another reason for forging a connection between feminism and Obama—to put an end to "black male victimology."

⑬ Dickerson *counterargues* Obama's "tortured" statement about feminism by *acknowledging* the difficulty of "the world the way it is" but arguing that Obama can change black women's perception of feminism. She suggests how feminists' embrace of Obama could help black causes as well.

⑭ Dickerson concludes with more *counterarguments*, acknowledging that she is "seeking silver linings" in a "sad" situation for Obama but ending with a direct call for her to change the situation.

⑮ *Salon* provides a forum for readers' letters and links to bloggers' reactions, allowing readers, if they choose, to see the argument in a broad context. Below, note that the "About the writer" information includes a link to Dickerson's blog.

Analyze

1. *Find* an example of an online position paper.

2. *Check* to see which of the features of position papers it displays, such as presenting the issue, asserting a clear, unequivocal position, arguing directly for

the position, counterarguing objections and opposing positions, and establishing credibility.

3. *Note* any special online characteristics such as links, audio, or still or moving images.

Write

Write a paragraph or two describing what you have learned from this example of online position papers.

AMBER DAHLKE

Sex Education in Schools

> *Amber Dahlke wrote "Sex Education in Schools" for one of her college classes. Addressing the issue of whether and how sex education should be taught in U.S. public schools, she takes a clear position and documents her paper in MLA style, an appropriate citation format for academic writing.*
>
> *Before you read, think about your own sex education. Did you learn about sex from your schools, your parents, your friends, or other sources? What do you think the role of schools should be in sex education? As you read, annotate the passages where Dahlke states her claim and also where she restates it in another form.*

Few issues related to America's public secondary school system 1 arouse more hostility and encompass more conflicting opinions than the topic of sex education. It is strange that in an era when the public and the media speak so openly about sex, we still debate when and how to introduce preteens and teenagers to the topic. Children, parents, teachers, principals, religious leaders, and legislators are in a constant battle over what should be taught in schools and how it should be approached. Attempts to find a common solution only reveal how tangled the discussion has become (Coeyman).

On one side of the argument is the "abstinence-only" approach. 2 This curriculum requires teachers to teach that sexual intercourse out of wedlock is wrong, no matter what age the participants are. On the other side of the conflict is the "comprehensive sex education" approach. Teachers using this sex education style teach that abstinence is the best way to avoid sexually transmitted diseases and unwanted pregnancy but also instruct students about safe sex practices (Landry et al.). They teach about contraceptives, demonstrating how to use them, describing how they prevent sexually transmitted diseases and unwanted pregnancy, and telling students where they can be obtained (Coeyman). The debate centers on how public funds should be spent—in trying to convince teens not to engage in sexual activity or in educating them about the risks of unsafe sex (Landry et al.). Sex education in all junior and senior high schools in the United States should be comprehensive.

Sex education should be taught in a comprehensive style because 3 this approach teaches students that abstinence is the best way to avoid sexually transmitted diseases and unwanted pregnancies, while also teaching them tactics for reducing risks if they do engage in sexual activity. The American Medical Association, the American Academy of Pediatrics, and the National Academy of Sciences endorse comprehensive sex education for students because it encourages them to have fewer sexual partners and to use condoms, birth control, and other methods to prevent disease and pregnancy. Students are taught that having sex for the first time is something that they should wait until they are emotionally and physically ready for. According to a study in the journal *Perspectives on Sexual and Reproductive Health,* young people who are taught using comprehensive sex education methods are more likely to use protection when engaging in intercourse later in life (Landry et al.).

Another reason that comprehensive sex education should be taught is the number of unwed pregnant teenagers. The United States has twice the teenage pregnancies of any other Western industrialized country. At least one million American women between the ages of fifteen and nineteen become pregnant each year. Seventy-six percent of these women are unwed. The percentage of American mothers between ages fifteen and seventeen who were unmarried when they gave birth has more than tripled in the past fifty years to 84 percent. The average age at which young women go through puberty is twelve, and the average age they marry is twenty-five. This leaves a thirteen-year gap in which a young woman might have sex. Out-of-wedlock births are on the rise because many teenagers are not being taught the importance of contraception and other safe sex tactics (Koch).

A final reason that a comprehensive sex education is important is that teenagers as a class contract sexually transmitted diseases at the second highest rate in the United States; every fourth teenager is infected with a sexually transmitted disease by the age of twenty-one (DeCarlo). Teenagers in the United States are one hundred times more likely to contract a sexually transmitted disease than teenagers in any other industrialized country in the world. The number of HIV/AIDS infections among teenagers is rapidly rising. Studies show that three million new AIDS cases are being treated in thirteen- to twenty-four-year-olds per year. It is estimated that one in every four teenagers will contract the HIV/AIDS virus before reaching age twenty-two (DeCarlo). Teenagers also run the risk of contracting one of more than twenty new sexually transmitted diseases discovered in the last forty years (Koch). These staggering statistics proving that teenagers are having unprotected sex show that a comprehensive sex education style is necessary to disseminate knowledge about sexually transmitted diseases and their prevention.

Currently, conventional political leaders are supporting abstinence-only sex education as the best way to lower teen pregnancy rates and the occurrence of sexually transmitted diseases. President Bill Clinton signed the Welfare Reform Act of 1996, which provided $50 million per year to fund abstinence-only education. The Bush administration increased that amount to $135 million in 2004. Any state that uses the funds must agree to promote abstinence-only education. With 95 percent of schools teaching some sort of sex education, the percentage of abstinence-only education is increasing as the funds for sex education become increasingly earmarked for abstinence-only curricula (Coeyman). Only 65 percent of principals report that their schools teach comprehensive sex education, even though 85 percent of Americans prefer that teaching style ("Strategic Thinking"). The result of the increase in abstinence-only sex education is that students are being denied valuable health information that could improve or even save their lives (Van Dorn 1).

Many people believe that comprehensive sex education increases sexual activity among teenagers and that teaching kids about sex suggests that having sex at a young age is okay. Overwhelming numbers of studies confirm that this is a misconception (Koch). Still, out of the 95 percent of Americans who believe that some type of sex education should be taught in schools, 55 percent believe that providing adolescents and preadolescents with information about safe sex will make them curious and more likely to engage in sexual activities earlier than they would have otherwise ("Sex Education in America"). They claim that providing teenagers with information about sex and distributing condoms and information about where to obtain contraception without parental knowledge give them permission to have sex. On the contrary, studies done six to twelve months after a comprehensive sex education course show that teenagers are postponing sexual activity and reducing their numbers of sexual partners dramatically (Koch). As Douglas Kirby, who leads the Campaign to Prevent Teen Pregnancy, puts it, "Sexuality and HIV education curricula do not increase sexual intercourse, either by hastening the onset of intercourse, increasing the frequency of intercourse or increasing the number of sexual partners" (Koch). The research demonstrates that comprehensive sex education aids teenagers in making wise choices regarding sexual intercourse.

It is important to encourage adolescents to choose abstinence but also to provide those who do choose to engage in sexual activity with the information they need to do so safely. According to Betsey Van Dorn, "A national task force of health, education, and sexuality professionals believes that an issue as multi-faceted as sex requires a multi-targeted approach. Teaching abstinence is a significant piece of the puzzle, but 'just say no' may be lost on students who are already sexually active" (1). In many ways, the abstinence-only curriculum is the opposite of the comprehensive sex education that most people in the United States prefer. Seventy-seven percent of Americans believe that comprehensive sex education will encourage teens to practice safe sex practices now or later in life (Coeyman). Studies prove that teaching kids about sex will help them make better decisions concerning multiple partners, the use of condoms, and other methods for protecting against diseases (Koch).

The parents who prefer a comprehensive sex education believe   9
that their children should be taught more than the basic reproductive facts. The millions of teenage pregnancies and cases of sexually transmitted diseases point to the dire need for teenagers to have information about how to resist the pressure to have sex, how to protect themselves from unwanted pregnancy and sexually transmitted diseases, and where to go for counseling and support (Van Dorn 2). It is time for educators, parents, and policy makers to stop misconstruing ideas about sex education based on the numbers of sexually transmitted diseases and unwanted pregnancies. We can no longer ignore the need for education both on how to postpone involvement and on how to protect oneself when the time does come to engage in sex (DeCarlo).

Works Cited

Coeyman, Marjorie. "Schools Stumble over Sex Education." *Christian Science Monitor.* Christian Science Monitor, 22 July 2003. Web. 21 Oct. 2004.

DeCarlo, Pamela. "Does Sex Education Work?" *Center for AIDS Prevention Studies.* U of California San Francisco, June 1995. Web. 21 Oct. 2004.

Koch, Kathy. "Encouraging Teen Abstinence." *CQ Researcher* 8.25 (1998): 576. *General OneFile.* Web. 21 Oct. 2004.

Landry, David J., et al. "Factors Associated with the Context of Sex Education in U.S. Public Secondary Schools." *Perspectives on Sexual and Reproductive Health* 35.6 (2003): 261–69. *General OneFile.* Web. 21 Oct. 2004.

"Sex Education in America." *NPR.org.* Natl. Public Radio, 24 Feb. 2004. Web. 21 Oct. 2004.

"Strategic Thinking: Sex Education in America." *Communication Initiative.* The Communication Initiative Network, 23 Feb. 2004. Web. 21 Oct. 2004.

Van Dorn, Betsy. "Comprehensive Sex Education: A Multi-Targeted Approach." *FamilyEducation.* Family Education Network, n.d. Web. 21 Oct. 2004.

READING FOR MEANING

This section presents three activities that will help you reread Dahlke's essay with a critical eye. All three activities add up to between one and two pages of writing, but they lead you from basic comprehension to a response and an analysis that deepen your understanding and critical thinking about what you are reading. Your instructor may ask you to do one or more of these activities in class or as homework.

Read to Comprehend

Reread the selection, and write a few sentences briefly explaining why Dahlke favors "comprehensive" sex education in schools. The following definitions may help you understand Dahlke's vocabulary:

abstinence (paragraph 2): refraining from sexual intercourse.

contraceptives (2): substances or devices that prevent pregnancy.

tactics (3): plans to achieve a goal (i.e., ways to practice safe sex).

Identify three or more additional words that you don't understand, and find the best definitions from the dictionary that work with their context.

Read to Respond

Write several paragraphs exploring your initial thoughts and feelings about Dahlke's position argument. Focus on anything that stands out for you, perhaps because it resonates with your own experience or because you find a statement puzzling. You might consider writing about the following:

- your experiences with sex education;
- your response to the statistics Dahlke uses to support her argument, especially in paragraphs 4 to 8; or
- your concerns about sex education in schools.

To develop your response to Dahlke's position, you might use the following critical reading strategies that are explained and illustrated in Appendix 1: *evaluating the logic of an argument* and *using a Toulmin analysis*.

Read to Analyze Assumptions

Reread Dahlke's position essay, and write a paragraph or two exploring one or more of the assumptions you find in the text. The following suggestions may help:

- **assumptions about sexuality.** In paragraph 3, when she is demonstrating that "comprehensive" sex education has distinguished supporters such as the American Medical Association, the American Academy of Pediatrics, and the National Academy of Sciences, Dahlke argues directly that this kind of sex education "encourages [teens] to have fewer sexual partners and to use condoms, birth control, and other methods to prevent disease and pregnancy." She adds that teens also need to be emotionally and physically ready for sex. To think critically about the assumptions in this essay related to sexuality, ask yourself: What age do most adults you know seem to believe is appropriate for sexual activity to begin? What seem to be the common concerns that most people have about the consequences of sexual behavior? Why should schools be responsible for sex education? When Dahlke says that comprehensive sex education will lead to more responsible sexual behavior later in life, what belief is she hoping her audience will share?

- **assumptions about statistics.** Throughout her essay, Dahlke uses many statistics to make her case for comprehensive sex education in schools (see especially paragraphs 4 to 8). Clearly she thinks that her statistics will be convincing to her audience. To think critically about assumptions in this essay related to statistics, ask yourself: What kind(s) of statistics are most convincing in this essay? Why? Did you find any of the statistics shocking? Did Dahlke's statistics change any of your beliefs or make you less certain of them? If so, how? Or did they just confirm your existing beliefs? In general, how much weight do you think readers give to statistical evidence in an argument about an emotionally charged issue like sex education?

READING LIKE A WRITER
ASSERTING A CLEAR, UNEQUIVOCAL POSITION

The writer's statement of position is the sun that lights up a position paper. Like moons and planets, the other sentences reflect the light of this position statement. Without it, the essay might explain the debate on an issue but would not argue for a position on it.

Writers usually (but not always) assert their positions early in an essay. To keep readers in focus, they may reassert the position later in the essay and nearly always do so in the conclusion. Because readers must be able to understand the writer's position readily and unambiguously, it should be stated clearly and without waffling. Even so, however, the position should be carefully qualified if necessary. Key terms must be precisely defined unless there is little likelihood that readers will differ over what they mean.

Analyze

1. *Underline* Dahlke's statement, restatements, and qualifications of her position (you will find these sentences at the end of paragraph 2, the beginnings

of paragraphs 3, 4, and 5, the middle of paragraph 7, and the end of paragraphs 7 and 9).

2. *Consider* whether the writer's position statements are clear and unequivocal. *Think about* where they are located in relation to the other parts of her argument.

Write

Write several sentences reporting what you have learned about how Dahlke asserts her position on the issue of comprehensive sex education in schools. Point to places where she restates or qualifies her position. What does each statement add to the others? Then *add a few sentences* evaluating how effectively Dahlke asserts her position for her particular readers. *Make judgments* about the clarity of the statements.

CONSIDERING IDEAS FOR YOUR OWN WRITING

Consider writing a position paper on a controversial educational issue, such as the following: Should there be exit exams in schools? Should there be reforms in the way classes are conducted, such as lengthening the time of classes but holding them less often or taking the classroom into the field so that students get more hands-on learning? Should subjects such as art, music, physical education, and similar nonacademic topics be reinstated in schools that have discontinued them to save money? (You could also argue the opposite.) Are there subjects currently not taught in schools that you think should be the schools' responsibility? Should school be mandatory year-round? Should after-school programs be expanded? Should there be general education classes in college? (Or the reverse: Should we abolish general education in colleges and universities?) Should we expand our notion of what constitutes a "major" in college?

A SPECIAL READING STRATEGY

Using a Toulmin Analysis

To analyze the logic of Dahlke's essay, perform a Toulmin analysis on it. Identify her claim and the reasons and evidence she gives to support it. Then try to discover the beliefs, values, and assumptions that connect her reasons and evidence to her claim—that is, the underlying ideas that lead her to use these reasons and this evidence to justify this claim. (Stephen Toulmin, who developed this system of analysis, called evidence "grounds," and assumptions "warrants.")

A useful approach is to list the claim and reasons using a sentence with a "because" clause. In this case, Dahlke has provided such a sentence herself at the beginning of paragraph 3:

Claim: "Sex education should be taught in a comprehensive style . . ."

Reason 1: ". . . because this approach teaches students that abstinence is the best way to avoid sexually transmitted diseases and unwanted pregnancies, . . ."

Reason 2: ". . . while also teaching them tactics for reducing risks if they do engage in sexual activity."

Although the two reasons that Dahlke gives for her claim are closely related, single them out so that you can analyze the reasoning behind each one. First, list the evidence—or grounds—provided to support Reason 1: "because this approach teaches students that abstinence is the best way to avoid sexually transmitted diseases and unwanted pregnancies." Use as much of the writer's own wording as possible, because doing so will help you identify her assumptions and beliefs.

Grounds:

1. Authorities like *the American Medical Association, the American Academy of Pediatrics, and the National Academy of Sciences endorse comprehensive sex education* because this approach *encourages having fewer sexual partners.*

2. Comprehensive sex education teaches students that *having sex for the first time is something that they should wait until they are emotionally and physically ready for.*

Now consider the denotations and connotations—the basic meanings and the emotional associations—of key words and phrases used by the writer in the reason and grounds. For example, consider her reference to "the American Medical Association, the American Academy of Pediatrics, and the National Academy of Sciences" and her use of the phrases "the best way to avoid," "sexually transmitted diseases," "abstinence," "fewer sexual partners," and "emotionally and physically ready." Why does Dahlke use this language, or any other particular language you note? What comes to *your* mind when you hear these words and phrases?

For example, you can tell that Dahlke values the opinions of medical and scientific authorities, such as the American Medical Association, and that she expects her readers to share this belief. She also seems to value—and to expect that her readers value—the idea of sexual abstinence for religious or cultural reasons, the idea that people should have few sexual partners (not many), and the idea that sexual behavior is special, something worth waiting for, and not something to be casually indulged in. *Comprehensive* seems to assume the value of an approach to sex education that deals with all aspects of the issue.

Once you have stated in your own words what the key terms tell you about Dahlke's values, speculate about what alternative assumptions or different values some readers might find in the connotations of these terms. For example, many people and cultural groups do not believe that the number of sexual partners a person has makes any difference or believe that sex education should present sex in a generally positive way. Such readers may be put off by the way that Dahlke makes her argument using language about abstaining and avoiding disease and pregnancy. On the other hand, many other people and groups believe that sexual behavior should be saved only for marriage or should not begin until people are older. To them, wording like "encourages . . . fewer sexual partners" may sound too weak and permissive, not really evidence that a comprehensive approach leads students to limit or delay sex to the extent these readers prefer.

Finally, compare your own values and beliefs with Dahlke's. Do you share the same views, or do you find some differences? What are they?

Once you have completed this analysis for Dahlke's first reason, try doing the same kind of analysis for Reason 2.

Appendix 1 (pp. 627–31) provides detailed guidelines on using a Toulmin analysis.

JESSICA STATSKY

Children Need to Play, Not Compete

Jessica Statsky was a college student when she wrote this position paper, in which she argues that organized sports are not good for children between the ages of six and twelve. Before you read, recall your own experiences as an elementary school student playing competitive sports, either in or out of school. If you were not actively involved yourself, did you know anyone who was? Do you recall whether winning was unduly emphasized? What value was placed on having a good time? On learning to get along with others? On developing athletic skills and confidence? As you read, notice how Statsky supports the reasons for her position and how she handles readers' likely objections to her argument. Also pay attention to the visible cues that Statsky provides to guide you through her argument step by step. You may want to add your own annotations to the text, paying special attention to the features of a position paper—such as presenting the issue, asserting a clear, unequivocal position, arguing directly for the position, counterarguing objections and opposing positions, and establishing credibility.

The other readings in this chapter are followed by reading and writing activities. Following this reading, however, you are on your own to decide how to read for meaning and read like a writer.

Statsky *presents the issue* in sentence 2 and *asserts a clear unequivocal position* at the end of sentence 2 and in all of sentence 3.

Over the past several decades, organized sports for children have increased dramatically in the United States. And though many adults regard Little League Baseball and Peewee Football as a basic part of childhood, the games are not always joyous ones. When overzealous parents and coaches impose adult standards on children's sports, the result can be activities that are neither satisfying nor beneficial to children.

1

Statsky further *defines* her terms and *forecasts* her reasons for opposing organized sports activities for children under age thirteen.

I am concerned about all organized sports activities for children between the ages of six and twelve. The damage I see results from noncontact as well as contact sports, from sports organized locally to those organized nationally. Highly organized competitive sports such as Peewee Football and Little League Baseball are too often played to adult standards, which are developmentally inappropriate for children and can be both physically and psychologically harmful. Furthermore, because they eliminate many children from organized sports before they are ready to compete, they are actually counterproductive for developing either future players or fans. Finally, because they emphasize competition and winning, they unfortunately provide occasions for some parents and coaches to place their own fantasies and needs ahead of children's welfare.

2

3   One readily understandable danger of overly competitive sports is that they entice children into physical
actions that are bad for growing bodies. Although the
official Little League Online Web site acknowledges
that children do risk injury playing baseball, the league
insists that "severe injuries . . . are infrequent" — "far
less than the risk of riding a skateboard, a bicycle, or
even the school bus" ("What about My Child?"). Nevertheless, Leonard Koppett in *Sports Illusion, Sports Reality* claims that a twelve-year-old trying to throw a curve
ball, for example, may put abnormal strain on developing arm and shoulder muscles, sometimes resulting in
lifelong injuries (294). Contact sports like football can
be even more hazardous. Thomas Tutko, a psychology
professor at San Jose State University and coauthor of
the book *Winning Is Everything and Other American
Myths*, writes:

> I am strongly opposed to young kids playing
> tackle football. It is not the right stage of develop-
> ment for them to be taught to crash into other kids.
> Kids under the age of fourteen are not by nature
> physical. Their main concern is self preservation.
> They don't want to meet head on and slam into each
> other. But tackle football absolutely requires that
> they try to hit each other as hard as they can. And it
> is too traumatic for young kids. (qtd. in Tosches A1)

4   As Tutko indicates, even when children are not
injured, fear of being hurt detracts from their enjoyment of the sport. Little League Online ranks fear of
injury as the seventh of seven reasons children quit
("What about My Child"). One mother of an eight-
year-old Peewee Football player explained, "The kids
get so scared. They get hit once and they don't want
anything to do with football anymore. They'll sit on the
bench and pretend their leg hurts" (qtd. in Tosches A1).
Some children are driven to even more desperate measures. For example, in one Peewee Football game, a
reporter watched the following scene as a player took
himself out of the game:

> "Coach, my tummy hurts. I can't play," he said.
> The coach told the player to get back onto the field.
> "There's nothing wrong with your stomach," he

*Arguing directly for the
position, Statsky presents
her first reason — the danger of physical harm to
growing bodies. She anticipates objections and counterargues by citing reliable
sources.*

*Statsky makes a transition
to her second reason — the
psychological harm caused
by organized sports. She
provides several examples
from authorities in the field
to support each of her
points and help establish
her credibility.*

said. When the coach turned his head, the seven-year-old stuck a finger down his throat and made himself vomit. When the coach turned back, the boy pointed to the ground and told him, "Yes there is, coach. See?" (Tosches A33)

Besides physical hazards and anxieties, competitive 5 sports pose psychological dangers for children. Martin Rablovsky, a former sports editor for the *New York Times*, says that in all his years of watching young children play organized sports, he has noticed very few of them smiling. "I've seen children enjoying a spontaneous pre-practice scrimmage become somber and serious when the coach's whistle blows," Rablovsky says. "The spirit of play suddenly disappears, and sport becomes joblike" (qtd. in Coakley 94). The primary goal of a professional athlete—winning—is not appropriate for children. Their goals should be having fun, learning, and being with friends. Although winning does add to the fun, too many adults lose sight of what matters and make winning the most important goal. Several studies have shown that when children are asked whether they would rather be warming the bench on a winning team or playing regularly on a losing team, about 90 percent choose the latter (Smith, Smith, and Smoll 11).

Note how Statsky *counterargues* the objection that since winning and losing are part of life, they should be part of childhood. She disagrees with this assumption and explains why.

Winning and losing may be an inevitable part of 6 adult life, but they should not be part of childhood. Too much competition too early in life can affect a child's development. Children are easily influenced, and when they sense that their competence and worth are based on their ability to live up to their parents' and coaches' high expectations—and on their ability to win—they can become discouraged and depressed. Little League advises parents to "keep winning in perspective" ("Your Role"), noting that the most common reasons children give for quitting, aside from change in interest, are lack of playing time, failure and fear of failure, disapproval by significant others, and psychological stress ("What about My Child"). According to Dr. Glyn C. Roberts, a professor of kinesiology at the Institute of Child Behavior and Development at the University of Illinois, 80 to 90 percent of children who play competitive sports at a young age drop out by sixteen (Kutner C8).

7   This statistic illustrates another reason I oppose competitive sports for children: because they are so highly selective, very few children get to participate. Far too soon, a few children are singled out for their athletic promise, while many others who may be on the verge of developing the necessary strength and ability are screened out and discouraged from trying out again. Like adults, children fear failure, and so even those with good physical skills may stay away because they lack self-confidence. Consequently, teams lose many promising players who with some encouragement and experience might have become stars. The problem is that many parent-sponsored, out-of-school programs give more importance to having a winning team than to developing children's physical skills and self-esteem.

Statsky makes a smooth transition to another reason: most children never get the chance to participate and enjoy sports because of the selection process.

8   Indeed, it is no secret that too often scorekeeping, league standings, and the drive to win bring out the worst in adults who are more absorbed in living out their own fantasies than in enhancing the quality of the experience for children (Smith, Smith, and Smoll 9). The news provides plenty of horror stories. *Los Angeles Times* reporter Rich Tosches, for example, tells the story of a brawl among seventy-five parents that began following a Peewee Football game when a parent from one team confronted a player from the other team (A33). Another example is provided by a *Los Angeles Times* editorial about a Little League manager who intimidated the opposing team by setting fire to one of its jerseys on the pitching mound before the game began. As the editorial writer commented, the manager showed his young team that "intimidation could substitute for playing well" ("The Bad News" B6). In addition, the Web site of the National Association of Sports Officials lists an appalling number of incidences of attacks on referees and field supervisors, including Thomas Juntas's fatal beating of a Massachusetts man who had been supervising a pick-up hockey game in which Juntas's son was playing (Topp).

Statsky's final reason for opposing organized sports for children: they bring out the worst in adults. She continues to establish her credibility by providing examples from a reputable newspaper and a Web site.

9   Although not all parents or coaches behave inappropriately, the seriousness of the problem is illustrated by the fact that Adelphi University in Garden City, New York, offers a sports psychology workshop for Little League coaches that is designed to balance their "animal instincts" with "educational theory" in

hopes of reducing the "screaming and hollering," in the words of Harold Weisman, manager of sixteen Little Leagues in New York City (Schmitt B2). In a three-and-one-half-hour Sunday morning workshop, coaches learn how to make practices more fun, treat injuries, deal with irate parents, and be "more sensitive to their young players' fears, emotional frailties, and need for recognition." Little League is to be credited with recognizing the need for such workshops.

Some parents would no doubt argue that children 10 cannot start too soon preparing to live in a competitive free-market economy. After all, secondary schools and colleges require students to compete for grades, and college admission is extremely competitive. And it is obvious how important competitive skills are in finding a job. Yet the ability to cooperate is also important for success in life. Before children are psychologically ready for competition, maybe we should emphasize cooperation and individual performance in team sports rather than winning.

Many people are ready for such an emphasis. One 11 New York Little League official who had attended the Adelphi workshop tried to ban scoring from six- to eight-year-olds' games—but parents wouldn't support him (Schmitt B2). An innovative children's sports program in New York City, City Sports for Kids, emphasizes fitness, self-esteem, and sportsmanship. In this program's basketball games, every member on a team plays at least two of six eight-minute periods. The basket is seven feet from the floor rather than ten feet, and a player can score a point just by hitting the rim (Bloch C12). I believe this kind of local program should replace overly competitive programs like Pee-wee Football and Little League Baseball. For example, childhood-fitness expert Stephen Virgilio of Adelphi University recommends "positive competition," which encourages children to strive to do their best without comparing themselves to an opponent. Virgilio also suggests that improvements can come from a few simple rule changes, such as rotating players to different positions several times during each game to show that "you're more interested in skill development than just trying to win a game" (qtd. in Rosenstock).

Authorities have clearly documented the excesses 12 and dangers of many competitive sports programs for

Statsky acknowledges another objection—that children must prepare for a competitive world—but she points out that cooperation is equally (or more) important. To support her counterargument, *she gives examples in paragraph 11 of alternative approaches to sports for children.*

children. It would seem that few children benefit from these programs and that those who do would benefit even more from programs emphasizing fitness, cooperation, sportsmanship, and individual performance. Thirteen- and fourteen-year-olds may be eager for competition, but few younger children are. These younger children deserve sports programs designed specifically for their needs and abilities.

Statsky concludes by reminding readers of her credible sources and reaffirming her thesis, again carefully limiting its scope to younger children.

Works Cited

"The Bad News Pyromaniacs?" Editorial. *Los Angeles Times* 16 June 1990: B6. Print.

Bloch, Gordon B. "Thrill of Victory Is Secondary to Fun." *New York Times* 2 Apr. 1990, late ed.: C12. Print.

Coakley, Jay J. *Sport in Society: Issues and Controversies.* St. Louis: Mosby, 1982. Print.

Koppett, Leonard. *Sports Illusion, Sports Reality.* Boston: Houghton, 1981. Print.

Kutner, Lawrence. "Athletics, through a Child's Eyes." *New York Times* 23 Mar. 1989, late ed.: C8. Print.

Rosenstock, Bonnie. "Competitive Sports for Kids: When Winning Becomes Cumbersome Instead of Fun." *Parentsknow.com.* NY Metro Parents Magazine, June 2002. Web. 28 June 2004.

Schmitt, Eric. "Psychologists Take Seat on Little League Bench." *New York Times* 14 Mar. 1988, late ed.: B2. Print.

Smith, Nathan, Ronald Smith, and Frank Smoll. *Kidsports: A Survival Guide for Parents.* Reading: Addison, 1983. Print.

Topp, Bill. "Poor Sporting Behavior Reported to NASO." *Naso.org.* National Association of Sports Officials, Feb. 2004. Web. 29 June 2004.

Tosches, Rich. "Peewee Football: Is It Time to Blow the Whistle?" *Los Angeles Times* 3 Dec. 1988: A1+. Print.

"What about My Child?" *Little League Online.* Little League, n.d. Web. 30 June 2004.

"Your Role as a Little League Parent." *Little League Online.* Little League, n.d. Web. 30 June 2004.

Statsky uses MLA style to document her sources.

READING FOR MEANING

Reading for meaning involves three activities:

- reading to comprehend,
- reading to respond, and
- reading to analyze assumptions.

Reread Statsky's essay, and then write a page or so explaining your understanding of its basic meaning or main point, a personal response you have to it, and one of its underlying assumptions.

READING LIKE A WRITER

Writers of position papers

- present the issue,
- assert a clear, unequivocal position,
- argue directly for the position,
- counterargue objections and opposing positions, and
- establish credibility.

Focus on one of these strategies in Statsky's essay, and analyze it carefully through close rereading and annotating. Then write several sentences explaining what you have learned about the strategy, giving specific examples from the reading to support your explanation. Add a few sentences evaluating how successfully Statsky uses the strategy to argue convincingly for her position.

REVIEWING WHAT MAKES POSITION PAPERS EFFECTIVE

In this chapter, you have been learning how to read position papers for meaning and how to read them like a writer. Before going on to write a position paper, pause here to review and contemplate what you have learned about the elements of effective position arguments.

Analyze

Choose one reading from this chapter that seems to you especially effective. Before rereading the selection, *jot down* one or two reasons you remember it as an example of an effective position paper.

Reread your chosen selection, adding further annotations about what makes it a particularly effective example of the genre. *Consider* the selection's purpose and the ways that it achieves that purpose for its intended readers. (You can make an informed guess about the intended readers and their expectations by noting the publication source of the essay.) Then *focus* on how well the essay

- presents the issue,
- asserts a clear, unequivocal position,
- argues directly for the position,

- counterargues objections and opposing positions, and

- establishes credibility.

You can review all of these basic features in the Guide to Reading Position Papers (p. 520).

Your instructor may ask you to complete this activity on your own or to work with a small group of other students who have chosen the same reading. If you work with others, allow enough time initially for all group members to reread the selection thoughtfully and to add their annotations. Then *discuss* as a group what makes the essay effective. *Take notes* on your discussion. One student in your group should then report to the class what the group has learned about the effectiveness of position papers. If you are working individually, write up what you have learned from your analysis.

Write

Write at least a page supporting your choice of this reading as an example of an effective position paper. *Assume* that your readers—your instructor and classmates—have read the selection but will not remember many details about it. They also might not remember it as especially successful. Therefore, you will need to *refer* to details and specific parts of the essay as you explain how it works and as you justify your evaluation of its effectiveness. You need not argue that it is the best essay in the chapter or that it is flawless, only that it is, in your view, a strong example of the genre.

■ A Guide to Writing Position Papers

The readings in this chapter have helped you learn a great deal about position papers. Now that you have seen how writers construct arguments supporting their position on issues for their particular readers, you can approach this type of writing confidently. The readings will remain an important resource for you as you develop your own position paper. Use them to review how other writers solved the types of problems you will encounter in your writing.

This Guide to Writing is designed to assist you in writing your position paper. Here you will find activities to help you choose an issue and discover what to say about it, organize your ideas and draft the essay, read the draft critically, revise the draft to strengthen your argument, and edit and proofread the essay to improve readability.

INVENTION AND RESEARCH

The following activities will help you choose an issue to write about and develop an argument to support your position on the issue. You will also explore what you already know about the issue and determine whether you need to learn more about it through extended research. A few minutes spent completing each writing activity will improve your chances of producing a detailed and convincing first draft.

Choosing an Issue

Rather than limiting yourself to the first issue that comes to mind, widen your options by making a list of the issues that interest you. List the most promising issues you can think of, beginning with any you listed for the Considering Ideas for Your Own Writing activities following the readings in this chapter. Continue listing other possible issues. Making such a list often generates still other ideas: As you list ideas, you will think of new issues you cannot imagine now.

List the issues in the form of questions like these:

- Should local school boards have the power to ban such books as *The Adventures of Huckleberry Finn* and *Of Mice and Men* from school libraries?

- Should teenagers be required to get their parents' permission to obtain birth-control information and contraceptives?

- Should businesses remain loyal to their communities, or should they move to wherever labor costs, taxes, and other conditions are more favorable?

After you have completed your list, reflect on the possible issues you have compiled. Choose an arguable issue, one that people disagree about but that cannot be resolved simply with facts or by authorities. Your choice also may be influenced by whether you have time for research and whether your instructor requires it. Issues that have been written about extensively—such as whether weapons searches should be conducted on high-school campuses or affirmative action should be continued in college admissions—make excellent topics for extended research. Other issues—such as whether students should be required to perform community service or be discouraged from taking part-time jobs that interfere with their studies—may be confidently based on personal experience.

Developing Your Argument

The writing and research activities that follow will enable you to test your choice of an issue and discover good ways to argue for your position on the issue.

Defining the Issue.   *To see how you can define the issue, write nonstop for a few minutes.* This brief but intensive writing will help stimulate your memory, letting you see what you already know about the issue and whether you will need to do research to discover more about it.

Considering Your Own Position and Reasons for It.   *Briefly state your current position on the issue and give a few reasons you take this position.* You may change your position as you develop your ideas and learn more about the issue, but for now say as directly as you can where you stand and why.

Researching the Issue.   *If your instructor requires you to research the issue, or if you decide your essay would benefit from research, consult Appendix 2, Strategies for Research and Documentation, for guidelines on finding library and Internet sources.* Research can help you look critically at your own thinking and help you anticipate your readers' arguments and possible objections to your argument.

RESEARCHING YOUR SUBJECT ONLINE

To learn more about opposing positions, search for your issue online. To do so, enter a key term—a word or brief phrase—of your issue into a search tool such as Google <http://www.google.com> or Yahoo! Directory <http://dir.yahoo.com>. If possible, identify at least two positions different from your own. No matter how well argued, they need not weaken your confidence in your position. Your purpose is to understand opposing positions so well that you can represent one or more of them accurately and counterargue them effectively.

Bookmark or keep a record of promising sites. Download any materials that may help you represent and counterargue opposing positions.

Analyzing Your Readers.   *Write for a few minutes identifying who your readers are, what they know about the issue, and how they can be convinced that your position may be plausible.* Describe your readers briefly. Mention anything you know about them as a group that might influence the way they would read your position paper. Speculate about how they will respond to your argument.

Rehearsing the Argument for Your Position.   *Consider the reasons you could give for your position, and then write for a few minutes about the one reason you think would be most convincing to your readers.* Which reason do you think is the strongest? Which is most likely to appeal to your readers? As you write, try to show your readers why they should take this reason seriously.

Rehearsing Your Counterargument.   *List what will likely be the one or two strongest opposing arguments or objections to your argument, and then write for a few minutes either conceding or refuting each one.* Try to think of arguments or objections your readers will expect you to know about and respond to, especially any criticism that could seriously undermine your argument.

Testing Your Choice.   *Pause now to decide whether you have chosen an issue about which you will be able to make a convincing argument.* At this point, you have some insights into how you will attempt to present the issue and argue to support your position on it for your particular readers. If your interest in the issue is growing and you are gaining confidence in the argument you want to make, you have probably made a good choice. However, if your interest in the issue is waning and you have been unable to come up with at least two or three plausible reasons why you take the position you do, you may want to consider choosing another issue. If your issue does not seem promising, return to your list of possible subjects to select another.

Considering Visuals.   *Consider whether visuals—drawings, photographs, tables, or graphs—would strengthen your argument.* You could construct your own visuals, scan materials from books and magazines, or download them from the Internet. If you submit your essay electronically to other students and your instructor or if you post it on a Web site, consider including photographs as well as snippets of film or sound. Visual and auditory materials are not at all a requirement of a successful position paper, as you can tell from the readings in this chapter, but they could add a new dimension to your writing. If you want to use photographs or recordings of people, though, be sure to obtain their permission.

Considering Your Purpose.   *Write for several minutes about your purpose for writing this position paper.* The following questions will help you think about your purpose:

- What do I hope to accomplish with my readers? How do I want to influence their thinking? What one big idea do I want them to grasp and remember?

- How much resistance to my argument should I expect from my readers? Will they be largely receptive? Skeptical but convincible? Resistant and perhaps even antagonistic?

- How can I interest my readers in the issue? How can I help my readers see its significance — both to society at large and to them personally?

Formulating a Working Thesis.   *Draft a thesis or position statement.* A working thesis — as opposed to a final or revised thesis — will help you bring your invention writing into focus and begin your draft with a clear purpose. As you draft and revise your essay, you may decide to modify your position and reformulate your thesis. Remember that the thesis for a position paper should assert your position on the issue and may define or qualify that position. In addition, the thesis usually forecasts your argument; it might also forecast your counterargument. The thesis and forecasting statements, therefore, may occupy several sentences. Here are three examples from the readings:

- "I believe we can replace most of our gasoline needs in 25 years with biomass from our farmlands and municipal waste, while creating a huge economic boom cycle and a cheaper, cleaner fuel for consumers" (Khosla, paragraph 4).

- "Sex education in all junior and senior high schools in the United States should be comprehensive.

    "Sex education should be taught in a comprehensive style because this approach teaches students that abstinence is the best way to avoid sexually transmitted diseases and unwanted pregnancies, while also teaching them tactics for reducing risks if they do engage in sexual activity" (Dahlke, paragraphs 2 and 3).

- "When overzealous parents and coaches impose adult standards on children's sports, the result can be activities that are neither satisfying nor beneficial to children.

    "I am concerned about all organized sports activities for children between the ages of six and twelve. The damage I see results from noncontact as well as contact sports, from sports organized locally to those organized nationally. Highly organized competitive sports such as Peewee Football and Little League Baseball are too often played to adult standards, which are developmentally inappropriate for children and can be both physically and psychologically harmful. Furthermore, because they eliminate many children from organized sports before they are ready to compete, they are actually counterproductive for developing either future players or fans. Finally, because they emphasize competition and winning, they unfortunately provide occasions for some parents and coaches to place their own fantasies and needs ahead of children's welfare" (Statsky, paragraphs 1 and 2).

DRAFTING

The following guidelines will help you set goals for your draft, plan its organization, and consider a useful sentence strategy.

Setting Goals

Establishing goals for your draft before you begin writing will enable you to make decisions and work more confidently. Consider the following questions now, and keep them in mind as you draft. They will help you set goals for drafting as well as recall how the writers you have read in this chapter tried to achieve similar goals.

- *How can I present the issue in a way that will interest my readers?* Should I open with an anecdote as Khosla and Brooks do, a response to a debate under way as Brooks does, or a connection to my personal experience as Khosla and Stabiner do? Do I need to define the issue explicitly, perhaps by distinguishing between terms like Moberg? Should I present the issue in a historical context, as Stabiner, Brooks, and Moberg do? Or should I start with alarming statistics, as Khosla does?

- *How can I support my argument in a way that will win the respect of my readers?* Should I quote authorities or offer statistics from research studies, as Khosla, Stabiner, Moberg, Dahlke, and Statsky do? Should I argue that my position is based on shared values, as all the writers in this chapter do? Should I create analogies, as Khosla and Brooks do? Should I provide examples or speculate about consequences, like all the writers? Should I support my argument with personal experience, as Khosla and Stabiner do?

- *How can I counterargue effectively?* Should I introduce my argument by reviewing readers' opposing positions and likely objections, as all the writers do? Should I concede the wisdom of readers' views, as Stabiner does? Or should I attempt to refute readers' views, as all the writers do?

- *How can I establish my authority and credibility on the issue?* Should I support my argument through research, as all the writers in this chapter do? Should I risk bringing in my personal experience, as Khosla and Stabiner do? How can I refute readers' views without attacking them, as Stabiner and Brooks manage to do? Should I make an appeal to possible shared moral values with readers, as Brooks and Moberg do?

Organizing Your Draft

With goals in mind and invention notes in hand, you are ready to make a tentative outline of your draft. First, list the reasons you plan to use as support for your argument. Decide how you will sequence these reasons. Writers of position papers often end with the strongest reasons because this organization gives the best reasons the greatest emphasis. Then add to your outline the opposing positions or objections that you plan to counterargue.

WORKING WITH SOURCES

Quoting and Paraphrasing

How you represent the views of those who disagree with your position is especially important because it affects your credibility with readers. If you do not represent your opponents' views fairly and accurately, readers very likely will—and probably should—question your honesty. One useful strategy is to insert quoted words and phrases into your summary of the source.

But how do you decide which elements to quote and which to put in your own words? The following sentences from Jessica Statsky's essay illustrate how you might make this decision. Compare the sentence below from paragraph 3 of Statsky's essay to the passage from her source, the Little League Baseball Web site. The words Statsky quotes are highlighted:

> **Statsky:** Although the official Little League Web site acknowledges that children do risk injury playing baseball, the league insists that "severe injuries . . . are infrequent"—"far less than the risk of riding a skateboard, a bicycle, or even the school bus" ("What about My Child?").

> **Little League Baseball:** We know that injuries constitute one of parents' foremost concerns, and rightly so. Injuries seem to be inevitable in any rigorous activity, especially if players are new to the sport and unfamiliar with its demands. But because of the safety precautions taken in Little League, severe injuries such as bone fractures are infrequent. Most injuries are sprains and strains, abrasions and cuts and bruises. The risk of serious injury in Little League Baseball is far less than the risk of riding a skateboard, a bicycle, or even the school bus.

Statsky summarizes Little League's acknowledgment that playing competitive sports can be harmful by condensing the second sentence ("Injuries seem to be inevitable in any rigorous activity, especially if players are new to the sport and unfamiliar with its demands") into one simple clause ("children do risk injury playing baseball"). Note what her summary leaves out—Little League's explanation that injuries are "inevitable in any rigorous activity," its emphasis on the increased likelihood of injury when the sport is "new" and "unfamiliar," and the claim that Little League takes "safety precautions" to prevent serious injury. Statsky omitted these statements because they try to explain away the basic fact she wants to emphasize—that "children do risk injury playing baseball." Demonstrating that Little League—renowned as the first and probably the most famous provider of organized sports for children—agrees with her about this basic fact lends credibility to Statsky's argument.

But when you omit language and ideas from your summary, you must take care not to misrepresent your source. Statsky makes clear in the second part of her sentence that although Little League agrees with her on the risk of injury, it disagrees about the seriousness of that risk. By quoting ("it insists that 'severe injuries . . . are infrequent'—'far less than the risk of riding a skateboard, a bicycle, or even the school bus'"), she assures readers she has not distorted Little League's position.

Using Ellipsis Marks in Quotations to Avoid Plagiarism

In an earlier draft, Statsky omitted the quotation marks around the phrase "severe injuries . . . are infrequent"—either because she did not know how to make the language from the original fit smoothly into her sentence or because she did not realize she could have multiple separate quotations from the same source in one sentence. Below is part of her original sentence, followed by the source with the quoted words highlighted.

Statsky: the league insists that severe injuries are infrequent—"far less than the risk of riding a skateboard, a bicycle, or even the school bus" ("What about My Child?").

Little League Baseball: severe injuries such as bone fractures are infrequent. Most injuries are sprains and strains, abrasions and cuts and bruises. The risk of serious injury in Little League Baseball is far less than the risk of riding a skateboard, a bicycle, or even the school bus.

Even though Statsky cites the source, this failure to use quotation marks around language that is borrowed amounts to plagiarism. A simple way to avoid plagiarizing is to use ellipsis marks (. . .) to indicate that words have been omitted: "severe injuries . . . are infrequent." When you cite sources in a position paper, use quotation marks whenever you use phrases from your source, *and* indicate your source. Doing one or the other is not enough; you must do both. For more information on quoting and using ellipses to integrate language from sources into your own sentences, see pages 670–79 in Appendix 2, Strategies for Research and Documentation.

Considering a Useful Sentence Strategy

As you draft your essay, you will need to move back and forth smoothly between direct arguments for your position and counterarguments for your readers' likely objections, questions, and preferred positions. One useful strategy for making this move is to concede the value of a likely criticism and then attempt to refute it immediately, either in the same sentence or in the next one. Here are two examples from Statsky's essay that illustrate ways to use concessions (shown in italics) and refutations (shown in bold):

> The primary goal of a professional athlete—winning—is not appropriate for children. Their goals should be having fun, learning, and being with friends. *Although winning does add to the fun,* **too many adults lose sight of what matters and make winning the most important goal.** (paragraph 5)

> *And it is obvious how important competitive skills are in finding a job.* **Yet the ability to cooperate is also important for success in life.** (10)

In these examples from different stages in her argument, Statsky concedes the importance or value of some of her readers' likely objections, but then firmly refutes them. (Because these illustrations are woven into an extended argument, you may better appreciate them if you look at them in context by turning to the paragraphs where they appear.)

Here are two examples from other readings in the chapter:

> Of course, 25 million gallons of ethanol is a drop in the tanker when it comes to our 140 billion-a-year oil habit. And ethanol itself is a subject of controversy for all sorts of reasons. Many of the criticisms, while true in some small ways, are aggressively promoted by the oil lobby and other interested parties in an effort to forestall change. Most are myths. *Challenges certainly exist with ethanol,* **but none are insurmountable, and—with apologies to Al Gore—the convenient truth is that corn ethanol is a crucial first step toward kicking our oil addiction.** (Khosla, paragraph 4)

> Educators at single-sex schools already get it: Equality is the goal, not the process. *There may be more than one path to the destination—***but it is the arrival, not the itinerary, that counts.** (Stabiner, paragraph 12)

This important counterargument strategy sometimes begins not with concession but with acknowledgment; that is, the writer simply restates part of an opponent's argument without conceding the wisdom of it. Here are some examples:

> *There are other scenarios we can imagine—say, wind-driven hydrogen generators powering our cars—***but they are just that: blue-sky flights of imagination from academics and dreamers with no notion of reality.** (Khosla, paragraph 11)

> *What is this misplaced reverence for the coed school?* **Do not think that it was designed with the best interests of all children at heart.** (Stabiner, paragraph 15)

> *We think of the Horatio Alger stories as rags-to-riches tales.* **In fact they are not.** The Alger heroes are almost never plucky young boys who become millionaires or moguls. (Brooks, paragraph 12)

But even if there were mobility, **such inequality would be problematic.** *Is it fair that society's wealth be divided so unevenly?* (Moberg, paragraph 7)

Many people believe that comprehensive sex education increases sexual activity among teenagers and that teaching kids about sex suggests that having sex at a young age is okay. **Overwhelming numbers of studies confirm that this is a misconception.** (Dahlke, paragraph 7)

The concession-refutation move, sometimes called the "yes-but" strategy, is important in most arguments. Following is a list of some of the other language this chapter's authors rely on to introduce their concession-refutation moves:

Introducing the Concession	*Introducing the Refutation That Follows*
There are folks who don't . . .	I hope they realize soon . . .
We don't have . . .	We have . . .
The first objections came . . .	But brain research has shown . . .
Some complain . . .	might be beside the point . . .
But if this is about . . .	then it is . . .
Most people . . .	But success didn't come quickly . . .
Their experience is not typical . . .	Most people . . .
There is less . . .	Yet . . .
If we want . . .	But . . .
On one side . . .	On the other side . . .
It is important to encourage . . .	but also to provide . . .
Although . . .	the seriousness of the problem . . .

In addition to using concession and refutation, you can strengthen your position paper with other rhetorical strategies. You may want to review the section on using appositives to identify or establish the authority of a source in Chapter 5 (pp. 291–93).

READING A DRAFT CRITICALLY

Getting a critical reading of your draft will help you see how to improve it. Your instructor may schedule class time for reading drafts, or you may want to ask a class-mate or a tutor in the writing center to read your draft. Ask your reader to use the following guidelines and to write out a response for you to consult during revision.

Read for a First Impression

1. Read the draft without stopping to annotate or comment, and then write two or three sentences giving your general impression.

2. Identify one aspect of the draft that seems particularly effective.

Read Again to Suggest Improvements

1. Suggest ways of presenting the issue more effectively.

   - Read the paragraphs that present the issue, and tell the writer how they help you understand the issue or fail to help you.

   - Point to any key terms used to present the issue that seem surprising, confusing, antagonizing, or unnecessarily loaded.

2. Recommend ways of asserting the position more clearly and unequivocally.

   - Find the writer's thesis, or position statement, and underline it. If you cannot find a clear thesis, let the writer know.

   - If you find several restatements of the thesis, examine them closely for consistency.

   - If the position seems extreme or overstated, suggest how it might be qualified and made more reasonable.

3. Help the writer argue more directly for the position and strengthen the argument.

   - Indicate any reasons that seem unconvincing, and explain briefly why you think so.

   - Look at the support the writer provides for each reason. If you find any of it ineffective, briefly explain why you think so and how it could be strengthened.

   - If you find places in the draft where support is lacking, suggest what kinds of support (facts, statistics, quotations, anecdotes, examples, or analogies) the writer might consider adding—and why.

4. Suggest ways of improving the counterargument.

   - If any part of the refutation could be strengthened, suggest what the writer could add or change.

   - If only the weakest objections or opposing positions have been acknowledged, remind the writer of the stronger ones that should be taken into account.

5. Suggest how credibility can be enhanced.

- Tell the writer whether the intended readers are likely to find the essay authoritative and trustworthy. Point to places where the argument seems most and least trustworthy.

- Identify places where the writer seeks to establish a common ground of shared values, beliefs, and attitudes with readers. Point to other places where the writer might attempt to do so without undermining the position being argued.

6. Suggest ways of improving readability.

- Consider whether the beginning adequately sets the stage for the argument, perhaps by establishing the tone or forecasting the argument.

- If the organization does not seem to follow a logical plan, suggest how it might be rearranged or where transitions could be inserted to clarify logical connections.

- Note whether the ending gives the argument a satisfactory sense of closure.

7. Evaluate the effectiveness of visuals.

- Look at any visuals in the essay, and tell the writer what they contribute to your understanding of the argument.

- If any visuals do not seem relevant or if there seem to be too many visuals, identify the ones that the writer could consider dropping, explaining your thinking.

- If a visual does not seem appropriately placed, suggest a better place for it.

REVISING

This section offers suggestions for revising your draft. Revising means re-envisioning your draft—trying to see it in a new way, given your purpose and readers, to develop a well-argued position paper.

The biggest mistake you can make while revising is to focus initially on words or sentences. Instead, first try to see your draft as a whole to assess its likely impact on your readers. Think imaginatively and boldly about cutting unconvincing material, adding new material, and moving material around to enhance clarity and strengthen your argument. Your computer makes even drastic revisions physically easy, but you still need to make the mental effort and decisions that will improve your draft.

You may have received help with this challenge from a classmate or tutor who gave your draft a critical reading. If so, keep this valuable feedback in mind as you decide which parts of your draft need revising and what specific changes you could make. The following suggestions will help you solve problems and strengthen your essay.

To Present the Issue More Effectively

- If readers do not fully understand what is at stake in the issue, consider adding anecdotes, examples, or facts to make the issue more specific and vivid, or try explaining more systematically why you see the issue as you do.

- If the terms you use to present the issue are surprising, antagonizing, or unnecessarily loaded, consider revising your presentation of the issue in more familiar or neutral terms, perhaps by using the sentence strategy of concession and refutation or acknowledgment and refutation.

To Assert the Position More Clearly and Unequivocally

- If your position on the issue seems unclear to readers, try reformulating it or spelling it out in more detail.

- If your thesis statement is not easy for readers to find, try stating it more directly to avoid misunderstanding.

- If your thesis is not appropriately qualified to account for valid opposing arguments or objections, modify it by limiting its scope.

To Argue More Directly for the Position and Strengthen the Argument

- If a reason seems unconvincing, try clarifying its relevance to the argument.

- If you need better support, review your invention notes or do more research to find facts, statistics, quotations, examples, or other types of support that will help bolster your argument.

To Improve the Counterargument

- If your refutation seems unconvincing, provide more or better support (such as facts and statistics from reputable sources) to convince readers that your counterargument is not idiosyncratic or personal. Avoid attacking your opponents on a personal level; refute only their ideas.

- If your counterargument ignores any strong opposing positions or reasonable objections, revise your essay to address them directly, perhaps using the sentence strategy of concession and refutation. If you cannot refute an opposing position, acknowledge its validity—and, if necessary, modify your position to accommodate it.

- If you can make any concessions without doing injustice to your own views, consider doing so now.

To Enhance Credibility

- If readers find any of your sources questionable, either establish these sources' credibility or choose more reliable sources to back up your argument.

- If readers think you ignore any opposing arguments, demonstrate to readers that you know and understand, even if you do not accept, these different points of view on the issue. Consider using the sentence strategy of concession and refutation or acknowledgment and refutation.

- If readers find your tone harsh or off-putting, consider the implications and potential offensiveness of your word choices. Then look for ways to show respect for and establish common ground with readers, revising your essay to achieve a more accommodating tone. Again, consider using the concession-refutation strategy.

To Improve Readability

- If the beginning seems dull or unfocused, rewrite it, perhaps by adding a surprising or vivid anecdote.

- If readers have trouble following your argument, consider adding a brief forecast of your main points at the beginning of your essay.

- If the reasons and counterarguments are not logically arranged, reorder them. Consider announcing each reason more explicitly or adding transitions to make the connections clearer.

- If the ending seems weak, search your invention and research notes for a memorable quotation or a vivid example that will strengthen your ending.

EDITING AND PROOFREADING

After you have revised the essay, be sure to spend some time checking for errors in usage, punctuation, and mechanics and considering matters of style. If you keep a list of errors you typically make, begin by checking your draft against this list. Ask someone else to proofread your essay before you print out a copy for your instructor or send it electronically.

From our research on student writing, we know that essays arguing positions have a high percentage of sentence fragment errors involving subordinating conjunctions as well as punctuation errors involving conjunctive adverbs. Because arguing a position often requires you to use subordinating conjunctions (such as *because*, *although*, and *since*) and conjunctive adverbs (such as *therefore*, *however*, and *thus*), you want to be sure you know the conventions for punctuating sentences that include these types of words. Check a writer's handbook for help with avoiding sentence fragments and using punctuation correctly in sentences with subordinating conjunctions and conjunctive adverbs.

REFLECTING ON WHAT YOU HAVE LEARNED

Position Paper

In this chapter, you have read critically several position papers and have written one of your own. To better remember what you have learned, pause now to reflect on the reading and writing activities you completed in this chapter.

1. *Write* a page or so reflecting on what you have learned. *Begin* by describing what you are most pleased with in your essay. Then *explain* what you think contributed to your achievement. *Be specific* about this contribution.

   - If it was something you learned from the readings, *indicate* which readings and specifically what you learned from them.

   - If it came from your invention writing, *point out* the section or sections that helped you most.

   - If you got good advice from a critical reader, *explain* exactly how the person helped you—perhaps by helping you understand a particular problem in your draft or by adding a new dimension to your writing.

   - *Try to write* about your achievement in terms of what you have learned about the genre.

2. Now *reflect* more generally on position papers, a genre of writing that plays an important role in our society. *Consider* some of the following questions: As a reader and writer of position papers, how important are reasons and supporting evidence? When people argue their positions on television, on radio talk shows, and in online discussion forums like blogs, do they tend to emphasize reasons and support? If not, what do they emphasize? How do you think their purpose differs from the purpose of the writers you read in this chapter and from your own purpose in writing a position paper? What contribution might position papers make to our society that other genres of writing cannot make?

A Catalog of Critical Reading Strategies

Serious study of a text requires a pencil in hand—
how much pride that pencil carries.

IRVING HOWE

Here we present seventeen specific strategies for reading critically, strategies that you can learn readily and then apply to the selections in this book as well as to your other college reading. Mastering these strategies will make reading much more satisfying and productive for you and help you handle difficult material with confidence:

- *Annotating:* recording your reactions to and questions about a text directly on the page

- *Previewing:* learning about a text before reading it closely

- *Outlining:* listing the main idea of each paragraph to see the organization of a text

- *Summarizing:* briefly presenting the main ideas of a text

- *Paraphrasing:* restating and clarifying the meaning of a few sentences from a text

- *Synthesizing:* combining ideas and information selected from different texts

- *Questioning to understand and remember:* inquiring about the content

- *Contextualizing:* placing a text within an appropriate historical and cultural framework

- *Reflecting on challenges to your beliefs and values:* examining your responses to reveal your own unexamined assumptions and attitudes

- *Exploring the significance of figurative language:* seeing how metaphors, similes, and symbols enhance meaning

- *Looking for patterns of opposition:* discovering what a text values by analyzing its system of binaries or contrasts

- *Evaluating the logic of an argument:* testing the argument of a text to see whether it makes sense

- *Using a Toulmin analysis:* evaluating the underlying assumptions of an argument

- *Recognizing logical fallacies:* looking for errors in reasoning

- *Recognizing emotional manipulation:* looking for false or exaggerated appeals

- *Judging the writer's credibility:* determining whether a text can be trusted

- *Comparing and contrasting related readings:* exploring likenesses and differences between texts to understand them better

ANNOTATING

For each of these strategies, annotating directly on the page is fundamental. *Annotating* means underlining key words, phrases, or sentences; writing comments or questions in the margins; bracketing important sections of the text; connecting ideas with lines or arrows; numbering related points in sequence; and making note of anything that strikes you as interesting, important, or questionable. (If writing on the text itself is impossible or undesirable, you can annotate a photocopy.)

Most readers annotate in layers, adding further annotations on second and third readings. Annotations can be light or heavy, depending on a reader's purpose and the difficulty of the material.

For several of the strategies in this appendix, you will need to build on and extend annotating by *taking inventory*: analyzing and classifying your annotations, searching systematically for patterns in the text, and interpreting their significance. An inventory is basically a list. When you take inventory, you make various kinds of lists in order to find meaning in a text. As you inventory your annotations on a particular reading, you may discover that the language and ideas cluster in various ways.

Inventorying annotations is a three-step process:

1. Examine your annotations for patterns or repetitions of any kind, such as recurring images or stylistic features, related words and phrases, similar examples, or reliance on authorities.

2. Try out different ways of grouping the items.

3. Consider what the patterns you have found suggest about the writer's meaning or rhetorical choices.

The patterns you discover will depend on the kind of reading you are analyzing and on the purpose of your analysis. (See Exploring the Significance of Figurative Language, p. 617, and Looking for Patterns of Opposition, p. 620, for examples of inventorying annotations.) These patterns can help you reach a deeper understanding of the text.

The following selection has been annotated to demonstrate the processes required by the critical-reading strategies we describe in the remainder of Appendix 1. As you read about each strategy, you will refer back to this annotated example.

MARTIN LUTHER KING JR.

An Annotated Sample from "Letter from Birmingham Jail"

Martin Luther King Jr. (1929–1968), a Baptist minister, first came to national notice in 1955, when he led a successful one-year bus boycott in Montgomery, Alabama, against state and city laws requiring racial segregation on public buses. He subsequently formed a national organization, the Southern Christian Leadership Conference, that brought people of all races from across the country to the South to fight nonviolently for racial integration. In 1963, King led demonstrations that protested segregation in Birmingham's downtown stores and restaurants. He was arrested in April and spent eight days in jail. Some of the peaceful demonstrations were met with violence: in September, members of the Ku Klux Klan bombed a black church, killing four little girls. While King was in jail, he wrote this famous "Letter from Birmingham Jail" to answer local clergy's criticism. King begins by discussing his disappointment with the lack of support he received from white moderates, such as the group of clergymen who published their criticism in the local newspaper (the complete text of the clergymen's published criticism appears at the end of this appendix).

The following brief excerpt from King's "Letter" is annotated to illustrate some of the ways you can annotate as you read. Since annotating is the first step for all critical-reading strategies in this catalog, these annotations are referred to throughout this appendix. As you read, add your own annotations in the right-hand margin.

¶1 White moderates block progress	. . . I must confess that over the past few years I have been 1 gravely disappointed with the <u>white moderate</u>. I have almost reached the regrettable conclusion that the Negro's [great stumbling block in his stride toward freedom] is not the White Citizen's Counciler or the Ku Klux Klanner, but the
Order vs. justice	white moderate, who is more devoted <u>to "order"</u> than to
Negative vs. positive	justice; who prefers a <u>negative peace</u> which is the absence of <u>tension</u> to a <u>positive peace</u> which is the <u>presence of justice</u>;
Ends vs. means	who constantly says: "I agree with you in the <u>goal</u> you seek, but I cannot agree with your <u>methods</u> of direct action"; who
Treating others like children	(paternalistically) believes he can set the timetable for another

man's freedom; who lives by a mythical concept of time and who constantly advises the Negro to wait for a "more convenient season." Shallow understanding from people of good will is more frustrating than absolute misunderstanding from people of ill will. [Lukewarm acceptance is much more bewildering than outright rejection.]

2   I had hoped that the white moderate would understand that law and order exist for the purpose of establishing justice and that when they fail in this purpose they become the [dangerously structured dams that block the flow of social progress.] I had hoped that the white moderate would understand that the present tension in the South is a necessary phase of the transition from an [obnoxious negative peace,] in which the Negro passively accepted his unjust plight, to a [substantive and positive peace,] in which all men will respect the dignity and worth of human personality. Actually, we who engage in nonviolent direct action are not the creators of tension. We merely bring to the surface the hidden tension that is already alive. We bring it out in the open, where it can be seen and dealt with. [Like a boil that can never be cured so long as it is covered up but must be opened with all its ugliness to the natural medicines of air and light, injustice must be exposed, with all the tension its exposure creates, to the light of human conscience and the air of national opinion before it can be cured.]

3   In your statement you assert that our actions, even though peaceful, must be condemned because they precipitate violence. But is this a logical assertion? Isn't this like condemning [a robbed man] because his possession of money precipitated the evil act of robbery? Isn't this like condemning [Socrates] because his unswerving commitment to truth and his philosophical inquiries precipitated the act by the misguided populace in which they made him drink hemlock? Isn't this like condemning [Jesus] because his unique God-consciousness and never-ceasing devotion to God's will precipitated the evil act of crucifixion? We must come to see that, as the federal courts have consistently affirmed, it is wrong to urge an individual to cease his efforts to gain his basic constitutional rights because the question may precipitate violence. [Society must protect the robbed and punish the robber.]

4   I had also hoped that the white moderate would reject the myth concerning time in relation to the struggle for freedom. I have just received a letter from a white brother in

¶2 Tension necessary for progress

Tension already exists

Simile: hidden tension is "like a boil"

True?

¶3 King questions clergymen's logic of blaming the victim

Yes!

¶4 Justifies urgency

Texas. He writes: "All Christians know that the colored people will receive equal rights eventually, but it is possible that you are in too great a religious hurry. It has taken Christianity almost two thousand years to accomplish what it has. The teachings of Christ take time to come to earth." Such an attitude stems from a tragic misconception of time, from the strangely irrational notion that there is something in the very flow of time that will inevitably cure all ills. [Actually, time itself is neutral; it can be used either destructively or constructively.] More and more I feel that the people of ill will have used time much more effectively than have the people of good will. We will have to repent in this generation not merely for the [hateful words and actions of the bad people] but for the [appalling silence of the good people.] Human progress never rolls in on [wheels of inevitability;] it comes through the tireless efforts of men willing to be co-workers with God, and without this hard work, time itself becomes an ally of the forces of social stagnation. [We must use time creatively, in the knowledge that the time is always ripe to do right.] Now is the time to make real the promise of democracy and transform our pending [national elegy] into a creative [psalm of brotherhood.] Now is the time to lift our national policy from the [quicksand of racial injustice] to the [solid rock of human dignity.]

You speak of our activity in Birmingham as extreme. At   5
first I was rather disappointed that fellow clergymen would see my nonviolent efforts as those of an extremist. I began thinking about the fact that I stand in the middle of two opposing forces in the Negro community. One is a [force of complacency,] made up in part of Negroes who, as a result of long years of oppression, are so drained of self-respect and a sense of "somebodiness" that they have adjusted to segregation; and in part of a few middle-class Negroes, who because of a degree of academic and economic security and because in some ways they profit by segregation, have become insensitive to the problems of the masses. The other [force is one of bitterness and hatred,] and it comes perilously close to advocating violence. It is expressed in the various black nationalist [groups that are springing up] across the nation, the largest and best-known being Elijah Muhammad's Muslim movement. Nourished by the Negro's frustration over the continued existence of racial discrimination, this movement is made up of people who have lost faith in America, who have absolutely repudiated Christianity, and who have concluded that the white man is an incorrigible "devil."

Marginal annotations:

Quotes white moderate as example

Critiques assumptions

Silence is as bad as hateful words and actions

Not moving

Elegy = mourning; psalm = celebration

Metaphors: quicksand, rock

¶5 Refutes criticism, King not an extremist

Complacency vs. hatred

Malcolm X?

6   I have tried to stand between these two forces, saying that we need emulate neither the "do-nothingism" of the complacent nor the hatred and despair of the black nationalist. For there is the more excellent way of love and nonviolent protest. I am grateful to God that, through the influence of the Negro church, the way of nonviolence became an integral part of our struggle.

¶6 Claims to offer better choice

7   If this philosophy had not emerged, by now many streets of the South would, I am convinced, be flowing with blood. And I am further convinced that if our white brothers dismiss as "rabble-rousers" and "outside agitators" those of us who employ nonviolent direct action, and if they refuse to support our nonviolent efforts, millions of Negroes will, out of frustration and despair, seek solace and security in black-nationalist ideologies — a development that would inevitably lead to a frightening racial nightmare.

¶7 Claims his movement prevents racial violence

if . . . then . . . Veiled threat?

8   [Oppressed people cannot remain oppressed forever.] The yearning for freedom eventually manifests itself, and that is what has happened to the American Negro. Something within has reminded him of his birthright of freedom, and something without has reminded him that it can be gained. Consciously or unconsciously, he has been caught up by the Zeitgeist, and with his black brothers of Africa and his brown and yellow brothers of Asia, South America and the Caribbean, the United States Negro is moving with a sense of great urgency toward the [promised land of racial justice.] If one recognizes this [vital urge that has engulfed the Negro community,] one should readily understand why public demonstrations are taking place. The Negro has many [pent-up resentments] and latent frustrations, and he must release them. So let him march; let him make prayer pilgrimages to the city hall; let him go on freedom rides — and try to understand why he must do so. If his repressed emotions are not released in nonviolent ways, they will seek expression through violence; this is not a threat but a fact of history. So I have not said to my people: "Get rid of your discontent." Rather, I have tried to say that this normal and healthy discontent can be [channeled into the creative outlet of non-violent direct action.] And now this approach is being termed extremist.

¶8 Change inevitable: evolution or revolution?

Spirit of the times

Worldwide uprising against injustice

Why "he," not "I"? Repeats "let him"

Not a threat? "I" channel discontent

9   But though I was initially disappointed at being categorized as an extremist, as I continued to think about the matter I gradually gained a measure of satisfaction from the label. Was not Jesus an extremist for love: "Love your enemies, bless them that curse you, do good to them that hate you,

¶9 Justifies extremism for righteous ends

and pray for them which despitefully use you, and persecute you." Was not Amos an extremist for justice: "Let justice roll down like waters and righteousness like an ever-flowing stream." Was not Paul an extremist for the Christian gospel: "I bear in my body the marks of the Lord Jesus." Was not Martin Luther an extremist: "Here I stand; I cannot do otherwise, so help me God." And John Bunyan: "I will stay in jail to the end of my days before I make a butchery of my conscience." And Abraham Lincoln: "This nation cannot survive half slave and half free." And Thomas Jefferson: "We hold these truths to be self-evident, that all men are created equal. . . ." [So the question is not whether we will be extremists, but what kind of extremists we will be.] Will we be extremists for hate or for love? Will we be extremists for the preservation of injustice or for the extension of justice? In that dramatic scene on Calvary's hill three men were crucified. We must never forget that all three were crucified for the same crime—the crime of extremism. Two were extremists for immorality, and thus fell below their environment. The other, Jesus Christ, was an extremist for love, truth and goodness, and thereby rose above his environment. Perhaps the South, [the nation and the world are in dire need of creative extremists.]

¶10 I had hoped that the white moderate would see this need. Perhaps I was too optimistic; perhaps I expected too much. I suppose I should have realized that few members of the oppressor race can understand the deep groans and passionate yearnings of the oppressed race, and still fewer have the vision to see that [injustice must be rooted out] by strong, persistent and determined action. I am thankful, however, that some of our white brothers in the South have grasped the meaning of this social revolution and committed themselves to it. They are still all too few in quantity, but they are big in quality. Some—such as Ralph McGill, Lillian Smith, Harry Golden, James McBride Dabbs, Ann Braden and Sarah Patton Boyle—have written about our struggle in eloquent and prophetic terms. Others have marched with us down nameless streets of the South. They have languished in filthy, roach-infested jails, suffering the abuse and brutality of policemen who view them as "dirty nigger-lovers." Unlike so many of their moderate brothers and sisters, they have recognized the urgency of the movement and sensed the need for powerful ["action" antidotes] to combat the [disease of segregation.]

Hebrew prophet

Apostle

Founded Protestantism

English preacher

Freed slaves

Wrote Declaration of Independence

No choice but to be extremists, but what kind?

¶10 Disappointed in white moderate critics; thanks supporters

Who are they?

Left unaided

Framing—recalls boil simile

Annotating

To annotate a reading,

1. Mark the text using notations.

- Circle words to be defined in the margin.

- Underline key words and phrases.

- Bracket important sentences and passages.

- Use lines or arrows to connect ideas or words.

- Use question marks to note any confusion or disagreement.

2. Write marginal comments.

- Number each paragraph for future reference.

- State the main idea of each paragraph.

- Define unfamiliar words.

- Note responses and questions.

- Identify interesting writing strategies.

- Point out patterns.

3. Layer additional markings on the text and comments in the margins as you reread for different purposes.

PREVIEWING

Previewing enables you to get a sense of what the text is about and how it is organized before reading it closely. This simple critical-reading strategy includes seeing what you can learn from headnotes, biographical notes about the author, or other introductory material; skimming to get an overview of the content and organization; and identifying the genre and rhetorical situation.

Learning from Headnotes

Many texts provide some introductory material to orient readers. Books often have brief blurbs on the cover describing the content and author, as well as a preface, an introduction, and a table of contents. Articles in professional and academic journals usually provide some background information. Scientific articles, for example, typically begin with an abstract summarizing the main points. In this book, as in many textbooks, headnotes introducing the author and identifying the circumstances under which the selection was originally published precede the reading selections.

Because Martin Luther King Jr. is a well-known figure, the headnote might not tell you anything you do not already know. If you know something else about the author that could help you better understand the selection, you might want to make a note of it. As a critical reader, you should think about whether the writer has authority and credibility on the subject. Information about the writer's education, professional experience, and other publications can help. If you need to know more about a particular author, search Google, Wikipedia, or biographical sites on the Web, such as Lives, the Biography Resource <http://amillionlives.com>. In the library or using your library's Web site as a portal, you could also consult a biographical dictionary or encyclopedia such as *Who's Who*, *Biography Index*, *Current Biography*, *American National Biography*, or *Contemporary Authors*.

Skimming for an Overview

When you *skim* a text, you give it a quick, selective, superficial reading. For most explanations and arguments, a good strategy is to read the opening and closing paragraphs. The first usually introduces the subject and may forecast the main points, while the last typically summarizes what is most important in the essay. You should also glance at the first sentence of every internal paragraph because it may serve as a topic sentence, introducing the point discussed in the paragraph. Because narrative writing is usually organized chronologically rather than logically, often you can get a sense of the progression by skimming for time markers such as *then*, *after*, and *later*. Heads and subheads, figures, charts, and the like also provide clues for skimming.

To illustrate, turn back to the King excerpt, and skim it. Notice that the opening paragraph establishes the subject: the white moderate's criticism of King's efforts. It also forecasts many of the main points that are taken up in subsequent paragraphs—for example, the moderate's greater devotion to order than to justice (paragraph 2), the moderate's criticism that King's methods, though nonviolent, precipitate violence (3), and the moderate's "paternalistic" timetable (1).

Identifying the Genre and Rhetorical Situation

Reading an unfamiliar text is like traveling in unknown territory: you can use a map to check what you see against what you expect to find. In much the same way, previewing for genre equips you with a set of expectations to guide your reading. *Genre*, meaning "kind" or "type," is generally used to classify pieces of writing according to their particular social function. Nonfiction prose genres include autobiography, observation, reflection, explanations of concepts, and various forms of argument, such as evaluation, analysis of causes or effects, proposals to solve a problem, and position papers on controversial issues. These genres are illustrated in Chapters 2 through 9 with guidelines to help you analyze and evaluate their effectiveness. After working through these chapters, you will be able to identify the genre of most unfamiliar pieces of writing you encounter.

You can make a tentative decision about the genre of a text by first looking at why the piece was written and to whom it was addressed. These two elements — purpose and audience — constitute the rhetorical or writing situation. Consider the writing of "Letter from Birmingham Jail." The title explicitly identifies this particular selection as a letter. We know that letters are usually written with a particular reader in mind but can also be written for the reading public (as in a letter to the editor of a magazine), that they may be part of an ongoing correspondence, and that they may be informal or formal.

Read the clergymen's statement at the end of this appendix (pp. 644–46) to gain some insights into the situation in which King wrote his letter and some understanding of his specific purpose for writing. As a public letter written in response to a public statement, "Letter from Birmingham Jail" may be classified as a position paper — one that argues for a particular point of view on a controversial issue.

Even without reading the clergymen's statement, you can get a sense of the rhetorical situation from the opening paragraph of the King excerpt. You would not be able to identify the "white moderate" with the clergymen who criticized King, but you would see clearly that he is referring to people he had hoped would support his cause but who, instead, have become an obstacle. King's feelings about the white moderate's lack of support are evident in the first paragraph, where he uses such words as "gravely disappointed," "regrettable conclusion," "frustrating," and "bewildering." The opening paragraph, as noted earlier, also identifies the white moderate's specific objections to King's methods. Therefore, you learn quickly the essay's genre (position paper), the points of disagreement between the two sides, and the writer's attitude toward those with whom he disagrees.

Knowing that this is an excerpt from a position paper allows you to appreciate the controversiality of the subject King is writing about and the sensitivity of the rhetorical situation. You can see how he asserts his own position at the same time that he tries to bridge the gap separating him from his critics. You can then evaluate the kinds of points King makes and the persuasiveness of his argument.

CHECKLIST

Previewing

To orient yourself before reading closely,

1. See what you can learn from headnotes or other introductory material.

2. Skim the text to get an overview of the content and organization.

3. Identify the genre and rhetorical situation.

OUTLINING

Outlining is an especially helpful critical-reading strategy for understanding the content and structure of a reading. Outlining, which identifies and organizes the text's main ideas, may be done as part of the annotating process, or it may be done separately. Writing an outline in the margins of the text as you read and annotate makes it easier to find information later. Writing an outline on a separate piece of paper gives you more space to work with and thus usually includes more detail.

The key to effective outlining is distinguishing between the main ideas and the supporting material, such as examples, factual evidence, and explanations. The main ideas form the backbone that holds the various parts and pieces of the text together. Outlining the main ideas helps you uncover this structure.

Making an outline, however, is not simple. The reader must exercise judgment in deciding which are the most important ideas. Reading is never a passive or neutral act; the process of outlining shows how active reading can be.

You may make either a *formal, multileveled outline* with roman (I, II) and arabic (1, 2) numerals together with capital and lowercase letters, or an *informal, scratch outline* that lists the main idea of each paragraph. A formal outline is harder and more time-consuming to create than a scratch outline. You might choose to make a formal outline of a reading about which you are writing an in-depth analysis or evaluation. For example, on the next two pages is a formal outline that a student wrote for a paper evaluating the logic of the King excerpt. Notice the student's use of roman numerals for the main ideas or claims, capital letters for the reasons, and arabic numerals for supporting evidence and explanation.

Making a scratch outline takes less time than creating a formal outline but still requires careful reading. A scratch outline records less information than a formal outline, but it is sufficient for most critical reading purposes. To make a scratch outline, you need to locate the topic of each paragraph. The topic is usually stated in a word or phrase, and it may be repeated or referred to throughout the paragraph. For example, the opening paragraph of the King excerpt (pp. 598–99) makes clear that its topic is the white moderate.

After you have found the topic of the paragraph, figure out what is being said about it. To return to our example: If the white moderate is the topic of the opening paragraph, then what King says about the topic can be found in the second sentence, where he announces the conclusion he has come to — namely, that the white moderate is "the Negro's great stumbling block in his stride toward freedom." The rest of the paragraph specifies the ways the white moderate blocks progress.

When you make an outline, you can use the writer's words, your own words, or a combination of the two. A paragraph-by-paragraph outline appears in the margins of the selection, with numbers for each paragraph (see pp. 599–602). Here is the same outline as it might appear on a separate piece of paper, slightly expanded and reworded:

Paragraph Scratch Outline

¶1 White moderates block progress in the struggle for racial justice.

¶2 Tension is necessary for progress.

¶3 The clergymen's criticism is not logical.

¶4 King justifies an urgent use of time.

¶5 Clergymen accuse King of being extreme, but he claims to stand between two extreme forces in the black community.

¶6 King offers a better choice.

¶7 King's movement has prevented racial violence by blacks.

¶8 Discontent is normal and healthy but must be channeled creatively rather than destructively.

¶9 Creative extremists are needed.

¶10 Some whites have supported King.

CHECKLIST

Outlining

To make a scratch outline of a text,

1. Reread each paragraph systematically, identifying the topic and what is being said about it. Do not include examples, specific details, quotations, or other explanatory and supporting material.

2. List the main ideas in the margin of the text or on a separate piece of paper.

Formal Outline

I. The Negro's great stumbling block in his stride toward freedom is . . . the white moderate

  A. *Because* the white moderate is more devoted to "order" than to justice (paragraph 2)

    1. Law and order should exist to establish justice

    2. Law and order compare to dangerously structured dams that block the flow of social progress

  B. *Because* the white moderate prefers a negative peace (absence of tension) to a positive peace (justice) (paragraph 2)

    1. The tension already exists

    2. It is not created by nonviolent direct action

    3. Society that does not eliminate injustice compares to a boil that hides its infections. Both can be cured only by exposure (boil simile)

    C. *Because* even though the white moderates agree with the goals, they do not support the means to achieve them (paragraph 3)
      1. The argument that the means—nonviolent direct action—are wrong because they precipitate violence is flawed
      2. Analogy of the robbed man condemned because he had money
      3. Comparison with Socrates and Jesus
    D. *Because* the white moderates paternalistically believe they can set a time-table for another man's freedom (paragraph 4)
      1. Rebuts the white moderate's argument that Christianity will cure man's ills and man must wait patiently for that to happen
      2. Argues that time is neutral and that man must use time creatively for constructive rather than destructive ends

II. Creative extremism is preferable to moderation
    A. Classifies himself as a moderate (paragraphs 5–8)
      1. I stand between two forces: the white moderate's complacency and the black Muslim's rage
      2. If nonviolent direct action were stopped, more violence, not less, would result
      3. "[M]illions of Negroes will, out of frustration and despair, seek solace and security in black-nationalist ideologies" (paragraph 7)
      4. Repressed emotions will be expressed—if not in nonviolent ways, then through violence (paragraph 8)
    B. Redefines himself as a "creative extremist" (paragraph 9)
      1. Extremism for love, truth, and goodness is creative extremism
      2. Identifies himself with the creative extremists Jesus, Amos, Paul, Martin Luther, John Bunyan, Abraham Lincoln, and Thomas Jefferson
    C. Not all whites are moderates; many are creative extremists (paragraph 10)
      1. Lists names of white writers
      2. Refers to white activists

SUMMARIZING

Summarizing is one of the most widely used strategies for critical reading because it helps you understand and remember what is most important in a text. Another advantage of summarizing is that it creates a condensed version of the reading's ideas and information, which you can refer to later or insert into your own written text. Along with quoting and paraphrasing, summarizing enables you to refer to and integrate other writers' ideas into your own writing.

A summary is a relatively brief restatement, primarily in the reader's own words, of the reading's main ideas. Summaries vary in length. Some are very brief—a sentence or even a subordinate clause. For example, if you were referring to the excerpt from "Letter from Birmingham Jail" and simply needed to indicate how it relates to your other sources, your summary might focus on only one aspect of the reading. It might look something like this:

> There have always been advocates of extremism in politics. Martin Luther King Jr., in "Letter from Birmingham Jail," for instance, defends nonviolent civil disobedience as an extreme but necessary means of bringing about racial justice.

If, however, you were surveying the important texts of the civil rights movement, you might write a longer, more detailed summary, one that not only identifies the reading's main ideas but also shows how the ideas relate to one another.

Many writers find it useful to outline the reading as a preliminary to writing a summary. A paragraph-by-paragraph scratch outline (like the one illustrated in the preceding section) lists the reading's main ideas following the sequence in which they appear in the original. But writing a summary requires more than merely stringing together the entries in an outline. A summary has to make explicit the logical connections between the ideas. Writing a summary shows how reading critically is a truly constructive process of interpretation involving both close analysis and creative synthesis.

To summarize, you need to segregate the main ideas from the supporting material, usually by making an outline of the reading. You want to use your own words for the most part because doing so confirms that you understand the material you have read, but you may also use key words and phrases from the reading. You may also want to cite the title and refer to the author by name, using verbs like *expresses*, *acknowledges*, and *explains* to indicate the writer's purpose and strategy at each point in the argument.

Following is a sample summary of the King excerpt. It is based on the outline on pages 607–08 but is much more detailed. Most important, it fills in connections between the ideas that King left for readers to make:

> King expresses his disappointment with white moderates who, by opposing his program of nonviolent direct action, have blocked progress toward racial justice. He acknowledges that his program has raised tension in the South, but he explains that tension is necessary to bring about change. Furthermore, he argues that tension already exists. But because it has been unexpressed, it is unhealthy and potentially dangerous.
>
> He defends his actions against the clergymen's criticisms, particularly their argument that he is in too much of a hurry. Responding to charges of extremism, King claims that he has actually prevented racial violence by channeling the natural frustrations of oppressed blacks into nonviolent protest. He asserts that extremism is precisely what is needed now—but it must be creative, rather than destructive, extremism. He concludes by again expressing disappointment with white moderates for not joining his effort as many other whites have.

CHECKLIST

Summarizing

To restate briefly the main ideas in a text,

1. Make an outline.

2. Write one or more paragraphs that present the main ideas largely in your own words. Use the outline as a guide, but reread parts of the original text as necessary.

3. To make the summary coherent, fill in connections between ideas.

PARAPHRASING

Unlike a summary, which is much briefer than the original text, a *paraphrase* is generally as long as the original and often longer. Whereas summarizing seeks to present the gist or essence of the reading and leave out everything else, paraphrasing tries to be comprehensive and leave out nothing that contributes to the meaning. (For more on summarizing, see the preceding section.)

Paraphrasing works as a critical reading strategy for especially complex and obscure passages. Because it requires a word-for-word or phrase-by-phrase rewording of the original text, paraphrasing is too time-consuming and labor intensive to use with long texts. But it is perfect for making sure you understand the important passages of a difficult reading. To paraphrase, you need to work systematically through the text, looking up in a good college dictionary many of the key words, even those you are somewhat familiar with. If you quote the author's words, put quotation marks around them, and be sure to define them.

Following are two passages. The first is excerpted from paragraph 2 of "Letter from Birmingham Jail." The second passage paraphrases the first.

Original

I had hoped that the white moderate would understand that law and order exist for the purpose of establishing justice and that when they fail in this purpose they become the dangerously structured dams that block the flow of social progress. I had hoped that the white moderate would understand that the present tension in the South is a necessary phase of the transition from an obnoxious negative peace, in which the Negro passively accepted his unjust plight, to a substantive and positive peace, in which all men will respect the dignity and worth of human personality.

Paraphrase

King writes that he had hoped for more understanding from the white moderates — specifically that they would recognize that law and order are not ends in themselves but means to the greater end of establishing justice. When law and order do not serve this greater end, they stand in the way of progress. King expected the white moderates to recognize that the current tense situation in the South is part of a transition that is necessary for progress. The current situation is bad because although there is peace, it is an "obnoxious" and "negative" kind of peace based on blacks passively accepting the injustice of the status quo. A better kind of peace, one that is "substantive," real and not imaginary, as well as "positive," requires that all people, regardless of race, be valued.

When you compare the paraphrase to the original, you can see that the paraphrase tries to remain true to the original by including *all* the important information and ideas. It also tries to be neutral — to avoid inserting the reader's opinions or distorting the original writer's ideas. But because paraphrasing requires the use of different words and putting those words together into different sentences, the resulting paraphrase will be different from the original. The paraphrase always, intentionally or not, expresses the reader's interpretation of the original text's meaning.

CHECKLIST

Paraphrasing

To paraphrase information in a text,

1. Reread the passage to be paraphrased, looking up unfamiliar words in a college dictionary.

2. Relying on key words in the passage, translate the information into your own sentences.

3. Revise to ensure coherence.

SYNTHESIZING

Synthesizing involves combining ideas and information gleaned from different sources. As a critical-reading strategy, synthesizing can help you see how different sources relate to one another — for example, by offering supporting details or opposing arguments.

When you synthesize material from different sources, you construct a conversation among your sources, a conversation in which you also participate. Synthesizing contributes most to critical thinking when writers use sources not only to support their ideas but to challenge and extend them as well.

In the following example, the reader uses a variety of sources related to the King passage (pp. 598–602). The synthesis brings the sources together around a central idea. Notice how quotation, paraphrase, and summary are all used to present King's and the other sources' ideas:

> When King defends his campaign of nonviolent direct action against the clergymen's criticism that "our actions, even though peaceful, must be condemned because they precipitate violence" (King excerpt, paragraph 3), he is using what Vinit Haksar calls Mohandas Gandhi's "safety-valve argument" ("Civil Disobedience and Non-Cooperation" 117). According to Haksar, Gandhi gave a "non-threatening warning of worse things to come" if his demands were not met. King similarly makes clear that advocates of actions more extreme than those he advocates are waiting in the wings: "The other force is one of bitterness and hatred, and it comes perilously close to advocating violence" (King excerpt, paragraph 5). King identifies this force with Elijah Muhammad, and although he does not name him, King's contemporary readers would have known that he was referring also to Malcolm X, who, according to Herbert J. Storing, "urged that Negroes take seriously the idea of revolution" ("The Case against Civil Disobedience" 90). In fact, Malcolm X accused King of being a modern-day Uncle Tom, trying "to keep us under control, to keep us passive and peaceful and nonviolent" (*Malcolm X Speaks* 12).

CHECKLIST

Synthesizing

To synthesize ideas and information,

1. Find and read a variety of sources on your topic, annotating the passages that give you ideas about the topic.

2. Look for patterns among your sources, possibly supporting or refuting your ideas or those of other sources.

3. Write one or more paragraphs synthesizing your sources, using quotation, paraphrase, and summary to present what they say on the topic.

QUESTIONING TO UNDERSTAND AND REMEMBER

As a student, you are accustomed to having teachers ask you questions about your reading. These questions are designed to help you understand a reading and respond to it more fully. However, when you need to understand and use new information, it may be more beneficial for *you* to write the questions. This strategy, *questioning to understand and remember*, involves writing questions while you read a text the first time. In difficult academic reading, you will understand the material better and remember it longer if you write a question for every paragraph or brief section.

We can demonstrate how this strategy works by returning to the excerpt from "Letter from Birmingham Jail" and examining, paragraph by paragraph, some questions that might be written about it. Reread the King selection (pp. 598–602). When you finish each paragraph, look at the question numbered to match that paragraph in the following list. Assume for this rereading that your goal is to comprehend the information and ideas. Notice that each question in the list asks about the content of a paragraph and that you can answer the question with information from that paragraph.

Paragraph	Question
1	How can white moderates be more of a barrier to racial equality than the Ku Klux Klan?
2	How can community tension resulting from nonviolent direct action benefit the civil rights movement?
3	How can peaceful actions be justified even if they cause violence?
4	Why should civil rights activists take action now instead of waiting for white moderates to support them?
5	How are complacent members of the community different from black nationalist groups?
6	What is King's position in relation to these two forces of complacency and anger?
7	What would have happened if King's nonviolent direct action movement had not started?
8	What is the focus of the protest, and what do King and others who are protesting hope to achieve?
9	What other creative extremists does King associate himself with?
10	Who are the whites who have supported King, and what has happened to some of them?

Each question focuses on the main idea in the paragraph, not on illustrations or details. Note, too, that each question is expressed partly in the reader's own words, not just copied from parts of the paragraph.

How can writing questions during reading help you understand and remember the content—the ideas and information—of the reading? Researchers studying the ways people learn from their reading have found that writing questions during reading enables readers to remember more than they would by reading the selection twice. Researchers who have compared the results of readers who write brief summary sentences for a paragraph with readers who write questions have found that readers who write questions learn more and remember the information longer. These researchers conjecture that writing a question involves reviewing or rehearsing information in a way that allows it to enter long-term memory, where it is more easily recalled. The result is that you clarify and "file" the information as you go along. You can then read more confidently because you have more of a base on which to build your understanding, a base that allows meaning to develop and that enables you to predict what is coming next and add it readily to what you have already learned.

This way of reading informational material is very slow, and at first it may seem inefficient. In those reading situations where you must use the information in an exam or a class discussion, it can be very efficient, however. Because this reading strategy is relatively time-consuming, you will want to use it selectively.

CHECKLIST

Questioning to Understand and Remember

To use questioning to understand and remember a reading, especially one that is unfamiliar or difficult,

1. Pause at the end of each paragraph to review the information.

2. Try to identify the most important information—the main ideas or gist of the discussion.

3. Write a question that can be answered by the main idea or ideas in the paragraph.

4. Move on to the next paragraph, repeating the process.

CONTEXTUALIZING

The texts you read were written in the past and often embody historical and cultural assumptions, values, and attitudes different from your own. To read critically, you need to become aware of these differences. *Contextualizing* is a critical reading strategy that involves making inferences about a reading's historical and cultural contexts and examining the differences between those contexts and your own.

We can divide the process of contextualizing into two steps:

1. Reread the text to see how it represents the historical and cultural situation. Compare the way the text presents the situation with what you know about the situation from other sources—such as what you have read in other books and articles, seen on television or in the movies, and learned in school or from talking with people who were directly involved.

   Write a few sentences describing your understanding of what it was like at that particular time and place. Note how the representation of the time and place in the text differs in significant ways from the other representations with which you are familiar.

2. Consider how much and in what ways the situation has changed. Write another sentence or two exploring the historical and cultural differences.

The excerpt from "Letter from Birmingham Jail" is a good example of a text that benefits from being read contextually. If you knew little about the history of slavery and segregation in the United States, Martin Luther King Jr., or the civil rights movement, it would be very difficult to understand the passion for justice and the impatience with delay expressed in the King selection. Most Americans, however, have read about Martin Luther King Jr. and the civil rights movement, or they have seen films such as Spike Lee's *Malcolm X*.

Here is how one reader contextualized the excerpt from "Letter from Birmingham Jail":

> 1. I am not old enough to remember what it was like in the early 1960s when Dr. King was leading marches and sit-ins, but I have seen television documentaries of newsclips showing demonstrators being attacked by dogs, doused by fire hoses, beaten and dragged by helmeted police. Such images give me a sense of the violence, fear, and hatred that King was responding to.
>
> The tension King writes about comes across in his writing. He uses his anger and frustration creatively to inspire his critics. He also threatens them, although he denies it. I saw a film on Malcolm X, so I could see that King was giving white people a choice between his nonviolent way and Malcolm's more confrontational way.
>
> 2. Things have certainly changed since the sixties. Legal segregation has ended. The term *Negro* is no longer used, but there still are racists like Don Imus on the radio. African Americans like Oprah Winfrey and Barack Obama are highly respected and powerful. The civil rights movement is over. So when I'm reading King, I'm reading history.
>
> Things seem better than when police officers beat black men like Rodney King or extremists like Ice T threatened violence. Don Imus, after all, lost his job for what he said. But in the ghetto, black children are still dying: where there were riots, there's now gang violence. I don't know who's playing Dr. King's role today.

Contextualizing

To contextualize,

1. Describe the historical and cultural situation as it is represented in the reading and in other sources with which you are familiar.

2. Compare the text's historical and cultural contexts to your own historical and cultural situations.

REFLECTING ON CHALLENGES TO YOUR BELIEFS AND VALUES

Reading often challenges our attitudes, our unconsciously held beliefs, or our positions on current issues. We may feel anxious, irritable, or disturbed; threatened or vulnerable; ashamed or combative. We may feel suddenly wary or alert. When we experience these feelings as we read, we are reacting in terms of our personal or family values, religious beliefs, racial or ethnic group, gender, sexual orientation, social class, or regional experience.

You can grow intellectually, emotionally, and in social understanding if you are willing (at least occasionally) to *reflect on challenges to your beliefs and values* instead of simply resisting them. Learning to question your unexamined assumptions and attitudes is an important part of becoming a critical thinker.

This reading strategy involves marking the text where you feel challenged and then reflecting on why you feel challenged. As you read a text for the first time, mark an X in the margin at each point where you sense a challenge to your attitudes, beliefs, or values. Make a brief note in the margin about what you feel at that point or about what in the text seems to create the challenge. The challenge you feel may be mild or strong. It may come frequently or only occasionally.

Review the places you have marked in the text where you felt challenged in some way. Consider what connections you can make among these places or among the feelings you experienced at each place. For example, you might notice that you object to only a limited part of a writer's argument, resist nearly all of an authority's quoted statements, or dispute implied judgments about your gender or social class.

Write about what you have learned. Begin by describing briefly the part or parts of the text that make you feel challenged. Then write several sentences, reflecting on your responses. Keep the focus on your feelings. You need not defend or justify your feelings. Instead, try to give them a voice. Where do they come from? Why are they important to you? Although the purpose is to explore why you feel as you do, you may find that thinking about your values, attitudes, and beliefs sends you back to the text for help with defining your own position.

Here, for example, is how one writer responded to the excerpt from "Letter from Birmingham Jail":

> I'm troubled and confused by the way King uses the labels *moderate* and *extremist*. He says he doesn't like being labeled an extremist but he labels the clergymen moderate. How could it be okay for King to be moderate and not okay for the clergymen? What does *moderate* mean anyway? My dictionary defines *moderate* as "keeping within reasonable or proper limits; not extreme, excessive, or intense." Being a moderate sounds a lot better than being an extremist. I was taught not to act rashly or to go off the deep end. I'm also troubled that King makes a threat (although he says he does not).

CHECKLIST

Reflecting on Challenges to Your Beliefs and Values

To reflect on challenges to your beliefs and values,

1. Identify the challenges by marking where in the text you feel your beliefs and values are being opposed, criticized, or unfairly characterized.

2. Select one or two of the most troubling challenges you have identified, and write a few sentences describing why you feel as you do. Do not attempt to defend your feelings; instead, analyze them to see where they come from.

EXPLORING THE SIGNIFICANCE OF FIGURATIVE LANGUAGE

Figurative language—metaphors, similes, and symbols—takes words literally associated with one object or idea and applies them to another object or idea. Because it embodies abstract ideas in vivid images, figurative language can often communicate more dramatically than direct statement. Figurative language also enriches meaning by drawing on a complex of feeling and association, indicating relations of resemblance and likeness. Here are definitions and examples of the most common figures of speech.

Metaphor implicitly compares two things by identifying them with each other. For instance, when King calls the white moderate "the Negro's great stumbling block in his stride toward freedom" (paragraph 1), he does not mean that the white moderate literally trips the Negro who is attempting to walk toward freedom. The sentence makes sense only when it is understood figuratively: the white moderate trips up the Negro by frustrating every effort to eliminate injustice. Similarly, King uses the image of a dam to express the abstract idea of the blockage of justice (paragraph 2).

Simile, a more explicit form of comparison, uses *like* or *as* to signal the relation of two seemingly unrelated things. King uses simile when he says that injustice is "like a boil that can never be cured so long as it is covered up" (paragraph 2). This simile makes several points of comparison between injustice and a boil. It suggests that injustice is a disease of society, just as a boil is a disease of the body, and that injustice, like a boil, must be exposed or it will fester and worsen. A simile with many points of comparison is called an *extended simile* or *conceit*.

A *symbol* is something that stands for or represents something else. Critics do not agree about the differences between a metaphor and a symbol, but one popular line of thought is that a symbol relates two or more items that already have a strong recognized alliance or affinity, whereas metaphor involves a more general association of two related or unrelated items. By this definition, King uses the white moderate as a symbol for supposed liberals and would-be supporters of civil rights who are actually frustrating the cause.

How these figures of speech are used in a text reveals something of the writer's feelings about the subject and attitude toward prospective readers and may even suggest the writer's feelings about the act of writing. Annotating and taking inventory of patterns of figurative language can thus provide insight into the tone and intended emotional effect of the writing.

Exploring the significance of figurative language involves (1) annotating and then listing all the metaphors, similes, and symbols you find in the reading; (2) grouping the figures of speech that appear to express similar feelings and attitudes, and labeling each group; and (3) writing to explore the meaning of the patterns you have found.

The following sample inventory and analysis of the King excerpt demonstrate the process of exploring the significance of figurative language.

Listing Figures of Speech

Step 1 produced the following inventory:

order is a dangerously structured dam that blocks the flow

social progress should flow

stumbling block in the stride toward freedom

injustice is like a boil that can never be cured

the light of human conscience and air of national opinion

time is something to be used, neutral, an ally, ripe

quicksand of racial injustice

the solid rock of human dignity

human progress never rolls in on wheels of inevitability

men are coworkers with God

groups springing up

promised land of racial justice

vital urge engulfed

pent-up resentments

normal and healthy discontent can be channeled into the creative outlet of nonviolent direct action

root out injustice

powerful action is an antidote

disease of segregation

Grouping Figures of Speech

Step 2 yielded three common themes:

Sickness: segregation is a disease; action is healthy, the only antidote; injustice is like a boil

Underground: tension is hidden; injustice must be rooted out; extremist groups are springing up; discontent can be channeled into a creative outlet

Blockage: forward movement is impeded by obstacles—the dam, stumbling block; human progress never rolls in on wheels of inevitability; social progress should flow

Exploring Patterns

Step 3 entailed about ten minutes of writing to explore the themes listed in step 2:

The patterns of *blockage* and *underground* suggest a feeling of frustration. Inertia is a problem; movement forward toward progress or upward toward the promised land is stalled. There seems to be a strong need to break through the resistance, the passivity, the discontent, and to be creative, active, vital. These are probably King's feelings both about his attempt to lead purposeful, effective demonstrations and his effort to write a convincing letter.

The simile of injustice being like a boil links the two patterns of *underground* and *sickness*, suggesting something bad, a disease, is inside the people or the society. The cure is to expose the blocked hatred and injustice, root it out, and release the tension or emotion that has so long been repressed. This implies that repression itself, not simply what is repressed, is the evil.

CHECKLIST

Exploring the Significance of Figurative Language

To understand how figurative language—metaphors, similes, and symbols—contributes to a reading's meaning,

1. Annotate and then list all the figures of speech you find.

2. Group them, and label each group.

3. Write to explore the meaning of the patterns you have found.

LOOKING FOR PATTERNS OF OPPOSITION

All texts contain *voices* or *patterns of opposition*. These voices may echo the views and values of critical readers the writer anticipates or predecessors to which the writer is responding; they may even reflect the writer's own conflicting values. You may need to look closely for such a dialogue of opposing voices within the text.

When we think of oppositions, we ordinarily think of polarities such as *yes* and *no*, *up* and *down*, *black* and *white*, *new* and *old*. Some oppositions, however, may be more subtle. The excerpt from "Letter from Birmingham Jail" is rich in such oppositions: *moderate* versus *extremist*, *order* versus *justice*, *direct action* versus *passive acceptance*, *expression* versus *repression*. These oppositions are not accidental; they form a significant pattern that gives a critical reader important information about King's letter.

A careful reading shows that one of the two terms in an opposition is nearly always valued over the other. In the King excerpt, for example, *extremist* is valued over *moderate* (paragraph 9). This preference for extremism is surprising. The critical reader should ask why, when white extremists like the Ku Klux Klan have committed so many outrages against black Southerners, King would prefer extremism. If King is trying to convince his readers to accept his point of view, why would he represent himself as an extremist? Moreover, why would a clergyman advocate extremism instead of moderation?

By studying the patterns of opposition, you can answer these questions more fully. You can see that King sets up this opposition to force his readers to examine their own values and realize that they are in fact misplaced. Instead of working toward justice, he says, those who support law and order maintain the unjust status quo. Getting his readers to think of the white moderate as blocking rather than facilitating peaceful change brings them to align themselves with King and perhaps even embrace his strategy of nonviolent resistance.

Looking for patterns of opposition is a four-step method of analysis:

1. Divide a piece of paper in half lengthwise or select two-column formatting in your word-processing program. In the left-hand column, list those words and phrases from the text that you have annotated as indicating oppositions. In the right-hand column, enter the word or phrase that seems, according to this writer, the opposite of each word or phrase in the left-hand column. You may have to paraphrase or even supply this opposite word or phrase if it is not stated directly in the text.

2. For each pair of words or phrases, put an asterisk next to the one that seems to be preferred by the writer.

3. Study the list of preferred words or phrases, and identify what you think is the predominant system of values put forth by the text. Do the same for the other list, identifying the alternative system or systems of values implied in the text. Take about ten minutes to describe the oppositions in writing.

4. To explore these conflicting points of view, write a few sentences presenting one side, and then write a few more sentences presenting the other side. Use as many of the words or phrases from the list as you can—explaining, extending, and justifying the values they imply. You may also, if you wish, quarrel with the choice of words or phrases on the grounds that they are loaded or oversimplify the issue.

The following sample inventory and analysis of the King excerpt demonstrate the method for exploring patterns of opposition in a text.

Listing Oppositions

Steps 1 and 2: This list of oppositions uses asterisks to identify King's preferred word or phrase in each pair:

white moderate	*extremist
order	*justice
negative peace	*positive peace
absence of justice	*presence of justice
goals	*methods
*direct action	passive acceptance

*exposed tension	hidden tension
*robbed	robber
*individual	society
*words	silence
*expression	repression
*extension of justice	preservation of injustice
*extremist for love, truth, and justice	extremist for immorality

Analyzing Oppositions

Step 3 produced the following description of the conflicting points of view:

> In this reading, King addresses as "white moderates" the clergymen who criticized him. He sees the moderate position in essentially negative terms, whereas extremism can be either negative or positive. Moderation is equated with passivity, acceptance of the status quo, fear of disorder, perhaps even fear of any change. The moderates believe justice can wait, whereas law and order cannot. Yet, as King points out, there is no law and order for blacks who are victimized and denied their constitutional rights.
>
> The argument King has with the white moderates is basically over means and ends. Both agree on the ends but disagree on the means that should be taken to secure those ends. What means are justified to achieve one's goals? How does one decide? King is willing to risk a certain amount of tension and disorder to bring about justice; he suggests that if progress is not made, more disorder, not less, is bound to result. In a sense, King represents himself as a moderate caught between the two extremes—the white moderates' "do-nothingism" and the black extremists' radicalism.
>
> At the same time, King replaces the opposition between moderation and extremism with an opposition between two kinds of extremism—one for love and the other for hate. In fact, he represents himself as an extremist willing to make whatever sacrifices—and perhaps even to take whatever means—are necessary to reach his goal of justice.

Considering Alternative Points of View

Step 4 entailed a few minutes of exploratory writing about the opposing point of view and then several more minutes of writing about King's possible response to the opposition's argument:

> *The moderates' side:* I can sympathize with the moderates' fear of further disorder and violence. Even though King advocates nonviolence,

violence does result. He may not cause it, but it does occur because of him. Moderates do not really advocate passive acceptance of injustice but want to pursue justice through legal means. These methods may be slow, but since ours is a system of law, the only way to make change is through that system. King wants to shake up the system and force it to move quickly for fear of violence. That strikes me as blackmail, as bad as if he were committing violence himself. Couldn't public opinion be brought to bear on the legal system to move more quickly? Can't we elect officials who will change unjust laws and see that the just ones are obeyed? The *vote* should be the weapon in a democracy, shouldn't it?

King's possible response: He would probably have argued that the opposing viewpoint was naive. One of the major injustices at that time was that blacks were prevented from voting, and no elected official would risk going against those who voted for him or her. King would probably have agreed that public opinion needed to be changed, that people needed to be educated, but he would also have argued that education was not enough when people were being systematically deprived of their legal rights. The very system of law that should have protected people was being used as a weapon against blacks in the South. The only way to get something done was to shake people up, make them aware of the injustice they were allowing to continue. Seeing their own police officers committing violence should have made people question their own values and begin to take action to right the wrongs.

CHECKLIST

Looking for Patterns of Opposition

To explore and analyze the patterns of opposition in a reading,

1. Annotate the selection to identify the oppositions, and list the pairs on a separate page.

2. Put an asterisk next to the writer's preferred word or phrase in each pair of opposing terms.

3. Examine the pattern of preferred terms to discover the system of values the pattern implies; then do the same for the unpreferred terms.

4. Write to analyze and evaluate the opposing points of view or, in the case of a reading that does not take a position, the alternative systems of value.

EVALUATING THE LOGIC OF AN ARGUMENT

An *argument* has two essential parts—the claim and the support. The *claim* asserts a conclusion—an idea, an opinion, a judgment, or a point of view—that the writer wants readers to accept. The *support* includes *reasons* (shared beliefs, assumptions, and values) and *evidence* (facts, examples, statistics, and authorities) that give readers the basis for accepting the writer's conclusion.

When you *evaluate the logic of an argument,* you are concerned about the process of reasoning as well as the argument's truthfulness. Three conditions must be met for an argument to be considered logically acceptable—what we call the ABC test:

A. The support must be *appropriate* to the claim.
B. All of the statements must be *believable.*
C. The argument must be *consistent* and *complete.*

In addition to the ABC test, you can also use other ways to evaluate the logic of an argument. The next two sections of this appendix explain how to use a specific method called a Toulmin analysis to determine the underlying assumptions in an argument (p. 627) and ways to recognize specific kinds of errors in reasoning, or logical fallacies (p. 631).

A. Testing for Appropriateness

To assess whether a writer's reasoning is *appropriate,* you look to see if all of the evidence is relevant to the claim it supports. For example, if a writer claims that children must be allowed certain legal rights, readers could readily accept as appropriate support quotations from Supreme Court justices' decisions but might question quotations from a writer of popular children's books. Readers could probably accept the reasoning that if women have certain legal rights then so should children, but few readers would agree that all human rights under the law should be extended to animals.

As these examples illustrate, appropriateness of support comes most often into question when the writer is invoking authority or arguing by analogy. For example, in the excerpt from "Letter from Birmingham Jail," King argues by analogy and, at the same time, invokes authority: "Isn't this like condemning Socrates because his unswerving commitment to truth and his philosophical inquiries precipitated the act by the misguided populace in which they made him drink hemlock?" (paragraph 3). Readers must judge the appropriateness (1) of comparing the Greek populace's condemnation of Socrates to the white moderates' condemnation of King's action and (2) also of accepting Socrates as an authority on this subject. Because Socrates is generally respected for his teaching on justice, his words and actions are likely to be considered appropriate to King's situation in Birmingham.

In paragraph 2, King argues that if law and order fail to establish justice, "they become the dangerously structured dams that block the flow of social progress."

The analogy asserts a logical relationship—that law and order are to social justice what a dam is to water. If readers do not accept this analogy, then the argument fails the test of appropriateness. Arguing by analogy is usually considered a weak kind of argument because most analogies are parallel only up to a point, beyond which they may fail.

B. Testing for Believability

Believability is a measure of the degree to which readers are willing to accept the assertions supporting the claim. Whereas some assertions are obviously true, most depend on the readers' sharing certain values, beliefs, and assumptions with the writer. Readers who agree with the white moderate that maintaining law and order is more important than establishing justice are not going to accept King's claim that the white moderate is blocking progress.

Other statements, such as those asserting facts, statistics, examples, and authorities, present evidence to support a claim. Readers must put all of these kinds of evidence to the test of believability.

Facts are statements that can be proven objectively to be true. The believability of facts depends on their *accuracy* (they should not distort or misrepresent reality), their *completeness* (they should not omit important details), and the *trustworthiness* of their sources (sources should be qualified and unbiased). In the excerpt from "Letter from Birmingham Jail," for instance, King asserts as fact that African Americans will not wait much longer for racial justice (paragraph 8). His critics might question the factuality of this assertion by asking: Is it true of all African Americans? How much longer will they wait? How does King know what African Americans will and will not do?

Statistics are often assumed to be factual, but they are really only interpretations of numerical data. The believability of statistics depends on the *accuracy* of the methods of gathering and analyzing data (representative samples should be used and variables accounted for), the *trustworthiness* of the sources (sources should be qualified and unbiased), and often the *comparability* of the data (are apples being compared to oranges?).

Examples and *anecdotes* are particular instances that if accepted as believable lead readers to accept the general claim. The power of examples depends on their *representativeness* (whether they are truly typical and thus generalizable) and their *specificity* (whether particular details make them seem true to life). Even if a vivid example or gripping anecdote does not convince readers, it strengthens argumentative writing by bringing home the point dramatically. In paragraph 5, for example, King supports his generalization that there are black nationalist extremists motivated by bitterness and hatred by citing the specific example of Elijah Muhammad's Muslim movement. Conversely, in paragraph 9, he refers to Jesus, Paul, Luther, and others as examples of extremists motivated by love. These examples support his assertions that extremism is not in itself wrong and that any judgment must depend on the cause for which one is an extremist.

Authorities are people whom the writer consults for expertise on a given subject. Such authorities must be not only appropriate, as mentioned earlier, but believable as well. The believability of authorities, their *credibility*, depends on whether the reader accepts them as experts on the topic. King cites authorities repeatedly throughout the essay, referring to religious leaders such as Jesus and Luther and to American political leaders such as Lincoln and Jefferson. These figures are certain to have a high degree of credibility among King's readers.

C. Testing for Consistency and Completeness

Be sure that all the support works together, that no supporting statement contradicts any of the others, and that no important objection or opposing argument is unacknowledged. To test for *consistency* and *completeness*, ask yourself: Are any of the supporting statements contradictory? Are any likely objections or opposing arguments not refuted?

In his essay, a potential contradiction is King's characterizing himself first as a moderate between the forces of complacency and violence and later as an extremist opposed to the forces of violence. King attempts to reconcile this apparent contradiction by explicitly redefining extremism in paragraph 9. Similarly, the fact that King fails to examine and refute every legal recourse available to his cause might allow a critical reader to question the sufficiency of his supporting arguments.

Following is one student's evaluation of the logic of King's argument. The student wrote these paragraphs after applying the ABC test to evaluate the appropriateness, believability, consistency, and completeness of King's supporting reasons and evidence:

> King writes both to the ministers who published the letter in the Birmingham newspaper and to the people of Birmingham. He seems to want to justify his group's actions. He challenges white moderates, but he also tries to avoid antagonizing them. Given this purpose and his readers, his supporting statements are generally appropriate. He relies mainly on assertions of shared belief with his readers and on memorable analogies. For example, he knows his readers will accept assertions like "law and order exist for the purpose of establishing justice"; it is good to be an extremist for "love, truth, and goodness"; and progress is not inevitable but results from tireless work and creativity. His analogies also seem acceptable and are based on appropriate comparisons. For example, he compares injustice to a boil that nonviolent action must expose to the air if it is to be healed.
>
> Likewise, his support is believable in terms of the well-known authorities he cites (Socrates, Jesus, Amos, Paul, Luther, Bunyan, Lincoln, Jefferson), the facts he asserts (for example, that racial tension results from injustice, not from nonviolent action), and the examples he offers (such as his assertion that extremism is not in itself wrong—as exemplified by Jesus, Paul, and Luther). If there is an inconsistency in the argument, it is the contradiction between King's portraits of himself both as a moderat-

ing force and as an "extremist for love," but his redefinition of extremism as a positive value for any social change is central to the overall persuasiveness of his logical appeal to white moderates.

USING A TOULMIN ANALYSIS

In addition to the ways of evaluating the logic of an argument that are discussed in the previous section, scholars have developed various formal systems for doing so. In *The Uses of Argument* (1964), Stephen Toulmin sets out a popular approach to reading, writing, and critical thinking that is widely used to discover and assess the logical structure of arguments. Students of legal writing frequently use Toulmin analysis, and you may find it helpful in your own reading and writing. As a user of this book, you may find that the most useful part of Toulmin's analysis is uncovering the underlying assumptions in an argument (or in any piece of writing) — the focus of the third part of the Reading for Meaning activities that follow the readings in Chapters 2 through 9.

Toulmin's specialized terms — *claim, data* and *grounds,* and *warrant* — are defined as follows:

- *Claim:* the thesis or main point of the argument.

- *Data* and *grounds:* the reasons and evidence that support the claim.

- *Warrant:* the beliefs, values, and assumptions that "warrant" or justify the claim based on the evidence. Often the warrant is unstated or implicit.

To find the warrant, you must figure out the belief or value system that enables the author to make the claim or draw the conclusion from the reasons and evidence set forth. The following strategies will help you identify the warrant underlying the argument. Once you uncover the warrant or assumption, you can determine whether the evidence—in Toulmin's words—"authorizes, entitles, or justifies the writer to make the claim based on the data," which basically means that the warrant helps you judge whether the writer's claim is justified by the evidence provided.

Identifying the Warrant

Let's look again at the beginning of the excerpt from King's "Letter from Birmingham Jail":

> . . . I must confess that over the past few years I have been gravely disappointed with the white moderate. I have almost reached the regrettable conclusion that the Negro's great stumbling block in his stride toward freedom is not the White Citizen's Counciler or the Ku Klux Klanner, but the white moderate, who is more devoted to "order" than to justice; who prefers a negative peace which is the absence of tension to a positive peace which is the presence of justice; who constantly says: "I agree with you in the goal you seek, but I cannot agree with your methods of direct action"; who paternalistically believes he can set the timetable for another man's freedom; who lives by a mythical concept of time and who constantly advises the Negro to wait for a "more convenient season." Shallow understanding from people of good will is more frustrating than absolute misunderstanding from people of ill will. Lukewarm acceptance is much more bewildering than outright rejection.
>
> I had hoped that the white moderate would understand that law and order exist for the purpose of establishing justice and that when they fail in this purpose they become the dangerously structured dams that block the flow of social progress. I had hoped that the white moderate would understand that the present tension in the South is a necessary phase of the transition from an obnoxious negative peace, in which the Negro passively accepted his unjust plight, to a substantive and positive peace, in which all men will respect the dignity and worth of human personality.

STEP 1. To apply a Toulmin analysis to King's argument, you first need to *find the claim and reasons* in the passage. What is the author's assertion? What point is the author trying to make? The answer to these questions is the claim. Then ask why the author thinks this claim is true: What reasons are offered to support it? Often you can paraphrase the passage as a *because* statement that is completed by those reasons: This claim is true because of reason one, reason two, and so on. It is helpful to use as much of the writer's own language as possible because the writer's choice of words will be important when you try to analyze the assumptions and discover the warrant. It is also helpful to underline or highlight words and phrases that seem to have a great deal of importance to the author.

A Toulmin analysis of the preceding passage might look like this:

- *Claim:* White moderates impede the African American's progress toward freedom

- *Reason 1:* because they care more for *order* than *justice* and

- *Reason 2:* because they prefer "a *negative peace* which is the *absence of tension* to a *positive peace* which is the *presence of justice*."

STEP 2. *Uncover the warrant* by discovering the assumptions of the writer. Write a few sentences exploring the values and beliefs implied by each key term or phrase. Ask yourself these questions: What are the connotations of these words? What do they mean beyond their literal meaning? How does their context in this passage affect my understanding of their meaning?

Let's look first at the argument based on reason 1. King apparently assumes that his readers believe, as he does, that justice is more important than order. Readers would have to ask themselves what these two key terms, *order* and *justice*, mean to King. How would you define these terms as King uses them? After you identify key terms, look up their dictionary meanings (*denotations*). Then write out the emotional or cultural associations (*connotations*) the words carry within the context of the passage. For example, the Dictionary.com definition of *order* is "a state of public peace or conformity to law." Clearly King believes that a state of public peace exists at the expense of African Americans' march toward freedom. He is troubled that white moderates prefer "a negative peace which is the absence of tension to a positive peace which is the presence of justice." An *order* that does not include justice, then, leads to his connotative definition: that the current *order* means a state of stagnation and a force for inertia (or not making any change or progress). However, in the next few lines, King adds to his connotative definition by criticizing white moderates for "prefer[ring] a negative peace," for "paternalistically believ[ing they] can set the timetable for another man's freedom," for suffering from a "shallow understanding" of the problem and for not understanding "that law and order exist for the purpose of establishing justice and that when they fail in this purpose they become the dangerously structured dams that block the flow of social progress."

The Dictionary.com definition for *justice* is "the quality of conforming to principles of reason, to generally accepted standards of right and wrong, and to the stated terms of laws, rules, agreements, etc. in matters affecting persons who could be wronged or unduly favored." Here King's connotative meaning is complex: he questions the laws that keep order, if the laws are not just. (That is why he later carefully defines just and unjust laws.) When he writes that "law and order exist for the purpose of establishing justice and . . . when they fail in this purpose they become the dangerously structured dams that block the flow of social progress," he is adding to the connotations of the word *justice* (as well as *order*) by arguing how tightly linked order must be to justice — that order for its own sake can prevent society from changing in ways that it needs to change.

Once you define the denotative and connotative meanings of key terms in a passage, write a few sentences summarizing the beliefs and values you have discovered in these meanings. For example, King believes that justice can be achieved only by disturbing the current order or, to put it another way, that a preference for order keeps people from making progress. Order means the status quo, as opposed to change or "progress towards freedom." By uncovering this warrant, you know that King believes that a disturbance of order is necessary to foster African Americans' progress. He does not believe that order is what is most important. Rather, he believes a disturbance of order is justified by the goal of progress toward freedom. King also believes that justice cannot be achieved without disturbing order and that justice is more important than order.

STEP 3. *Consider alternative assumptions* readers might have about the key terms in King's argument. If you know anything about the context of the period when the passage was written, or if the author gives you any clues or direct information about the audience, you will be able to figure out these assumptions from the text. For example, whereas King values justice over order, he clearly assumes that white moderates and other readers in 1963 would think the opposite. Write a few sentences exploring the meanings of *order* and *justice* that might lead someone to value order more than justice. King's readers may not feel quite the same way about the concepts embodied in these terms: *order* could mean "safety," or if justice can come only at the price of social chaos, perhaps (as King worries) readers might conclude that it is better to wait for justice than to risk social upheaval.

STEP 4. *Restate the warrants underlying the argument (the claim and the reasons)* using the denotations and connotations of the key terms. One way to do this is to phrase the beliefs of the author in *that* clauses. King expects his readers to believe, as he does:

— that justice for African Americans in the 1960s requires progress toward freedom

— that anyone who stops or slows this progress is a stumbling block

— that peace is less important than justice

— that order is less important than justice

— that safety is less important than justice

— that progress is more important than maintaining the status quo

— that social unrest and disorder are necessary to achieve justice

—that although breaking the law (what King calls "direct action" and we know as "civil disobedience") disrupts order, peace, and safety, it is necessary to achieve justice

STEP 5. *Explore your own values and beliefs* in relation to those uncovered in your Toulmin analysis. How do you feel about the warrants you identified, given your own experience? Given the difference (if any) between the time the passage was written and the present?

CHECKLIST

Using a Toulmin Analysis

To perform a Toulmin analysis,

1. Identify the author's claim. Identify the reasons and evidence that support that claim.

2. Consider how key terms reflect the author's beliefs and values by defining those terms denotatively and connotatively.

3. Consider alternative assumptions readers might have about the key terms.

4. Restate the author's warrants—the beliefs, values, and assumptions that "warrant" the claim.

5. Compare your own values and beliefs with the author's.

RECOGNIZING LOGICAL FALLACIES

A *logical fallacy* is an error or a distortion in the reasoning process. Sometimes writers are unaware that they have committed a logical fallacy: they believe their logic is correct and don't understand why it is faulty. In many cases, however, writers use a fallacy deliberately because they want to avoid reasoning that might undermine their argument or because they want to divert the reader into a different line of reasoning. As you learn to spot logical fallacies in your reading (and in what you hear on radio and television), you will learn also to avoid them in your writing. Students who study formal debate in a speech course or debate club often learn fallacies so they can call attention to and refute the false logic in an opponent's argument. Ethical writers should beware of using fallacies, but they should know how to recognize them and how to refute them.

Identifying fallacies can be tricky, however. Many of them involve subtle and complex issues of reasoning that require careful thought and analysis. In addition, in many cases reasoning becomes fallacious or false only when it is taken too far—when it has become extreme—and reasonable people can disagree about when that point is reached. In logic, as in life, the line between truth and falsehood is often not clearly defined. In fact, one of the most common logical fallacies is the belief that there are only two choices in particular situations.

In general, though, you should suspect that you might be reading a logical fallacy when you stop to think "wait a minute—that doesn't make sense" or when you believe the writer has "gone too far." Recognizing the following common fallacies is an important step in learning to be a critical reader.

Slippery Slope

A *slippery-slope* fallacy occurs when someone asserts that if one thing happens, then a series of bad related consequences will *necessarily* follow. The name comes from the idea that if a person takes one step down a slippery slope, he or she cannot help sliding all the way to the bottom. Here are a few examples of this type of faulty reasoning:

- Often when people start making improvements to their homes, the work leads to the need for more improvements. If you paint one room, then it makes the rest of the rooms look dingy, so you have to paint them, too; then the windows need replacing; and so on. This is a valid slippery-slope argument because a particular chain of events does often or usually result from the initial action (though not necessarily in every case).

- Antidrug campaigns often claim that if someone smokes marijuana, then he or she will likely become addicted to other illegal drugs. While there is some evidence that marijuana use may lead to additional drug use, this is not true of most people.

- A common argument against euthanasia is that if we allow people to take their own lives (or allow doctors or relatives to help them do so) to avoid extraordinary misery in their final days, then down the line we will allow or encourage assisted suicide for matters that might not be devastating or fatal. Given the relatively brief time in which euthanasia has been practiced legally anywhere in the world, it seems too early to judge whether this argument is based on sound reasoning or is a slippery-slope fallacy.

Post hoc, ergo propter hoc

One of the most common fallacies has the Latin name *post hoc, ergo propter hoc,* which means "after this, therefore because of this." A *post hoc* fallacy wrongly assumes that an event that occurs *after* another event is *caused* by the first event. In many cases, there is no connection at all between the events; in others, a connection does exist, but it is more complicated than the person making it realizes or admits. This fallacy in causal analysis often occurs when writers try to attribute to one cause something that has several or many causes. When complex issues are made to seem simple, look for this fallacy. Here are some examples:

- If you took medicine prescribed by your doctor for a cold and then broke out in hives, you might assume that the medicine caused the hives. However, if you took the medicine with a drink you had never had before, it could have been the drink or the combination of the drink and the medicine that caused the hives. Or the hives might be from a case of nerves or another cause completely unrelated to the medicine, the drink, or anything else you ingested.

- Some people argue that depictions of violence on television and in films cause teenagers to act violently. But most teenagers do not become violent even if they watch a great deal of violence on the screen. To avoid the *post hoc* fallacy, someone making this argument would have to show a clear connection between the amount of violence teenagers watch and the likelihood that they will become violent themselves. The person would also need to consider other possible causes, such as membership in gangs, alienation at school, parental abuse, and so on.

False Dilemma (Either/Or Reasoning)

One of the most common fallacies, the *false dilemma* or *either/or reasoning*, puts readers in the position of having to choose one of two options as if there were no other choices — but rarely in life are options narrowed down to only two. Writers who employ the false dilemma fallacy are usually trying to make the reader choose an option they favor by making the reader believe there are only two choices. Their reasoning avoids the complexities of most issues. Here are some examples:

- Martin Luther King Jr., in paragraph 5 of the excerpt from "Letter from Birmingham Jail" (p. 600), refutes an either/or argument made by others. Arguing that the choice between a "force of complacency" or a force "of bitterness and hatred" is a false dilemma, King points out that there are other alternatives, among them the option of nonviolent protest that he represents.

- A candidate for governor argues that the way to solve traffic congestion is to turn freeways into toll roads, because building a subway system would be too expensive. This argument sets up a fallacious either/or opposition. In fact, toll roads could help raise funds to pay for a subway system, which would give commuters an alternative means of transportation.

Mistaking the Part for the Whole (Nonrepresentative Sample)

The *nonrepresentative sample* fallacy occurs when a writer assumes that if something is true of a part of a larger whole, then it is true of the whole, or vice versa. Sometimes this is indeed the case, but often it is not because the part is not representative — it does not have the typical characteristics — of the whole. This fallacy often occurs in connection with public opinion polls, especially online polls, when no effort is made to ensure that respondents accurately represent the characteristics of the larger group whose opinion they are said to reflect. Here are some examples of this fallacy:

- One of the best-known examples of a nonrepresentative sample in political polling occurred in the 1936 presidential election, when *Literary Digest* magazine conducted a telephone poll that predicted President Franklin D. Roosevelt would be defeated for reelection by his Republican opponent, Alfred P. Landon. On Election Day, Roosevelt won reelection in a landslide. The main explanation for this faulty forecast was the way in which the poll was conducted: because Republican voters tended to be wealthier than Democratic ones and because during the Depression of the 1930s many Democratic voters could not afford telephones, the magazine surveyed a disproportionately large number of Republicans.

- Suppose that your school has the best football team in its conference. That does not necessarily mean that the quarterback, the kicker, or the defensive line is the best in the conference, because putting the various members of the team together gives the team as a whole qualities that are different from those of the individuals involved.

Hasty Generalization

A *hasty generalization* leaps to a conclusion without providing enough evidence to support the leap. Here are some examples:

- Government leaders think that the appearance of troop maneuvers in a border town of a neighboring country signals an immediate invasion of the nearby territory. However, in the absence of other, confirming information, it could be just as likely that a leader had not planned an invasion but had decided that the border town was a good place to practice troop maneuvers, especially if the goal was to impress the neighbor with their military might.

- "Crime in this city is getting worse and worse. Just yesterday, two people were held up at ATMs downtown." Two crimes, no matter how serious, do not indicate that the overall *rate* of crime is rising. This may indeed be the case, but proving it would require statistics, not just a couple of examples.

Bandwagon Appeal

This fallacy can be recognized when someone is appealing to the notion that "since everyone else does it, you should too." *Bandwagon appeals* are probably most common in advertising and political rhetoric. Here are some examples:

- "Join the thousands who've found relief from arthritis pain with Ache-No-More."

- "A powerful new political tide is surging through America. Want to come together with millions of your fellow citizens in a movement to change our nation's priorities? Volunteer for Americans for National Renewal."

Ad hominem (or *ad personam*) Attack

These Latin names mean "to the man" or "to the person." An *ad hominem* or *ad personam attack* occurs when writers attack the person who propounds the ideas with which they disagree, rather than attack the ideas themselves. Certainly the character and credibility of the writer making the argument affect how persuasive a reader finds it, but they do not affect the underlying soundness of the argument. Here are some examples:

- Whenever a writer attacks a person, be alert for a logical fallacy. Martin Luther King Jr. could have attacked the clergy who wrote the letter he is addressing in "Letter from Birmingham Jail." He could have called them intolerant or foolish, for example. Instead, he carefully addresses their arguments step by step and shows how his logic is superior to theirs. Some readers might think King does fall victim to this fallacy when he says that the white moderate has only a "shallow understanding" (paragraph 1) of the problem, but he goes on to show how complex the problem is and how the white moderate needs to become more engaged and active in implementing change.

- "My opponent, one of the richest men in the state, wants to cut taxes for himself and his rich friends." "Of course my opponent favors raising corporate taxes. He's just a political hack who's never had to meet a payroll." A proposal's value does not depend on whether the person making it will personally benefit from it or has personal experience with the issue involved. Something that benefits the person who proposes it may well (although not necessarily) benefit society in general, and someone with an outsider's perspective on an issue may well (although not necessarily) have better ideas about it than someone with experience. Again, note that sound reasoning is not the same as credibility. Those with something personal to gain from a proposal or with no experience in the issue may carry less credibility with the people they are trying to persuade, but that does not mean that their views are any less logical. An important part of becoming a critical reader is learning to disregard personal attacks on (or ridicule of) the person making an argument and to focus on the logic of the argument.

Straw Man (or Straw Person)

In a straw-man fallacy, the writer portrays an opponent's position as more extreme than it actually is so that it can be refuted more easily, as one would be able to knock down a straw scarecrow more easily than a live human being. As with many other fallacies, however, the line between what is and is not a straw-man argument is not always clear. Sometimes the writer claims that the opponent's position is part of a plan to achieve a more extreme position—and this claim could be considered either a straw-man argument (which would be fallacious) or a slippery-slope argument (which might be fallacious or might not). Here is an example:

- If a political candidate supports partial privatization of Social Security, an opponent who simply claims that the candidate "proposes doing away with Social Security" is creating a straw-man fallacy. If the opponent simply claims that "partial privatization would be a first step toward doing away with Social Security," this would be a slippery-slope argument—which may or may not be fallacious in itself but is not a straw-man argument because it does not actually misrepresent the candidate's position. Finally, if the opponent argues that the candidate "supports partial privatization as a first step toward doing away with Social Security," the reader would have to consider other evidence (such as other positions the candidate has taken or his or her voting record) to judge whether this is a fallacious straw-man argument or a sound slippery-slope one.

Begging the Question (Circular Reasoning)

In *begging the question*, the writer makes an argument that assumes the truth of what is theoretically the point at issue. In other words, to believe what the argument is trying to prove, the reader has to already believe it. Here are some examples:

- "We shouldn't do that because it's a bad idea." This statement essentially just says, "That's a bad idea because it's a bad idea."

- "God created the world in seven days; this has to be true because the Bible says so, and the Bible is the word of God." This example shows why this fallacy is often called *circular reasoning*: the reasoning simply circles back to the original underlying claim that God is all-powerful. If the reader already believes that the Bible is the word of God and therefore is sufficient evidence for God's creation of the world in seven days, then there is no need to make this claim. If not, then he or she will not be convinced by this argument for it.

- When the U.S. Supreme Court was deciding whether to hear the case of *Bush v. Gore*, an appeal of a decision by the Florida Supreme Court after the disputed presidential election of 2000, Justice Antonin Scalia argued that the Court should accept the case to avoid "casting a cloud" over the election of

George W. Bush as president. But the point at issue in the case—the claim that was being argued—was whether Bush had indeed been elected president. Gore supporters pointed out that Scalia's argument, based on the assumption that the claim had already been established, was an example of circular reasoning.

Red Herring

You can remember this fallacy by the picture it presents—dragging a dead fish across a trail to distract dogs from pursuing the scent of their real target. In this case, writers use irrelevant arguments to distract readers from the real issue, perhaps because their own argument is weak and they don't want the reader to notice. Red herrings often occur in political debates when one debater does not really want to address an issue raised by the other debater. Here are some examples:

- "My opponent tries to blame my administration for the high price of prescription drugs, but he supports a government takeover of health care." That the opponent supports a government takeover of health care (whether true or false) has nothing to do with whether the policies of the speaker's administration are responsible for the high price of prescription drugs.

- In a U.S. Senate race in 2004, a candidate argued that gay people should not be allowed to adopt children because incest may result if adopted siblings unknowingly marry each other. The risk the candidate mentions is real (if remote), but it is no more likely for children adopted by gay people than for those adopted by heterosexuals. In trying to make an argument against gay adoption, the candidate was making an argument against adoption in general (also implying another kind of incest is likely to occur—between parent and child).

CHECKLIST

Recognizing Logical Fallacies

To determine whether the writer succumbs to any logical fallacies,

1. Annotate places in the text where you stop to think "wait a minute—that doesn't make sense" or where you think the writer has "gone too far."

2. Analyze these places to see if they represent any of the fallacies discussed in this section.

3. Write a few sentences exploring what you discover.

RECOGNIZING EMOTIONAL MANIPULATION

Writers often try to arouse emotions in readers—to excite their interest, make them care, move them to action. Although nothing is wrong with appealing to readers' emotions, it is wrong to manipulate readers with false or exaggerated emotional appeals.

Many words have connotations, associations that enrich their meaning and give words much of their emotional power. For example, we use the word *manipulation* in naming this particular critical reading strategy to arouse an emotional response in readers like you. No one wants to be manipulated. Everyone wants to feel in control of his or her attitudes and opinions. This is especially true in reading arguments: we want to be convinced, not tricked.

Emotional manipulation often works by distracting readers from relevant reasons and evidence. To keep from being distracted, you want to pay close attention as you read and try to distinguish between emotional appeals that are acceptable and those that you consider manipulative or excessive.

Here is an example of one student's reaction to the emotional appeal of the excerpt from "Letter from Birmingham Jail":

> As someone King would probably identify as a white moderate, I can't help reacting negatively to some of the language he uses in this reading. For example, in the first paragraph, he equates white moderates with members of the Ku Klux Klan even though he admits that white moderates were in favor of racial equality and justice. He also puts down white moderates for being paternalistic. Finally, he uses scare tactics when he threatens "a frightening racial nightmare."

CHECKLIST

Recognizing Emotional Manipulation

To assess whether emotional appeals are unfair and manipulative,

1. Annotate places in the text where you sense emotional appeals are being used.

2. Write a few sentences identifying the kinds of appeals you have found and exploring your responses to them.

JUDGING THE WRITER'S CREDIBILITY

Writers often try to persuade readers to respect and believe them. Because readers may not know them personally or even by reputation, writers must present an image of themselves in their writing that will gain their readers' confidence. This image cannot be made directly but must be made indirectly, through the arguments, language, and system of values and beliefs implied in the writing. Writers establish *credibility* in several ways:

- by showing their knowledge of the subject,
- by building common ground with readers, and
- by responding fairly to objections and opposing arguments.

Testing for Knowledge

Writers demonstrate their knowledge of the subject through the facts and statistics they marshal, the sources they rely on for information, and the scope and depth of their understanding. As a critical reader, you may not be sufficiently expert on the subject yourself to know whether the facts are accurate, the sources reliable, and the understanding sufficient. You may need to do some research to see what others are saying about the subject. You can also check credentials — the writer's educational and professional qualifications, the respectability of the publication in which the selection first appeared, any reviews of the writer's work — to determine whether the writer is a respected authority in the field. King brings with him the authority that comes from being a member of the clergy and a respected leader of the Southern Christian Leadership Conference.

Testing for Common Ground

One way that writers can establish common ground with their readers is by basing their reasoning on shared values, beliefs, and attitudes. They use language that includes their readers (*we*) rather than excludes them (*they*). They qualify their assertions to keep them from being too extreme. Above all, they acknowledge differences of opinion and try to make room in their argument to accommodate reasonable differences. As a reader, you will be affected by such appeals.

King creates common ground with readers by using the inclusive pronoun *we*, suggesting shared concerns between himself and his audience. Notice, however, his use of masculine pronouns and other references ("the Negro . . . he," "our brothers"). Although King intended this letter to be published in the local newspaper, where it would be read by an audience of both men and women, he addressed it to male clergy. By using language that excludes women, King missed the opportunity to build common ground with half his readers.

Testing for Fairness

Writers display their character by how they handle objections to their arguments. As a critical reader, you want to pay particular attention to how writers treat possible differences of opinion. Be suspicious of those who ignore differences and pretend everyone agrees with their viewpoints. When objections or opposing views are represented, you should consider whether they have been distorted in any way; if they are refuted, you want to be sure they are challenged fairly—with sound reasoning and solid evidence.

One way to gauge an author's credibility is to identify the tone of the argument. *Tone*, the writer's attitude toward the subject and toward the reader, is concerned not so much with what is said as with how it is said. By reading sensitively, you should be able to detect the writer's tone. To identify the tone, list whatever descriptive adjectives come to mind in response to either of these questions: How would you characterize the attitude of this selection? What sort of emotion does the writer bring to his or her writing? Judging from this piece of writing, what kind of person does the author seem to be?

Here is one student's answer to the second question, based on the excerpt from "Letter from Birmingham Jail":

> I know something about King from television programs on the civil rights movement. But if I were to talk about my impression of him from this passage, I'd use words like *patient, thoughtful, well educated, moral, confident.* He doesn't lose his temper but tries to convince his readers by making a case that is reasoned carefully and painstakingly. He's trying to change people's attitudes; no matter how annoyed he might be with them, he treats them with respect. It's as if he believes that their hearts are right, but they're just confused. If he can just set them straight, everything will be fine. Of course, he also sounds a little pompous when he compares himself to Jesus and Socrates, and the threat he appears to make in paragraph 8 seems out of character. Maybe he's losing control of his self-image at those moments.

CHECKLIST

Judging the Writer's Credibility

To decide whether you can trust the writer,

1. As you read and annotate, consider the writer's knowledge of the subject, the ways that the writer establishes common ground with readers, and the ways that the writer deals fairly with objections and opposing arguments.

2. Write a few sentences exploring what you discover.

COMPARING AND CONTRASTING RELATED READINGS

When you *compare* two reading selections, you look for similarities. When you *contrast* them, you look for differences. As critical reading strategies, comparing and contrasting enable you to see both texts more clearly.

Both strategies depend on how imaginative you are in preparing the grounds or basis for comparison. We often hear that it is fruitless, so to speak, to compare apples and oranges. It is true that you cannot add or multiply them, but you can put one against the other and come up with some interesting similarities and differences. For example, comparing apples and oranges in terms of their roles as symbols in Western culture (say, the apple of Adam and Eve compared to the symbol for Apple computers) could be quite productive. The grounds or basis for comparison, like a camera lens, brings some things into focus while blurring others.

To demonstrate how this strategy works, we compare and contrast the excerpt from "Letter from Birmingham Jail" (pp. 598–602) with the following selection by Lewis H. Van Dusen Jr.

LEWIS H. VAN DUSEN JR.

Legitimate Pressures and Illegitimate Results

A respected attorney and legal scholar, Lewis H. Van Dusen Jr. has served as chair of the American Bar Association Committee on Ethics and Professional Responsibility. This selection comes from the essay "Civil Disobedience: Destroyer of Democracy," which first appeared in the American Bar Association Journal *in 1969. As you read, notice the annotations we made comparing this essay with the one by King.*

1   There are many civil rights leaders who show impatience with the process of democracy. They rely on the sit-in, boycott, or mass picketing to gain speedier solutions to the problems that face every citizen. But we must realize that the legitimate pressures that [won concessions in the past] can easily escalate into the illegitimate power plays that might [extort] demands in the future.] The victories of these civil rights leaders must not shake our confidence in the democratic procedures, as the pressures of demonstration are desirable only if they take place within the limits allowed by law. Civil rights gains should continue to be won by the persuasion of Congress and other legislative bodies and by the decision of courts. Any illegal entreaty for the [rights of some] can be an injury to the [rights of others,] for mass demonstrations often trigger violence.

> To get something by force or intimidation

Those who advocate [taking the law into their own hands] 2
should reflect that when they are disobeying what they consider to be an immoral law, they are deciding on a possibly immoral course. Their answer is that the process for democratic relief is too slow, that only mass confrontation can bring immediate action, and that any injuries are the inevitable cost of the pursuit of justice. Their answer is, simply put, that the end justifies the means. It is this justification of any form of demonstration as a form of dissent that threatens to destroy a society built on the rule of law.

King's concern with time

Ends vs. means debate

Any form?

Our Bill of Rights guarantees wide opportunities to use 3
mass meetings, public parades, and organized demonstrations to stimulate sentiment, to dramatize issues, and to cause change. The Washington freedom march of 1963 was such a call for action. But the rights of free expression cannot be mere force cloaked in the garb of free speech. As the courts have decreed in labor cases, free assembly does not mean mass picketing or sit-down strikes. These rights are subject to limitations of time and place so as to secure the rights of others. When militant students storm a college president's office to achieve demands, when certain groups plan rush-hour car stalling to protest discrimination in employment, these are not dissent, but a denial of rights to others. Neither is it the lawful use of mass protest, but rather the unlawful use of mob power.

These are legal

Right to demonstrate is limited

Can't deny others' rights

Justice Black, one of the foremost advocates and defenders 4
of the right of protest and dissent, has said:

> . . . Experience demonstrates that it is not a far step from what to many seems to be the earnest, honest, patriotic, kind-spirited multitude of today, to the fanatical, threatening, lawless mob of tomorrow. And the crowds that press in the streets for noble goals today can be supplanted tomorrow by street mobs pressuring the courts for precisely opposite ends.

Society must censure those demonstrators who would 5
trespass on the public peace, as it must condemn those rioters whose pillage would destroy the public peace. But more ambivalent is society's posture toward the civil disobedient. Unlike the rioter, the true civil disobedient commits no violence. Unlike the mob demonstrator, he commits no trespass on others' rights. The civil disobedient, while deliberately violating a law, shows an oblique respect for the law by voluntarily submitting to its sanctions. He neither resists arrest

nor evades punishment. Thus, he breaches the law but not the peace.

6   But civil disobedience, whatever the ethical rationalization, is still an assault on our democratic society, an affront to our legal order, and an attack on our constitutional government. To indulge civil disobedience is to invite anarchy, and the permissive arbitrariness of anarchy is hardly less tolerable than the repressive arbitrariness of tyranny. Too often the license of liberty is followed by the loss of liberty, because into the desert of anarchy comes the man on horseback, a Mussolini or a Hitler.

Isn't he contradicting himself?

Threatens repression as retaliation

We had already read and annotated the King excerpt, so we read the Van Dusen selection looking for a basis for comparison. We decided to base our contrast on the writers' different views of nonviolent direct action. We carefully reread the Van Dusen selection, annotating aspects of his argument against the use of nonviolent direct action. These annotations led directly to the first paragraph of our contrast, which summarizes Van Dusen's argument. Then we reread the King excerpt, looking for how he justifies nonviolent direct action. The second paragraph of our contrast presents King's defense, plus some of our own ideas on how he could have responded to Van Dusen.

King and Van Dusen present radically different views of legal, nonviolent direct action, such as parades, demonstrations, boycotts, sit-ins, or pickets. Although Van Dusen acknowledges that direct action is legal, he nevertheless fears it; and he challenges it energetically in these paragraphs. He seems most concerned about the ways direct action disturbs the peace, infringes on others' rights, and threatens violence. He worries that, even though some groups make gains through direct action, the end result is that everyone else begins to doubt the validity of the usual democratic procedures of relying on legislation and the courts. He condemns advocates of direct action like King for believing that the end (in this case, racial justice) justifies the means (direct action). Van Dusen argues that demonstrations often end violently and that an organized movement like King's can in the beginning win concessions through direct action but then end up extorting demands through threats and illegal uses of power.

In contrast, King argues that nonviolent direct action preserves the peace by bringing hidden tensions and prejudices to the surface where they can be acknowledged and addressed. Direct action enhances democracy by changing its unjust laws and thereby strengthening it. Since direct action is entirely legal, to forgo it as a strategy for change would be to turn one's back on a basic democratic principle. Although it may inconvenience people, its end (a more just social order) is entirely justified by its means (direct action). King would no doubt insist that the occasional violence that follows direct action results always from aggressive, unlawful interference with demonstrations—interference sometimes led by police officers. He might also argue that neither anarchy nor extortion followed from his group's actions.

Notice that these paragraphs address each writer's argument separately. An alternative plan would have been to compare and contrast the two writers' arguments point by point.

CHECKLIST

Comparing and Contrasting Related Readings

To compare and contrast two related readings,

1. Read them both to decide on a basis or grounds for comparison or contrast.

2. Reread and annotate one selection to identify points of comparison or contrast.

3. Reread the second selection, annotating for the points you have already identified.

4. Write up your analyses of the two selections, revising your analysis of the first selection to reflect any new insights you have gained. Or write a point-by-point comparison or contrast of the two selections.

Martin Luther King Jr. wrote "Letter from Birmingham Jail" in response to the following public statement by eight Alabama clergymen.

Public Statement by Eight Alabama Clergymen

April 12, 1963

We the undersigned clergymen are among those who, in January, issued "An Appeal for Law and Order and Common Sense," in dealing with racial problems in Alabama. We expressed understanding that honest convictions in racial matters could properly

1

be pursued in the courts, but urged that decisions of those courts should in the meantime be peacefully obeyed.

Since that time there has been some evidence of increased forebearance and a willingness to face facts. Responsible citizens have undertaken to work on various problems which cause racial friction and unrest. In Birmingham, recent public events have given indication that we all have opportunity for a new constructive and realistic approach to racial problems.

However, we are now confronted by a series of demonstrations by some of our Negro citizens, directed and led in part by outsiders. We recognize the natural impatience of people who feel that their hopes are slow in being realized. But we are convinced that these demonstrations are unwise and untimely.

We agree rather with certain local Negro leadership which has called for honest and open negotiation of racial issues in our area. And we believe this kind of facing of issues can best be accomplished by citizens of our own metropolitan area, white and Negro, meeting with their knowledge and experience of the local situation. All of us need to face that responsibility and find proper channels for its accomplishment.

Just as we formerly pointed out that "hatred and violence have no sanction in our religious and political traditions," we also point out that such actions as incite to hatred and violence, however technically peaceful those actions may be, have not contributed to the resolution of our local problems. We do not believe that these days of new hope are days when extreme measures are justified in Birmingham.

We commend the community as a whole, and the local news media and law enforcement officials in particular, on the calm manner in which these demonstrations have been handled. We urge the public to continue to show restraint should the demonstrations continue, and the law enforcement officials to remain calm and continue to protect our city from violence.

We further strongly urge our own Negro community to withdraw support from these demonstrations, and to unite locally in working peacefully for a better Birmingham. When rights are consistently denied, a cause should be pressed in the courts and in negotiations among local leaders, and not in the streets. We appeal to both our white and Negro citizenry to observe the principles of law and order and common sense.

Signed by:
C. C. J. CARPENTER, D.D., LL.D., *Bishop of Alabama*
  JOSEPH A. DURICK, D.D., *Auxiliary Bishop, Diocese of Mobile–Birmingham*

Rabbi MILTON L. GRAFMAN, *Temple Emanu-El, Birmingham, Alabama*

Bishop PAUL HARDIN, *Bishop of the Alabama-West Florida Conference of the Methodist Church*

Bishop NOLAN B. HARMON, *Bishop of the North Alabama Conference of the Methodist Church*

GEORGE M. MURRAY, D.D., LL.D., *Bishop Coadjutor, Episcopal Diocese of Alabama*

EDWARD V. RAMAGE, *Moderator, Synod of the Alabama Presbyterian Church in the United States*

EARL STALLINGS, *Pastor, First Baptist Church, Birmingham, Alabama*

Strategies for Research and Documentation

As many of the essays in *Reading Critically, Writing Well* show, writers often rely on research to expand and test their own ideas about a topic. This appendix offers advice on conducting research, evaluating potential sources, integrating source material you decide to use with your own writing, and documenting this material in an acceptable way.

CONDUCTING RESEARCH

In your college career, you may have opportunities to do many different kinds of research, including laboratory experiments and statistical surveys. Here we introduce the three basic types of research you are most likely to use to satisfy the assignments in *Reading Critically, Writing Well* and to fulfill requirements of other lower-division courses: field research using observation and interview, library research, and Internet research.

Field Research

Observation and *interview* are the two major kinds of *field* or *ethnographic research*. The observational essays in Chapter 3 illustrate some of the ways you might use field research. You might also use these research techniques when proposing a solution to a problem (Chapter 8) or when arguing a position on a controversial issue (Chapter 9). You may be asked to read and write essays based on field research in other courses as well, such as in sociology, political science, anthropology, psychology, communication, or business.

Observation

Following are guidelines for planning an observational visit, taking notes on your observations, and reflecting on what you observed.

PLANNING THE VISIT

To ensure that you use your time productively during observational visits, you must plan them carefully.

GETTING ACCESS. If the place you propose to visit is public, you probably will have easy access to it. Ask yourself whether everything you need to see is within casual view. If not, you have encountered a potential problem of access. If you require special access or permission, you will need to call ahead or make a get-acquainted visit to introduce yourself and explain your purpose.

ANNOUNCING YOUR INTENTIONS. Explain politely who you are, where you are from, and why you would like access. You may be surprised at how receptive people can be to a student on assignment from a college course. Not every place you wish to visit will welcome you, however. A variety of constraints on outside visitors exist in private businesses as well as public institutions. But generally, if people know your intentions, they may be able to tell you about aspects of a place or an activity you would not have thought to observe.

BRINGING TOOLS. Take a notebook with a firm back so that you will have a steady writing surface, perhaps a small pad with a spiral binding across the top. Take a few pens or pencils. If you prefer to use a tape recorder to record your observations, bring along extra tapes and batteries. Also take a notebook in case something goes wrong with the tape recorder.

OBSERVING AND TAKING NOTES

Here are some practical suggestions for making observations and taking notes.

OBSERVING. Some activities invite multiple vantage points, whereas others seem to limit the observer to a single perspective. Explore the space as much as possible, taking advantage of every vantage point available to you. Consider it from different angles, both literally and figuratively. Since your purposes are to analyze as well as to describe your subject, look for its typical and atypical features, how it is like and unlike similar subjects. Think also about what would make the subject interesting to your readers.

NOTETAKING. You undoubtedly will find your own style of notetaking, but here are a few pointers:

- Write only on one side of the page. Later, when you organize your notes, you may want to cut up the pages and file notes under different headings.

- Along with writing words, phrases, or sentences, draw diagrams and sketches that will help you see and recall the place later on.

- Use abbreviations as much as you like, but use them consistently and clearly.

- Note any ideas or questions that occur to you.

- Use quotation marks around any overheard conversation you take down.

Because you can later reorganize your observational notes easily, you do not need to record them in any planned or systematic way. Your notes should include information about the place, the people, and your personal reactions to both.

The Place. Begin by listing objects you see. Then add details of some of these objects—color, shape, size, texture, function, relation to similar or dissimilar objects. Although visual details will probably dominate your notes, you might also want to note sounds and smells. Be sure to include some notes about the shape, dimensions, and layout of the place. How big is it? How is it organized?

The People. Note the number of people and their activities, movements, and behavior. Describe their appearance or dress. Record parts of overheard conversations. Note whether you see more men than women, more people of one racial group than of another, more older than younger people. Most important, note anything surprising or unusual about people in the scene and how they interact with one another.

Your Impressions. Include in your notes the feelings, ideas, or insights you have about what you observe.

REFLECTING ON YOUR OBSERVATIONS

Immediately after your visit (within a few minutes, if possible), find a quiet place to reflect on what you saw, review your notes, and add any images, details, insights, or questions you now recall. Give yourself at least a half hour for quiet thought. Finally, review all your notes, and write a few sentences about your main impressions of the place. What did you learn? How did this visit change or confirm your preconceptions? What impression of the place and people would you like to convey to readers?

Interview

Here are guidelines for planning and setting up an interview, conducting an interview, and reflecting on what you learned.

PLANNING THE INTERVIEW

CHOOSING AN INTERVIEW SUBJECT. If you will be interviewing a person who is the focus of your research, consider beginning with one or two background interviews with other people. If several people play important roles, be sure to interview as many of them as possible. Try to be flexible, however, because you may be unable to speak with the people you targeted initially and may wind up interviewing someone else—an assistant, perhaps. You might even learn more from an assistant than you would from the person in charge.

ARRANGING AN INTERVIEW. You may be nervous about phoning or e-mailing a busy person and asking for some of his or her time. Indeed, you may get turned down. If so, do ask if someone else might talk with you: many people are genuinely flattered to be asked about themselves and their work. Moreover, because you are a college student on assignment, some people may feel that they are doing a public service by allowing you to interview them. When arranging the interview, introduce yourself with a short, simple, and enthusiastic description of your project.

Keep in mind that the person you want to interview will be donating time to you. When you call or e-mail ahead to arrange a specific time for the interview, be sure to ask what time is most convenient. Arrive at the appointed time, and bring all the materials you will need to conduct the interview. Remember, too, to express your thanks when the interview has ended.

PREPARING FOR THE INTERVIEW. Make any necessary observational visits, and do any essential background reading before the interview. Consider your objectives: for example, do you want the "big picture," answers to specific questions, or clarification of something you observed, read, or heard about in another interview?

The key to good interviewing is flexibility. You may be looking for facts, but your interview subject may not have any to offer. In that case, you should be willing to shift gears and go after whatever insight your subject does have to offer.

COMPOSING INTERVIEW QUESTIONS. You probably will want to mix *specific questions* requesting factual information with *open-ended questions*, which are likely to generate anecdotes and reveal attitudes that could lead to other, more penetrating questions. In interviewing a small-business owner, for example, you might begin with a specific question about when the business was established and then follow up with an open-ended question, such as "Could you take a few minutes to tell me something about your early days in the business? I'd be interested to hear about how you got started, what your hopes were, and what problems you had to face." Also consider asking directly for an anecdote ("What happened when your employees threatened to strike?"), encouraging reflection ("What do you think has helped you most? What has hampered you?"), or soliciting advice ("What advice would you give someone trying to start a new business today?").

The best questions encourage the interview subject to talk freely but to the point. If the answer strays too far from the point, a follow-up question may be necessary to refocus the talk. Another way to direct the conversation is to rephrase the subject's answer, saying something like "Let me see if I have this right . . ." or "Am I correct in saying that you feel . . . ?" Often, the interview subject will take this opportunity to amplify the original response by adding just the anecdote or quotation you have been looking for.

One type of question to avoid during interviewing is the *leading question*. Such questions assume too much. Consider, for example, this question: "Do you think the increase in the occurrence of rape is due to the fact that women are perceived as competitors in a severely depressed economy?" The question makes several assumptions, including that there is an increase in the occurrence of rape, that women are perceived (apparently by rapists) as competitors, and that the economy is severely depressed. A better way of asking the question might be to make the assumptions more explicit by dividing the question into its parts: "Do you think there is an increase in the occurrence of rape? What could have caused it? I've heard some people argue that the economy has something to do with it. Do you think so? Do you think rapists perceive women as competitors? Could the current economic situation have made this competition more severe?" This form of questioning allows you to voice what others have said without bullying your subject into echoing your terms.

BRINGING TOOLS. You will need several pencils or pens and a notebook with a firm back so you can write without a table. We recommend dividing the page into two columns. Use the left-hand column (one-third of the page) to note your impressions and descriptions of the scene, the person, and the mood of the interview. Title this column *Impressions*. Title the wider right-hand column *Information*. Before the interview, write down a few basic questions to jog your memory. During the interview, however, listen and ask questions based on what your interview subject says. Do not mechanically go through your list of questions.

TAKING NOTES DURING THE INTERVIEW

Your interview notes might include a few full quotations, key words, and phrases to jog your memory, as well as descriptive jottings about the scene, the person, and the mood of the interview. Remember that how something is said may be as important as what is said. Do not try to record everything your subject says during the interview. Except for the occasional quotation that you will cite directly, you do not want to make a verbatim transcript of the interview. You may not have much confidence in your memory, but if you pay close attention to your subject you are likely to recall a good deal of the conversation immediately after the interview, when you should take the time to add to your notes.

REFLECTING ON THE INTERVIEW

Soon after the interview has concluded, find a quiet place to review your notes. Spend at least half an hour adding to your notes and thinking about what you learned. At the end of this time, write a few sentences about your main impressions from the interview:

- What were the highlights of the interview for you?

- Which questions did not get as much of a response as you anticipated or seem less important to you now?

- How did the interview change your attitude toward or understanding of the subject?

- How has this experience influenced your plans to interview others or to reinterview this person?

Integrating Library and Internet Research

Although this appendix includes separate sections on library and Internet research, these two methods of researching information are closely intertwined. You can often use the Internet to access your library's resources—the catalog of books and other items, indexes to periodical articles, and other kinds of electronic databases—from your own computer in your home or dorm room. On the other hand, you will need or want to go through the library's computers rather than your own to access many Web-based resources, including those that charge fees for subscriptions or for downloading and printing documents.

For most research topics, finding source materials will entail both library and Internet research because each offers material not available from the other. The vast majority of books and articles published in print are not available online, and so you will almost certainly need to consult some of these print sources to avoid getting a skewed perspective on your topic, especially if it deals with events that occurred more than a few years ago. Keep in mind that print sources also tend to offer more reliable information than online sources (for the reasons listed on pp. 663–66). Likewise, though, very little online material ever appears in print, and especially for current topics, you will almost certainly want to check the Web as well as the electronic sources to which your campus library subscribes for the latest developments or research findings. In addition, compared with print sources, online sources usually take less time and effort both to find and to integrate into your own writing. While in these ways online sources can help you do a more thorough job of research within a limited period of time, be careful not to rely too heavily on the Web just because it is easy to use.

Library Research

Library research involves a variety of activities: checking the library catalog, browsing in the stacks, consulting bibliographical indexes, and evaluating sources. Although librarians are there to help, all college students should learn basic library research skills. You should familiarize yourself with your college library's resources and keep careful notes as you research so that you will not have to go back over the same ground later on.

Library research can be useful at various stages of the writing process, depending on the kind of essay you are writing and the special needs of your subject. You may, for example, need to do research immediately to choose a subject. Or you may choose a topic without the benefit of research, and then use the library to find specific information to develop and support your thesis. But no matter when you enter the stacks, you need to follow a systematic strategy: keep a working bibliography; prepare to search for sources by determining the appropriate subject headings or other criteria; consult standard reference works, such as bibliographical indexes and computer databases; and search for books, articles, and other sources on your topic. Later in this appendix, in Evaluating Sources Critically (pp. 666–70), you will find guidelines to help you evaluate the relevancy and credibility of these and other sources.

Keep a Working Bibliography

A *working bibliography* is a preliminary, ongoing record of all the references you consult as you research, even including those that you do not plan to cite in your essay. Encyclopedias, bibliographies, and indexes, for example, should go into the working bibliography, though you will not list these resources in your final bibliography. The working bibliography is a record of the *research process* as a whole; the final bibliography is a record of the *research paper* that you ultimately write.

Since the working bibliography is a first draft of your final list of sources, it is a good idea to use the same documentation style from the start. In Acknowledging Sources (pp. 680–702), later in this appendix, two styles of documentation are discussed and illustrated: the style adopted by the Modern Language Association (MLA) and widely used in the humanities and the style advocated by the American Psychological Association (APA) for use in the social sciences. Individual disciplines often have their own preferred styles of documentation, which your instructor may wish you to use.

You can keep your working bibliography on index cards, in a notebook, or in a computer file. Whatever method you choose, make your entries accurate and complete. If the call number for a book is missing a single digit, for example, you might not be able to find the book in the stacks.

Consult Standard Reference Works

To get an overview of your topic, look up your subject headings in *standard reference works*. Usually, these resources are found in the reference section of the library and cannot be checked out, so budget your library time for consulting reference works accordingly.

The most useful standard reference works include *specialized encyclopedias, disciplinary guides, government publications*, and *bibliographies*. In addition, a general encyclopedia such as *Encyclopedia Americana* might help provide a general overview of your topic, while almanacs, atlases, and dictionaries are sometimes useful as well.

SPECIALIZED ENCYCLOPEDIAS

A specialized encyclopedia, such as *Encyclopedia of Crime and Justice*, or a disciplinary guide, such as *Social Sciences: A Cross-Disciplinary Guide to Selected Sources*, can offer background on your subject and starting points for further research. Specialized encyclopedias often include an explanation of issues related to the topic, definitions of specialized terminology, and selective bibliographies naming additional sources. Specialized encyclopedias can be found in the catalog under the subject heading for the discipline, such as "psychology," and the subheading "dictionaries and encyclopedias." Three particular reference sources can help you identify specialized encyclopedias covering your topic:

- *ARBA Guide to Subject Encyclopedias and Dictionaries*, 2nd ed. (1997). Lists specialized encyclopedias by broad subject category, with descriptions of coverage, focus, and any special features. Also available online through library portals.

- *Subject Encyclopedias: User Guide, Review Citations, and Keyword Index* (1999). Lists specialized encyclopedias by broad subject category and provides access to individual articles within them. By looking under the key terms that describe a topic, you can find references to specific articles in any of over four hundred specialized encyclopedias.

- *Kister's Best Encyclopedias: A Comparative Guide to General and Specialized Encyclopedias*, 2nd ed. (1994). Describes over a thousand encyclopedias, both print and electronic. Includes major foreign-language encyclopedias.

DISCIPLINARY GUIDES

Disciplinary guides can help you locate the major handbooks, encyclopedias, bibliographies, journals, periodical indexes, and computer databases in various academic fields. These types of works are published rarely and are not known for their currency. However, they can be valuable references, if you take the time to check dates and supplement your sources as needed. Here is a sample of disciplinary guides:

- *The Humanities: A Selective Guide to Information Sources*, 5th ed. (2000). By Ron Blazek and Elizabeth S. Aversa. Also available online through library portals.

- *Introduction to Library Research in Anthropology*, 2nd ed. (1998). By John M. Weeks.

- *The American Historical Association's Guide to Historical Literature*, 3rd ed. (1995). Edited by Mary Beth Norton and Pamela Gerardi.

- *Political Science: A Guide to Reference and Information Sources* (1990). By Henry E. York.

- *Literary Research Guide: A Guide to Reference Sources for the Study of Literatures in English and Related Topics*, 4th ed. (2002). By James L. Harner.

GOVERNMENT RESOURCES

Some government publications and statistical reports may be found in the reference section or in a special government documents section of your college library. If you are researching current issues, for example, you might want to consult *Congressional Quarterly Almanac* or *CQ Weekly*. On the Internet, try the home page of the U.S. Congress for the *Congressional Record* <http://thomas.loc .gov/home/thomas2.html>. For compilations of statistics, try *Statistical Abstract of the United States, Statistical Reference Index*, and *The Gallup Poll: Public Opinion*. The Gallup Web site <http://www.gallup.com> provides descriptions of some of its most recent polls.

BIBLIOGRAPHIES

A bibliography is simply a list of books on a given topic, which can be more or less exhaustive depending on its purpose. (To discover how selections were made, check the bibliography's preface or introduction.) A good way to locate a comprehensive, up-to-date bibliography on your subject is to look in the *Bibliographic Index*. A master list of bibliographies that contain fifty or more titles, the *Bibliographic Index* draws from articles, books, and government publications. The index, published yearly, is not cumulative, so check the most recent volume for current information.

Identify Subject Headings and Keywords

To extend your research beyond standard reference works, you need to find appropriate subject headings and keywords. *Subject headings* are specific words and phrases used in library catalogs, periodical indexes, and other databases to categorize the contents of books and articles so that people can look for materials about a particular topic. One way to begin your search for subject headings is to consult the *Library of Congress Subject Headings* (LCSH), which your library probably makes available both in print and online. This work lists the standard subject headings used in library catalogs. Here is an example from the LCSH:

Home schooling *(May Subd Geog)* ◄─────────── Place names may follow heading
  Here are entered works on the provision of compulsory education in the home by parents as an alternative to traditional public or private schooling. General works on the provision of education in the home by educational personnel are entered under Domestic Education.

Used for ──────► UF Education, Home
          Home-based education
          Home education   NT = Narrower term
          Home instruction   SA = See also
          Home teaching by parents
          Homeschooling
          Instruction, Home
          Schooling, Home
Broader Term ──────► BT Education
Related Term ──────► RT Education—United States
          Education—Parent participation

This sample entry proved particularly useful because when the student research-ing this topic found nothing listed in the library catalog under "Home schooling," she tried the other headings until "Education—Parent participation" and "Edu-cation—United States" yielded information on three books. Note, too, that this entry explains the types of books that would be found under these headings and those that would be found elsewhere.

Instead of looking for likely headings in the LCSH, however, you can usually locate useful subject headings faster by searching the catalog or other database using *keywords*, words or phrases that you think describe your topic. As you read about your subject in an encyclopedia or other reference book, you should keep a list of keywords that may be useful. As you review the results of a keyword search, look for the titles that seem to match most closely the topics that you are looking for. When you call up the detailed information for these titles, look for the section labeled "Subject" or "Subject Heading," which will show the headings under which the book or article is classified. (In the example that follows, this section is abbreviated as "Subj-lcsh.") In many computerized catalogs and databases, these subject headings are links that you can click on to get a list of other materials on the same subject. Keep a list in your working bibliography of all the subject head-ings you find that relate to your topic, so that you can refer to them each time you start looking for information. Here is an example of an online catalog listing for a book on home schooling:

| Title: | Kingdom of children: culture and controversy in the homeschooling movement/ Mitchell L. Stevens |
| Imprint: | Princeton, NJ: Princeton University Press, c2001. |

LOCATION	CALL NO	STATUS
Coe	LC40.S74 2001	NOT CHCKD OUT

Description:	xiii, 228 p.; 24 cm
Series:	Princeton studies in cultural sociology
Subj-lcsh	**Home Schooling—United States**
	Educational sociology—United States
Note(s):	Includes bibliographical references (p. 199–224) and index

DETERMINING THE MOST PROMISING SOURCES

As you follow a subject heading into the library catalog and periodical indexes, you will discover many seemingly relevant books and articles. How do you decide which ones to track down and examine? You may have little to go on but author, title, date, and publisher or periodical name, but these details actually provide useful clues. Look again, for example, at the online catalog reference to a book on home schooling. The title, *Kingdom of Children: Culture and Controversy in the Homeschooling Movement,* is the first clue to the subject coverage of the book. Note that the publication date, 2001, is fairly recent. From the subject headings, you can see that this book focuses on sociological aspects of home schooling and that its geographic focus is the United States. Finally, from the notes, you can see that the book includes an extensive bibliography that could lead you to other sources.

Now look at search results from ERIC, an electronic periodical database, searched through EBSCOhost:

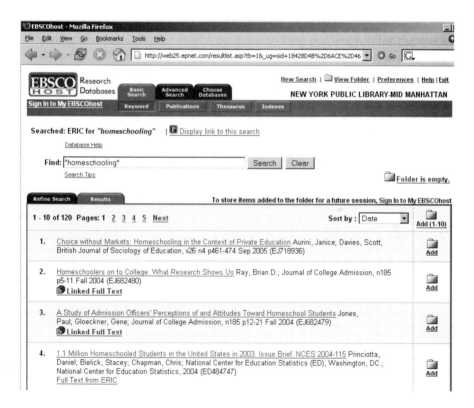

This screen lists articles that address different aspects of home schooling. You can see that the first article deals with the issue from a British point of view, which might provide an interesting cross-cultural perspective for your essay. The second and third articles, both from a journal devoted to the topic of college admissions, might give you a sense of how well home schooling prepares students for college. Be careful, though, to stay focused on your specific research topic or thesis, especially if you are pressed for time and cannot afford to become distracted exploring sources that sound interesting but are unlikely to be useful.

In addition, each entry contains the information that you will need to locate it in a library, and some entries provide a link to the full text of the article. Going back to the second article, here is what each piece of information means:

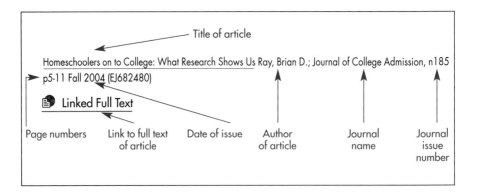

When you look in catalogs and indexes, consider the following points when deciding whether you should track down a particular source:

- *Relevance to your topic:* Do the title, subtitle, description, subject headings, and abstract help you determine how directly the particular source addresses your topic?

- *Publication date:* How recent is the source? For current controversies, emerging trends, and scientific or technological developments, you must consult recent material. For historical or biographical topics, you will want to start with present-day perspectives but eventually explore older sources that offer authoritative perspectives. You may also want or need to consult sources written at the time of the events or during the life of the person you are researching.

- *Description:* Does the length indicate a brief treatment of the topic or an extended treatment? Does the work include illustrations that may elaborate on concepts discussed in the text? Does it include a bibliography that could lead you to other works or an index that could give you an overview of what is discussed in the text? Does the abstract indicate the focus of the work?

From among the sources that look promising, select publications that seem by their titles to address different aspects of your topic or to approach it from different perspectives. Try to avoid selecting sources that are mostly by the same author, from the same publisher, or in the same journal. Common sense will lead you to an appropriate decision about diversity in source materials.

Search Online Library Catalogs and Databases

Computerized library catalogs and other databases consist of thousands or millions of records, each representing an individual item such as a book, an article, or a government publication. The record is made up of different fields describing the item and allowing users to search for it and retrieve it from the database.

USING DIFFERENT SEARCH TECHNIQUES

Basic search strategies include author, title, and subject searches. When you request an *author search*, the computer looks for a match between the name you type and the names listed in the author field of all the records in the online catalog or other database. When you request a *title search* or a *subject search*, the computer looks for a match in the title field or the subject field, respectively. Computers are very literal. They try to match only the exact terms you enter, and most do not recognize variant or incorrect spellings. That is an incentive to become a good speller and a good typist. However, because most library catalogs and databases also offer the option of searching for titles and subjects by keywords, you need not enter the full exact title or subject heading. In addition, you can be flexible where the computer cannot. For instance, if you were researching the topic of home schooling, you could do a subject search not only for "home schooling" but also for "homeschooling" and "home-schooling."

DOING ADVANCED SEARCHES AND USING BOOLEAN OPERATORS

The real power of using a computerized library catalog or other database is demonstrated when you need to look up books or articles using more than one keyword. For example, suppose you want information about home schooling in California. Rather than looking through an index listing all the articles on home schooling and picking out those that mention California, you can ask the computer to do the work for you by linking your two keywords. Many online catalogs and databases now offer the option of an *advanced search*, sometimes on a separate page from the main search page, that allows you to search for more than one keyword at a time, search for certain keywords while excluding others, or search for an exact phrase. Or you may be able to create this kind of advanced search yourself by using the *Boolean operators* AND, OR, and NOT along with quotation marks and parentheses.

To understand the operation of *Boolean logic* (developed by and named after George Boole, a nineteenth-century mathematician), picture one set of articles about home schooling and another set of articles about California. A third set is formed by articles that are about both home schooling and California. The diagrams on page 660 provide an illustration of how each Boolean operator works.

USING TRUNCATION

Another useful search strategy is *truncation*. With this technique, you drop the ending of a word or term and replace it with a symbol, which indicates you want to retrieve records containing any term that begins the same way as your term. For example, by entering the term "home school#" you would retrieve all the records that have terms such as "home school," "home schooling," "home schools," "home schooled," or "home schoolers." Truncation is useful when you want to retrieve both the plural and singular forms of a word or any word for which you are not sure of the ending. Truncation symbols vary with the catalog or database. The question mark (?), asterisk (*), and pound sign (#) are frequently used.

The Boolean Operators: AND, OR, and NOT

AND

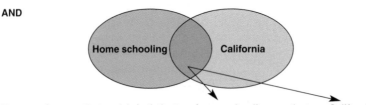

Returns references that contain both the term **home schooling** AND the term **California**

- Narrows the search
- Combines unrelated terms
- Is the default used by most online catalogs and databases

OR

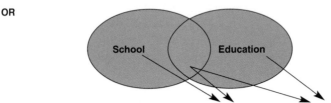

Returns all references that contain either the term **school** OR the term **education** OR both terms
- Broadens the search (**"OR is more"**)
- Is useful with synonyms and variant spellings: ("home schooling" and "homeschooling")

NOT

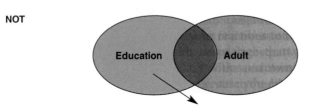

Returns references that include the term **education** but NOT the term **adult**
- Narrows the search
- May eliminate relevant material

Search for Books

The primary source of information on books is the library's *online catalog*. The online catalog provides flexibility in searching by keyword or subject heading and often tells you whether the book is available or checked out. Another distinct advantage is that you can print out source information rather than having to copy it by hand. You should, however, check to make sure that the online catalog goes far enough back in time for your purposes. If not, see whether your library has maintained its hard-copy card catalog for the period in question.

Each catalog or computer entry gives the same basic information: the author, the title, the publication information and physical description of the book (including the number of pages), the subject heading(s) related to the book, and the call number you will need to find the book on the library shelves. Most libraries provide a map showing where the various call numbers are shelved. Look again at the sample catalog entry for a book on home schooling:

Title:	Kingdom of children: culture and controversy in the homeschooling movement/ Mitchell L. Stevens
Imprint:	Princeton, NJ: Princeton University Press, c2001.

LOCATION	CALL NO	STATUS
Coe	LC40.S74 2001	NOT CHCKD OUT

Description:	xiii, 228 p.; 24 cm
Series:	Princeton studies in cultural sociology
Subj-lcsh	**Home Schooling — United States**
	Educational sociology — United States
Note(s):	Includes bibliographical references (p. 199–224) and index

Even if you attend a large research university, your library is unlikely to hold every book or journal article you might need. Remember that your library's online catalog and serial record (a list of the periodicals the library holds) include only records of the books and periodicals it holds. As you will learn in the following section on Internet research, you can access the online catalogs of other libraries to find sources not within your library's holdings. At that point, you can request an interlibrary loan from another college library, a procedure handled by e-mail or in person at the reference desk. Keep in mind, however, that it may take up to a couple of weeks to obtain a source by way of interlibrary loan.

Search for Articles

Articles published in periodicals (magazines, journals, and newspapers) usually are not listed in the library catalog. To find them, you will want to use *periodical indexes*, which originally appeared only in print form but today are likely to take the form of a CD-ROM, an online database, or a hybrid of the two. In addition to listing the kind of basic information about articles that online library catalogs do about books, many periodical indexes offer *abstracts*, which summarize the articles, and *full-text retrieval*, meaning that you can view an entire article online and potentially download it (often excluding graphics) for reading offline.

Following is a list of some of the periodical indexes that your library might subscribe to or that provide free access to their contents:

- *Readers' Guide to Periodical Literature* (1900–; CD-ROM, 1983–; online). The classic index for periodicals, updated quarterly, offering about two hundred popular periodicals. <http://www.hwwilson.com/Databases/Readersg.htm>

- *ERIC (Education Resources Information Center)* (1966–; online). Houses indexes, abstracts, and the full text of selected articles from 750 education journals. <http://www.eric.ed.gov>

- *Business Periodicals Ondisc* (1988–), and *ABI/INFORM* (1988–). Provide the full text of articles from business periodicals, including illustrations.

- *Humanities Index* (1974–; online, 1984–). Covers more than five hundred periodicals in archaeology, history, classics, literature, performing arts, philosophy, and religion.

- *Ingenta* (1998–; online). An online document-delivery service that lists articles from more than 5,400 online journals and 26,000 other publications. For a fee, you can receive the full text of the article, online or by fax. <http://www.ingenta.com>

- *Lexis-Nexis* (1973–; online and CD-ROM). An information service for journalists, lawyers, and financial analysts. <http://www.lexis-nexis.com>

- *InfoTrac* (online and CD-ROM). An information supplier that provides access to the following three indexes: (1) *General Periodicals Index*, which lists information on over twelve hundred general-interest publications; (2) *Academic Index*, which provides the full text of articles from five hundred popular and academic periodicals; and (3) *National Newspaper Index*, which covers the *Christian Science Monitor, Los Angeles Times, New York Times, Wall Street Journal*, and *Washington Post*. <http://www.infotrac-college.com/ wadsworth/access.html>

- *Social Sciences Index* (1974–; online, 1983–). Covers more than five hundred periodicals in economics, geography, law, political science, psychology, public administration, and sociology.

- *Public Affairs Information Service Bulletin* (1915–; online, 1972–). Covers articles and other publications by public and private agencies on economic and social conditions, international relations, and public administration. Subject listings only.

For current events and topics in the news, you can use news-specific databases, including *NewsBank, Newspaper Abstracts*, and *Alternative Press Index*. Most of these resources use the Library of Congress subject headings, but some have their own systems of classification. To see how subjects are classified in the index or abstract you are using, check the opening page or screen.

When you look for the print periodicals in your library, you will typically find them arranged alphabetically by title in a particular section of the building. For previous years' collections of popular magazines and many scholarly journals, look for bound annual volumes rather than individual issues. Some older periodicals may be stored on microfilm (reels) or microfiche (cards) that must be read in viewing machines.

You might also want to check the Web sites of local or national newspapers whose coverage you respect. Here are some possibilities:

Chicago Tribune	http://www.chicagotribune.com
Los Angeles Times	http://www.latimes.com
New York Times	http://www.nytimes.com
San Francisco Chronicle	http://www.sfgate.com/chronicle
San Jose Mercury News	http://www.mercurynews.com
Washington Post	http://www.washingtonpost.com

Be warned, though, that some online news publishers now charge a fee for the full-text retrieval of articles. Finding the article is usually free of charge, but downloading the full text of an article to your computer will likely cost a small fee.

Internet Research

By now, most of you are familiar with searching the Internet. This section introduces you to some tools and strategies that will help you use the Net more efficiently to find information on a topic.

As you use the Internet for conducting research, keep the following concerns and guidelines in mind:

- *The Internet has no central system of organization.* On the Internet, a huge amount of information is stored on many different networks and servers and in many different formats, each with its own system of organization. The Internet has no central catalog, reference librarian, or standard classification system for the vast resources available there.

- *Many significant electronic sources are not part of the Internet or require a paid subscription or other fees.* Computerized library catalogs, electronic periodical indexes, full-text article databases, and other electronic resources are often stored on CD-ROMs or on campus computer networks rather than on the Internet and so are available to students only through the library or other campus computers. Furthermore, some databases on the Web charge for a subscription or for downloading or printing out content. For these reasons (as well as the one discussed below), you should plan to use the library or campus computer system for much of your electronic research, since it will give you access to more material at a lower cost. You will not need to pay for subscriptions, and you may be able to download or print out material for free as well.

■ *Internet sources that you find on your own are generally less reliable than print sources or than electronic sources to which your library or campus subscribes.* Because it is relatively easy for anyone to publish on the Internet, judging the reliability of online information is a special concern. Depending on your topic, purpose, and audience, the sources you find on the Internet may not be as credible or authoritative as print sources or subscription electronic sources, which have usually been screened by publishers, editors, librarians, and authorities on the topic. For some topics, most of what you find on the Internet may be written by highly biased or amateur authors, so you will need to balance or supplement these sources with information from your library or campus and print sources. When in doubt about the reliability of an online source for a particular assignment, check with your instructor.

■ *Internet sources are not as stable as print sources or as the electronic sources to which your library or campus subscribes.* A Web site that existed last week may no longer be available today, or its content may have changed.

■ *Internet sources must be documented, and so you need to include them in your working bibliography.* A working bibliography is an ongoing record of all the possible sources you discover as you research your subject. The working bibliography becomes the draft for the list of references or works cited at the end of your essay, even if you do not include all these sources in your final list. You will need to follow appropriate conventions for quoting, paraphrasing, summarizing, and documenting the online sources you use, just as you do for print sources. Because an Internet source can change or disappear quickly, be sure to record the information for the working-bibliography entry when you first find the source. Whenever possible, download and print out the source to preserve it. Make sure your download or printout includes all the items of information required for the entry or at least all those you can find. Citation forms for Internet sources typically require more information than those for print sources, but the items are often harder (or impossible) to identify because Internet sources do not appear in the kinds of standard formats that print sources do.

Finding the Best Information Online

Because the World Wide Web does not have a central directory, *search tools* like Google and Yahoo! are important resources for finding relevant information on your topic. To use these tools effectively, you should understand their features, strengths, and limitations.

Many search tools now allow you to look for sources using both search engines and subject directories. *Search engines* are based on keywords. They are simply computer programs that scan the Web—or that part of the Web that is in the particular search engine's database—looking for the keywords you have entered. *Subject directories* are based on categories, like the subject headings in a library catalog or periodical index. Beginning with a menu of general subjects, you click on increasingly narrow subjects (for example, from "science" to "biology" to "genetics" to "DNA mapping") until you reach either a list of specific Web sites or a point where you have to do a keyword search within the narrowest subject you have chosen. Search engines are most useful when you have a good idea of the appropriate keywords for your topic or when you are not sure under what category the topic falls. But subject directories can help quickly narrow your search to those parts of the Web that are likely to be most productive, thereby avoiding keyword searches that produce hundreds or thousands of results.

Always click on the help, hints, or tips link on a search tool's home page to find out more about its recognized commands and advanced-search techniques. Most search tools allow searches using Boolean operators (see pp. 659–60) or incorporate Boolean logic into an advanced-search page. Many also let you limit a search to specific dates, languages, or other criteria.

As with searches of library catalogs and databases, the success of a Web search depends to a great extent on the keywords you choose. Remember that many different words often describe the same topic. If your topic is ecology, for example, you may find information under the keywords *ecosystem, environment, pollution,* and *endangered species,* as well as a number of other related keywords, depending on the focus of your research. When you find a source that seems promising, be sure to create a bookmark for the Web page so that you can return to it easily later on.

No matter how precise your keywords are, search engines can be unreliable, and you may not find the best available resources. You might instead begin your search at the Web site of a relevant and respected organization. If you want photos of constellations, go to the NASA Web page. If you want the text of laws, go to a government Web page like GPO Access. In addition, be sure to supplement your Internet research with other sources from your library, including books, reference works, and articles from appropriate periodicals.

Two other, more recent sources of online information are *blogs* and *RSS*. Because blogs are not subjected to the same editorial scrutiny as published books or periodical articles and may reflect just one person's opinions and biases, it's a good idea to find several blogs from multiple perspectives about your subject. Some Web sites, such as Blogwise <www.blogwise.com> and Blogger <www.blogger.com>, provide directories and search functions to help you find blogs on a particular topic.

If you are researching a very current topic and need to follow constantly updated news sites and blogs, you can use a program called an *aggregator*, which obtains news automatically from many sources and assembles it through a process called RSS (really simple syndication). Using an aggregator, you can scan the information from a variety of sources by referring to just one Web page and then click on links to the news stories to read further. Many aggregators, such as NetNewsWire, NewsGator, and SharpReader, are available as software that you can download to your computer; others are Web sites you can customize to your own preferences, such as Bloglines <www.bloglines.com> and NewsIsFree <www.newsisfree.com>.

Use E-mail and Online Discussion Forums

You may be able to contact other researchers and experts directly through *e-mail* (electronic mail). Some authors include their e-mail addresses with their articles, allowing you to write to them for further information. Web pages often include e-mail links to individuals who have further information on specific topics.

Another important resource for some projects, *online discussion forums*, are interest groups in which people post messages in a public forum for discussion. The messages are usually posted on the Internet for anyone to read and respond to, much like a public bulletin board. An *e-mail discussion list (listserv)* is like a discussion forum except that messages are not posted in a public forum but are sent automatically to all subscribers of the group by private e-mail. In addition, the discussion that takes place through discussion lists tends to be more serious and focused than that of discussion forums. One student researching language acquisition, for instance, subscribed to a discussion list made up primarily of teachers of English as a second language. She read the group's e-mail discussions for a while to determine whether her questions would be appropriate to the list rather than posting her message immediately. She decided to post a message with questions related to her research. In return, she received a great deal of useful information from professionals in the field.

Finally, note that most discussion forums and some discussion lists maintain searchable archives of previous postings. Contact a reference librarian for help in identifying these useful research tools, or start with a search engine that specializes in online groups, such as Google Groups <http://www.groups.google.com>. If all else fails, you can try a keyword search online combining the keyword *listserv* or *discussion forum* with your topic to see what you can find.

EVALUATING SOURCES CRITICALLY

From the very beginning of your search for sources, you should evaluate each potential source to determine whether it will be useful and relevant to your essay. You must decide which sources provide information relevant to the topic, but you also must read sources with a critical eye to decide how credible or trustworthy they are. Just because a book or an essay appears in print or an article is posted on a Web site does not necessarily mean the information or opinions within it are reliable.

Criteria for Evaluating Sources

To help you evaluate the sources you have found, try using the following criteria. Your goal is to determine the relevance, currency, range of viewpoints, and authoritativeness of each potential source. In addition, you want to take special care when evaluating sources gathered from the Internet.

Determine the Relevance of Potential Sources

Begin your evaluation of sources by narrowing your working bibliography to the most relevant works. To decide how relevant a particular source is to your topic, you need to examine the source in depth. Do not depend on title alone, for it may be misleading. If the source is a book, check its table of contents and index to see how many pages are devoted to the precise subject you are exploring. In most cases you will want an in-depth, not a superficial, treatment of the subject. Read the preface or introduction to a book, the abstract or opening paragraphs of an article, and any biographical information given about the author to determine the author's basic or distinctive approach to the subject. As you look at all these elements, consider the following questions:

- Does the source provide a general overview or a specialized point of view? General sources are helpful early in your research, but ultimately you will need the authoritative and up-to-date coverage of specialized sources (excluding those that are overly technical).

- Is the source long enough to provide adequate detail?

- Is the source written for general readers or specialists? Advocates or critics?

- Is the author an expert on the topic? Does the author's way of looking at the topic support or challenge other views?

- Is the information in the source substantiated elsewhere? Does its approach seem to be comparable to, or a significant challenge to, the approaches of other credible sources?

Determine the Currency of Potential Sources

Although you should always consult the most up-to-date sources available on your subject, older sources often establish the principles, theories, and data on which later work is based and may provide a useful perspective for evaluating it. If older works are considered authoritative, you may want to become familiar with them. To determine which sources are authoritative, note the ones that are cited most often in encyclopedia articles, bibliographies, and recent works on the subject. If your source is on the Web, consider whether it has been regularly updated.

Determine the Viewpoint of Potential Sources

Your sources should represent multiple viewpoints on the topic. Just as you would not depend on a single author for all of your information, you would not want to use authors who all belong to the same school of thought. Authors come to their subjects with particular viewpoints derived from their philosophies, experiences, educational backgrounds, and affiliations. In evaluating your sources, then, consider carefully how these viewpoints are reflected in the writing and how they affect the way authors present their arguments.

Although the text of a source gives you the most precise indication of the author's viewpoint, you can often get a good idea of it by also looking at the preface or introduction or at the sources the author cites. You will want to determine whether the document fairly represents other views on the topic with which you are familiar. When you examine a reference, you can often determine the point of view it represents by considering the following elements:

- *Title:* Look closely at the title and subtitle to see if they use words that indicate a particular viewpoint. Keep in mind, however, that titles and subtitles are often determined by editors or publishers rather than authors, especially in the case of newspaper and magazine articles.

- *Author:* Consider how the author's professional affiliation might affect his or her perspective on the topic. Look at the tone of the writing and any biographical information provided about the author. Also try entering the author's name into a search engine to see what you can learn from online sources.

- *Editorial slant:* Notice where the selection was published. To determine the editorial slant of a newspaper or periodical, all you have to do is read some of its editorials, opinion columns, or letters to the editor. You can also check such sources as the *Gale Directory of Publications and Broadcast Media* (2003) and *Magazines for Libraries* (2003). For books, read the preface or introduction as well as the acknowledgments and sources cited to get an idea of how the authors position themselves in relation to other specialists in the field. For Internet sources, notice what organization, if any, stands behind the author's work.

Determine Whether the Sources Are Authoritative

To help determine whether a source is reliable and authoritative, check the author's professional credentials, background, and publication history to verify that he or she is an established voice in the field. To help determine which authors are established, note whether they are cited in encyclopedia articles, bibliographies, and recent works on the subject. For books, you can also look up reviews in newspapers or academic journals.

Experts will (and should) disagree on topics, and each author will naturally see the topic in his or her own way. Yet authoritative authors explain and support, not just assert, their opinions. They also cite their sources. Because articles published in most academic journals and books published by university presses are judged by other experts in the field, you can assume that these authors' views are respected even if they are controversial. Allowing for differences of viewpoint, information about the topic provided in the source should be consistent with information you have found on the topic in other sources.

Use Special Care in Evaluating Internet Sources

Unlike most published print resources, which have been selected and reviewed by editors in a "filtering" process to ensure their accuracy and credibility, most publications on the Internet have been through no comparable filtering process. Anyone who can upload material to a server can publish on the Internet. Web sites may be sponsored by academic institutions, government agencies, companies, organizations, clubs, or individuals — for recreational or professional use. This variety makes it essential that you take extra care in evaluating the credentials of the author and the credibility of the information before you use an Internet publication as a source.

The information needed to evaluate Internet sources is often more difficult to locate than it is for print sources. Books, for example, display the name of their publisher on the spine and the title page, include information about the author in the beginning or at the end of the book, and often make the purpose of the work clear in a preface or introduction. Determining the publisher, the purpose, and sometimes even the author of a Web page, however, can often be more difficult because of the technical differences between print and online media. For example, Web pages that are part of a larger Web site might — when they are accessed by a search engine — give few pointers to the rest of the site. These Web pages may carry little or no indication of who published or sponsored the site or of its overall purpose or author. In this situation, you should not use the source unless more information about the Web site can be tracked down.

The following techniques will help you evaluate Internet sources:

- *Look for the following information on online articles you retrieve:* the author's professional title, affiliation, and other credentials; the sponsor of the page and the Web site; a link to the site's home page; and the date the site was created or last revised. Check the title, headers, and footers of the Web page for this information. If it is provided, it may indicate a willingness to publish in a professional manner, and it will help you evaluate the source according to the criteria discussed earlier. Checking the home page of the Web site will help you discover, for example, if its purpose is commercial (a site published to sell radar detectors) or one of public safety (a site established by the Highway Patrol to give information on speed limits).

- *Try to contact the sponsoring institution.* By deleting all but the initial directory from a lengthy URL, you may be able to determine the sponsoring institution for the Web page. For example, in <http://loc.gov/z3950/gateway.html>, taking away the subdirectory name (z3950) and the filename (gateway.html) will reveal the sponsoring computer's address: <http:// loc.gov> (which in this case is the Library of Congress home page). Enter the abbreviated URL address in your browser to access the site and to determine where the information comes from.

- *Follow links out from the site to others.* Internet sources sometimes provide direct links to other sources so you can see the context from which a fact, statistic, or quotation has been taken. Many also link to Web site "consumer reports" that have rated the site favorably, but you need to consider whether the site doing the ratings is trustworthy.

- *Use any other evaluation techniques available.* Even if you cannot discover the author's credentials, you can check his or her facts, details, and presentation: Does the information make sense to you? Can you verify the facts? You may find that, even though the author is not a recognized expert in the field, he or she offers information valuable to your project. One advantage of the Web is that anyone, not just recognized experts, can express views and relate first-hand experiences that may be useful in developing your topic.

INTEGRATING SOURCES WITH YOUR OWN WRITING

Writers commonly use sources by quoting directly, by paraphrasing, and by summarizing. This section provides guidelines for deciding when to use each of these three methods and how to do so effectively.

Deciding Whether to Quote, Paraphrase, or Summarize

As a general rule, quote only in these situations: (1) when the wording of the source is particularly memorable or vivid or expresses a point so well that you cannot improve it without destroying the meaning, (2) when the words of reliable and respected authorities would lend support to your position, (3) when you wish to highlight the author's opinions, (4) when you wish to cite an author whose opinions challenge or vary greatly from those of other experts, or (5) when you are going to discuss the source's choice of words. Paraphrase passages whose details you wish to note completely but whose language is not particularly striking. Summarize any long passages whose main points you wish to record selectively as background or general support for a point you are making.

Quoting

A *quotation* duplicates the source exactly, word for word. If the source has an error, copy it and add the notation *sic* (Latin for "thus") in brackets immediately after the error to indicate that it is not your error but your source's:

According to a recent newspaper article, "Plagirism [sic] is a problem among journalists and scholars as well as students" (Berensen 62).

However, you can change quotations (1) to emphasize particular words by underlining or italicizing them, (2) to omit irrelevant information or to make the quotation conform grammatically to your sentence by using ellipsis marks, and (3) to make the quotation conform grammatically or to insert information by using brackets.

Use Italicizing for Emphasis

You may italicize any words in the quotation that you want to emphasize; add a semicolon and the words *emphasis added* (in regular type, not italicized or underlined) to the parenthetical citation.

In her 2001 exposé of the struggles of the working class, Ehrenreich writes, "The wages Winn-Dixie is offering--*$6 and a couple of dimes to start with*--are not enough, I decide, to compensate for this indignity" (14; emphasis added).

Use Ellipsis Marks for Omissions

A writer may decide to leave certain words out of a quotation because they are not relevant to the point being made or because they add information readers will not need in the context in which the quotation is being used. When you omit words from within a quotation, you must use ellipsis marks—three spaced periods (. . .)—in place of the missing words. When the omission occurs within the sentence, include a space before the first ellipsis mark and after the closing mark. There should also be spaces between the three marks.

Ellen Ruppel Shell claims in "Does Civilization Cause Asthma?" that what asthma "lacks in lethality, it more than makes up for in morbidity: it wears people down . . . and threatens their livelihood" (90).

When the omission falls at the end of a sentence, place a sentence period *directly after* the final word of the sentence, followed by a space and three spaced ellipsis marks.

But Grimaldi's commentary contends that for Aristotle, rhetoric, like dialectic, had "no limited and unique subject matter upon which it must be exercised. . . . Instead, rhetoric as an art transcends all specific disciplines and may be brought into play in them" (6).

A period plus ellipsis marks can indicate the omission of the rest of the sentence as well as whole sentences, paragraphs, or even pages.

When a parenthetical reference follows the ellipsis marks at the end of a sentence, place the three spaced periods after the quotation, and place the sentence period after the final parenthesis:

But Grimaldi's commentary contends that for Aristotle, rhetoric, like dialectic, had "no limited and unique subject matter upon which it must be exercised . . ." (6).

When you quote only single words or phrases, you do not need to use ellipsis marks because it will be obvious that you have left out some of the original.

According to Geoffrey Nunberg, many people believe that the Web is "just one more route along which English will march on an ineluctable course of world conquest" (40).

For the same reason, you need not use ellipsis marks if you omit the beginning of a quoted sentence unless the rest of the sentence begins with a capitalized word and still appears to be a complete sentence.

Use Brackets for Insertions or Changes

Use brackets around an insertion or other change needed to make a quotation conform grammatically to your sentence, such as a change in the form of a verb or pronoun or in the capitalization of the first word of the quotation. In this example from an essay on James Joyce's "Araby," the writer adapts Joyce's phrases "we played till our bodies glowed" and "shook music from the buckled harness" to fit the grammar of her sentences:

In the dark, cold streets during the "short days of winter," the boys must generate their own heat by "play[ing] till [their] bodies glowed." Music is "[shaken] from the buckled harness" as if it were unnatural, and the singers in the market chant nasally of "the troubles in our native land" (30).

You may also use brackets to add or substitute explanatory material in a quotation:

Guterson notes that among Native Americans in Florida, "education was in the home; learning by doing was reinforced by the myths and legends which repeated the basic value system of their [the Seminoles'] way of life" (159).

Some changes that make a quotation conform grammatically to another sentence may be made without any signal to readers: (1) A period at the end of a quotation may be changed to a comma if you are using the quotation within your own sentence, and (2) double quotation marks enclosing a quotation are changed to single quotation marks when the quotation is enclosed within a longer quotation.

Integrating Quotations

Depending on its length, a quotation may be incorporated into your text by being enclosed in quotation marks or set off from your text in a block without quotation marks. In either case, be sure to blend the quotation into your essay rather than drop it in without appropriate integration.

In-Text Quotations

Incorporate brief quotations (no more than four typed lines of prose or three lines of poetry) into your text. You may place the quotation virtually anywhere in your sentence:

At the Beginning

"To live a life is not to cross a field," Sutherland quotes Pasternak at the beginning of her narrative (11).

In the Middle

Anna Quindlen argues that "booze and beer are not the same as illegal drugs. They're worse" (88)--a claim that meets much resistance from students and parents alike.

At the End

In *The Second Sex,* Simone de Beauvoir describes such an experience as one in which the girl "becomes as object, and she sees herself as object" (378).

Divided by Your Own Words

"Science usually prefers the literal to the nonliteral term," Kinneavy writes, "--that is, figures of speech are often out of place in science" (177).

When you quote poetry within your text, use a slash (/) with spaces before and after to signal the end of each line of verse:

Alluding to St. Augustine's distinction between the City of God and the Earthly City, Lowell writes that "much against my will / I left the City of God where it belongs" (4-5).

Block Quotations

In MLA documentation style, use block form for prose quotations of five or more typed lines and poetry quotations of four or more lines. Indent the quotation an inch (ten character spaces) from the left margin, as shown in the following example. In APA style, use block form for quotations of forty words or more. Indent the block quotation five to seven spaces, keeping your indents consistent throughout your paper.

In a block quotation, double-space between lines just as you do in your text. *Do not* enclose the passage within quotation marks. Use a colon to introduce a block quotation, unless the context calls for another punctuation mark or none at all. When quoting a single paragraph or part of one in MLA style, do not indent the first line of the quotation more than the rest. In quoting two or more paragraphs, indent the first line of each paragraph an extra quarter inch (three spaces). If you are using APA style, the first line of subsequent paragraphs in the block quotation indents an additional five to seven spaces from the block quotation indent.

In "A Literary Legacy from Dunbar to Baraka," Margaret Walker says of Paul Lawrence Dunbar's dialect poems:

> He realized that the white world in the United States tolerated his literary genius only because of his "jingles in a broken tongue," and they found the old "darky" tales and speech amusing and within the vein of folklore into which they wished to classify all Negro life. This troubled Dunbar because he realized that white America was denigrating him as a writer and as a man. (70)

Introducing Quotations

Statements that introduce in-text quotations take a range of punctuation marks and lead-in words. Here are some examples of ways writers typically introduce quotations.

Introducing a Quotation Using a Colon

A colon usually follows an independent clause that introduces a quotation.

Richard Dyer argues that racism will disappear only when whites stop thinking of themselves as raceless: "White people need to learn to see themselves as white, to see their particularity" (12).

Introducing a Quotation Using a Comma

A comma usually follows an introduction that incorporates the quotation in its sentence structure (an introduction that could not stand on its own as a sentence).

Similarly, Duncan Turner asserts, "As matters now stand, it is unwise to talk about communication without some understanding of Burke" (259).

Introducing a Quotation Using *that*

No punctuation is generally needed with *that*, and no capital letter is used to begin the quotation.

Noting this failure, Alice Miller asserts that "the reason for her despair was not her suffering but the impossibility of communicating her suffering to another person" (255).

Punctuating within Quotations

Although punctuation within a quotation should reproduce the original, some adaptations may be necessary. Use single quotation marks for quotations within the quotation:

Original from Guterson (16–17)

E. D. Hirsch recognizes the connection between family and learning, suggesting in his discussion of family background and academic achievement "that the significant part of our children's education has been going on outside rather than inside the schools."

Quoted Version

Guterson claims that E. D. Hirsch "recognizes the connection between family and learning, suggesting in his discussion of family background and academic achievement 'that the significant part of our children's education has been going on outside rather than inside the schools'" (16–17).

If the quotation ends with a question mark or an exclamation point, retain the original punctuation:

"Did you think I loved you?" Edith later asks Dombey (566).

If a quotation ending with a question mark or an exclamation point concludes your sentence, retain the question mark or exclamation point, and put the parenthetical reference and sentence period outside the quotation marks:

Edith later asks Dombey, "Did you think I loved you?" (566).

Avoiding Grammatical Tangles

When you incorporate quotations into your writing, and especially when you omit words from quotations, you run the risk of creating ungrammatical sentences. Three common errors you should try to avoid are *verb incompatibility, ungrammatical omissions*, and *sentence fragments*.

Verb Incompatibility

When this error occurs, the verb form in the introductory statement is grammatically incompatible with the verb form in the quotation. When your quotation has a verb form that does not fit in with your text, it is usually possible to use just part of the quotation, thus avoiding verb incompatibility.

The narrator suggests his bitter disappointment when ~~"I saw myself~~ "as a creature driven [*he describes seeing himself*] and derided by vanity" (35).

As this sentence illustrates, use the present tense when you refer to events in a literary work.

Ungrammatical Omission

Sometimes omitting text from a quotation leaves you with an ungrammatical sentence. Two ways of correcting the grammar are (1) to adapt the quotation (with brackets) so that its parts fit together grammatically and (2) to use only one part of the quotation.

From the moment of the boy's arrival in Araby, the bazaar is presented as a commercial enterprise: "I could not find any sixpenny entrance and . . . ~~handing~~ [hand[ed]] a shilling to a weary-looking man" (34).

From the moment of the boy's arrival in Araby, the bazaar is presented as a commercial enterprise: "~~I~~ [He] could not find any sixpenny entrance [,] and ~~. . . handing a shilling to a weary-looking man" (34).~~ [so had to pay a shilling to get in (34).]

Sentence Fragment

Sometimes when a quotation is a complete sentence, writers neglect the sentence that introduces the quote — for example, by forgetting to include a verb. It is important to make sure that the quotation is introduced by a complete sentence.

The girl's interest in the bazaar ~~leading~~ [leads] the narrator to make what amounts to a sacred oath: "If I go . . . I will bring you something" (32).

Paraphrasing and Summarizing

In addition to quoting sources, writers have the option of paraphrasing or summarizing what others have written.

Paraphrasing

In a *paraphrase*, the writer restates primarily in his or her own words all the relevant information from a passage, without offering any additional comments or any suggestion of agreement or disagreement with the source's ideas. Paraphrasing is useful for recording details of the passage when the order of the details is important but the source's wording is not. It also allows you to avoid quoting too much — or at all when the author's choice of words is not worth special attention. Because all the details of the passage are included in a paraphrase, it is often about the same length as the original passage.

Here are a passage from a book on home schooling and an example of an acceptable paraphrase of it:

Original Passage

Bruner and the discovery theorists have also illuminated conditions that apparently pave the way for learning. It is significant that these conditions are unique to each learner, so unique, in fact, that in many cases classrooms can't provide them. Bruner also contends that the more one discovers information in a great variety of circumstances, the more likely one is to develop the inner categories required to organize that information. Yet life at school, which is for the most part generic and predictable, daily keeps many children from the great variety of circumstances they need to learn well.

— David Guterson, *Family Matters: Why Homeschooling Makes Sense*, p. 172

Acceptable Paraphrase

According to Guterson, the "discovery theorists," particularly Bruner, have found that there seem to be certain conditions that help learning to take place. Because each individual requires different conditions, many children are not able to learn in the classroom. When people can explore information in many different situations, Bruner's argument goes on, they learn to classify and order what they discover. The general routine of the school day, however, does not provide children with the diverse activities and situations that would allow them to learn these skills (172).

Readers assume that some words in a paraphrase are taken from the source. Indeed, it would be nearly impossible for paraphrasers to avoid using any key terms from the source, and it would be counterproductive to try to do so because the original and paraphrase necessarily share the same information and concepts. Notice, though, that of the total of eighty-seven words in the paraphrase, the paraphraser uses only a name ("Bruner") and a few key nouns and verbs ("discovery theorists," "conditions," "children," "learn[ing]," "information," "situations") for which it would be awkward to substitute other words or phrases. If the paraphraser had wanted to use other kinds of language from the source, such as the description of life at school as "generic and predictable," these adjectives should have been enclosed in quotation marks. In fact, the paraphraser does put quotation marks around the term "discovery theorists," a technical term likely to be unfamiliar to readers.

The source of all the material in the paraphrase is identified by the author's name in the first sentence and by the page number in the last sentence, which indicates where the paraphrased material appears in David Guterson's book. This source citation follows the style of the Modern Language Association (MLA). Notice that placing the citation information in this way indicates clearly to readers where the paraphrase begins and ends, so that they understand where the text is expressing ideas taken from a source and where it is expressing the writer's own ideas (or ideas from a different source). Should readers want to check the accuracy or completeness of the paraphrase, they could turn to the alphabetically arranged list of works cited at the end of the essay, look for Guterson's name, and find there all the information they would need to locate the book and check the source.

Although it is acceptable and often necessary to reuse a few key terms or to quote striking or technical language from a source, paraphrasers must avoid borrowing too many words or repeating the same sentence structure. Notice in the following paraphrase of Guterson's first sentence that the paraphraser repeats too many of the author's own words and phrases:

Unacceptable Paraphrase:
Too Many Borrowed Words and Phrases

Apparently, some conditions, which have been illuminated by Bruner and other discovery theorists, pave the way for people to learn.

By comparing the source's first sentence and this paraphrase of it, you can see that the paraphraser borrows almost all of the key terms from the original sentence, including the entire phrase "pave the way for." Even if you cite the source, this sort of heavy borrowing is an example of *plagiarism*—using the ideas and words of others as though they were your own (see p. 680).

The following paraphrase of the same sentence is unacceptable because it too closely resembles the structure of the original sentence:

Unacceptable Paraphrase:
Sentence Structure Repeated Too Closely

Bruner and other researchers have also identified circumstances that seem to ease the path to learning.

Here the paraphraser borrows the phrases and clauses of the source and arranges them in an identical sequence, merely substituting synonyms for Guterson's key terms: "researchers" for "theorists," "identified" for "illuminated," "circumstances" for "conditions," "seem to" for "apparently," and "ease the path to" for "pave the way for." Even though most key terms have been changed, this paraphrase is also an example of plagiarism because it duplicates the source's sentence structure.

Summarizing

Like a paraphrase, a *summary* may use key terms from the source, but it is made up mainly of words supplied by the writer. A summary presents only the main ideas of the source, leaving out examples and details. Consequently, summaries allow you to bring concisely into your writing large amounts of information from source material.

Here is an example of a summary of five pages from Guterson's book. You can see at a glance how drastically some summaries condense information, in this case from five pages to five sentences. Depending on the summarizer's purpose, however, the same five pages could be summarized in one sentence or in two dozen sentences.

Summary

In looking at different theories of learning that discuss individual-based programs (such as home schooling) versus the public school system, Guterson describes the disagreements among "cognitivist theorists." One group, the "discovery theorists," believes that individual children learn by creating their own ways of sorting the information they take in from their experiences. Schools should help students develop better ways of organizing new material, not just present them with material that is already categorized, as traditional schools do. "Assimilationist theorists," by contrast, believe that children learn by linking what they don't know to information they already know. These theorists claim that traditional schools help students learn when they present information in ways that allow children to fit the new material into categories they have already developed (171–75).

Notice that the source of the summarized material is identified by the author's name in the first sentence and that the page numbers from the source are cited parenthetically in the last sentence, following MLA citation style. As with a paraphrase, putting the citation information at the beginning and the end of the summary in this way makes clear to the reader the boundaries between the ideas in the source and the writer's own ideas (or the ideas in a different source).

Although this summarizer encloses in quotation marks three technical terms from the original source, summaries usually do not include quotations: Their purpose is not to display the source's language but to present its main ideas. Even a lengthy summary is more than a dry list of main ideas from a source; it is a coherent, readable new text composed of the source's main ideas. An effective summary provides balanced coverage of the source, following the same sequence of ideas while avoiding any hint of agreement or disagreement.

ACKNOWLEDGING SOURCES

Notice in the preceding examples that the source is acknowledged by name. Even when you use your own words to present someone else's information, you must acknowledge that you borrowed the information. The only types of information that do not require acknowledgment are common knowledge (John F. Kennedy was assassinated in Dallas), facts widely available in many sources (before 1933, U.S. presidents were inaugurated on March 4 rather than on January 20), well-known quotations ("To be, or not to be: that is the question"), and material you created or gathered yourself, such as your own photographs or survey data. Remember to acknowledge the source of visuals (photographs, tables, charts, graphs, diagrams, drawings, maps, screen shots) that you do not create yourself as well as the source of any information that you use to create your own visuals. (You should also request permission from the source of every visual you want to borrow if your essay will be posted on the Web.) When in doubt about the need to acknowledge a source, it is always safer to include a citation.

The documentation guidelines later in this appendix (pp. 681–702) present various styles for citing sources. Whichever style you use, your readers must be able to tell where words or ideas that are not your own begin and end. You can accomplish this most readily by taking and transcribing notes carefully, by placing parenthetical source citations correctly, and by separating your words from those of the source with *signal phrases,* such as "According to Smith," "Peters claims," and "As Olmos asserts." (When you cite a source for the first time in a signal phrase, you may use the author's full name; after that, use just the last name.)

Avoiding Plagiarism

Writers—students and professionals alike—occasionally fail to acknowledge sources properly. The word *plagiarism,* which derives from the Latin word for "kidnapping," refers to the unacknowledged use of another's words, ideas, sentence structure, or information. Students sometimes get into trouble because they mistakenly assume that plagiarizing occurs only when another writer's exact words are used without acknowledgment. In fact, plagiarism applies to such diverse forms of expression as musical compositions and visual images as well as ideas and statistics. So keep in mind that, with the exceptions listed above, you must indicate the source of any borrowed information or ideas you use in your essay—whether you have paraphrased, summarized, or quoted directly from the source or have reproduced it or referred to it in some other way.

Remember especially the need to document electronic sources fully and accurately. Perhaps because it is so easy to access and distribute text and visuals online and to copy material from one electronic document and paste it into another, many students do not realize—or may forget—that information, ideas, and images from electronic sources require acknowledgment in even more detail than those from print sources do (and are often easier to detect if they are not acknowledged).

Some people plagiarize simply because they do not know the conventions for using and acknowledging sources. This appendix makes clear how to incorporate sources into your writing and how to acknowledge your use of those sources. Others plagiarize because they keep sloppy notes that fail to distinguish between their own and their sources' ideas. Either they neglect to enclose their sources' words in quotation marks, or they fail to indicate when they are paraphrasing or summarizing a source's ideas and information. If you keep a working bibliography and careful notes, you will not make this serious mistake.

Another reason some people plagiarize is that they doubt their ability to write the essay by themselves. They feel intimidated by the writing task, the deadline, or their own and others' expectations. If you experience this same anxiety about your work, speak to your instructor. Do not run the risk of failing a course or being expelled because of plagiarism. If you are confused about what is and what is not plagiarism, be sure to ask your instructor.

Understanding Documentation Styles

Although there are several systems for acknowledging sources, most documentation styles use short in-text citations that are keyed to a separate bibliography. The information required in the in-text citations and the order and content of the bibliography vary across academic disciplines. The following guidelines present the basic features of two styles: the *Modern Language Association (MLA)* system, which is widely used in the humanities, and the *American Psychological Association (APA)* system, which is widely used in the social sciences. Earlier in this book, you can find student-written essays that follow MLA style (Linh Kieu Ngo, Chapter 5; Amber Ripplinger, Chapter 7; Jeff Varley, Chapter 8; and Amber Dahlke and Jessica Statsky, Chapter 9) and APA style (Patrick O'Malley, Chapter 8).

Documenting Sources Using MLA Style

The following guidelines are sufficient for most college research assignments in English and other humanities courses that call for MLA-style documentation. For additional information, see the *MLA Handbook for Writers of Research Papers*, seventh edition (2009), or check the MLA Web site <http://www.mla.org>.

Use In-Text Citations to Show Where You Have Used Material from Sources

The MLA author-page system requires parenthetical in-text citations that are keyed to a list of works cited in the paper. In-text citations generally include the author's last name and the page number of the passage being cited. There is no punctuation between author and page. The parenthetical citation should follow the quoted, paraphrased, or summarized material as closely as possible without disrupting the flow of the sentence.

Dr. James is described as a "not-too-skeletal Ichabod Crane" (Simon 68).

Note that the parenthetical citation comes before the final period. With block quotations, however, the citation comes after the final period, preceded by a space (see p. 674 for an example).

If you mention the author's name in your text, supply just the page reference in parentheses.

Simon describes Dr. James as a "not-too-skeletal Ichabod Crane" (68).

USE THE FOLLOWING MODELS FOR IN-TEXT CITATIONS

1. When the source has more than one author

Dyal, Corning, and Willows identify several types of students, including the "Authority-Rebel" (4).

Authority-rebels see themselves as "superior to other students in the class" (Dyal, Corning, and Willows 4).

The drug AZT has been shown to reduce the risk of transmission from HIV-positive mothers to their infants by as much as two-thirds (Van de Perre et al. 4-5).

For four or more authors, use all the authors' names or only the first author's name followed by *et al.* ("and others"), as in the example above.

2. When the author is not named

In 1992, five years after the Symms legislation, the number of deaths from automobile accidents reached a thirty-year low ("Highways" 51).

3. When the source has a corporate or government author

A tuition increase has been proposed for community and technical colleges to offset budget deficits from Initiative 601 (Washington State Board for Community and Technical Colleges 4).

4. When two or more works by the same author are cited

When old paint becomes transparent, it sometimes shows the artist's original plans: "A tree will show through a woman's dress" (Hellman, *Pentimento* 1).

Because more than one of Hellman's works is included in the list of works cited, the title follows the author's name in the parentheses.

5. When two or more authors have the same last name

According to Edgar V. Roberts, Chaplin's *Modern Times* provides a good example of montage used to make an editorial statement (246).

Chaplin's *Modern Times* provides a good example of montage used to make an editorial statement (E. V. Roberts 246).

Note that Roberts's first and middle initials are included in the parentheses because another author with the same last name is included in the list of works cited.

6. When a work without page numbers is cited

The average speed on Montana's interstate highways, for example, has risen by only 2 miles per hour since the repeal of the federal speed limit, with most drivers topping out at 75 (Schmid).

There is no page number available for this source because it comes from the Internet.

7. When a quotation is taken from a secondary source

Chancellor Helmut Kohl summed up the German attitude: "For millions of people, a car is part of their personal freedom" (qtd. in Cote 12).

Create a works-cited entry for the secondary source in which you found the quote, rather than for the original source (for this example, an entry for Cote, not Kohl, would appear in the list of works cited).

8. When a citation comes from a multivolume work

"Double meaning," according to Freud, "is one of the most fertile sources for . . . jokes" (8: 56).

In the parentheses, the number *8* indicates the volume and *56* indicates the page. (For a works-cited entry for a single volume in a multivolume work, see p. 686, entry 8.)

9. When the source is a literary work

For a novel or other prose work available in various editions, provide the page numbers from the edition used. To help readers locate the quotation in another edition, add the part and/or chapter number.

In Hard Times, Tom reveals his utter narcissism by blaming Louisa for his own failure: "'You have regularly given me up. You never cared for me'" (Dickens 262; bk. 3, ch. 9).

For a play in verse, such as a Shakespearean play, indicate the act, scene, and line numbers instead of the page numbers.

At the beginning, Regan's fawning rhetoric hides her true attitude toward Lear: "I profess / Myself an enemy to all other joys / . . . / And find I am alone felicitate / In your dear highness' love" (*King Lear* 1.1.74-75, 77-78).

For a poem, indicate the line numbers and stanzas (if they are numbered) instead of the page numbers.

In "Song of Myself," Whitman finds poetic details in busy urban settings, as when he describes "the blab of the pave, tires of carts . . . / . . . the driver with his interrogating thumb" (8.153-54).

If the source gives only line numbers, use the word *lines* in the first citation; in subsequent citations, give only the numbers.

10. When the citation comes from a work in an anthology

In "Six Days: Some Rememberings," Grace Paley recalls that when she was in jail for protesting the Vietnam War, her pen and paper were taken away and she felt "a terrible pain in the area of my heart--a nausea" (191).

If you are discussing the editor's preface or introduction, name the editor.

11. When two or more works are cited in the same parentheses

When two or more different sources are used in the same passage, it may be necessary to cite them in the same parentheses. Separate the citations with a semicolon.

A few studies have considered differences between oral and written discourse production (Scardamalia, Bereiter, and Goelman; Gould).

The scene registers conflicts in English law as well, for while the medieval Westminster statutes also distinguish between lawful and unlawful exchanges of women, sixteenth-century statutes begin to redefine rape as a violent crime against a woman rather than as a property crime against her guardians (Maitland 2:490–91; Post; Bashar; Gossett).

12. When an entire work is cited

In *The Structure of Scientific Revolutions*, Thomas Kuhn discusses how scientists change their thinking.

No parenthetical citation is necessary.

13. When material from the Internet is cited

In handling livestock, "many people attempt to restrain animals with sheer force instead of using behavioral principles" (Grandin).

If the author is not named, give the document title. Include page or paragraph numbers, if available.

Include All of Your Sources in a Works-Cited List at the End of Your Essay

In MLA style, every source referred to in the text of your essay must have a corresponding entry in the list of works cited at the end of your essay. Conversely, every entry in the works-cited list must correspond to at least one in-text citation in the essay. The information provided in this list enables readers to find the sources cited in the essay. The MLA recommends that the list of works cited be placed at the end of the paper, beginning on a new page with pages numbered consecutively; that the first line of each entry begins flush with the left margin; that subsequent lines of the same entry indent five character spaces; and that the entire list be double-spaced, between and within entries.

Do not worry about including information that is unavailable within the source, such as the author's middle initial or the issue number for a periodical. The MLA now requires the medium of publication in all works-cited entries. The medium usually appears at the end of the citation (but see specific models in this section, especially those for electronic entries, for exact placement).

BASIC ENTRY FOR A BOOK

Author's last name, First name, Middle initial. *Book Title*. City of publication: Publisher's name, year published. Medium.

USE THE FOLLOWING MODELS FOR BOOKS

1. A book by a single author

Ehrenreich, Barbara. *Nickel and Dimed: On (Not) Getting By in America*. New York: Metropolitan, 2001. Print.

2. Multiple works by the same author (or same group of authors)

Kingsolver, Barbara. *High Tide in Tucson: Essays from Now or Never*. New York: HarperCollins, 1995. Print.

---. *Small Wonder*. New York: HarperCollins, 2002. Print.

3. A book by an agency, organization, or corporation

American Medical Association. *Family Medical Guide*. 4th ed. Hoboken: Wiley, 2004. Print.

4. A book by two or more authors

For two or three authors:

Saba, Laura, and Julie Gattis. *The McGraw-Hill Homeschooling Companion*. New York: McGraw, 2002. Print.

For three or more authors, name all the authors *or* only the first author followed by *et al.* ("and others"):

Belenky, Mary F., Blythe M. Clinchy, Nancy R. Goldberger, and Jill M. Tarule. *Women's Ways of Knowing: The Development of Self, Voice, and Mind*. New York: Basic, 1986. Print.

Belenky, Mary F., et al. *Women's Ways of Knowing: The Development of Self, Voice, and Mind*. New York: Basic, 1986. Print.

5. A book with an unlisted author

Rand McNally Commercial Atlas and Marketing Guide. Skokie: Rand, 2003. Print.

6. A book with one or more editors

Axelrod, Steven Gould, and Helen Deese, eds. *Robert Lowell: Essays on the Poetry*. Cambridge: Cambridge UP, 1986. Print.

7. A book with an author and an editor

If you refer to the work itself:

Arnold, Matthew. *Culture and Anarchy*. Ed. Samuel Lipman. New Haven: Yale UP, 1994. Print.

If you discuss the editor's work in your essay:

Lipman, Samuel, ed. *Culture and Anarchy*. By Matthew Arnold. 1869. New Haven: Yale UP, 1994. Print.

8. One volume of a multivolume work

If only one volume from a multivolume set is used, indicate the volume number after the title:

Freud, Sigmund. *The Standard Edition of the Complete Psychological Works of Sigmund Freud*. Vol. 8. Trans. and ed. James Strachey. New York: Norton, 2000. Print.

9. Two or more volumes of a multivolume work

Sandburg, Carl. *Abraham Lincoln*. 6 vols. New York: Scribner's, 1939. Print.

10. A book that is part of a series

After the medium of publication, include the series name, without italics or quotation marks, followed by the series number. If the word *Series* is part of the name, include the abbreviation *Ser.* before the number.

Zigova, Tanya, et al. *Neural Stem Cells: Methods and Protocols*. Totowa: Humana, 2002. Print. Methods in Molecular Biology 198.

11. A republished book

Provide the original publication date after the title of the book, followed by normal publication information for the current edition:

Alcott, Louisa May. *An Old-Fashioned Girl*. 1870. New York: Puffin, 1995. Print.

12. A later edition of a book

Rottenberg, Annette T., and Donna Haisty Winchell. *The Structure of Argument*. 5th ed.
Boston: Bedford, 2006. Print.

13. A book with a title in its title

Do not italicize a title normally italicized when it appears within the title of a
book or other work that is italicized:

Hertenstein, Mike. *The Double Vision of* Star Trek*: Half-Humans, Evil Twins, and Science
Fiction*. Chicago: Cornerstone, 1998. Print.

O'Neill, Terry, ed. *Readings on* To Kill a Mockingbird. San Diego: Greenhaven, 2000. Print.

Use quotation marks around a work normally enclosed in quotation marks when
it appears in the title of a book or other work that is italicized:

Miller, Edwin Haviland. *Walt Whitman's "Song of Myself": A Mosaic of Interpretations*. Iowa
City: U of Iowa P, 1989. Print.

14. A work in an anthology or a collection

Fairbairn-Dunlop, Peggy. "Women and Agriculture in Western Samoa." *Different Places,
Different Voices*. Ed. Janet H. Momsen and Vivian Kinnaird. London: Routledge, 1993.
211-26. Print.

15. A translation

If you refer to the work itself:

Tolstoy, Leo. *War and Peace*. Trans. Constance Garnett. New York: Modern, 2002. Print.

If you discuss the translation in your essay:

Garnett, Constance, trans. *War and Peace*. By Leo Tolstoy. New York: Modern, 2002. Print.

16. An article in a reference book

Rowland, Lewis P. "Myasthenia Gravis." *The Encyclopedia Americana*. 2001 ed. Print.

17. An introduction, preface, foreword, or afterword

Graff, Gerald, and James Phelan. Preface. *Adventures of Huckleberry Finn*. By Mark Twain. 2nd
ed. New York: Bedford, 2004. iii-vii. Print.

BASIC ENTRY FOR AN ARTICLE

Author's last name, First name, Middle initial. "Title of the Article." *Journal Name* Volume
number.Issue number (year published): page range. Medium.

USE THE FOLLOWING MODELS FOR ARTICLES

18. An article from a newspaper

Peterson, Andrea. "Finding a Cure for Old Age." *Wall Street Journal* 20 May 2003:
    D1+. Print.

19. An article from a weekly or biweekly magazine

Gross, Michael Joseph. "Family Life during Wartime." *Advocate* 29 Apr. 2003:
    42-48. Print.

20. An article from a monthly or bimonthly magazine

Stacey, Patricia. "Floor Time." *Atlantic Monthly* Jan.-Feb. 2003: 127-34. Print.

21. An article in a scholarly journal with continuous annual pagination

Shan, Jordan Z., Alan G. Morris, and Fiona Sun. "Financial Development and Economic
    Growth: An Egg and Chicken Problem?" *Review of International Economics* 9 (2001):
    443-54. Print.

22. An article in a scholarly journal that paginates each issue separately

Epstein, Alexandra. "Teen Parents: What They Need to Know." *High/Scope Resource* 1.2
    (1982): 6. Print.

23. An editorial

"The Future Is Now." Editorial. *National Review* 22 Apr. 2002: 15-16. Print.

24. A letter to the editor

Orent, Wendy, and Alan Zelicoff. Letter. *New Republic* 18 Nov. 2002: 4-5. Print.

25. A review

If the review is titled:

Cassidy, John. "Master of Disaster." Rev. of *Globalization and Its Discontents*, by Joseph
    Stiglitz. *New Yorker* 12 July 2002: 82-86. Print.

If the review is untitled:

Lane, Anthony. Rev. of *The English Patient*, dir. Anthony Minghella. *New Yorker* 25 Nov. 1996:
    118-21. Print.

If the review has no title and no named author, start with the words *Rev. of* and the title of the work being reviewed.

26. An unsigned article

"A Shot of Reality." *US News and World Report* 1 July 2003: 13. Print.

Alphabetize the entry according to the first word after any initial *A, An,* or *The.*

BASIC ENTRY FOR AN ELECTRONIC SOURCE

Although there are many varieties of works-cited entries for Internet sources, the information generally follows this order:

Author's last name, First name, Middle initial. "Title of Short Work." *Title of Book, Periodical, or Web Site.* Name of sponsoring institution or organization, Publication date or date of last revision. Medium. Date of access.

USE THE FOLLOWING MODELS FOR ELECTRONIC SOURCES

Citations of electronic sources require information normally included in citations of print sources (author, document title, and publication date) as well as information specific to electronic sources, including the following:

- Name of the Web site or database, italicized.
- Name of any institution or organization that sponsors the site (usually found at the bottom of the home page).
- Date of electronic publication or most recent update.
- Medium (Web).
- Date you most recently accessed the source.

If you cannot locate all of this information, include what you do find. You can learn more about citing electronic sources at the MLA Web site at <www .mla.org>.

27. An entire Web site

Professional Web site:

International Virginia Woolf Society. Intl. Virginia Woolf Soc., 31 Aug. 2002.
   Web. 7 Oct. 2005.

Personal Web site:

Chesson, Frederick W. Home page. Frederick W. Chesson, 1 Apr. 2003. Web. 21 Feb. 2006.

28. A book or short work within a scholarly project

Book:

Corelli, Marie. *The Treasure of Heaven.* London: Constable, 1906. *Victorian Women Writers Project.* Ed. Percy Willett. Web. 10 Sept. 2005.

Short work:

Heims, Marjorie. "The Strange Case of Sarah Jones." *Free Expression Policy Project.* Free Expression Policy Project, 24 Jan. 2003. Web. 13 Mar. 2006.

29. An article from an online journal

Cesarini, Paul. "Computers, Technology, and Literacies." *Journal of Literacy and Technology* 4.1 (2004/2005): n. pag. Web. 12 Oct. 2005.

30. An article from an online magazine

If you accessed the article through a personal subscription:

Weeks, W. William. "Beyond the Ark." *Nature Conservancy* Mar.-Apr. 1999. *America Online.* Web. 20 Aug. 2005.

If you accessed the article through a library subscription:

Hillenbrand, Laura. "A Sudden Illness: Personal History." *New Yorker* 7 July 2003: 56. *ProQuest.* Web. 14 June 2005.

31. A posting to a discussion group or listserv

A discussion group posting:

Willie, Otis. "In the Heat of the Battle." *Google Groups: US Revolution.* Google, 27 Sept. 2005. Web. 7 Oct. 2005.

A listserv posting:

Martin, Francesca Alys. "Wait—Did Somebody Say 'Buffy'?" *CULTSTUD-L.* U of Minnesota, 8 Mar. 2000. Web. 16 Mar. 2000.

32. An online scholarly project

Darwin Correspondence Project. U of Cambridge, 2007. Web. 28 Nov. 2009.

33. Material from a periodically published database on CD-ROM

Braus, Patricia. "Sex and the Single Spender." *American Demographics* 15.11 (1993): 28-34. CD-ROM. *ABI/INFORM.* UMI-ProQuest. 1993.

If no print version is available, include the author, title, and date (if provided), along with information about the electronic source.

34. A nonperiodical publication on CD-ROM, magnetic tape, or diskette

Picasso: The Man, His Works, the Legend. Danbury: Grolier Interactive, 1996. CD-ROM.

USE THE FOLLOWING MODELS FOR OTHER SOURCES

35. An interview

Published interview:

Lowell, Robert. "Robert Lowell." Interview with Frederick Seidel. *Paris Review* 25 (1975): 56-95. Print.

Personal interview:

Franklin, Ann. Personal interview. 3 Sept. 2002.

Broadcast interview:

Calloway, Cab. Interview by Rich Conaty. *The Big Broadcast.* WFUV, New York, 10 Dec. 1990. Radio.

36. A lecture or public address

Birnbaum, Jack. "The Domestication of Computers." Conf. of the Usability Professionals Association. Hyatt Grand Cypress Resort, Orlando. 10 July 2002. Lecture.

37. A government document

United States. Dept. of Health and Human Services. *Building Communities Together: Federal Programs Guide, 1999-2000.* Washington: GPO, 1999. Print.

If the author is known, the author's name may either come first or be placed after the title and introduced with the word *By.*

38. A pamphlet

BoatU.S. Foundation for Boating Safety and Clean Water. *Hypothermia and Cold Water Survival.* Alexandria: Boat U.S. Foundation, 2001. Print.

39. A published doctoral dissertation

Hilfinger, Paul N. *Abstraction Mechanisms and Language Design.* Diss. Carnegie Mellon U, 1981. Cambridge: MIT P, 1983. Print.

40. An unpublished doctoral dissertation

Bullock, Barbara. "Basic Needs Fulfillment among Less Developed Countries: Social Progress over Two Decades of Growth." Diss. Vanderbilt U, 1986. Print.

41. A dissertation abstract

Bernstein, Stephen David. "Fugitive Genre: Gothicism, Ideology, and Intertextuality." Diss. Yale U, 1991. *DAI* 51.9 (1991): 3078–79A. Print.

42. Published proceedings of a conference

Duffett, John, ed. *Against the Crime of Silence: Proceedings of the International War Crimes Tribunal,* Nov. 1967, Stockholm. New York: Clarion-Simon, 1970. Print.

If the name of the conference is part of the title of the publication, it need not be repeated. Use the format for a work in an anthology (see entry 14 on p. 687) to cite an individual presentation.

43. A letter

Hamilton, Alexander. "To William Seton." 3 Dec. 1790. *The Papers of Alexander Hamilton.* Ed. Harold C. Syrett. Vol. 7. New York: Columbia UP, 1969. 190. Print.

For handwritten or typed letters, use the designation *MS* or *TS,* respectively.

Rogers, Katherine. Letter to the author. 22 Mar. 2003. TS.

44. A map or chart

Map of Afghanistan and Surrounding Territory. Map. Burlington: GiziMap, 2001. Print.

45. A cartoon or comic strip

Provide the title (if given) in quotation marks directly following the artist's name.

Cheney, Tom. Cartoon. *New Yorker* 10 Oct. 2005: 55. Print.

46. An advertisement

City Harvest Feed the Kids 2003. Advertisement. *New York* 26 May 2003: 15. Print.

47. A work of art or a musical composition

Beethoven, Ludwig van. Violin Concerto in D Major, op. 61.

Gershwin, George. *Porgy and Bess.* 1935.

For a work of art, include the medium of composition after the year.

De Goya, Francisco. *The Sleep of Reason Produces Monsters.* 1799. Etching and Aquatint. Norton Simon Museum, Pasadena.

48. A performance

Proof. By David Auburn. Dir. Daniel Sullivan. Perf. Mary-Louise Parker. Walter Kerr Theatre, New York. 9 Sept. 2001. Performance.

Include the names of any performers or other contributors who are relevant to or cited in your essay.

49. A television or radio program

"Murder of the Century." *American Experience*. Narr. David Ogden Stiers. Writ. and prod. Carl Charlson. PBS. WEDU, Tampa, 14 July 2003. Television.

Include the names of any contributors who are relevant to or cited in your essay. If you are discussing the work of a particular person (for example, the director or writer), begin the entry with that person's name.

50. A film or video recording

Space Station. Prod. and dir. Toni Myers. Narr. Tom Cruise. IMAX, 2002. Film.

Casablanca. Dir. Michael Curtiz. Perf. Humphrey Bogart. 1942. MGM-UA Home Video, 1992. Videocassette.

Include the names of any performers or other contributors who are relevant to or cited in your essay. If you are discussing the work of a particular person (for example, an actor), begin the entry with that person's name:

Bogart, Humphrey, perf. *Casablanca*. Dir. Michael Curtiz. 1942. MGM-UA Home Video, 1992. Videocassette.

51. A sound recording

Bach, Johann Sebastian. Italian Concerto in F, Partita no. 1, and Toccata in D. Dubravka Tomsic, piano. Polyband, 1987. LP.

Jane's Addiction. "Been Caught Stealing." *Ritual de lo Habitual*. Warner Brothers, 1990. Audiocassette.

If the year of issue is not known, add *n.d.*

52. An interview

Ashrawi, Hanan. "Tanks vs. Olive Branches." Interview with Rose Marie Berger. *Sojourners Magazine* Feb. 2005: 22-26. Print.

Franklin, Ann. Personal interview. 3 Sept. 2005.

Documenting Sources Using APA Style

The following guidelines are sufficient for most college research reports that call for APA-style documentation. For additional information, see the *Publication Manual of the American Psychological Association*, sixth edition (2010), or check the APA Web site <http://apastyle.apa.org>. APA style requires parenthetical in-text citations that are keyed to a list of references mentioned in the paper.

Use In-Text Citations to Show Where You Have Used Material from Sources

The APA author-year system calls for the last name of the author and the year of publication of the original work in the citation. If the cited material is a quotation, you also need to include the page number(s) of the original. If the cited material is not a quotation, the page reference is optional. Use commas to separate author, year, and page in a parenthetical citation. The page number is preceded by *p.* for a single page or *pp.* for a range. Use an ampersand (&) to join the names of multiple authors.

The conditions in the stockyards were so dangerous that workers "fell into the vats; and when they were fished out, there was never enough of them left to be worth exhibiting" (Sinclair, 2005, p. 134).

Racial bias does not necessarily diminish merely through exposure to individuals of other races (Johnson & Tyree, 2001).

If you are citing an electronic source without page numbers, give the paragraph number if it is provided, preceded by the abbreviation *para.* If no paragraph number is given, give the heading of the section and the number of the paragraph within it where the material appears, if possible.

The subjects were tested for their responses to various stimuli, both positive and negative (Simpson, 2002, para. 4).

If the author's name is mentioned in your text, cite the year in parentheses directly following the author's name, and place the page reference in parentheses before the final sentence period. Use *and* to join the names of multiple authors.

Sinclair (2005) wrote that workers sometimes "fell into the vats; and when they were fished out, there was never enough of them left to be worth exhibiting" (p. 134).

As Johnson and Tyree (2001) have found, racial bias does not diminish merely through exposure to individuals of other races (Conclusion section, para. 2).

USE THE FOLLOWING MODELS FOR IN-TEXT CITATIONS

1. **When the source has three or more authors**

First citation for a source with three to five authors:

Rosenzweig, Breedlove, and Watson (2005) wrote that biological psychology is an interdiscipinary field that includes scientists from "quite different backgrounds" (p. 3).

Subsequent citations for a source with three to five authors:

Biological psychology is "the field that relates behavior to bloody processes, especially the workings of the brain" (Rosenzweig et al., 2005, p. 3).

For a source with six or more authors, use the last name of the first author and *et al.* in all in-text citations.

2. When the author is not named

As reported in the 1994 *Economist* article "Classless Society," estimates as late as 1993 placed the number of home-schooled children in the 350,000 to 500,000 range.

An international pollution treaty still to be ratified would prohibit all plastic garbage from being dumped at sea ("Awash," 1987).

3. When the author is an agency or a corporation

First in-text or parenthetical citation:

According to the Washington State Board of Community and Technical Colleges (WSBCTC), (1995), a tuition increase has been proposed to offset budget deficits from Initiative 601.

Tuition increases proposed for Washington community and technical colleges would help offset budget deficits brought about by Initiative 601 (Washington State Board of Community and Technical Colleges [WSBCTC], 1995).

Subsequent parenthetical citations for the same source:

The tuition increases would amount to about 3 percent and would still not cover the loss of revenue (WSBCTC, 1995).

4. When two or more authors have the same last name

"Women are more in the public world, the heretofore male world, than at any previous moment in history," transforming "the lives of women and men to an extent probably unparalleled by any other social or political movement" (W. Brown, 1988, pp. 1, 3).

If two or more primary authors with the same last name are listed in the references, include the authors' first initial in all text citations, even if the year of publication of the authors' works differs.

5. When two or more works are cited in the same parentheses

Through support organizations and programs offered by public schools, home-schooled children are also able to take part in social activities outside the home, such as field trips and sports (Guterson, 1992; Hahn & Hasson, 1996).

When citing two or more works by different authors, arrange them alphabetically by the authors' last names, as in the preceding example. However, when citing multiple works by the same author in the same parentheses, order the citations by date, with the oldest reference first: (*Postman, 1979, 1986*).

6. When two or more works by the same author share the same publication year

Middle-class unemployed workers are better off than their lower-class counterparts, because "the white collar unemployed are likely to have some assets to invest in their job search" (Ehrenreich, 2005b, p. 16).

When two or more works by the same author or authors are cited, the years of publication are usually enough to distinguish them. An exception occurs when the works share the same publication date. In this case, arrange the works alphabetically by title, and then add *a, b, c,* and so on after the year to distinguish works published in the same year by the same author(s).

7. When a quotation is taken from a secondary source

Forster says "the collapse of all civilization, so realistic for us, sounded in Matthew Arnold's ears like a distant and harmonious cataract" (as cited in Trilling, 1955, p. 11).

Create an entry in the list of references for the secondary source in which you found the quote, not for the original source.

8. When material from the Internet is cited

Each type of welfare recipient "requires specific services or assistance to make the transition from welfare to work" (Armato & Halpern, 1996, para. 7).

9. When an e-mail or other personal communication is cited

According to L. Jones (personal communication, May 2, 2001), some parents believe they must maximize their day-care value and leave their children at day-care centers for up to ten hours a day, even on their days off.

In addition to e-mail messages, personal communications include letters, memos, personal interviews, telephone conversations, and online discussion group postings that are not archived. Give the initial(s) as well as the surname of the communicator, and provide as exact a date as possible. Personal communications are cited only in the text; do not include them in the list of references.

Include All of Your Sources in a References List at the End of Your Essay

In APA style, every source referred to in the text of your essay (except personal communications) must have a corresponding entry in the list of references at the end of your essay. Conversely, every entry in the references list must correspond to at least one in-text citation in the essay. The information provided in this list enables readers to find the sources cited in the essay. If you want to show the sources you consulted but did not cite in the essay, list them on a separate page titled *Bibliography*.

The APA recommends that all references be double-spaced and that students use a *hanging indent*: the first line of the entry is not indented, but subsequent lines are indented five to seven spaces. The examples in this section demonstrate the hanging-indent style. The APA encourages use of italics, as shown in the following model entries, but your instructor may permit or even prefer underlining instead.

Copy the author's name and the title from the first or title page of the source, but use only initials, not first names. Do not worry about including information that is unavailable, such as the author's middle initial or the issue number for a journal article.

BASIC ENTRY FOR A BOOK

Author's last name, First initial. Middle initial. (year published). *Book title*. City and state of publication: Publisher's name.

USE THE FOLLOWING MODELS FOR BOOKS

1. A book by a single author

Ehrenreich, B. (2001). *Nickel and dimed: On (not) getting by in America*. New York, NY: Metropolitan.

2. A book by two to seven authors

Hunt, L., Po-Chia Hsia, R., Martin, T. R., Rosenwein, B. H., Rosenwein, H., & Smith, B. G. (2001). *The making of the West: Peoples and cultures*. Boston, MA: Bedford/ St. Martin's.

Saba, L., & Gattis, J. (2002). *The McGraw-Hill homeschooling companion*. New York, NY: McGraw-Hill.

3. A book by an agency, organization, or corporation

American Medical Association. (2004). *Family medical guide*. Hoboken, NJ: Wiley.

4. A book with an unlisted author

Rand McNally commercial atlas and marketing guide. (2003). Skokie, IL: Rand McNally.

When the word *Anonymous* appears on the title page, cite the author as *Anonymous*.

5. A later edition of a book

Lewis, I. M. (1996). *Religion in context: Cults and charisma* (2nd ed.). New York, NY:
Cambridge University Press.

6. Multiple works by the same author (or same group of authors)

Ritzer, G. (1993). *The McDonaldization of society*. Newbury Park, CA: Pine Forge Press.

Ritzer, G. (1994). *Sociological beginnings: On the origins of key ideas in sociology*. New York,
NY: McGraw-Hill.

Two or more books published by the same author or authors are listed in chronological order, as shown above.

However, when the books also have the same publication date, arrange them
alphabetically by title and add a lowercase letter after the date: *1996a, 1996b*. (See
item 22 on p. 700 for examples.)

7. A multivolume work

Sandburg, C. (1939). *Abraham Lincoln: Vol. 2. The war years*. New York, NY: Scribner's.

Sandburg, C. (1939). *Abraham Lincoln* (Vols. 1–6). New York, NY: Scribner's.

8. A book with an author and an editor

Baum, L. F. (1996). *Our landlady* (N. T. Koupal, Ed.). Lincoln, NE: University of Nebraska Press.

9. An edited collection

Waldman, D., & Walker, J. (Eds.). (1999). *Feminism and documentary*. Minneapolis:
University of Minnesota Press.

10. A work in an anthology or a collection

Fairbairn-Dunlop, P. (1993). Women and agriculture in western Samoa. In J. H. Momsen &
V. Kinnaird (Eds.), *Different places, different voices* (pp. 211–226). London, England:
Routledge.

11. A republished book

Arnold, M. (1966). *Culture and anarchy* (J. D. Wilson, Ed.). New York, NY: Cambridge
University Press. (Original work published 1869)

Note: Both the original and the republished dates are included in the in-text citation, separated by a slash: *(Arnold, 1869/1966)*.

12. A translation

Tolstoy, L. (2002). *War and peace* (C. Garnett, Trans.). New York, NY: Modern Library.
(Original work published 1869)

Note: Both the original publication date and the publication date for the translation are included in the in-text citation, separated by a slash: *(Tolstoy, 1869/1972).*

13. An article in a reference book

Rowland, R. P. (2001). Myasthenia gravis. In *Encyclopedia Americana* (Vol. 19, p. 683). Danbury, CT: Grolier.

14. An introduction, preface, foreword, or afterword

Graff, G., & Phelan, J. (2004). Preface. In M. Twain, *Adventures of Huckleberry Finn* (pp. iii–vii). New York, NY: Bedford/St. Martin's.

BASIC ENTRY FOR AN ARTICLE

Author's last name, First initial. Middle initial. (publication date). Title of the article. *Journal Name, volume number*(issue number), page range.

USE THE FOLLOWING MODELS FOR ARTICLES

15. An article in a scholarly journal with continuous annual pagination

Shan, J. Z., Morris, A. G., & Sun, F. (2001). Financial development and economic growth: A chicken and egg problem? *Review of Economics, 9*, 443–454.

16. An article in a scholarly journal that paginates each issue separately

Tran, D. (2002). Personal income by state, second quarter 2002. *Current Business, 82*(11), 55–73.

17. An article from a newspaper

Peterson, A. (2003, May 20). Finding a cure for old age. *The Wall Street Journal*, pp. D1, D5.

18. An article from a magazine

Stacey, P. (2003, January/February). Floor time. *The Atlantic, 291*(1), 127–134.

19. An unsigned article

Communities blowing whistle on street basketball. (2003, November 9). *USA Today*, p. 20A.

20. A review

Cassidy, J. (2002, July 12). Master of disaster [Review of the book *Globalization and its discontents*]. *The New Yorker*, 82–86.

If the review is untitled, use the bracketed information as the title, retaining the brackets.

21. An editorial or a letter to the editor

Meader, R. (1997, May 11). Hard to see how consumers will benefit from deregulation [Letter to the editor]. *Seattle Post-Intelligencer*, p. E3.

22. Two or more articles by the same author published in the same year

Selimuddin, A. K. (1989a, March 25). The selling of America. *USA Today*, pp. 12–14.

Selimuddin, A. K. (1989b, September). Will America become #2? *USA Today Magazine*, 14–16.

USE THE FOLLOWING MODELS FOR ELECTRONIC SOURCES

The APA's guidelines require that citations of electronic sources be detailed enough to let readers retrieve the source, and they recommend that you check URLs frequently to make sure they still provide access to the source, updating them as necessary. For undated online content, use "(n.d.)" where the publication date would appear and include a retrieval date; also include a retrieval date for content that could change, as opposed to "final" content like journal articles or archived material. For sources that are not from periodicals, give the name of the online publisher only when its identity is not obvious from the author name, URL, or database name, as in item 30 (p. 701).

23. A journal article with a DOI assigned

For journals that assign each article a Digital Object Identifier (DOI)—a string of computer-generated letters and numbers that serves as a more permanent identifier than a URL—use the article's DOI instead of its URL.

Konig, A., Lating, J., & Kirkhart, M. W. (2007). Content of disclosure and health: Autonomic response to talking about a stressful event. *Brief Treatment and Crisis Intervention, 7*(3), 176–183. doi:10.1093/brief-treatment/mhm012

24. A journal article with no DOI assigned

Gruenert, S., & Galligan, R. (2007). The difference dads make: Young adult men's experiences with their fathers. *E-Journal of Applied Psychology, 3*(1), 3–15. Retrieved from http://ojs.lib.swin.edu.au/index.php/ejap/article/view/75/102

If access to the journal requires a subscription, use the URL of the journal's home page rather than that of the article.

25. An abstract retrieved from a database

Kerlikowske, R. G., & Wilson, M. (2007). *NetSmartz: a comprehensive approach to internet safety and awareness* (NCJ No. 219566). Abstract retrieved from National Criminal Justice Reference Service abstracts database: http://www.ncjrs.gov/App /AbstractsDBSearch.aspx

26. A U.S. government report

U.S. Department of Labor Bureau of Labor Statistics. (n.d.). *Occupational outlook handbook 2000–01*. Retrieved from http://stats.bls.gov/ocohome.htm

27. An online encyclopedia article

Chad. (2007). In *Encyclopædia Britannica*. Retrieved from http://www.britannica.com/eb

Begin the entry with the author if one is listed.

28. A newspaper article

Hauser, C. (2007, September 24). Amid protests, president of Iran speaks at Columbia. *The New York Times*. Retrieved from http://www.nytimes.com

29. Online magazine content not available in print

Gordon, P. H. (2007, September 24). Should there be a "War on Terror"? A TNR online debate [Online exclusive]. *The New Republic*. Retrieved from http://www.tnr.com

30. An article on a Web site

Manino, L., & C. Newman. (2007, September). *Time is money . . . and dinner!* Retrieved from U.S. Department of Agriculture Amber Waves website: http://www.ers.usda.gov /AmberWaves

31. A posting to an electronic mailing list

Crispin, P. (2001, September 2). The Hunger Site/Windows RG/WebElements [Electronic mailing list message]. Retrieved from http://www.tourbus.com/cgi-bin/archive .pl/2001/TB090201.HTM

32. A blog posting

Frappe. (2007, September 25). Re: Senate Dems reluctant to de-authorize Iraq war [Web log post]. Retrieved from http://www.huffingtonpost.com

33. An e-mail message

The APA's *Publication Manual* discourages including e-mail messages in the list of references. Cite an e-mail message only in the text as a personal communication (see entry 9 on p. 696).

USE THE FOLLOWING MODELS FOR OTHER SOURCES

34. A government document

U.S. Department of Health and Human Services. (1999). *Building communities together: Federal programs guide, 1999–2000*. Washington, DC: Government Printing Office.

35. An unpublished doctoral dissertation

Bullock, B. (1986). *Basic needs fulfillment among less developed countries: Social progress over two decades of growth* (Unpublished doctoral dissertation). Vanderbilt University, Nashville, TN.

36. A television program

Charlson, C. (Writer/Producer). (2003, July 14). Murder of the century [Television series episode]. In M. Samels (Executive producer), *American experience*. Tampa, FL: WEDU.

37. A film or video recording

Myers, T. (Producer/Director). (2002). *Space station* [Motion picture]. New York, NY: IMAX.

For a film on DVD or videocassette, list this medium instead of *Motion picture* in the brackets.

38. A music recording

Beethoven, L. van. (1806). Violin concerto in D major, op. 61 [Recorded by USSR State Orchestra]. (Cassette Recording No. ACS 8044). New York, NY: Allegro. (1980)

Springsteen, B. (1984). Dancing in the dark. On *Born in the U.S.A.* [CD]. New York, NY: Columbia.

If the recording date differs from the copyright date, it should appear in parentheses after the name of the label. When it is necessary to include a number for the recording, use parentheses for the medium; otherwise, use brackets.

39. An interview

Do not list personal interviews in your APA-style references list. Simply cite the person's name (last name and initials) in your text, and in parentheses give the notation *personal communication* (in regular type, not italicized or underlined) followed by a comma and the date of the interview. For published interviews, use the appropriate format for an article.

Acknowledgments (continued from copyright page)

Beth L. Bailey. "Dating." From *Front Porch to Back Seat: Courtship in Twentieth-Century America*, pp. 25–26. © 1988 The Johns Hopkins University Press. Reprinted with permission of The Johns Hopkins University Press.

Gary Beck. "Not Your Everyday Homeless Proposal." First published in *Outcry Magazine*, April 2006, Issue 4, Volume 6. Copyright © 2006. Reprinted by permission of the author.

David Brooks. "A Nation of Grinders." From *The New York Times*, June 29, 2003. Copyright © 2003 The New York Times Company. Reprinted by permission.

Helena Curtis and N. Sue Barnes. "Parthenogenesis." Excerpt from *Biology 5th edition*, by Helena Curtis and N. Sue Barnes, p. 1103, Chapter 52. Copyright © 1968, 1975, 1979, 1983, 1989 by Worth Publishers, Inc. Reprinted by permission of the publisher. All rights reserved.

Annie Dillard. Excerpt from pp. 45–49 from *An American Childhood*, by Annie Dillard. Copyright © 1987 by Annie Dillard. Reprinted by permission of HarperCollins Publishers, Inc.

Steven Doloff. "A Universe Lies on the Sidewalks of New York." Originally published in *Newsday* (City Edition), July 24, 2002. Copyright © 2002 by the author. Reprinted by permission of the author.

John Dutton. "Toxic Soup." Originally published in *The Patagonia* (Winter 2006) Catalog. Copyright © John Dutton. Reprinted by permission of the author.

John T. Edge. "I'm Not Leaving Until I Eat This Thing." Originally published in *The Oxford American*, September/October 1999. Copyright © 1999 by John T. Edge. Reprinted with permission of the author.

Amitai Etzioni. "Working at McDonald's." Originally published in *The Miami Herald*, August 24, 1986. Copyright © 1986 by Amitai Etzioni, author of *The Spirit of Community*. Director, George Washington University Center for Communitarian Policy Studies. Reprinted with permission of the author.

Anne Gray. "Daddy's Loss." Originally published in *Creative Non Fiction No. 5*. Copyright © 1996 by Anne Gray. Reprinted by permission of the author in honor of her father, Powell Overton Morgan.

William L. Hamilton. "At Ole Miss, the Tailgaters Never Lose." From *The New York Times*, September 29, 2006. Copyright © 2006 The New York Times Company. Reprinted by permission.

Chip Heath and Dan Heath. From *Made to Stick*, by Chip Heath and Dan Heath. Copyright © 2007 by Chip Heath and Dan Heath. Used by permission of Random House, Inc.

Virginia Holman. "Their First Patient," from *DoubleTake* (Winter 2000). Copyright © 2000 by Virginia Holman. Reprinted with the permission of the author.

Vinod Khosla. "My Big Biofuels Bet." From *Wired*, October 2006, issue 14.10. Copyright © 2006. Reprinted by permission of the author.

Martin Luther King Jr. "Letter From Birmingham Jail." Copyright © 1963 by Martin Luther King Jr., copyright renewed 1991 by Coretta Scott King. Reprinted by arrangement with The Heirs to the Estate of Martin Luther King Jr., c/o Writers House, as agent for the proprietor.

Stephen King. "Why We Crave Horror Movies." Reprinted with permission. © Stephen King. All rights reserved. Originally appeared in *Playboy* (1982).

Karen Kornbluh. "Win-Win Flexibility." Originally published in *New American Foundation*, June 29, 2005. Copyright © 2005 by Karen Kornbluh. Reprinted by permission of the author.

Jonathan Kozol. "The Human Cost of an Illiterate Society." From *Illiterate America*, by Jonathan Kozol. Copyright © 1985 by Jonathan Kozol. Used by permission of Doubleday, a division of Random House, Inc.

Photo Credits

pp. 49–51. From "Playing B-Ball with Barack Obama, 1988/1989," by Marshall Poe, http://www.memoryarchive.org. For license terms of this work, see http://creativecommons.org/licenses/by/3.0.

p. 94. Shannon Brinkman.

pp. 101, 103, 105. Rollin Riggs/The New York Times/Redux Pictures.

p. 102. The New York Times.

pp. 120–121 (screenshot of "Behind the Scenes with Walter Murch"). © 2007, National Public Radio, Inc.

p. 120 (photograph of Walter Murch). Sean Cullen.

p. 121 (scene from *The English Patient*). Miramax Home Entertainment.

p. 121 (scene from *Apocalypse Now*). Copyright © 2000 Zoetrope Corp.

p. 131. AP IMAGES/Alik Keplicz

p. 180. Joshua Gorchov.

p. 186–88 (screenshot of "Global Voices Delhi Summit"). From "Global Voices Delhi Summit" by Rebecca MacKinnon, December 19, 2006, http://rconversation.blogs.com.

p. 267–68. From Wikipedia, http://en.wikipedia.org/wiki/Flow_(psychology). This work is released under the terms of the GNU Free Documentation License, http://www.gnu.org/licenses/fdl.html.

p. 315. Photofest.

p. 329. Philippe Petit-Roulet.

pp. 412–14. © 2007 by Kathy Belge (http://lesbianlife.about.com). Used with permission of About, Inc., which can be found online at www.about.com. All rights reserved.

p. 483–86. From "When (And How) The Shooting Stops," by Elayne Boosler, HuffingtonPost.com, April 26, 2007.

p. 522. Copyright © Condé Nast Publications Inc.

p. 560–63 (screenshot of "Michelle Obama's Sacrifice"). This article first appeared in Salon.com at http://www.salon.com. An online version remains in the Salon archives. Reprinted with permission.

p. 560 (photograph of Michelle Obama). AP Images/Charles Rex Arbogast.

p. 655. By permission of EBSCO Publishing.

Index to Methods of Development

This index lists the readings in the text according to the methods of writing the authors used to develop their ideas. For readings relying predominantly on one method or strategy, we indicate the first page of the reading. If a method plays a minor role in a reading, we provide both the first page of the reading as well as the paragraph number(s) where the method is put to use.

Comparison and Contrast

Definition

Narration

Process

Index of Authors, Titles, and Terms